Lower Norfolk County, Virginia Court Records

Book "A" 1637-1646 & Book "B" 1646-1651/2

Alice Granbery Walter

CLEARFIELD

Reprinted for
Clearfield Company, Inc. by
Genealogical Publishing Co., Inc.
Baltimore, Maryland
1994, 1995, 2002

International Standard Book Number: 0-8063-4560-8

Made in the United States of America

NOTICE

This work was reproduced from the original edition. A characteristic of this copy, from which the printer worked, was that the image was uneven. Every effort has been made by the printer to produce as fine a reprint of the original edition as possible.

BOOK "A"

LOWER NORFOLK COUNTY VIRGINIA

COURT RECORDS
1637 -- 1646

Transcribed from the 1950 film of
the original Journal 1978

PREFACE

Work on this first, still extant, book of Court Records of Lower Norfolk County, Virginia was started in 1978 after publishing Book B the second book of Court Records of the same County.

This is as true a copy of the original Book A as it was possible to do. Holes in the paper, water damage, and various other causes making a lot of the script impossible to read. Having completed a longhand copy, complete with the various clerk's mispellings of names and words it must be remembered that the various clerks wrote what they heard.

Some illustrations of the script are given throughout the book, however, no assumptions or guesses have been as to the correct spellings etc.

Notes signed AGW are by the Editor. Some of these give a reference to NU which refers to Nell Marion Nugents volume one of Cavaliers and Pioneers. In the case of certificates being awarded for the transportation of various persons a comparison is made to her interpretation of the patent from the patent books. It was believed that this would help anyone researching the names.

The original folio and page number are given with the page number added when the book was restored by the Tidewater Chapter of the Colonial Dames. The page numbers of this manuscript are at the bottom of the page and are the page numbers given in the index. The original numbers of pages and folios are to make it easier to obtain copies of the original book from any institution which may have a microfilm of the original.

Some names have been spelled four or five different ways and have not been corrected. As previously noted nothing has been assumed.

Being aware of the transcript of the 36 pages of this book A which appeared in the Virginia Historical Magazine volume 39, pp 1-20,118-125, and pp 239-249 in January 1931 their presentation of these records does leave out some of the less palatable events and have been corrected to the true Court Records. Every word of their extracts has been compared to the original record and changed if not conforming to the original.

After months of deciphering the script from microfilm and photostats it was possible to get these records in long hand. Then came the tedious task of typewriting It was not easy mispelling so many words. The time came when it was decided to quit, and it was decided to cease publication being worn out with it, and to go on to other publications. That was about 12 years ago. Now it is finished at long last.

The original Court Record Book is turned upside down about midway but this manuscript has continued as it should have been written.

The original spelling is used except where it becomes confusing and some words being spelled right unintentionaly Some words corrected are: ffor for for, p for per,pro,etc. Pish is, of course Parish which often has an added e.

The word Further is usually spelled ffarther. This should alert us to the broad A was most likely used. Thus changing many names - as an example Mackfarson for McPherson which name may not even appear in this book.

EXAMPLES-

Missing words = xxxxx or ....

Words underlined = most often mispelled but written as the Clerk heard them and entered.

p = per, pre, pro

(XX) Initials in brackets are the marks of persons who could not write

() = comments by the Editor also Initialed AGW

X = Christ - Xmas, Xopher for Christopher

All months have been reduced to 3 letters ie Jan,Feb etc.

Two examples of spelling:

Such = Such

that = That

Alice Granberry Walter

COURT DATES

AT A COURT HOULDEN
IN THE LOWER COUNTY OF NEW NORFOLKE THE
15th of MAE 1637

PRESENT: CAPT: ADAM THOROWGOOD ESQR:

CAPT: JOHN SIBSEY
MR: EDWARD WINDHAM MR: ffRANCIS MASON
MR: WM: JULIAN MR: ROBT: CAME

The deposition of GILBERT GUY aged 28 yeares or thereabouts - sworne and examined, sayeth that he being at the house of WILLIAM ffOULER, discoursing with him concerning certain cask found by the servants of CAPT: ADAM THOROWGOOD by the seaside, but afterwards being seized and fetched away by the aforesaid WILLIAM ffOULER, the aforesaid deponent told him it would vex him to have the casks taken away from him, whereupon the wife of the said WILLIAM ffOULER asked, who would take them from him? The said deponent answered, CAPT: THOROWGOOD, upon which she, the said ANNE ffOULER, answered, "Let CAPT: THOROWGOOD have *****

WILLIAM TANNER, aged 36 yeares or thereabouts, sworne and examined sayeth - That being in the company with GILBERT GUY at the house of WILLIAM ffOULER, he, the said deponent heard GILBERT GUY tell WILLIAM ffOULER that it would vex him to have the casks which he had fetched home taken from him whereupon the wife of the said ffOULER asked who would take them from him? The said GILBERT answered, CAPT: THOROWGOOD. Upon which she, the said ANNE ffOULER answered "Let CAPT: THOROWGOOD *****

Whereas it doth appear to this Court by the oaths of severa witnesses, that ANNE ffOULER the wife of WILLIAM ffOULER of Linhaven, Planter, did, in a shameful uncomely and irreverant manner, bid CAPT: THOROWGOOD ***** , with the aggravation of many unusual terms - It is therefore ordered that the said ANNE ffOULER shall, for her offense, receive twenty stripes upon her bare shoulders and ask forgiveness of the said CAPT: THOROWGOOD here now in Court and also the ensueing Sunday at Linhaven.

GILBERT GUY, aged 28 yeares, or thereabouts - sworne and examined, sayeth that, being at the house of WILLIAM ffOULER when THOMAS KEELING, agent of CAPT: ADAM THOROWGOOD. came to demand certain Cask which were found and marked by servants of the said CAPT: THOROWGOOD. he heard MRS. ffOULER, the wife of WILLIAM ffOULER, in a most railing manner, call the said THOMAS KEELING, Jackanapes, Newgate rogue and brigand and told him if he did not get him out of doors she would break his head.

JAMES STARLING aged 24 yeares or thereabouts, sworn and examined saith - that being at the house of WILLIAM ffOULER when THOMAS KEELING agent of CAPT: ADAM THOROWGOOD came to demand certain cask which were found and marked by the servants of CAPT: THOROWGOOD, he heard ANNE ffOULER, the wife of WILLIAM ffOULER in a most railing manner, call the said THOMAS KEELING, Jackanapes, Newgate rogue and brigand and told him if he did not get out of doors she would break his head.

(End of folio 1 and/or page 1)

Whereas it doth appear to this Court that ANNE ffouler, the wife of WILLIAM ffOULER, of Linhaven, Planter, hath in a most shameful and reproachful manner, defamed THOMAS KEELING of Linhaven aforesaid, with abusive names and promiscuous speeches, it is therefore ordered that the said ANNE ffOULER shall ask THOMAS KEELING forgiveness here in this Court and the next Sabbath at the dwelling house of CAPT: THOROWGOOD.

Whereas SARAH PURSLIT (written thusly: Purslit) widow, being big with child and destitute of any place of abiding, did complain of the same unto the right worshipful SIR JOHN HARVEY Knight, Governor &c who did order that the aforesaid SARAH should forthwith be married unto THOMAS HUGHS, the reported father of her child, man-servant to CAPT: WILLOBE, the same being first lawfully asked, it is therefore ordered that MR. JOHN WILSON, minister of Elizabeth River, after lawful publication of the bans, shall solemnize matrimony them - it is also further ordered that ROBERT DARBY, agent of CAPT: THOMAS WILLOBE, shall give towards the maintenance of the said SARAH, one bushel of corn in the behalf of CAPT: WILLOBE, and likewise to give leave unto the aforsd THOMAS HUGHS to go to the said SARAH PURSLIT at convenient times, not hindering his master's business.

Whereas JOHN BURNET, merchaunt, hath left a parcel of goods in the custody of CAPT: SIBSEY and has likewise given him order to have them appraised, it is therefore ordered that HENRY SEAWELL, CORNELIUS LOYD, JOHN GATER (written: Gator), and JOHN WATKINGS shall be sworne to make due appraisement of them and to give in a true accompt at the next Court of the appraysement by them made.

WILLIAM RAMSHEIR (Ramsha ?), one certificate for five servants videlitz SAVILL GASKING in the Merchants Hope, 1635; WILLIAM BREWER in the Marmaduke 1634; HENERY JOANES in the George 1636; RICHARD STERNILL in the Bonaventure 1634; JOHN (written: Harly) (Note by Ed: Va. Mag gives this name as Hawley while Nugent gives the same name as Hackley and to your editor it looks like Harly?) in the American 1633; and JOHN WELLS in the George, 1636.

AT A COURT HOULDEN
AT LYNNEHAVEN in THE LOWER COUNTY OF NORFOLKE THE
7th of JULY 1637

PRESENT: CAPT: ADAM THOROWGOOD ESQR:
CAPT: JOHN SIBSEY
MR. EDWARD WINDHAM MR. ffRANCIS MASON
MR. WILLM: JULIAN MR. ROBT: CAME

HENRY HAWKINGS, aged 22 yeares or thereabouts being sworne and examined saith that being at the Warrikesquiacke Plantation they were there jesting concerning rare ripe pumpkins whereupon GEORGE LOCKE told him that THOMAS DAVIS told him likewise that he did have the use of ANNE CLARKE to lie with her and her answer was that she would not but (there?) in his house she might better do it.

GEORGE LOCKE aged -(faded)- yeares sworne & examined (end f 1a) saith that he heard ROBT: PIERCE say that THOMAS DAVIS tould him that he had the use of ANNE CLARKE and would have done it again but could not. f 2

THOMAS RIVERS, alias MARSH, aged 21 yeares or thereabouts sworne & examined saith that he did see THOMAS DAVIS with his hand under ANNE CLARKE's apron and furder that THOMAS DAVIS did say he had the use of her and would have done it againe but could not and likewise this deponent saith that he heard somebody talke with the sd ANNE CLARKE and she answered that three weeks home was time enough.

Whereas it doth appear to this Court that THOMAS DAVIS, of Elizabeth River, tailor, did report that he had the use of ANNE CLARKE to the great impeaching and acandalizing of her credit, and no truth or likelihood of the said report appearing, It is therefore ordered that said THOMAS DAVIS shall pay the fees and charges of the Court.

Whereas the aforsd THOMAS DAVIS did confess and acknowledge himself to be drunk at the same time when he did scandalize the said ANNE CLARKE, It is therefore ordered that the said THOMAS DAVIS, shall, for his said offence, pay unto the sheriff of this County for the building of a pair of stockes.

Whereas it doth appear that OLIVER HANKOCKE of the eastern side of Linnehaven, Planter, did borrow of THOMAS CHEELY, half a barrel of corn, in his great necessity, and now denying to pay the said corn, It is therefore ordered that the said OLIVER HANKOCKE shall within this ten days, pay the said corn, otherwise to pay so much tobacco as the said corn would produce at this instant.

ROBERT HAYES, one certificate for the transportation of eight persons, viz: himself, and his wife, AMOS WORTMAN, MARY WORTMAN, THOMAS WORTMAN, JOHN WORTMAN (this name should be Workman), ALEXANDER HAYES & NATHANIEL HAYES.

AT A COURT HOULDEN
IN THE LOWER COUNTY OF NEW NORFOLKE THE
26th of OCTOBER 1637

PRESENT: CAPT: ADAM THOROWGOOD ESQR:

CAPT: JOHN SIBSEY	MR. WILLM: JULIAN
MR. EDWARD WINDHAM	MR. ffRANCIS MASON

Whereas it doth appear to this Court that JOHN PENRICE of the County of Elizabeth City, Carpenter, is indebted unto CORNELIUS LLOYD in the sum of 800 weight of Virginia Tobacco as by specialty appeareth, it is ordered that the said JOHN PENRICE shall pay the said sum of tobacco at or before the first of December next ensuing or else execution to be awarded. (end of f 2 & p 3)

Whereas it doth appear to this Court that THOMAS ALLEN of the County of Elizabeth City, Merchant, did transport the goods and servants of HENERY SOUTHERNE and WILLM: LATON of the aforesaid County, Planter, from the Back River at Kequotan into Linnehaven, f 2a p 4 no freight being agreed upon, It is therefore ordered that the said WILLIAM LATON shall pay unto the said THOMAS ALLEN the sum of 500 weight of Virginia tobacco in leaf, at or before the 20th of November next ensuing provided that the said WILLIAM LATON cannot provide former agreement for the transportation of the said goods and servants betwixt the aforesaid HENERY SOUTHERNE and THOMAS ALLEN.

Whereas it doth appear that JOHN BOULTER did buy of MATTHEW HEYWARD four barrels of Indian Corne being in the house of ROBT: JOANES the which JOANES, the aforesaid BOULTER coming to demand a while after without any notice or token from under HEYWARD's hand, the said JOANES denied to deliver, but being very earnest for it, the said JOANES delivered two barrels and a bushel of it. It is therefore ordered that the said ROBT: JOANES shall repay the aforesd corn by the first of January or else execution to be awarded.

Whereas it doth appear that WILLIAM SHIPPE of the Lower County of Norfolke, Planter, doth stand indebted unto GEORGE WHITE of Nansemund, Clerk, in the sum of 115 pounds of tobacco and four barrels of Indian corn, as per specialty appeareth, it is therefore ordered that the aforesaid WILLIAM SHIPPE shall pay the aforesd sum of tobacco and corn by the 1st of January or else execution be awarded.

WHEREAS it doth appear that WILLIAM JULIAN of the Lower County of Norfolke, Planter, doth owe and stand indebted unto HENERY HALL, of the aforesaid county, Planter, one sow shoat as by sufficient proof appeareth, it is therefore ordered that the aforesaid WILLIAM JULIAN shall pay unto the said RICHARD HALL (in original) one sow shoat or 100 weight of tobacco in leaf by the 25th of December next ensuing, otherwise execution to be awarded.

AT A COURT HOULDEN
IN THE LOWER COUNTY OF NORFOLKE THE 10 Jan 1637

PRESENT: CAPT: ADAM THOROWGOOD ESQR:
CAPT: JOHN SIBSEY MR. WILLIAM JULIAN
MR. EDWARD WINDH(AM) MR. ffRANCIS MASON

Whereas it doth appear that ROBT: EIRES of Elizabeth City River Planter, is indebted unto JOHN ANGOOD, Merchant, the sum of 2000 pound of tobacco in leaf, as by specialty appeareth, It is therefore ordered that the aforesaid ROBT: EIRES shall pay the said sum of tobacco unto the said JOHN ANGOOD or his assignes, within 15 dayes after the date hereof, otherwise execution awarded.(end f 2a)

Whereas it doth appear to this Court that THOMAS BULLOCKE, Chirugeon, is indebted unto WILLM: PARRY of the County of Elizabeth City the sum of 530 pounds of tobacco in leaf, It is therefore ordered that the aforesaid THOMAS BULLOCK shall pay unto WILLM: PARRY or his assignes, the aforesaid sum of tobacco within ten dayes after the date hereof. f 3 p 5

Whereas it doth appear that THOMAS DAVIS of Elizabeth River,

Tailor, doth owe unto THOMAS RUDDER of Linnehaven, Planter, the sum of 700 weight of tobacco in leaf, It is therefore ordered that the aforesaid THOMAS DAVIS shall within the space of ten days after the date hereof, pay aforesaid sum of tobacco or else execution to be awarded.

Whereas THOMAS DAVIS, Tailor, hath produced an account upon oath heere now in Court containing 970 weight of tobacco due from THOMAS CODDE Planter, It is therefore ordered that the aforenamed THOMAS CODDE shall within ten dayes after the date hereof pay the tobacco due upon the sd account unlesse he the sd THOMAS CODDE can prove aforesd sum of tob. to be discounted.

Whereas PETER PORTER, Carpenter, did buy of DANIELL TANNER of Elizabeth Citty, Carpenter, two kiddes without bargaining for the price thereof, but now refusing to pay according as the sd. DANIELL TANNER sold kiddes at the same time he bought these. It is therefore ordered that the aforesd PETER PORTER shall for the said two kiddes pay 120 weight of tobacco. Further it is ordered that DANIELL TANNER shall, within this ten dayes, pay unto the said PETER PORTER the sum of 72 pounds of tobacco being due for six days work.

Whereas it doth appear that WILLIAM JULIAN doth stand indebted unto RICHARD KENNER, Chircurgeon, in the quantity of 700 weight of tobacco in leaf. It is therefore ordered that the aforesaid WILLIAM JULIAN shall, within ten days after the date hereof, pay the aforesaid sum of tobacco or else execution to be awarded.

Whereas it doth appear by sufficient testimony that CHRISTOPHER BURROWS of Linnehaven, Planter, hath chaffered and bargained with Indians without license from the Governor or Council. It is therefore ordered that the aforesd CHRISTOPHER BURROWS shall pay as a fine for the said offense the sum of 500 weight of tobacco by the 1st of October next ensuing, 1638, to be employed in what use the Court shall see fit.

Whereas DANIELL TANNER of Elizabeth Citty, Carpenter, stands bound with JOHN PENRICE of Yorke, Carpenter, for the performance of certaine building due to CAPT: ADAM THOROWGOOD but the said buildings not being finished according to specialty, whereby the aforesd CAPT: THOROWGOOD was constrained to hire men to finish the sd worke. It is therefore ordered that the aforesd DANIELL TANNER shall pay unto CAPT: THOROWGOOD the tobacco he hath disbursed in men's wages to finish the sd buildings - It is likewise ordered that the aforesd DANIELL TANNER shall, within ten days after the date hereof, pay unto the said CAPT: ADAM THOROWGOOD 3 barrels of Indian corne, being -(corner torn off page)- (an account of the bill ? -39V8) wherein he standeth bound with the aforesaid PENRICE.

(end of f 3, p 5)

f 3a
p 6

Whereas ROBERT WARD, Planter, hath justly and truly served WILLIAM JULIAN of the Lower County of Norfolke, Planter, from the 20th of September to the 20th of December next ensuing, as p(er) sufficient proof appeareth. It is therefore ordered that the aforesaid WILLIAM JULIAN shall pay unto ROBERT WARD the sum of 300 waight of tobacco in leafe within ten dayes after the date hereof.

Deposition of ROBERT WEST aged 24 yeares or thereabouts, taken the 16th day of January 1637/8. This deponent being sworne and examined saith; that he spoke to the Indian that lived with CHRISTOPHER BURROWS to make him a ware (pottery?) who promised he would. But the Indian neglecting his promise and putting him off with divers delays the aforesd deponent demanded of CHRISTOPHER BURROWS why the Indian came not to make him a ware who answered, he should make him none unless he would give him a pair of breeches and a pair of shooes and stockings.

THOMAS CHEELY age 40 yeares or thereabouts, sworne and examined, saith; that the Indian which did usually abide at CHRISTOPHER BURROWS, his house, did there remain 40 days after the Act of Assembly were read at CAPT: THOROWGOODS and that he went away then but came again about two months after and was entertained by the aforesd CHRISTOPHER BURROWS, thinking there had been peace between them and the English but so soon as CAPT: HOWELL came and told CHRISTOPHER BURROWS that CAPT: SIBSEY's boy was hurt with the Indians, the aforesd Indian went forth of the doores and was never seen since.

THOMAS KEELING aged 24 yeares or thereabouts, sworne and examined saith; That CHRISTOPHER BURROWS told him the said deponent, that if he did not pay unto CAPT: ADAM THOROWGOOD the tobacco which he owed him for a negro, within ten days after the date thereof that then he, the said CHRISTOPHER BURROWS, would restore unto CAPT: ADAM THOROWGOOD his negro again.

ROBERT HAYES aged 44 yeares or thereabouts, sworne and examined saith; that he heard CAPT: ADAM THOROWGOOD demaund of CHRISTOPHER BURROWS, the tobacco which he owed him for a negro, who answered, if he did not pay the aforesd tobacco within ten days that then, he, the sd CHRISTOPHER BURROWS, would restore the negro again.

ffRANCIS MASON aged 42 yeares or thereabouts sworne and examined saith that he, the said deponent, did see CAPT: JOHN SIBSEY about the middle of May last past, deliver one firking (firkin = 1/4 barrel) of butter to JAMES HAWLY who received it for the use of GABRIELL HAWLY. (name should probably be Hawley?)

(end of f 3a, p 6)

f 4 p 7

DANIELL TANNER aged 56 yeares or thereabouts sworne and examined saith; that about the 4th of Aprill last past, the said deponent, by the appointment of GABRIELL HAWLY, did demaund twelve paire of shooes of CAPT: JOHN SIBSEY for the aforesd HAWLY's use and received them.

(JARVIS ?) MASON aged 26 yeares or thereabouts, sworne and examined, saith; that he the sd deponent about the middle of March last past (1636/7) did by the appointment of CAPT: JOHN SIBSEY carry over to Kequotan two barrels of Indian corne and delivered it to JAMES HAWLY for the use of GABRIELL HAWLY.

(Note: Your Ed. wonders if this Jarvis Mason could have been the son of ffrancis Mason? or Could he have been the James Mason of Surry County who had a son Francis Mason? see illustration AGW)

= John

r r r ffrancis Mason

The above illustration of the name Jarvis and the name John clearly show that this name begins with a J, however, the lower case r in Jarvis is not made like any other r on the page. Is this name Jamis, James or Jarvis? AGW

HENERY TOMPSON aged 26 yeares or thereabouts, sworne and examined, saith; that he, the sd deponent, by the appointment of CAPT: SIBSEY, did deliver unto GABRIELL HAWLY one firkine of butter and about 20 pounds of soap.

AT A COURT HOULDEN
IN THE LOWER COUNTY OF NEW NORFOLKE THE
2nd of APRILL 1638

PRESENT: CAPT: ADAM THOROWGOOD ESQR:
CAPT: JOHN SIBSEY MR. WILLIAM JULIAN
MR. EDWARD WINDHAM MR. ffRANCIS MASON

Whereas it doth appear that certain of the servants of CAPT: JOHN SIBSEY have, in the time of his absence, raised a mutiny against WILLIAM EDWARDS, the agent of the aforesd CAPT: SIBSEY, It is therefore ordered that the said servants shall for their offence so committed receive 100 strippes apiece, severally upon the bare shoulders.

Whereas ROBT: EIRES did cause the body of ROBT: WARD to be arrested to this Court, which he hath performed in personal appearance according to the tenor of the warrant to their great trouble and hindrance, the said ROBERT EIRES not being present in person nor yet by attorney to prosecute his suit; It is therefore ordered that the aforesd ROBERT EIRES shall stand and remain nonsuited and also pay his damages and the charges of the Court.

Whereas there was an order passed at this Court the 16th of Jan last (1637/8) that WILLIAM JULIAN of the Lower County of Norfolke, Planter, the sum of 300 weight of tobacco for wages due unto the aforesd ROBERT WARD but the said JULIAN not having performed the foregoing order, It is therefore ordered that the aforesd WILLIAM JULIAN shall, by the 1st of October next ensuing pay the sum of 360 pounds of tobacco unto the aforesd WARD, or else execution &c.

Whereas there was a difference between GEORGE LOVE and THOMAS MARSH concerning a parcell of land which is now in the possession of RICHARD (sic) and it now appeareth that the said land belongeth no more to one than to the other; It is therefore ordered that the sd land be equally divided betwixt the aforesd 3 persons viz: 50 acres per poll ....

AT A COURT HOULDEN
IN THE LOWER COUNTY OF NEW NORFOLKE THE
18th of MAY 1638

PRESENT: CAPT: ADAM THOROWGOOD ESQR:
CAPT: JOHN SIBSEY MR. WILLIAM JULIAN
MR. EDWARD WINDHAM MR. ffRANCIS MASON

Whereas it doth appear that RICHARD LOE (Lowe?) Eliz: river, Planter, hath most falsely and after a most reproachfull manner scandalized ANNE BUTKINGS the wife of HENERY BUTKINGS of the afor-sd County, Planter to the great impeaching of the foresd ANNE BUTKINGS credit; It is therefore ordered that the aforesd RICHARD LOE shall for the sd offence, aske forgivenes the next Sabbath at the Parish Church of the Lower Norfolke County and the next ensu-ing Sabbath at Elizabeth River and further that the sd RICHARD LOE shall pay for the building of a pair of stockes.

(Note: the name above is given in 39V12 as Ruskings. Your ed-itor reads it as BUTKINGS, but wonders if the name could be Nutkin which appears in later Norfolk County Records?)

Whereas it doth appeare that ROBT: JOANES, Planter, hath not giving (given) a true and iust (just) acount unto TRISTRAM MASON copartiner with the sd JOANES of the disbursement of their cropp It is therefore ordered that the said JOANES shall stand bound in the forfeiture of 1000 weight of tobacco to produce a general ac-count from the beginning of their copartnershipe of all affaires charges and disbursements that have been betweene them, the sd 2 partners at the next Court houlden at CAPT: JOHN SIBSEYS of else-where.

Whereas THOMAS DAVIS of Eliz: river Taylor, hath produced an account here in Court amounting to the sum of 128 pounds of tobac-co due from RICHARD LOE of the foresd County, Planter; It is therefore ordered that the aforesd RICHARD LOE shall pay the sd sum of tobacco unless he can, by sufficient testimony prove the payment thereof by the 1st of October next ensuing. (1638)

Whereas it doth appeare that RICHARD LOE, Planter, hath bought of THOMAS MARSH, Planter, all his estate whatsomever (sic) heere resident in Virginia but the sd LOE now denying to put in security for the payment of the tobacco due him upon the sd bargain; It is therefore ordered that the aforesd THOMAS MARSH shall detain and keep in his custody the estate untill such time as the aforesd RICHARD LOE shall pay the tobacco.

Whereas it doth appeare that DEBORA GLASCOCKE wife of ROBT: GLASCOCKE of New Norfolke, Carpenter, hath most falsely and after an abusive manner scandalized CAPT: SIBSEY in saying his maide servant was with child by him and she now not making the same appeare by any proofe to be reported to her by any other it is therefore ordered that the sd DEBORA shall receive 100 stripes on the bare shoulders and likewise aske the sd CAPT: SIBSEY forgive-nes heere now in Court and the next Saboth at the parish Church at the time of divine Service.

AT A COURT HOULDEN
IN THE LOWER COUNTY OF NEW NORFOLKE THE
10th of SEPTEMBR 1638

PRESENT: CAPT: ADAM THOROWGOOD ESQR:
CAPT: JOHN SIBSEY MR. WILLIAM JULIAN
MR. EDWARD WINDHAM MR. ffRANCIS MASON

The deposition of WILLIA (sic) WHITBY aged 24 yeares of thereabouts sworne and examined saith: that MARGARET HARRINGTON servant to WILLIAM JULIAN told him, the sd deponent, that her mistres SARAH JULIAN had divers times abused her body with CORNELIUS LOYD she the sd MARGARET saying likewise that her mistris had often misused her but now she would be even with her. WILLIA BERRY servant to MR. WILLIAM JULIAN doth likewise testifie that he heard the aforesd MARGARET say that CORNELIUS LOYD had used her Mistris SARAH JULIAN as above written.

Whereas it doth appear that THOMAS COOPER, Joyner, did borrow of THOMAS LAMBERT, Planter, a boate to fetch some planke from Nansamund to finish certaine worke which he was to do for the sd THOMAS LAMBERT and the boate being in the sd service accidentilly lost; It is therefore ordered that the sd THOMAS COOPER shall the last of December next ensuing (1638), pay unto the foresd THOMAS LAMBERT, the sum of 400 pounds of tobacco being the one half of the appraisement of the foresd boate the other halfe to be borne by THOMAS LAMBERT.

Whereas WILLIAM BERRY and ANTHONY HEWETT servants to MR. WILLM: JULIAN did depose against WILLM: WHITBY in a case altogether false and fained, and being thereof lawfully convicted by sufficient proofe and testimony and having also spoken certain scandalous words concerning CAPT: THOROWGOOD and CAPT: SIBSEY to the great impeachment of their credits; It is therefore ordered that the said offenders shall receive 50 lashes apiece upon the bare shoulders.

Whereas it doth appeare that MARGARET HARRINGTON servant to MR: WILLIAM JULIAN, hath most infamously and maliciously scandalized and defamed her mistress, SARAH JULIAN, by reporting that she had often seene CORNELIUS LOYD use her sd Mistris in Carnall Capulation. But now being not able to prove or justify the same; It is therefore ordered that she the sd MARGARET, shall receive 100 stripes upon the bare shoulders and also ask her said mistress forgivenes heere now in Court.

AT A COURT HOULDEN
IN THE LOWER COUNTY OF NEW NORFOLKE THE
21 of NOVEMBR 1638

PRESENT: CAPT: ADAM THOROWGOOD ESQR:
CAPT: JOHN SIBSEY MR. WILLM: JULIAN
MR. EDWARD WINDHAM MR. ffRANCIS MASON
MR. HENERY SEAWELL

THOMAS MELTON, one Certificate for the transportation of foure persons viz: himselfe in the Hopewell 1632, ANNE WALLINGTON in the Safety 1635, GOWIN LANCASTER in the Transport 1635, EDWARD COOPER in the Blessinge 1637.
(end of f 5)

f 5a

It is ordered by this Court that the sheriff of this County shall levy and receive now, this Winter, ten pounds of Tobacco per poll of all tithable persons inhabiting within this said County according to a list made this present court and to be accountable for the same to CAPT: JOHN SIBSEY and ROBT: HAYES in satisfaction for their charges, being Burgesses for the last Grand Assembly. It is likewise further ordered that the said Sheriff shall levy two pounds of tobacco per poll according to the aforesd list and to be accountable for the same to MR. ROBT: HAYES it being due to him for keeping a Ferry at the Little Creeke at Linnehaven the last yeare.

Whereas JOHN BEADLE, Planter, hath informed this Court that he was hired by PETER PORTER and MOYSES STONE to serve but unto (the) middle of this moneth and being by sufficient proofe found to be hired untill the last of this moneth; It is therefore ordered that, for misinforming the Court and troubling of his said masters he shall serve them one fortnight complete after the expiration of this present November and also pay the charges of the Court.

Whereas JOHN YATES did cause the bodyes of THOMAS TODDE, THOMAS COOPER and ffRANCIS LINCH to be arrested to this Court, which they have performed in personall appearance according to the tennor of the warrant, to their great trouble and detriment, the said JOHN YATES not being present in person nor yet by attorney, to prosecute his suite; It is therefore ordered that the said JOHN YATES shall stand and remain non suited and also pay their damages and the charges of the Court.

Whereas there has been an order of Court granted by the Governor and Council for the building and erecting of a Church in the upper part of this County with a reference to the Commander and Commissioners of the said County for the appointing of a place fitting and convenient for the situation and building thereof, the said order being in part not accomplished but standing now in election to be voyde and the work to fall into ruine, we now, the said Commissioners taking it into consideration, do appoint CAPT: JOHN SIBSEY and HENERY SEAWELL to procure workmen for the finishing of the same and what they shall answer for with the said workmen, to be levied by the appointment of us the Commissioners.

Whereas all, or the most part of the inhabitants resident within this County do sustain many inconveniences for want of free passage over these creekes viz: the Creeke at DANIELL TANNERS, the two Creekes at LIEUTENNANT MASONS and the Little Creeke at Linnehaven; It is therefore ordered that the sheriff shall levy of all tithable persons within this county two pounds of tobacco per poll for the maintenance of a Ferry at DANIELL TANNERS, four pounds of tobacco per poll for a Ferry at LIEUTENNANT MASONS and two pounds of tobacco per poll for a Ferry at the Little Creeke at Linnehaven to be paid unto such as shall undertake the keeping of the said Ferries, provided that they keep sufficient Boates and give good attendance for the transportation of passengers - Passengers being likewise bound by the said order to come for their passage between sun rising and sitting otherwise pay for their passage over and besides the aforesaid levies; The said ferries to begin the first of January next ensuing (1638/9). (End of f 5a)

f 6
p 11

AT A COURT HOULDEN
IN THE LOWER COUNTY OF NEW NORFOLKE THE
6th of ffEBRUARY 1638/9

PRESENT: CAPT: JOHN SIBSEY — MR: WILLM: JULIAN
MR: EDWARD WINDH: — MR: ffRANCIS MASON
MR: HENERY SEAWELL

Whereas it doth appeare that THOMAS HAYES, Planter, of Linnehaven is indebted unto THOMAS BULLOCKE, Chirurgeon, the sum of 300 weight of tobacco but he the sd THOMAS HAYES, now denying the payment thereof, saying that the aforesd THOMAS BULLOCKE did promise to the contrary; It is therefore ordered that the aforesd THOMAS BULLOCKE can, by sufficient witnesses before CAPT: THOROWGOOD prove the contrary, That then the said THOMAS HAYES shall, within ten dayes after the date hereof pay the said sum of tobacco.

Whereas GEORGE LOCKE and SIMON HANCOCKE, Planters, are indebted unto BARTHOLOMEW HOSKINGS, Planter, 1067 pounds of tobacco and cask, due to be paid this yeare as by specialty appeareth; It is therefore ordered that the aforesd parties shall within ten dayes after the date hereof, pay the aforesd sum of tobacco or else execution to be awarded.

Whereas it doth appeare that LANCASTER LOVET, Planter, is indebted unto THOMAS BULLOCKE, Chirurgeon, the sum of 620 pounds of tobacco, the which tobacco was to be paid upon all demaunds; It is therefore ordered that the aforesd LANCASTER shall pay the said sum of tobacco within ten dayes after the order hereof or else execution to be awarded; It is likewise further ordered that the aforesd LANCASTER LOVET shall out of HENERY COLEMANS croppe pay the sum of 400 pounds of tobacco unto THOMAS BULLOCKE, Chirurgeon, it being for the cure of the said COLEMANS servants.

Whereas it doth appeare to this Court that ROBERT EIRES and GEORGE ffADON are indebted unto SIMON HANCOCKE the sum of 516 pounds of tobacco for goods sold unto the aforesd parties; It is therefore ordered that ROBERT EIRES and GEORGE ffADON shall within ten dayes after the date hereof pay the aforesd tobacco or else execution be awarded.

Whereas JOHN CLARKE, Planter, hath bought of ROBT: PAGE, Merchaunt, so many goods as did amount to the value of 714 pounds, but the sd CLARKE being now found not able to satisffie the whole sum of the sd tob. It is therefore ordered he shall pay the one halfe thereof within ten dayes after the date hereof and put in sufficient security to pay the other halfe by the 1st of Novembr:

next ensuing (1639) otherwise to serve so long as that his wages shall produce the aforesd sum of tob:

Whereas ROBT: GLASCOCKE, Planter, is indebted unto WILLIAM HODGES, Mariner, the sum of 400 pounds of tobacco, being due for goods bought of the sd HODGES; It is therefore ordered that the aforesd GLASCOCKE shall, within ten dayes after the date hereof, pay the said sum of tobacco or else execution to be awarded.

Whereas ROBT: EYRES of Eliza: river, Planter, is (indebted) unto THOMAS BULLOCKE, Chirurgeon, (the) quantity of 410 pounds of tob. to be paid upon all demaunds, as by specialty appeareth; It is therefore ordered that the aforsd ROBT: EIRES shall pay the tob within ten dayes after the date hereof or else execution to be awarded. (end of f 6 & p 11)

f 6a
p 12 Whereas it doth appeare that JOHN WILSON of the Lower County of Norfolke, Clarke, hath bought of ROBT: PAGE, Merchaunt, as many goods as do amount to the value of 849 (pounds of tob?) as p(er) specialty appeareth; It is therefore ordered that the aforesd JOHN WILSON shall within ten dayes after the date hereof pay the aforesd sum of tob or else execution to be awarded. It is likewise further ordered that the aforesd JOHN WILSON shall pay unto NATHAN STAINESMORE the sum of 208 pounds of tobacco within the space of ten dayes after the date hereof being due p(er) account the last yeare.

Whereas ROBT: EIRES and GEORGE ffADON are indebted unto THOMAS MARSH of Eliza: River, Planter, the quantity of 1300 pounds of tob as p(er) specialty appeareth; It is therefore ordered that the sd two parties shall, within ten dayes after the date hereof, pay the tob unless they can by sufficient testimony prove the said tob to be already paid.

Whereas HENERY SEAWELL hath made appeare to this Court that THOMAS JVIE (IVIE) is indebted unto him, the sd HENERY SEAWELL the sum of 200 weight of tob; It is therefore ordered that the aforesd THOMAS IVIE shall within ten dayes after the date hereof pay the aforesd sum of tob or else execution to be awarded.

Whereas THOMAS MARSH, Planter, is indebted unto NATHAN STAINSMORE, Merchaunt, the sum of 1474 pounds of tob as p(er) specialty appeareth; It is therefore ordered that the aforesd THOMAS MARSH shall within ten dayes after the date hereof pay the sd sum of tob else execution to be awarded.

Whereas THOMAS SAWYER, Planter, is indebted unto THOMAS IVIE, Planter, the sum of 150 pounds of tob as p(er) specialty appeareth It is therefore ordered that the aforesd THOMAS SAWYER shall pay the sd tob within ten dayes after the date hereof or else execution to be awarded.

Whereas it doth appeare that THOMAS SAWYER, Planter, hath bought of NATHAN STAINESMORE as many goodes as do amount to the value of 500 weight of tob, which tob by specialty the sd SAWYER was bound to pay upon all demaunds but not having performed the aforesd specialty; It is therefore ordered that he the sd SAWYER shall within ten dayes after the date hereof pay the aforsd tob or else execution to be awarded.

Whereas it doth appeare that THOMAS IVIE is indebted unto CAPT: JOHN SIBSEY and ROBT: PAGE, Merchaunts, the sum of 483 pounds of tob for commodities bought of the said two parties and by specialty being bound to pay the same upon all demaunds but not having performed the same; It is therefore ordered that the aforesd THOMAS IVIE shall within ten dayes after the date hereof pay the tob or else execution &c.

Whereas WILLIAM SHIPPE, Planter, hath made it appeare that he hath according to the conditions of his lease made with CAPT: THOMAS WILLOBY proffered the sale on his ground unto the agent of the aforesd CAPT: WILLOBY and the said agent having refused it hath now sold the sd land unto JOHN HOLMES, Planter; It is therefore ordered that the sd JOHN HOLMES shall peaceably enjoy the sd ground. (End of f 6a & p 12)

f 7

Whereas ANTHONY DELEMONS, Servant, unto CAPT: JOHN SIBSEY hath conveyed and made away the goods of his said master, and bartered and bargained contrary to the lawes and customes of the country in that case made and provided; It is therefore ordered that the sd ANTHONY DELEMONS shall receive 30 stripes on the bare shoulders. p 13

AT A COURT HOULDEN
IN THE LOWER COUNTY OF NORFOLKE THE
fourth of MARCH 1638/9

PRESENT: CAPT: ADAM THOROWGOOD ESQR:

CAPT: JOHN SIBSEY	MR: ffRANCIS MASON
MR: WILLM: JULIAN	MR: HENERY SEAWELL

The deposition of ELIZABETH LATON (Layton?) aged 24 yeares or thereabouts sworne and examined saith that being at the house of JOHN LANCFIELD (Lanckfield?) speaking with GEOPHRY WITE about serving her husband the sd GEOPHRY replied he would willingly serve him but that he knew the sd WILLM: LATON would gain CAPT: THOROWGOODS ill will thereby. Further this deponent saith that she heard the said GEOPHRY swear that CAPT: THOROWGOOD had bound him, the sd GEOPHRY, in the forfeiture of 7 yeares not to serve the aforesd WILLM: LATON for feare of which he durst not serve him. Further this deponent saith that at another time he the sd GEOPHRY being at her house said that MRS: THOROWGOOD did in a threatening way bid him, the sd GEOPHRY take heed that he did never come to her for so much as a paire of shooes.

JAMES SMITH aged 25 yeares or thereabouts sworne and examined testif(ied) idem.

EDWARD WILLIAMS aged 24 yeares or thereabouts sworne and examined saith that when he, the sd EDWARD WILLIAMS was CAPT: THOROWGOODS cow keeper, the cows then going into a penne (pen) adjoining to the goats penne, he, the deponent did after and divers times see GEOPHRY WITE, then keeper of CAPT: THOROWGOODS goats, beat ye sd goats after such an excessive manner with the barres of the cow penne.

EDWARD COLEMAN aged 26 yeares or thereabouts sworne and examined testified idem.

JOHN WEBBE aged 23 yeares or thereabouts sworne and examined saith that when he the sd deponent was building a house for CAPT: THOROWGOOD at the goate penne he did often and divers times see GEOPHRY WITE then keeper of CAPT: THOROWGOODS goates beat sd goates after such an excessive manner that they would cry as if they had been killed. Further this deponent saith that he hath heard the aforesaid GEOPHRY beat the goates from the cow penne on the farther side of the pond to the tobacco house which stands in CAPT: THOROWGOODS yard.

ANDREW HILL aged 23 yeares or thereabouts sworne and examined saith that going to the house of ROBT: MARTIN in the company of GILBERT GUY he the sd deponent asked the wife of ROBT: MARTIN where her husband was, who answered, her husband was not at home, neither had been at home that week whereupon sd deponent told her there was a warrant out for her husband. She answered if MR. MEARES had a warrant for him he might keepe it if he would in his pocket for her husband should not be found till after the Court.

f 7a (end of f 7 & p 13)

p 14 GEORGE HUNTER aged 36 yeares or thereabouts sworne and examined testified idem.

Whereas it doth appeare that JOHN WILSON of the Lower Norfolke, Clarke, was indebted unto JOHN HILL the last yeare 5 barrels of corne by non payment the said JOHN HILL was enforced to buy corne at the rate of 100 pounds of tob a barrel; It is therefore ordered that the aforesd JOHN WILSON shall pay the sum of 300 weight of tob and 2 barrels of corne unto the sd JOHN HILL within the space of ten dayes after the date hereof or else execution &c.

Whereas it doth appeare that JOHN HILL, Planter, is indebted unto JOHN MEARES, Merchaunt, the sum of 500 pounds of tob and cask It is therefore ordered that the aforesd JOHN HILL shall within ten dayes after the date hereof pay the aforesd sum of tob unto JOHN MEARES or else execution &c.

Whereas it doth appeare by sufficient witnesse that ROBT: MARTIN hath purposely absented himselfe from appearing to answer the suit of NATHAN STAINESMORE the debt being proved to be due; It is therefore ordered that the aforesd MARTIN shall pay the said debt within the space of ten dayes after the date hereof unto the sd STAINESMORE or else execution &c.

Whereas WILLM: DURFORD of Eliza: River, Boaterite, is indebted unto ROBT: PAGE, Merchaunt, the sum of 1302 pounds of tob as by specialty appeareth; It is therefore ordered that the aforesd WILLM: DURFORD shall satisfy the sd sum within the space of ten dayes after the date hereof or else execution &c.

Whereas it doth appeare that WILLM: RAMSHEIR hath bought as many goods of ROBT: PAGE, Merchaunt, as do amount to the value of 1029 pounds of tob and being now found not able to satisffy the total this yeare; It is therefore ordered that the aforesd RAIMSHEIR shall within the space of ten dayes after the date hereof pay one hogshead of tob containing 300 weight unto the aforesd ROBT: PAGE or else execution to be awarded on the whole sum.

Whereas it doth appeare that WILLM: DURFORD is indebted unto

NATHAN STAINESMORE the sum of 1130 pounds of tob; It is therefore ordered that the aforesd WILLM: DURFORD shall, within the space of ten dayes after the date hereof satisffie the aforesd sum or else execution &c.

Whereas JOHN GOOGE (or Hooge?) of the Lower Norfolke, Planter, is indebted unto NATHAN STAINESMORE the sum of 549 pounds of tob as by specialty appeareth; It is therefore ordered that the aforesd JOHN GOOGE shall within the space of ten dayes after the date hereof satisffie the said sum or else execution &c.

Whereas DANIELL HOPKINGSON hath made it appeare p(er) account that THOMAS CODDE of Eliza: river, Planter, is indebted unto him, the sd DANIELL HOPKINGSON the sum of 1223 pounds of tob; It is therefore ordered that the aforesd THOMAS CODDE shall within the space of ten days after the date hereof satisffie the aforesd sum unless he can in the interim discount any part thereof.(end of f7a)

f 8

Whereas THOMAS MARSH hath made it appeare to this Court that JOHN GOOGE is indebted unto him the aforesd THOMAS MARSH the sum of 560 pounds of tob; It is therefore ordered that the aforesd JOHN GOOGE shall within the space of ten dayes after the date hereof satisffie the aforesd sum or else execution to be awarded. p 15

Whereas JOHN DRAITON (Drayton?) of Eliza: River, Cooper, is indebted unto WILLIAM ATTERBURY (Note: this name is indexed in the original Norfolk Co. books as A. Herbury), Merchaunt, the sum of 210 pounds of tob as p(er) specialty appeareth; It is therefore ordered that the aforesd JOHN DRAITON shall within the space of ten dayes after the date hereof satisffie the aforesd sum or else execution &c.

Whereas it doth appeare that THOMAS CODDE of Eliza: River, Planter, is indebted unto THOMAS MARSH the sum of 510 pounds of tob for commodities bought of the said THOMAS MARSH and not having satisffied the sd sum; It is therefore ordered that the sd THOMAS CODDE shall within the space of ten dayes after the date hereof satisffie the sd sum or else execution &c.

Whereas THOMAS CHEELY of Linnehaven, Planter, is indebted unto ROBT: FREEMAN, late deceased the sum of 367 weight of tob as by specialty appeareth; It is therefore ordered that the said THOMAS CHEELY shall pay the sd debt unto CAPT: WILLIAM BROCAS administrator of the sd FREEMANS estate within the space of ten dayes &c

Whereas it doth appeare that HENERY HAWKINGS of Eliza: River, Planter, hath transported THOMAS PAGE, servant unto ANTHONY LINES without the consent or knowledge of sd LINEY; It is therefore ordered that the said HENERY HAWKINGS shall, forthwith without delay fetch back the sd PAGE and deliver him to the aforesd LINEY or else suffer such punishment as shall be inflicted upon him.

Whereas it doth appeare that JOHN WILSON, Clarke, has received great loss and damage by not receiving his corne due the last yeare for tiths; It is therefore ordered that all such persons as the sd JOHN WILSON shall make appeare to have denied the payment thereof, shall pay unto the aforesd JOHN WILSON after the rate of 100 pounds of tob a barrel.

Whereas it doth appeare that JOHN CLARKE of Elizabeth River, planter stands indebted unto (JOHN?) MEARES, Merchaunt the sum of 72 pounds of tob which was due -(faded words)- last past but as yet unsatisfied it is therefore ordered that the sd JOHN CLARKE within the space of ten dayes after the date hereof satisffie the abovesd sume or else execution to be awarded.

Whereas it doth appeare that ROBT: MARTIN, planter, hath hired ffRANCIS LYNCH planter, to serve him, the foresaid MARTIN for the term of one year, but he, the foresaid ffRANCIS LYNCH being contrary to his covenant, gone away from the service of the said MARTIN shall detain in his custody, all such goods as appertain unto the said LYNCH until he shall either return or come to a further agreement.

Whereas GEOPHRY WITE of Linnhaven, planter, hath most falsly slandered CAPT. ADAM THOROWGOOD as per sufficient proof appeareth it is therefore ordered that the said GEOPHRY WITE shall receive forty lashes on the bare shoulders and likewise (ask?) his forgiveness here now in Court and the next Sabbath at Linnhaven. It is likewise ordered that whereas the said GEOPHRY did, in the time of his service, being hired by CAPT: THOROWGOOD to keep goats, beat and bruise the said goats after an excessive manner, that he the said GEOPHRY shall put in good security to pay 800 weight of tob unto the said CAPT: THOROWGOOD by the 12th of November next ensuing or else to serve him one complete year.

f 8a

p 16 SARAH JULIAN, aged 39 years or thereabouts, sworn and examined Sayeth: that, being at the house of WILLIAM RAINSHIER then dwelling at BLUNT POINT, she the said deponent saw the aforesd RAINSHEIR deliver a maid servant belonging to MR: PUSY, who had lived with the said RAINSHEIR about a fortnight, unto ROBERT FREEMAN, the said PUSIES (sic) assignee.

AT A COURT HOLDEN IN THE LOWER COUNTY OF NORFOLKE THE

8 APRIL 1639

PRESENT: CAPT: ADAM THOROUGHGOOD, ESQR:

CAPT: JOHN SIBSEY	MR: ffRANCIS MASON
MR: WILLIAM WINDHAM	MR: HENERY SEAWELL

Whereas JOHN GATER is indebted unto WILLIAM ATTERBURY the sum of 710 pounds of tob as by account appeareth, but it now appearing by sufficient proof that the said WILLIAM ATTERBURY did promise to accept of one hogshead of tobacco this year for payment made in part of the whole it is therefore ordered that the aforesaid WILLIAM ATTERBURY shall according to his promise accept of one hogshead of tob containing 360 pounds net, he the sd GATER putting in sufficient security for the payment of the remainder the next year.

Whereas WAMOUTH PHESY is indebted unto WILLIAM SHIPPE the sum of 200 pounds of tob, which tob is not yet paid it is therefore ordered that the said WAMOUTH PHESY shall within the space of ten days after the date hereof, pay the said sum or else execution to be awarded.

Court 4 Mar 1638/9 f 8a p 16

Whereas it doth appear that WAMOUTH PHESY hath sold unto HENERY COLEMAN as much corn as doth amount to the value of 250 pounds of tob which corn the said COLEMAN having transported to KEQUOTAN and the agent of the aforesaid COLEMAN now refusing to pay the tob it is therefore ordered that the aforesaid PHESY shall make stoppage of as much of the said COLEMAN's corn as shall satisfy the debt.

Whereas BARTHOLOMEW HOSKINGS planter bought of HENERY HAWKINS, ROBERT TAYLOR and WILLIAM RAINSHEIR a patent for 300 acres of land but the said patent being taken up (in) WILLIAM RAINSHEIRS name: It is therefore ordered that they the said three parties shall at the next Quarter Court held at James City, renew the aforesaid patent in all three names and assign it to the aforesaid BARTHOLOMEW HOSKINGS.

Whereas ANTHONY LINEY, millrite, is indebted to ROBERT JOHNS, merchant, the sum of fifteen pounds three shillings and a penny of lawful money of England as by specialty appeareth: It is therefore ordered that aforesaid ANTHONY LINEY shall by the tenth of May next ensuing satisfy the said sum or else execution to be awarded.

Whereas CATO GARISON mariner hath without occasion or cause wounded ROB CLAYTON mariner after a most desparate and dangerous manner, as by sufficient proof appeareth: It is therefore ordered that the aforesaid GARRISON shall forthwith put in sufficient security to pay, within ten days after the ship PELICAN's arrival in ENGLAND, ten pounds sterling unto JONATHAN LANGWORTH, chirurgeon, for the cure of the said wounds and damages by him received.

Whereas THOMAS DAVIS is indebted unto GEORGE PEWSEY, mariner deceased, the sum of 700 pounds of tob as by specialty appeareth, it is therefore (ordered) that the aforesaid THOMAS DAVIS shall put in sufficient security to pay the sum of 770 pounds of tobacco at the now dwelling house of CAPT: THOROWGOOD by the 10th of October next ensuing or else execution to be awarded.

f 9 p17

Whereas JOHN BARNET merchant is indebted unto ROBERT PAGE, WILLIAM WEBSTER and RICHARD WAKE the sum of 84 pounds and 16 shillings of lawful money of England, as by specialty appeareth, it being likewise proved by sufficient witnesses that the said JOHN BARNET is altogether careless and neglective in the receiving or seeking to receive any debt or debts due to him here in Virginia: It is therefore ordered that he shall authorize and appoint ROBERT PAGE, his heirs, executors or assigns, to receive all such parts or parcels of tob as are due to him, the aforesaid JOHN BARNET (or BURNET?) he being likewise to do his best endeavors in assisting the said ROBERT PAGE, provided always that the said ROBERT PAGE shall give a swift account of all such tobaccos he shall receive belonging unto the aforesaid BARNET - Further likewise it is ordered that in case the aforesaid ROBERT PAGE be not satisfied neither in tob or money by the last ship departing out of Virginia, that then he, the aforesaid ROBERT PAGE shall by virtue hereof make seizure of so much of the goods moveable and unmoveable of the aforesaid BURNET (sic) as shall satisfy the debt.

Whereas THOMAS SAWYER of Elizabeth River, planter, is indebted to CORNELIUS LOYD merchant, the sum of 1425 pounds of tob as by account appeareth, which tob being unpaid, the aforesaid CORNELIUS is like to sustain great loss and damage thereby: It is therefore ordered that the said THOMAS SAWYER shall within the space of six days after the date hereof, satisfy the aforesaid debt or else execution is to be awarded.

15 Jan 1638/9

MEMORANDA - that I CONSTANTINE WADDINGTON of Virginia Cooper, do hereby for myself, executors, administrators, attorneys and assigns utterly and absolutely acquit, exonerate, discharge and release CAPT: JNO: SIBSEY of Virginia, esqr: his heirs, executors, administrators and assigns from all manner of debts, duties, actual, real or personal suits, trespass, specialty, indenture, evidence and demand whatsoever from the beginning of the world until the day of the date hereof, but more especially and particularly of and from one certain writing or covenant in which the said CAPT: SIBSEY, by the act and deed of his attourney partner RICHARD WAKE of London, Marchant, is obliged to pay unto me the said CONSTANTINE WADDINGTON, ten pounds sterling yearly and successively for the term of three years and a half after my arrival in Virginia, as alsoe of and from the said debt itself of ten pounds sterling yearly according to the true intent & purpose hereof. In witness of which I the said CONSTANTINE WADDINGTON have hereunto set my hand and seal the day above written.

Witness: ANTH: LAWSON
XOP: BURROWES — Signed/ CONSTANTINE WADDINGTON
ROBERT WEST

f 9a
p 18 Whereas it appeareth to the Court that THOMAS HOULT was security for REYNOLDS FLEETE for ten pounds of Beaver (skins?) due unto JAMES; it is therefore ordered that the said THOMAS HOULT shall put in sufficient security or pay the said Beaver (skin) or so much tob as shall avail thereto after the weight of 30 per pound within the two days, and 90 pounds of tob to the said BOLTISWANE, and to pay the Sheriff -

Whereas it appeareth to the Court that HENRY WATTSONNE is indebted unto THOMAS BULLOCK, chirurgeon, the sum of 300 pounds of tob as by specialty appeareth; it is therefore ordered that the said HENRY WATSONNE shall pay the said sum of tob within twelve days or else execution to be awarded.

Whereas it appeareth to this Court that THOMAS HOULT hath carried THOMAS COOP (ER?) of ELIZABETH RIVER, carpenter for MARYLAND, he the said COOP(ER?) being much engaged in Virginia, It is therefore ordered that the said THOMAS HOULT shall procure the Governor of Virginia's letter to the Governor of Maryland for his present return.

Whereas it appeareth to this Court that WILLIAM DUFORD bought of RICHARD LEE certain work to be paid at all demands. It is therefore ordered that the said RICHARD LEE shall pay ten days work and 400 6 penny nails for all of the tobacco due to him the said WILLIAM DUFORD and charges for the loss of his time and also to bear part of the charges of the Court.

Whereas it appeareth to this Court that THOMAS TODD is indebted unto HENRY WATSONNE the sum of 300 l tob as by specialty appeareth, It is therefore ordered that the said TODD shall pay the said sum of tobacco, with cask, within ten days, of else execution.

Whereas it appeareth to this Court that ROBERT EARES is indebted unto THOMAS MARSH in the sum of 944 l tob as by specialty appeareth: It is therefore ordered that the said ROBERT EARES shall pay the said sum of tobacco within six days or else execution. f 10

Whereas it appeareth unto this Court that THOMAS MARSH is bound p 19
unto ROBERT EARES for the sum of 944 l tob due to CORNELIUS LOYD, the said THOMAS MARSH being to go for England and the said ROBERT EARES desiring to be released from the said debt; It is therefore ordered that the said ROBERT EARES shall bind over his cattle and goods for security to pay the said debt until he hath had a trial by Court. If the ROBT: EARES do cost the said CORNELIUS this bond to stand void, otherwise the said CORNELIUS shall possess as much of his goods as shall satisfy his debt.

Whereas it appeareth to this Court that JOHN YATES is indebted unto EUPHRANDITUS LAWSON the sum of 220 l tob as by account appeareth. It is therefore ordered that the said JOHN YATES shall pay the said sum of tobacco within ten dayes or else execution.

Whereas there was an order of Court granted at a Court held at Mr. HENRY SEAWELLS the 6 Feb that BARTHOLOMEW HOSKINS should stand to the loss of 150 l tob being the half or a hogshead lent to ROBERT EAIRES but taken into better consideration it is ordered that the aforesaid order shall be repealed and the said ROBERT EAIRES shall put in security to pay unto BARTHOLOMEW HOSKINS the 150 l tob next year.

AT A COURT HOLDEN AT LINNHAVEN IN LOWER COUNTY OF NORFOLKE
The 17th day of Jul 1639

PRESENT: CAPT: ADAM THORROWGOOD, ESQ:

CAPT. JOHN SIBSEY	MR: WILLIAM JULIAN
MR: EDWARD WINDHAM	MR: ffRANCIS MASON

Whereas at a Court holden by the Grand Council at Yorke the first of this present July there was ordered that there should be appointed fifteen sufficient men out of the Lower County of Norfolke to march against the Menticoke Indians, accordinge therefore to the said order, the Commander and Commissioners of this County have made choice of these men whose names are here mentioned to go the said March: f 10a

p 20

THOMAS RUDDER	GEORGE LOCKE	JOHN GATTER
HENRY MICHAELL	JOHN GILLAM	WILL: BERRY
GOWERING LANKESTER	ROBT: MASTERE	MARM: WARINGTON
MR: WEST	THO: LOVETT	JOHN GRAYGOSSE
ROBT: WARD	JAMES AT TO BROWNES	ROBT: SMITH

Every 20 persons beinge to provide 2 lbs of powder and 2 lbs of shot & 40 lbs of Bisquett and half a bushel of peas a man for them sent for the march.

Whereas it doth appear to this Court that HENRY CATLINGE did, about the 20th of Dec last seate upon the land of CORNELIUS LOYD, the said CORNELIUS giving the said CATLINGE warninge to the contrary, as by sufficient proof hath made appear the said CORNELIUS shall give satisfaction to the said CATLINGE for his work done upon the said land before the warning was given and then to enjoy his land.

Whereas there was a difference concerning a parcel of land between CORNELIUS LOYD and HENRY CATLINGE at the last Quarter Court held at Jamestown, the said CORNELIUS LOYD making it appear that the land was his, before the Governor and Council; It is therefore ordered as above mentioned, that, after satisfaction made, he shall enjoy the land.

Whereas it doth appear to this Court that ROBERT MARTIN doth owe unto ROBERT TAYLOR as by sufficient proof appeareth seven days work the said MARTINE denying to pay it; It is therefore ordered that the said MARTINE shall pay four days worke this weake and four next
f 11 weake.

p 25 WILLIAM LAYTON hath made it appeare to this Court that he hath land due to him for the transportation of the persons whose names are specified:GEORGE EARLE in the AMIRICAY (America) in 1637
CHRISTOPHER STOAXE in the SAFTIE in 1635
GEORGE WADE in the PRIMROSE in 1636
JOHN MOORE in the BLESSINGE in 1637
WILLIAM LAYTONNE in the HOPEWELL in 1627

AT A COURT HOLDEN AT MR. WILLM: JULIANS

the 18th of October 1639

PRESENT: CAPT: ADAM THORROWGOOD

CAPT: JOHN SIBSEY MR. HENRY SEAWELL
MR. WILLIAM JULIAN MR. ffRANCIS MASON

Whereas by an act of Court made by the Governor and Council at James City the 10th of this present October it is ordered the Commissioners of every county, with the consent of all the freemen, should choose Burdiges for their countie It is therefore thought fit by this Court as also with the consent of the freemen therein that MR: HENRY SEAWELL & MR: JOHN HILL shuld be Burdegesses for this countie. These are to certify that the Commissioners of the Lower Norfolk Countie have fownd by divers sufficient witnesses that ffRANCIS LAND could make no bargain whatsoever with COBB HOWELL without the consent of CAPT: ADAM THORROWGOOD. Further it is proved that the aforesaid FRANCIS LAND hath tooke an acquittance since the makinge of the artikells of agreement of the said COBB HOWELL without the consent of CAPT: ADAM THORROWGOOD. It is also further proved that the aforesaid ffRANCIS LAND was to make two hundred hogsheads, the one half for himself and the other half for COBB HOWELL - After all these aforesaid proofes the said ffRANCIS
f 11a LAND doth appeal to JamesTowne.

p 22 Whereas it doth appear to this Court that ffRANCIS LAND hath most falsely scandalized CAPT: ADAM THORROWGOOD as by sufficient witness appeareth; It is therefore ordered that the aforesaid ffRANCIS LAND shall, for the said offence ask the said CAPT: THORROWGOODS forgiveness here now in Court and on Sunday com sennight at the Parish Church in Linhaven.

Whereas there is a difference between JOHN DRAITON (Drayton or Layton?) and JOHN GATER concerning the sharing of certain casks belonging to the aforesaid DRAYTON. It is therefore ordered that the said Caskes shall be equally divided, the one half to the one party and the other half to the other party, the said DRAYTON allowing for the work of two men of the said TAYLORS being employed in getting of timber for 200 casks, as shall be thought fit by two sufficient men, the said GATER being to bring in the next Court an account of all the cask set up by the (said) DRAYTON the last year, 1638.

Whereas it doth appeare that there are divers and many damages done unto cattle in this Lower County of New Norfolke by the multitude of wolves which do frequent the woods and plantations, it is therefore ordered that what person whatsoever within the aforesaid county shall kill any wolf and bring in the head to any officer in the said County, the said person for every wolf so killed shall be paid by the Sheriff 50 pounds of tobacco.

The deposition of JOHN JOHNSON age 20 years examinds sayeth: That whereas LANCKES^r LEWETT (Lovett) bought of HENRY COLEMAN this deponent for the time he had to serve the said COLEMAN he the said COLEMAN selling the deponent unto LANCKES^r to serve until the 11th of January 1639. f 12

p 23

Deposition of RICHARD HORNER Age 44 years, examined sayeth: That HENRY COLEMAN sould unto LANCKES^r LEWETT (LOVETT) JOHN JOHNSONN servant for 800 lb tob and 20 barrels of corne but what time the said JOHNSONN had to serve the deponent knoweth not.

The deposition of COBB HOWELL aiged (sic) 32 years, examined sayeth that the said deponent heard ffRANCIS LAND say that he called CRISTOFER BURROUGHS to witness concerning the cattle but he would not go for fear of the said CAPT: THORROWGOODS displeasure.

p: mee RO: xxxxxxx

The Oath of the Sherriffe

You shall swear to serve his Matie truly in the office of Sherriffe to the best of your knowledge, not to exercise the same corruptly dureing the time you shall remain theirein neather shall accept, receave or take by any coulor, meanes pf device whatsoever, or consent to the takeing of any manner of Bribe, fee or reward of any person or persons for the impanelling, executeinge or returneing of any inquest, warrant, writt or any other precept whatsoever between party & party, above the vallue of such ffee or ffees as are appointed for the same, but you shall, according to your power truly and indifferantly serve and returne all such writts, warrants or other (process?) as shall be directed to you from the Governor or Council or any of them or any other his Majesty's Commissioners for this County, without favor or affection and any other pretense or evasion f 12 18 Oct 1639

as doth appertain to be done by your duty & office, during the time you shall remain therein, so helpe you God and the contents of the
f 12a Booke.
p 24 is blank

f 12^2 (This is the second folio 12 in the book numbered 27 at bottom of
p 25 page)

AT A COURT HOLDEN the 2nd DAY OF MARCH AT CAPT: JOHN SIBSEYS 1639/40
LOWER NORFOLK COUNTY

PRESENT: CAPT: THOS: WILLOUGHBIE, ESQ.

CAPT: JNO: SIBSEY	LEIFT: ffRANCIS MASON
MR: HENRY SEWELL	MR: WILLIAM JULIAN

It is ordered by this Court that whereupon CORNELIUS LLOYD did furnishe the inhabitants of this County with seven buffe Coates for NANTICOAKE MARCH, which said coates are now ordered to be served for the use of this said County that every person which was liable to set forth a man in that service shall pay his or their apporconable quantity of tobacco for the said coates and shall bringe or cause to bee brought to the house ~~of CAPT: JOHN SIBSEY~~ (scratched out in book) before the 10th of April next, the said coates being valued by this Court at 250 lbs of tobacco per coate.

It is ordered by this Court that whereas MR. STEPHEN COOPER is indebted unto MR: JNO: MEARE in the some of 15 pounds 10 shillings sterling as appeareth by his bill of Ex^c for the payment of the same and by another bill givinge order to his then assignee, MR: THOMAS MEARES, to pay unto the said MR: JNO: MEARES the quantity of 1560 lbs of tobacco in case of the none payment of the said sum of 15 pounds, 10 shillings sterling and whereas MR: JOHN GATHER, now atturney to the said STEPHEN COOPER and the said JOHN MEARES have referred themselvee to the order of this Court cond: the satisfying of the aforesaid debt. It is therefore agreed and concluded that the said JOHN GAITHER shall pay unto the said JOHN MEARES the aforesaid quantity of 1560 lbs of tobacco within one month next ensuing this order.

It is ordered by this Court that JOHN GATHER atturney to STEPHEN COOPER shall pay unto THOMAS MEARES 50 shillings after the burning of tobacco to bee payed in tobacco at 35 per lb which is for tobacco bought of MR: MEARES as per bill.

f 12a^2
p 26 It is ordered by this Court that JOHN GATHER atturney for STEPHEN COOPER shall pay to THOMAS SAYER twenty and five pownds of sugar which is owing by the said STEPHEN to MR: SAYER as by his bill appeareth.

It is ordered by this Court that MR: HENRIE CATLIN shall sattisfy and pay unto JOHN HATTON for one broad axe, one inch auger, 2 lbs of penny nayles, 150 six penny nayles and one new gimlett which were broken and spent about MR: CATLINS worke, etc.

It is ordered per Curis, that EDD SELBY shall pay to SERGEANT EDWARDS before the last of this month, 100 lbs of Virginia leafe tobacco and a pair of shooes and that the said SARGEANT EDWARDS shall pay & deliver to the aforesaid SELBY, one pair of drawers.

*It is ordered per Curia, that the goods of LAWRENCE PEETERS shall be stayed at his house until such time as he hath made satisfactcon for country duties and that he shall appear at the next Court holden for this county the 1 of April 1640.

The deposition of JOHN GILLIAM who sayeth that he heard MARRA MELLO say to MR: TOD that he would bet him as much timber as he could work off in a month but MR: TOD would not accept thereof and that afterwards he heardthe said MARRA MELLO say that when he had been about some business of his own, he would get MR: TOD some more timber but whether or not it was at the same time this deponent knoweth not.**
* to ** is very faint in the book and hard to transcribe. f 13

(NOTE: The second page number given is the one that appears at the bottom of the pages. It differs from the usual page number) p 27 p 28

Depositions of ROBT: BODIE,RICH: ffOSTER & ROBT: HARWOOD et sequiter

ROBT: BODIE sayeth that in 9ber last was two yeares BARTHOLOMEW HOSKINS did buy of ROBERT TAYLOR and HENRY HAWKINS 200 acres of land lyinge on the Eastern Branch of Elizabeth river for one cowe and two yearlings and gave six pence in earnest of the said bargain to one of the other parties but this deponent knoweth not to whither of them it was given.

RICHARD ffOSTER sayeth that his father BARTHOLOMEW HOSKINS did buy 200 acres of land of HENRY HAWKINS and ROBERT TAYLOR for one cowe with calfe and two yearlings about five weeks before Christmas was two yeares and that he gave sixpence in earnest of the said bargain to the said HENRY HAWKINS.

ROBTERT HARWOOD sayeth ut supra:

The last will and testament of JOHN GOUGE proved the 10 March 1639 before CAPT: THOMAS WILLOUGHTEY by the oaths of ROBERT POWES clerk and THOMAS TOD.

AT A COURT HOLDEN FOR LOWER NORFOLK COUNTY AT CAPT: JOHN SIBSEYS 17 of March 1639

PRESENT: CAPT: THOMAS WILLOUGHBY, ESQR:
CAPT JOHN SIBSEY MR. HENRY SEWELL
LIEUT: ffRANCIS MASON

It is ordered per Curia that the inhabitants of this County shall pay 23 lbs of tobacco per poll for the defrayinge of the Burgesses charges attending the Assembly held in 8ber last and att the Assembly held in January last, for the killinge of six wolves and the ferries.

AT A COURT HOLDEN AT MR: WILLIAM JULIANS the 30 March 1639/40

PRESENT: CAPT: THOMAS WILLOUGHBEY, ESQR:
CAPT. JOHN SIBSEY MR. HENRY SEWELL
LIEUT: ffRANCIS MASON MR: WILLIAM JULIAN

Whereas MR: THOMAS BULLOCKE hath made it appear unto this Court that there is 230 lbs of tobacco due him for physicke administered at severall times to a Negro servant of MR: ROBERT CARNE it is therefore ordered his agent, THOMAS KEELING shall satttisfy unto the said MR: THOMAS BULLOCKE the said quantity of 230 lb of tobacco.

Whereas RICHARD HORNER is indebted to LIEUTENANT ffRANCIS MASON 480 lbs tobacco as by his bill appeareth. It is therefore ordered by this Court that the said RICHARD HORNER shall satisfy the said debt within ten days next ensuing and also shall pay the charges of the Court, etc.

Whereas it appears that HENRY COLEMAN is indebted to CAPT: JOHN SIBSEY 200 lbs of tobacco (-illegible-) of cask it is therefore thought fitt and soe ordered that LANCASTER LOWETT shall sattisfy the said debt out of the tobacco of the said HENRY COLMAN within ten days after the date hereof and likewise the charges of the
f 14 Court.

p 29 Whereas it appeareth to this Court that RICHARD KENNER and THOMAS SMYTHE are indebted upto CAPT: JOHN SIBSEY 1750 lbs of tobacco It is therefore ordered that they shall pay the said debt within ten days after the date hereof and the charges of the Court.

It is ordered by this Court that THOMAS TUCKER shall pay unto RICHARD KEMPE and THOMAS SMYTH 1612 lbs of tobacco being two thirds of his debt due unto them according to the acte of Assembly 400 lbs tobacco being deducted out of the said 1612 for his labour and his servants the last winter.

Whereas it appeareth that SEVILL GASKIN is indebted unto THOMAS MARSHE 800 lbs of tobacco, which said GASKIN had covenanted with JOHN GOUGE deceased to become his servant for a certain tearme upon condition to pay all the said GASKINS debts and in case the said GOUGE die during the tearme agreed upon that then the said GASKIN should be free. Now, soe assuming as the said GOUGE hath not yet satisfied the debt nor left estate sufficient to pay it withall and the Court doth censure that the aforesaid contract was mearly fraudulent. It is therefore ordered that the said GASKIN shall pay his debts himselfe.

THOMAS MEARE age 38 years or Thereabouts deposed and Sayeth: that one MR: ffRANCIS being at this deponent's house, to take on a condition which was betweene SEVILL GASKIN and THOMAS MARSHE the said THOMAS MARSHE said unto MR: ffRANCIS I hope you will see mee sattisfied in tobacco, the said MR: ffRANCIS answered yes.

It is ordered by this Court that MR: ffRANCIS shall bee free from the debt which hee is now impleaded for, notwithstanding the aforesaid deposition in as much as it appeareth that he was noe ways interested in the estate of the aforesaid JOHN GOUGE.

f 14a

p 30 It is ordered by this Court that THOMAS TOD shall pay unto MARRA MELLO (this name could be WELLO or CELLO) 200 lbs tobacco over and besides his share of corne and tobacco due unto him for his last yeares work according to an agreement made between them, and also the charges of this Court.

It is ordered by this Court that JOHN GATHER shall satisfy and pay unto WILLIAM SHIPP out of the estate of JOHN DRAYTON deceased 479 lbs of tobacco which hee hath made appeare to bee due unto him for goods sold to the said DRAYTON.

It is thought fit and so ordered that HENRY RUTKINS shall pay the countrey duties which were due the last yeare for one HUMPHREY BEST who was then his servant.

Whereas it appeareth to this Court that JOHN DRAYTON, deceased was att the time of his death indebted unto MR: HENRY SEWELL 350 lbs of tobacco and cask for one case of strong water. It is therefore ordered that JOHN GATHER shall sattisfy and pay the said debt out of the deceadents estate.

Whereas it appeareth that THOMAS SAWYER did administer certain physick to the servants of JOHN DRAYTON deceased, amounting to the value of 200 lbs of tobacco. It is therefore ordered that JNO: GATHER shall sattisfy and pay the said quantity of 200 lbs tobacco out of the said DRAYTONS estate.

It is ordered by this Court that WILLM: CROUCH shall take an invoice of all the goods and debts of JOHN WHYTE deceased and shall likewise take the said goods and debts into his custody and with all convenient speed shall procure a letter of administration for his proceedings further therein. f 15

Whereas it appeareth that SIMON HANCOCKE hath formerly lent unto p 31 JOHN GATHER 17 hogsheads of Indian corne and that the said GATHER hath restored 7 hogsheads again of the said debt. It is therefore ordered by this Court that the said JOHN GATHER shall make payment of the remainder being ten hogsheads more of Indian Corne.

It is ordered by this Court that ROBT: GLASCOCKE shall pay and deliver before the last of Aprill one be ticke or else in lewe thereof one cowe calfe and one pair of shooes and the said JOHN GATHER shall pay and deliver to the saidROBT: GLASCOCKE before expiration of the afforesaid last of Aprill two yards of Holland and as much more as to make a band and alsoe two pounds of tobacco.

The wife of CAPT: JOHN SIBSEY informeth upon oath and sayeth that she formerly delivered unto MARY SOAMES, her then servant, three gould rings to keepe and demanding them agayne about two months after of the said MARY she denyed that she had any rings of her mistress, but the said MARY loo inge in divers places in the house she found one of the said 3 ringes and delivered to this informer and that sithence the said MARY beinge gone to live in another place, CHRISTOPHER BURROWES brought a gould ringe to this informer which the said BURROWES tould her he received from the said MARY and this informer further sayeth that the ringe which BURROWES brought unto her is one of those three ringes which shee formerly had delivered to the said MARY SOAMES and further informeth not.

The deposition of SEVILL GASKINS, age 24 years or thereabouts sayeth: That MARY SOAMES tould him this deponent that this ring for which she is now questioned was given her by one WILLIAM GOULD a seaman and further deponent sayeth not.

f 15a
p 32 MARIE (sic) SOAMES examined sayeth: That shee had this ringe now in question of JOHN DRAYTON deceased but denyeth that this is MRIS: SIBSEYS ringe or that shee hath any ringe of ringes of hers and further sayeth not.

Whereas THOMAS IVEY havinge bought a parcel of land from MR: WILLIAM JULIAN and now desyreth to have the same assured and confirmed unto him It is therefore thought fitt and soe ordered that the said MR: JULIAN shall (give) him an assurance of the said land according to their agreement provided that said MR: IVEY doe give MR: JULIAN due and ample satisfactcon for the same according to the said agreement.

MR: THOMAS IVEY aged 36 years or thereabouts Deposed Sayeth: that he bought a hog from MR: WILLIAM JULIAN which this deponents wief was to pay for in worke otherwise in case of non payment accordingly then this deponent was to pay to the said MR: JULIAN 140 lbs of tobacco for the said hog and further sayeth not.

It is therefore ordered by this Courte that MR THOMAS IVEY shall pay unto MR: WILLM: JULIAN 140 lbs of tobacco for one hog bought of and for butter milke and makinge fower shirts and smocks to some of eleven shillings, ten pence.

It is ordered by this Court that ROBERT GLASCOCK shall pay unto MR: JNO: MEARE the some of two pounds and ten shillings sterling for one case of stronge liquors and that the said MR: MEARE shall pay and deliver unto the said GLASCOCK one petticoate and one wast coate which shall be really worth twenty shillings starling in England which order is to bee performed on both the within one moneth after the date hereof.

f 16
p 33 It is ordered by this Courte that CORNELIUS LLOYD shall sattisfy and pay unto GILBERT GUY Under Sheriffe of this County of Lower Northfolke all such ffees as are due unto him for the serving of an attachment of twenty pounds starling upon MR: ROBERT PAGE for monyes pretended to bee in the hands of MR: JOHN ALLEN.

Sergeant WILLM: EDWARDS aged 36 years or thereabouts sworn and examined sayeth that there came a man from Linnhaven to the house of CAPT: JOHN SIBSEY about 9ber last past and demanded of the said CAPT: SIBSEY whether hee would parte from a servant of his beinge a Portingall called by the name of TAWNEY, whereupon the said CAPT: SIBSEY tould him that his said servant had a yeare longer to serve him whereunto the said TAWNEY being then present said that hee came into the country for fower yeares but MR: PAGE who brought him in tould him that he should bee but three yeares and further this deponent sayeth not.

vera copia EDWARD ffLETCHER
Cleric Cur.

25 May 1640 f 16

AT A COURT HOLDEN AT WM: SHIPPS the 25th DAY OF MAY 1640

PRESENT: CAPT: THOS: WILLOUGHBIE, ESQ^r^:
CAPT: JOHN SIBSEY LIEUT: ffFRANCIS MASON
MR: HENRIE SEWELL MR: WM: JULIAN

Whereas it appeareth to this Court that JACOB BRADSHAWE hath made up in rould 1200 lbs of tobacco for ENSIGNE THOMAS KEELINGE which said tobacco upon beinge found unmarketable was consumed and burned according to the acte of the last Assembly in respect whereof the said KEELINGE denyeth paymt: to the said JACOB BRADSHAWE 20 pownds of merchantable tobacco in every hundred soe by him made up or else five shillings in mony within ten dayes next ensueing and the charges in the suite or else execution to be awarded.

f 16a p 34

JACOB BRADSHAWE aged 29 yeares or thereabouts sworn and eaxamined Sayeth: that he the said deponent went to CAPT. JOHN SIBSEYS about 9ber last past to buy the tyme out which one TAWNEY, a Portingall, had then to serve the said CAPT: and demandinge of CAPT. SIBSEY how longe the said TAWNEY had to serve him, he told this deponent that the said TAWNEY had a yeare and as much as until March next to serve him whereupon this deponent would not meddle with him but TAWNEY said that though hee came into the country for fower yeares yet MR. PAGE promised him that in respect hee had coasted up and downe for him that he should bee servant but for three yeares and further sayeth not.

HENERY CATLIN recognovit se debere serenissimo duo regi Ct sub lac conditur: that hee shall personally appeare before the Governor and Councell att the next Quarter Court houlden at James Citty the 4th of June and (respond) for shippinge of tobacco contrary to the actof the last Assembly.

HENRY HAWKINS recognovit se debere deo duo regi C sat ead conditur

Whereas it appeareth to this Court that SERGEANT EDWARDS sould a servant which he had no power to dispose of to ffRANCIS LAND and whereas the said LAND did passe his bill to the said EDWARDS for payment of a certaine parcel of tobacco in satisfaccon of the said servant: It is therefore ordered by the consent of both parties that the sale of the said servant shall bee disannulled and that the said EDWARDS shall deliver the aforesaid bill to the said LAND and shall pay the charges of the Court.

It is ordered by this Court that JOHN RADFORD shall make as assurance of 150 acres of land to GIDEON TILLISSON lyinge on the Westerne Branch of Elizabeth River.

f 17 p 35 at bottom of page 32

It is ordered by this Court that TIMOTHIE IVEY shall pay the charges of the Court for a suit arbitrated betwixt him and MATHEW PHILLIPPS.

Whereas it appeareth to this Court that HENERY HAWKINS hath imployed GILBERT GUY under sheriffe of this County to execute a subpoena and five warrants on several persons the due ffees whereof amount to 140 lbs of tobacco: It is therefore ordered that the aforesaid HENERY HAWKINS shall forthwith satisfy the said 140 lbs of tobacco to the said GUILBERT GUY.

Whereas it appeareth to this Courte that JOHN DRAYTON deceased was indebted to WILLM: CROWCH in 200 lbs of tobacco it is therefore ordered that MR: JOHN GAITHER being administrator of the said DRAYTON of late shall satisfy and pay the said debt within ten dayes after the date hereof.

Whereas the inhabitants of this Parish being this day covenanted for the providinge of themselves an able minister to instruct them concerning their souls health MR: THOMAS HARRISON clerk hath tendered his services to God and the said Inhabitants in that behalfe which his said tender is well liked of, with the general approbation of the said inhabitante, the parishioners of the parish church at MR: SEWELLS POINTE who to testifie their zeale and willingness to promote Gods service doe hereby promise and the Court now sitting doth likewise order and establish the same to pay one hundred pounds sterling yearly to the said HARRISON so longe as he shall continue a minister to the said Parish in recompense of his paines and in full satisfaccon of his rites within his limitts which is to bee paid unto him is forthwith: CAPT: JOHN SIBSEY, LEIFT: ffRANCIS MASON, MR. HENERY SEWELL are to pay for themselves and the inhabitants of this parish from CAPT: WILLOUGHBIES plantation to DANIEL TANNERS Creek 32 pounds 10 shillings sterling: MR. CORNELIUS LLOYD, MR: HENERY CATLIN & JOHN HILL are to pay for the inhabitants of the Western Branch and Craney Point 33 pounds sterling: MR: WILLIAM JULIAN, MR: JOHN GAITHER, ENSIGN THOMAS LAMBERT, THOMAS SAWYER, THOMAS MEARE and JOHN WATKINS are to pay 36 pounds
f 17a sterling for the inhabitants from DANIEL TANNERS Creek and over all
p 36 the eastward and southward branches. In witness whereof we the said undertakers have hereunto subscribed our hands:

ENSIGN THO: LAMBERT	CORNELIUS LLOYD
JOHN GAITHER	HENRY CATLIN
JOHN WATKINS	JOHN HILL
WILLIAM JULIAN	JOHN SIBSEY
THOMAS SAWYER	ffRANCIS MASON
THOMAS MEARE	HENRY SEWELL

Whereas there is a difference among the inhabitants of the aforesaid Parish concerning the employing of a minister being now entertained to live among them the inhabitants from DANIEL TANNERS Creek & upwards, the three branches of Elizabeth River in respects they are the greatest number of tithable persons not thinking it fitt or equal that they should pay the greatest part of the 100 pounds which is by the aforesaid order allotted for the ministers annual stipend unless the said minister shall teache and instruct them as often as he shall teache att the Parish Church situated at MR: SEWELLS Point: It is therefore arranged among the said inhabitants that the said minister shall teache every other Sunday amongst the inhabitants of Elizabeth River at the house of ROBT: GLASCOCKE until a convenient Church be built and erected there for Gods service which is agreed to be finished at the charge of the inhabitants of Elizabeth River before the 1st day of May next ensueing.

Whereas it was formerly ordered that MR. JOHN GATHER should pay unto MR. JOHN MEARES 1560 lbs of tobacco & cask, in satisfaccon of a bill of 15 pounds 10 shillings sterling due from MR. STEPHEN COWPER as by the said order doth appeareth which the said MR. GATHER has accordingly performed but the said MR. MEARES nevertheless sent directions to England to secure more satisfaccon of and from the said STEPHEN COWPER for the said debt contendint that he received the said tobacco in part payment. Now the*Court farther explaining the said order have hereby ordered that MR. JOHN MEARE shall give the said MR. GATHER a full discharge for the said debt and shall likewise enter into 40 pounds bond to free the said STEPHEN COWPER and JOHN GATHER from all further trouble, charges and incumbrances which may arise to either of them for and by reason of the said debt, etc. *f18 p37

Whereas there is a difference between CAPT. JOHN SIBSEY and one TAWNEY, a Portingall, which the said CAPTAIN Alledgeth that the said TAWNEY hath yet to serve him, the said TAWNEY pleading that his service was expired in March last but cannot prove the same to this Court: It is therefore ordered that the said TAWNEY shall serve the said Captain as formerly until Candlemas next unless he can in the interim provide an evidence that he was to serve him but three years, which, if he can do the said CAPT. SIBSEY shall then give his full satisfaccon in tobacco and corne for one years service etc.

Whereas it appeareth to this Court that EADY HANKINGS hath served ROBT. GLASCOCKE for the space of five moneths which service shee hath not received satisfaccon for. It is therefore ordered that the said ROBERT GLASCOCKE shall pay unto the said EADY HANKINGS 150 lbs of regular tobacco and the charges of the Court, etc.

Whereas it appeareth to this Court that MARRA MELLO hath uttered divers scandalous speeches against AGNES the wife of JOHN HOLMES tending to her great defamation thereby, both depriving her of and depraving her former honor and good report which, because he cannot prove; It is ordered that he shall the next Sunday upon his knees at the Parish Church at MR: SEWELLS POINT confess that he hath done her wrong and openly ask God and her forgiveness.

WILLIAM DEARFORD aged 32 yeares or thereabouts, sworn & examined, sayeth that he came on Friday last with ROBERT BODIE, said to be under sheriffe of this county to MR. THOS. TODS house where he the said under sheriffe demanded 170 lbs *of tobacco for county duties and demanded 120 lbs of tobacco more but for what this depontnt knoweth not. But the said TOD answered that whatsoever the Court ordered him to pay on Monday next he would pay otherwise hee would not. Soe goind down to MR.TODS landing place the said sheriffe distrayned upon a boate for the county duties but this deponent knoweth not whether the intent of his distress was for the other demand of 120 lbs of tobacco and thereupon the said under sherriffe appointed him, this deponent, and SIMON HANCOCKE to appraise the said boate which they valued at 40 lbs of tobacco. Then MR. TOD *f18a p38

18a p 38 25 May 1640

bade the undersheriffe lett the boat alone and come up and receive his tobacco whereto the said sheriffe answered that hee has no stilyards but hee required the said MR: TOD that the boates should be forthcoming & he would go fetch stilyards but the said MR: TOD refused. "It may bee I will and may bee I will not" and therefore the said under sheriffe rowed the said boat away and as he departed bade MR: TOD bring his tobacco and he shall have his boate again and further this deponent sayeth not.

ATT A COURT HOLDEN ATT
WILLM: SHIPPS
the 6th of July 1640

PRESENT: CAPT: THOS: WILLOUGHBY, ESQR:

CAPT: JOHN SIBSEY MR: ffRANCIS MASON
MR: HENRY SEWELL MR: EDWARD WINDHAM
MR: WILLIAM JULIAN

Whereas it appeareth to this Court that THOMAS HAYES is indebted unto MR: OLIVER VANKECKE to six dayes work. It is therefore ordered that the said shall forthwith pay three dayes to the said VANKECKE and three dayes more in August next and the charges of the Court.

Whereas it appeareth to this Court that PARSON WILLSON was indebted in his lifetime to WILLIAM SHIPP seven barrels of corne which the said SHIPP did turn over to SAVILL GASKINE it is therefore ordered that the said GASKINE shall collect the said corne of all such persons as owe any tithes to the said PARSONNE WILLSON excepting MR: MEERES and MR: SAWER who have paid their tithes to MR: POWES Clerke for the last yeare.

f 19
p 39
bottm
of p
34

Whereas it appeares to this Court that ffRANCIS LAND hath confessed that he undertook to pay unto MR: THOMAS BULLOCK one barrel and a half of Indian corne which was debt due from one NICHOLAS WRITE. It is therefore ordered that the said ffRANCIS LAND shall pay the said barrel and a half of corne unto MR: THOMAS BULLOCK otherwise execution to be awarded 15 Jul 1640.

Whereas it appeareth to this Court that OLIVER VANKECKE hath paid for the use of THOMAS ALLEN 528 lb tobacco. It is therefore ordered that he shall proceede for the recoverie of the said debt by virtue of an execution granted him the 22 Apr 1640 at James Cittie upon the estate of THOMAS CAUSON who is indebted to the said ALLEN 500 lb tobacco by reason of marryinge the widdow LAYTON whose husband in his lifetime was indebted so much to the said ALLEN and also to pay charges of the Court otherwise execution.

Whereas it appeareth to this Court that EADY HANKINGE hath spoken divers reproachfull words against the wife of MATTHEW HOWARD which she cannot prove. It is therefore ordered that EADY HANKINGE shall ask the said HOWARD'S wife openly forgiveness bouth at the house of MR: WILLM: JULIAN on Friday next and also at the Parish Church the Sunday followinge and defray the charges of the Court.

Whereas it appeareth to this Court that TRISTRAM MASSON hath caused to summon ROBT: TAYLOR to have his affairs and to appear at this Court. It is therefore ordered that the said MASSON shall pay the said ROBT: TAYLOR for one days worke and his charges for his diett the said day and likewise the charges of the suite.

It is ordered per curiam that MR: JOHN RADFORD shall pay unto GIDEON TILLISONNE 300 weight of tobacco which is for his charges att Jamestowne Court and at this Court.

CHURCHWARDENS APPOINTED FOR THIS PARISH

LEIFTENT ffRANCIS MASSONE
MR: THOMAS MEERES CHRUCH WARDENS

MR: SAWER, sworne SHERIFFE
HENRY HAWKINS sworne CONSTABLE
ELIZABETH RIVER PISH

The deposition of WALTER HIGHWAYE age 20 yeares deposed sayeth that his master MR: JOHN MEARES sent him this deponent with 8 hogsheads of tobacco aboard MR: COALE'S shipp upon Whittsunn Monday last but comminge to the shipp MR: COALE was not aboard and his tob would not be received but the servants on the shipp sent the deponent to MR: CHANDLERS at Newporte Newes where MR: COALE was. Soe this deponent went thither where meetinge with MR: COALE and tellinge him whence he came MR: COALE askt him how many hogsheads he had brought. This deponent answered 8. MR: COALE told him that he promised him fraite but for four hogsheads and further said that he knew not how to dispose of the said hogsheads but bade this deponent put the tobacco ashore at MR: CHANDLERS howse where it now lieth & further sayeth not. f 19a p 40

MR: THOMAS MEARESage 38 years deposed sayeth that MR: JOHN MEARES and MR: JOHN COALE being at this deponents howse about May last this deponent asked the said JOHN MEARES if he had shipped any tobacco with MR: COALE who told him yes he had shipped two tunnes per six pounds per ton and wished the deponent to aske the said JOHN MEARES before MR: COALE whether he had undertaken to carrie so much tobacco for the said JOHN MEARES at such a rate, if so he might have wittnesses of the bargaine but MR: COALE made no answere to their conference and further sayeth not.

Whereas it appeareth to this Court that MR: COALE hath undertaken to fraite home one ton of tobacco for MR: JOHN MEARES which he hath not performed and whereas the said MR: JOHN MEARES hath made it appear that he hath been at 35 shillings charges about the followinge of the said businesse besides by the said COALES appoyntment 2 hogsheads of tobacco which the said MEARES pretendeth he should have shipped by condition with the said COALE and by layinge his tobacco at MR: CHANDLERS howse which is at Newport Newes being very remote from the said MEARES plantacon. It is therefore ordered that the said MR: JOHN COALE shall satisfie and pay 5 pounds to the said JOHN MEARES to be paid in tobacco regulated at 3 pence per pound in consideration of his damages and for want of fraite.

f 20 p 41 botm of p 35 6 July 1640

Whereas it appeareth to this Court that SAVELL GASKIN standeth indebted unto THOMAS HOULT in 120 lb tobacco which debt the said HOULT hath turned over to LANCKESTER LOWETT (Lovett). It is therefore ordered that the said GASKIN shall within this fortnight give securitie to the said LANCKESTER LOWETT for the payment of the said debt at the next Court and the charges of the Court accordinge to acts of Assembly.

It is ordered by this Court that MR: JOHN GATHER shall give to his late servant CHRISTOFER BURSTEN one barrel of eares, one sute of apparell, one shirt, one pare of shooes and one pair of stockins, etc.

The deposition of THOMAS BULLOCK age 28 yeares examined and sworn sayeth that EDWARD LILLIE being at the howse of the said BULLOCK being in discourse with him about MR: HAYES and concerninge the Church EDWARD LILLIE said that MR: HAYES did raile upon this deponent and M[r]: BOURROWGHS and MR: WM: DAVIS and said they weare a company of Jacknapesses and had nothinge but a littell chimney corner law amongst them and that MR: HAYES did pussuade them to do their worke slightly and an easier way.

JACOB BRADSHAW age 25 yeares deposeth sayeth that EDWARD LILLIE beinge at MR: HAYES Howse the said HAYES asked him why he did not gett forwarder the church worke. The said LILLIE answered that he could not go forward for want of nayles and other iron worke. The said HAYES furnished him presently with nayles and bid him hire CHRISTOFER the joiner to helpe for a month and also said HAYES told the said Lillie that he would come also and helpe him work a fortnight and by that time they shuld have done and finished the worke and further sayeth nott.

f 20a p 42 SIMON PEETER age 28 yeares deposed sayeth that he hard EADY HANKINGE say that MATTHEW HAYWARDS wife did live as brave a life as any woeman in Virginia for she could lie abed every morninge till her husband went a milkinge and came back againe and washe the dishes and skimmed the milk and then MR: EDWARD ffLOIDE would come in and say "Come neighboure will you walke" and soe they went abroad and left the children cryinge. That her husband was faine to come home and leave his worke to quiett the children - further sayeth nott.

PETER RIGLESWORTH declareth the same upon oath

ROBT: BODY age 23 yeares examined sayeth that BARTHOLOMEW HOSKINS received of THOMAS TODD the last cropp the some of 1000 lb of tobacco but concerninge the bill of ROBT: DAVIS to MR: HOSKINE he knoweth not what the some of it was and further sayeth not.

ATT A COURT HOLDEN AT THE HOUSE OF
WILLM: SHIPP upon the
3 August 1640

PRESENT: CAPT: THOMAS WILLOUGHBY, ESQR:

CAPT: JOHN SIBSEY	MR: EDWARD WINDHAM
MR: HENRY SEWELL	MR: WILLIAM JULIAN

3 Aug 1640 f 21 p 43 botm p 36

Whereas it appeareth to this Court that WILLIAM NASH is indebted to SIMOND HANCOCK in 2000 six penny nailes as by acknowledgement appeareth. It is therefore ordered that MR: SAWER shall upon Satterday next make payment of 1000 thereof and upon the Satterday following make payment of 500 more he the said MR: SAWER beinge indebted unto WILLIAM NASH the just sum of 1500 six penny nayles and that the said WILLIAM NASH shall make present payment of the remainder being 500 six penny nailes otherwise execution to be awarded.

Whereas it appeareth to this Court that RICHARD ffloide is indebted unto JOHN DIER the some of 200 lb tobacco as by acknowledgment appeareth. It is therefore ordered that after MR: EDWARD WINDHAM hath had a sufficient view of the tobacco of RICHARD ffLOIDE and findinge it to be marchantable that then the said JOHN DIER shall upon the tenderinge of the some of 200 lb of tobacco receive the faire debt but if not marchantable then the said ffLOIDE shall make payment the ensuing cropp accordinge to the acts of Assembly otherwise execution.

Whereas it appeareth to this Court that MR: BARTHOLOMEW HASKINE hath received and markt three hogsheads of tobacco of LAWRENCE PEETERS for coyntry levies it is therefore ordered that the said BARTHOLOMEW HOSKINE shall give a just account to the said LAWRENCE PEETERS of the aforesaid tobacco and if there shall anything remain due to the said LAWRENCE PEETERS that then the said BARTHOLOMEW HOSKINS (sic) shall make satisfaction thereof but if there shall contrarily any some or somes of tobacco be wantinge to satisfie the country levy then the said LAWRENCE PEETERS shall make present payment thereof and also the charges of the Court otherwise execution.

f 21a p 44

CHURCH WARDENS FOR THE PARISH OF LINHAVEN

MR: THOMAS TODD
JOHN STRATTON

the names of those who are chosen for the VESTRIE of the aforesaid Parish.

MR: EDWARD WINDHAM	MR: THOMAS BULLOCK
MR: HENRY WOODHOWSE	MR: THO: CAUSSONNE
MR: BARTHOLOMEW HOSKINS	MR: THOMAS KEELINGE
MR: THOMAS TODD	MR: ROBT: HAYES
MR: CHRISTOPHER BURROWES	MR: JOHN LANCKFEILD

It is ordered per Curiam that all such persons as have not according to the agreement of this Vestry brought in unto the places appointed three pecks of corne per poll shall now accordingly bring in the aforesaid quantity of corne unto the appointed places otherwise execution.

Whereas it appeareth to this Court that MR: JOHN MEARE hath bought of LIEUTENANT ffRANCIS MASSON the quantity of four barrels of corne at the price of 50 shillings sterling the said corne being a due debt from MR: GAYTER. It is therefore ordered that according to his proffer in court that the said JOHN GATHER shall discharge MR: JOHN MEARE of the payment of the said 50 shillings due unto LIEFTENANT ffRANCIS MASSON he paying unto LEIFTENANT MASSON the said debt with the charges of the Court otherwise execution.

Whereas it appeareth to this Court that THOS: TODD doth stand indebted unto JOHN HILL the sum of 432 lb tobacco as upon oath appeareth. It is therefore ordered that the said THOMAS TODD shall within six days make payment of the said debt with the charges of the court otherwise execution.

f 22 It is ordered per Curiam that if MR: CAUSSONNE shall not against
p 45 the next monthly court make appeare by two deposicons that suffi-
botm. cient payment hath made by him unto CAPT: ADAM THORROWGOOD of the
p 37 some of 40 shillings sterling that then the said THOMAS CAUSSONNE shall make present payment of the same otherwise execution.

ANNE KEELING age 22 yeares or thereabouts sworn & examined sayeth that being at MRS: THORROWGOODS house THOMAS CAUSON and ELIZABETH his wife came thither and MRS: THORROWGOOD fallinge into discourse with her concerninge a bill of ADAM BOWSERS and divers other things which this deponent doth not well remember at present she this deponent heard the said CAUSONS wife tell MRS: THORROWGOOD shee knew none that could ever gett any bills out of CAPT: THORROWGOODS hands to whom MRS: THORROWGOOD replied. "Why GOODY LAYTON could you never gett yours which shee answered Yes" Then MRS: THORROWGOOD bade her bring any other that could not at which the said CAUSONS wife turned her about in a scornfull maner and cried pish. Then said MRS: THORROWGOOD,"GOODY LAYTON you must think to put off with a pish for if you have wronged him you must answer for it for though he be dead I am heere in his behalfe to right him and further this deponent sayeth not."

DOROTHY MOY (or May) age 26 years or thereabouts sworn & examined sayeth that being at MRS: THORROWGOODS, MR: THOMAS CAUSON and his wife came thither and that MRS: THORROWGOOD and she fell into discourse concerning a bill of ADAM BOWSERS and many other things which this deponent hath now forgotten. She this deponent heard the said wife of THOMAS CAUSON tell MRS. THORROWGOOD that she knew none that could ever gett any bills out of CAPT: THORROWGOODS hands & further deponent sayeth not.

ROBERT BODY age 23 years or thereabouts sworn & examined sayeth that after he had arrested ELIZABETH CAUSON she wished that she were able to come to the court for if she weare she would make MRS: THORROWGOOD ashamed and also wished for one of her horses to carrie her and further this deponent sayeth not.

f 22a
p 46 Whereas it appeareth to this court that divers scandals hath binne raysed upon CAPT: ADAM THORROWGOOD deceased by the wife of THOMAS CAWSON as by two depositions positively appeareth. It is therefore ordered that the said wife of THOMAS CAWSON shall ask

the wife ofthe said CAPT: THORROWGOOD forgiveness on her kneese for the same before the congregacon heere present and also at the Parish Church of Linhaven on the next Sunday after the first lesson in Morning prayer.

It is ordered per Curiam that WILLIAM BURROUGH shall accordinge to condition kill for THOMAS CAUSON so many deere as there are weekes betweene this present date and Christmas killinge every weeke one deer and one turkey always provided that the said THOMAS CAUSON shall find him sufficient powder and shott likewise to allow him the said WILLIAM BURROUGH meate and drinke according as they provide for themselves at their own table.

Whereas it appeareth to this court by the oath of ffRANCIS LAND that MR: XPOFER BURROUGH hath transported three servants into the colony whose names are hereunder menchoned: JOHNATHAN EXTECKETER JAMES CAULDER, THOMAS HALL.

Whereas it appeareth to this court by acknowledgement that CHRISTOFER COOKE hath freely given unto GEORGE MEE two barrels of Indian Corne which said corne ELIZABETH CASSONN hath before the board promised to satisfy unto the said GEORGE MEA: It is therefore ordered the said ELIZABETH CASSONN shall within six days satisfy or pay the said two barrels of corne unto GEORGE MEA otherwise execution and also the charges of the court.

It is further ordered that the said ELIZABETH CAUSSONN shall this ensuing crop pay unto the aforesaid GEORGE MEA fower barrells of the like corne for damages done in his field of corne by the hoggs of the said ELIZABETH CASSONN and also the charges of the court otherwise execution. f 23

Whereas it appeareth to this court that there was a condition p 47
made between CONSTANTINE WADINGTON and WILLIAM LAYTON in his life- botm
time as followeth: That the said CONSTANTINE was to make caske for p 38
the said WILLIAM LAITON (sic) for the halfe thereof the said WILLM: beinge to find timber and gett it. Now the said CONSTANTINE hath made 208 caskes whereof he never receaved any account for any more than 80 caskes.

It is therefore ordered that the said wife of WILLIAM LAYTON shall satisfy the said CONSTANTINE for the remainder of the said casks beinge six tunne according as caske were sould the last year and if in case the said ELIZABETH **shall make it appear** that shee hath made no use of the six tunne of cask or any of them that then the said CONSTANTINE is to repaire **the said six tunnes of casks.**

It is further ordered that the said ELIZABETH LAYTON shall deliver unto CONSTANTINE WADINGTON his own two sowes with three sowes more of a twelve months ould apiece within six days after the date hereof and if in case the said sowes or any of them shall pigg before the delivery thereof that then likewise the sowes with their increase shall be delivered unto the said CONSTANTINE WADINGTON otherwise execution.

f 23 p 47 botm p 38 8 Sep 1640

AT A COURT
Holden for the Lower Norfolk at the house of CAPT: JNO: SIBSEY
8 September 1640

Whereas it appeareth to this court that JOHN RADFORD hath raysed divers scandals upon JOHN HILL to his greate disparagement. It is therefore ordered that the said JOHN RADFORD shall upon the next Sunday aske public forgiveness of the said JOHN HILL for the same at the parish Church at Seawells Point before the whole congregacon then present after the first lessone in morning prayer.

PRESENT: CAPT: THOS: WILLOUGHBY, ESQ:

CAPT: JOHN SIBSEY LEIFT: ffRANCIS MASSON)
MR: WILLIAM JULIAN MR: HENRY SEAWELL)- 8 Sep 1640

f 23a Whereas it appears to this court that GIDEAN TILLISSONNE hath
p 48 bought of JOHN RADFORD 150 acres of land out of a patent for 200 acres granted by SIR JOHN HARVEY upon 6th of May Anno Domini 1638 as by a deposition appeareth and by his own word is proved the said RADFORD saying that he shewed the said GIDEON a patent out of which he should have his land beinge at the time that the said RADFORD made sale of his land unto the said GIDEAN which appeareth to be the patent above menchoned the said RADFORD having no other patent at that time for land due to himselfe. It is therefore ordered that the said RADFORD shall first make a choice of 50 acres of land which will be surplus in the aforesaid patent and then make a firme assignment of the remainder unto the said GIDIAN (sic) TILLISON and to pay him, the said GIDEAN 3 pounds sterling for charges and damages besides to pay for one warrant and four subpoenies with the servinge of them accordinge to Acts of Assembly otherwise Execucon

Whereas it appeareth to this court that GIDEAN TILLISSON hath lost one cloake of JOHN RADFORDS as by acknowledgmt appeareth. It is therefore ordered that the said RADFORD shall abate 200 lb tobacco out of the damages which the said RADFORD is to pay unto the said GIDEAN and that the said GIDEAN shall pay unto the said JOHN RADFORD 15 shillings for the use of his man and his boate otherwise execution.

Whereas it appeareth to this Court that RICHARD OWINE is indebted unto JOHN WRIGHT the some of 80 lb of tobacco as by acknowledgment appeareth. It is therefore ordered that the aforesaid some of tobacco shall be satisfied in stripped and smoothed tobacco this present cropp with the charges of the court otherwise execution.

Whereas it appeareth to this court that JOHN BROWNE was arrested at the suite of GEORGE LOCK (or Cock) the said LOCK not appearing It is therefore ordered that the said LOCK shall be nonsuited and shall pay unto JOHN BROWNE 10 shillings for damages and also with the charges of the court otherwise execution.

f 24
p 49 Whereas it appeareth to this court that JOHN SPENCER was sub-
botm poenaed at the suite of XPOFER BURROWS the said CRISTOFER not
p 39 appearing. It is therefore ordered that the said XPOFER shall be non-suited and to paye 15 shillings to the said SPENCER for damages

and also the charges of the court otherwise execution.

Whereas it appeareth to this court that ROBT: HAYES was arrested at the sute of THOMAS BULLOCK he the said BULLOCK not appearinge It is therefore ordered that the (sic) THO: BULLOCK shall pay unto the said ROBT: HAYES 15 shillings for debt and damages and also the charges of the court otherwise execution.

The deposition of EDWARD BUTTLER age 22 years
or thereabouts examined sayeth

that whereas JOHN RADFORD had a certain parcel of land lying upon the Western Branch of Elizabeth River containing the quantitie of 200 acres or thereabouts holden by the said RADFORD by virtue of a patent out of which said land the said RADFORD did sell unto GID-DIAN TILLISON the quantity of 150 acres for and in consideration of 1250 lb tobacco which said parcel of land was confirmed by bill of saile given under the hand and seal of the said RADFORD to that end and purpose that the said land might be peaceably enjoyed by the said TILLISON or his heires forever without any trouble lett of molestation of him the said RADFORD or any other person or persons whatsoever through on by his meanes of procurement which said bill of saile was written by the deponent on or about July Anno 1639 and this deponent sayeth further that the said RADFORD did condicon into the aforesaid bargaine to lend the said TILLISON his boate two dayes to Nutmeg Quarter together with himselfe or a man to transport the said TILLISONS goods to the aforesaid land bought of him the said RADFORD and further this deponent sayeth not.

per Mea. EDWARD BUTLER

f 24a
p 50

ATT A COURT
Howldinge att MR: HENRY SEAWELLS upon the
28th September 1640

PRESENT: CAPT: THO: WILLOUGHBY, ESQ:
CAPT: JOHN SIBSEY MR: HENRY SEAWELL
LEIFT: ffRANCIS MASON MR: EDWARD WINDHAM
MR: WILL: JULLIAN

Whereas it appeareth to this count that ffRANCIS LAND is indebted unto XPOFER BURROUGH the just some of 1660 lb tobacco and 3 barrels of eares as by account appeareth. It is therefore ordered that the said ffRANCIS LAND shall satisfie the said XPOFER BURROUGH out of tobaccoes which are due from the said XOPHER unto ffRANCIS LAND otherwise execution.

Whereas it appeareth to this court that XOPFER YONGE and LANCK[r] LEWETT (Lovett) is indebted is (sic) indebted unto THO: SAVAGE 2500 lb tobacco as by bill appeareth. It is therefore ordered that the said LEWETT being security for the said XPOFER YONGE shall satisfy the atturney of the said SAVAGE, ffRANCIS LAND 200 lb tob-acco, the present crop upon the last of December and 200 lb tobacco the ensuing yeare accordinge to the former date otherwise execution

It is ordered per Curiam that ROBERT GLASSKOCK shall within 14 days provide one shirt for his servant ffRANCIS BRIGHT and pay the charges of the court otherwise execution.

Whereas it appeareth to this court that THO: BROWNE is indebted unto HENRY RUDKINS the quantity of 2 barrels of corne and two cocks as by bill appeareth. It is therefore ordered that the said THO: BROWNE shall make payment of the said corne and cocks by the last of October next with charges of the court otherwise execution.

It is ordered per Curiam that DANIELL NEALE (or Meale) shall make satisfaccon for three weeks worke the next Summer in this month to CAPT: JOHN SIBSEY with charges of the court otherwise execution.

f 25 The last will and Testament of JOHN LANCKFEILD deceased proved
p 51 by the oaths of WILLIAM EDWARDS and EDWARD HOLMES:

botm p 40 Whereas it appeareth to this court that CORNELIUS LLOYD hath forbiding the bannes of matremony between THOS: TUCKER and EDY HANTINGE not showinge any cause for the same but by a letter from CAPT: TUCKER to demand service from the said THOS: TUCKER which hath binn three yeares since freed from the said CORNELIUS by an atturney of the said CAPTAIN TUCKERS. It is therefore ordered that the said THO: TUCKER and EDY HANTINGE shall quietly and peacably proceed in the lawful course of marriage but if the said CORNELIUS shall hereafter show anye authoritye or indenture for service from the said THOMAS TUCKER that then the said THO: TUCKER shall satisfy any lawful atturney of CAPT: TUCKERS for the same.

Know all men by these presents that I CRISTOFER BURROUGH of Linhaven planter for divers good causes and considerings me thereunto moveing............have given, granted, sould confirmed and sett over unto my well beloved brother WILLIAM BURROUGH of the same place planter and to his heires and assignes all that whole plantation whereon I the said XPOFER do now live with all my goods tenements, hogs, household stuff whatsoever the boates, corne and tobacco and debts now owing unto me excepted togeather with all profits and commodities which shall from thence by my endeavors arrise duringe the time of my keepeing the same in my possession, excepting what shall arise from the before excepted. And I XPOFER do herebye covenant, promise and grant to surrender the said plantation and the rest upon all demands unto the said WILLIAM without fraud covin or delaye.

In witness whereof I have hereto sett my hand and seale this 6th day of January in the year of our Lord 1639/40

In presence of: XOP: BURROUGH
RALPH CLARKE with his seal

AT A COURT
Howldinge at Lieft. FFRANCIS MASSONS the
2nd November 1640

PRESENT: CAPT. JOHN SIBSEY LEIFT. ffRANCIS MASSON
MR. HENRY SEAWELL MR. WILL: JULIAN
MR. EDWARD WINDHAM

Whereas: it appeareth to this court that SAVILL GASKIN is indebted unto THO: MIRES the some of 4 ₤ 15.s sterlinge the which some is valuably to be satisfied in tobacco, accordinge as it shall passe in the collony or by specialty appeareth: It is therefore ordered that the said SAVILL GASKINS shall make payment of the debt within six weakes with charges of the Court, otherwise exec.

Whereas it appeareth to this Court that WILLIAM KETTELL hath conditioned with CAPT. THOMAS WILLOUGHBY to serve him three compleate years and to enter thereinto as soon as his cropp was finished, as by two deposicions positively appeareth, he the said KETTELL havinge receaved satisfaccion for the same, onely he is to have such apparell as the rest of the said CAPT. WILLOUGHBYS servants dureing his said terme and for corne, he is to save to the Captain's (courtesy?): it is therefore ordered that the said WILLIAM KETTELL shall enter into service upon the 1st of January next ensuing and continue in the same three compleate yeares without he the said KETTELL cann produce 20 ₤ sterling to be paid in England and also pay the charges of the Court.

Whereas: it appeareth to this Court that OWINE HAYES is indebted unto ROBT: SMITH the some of 96 L tob stripped and smooth as by specialty appeareth. It is therefore ordered that the said OWNIE shall make payment of the said some of tobacco within 30 dayes, otherwise execucion.

Whereas: THOMAS BULLOCK hath made appeare to this Court by two depositions, positively, that JOHN PHILLIPS sett doggs upon the hoges of the said BULLOCK and killed one of them. It is therefore ordered that the said JOHN PHILLIPS shall in satisfaction thereof pay unto the said THO: BULLOCK the some of 3 ₤ Sterlinge at or before the 1st of December next ensueing with charges of the Court otherwise execucion.

It is further ordered that for divers scandalizinge and tauntinge speeches which the said PHILLIPS hath given the said THOS: BULLOCK as well here in court as elsewhers he shall ask the said BULLOCK forgivenesse here in open Court before the Congregaccon here present. *f 26

* Whereas: it appeareth to this Court that WILLIAM BLAND hath entered into condicon with THOS: BULLOCK to serve his two months: It is therefore ordered that the said WILLM: BLAND shall enter into his covenanted service upon the 26th of this present month and upon performance thereof to have according to the tennore of his condicon he allowinge the said BULLOCK his charges in Court execucon. p 53 botm p 41

MR. BATHOLOMEW HASKINS hath, before this Court proffered satisfacon for two servants to MR. WOODHOWSE or to his attorney accordinge to order from the Governor and Councell from James City.

MR. JOHN GATER hath mede appeare to this court that by two sufficient witnesses, THO: LAMBERT and THO: IVEY , that he hath tendered 1000 l tob at his now dwelling howse the said some being due to the two brother's DINGMEN and tendered for their use.

Whereas it appeareth to this Court by condition that EDWARD LILLIE, Joynerwas to performe certaine worke due to HENRY HAWKINS he havinge given satisfaction for the same two yeares since which work is yett not performed: It is therefore ordered that the said LILLY (sic) shall restore out of the former satisfaction 148 l tob unto the said HENRY HAWKINS att or before the 1st of Dec ensuing with charges of the Court otherwise execucon.

Whereas it appeareth to this Court by Specialty that SAVILL GASKINE is indebted unto HENRY HAWKINS the sum of 160 l tob due the last yeare. It is therefore ordered that the said SAVIL GASKIN shall put him in sufficient security within 20 dayes for the payment of the said some this ensuinge yeare and also pay the charges of the Court, otherwise execucon

Whereas it appeareth to this court that THOS: CAUSSON is indebted unto CAPT: THO: WILLOUGHBY the sum of 9 ℔ 9s Sterlinge by specialty. It is therefore ordered that the said CAUSSON shall shipp such a quantity of tobacco abord any shipp or shipps which the said CAPT: WILLOUGHBY shall appoint as shall be thought fit by sufficient men to make sattisfaccon for the aforesaid some of mony and the bill of ladinge taken in his name otherwise execucon.

It doth appeare to this Court that THOS: KEELINGE hath transported into the Colony these fowre persons: ANNE KEELINGE in the John and Dority (Dorothy?) in 1634, THOMAS ALLEN in the Rebecca in 1636, RICHARD SMITH in the Blessinge in 1637, One Negro in Capt. Jonathan in 1637. Witness: EDWARD WINDHAM & HENRY SEAWELL.

JOHN HOLLMES hath maid appeare to this Court that he hath transported fowre persons into the Collony: GEORGE HORNER and his wife on the (ships name blank in record) EDWARD HOLMES in the (blank) and (Name blank) BROWNE in the (blank). Witness: HENRY SEAWELL.

f26a*
p 54 * Whereas it appeareth to this Court that THO: CAUSSON can not accordinge to former order produce two depositions from the records att JAMESTOWNE that he hath satisfied CAPT: ADAM THORROWGOOD a debt of 40 shillings due from ADAM BOWSER but after order made by this Court appealed to Jamestowne and then never answered the sute. It is therefore ordered that the said CAUSSON shall make payment of the said 40 shillings and likewise pay 30 shillings for charges to the said MRS. (Sic) THORROWGOOD within 20 dayes, the sute havinge been four times in this Court and over at Jamestowne - otherwise execucon

Whereas it appeareth to this court by sufficient witness that THO: CHEELY ia indebted unto OWINE HAYES the sum of 200 l tob it beinge for part of his share in the cropp about 2 yeares since: It is therefore ordered that the said THO: CHEELY shall make payment of the said some of tobacco accordinge to the Act of the last Grand Assembly beinge 40 l per 100 l out of the two thirds of his cropp of tobacco, within 30 days otherwise execucon.

THOMAS IVEY hath made appeare to this Court that he hath transported into the Colony three persons, himselfe & his wife in the Rebecca in 1637, WILLIAM BROWNE in the Blessinge in 1637. Witnesse JOHN SIBSEY.

Deposition of JOHN RICHARDSON age 20 yeares or thereabouts examined sayeth: That WILLIAM KETTELL, where he receaved the maides cloathes of CAPT: WILLOUGHBY lookeing of them over he tould the Captain he could find in his heart to serve the Captain 3 yeares and lett the bargain alone, to which the said Captain answered that if he would he might. ROBERT SMITH standing by at the same time said KETTELL have a care what you do for what is done before witnesses is as good as if it were under handwrittinge. Whereupon Kettell replied that he wouldserve the Captain 3 yeares if he would give him cloathes as the rest of his servants have and so the Captain and he agreed upon the same and after they had so agreed KETTELL putt in to have 3 barrels of corne. The said Captain answered that that was at his curtisy. Kettell told him hee would stand to his curtisy and further this deponent sayeth not.

The deposition of HENRY HAWKINS age 27 years sayeth: that he heard WILLIAM DAVIS ask EDWARD LILLY what he would do about the boate and that the said LILLY replied Cleare me and take all but whether he meant the boate or no this deponent knoweth not. And further this deponent sayeth not.

*JOHN DIER sworn and examined sayeth that he heard THOS: CHEELY tell OWINE HAYES that theire was a hogshead of tobacco at Mrs: THORROWGOOD's howse for him and that the said OWINE ANSWERED that he would not have it. And further this deponent sayeth not.

* f 27 p 55 botm p 42

The deposition of RICHARD ffLOYD age 23 yeares or thereabouts sworn and examined sayeth: that he heard JOHN PHILLIPS say that ANDREWE, MR: BURROW's his man saye that the said MR: BURROWS his dorg set foule of MR: BULLOCK's boare and that the said ANDREWE tooke the dogg (sic) off and that the dogg ranne towards MR: BULLOCKS but came presently back againe to him the said ANDREWE and died. This defendant further saith that he heard the said PHILLIPS say that when he had sett the doggs upon MR: BULLOCK's hoggs so the PHILLIPS said to MR: BULLOCK we have sett the doggs upon the hoggs SARA (or SIR?) BULLOCK take them you off & that he would say as much in open Court. And further this deponent sayeth not.

Deposition of NICHOLAS COUCH (or CRUCH) age 21 yeares or thereabouts sworn and examined sayeth: That he followed THO:BULLOCK into the grownd when he heard his hoggs aworrowinge and came up with him. CHRISTOPHERS BURROWS, his man, was in THO: BULLOCK;s grownd and PHILLIPS was on the other side. THO: BULLOCK said

f 27 p 55 botm 42 2nd November 1640

SIR PHILLIPS why doe you sett your doggs after my hoggs and PHILLIPS answered SIR*BULLOCK wee have sett them on, take you them off. (the SIR Bullock seems to read SIRRA here)* and so left then and suddenly after this deponent sawe a red dogg eating a shott (shoat) nigh MR: BULLOCK's howse. And further this deponent sayeth not.

An inventory of the goods and estate of SARAH TAYLOR widdow, taken and appraised by M: THOS: MEARES and THOS: SAWER (SAYER?) November 20th 1640.

	ʟ - s- d
Imprimis: one small sea bed, one rug, two pillows & a blanckett, one pair sheettes & pillober	01.0.0
5 ould smocks	01.0.0
1 box & 1 parcel of wearing lining	01.0.0
4 napkins, 4 towells	00.5.0
1 stuff petticoat & wastcoate, one sea greene aprone	01.4.0
1 ould gowne, 1 ould pettycoate & waistcoate	00.7.0
1 ould silk gowne and Taffity pettycoate and wastcoate	01.10.0
1 ould parcel of shooes & stockins	00.02.6
1 slick stone, 1 smoothing irone	00.01.0
1 lookeing glasse, combe & brush	00.01.0
2 spoones	0. 0.6
Fowre 1/2 of thread	0. 0.9
2 paires of gloves	0. 0.4
1 old hat	0. 4.0
TOTALL	6.16.1

*f 27a p 56

*ATT A COURT
Howldinge at the howse of CAPT: THO: WILLOUGHBY
November the last (30th) 1640

PRESENT: CAPT: THOS: WILLOUGHBY Esq:

CAPT: JOHN SIBSEY	MR: HENRY SEAWELL
MR: EDWARD WINDHAM	MR: ffRANCIS MASSON

Whereas it appeareth to this Court that RALPH CLARK deceased was indebted unto CAPT: THOS: WILLOUGHBY in his lifetime the some of ʟ 3.10 S. Sterlinge and 96 pounds of tobacco. It is therefore ordered that THOS: CAUSSON the executor of the said RALPH's estate shall put in sufficient security for the shippinge of such a quantity of tobacco as two sufficient men shall thinke fitt for to satisfie the said debt the said tobacco beinge to be shipt aboard any ship or ships which the said CAPT: WILLOUGHBY shall appoint as likewise for the some of 9 ʟ 9 S. which hath formerly been ordered in forme with this order verbatum: otherwise execucon.

Whereas it appeareth to this Court that JOHN WILLIAMS is indebed unto LANCKESTER LOVETT the just some of 50 1 tob and five barrels of corne as by specialty appeareth. It is therefore ordered that the said JOHN WILLIAMS shall remaine in the Sheriffes custidy untill such time as he shall put in security for the payment of the said debt according to the tennor of the bill and also to pay the charges of the Court. Otherwise execucon

30th November 1640 f 27a p 56

Whereas it appeareth to this Court that ROBERT ffEAKE (PEAKE?) borrowed a boate of MR: WOODHOWSE and the said boate was spoiled and made altogether unserviceable in the time the said ROBT: ffEAKE had hir (sic) in his possession, these two parties havinge referred themselves to this Court to decide the cause. It is therefore ordered that the aforesaid ROBT: ffEAKE shall make payment of the some of 20 ℔ sterling or else sufficient bill of exchange to be delivered to the said WOODHOWSE against such time as the first ship shall sett sail for England, otherwise - * f 28 p 57

* Whereas HUMPHREY PRICE AND ffRANCIS LAND standeth jointly indebt- btm
ed unto DANNELL TANER one heifer with calfe which was due to be paid p 43
uppon the feast of St. Mickhell last past as by specialty appeareth It is therefore ordered that the said ffRANCIS LAND shall deliver unto the said DANELL TANNER (sic) one heifer with calfe within 14 or else one heifer with a cow calfe by her side by the 1st of March next ensuinge with 40 pence charges heere and at Kequotan Court - Otherwise -

It is ordered per curiam that all such bills or accounts which shall be made to appeare in Court to be due from the deceased JOHN LANCKFIELD there shall be order granted that THO: BULLOCK & ROBT: HAYES shall be liable to make satisfaction for the same they being the executors of the said JOHN LANCKFIELD deceased.

Whereas it sppeareth to this Court that JOHN HOLLMES was indebted unto MARY BROWNE the just some of 24 ℔ sterlinge the which said some was left her by her father it being delivered into the possession of the said JOHN HOLLMES as by acknowledgment appeareth - and whereas JOHN HOLLMES hath made it appeare upon oath that he hath been at charges with NICHOLAS BROWNE father to the said MARY BROWNE in the some of 16 ℔ sterlinge which the Court alloweth on and likewise ordered that the said JOHN HOLLMES shall make payment of the some of 10 ℔ sterlinge to be paid valluably in goods and commodities - the one halfe to be paid the 1st of Jan next and the other halfe upon the last of November next ensuinge the date hereof with charges of the Court - otherwise exec.

Whereas it appeareth to this Court that NATHANELL DUTTON died in the house of MR: THO: SAYER and MR: JOHN MEARES have an order from the said NATHANELLS father to administer upon the estate of the said NATHANELL deceased: it is therefore ordered that the said MR: THOS: SAYER shall deliver up unto MR: JOHN MEARES a true inventory of the aforesaid estate and likewise it is further ordered that the said JOHN MEARES shall be liable to pay unto SAWER (SAYER) all such debts as he the said SAYER (sic) shall make appeare to be due to him for the said NATHANELL DUTTON deceased and also to pay the charges of the Court - Otherwise exec. f 28a p 58

* Whereas it appeareth to this Court that THOMAS HAYES is indebted unto DAVID WILLIAMS the quantity of 2 barrels and a half of Corne due from the said THO: HAYES for rent it is therefore ordered that the said THO: HAYES shall make payment of the said quantity of corne within ten daya - otherwise exec.

f 28a p58 30th November 1640

LANCKESTER LOVETT hath made appeare to this Court that he hath transported into this colloney fowre persons whose names are as followeth: EDWARD STONNE in the Pellican in 1618, THOMAS MASSON in Capt: Duglass Shipp in 1635, THEOPHELUS TOMSON with CAPT: PAINE in 1634, JOHN JOHNSONNE in CAPT: DUGLASS in 1635

An inventory of the goods and estate of JOHN LANCKFIELD deceased with that part thereof are sold and what kept in the hands of the executors for the benefit of the children. Delivered upon oath the 26 Oct 1640.

IMPRIMUS: a feather bed, a bolster, a rugg sold to MR: 2 pillowes, a matt cord and bedstead	BULLOCK for for 160 1 tob
An old Beaver hat, 4 pieces of earthen ware, 12 spoons, a brush, a salt, a pair of tongs, an iron pot & hooks, and a candlestick	to THO: DAVIS for 83 1 tob
4 pieces of earthenware, a pewter hand pot, a frying pan & 4 pot hooks & hangers	to WILL DAVIS for 10 1tob
1 iron kettle, 1 stock lock, 3 axes, 5 hoes, 2 calves, 1 pair silk garters	to THO: HAYES for 110 1 tob
2 old chests, a looking glass, a grind stone, a spit 2 hammers, a hand saw & a demi caster	to WILL DAVIS for 111 1 tob
7 napkins, a Bible, a testament, a Practice of Piety, a chamber pot, a pistol, a cutwork handkerchief & an old band	to THO:BULL-OCK for 74 1 tob
An iron pot, a skimmer, a gun, 2 pistols, some shot, a wash tub, a powder horn, belt & shot bag	to THOS:MARSH for 160 1 tob
3 pewter dishes, a comb, a corn barrel, 2 trays, a smoking iron & stick stone	to ROBT:HAYES for 167 1 tob

*f 29 p 59 btm 44 (this whole inventory in faded)

* 3 pewter dishes, 2 pillow bearers, a table fram, & two flasks	to WILL: ffANNE for 95 1 tob

Reserved for the childrens use:

3 Holland sheetts & a halfe, 3 coarse sheetts, 1 pair of pillows 3/4 yd of Broad Cloth, 1 cotton blanket, a cilver dram cup, a silver spoon, an apron, 3 yeards of silver twist, 7 goats, breeders, 3 rams, 10 ewe kids, one old sow, 2 heifers and a yearling heifer calfe, one great boar, 2 hogs, 5 pigs and a feather bed, 2 pillos and a rug, a chest and a case, one gold ringe, a bracelett with single Pence (?), a Maide servant, a plantacon his time of possession beinge 5 yeares to come.

One bill of ANTHONY LINNES of ould debt	500 1 tob
one bill of CRISTOFER NEADHAMS of this yeares debt	ƀ 1400.00.00
Due from MR: HILL 5 pownds sterlinge or tobacco as it shall passe.	5.00.00
Due from THOS: CAUSSON 20 shillings sterlinge	1.00.00
Also his cropp of corne being four barrels 1/2 due	

NOTE: DATE OUT OF ORDER

30 NOVEMBER 1640
15 March 1640/41
4 January 1640/41

f 29 p 59
btm 44

from EDWARD HOLLMES, 2 barrels of Corne, two indentures, one of JOHN SHAWES and one of THO: THOMSONNS to take up land for the children.

AT A COURT
HOLDING AT CAPT: JOHN SIBSEYS THE 15th OF MARCH 1640/41

PRESENT: CAPT: THOS: WILLOUGHBY ESQR
CAPT: JOHN SIBSEY LIEFT: ffRANCIS MASSON
MR: EDW: WINDHAM MR: HENRY SEWELL
MR: JULIAN

At a Court howldinge att James Citty the 4th Feb 1640 PRESENT: SIRffRANCIS WIATT knight, Governor etc, CAPT: JOHN WEST, CAPT: THO: WILLOUGHBY. MR: GEORGE MINIFREE, CAPT: SAMUELL MATTHEWES MR: ROGER WINGATE, CAPT: WILL: BROCAS, CAPT: WILM: PERCE, MR: ARGOLL YERLY (YEARDLEY) MR: AMBROSE HARMER.

The Court hath ordered that MRS: SARAH GOOYKINS shall deliver upon oath a true and perfect inventory in kind of the estate of CAPT: ADAM THOROWGOOD her late husband deceased and in regard of the great distance of her residence CAPT: THO: WILLOUGHBY shall have the power to administer the oath & that the said CAPT: WILLOUGHBY shall nominate and appoint two sufficient men upon their oaths before him taken to make just and indifferent prasure (appraisal) with the inventory to be returned to the Governor and Councell att the next Quarter Court.

Memoranda: that CAPT: THO: WILLOUGHBY hath disclamed in Court for himselfe and MR: HENRY SEAWELL the overseershipp of the last will and testament of CAPT: ADAM THOROWGOOD deceased.

Extrahit - et examinat by me
GEORGE READE PRESENT SECRETARY

AT A COURT
HOWLDINGE the 4th of JANUARY 1640 AT THE HOWSE OF MR: WILLM: JULLIAN - PRESENT:

CAPT: THO: WILLOUGHBY ESQR
MR: EDW: WINDHAM CAPT: JOHN SIBSEY
MR: HENRY SEAWELL LEIFT: ffRANCIS MASSON
MR: WILLM: JULLIAN

* f30 p 61
btm
p 45

*It is ordered per Curiam that JOHN GAYTER shall within three weekes provide for THO: HALL his servant one cloath sute of cloathes, 2 shirts, 1 pair of shooes and stockins, 1 pare of canvas breeches and one bed, boulster & blankett and all other particulars menchoned in his indenture - otherwise execucon

It is ordered per Curiam that ROBERT GLASCOCK, HENRY HAWKINS, and WILLIAM RAMSHAW shall perform all things to JASPER HOSKINS according to the tennor of a condicon made betweene them the above named unto the said JASPER bearinge date the 26 Feb 1639 and also pay the charges of the Court - Otherwise execucon

It is ordered per curiam that no order after the date hereof shall passe against the estate of JOHN NUTKINE until such time as a condicon be performed, made betweene the said NUTKINE and

THO: BRITTAINE the said condition bearing date the 15 Jun 1640.

It is ordered per Curiam that the next taxes which shall arise within this county, that MR: THOS: MEERES shall be satisfied out of the same for one shott the which the Burgesses had of him the last Grand Assembly.

Whereas it appears to this Court by Specialty that EDW: LILLY is indebted unto HENRY CATTLINE one milch cowe betweene 3 & 6 years old to be delivered unto the said HENRY at his now dwelling howse the 10 Oct last past. It is therefore ordered that the said LILLY shall within 14 dayes make payment of the said cow or else 9 £ sterlinge with charges of the Court - otherwise execucon

The last will and testament of GILBERT GUY proved by the oaths of THOS: BULLOCK, XOPHER BURROUGHS & ROBT: HAYES the said will bearing date the 2 May 1640

THOS: BROWN hath made it appear to this Court that hee hath due to him 450 acres of land for the transportating of nine persons into this Colony whose names are followeth: THOS: HALL, ELIZ: BAKER, THOS: BLEWETT, ANNE MORLEY, JAMES JAMES, OWINE MERREYDETH, THOS: ANDREWES, WILL: HICHKOCK and THO: BROWNE.

Whereas it appeareth to this Court that WILLIAM BURROUGH as Security for SAVILL GASKINS is indebted unto THO: MARSH the some of 800 1 tob due by specialty to be paid in June 1639. It is therefore ordered that the said WILL: BURROUGH shall make payment of the said debt accordinge to the tennor of the bill and to make the first payment within ten dayes with charges of the Court - Otherwise execucon.

*f 30a p 62 *Whereas it appeareth to this Court that THOMAS CAUSSON is indebted unto THO: CHEELY one barrel and a halfe of Corne and 36 1 tob stripted and smoothed. It is therefore ordered that the said THOMAS CAUSSON shall make payment of the said debts within 10 dayes with charges of the Court - Otherwise execucon

Whereas it appeareth to this Court by condition that XPOFER BURROUGH is indebted unto THO: DAVIS five ewe goats with kids or kids by their sides and one ram kidd of eight months old. It is therefore ordered that the said XPOFER shall make payment of the aforesaid particulars within 20 dayes and also to lett the said THOMAS DAVIS have the benefit of the which kidds and also to pay the charges of the Court. Otherwise execucon

Whereas it appeareth to this Court by specialty that THOS: TOOKER is indebted unto WILLM: KETTELL the quantity of fowre barrels and a half of Corne and the said WILLM: KETTELL hath assigned over the said bill unto JOHN SUTTON it is therefore ordered that the said THO: TOOKER shall restore unto the said JOHN one black gowne with one barrel of Corne upon demand in satisfaction of the said debt. Otherwise execucon.

It is ordered per Curiam that TRESTRAM MASSON shall detaine so much of the cropp of THO: TOOKERS as shall satisfy countie duties and taxes in the county.

Whereas it appeareth to this Court that RICH: ffOSTER is indebted unto SARAH GUY the quantity of 150 1 tob stripped and smoothed and one pair of worsted stockins & one shillinge as by condition under his hand. It is therefore ordered that the said RICH: ffOSTER shall within 20 days make payment of the said debt with charges of the Court. Otherwise execucon

Whereas it appeareth by account that GUILBERT GUY deceased was indebted unto CAPT: THOS: WILLOUGHBY the some of 14 shillings, 6 pence It is therefore ordered that the said CAPT: WILLOUGHBY shall be first satisfied out of the estate of the said GUILBERT GUY, other wise

Whereas it appeareth to this Court by Specialty that GUILBERT GUY deceased was indebted unto HENRY SEWEL the some of1 ₺ 10 sh It is therefore ordered that the said HENRY SEAWELL (sic) shall be satisfied out of the estate of said GUILBERT provided that an order of Court be first payd being granted unto CAPT: THOS: WILLOUGHBY for 14s 6d Otherwise ececucon

It is ordered that CORNELIUS LOYD shall be satisfied two barrels of corne out of the estate of GUILBERT GUY deceased all former orders being first satisfied, the debt having been proved by specialty and oath. *f 31 p 63 btm p 46

*Whereas it appeareth to this Court by specialty that GILBERT (sic) GUY deceased was indebted unto MR: CORKER the quantity of 90 1 tob due to be paid the 10 Oct anno 1639. the said CORKER havinge given order unto ROBT: SMITH to receave the said some. It is therefore ordered that the said ROBT: SMITH shall be satisfied out of the estate of the said GUILBERT GUY provided that an order be first paid granted unto MR: HENRY SEAWELL for 1 ₺ 10 sh sterling. Other wise execucon.

Whereas it appeareth by acknowledgement that GUILBERT GUY deceased was indebted unto JOHN WEBB one barrel of corne and one pair of hose and shooes. It is therefore ordered that the said JOHN WEBB shall be first satisfied out of the estate of the said GUILBERT GUY provided that an order of Court be first paid granted unto ROBT: SMITH for 90 1 tob. Otherwise execucon

Whereas it appeareth to this Court by the oaths of witnesses that ROBERT HAYES is indebted unto WILLM: PENN for satisfaction of 3 weekes worke. It is therefore ordered that the said ROBT: HAYES shall make payment unto the said PENN of 40 1 of stripped and smoothed tobacco within ten dayes. Otherwise execucon

It is ordered per Curiam that the sheriff of this county shall pay unto RICH: ffOSTER the quantity of 50 1 of stript smooth tob the which is due from SAVILL GASKINE as by bill appeareth, he the said SAVILL being arrested to appear at this Court at the sute of RICH: ffOSTER but hath not appeared to save his recognicance. It is therefore ordered as aforesaid for the better securing of the said RICH: ffOSTER his debt also the said sheriffe to pay the charges of the Court. Otherwise execucon

f 31 p 63 btm p 46   4 JANUARY 1640/41

Whereas it appeareth to this Court by speacialty that THOMAS MELTON is indebted unto GOWINE LANCKESTER the quantity of 15 barrels of corne it is therefore ordered that the said THOMAS MELLTON (sic) shall within 30 days make payment of the said corne with charges of the Court otherwise execucon

Whereas it appeareth to the Court by oath of ROBT: HAYES that JOHN LANCKFIELD deceased hath transported into this Collony two persons whose names are as followeth and 3 children borne in the Collony whose names are as followeth: Servants: JOHN TOMSON, JOHN SHAWE, children: ffran: LANCKFIELD, SARAH LANCKFIELD, ELIZ: LANCKFIELD

*f 31a p 64 *Whereas it appeareth to this Court by account that JOHN WHITE deceased was indebted unto TRESTRAM MASSON the some of 517 l tob It is therefore ordered that the said TRESTRAM MASSON shall be satisfied our of the estate of the said JOHN WHITE provided that the administrator of the said WHITES estate be first payd. Otherwise execucon

It is ordered per Curiam that GEORGE LOCK shall pay unto ROBT: BODY the some of 17 l of stript and smoothed tob it appearing to be due from the said LOCK for Burgesses charges the said BODY being employed by the sheriffe of the county for the recd of them Otherwise execucon

Whereas it appeareth to this Court by account upon oath that JOHN WHITE deceased was indebted unto HENRY SEAWELL the some of 655 l tob. It is therefore ordered that the said HENRY SEAWELL shall be satisfied out of the estate of the said WHITE provided that an order granted unto TRESTRAM MASSON be first payd. otherwise execucon

Whereas it appeareth to this Court by witnesses that GILBERT GUY deceased was indebted unto THO: SAYER the some of 50 l tob accordinge to the act of Assembly/ It is therefore ordered that THOMAS SAYER shall be satisfied out of the estate of the said GILBERT provided that an order granted unto JOHN WEBB for one barrel of corne and one paire of shooes and stockins. Otherwise execucon.

Whereas it appeareth to this Court by acknowledgment that GILBERT GUY deceased was indebted unto ROBT: HAYES the some of 44 l tob stript and smooth. It is therefore ordered that the said ROBT: HAYES shall be satisfied out of the estate of the said GILBERT provided that an order granted unto THOS: SAYER be first payd. Otherwise execucon

ROBERT HAYES hath maid appeale to this Court that he hath transported into this Collony two persons for which one he hath not taken up any land for whose names are as followeth: HUMPHREY CASSELL, NICHO: CRASSE.

MR: ffRANCIS MASSON & MR: HENRY SEAWELL Churchwardens doe present to this Court DANIELL NEALE & ELEANOR READE for committinge ffornicacion & Adultrie beinge the second time committed by them.

4 th JANUARY 1640/41 f 31a p 64

THOMAS MEERES & HENRY CATLINE Churchwardens doe present THOMAS TOOKER & EDY his (son or servant?) for beinge guilty of fornicacion

*MR: CODD & JOHN STRATTON Churchwardens doe present CHRISTOFER BURROUGH & MARY his wife for ffornicacion they beinge the 28th May theire child baptized the 25 Nov 1640. *f 32 p 65 btm p 47

And SAVILL GASKINE & ANNE his wife which weare maryed the 13th day of Sep & shee was Churched the 10th of November 1640.

JAMES SMITH & WITH ANNE his wife were married the 27th of Sep 1640 theire child baptized the 26th of Dec.

RICHARD ffOSTER and ANNE his wife were married the 19th day of Nov 1640 Shee the said ANNE as it is reported hath deserved (sic) for a child.

These are presented for ffornicacion

Deposition of ANNE GASKINE aged 20 yeares saith that beinge at the howse of RICHARD ffOSTER the night before the weding & beinge in bed with ANNE JACKSON to which one that sd RICH: ffOSTER was the next day to be married amongst theire discourse the said ANNE JACKSON tould this depont that shee was two months gonne with child &the next night being the wedding night this deponent did likewise lie there but had not longe in bedd before the said ffOSTER called this deponent desir(ing) her to come to his wife who who was very sick which this deponent did accordingly and askt the said ffosters wife how shee did & if she weare not with child her answer was noe but shee was very ill & had a greate payne in her back & bellie then this depont: sat downe & a little after askt her again how shee did who answered pretty well now & by and by aftere called this deponent & desired her to looke into the bedd for theire was some what come frome her whereupon this deponent rose & turning downethe bedd cloathes looked into the bedd and ffownd a peece or lumpe of flesh about the bignesses of her hand deformed & without any resemblance of a child att all then this ffOSTERS wife said to this deponent goe your waies not I am prity well so leaveinge the soreld (?) lump of flesh & turneinge downe the cloathes againe this deponent left her and went away but what became of it afterwards this deponent knoweth not and further saith not.

JACOB BRADSHAW age 25 years sworn and examined sayeth: that in the extremity of GUILBERT GUY his sicknesse this deponent beinge at his howse the said GUILBERT desired him to goe to RICHARD the surgon and desire him to come unto him and also to desire MR: MASSON to come and reckon with him and the said MR: MASSON tould this deponent that he would come about the middle of the weeke and farther this deponent sayeth not. * f 32a p 66

*ROBERT BODY age 23 yeares sworn and examined sayeth: that MR: ffRANCIS MASSON demanded of him when the sheriffe would pay him the rest of the some for the ferrie who answered him that GUILBERT GUY said that he had not more in his hand than would satisffie for the

ferrie. MR MASSON answered that he had been with GILBERT GUY and reckoned with him and how that GILBERT GUY was in his debt and would have persuaded this deponent that he was in the howse when he reckoned with GILBERT GUY and further this deponent sayeth not.

Deposicion of DAVID LEWELLINGE aged 22 yeares sworne and examined saith that being at the howse of RICHARD ffOSTER the next night aftere theire weddinge day he -(can't read - faded)- that the wife of RICH: ffOSTER was very sick and heard the said ffOSTER call the wife of one SAVILL GASKINE and desired her to helpe his wife and suddenly aftere the said ffOSTERS wife vomited & therewith was somewhat better as far as this deponent could preseave and farther said that he heard the wife of the sd GASKINE speake unto RICH: ffOSTER & bidd him goe to bed & keepe her warme & farther this deponent saith not.

Deposition of THOS: IVEY sworn and examined sayeth that he heard WILLIAM CRUCH and TRESTRAM MASSON agree about binige partners in the administration of JOHN WHITES estate provided that the said TRESTRAM should beare halfe the charges for taking out the letter of administration and further this deponent sayeth not.

Deposition of THO: DAVIS sworne & examined saith that SAVILL GASKINE tould him that he was at RICH: ffOSTERS weddinge and that he heard ffOSTERS wife cry out of her back & her bellie and that he thought that she had a miss chance whereupon this deponent asked the said GASKINE if she were delivered of anythinge who replied yes & that they put it under the boulster and that the wife of the said ffOSTER confessed unto his wife that the first night that the said ffoster lay with her was the night that JOHN LANCKFIELD was buried & further this deponent saith not 1640

* f33 p 67 btm p 48

* An Inventory of JOHN WHITES estate as it was sold in tobacco

to WILLM: CRUCH one patent for land	180 lbs
More to the said CRUCH (COUCH?) one gun, one old lock	165
to TRESTRAM MASSON one cloth suit and Holland Shirt	300
to MR: HOSKINS one chest	124
to SIMOND HANCOCK on square, one axe, one saw, one auger , one planing form, one stock, one hat, one old green suit, one old pair of canvas drawers, one old stack bed	104
	873

Debts owing to JOHN WHITE deceased in tobacco

CAPT: JOHN SIBSEY	080
MR: HENRY SEAWELL	450
MR: WILLM: JULLIAN	220
MR: WATKINES	277
Debts received of JOHN WHITES in tobacco	1027
of CAPT: SIBSEY	080
of MR: SEAWELL	370
of MR: JULLIAN	220
of MR: WATKINS	227
	947

4th JANUARY 1640/41 f 33 p 67 btm p 48

Rests due to pay from MR: SEAWELL	0080	
Debts due from JOHN WHITE unto WILLM: CRUCH & TRESTRAM MASSON By condition	600	
For work at MR: SEAWELLS	225	
For work at MR: JULIANS	110	
For work at MR: GAYTERS	200	
	1135	
Due to WILL: CRUCH in past winter		
Left unpaid of his freedome	425	lbs
For 10 weekes worke of his man by cond:	300	
For work his man did at MR: SEAWELLS	112	
For his mans work at MR: JULIANS	055	
For his mans work at MR: GAYTERS	100	
	992	

This is due to WILLIAM CRUCH of WHITES estate. *33a p 68

* LANCKSTER LOVETT exore maid pet: out depossion GASKINE ....(the rest of this page is blank)

* f 34 p 69 btm p 49

* AT A COURT

HOWLDINGE IN THE LOWER NORFOLKE AT THE HOWSE OF
CAPT: JOHN SIBSEY
March 15th 1640/41

PRESENT: CAPT THO: WILLOUGHBY ESQR
CAPT: JO: SIBSEY MR: WM: JULIAN
MR: EDW: WINDHAM MR: HENRY SEAWELL
LEIFT: ffRANCIS MASSON

Whereas it appeareth to the Court by specialty that THOMAS ffRANCIS is indebted unto LANCKESTER LOVETT the quantity of 10 pounds of powder and 50 pounds of swanne shot. It is therefore ordered that THOS: BULLOCK attorney for the said THO: ffRANCIS shall make payment of the like particulars within two months or else give satisfaction according to the rates that the said commodities shall be sould for the present yeare otherwise execucon to be awarded.

Whereas it appeareth to this Court by account upon oath that JOHN LANCKFIELD deceased was indebted unto CORNELIUS LLOYD the sum of 194 1 tob stripped and smooth It is therefore ordered that ROBERT HAYES administrator of the said some of 194 1 tob within 20 days otherwise ececution to be awarded.

Whereas it appeareth to this Court by bill that JOHN LANCKFIELD deceased was indebted unto CAPT: ADAM THOROWGOOD the just sum of 561 1 tob stript and smooth It is therefore ordered that the administrator of the said LANCKFIELDS estate shall pay unto MRS: SARAH THORROWGOOD wife to the said ADAM THORROWGOOD deceased the said some of 561 1 tob by the last of April next ensuing otherwise execution to be awarded.

Whereas it appeareth to this Court by specialty that JOHN

LANCKFIELD deceased was indebted unto WILLM: SHIPP the full sum of 330 l tob stript and smooth It is therefore ordered that the administrator of the said LANGFIELDS (sic) estate shall pay unto the said WILLM: SHIPP the said some of 330 l tob within ten days otherwise ececution to be awarded

Whereas it appeareth to this Court by sufficient testimony that JOHN ffOULER the full sum of 80 l tob stript and smooth and 16 shillings sterling money and 3 ells of canves It is therefore ordered that the administrator of the said LANCKFIELDS estate pay unto ANNE ffOULER wife of the said deceased WILLIAM ffOULER the said some of 80 l tob and 16 shillings to be paid according to the late act of Assembly and the canvas to be paid in kind within 10 days otherwise execution to be awarded (this whole item is faded)

Whereas it appeareth to this Court that JOHN DIER hath done certain work for ffRANCIS LAND and hath not received any satisfaction for the same It is therefore ordered that the said ffRANCIS LAND shall pay unto the said DIER the some of 50 l tob stript and to deliver the said DIER one canoe the which doth belong to him and also pay the charges of the Court otherwise execution.

* f 34a p 70

* Whereas it appeareth to this Court by specialty that OWINE HAYES is indebted unto JOHN DIER the some of one barrel and a halfe of corne: It is therefore ordered that the same OWINE HAYES shall make payment of the said quantity of corne unto the said DIER within 2 months otherwise execution to be awarded (this whole item is faded)

Whereas it appeareth to this Court by specialty that HUMPHREY BEST hath served JAMES WARNER the full term according to his indenture and that he hath not received any cloathes of the said WARNER accordinge to the custome of the country It is therefore ordered that the said JAMES WARNER shall within ten days or 14 days at the farthest provide for the said BEST cloathes and necessaries according to the custome of Virginia otherwise execution to be awarded

Whereas RICHARD STERNELL hath arrested to this Court HENRY HAWKINS who hath made his appearance according to the tennor of his bond but the said STERNELL hath not appeared to prosecute the said HAWKINS It is therefore ordered that the said STERNELL shall pay the charges of this Court and remain non suted

OLIVER VAN KECK hath made it appear to this Court that he hath transported into this Collony the four persons whose names are hereunder mentioned: OLIVER VAN KECK (or HECK), CATHERINE VAN KECK, PETER VAN KECK and JOHN WISE.

Whereas it appeareth to this Court by specialty that OWINE HAYES is indebted unto RICH: ffOSTER the quantity of 3 barrels of Corne and 20 l tob stript and smooth It is therefore ordered that the said OWINE HAYES shall within 30 days make payment of the said corne and tobacco according to the tennor of his bill with charges of the Court otherwise execution to be awarded

Whereas it appeareth to this Court that JOHN PAMER (PALMER?) heth cleared certain ground for GOWERINGE LANCKESTER and hath not received any satisfaction for the same It is therefore ordered that the said GOWERINGE (Gowine?) shall make payment unto the said PAMER the quantity of 50 1 tob stript and smooth within ten days with charges of the Court otherwise execution (this item if very faded and hard to check)

Whereas it appeareth to this Court by the oath of RICHARD KENNER that JOHN WHITE deceased did in his lifetime freely and voluntarily give unto JOHNATHAN LANGWORTH 12 days work and sent his servant JOHN NAT for to perform the same It is therefore ordered that the said JOHNATHAN LANGWORTH shall be discharged from any demand of satisfaction for the 12 days work and from the fear of any future pleas made by the administrator of the said WHITES estate o f any other

Whereas it appeareth to this Court by condition that JOHN NUTKINE is indebted unto THOMAS BRITAINE the quantity of 60 1 tob stript It is therefore ordered that the said JOHN NUTKINE shall within 10 days make payment of the said debt and the charges of this Court Otherwise execution to be ordered * f 35 p 71 btm p 50

* Whereas it appeareth to this Court by the oath of WILLM: EDWARDS that RICHARD KENNON (name previously spelled KENNER) is indebted unto JOHN MONDS the just some of 40 1 tob stript and smooth It is therefore ordered that the said RICHARD KENNON shall within 10 days make payment of the said debt unto the said JOHN MONDS otherwise execution to be awarded

It is ordered by this Court that every working hand and tithable person beginning at PETER PORTER and so along to CAPT: WILLOUGHBY for the ministers duties shall pay 10 shillings per poll which was by former agreement and it is further ordered that the said inhabitants shall satisfy and pay 24 1 tob per poll being for 52 persons as by the list appeareth and one bushel of corne per poll for and towards the new repairing and finishing of the church and lastly the sheriff shall have power to receive of MR: CORNELIUS LOYD and MR: ROBT: ffEAKE of each of them 100 1 tob the which given freely as a gift towards the church otherwise execution

Whereas it appeareth to this Court by bill that THOS: HAYES is indebted unto THOS: BULLOCK the some of 90 1 tob stript and smooth It is therefore ordered that the said THOS: HAYES shall make payment unto the said THOS: BULLOCK of the said some within ten days otherwise execution to be ordered

These are to certify that WILLM: DAVIS hath made appeare to this Court by oath of WILLM: SHIPP that he hath transported into this collony one WILLIAM COULDWIELL and hath not taken up land for him.

Whereas it appeareth to this Court that ROBERT MATHEWS is indebted unto LANCKESTER LOVETT the just some of 3 Ł sterlinge to be paid valuably in tobacco It is therefore ordered that the said ROBT: MATHEWS shall within ten days make a payment of the said debt according to acts of the Assembly otherwise execution

Whereas it appeareth to this Court by a note of particulars what charges the Burgesses have been att and is approved on by this Court It is therefore ordered that all the tithables, inhabitants shall pay for the defraying of theire charges 2 1 tob per poll to be levied by the Sheriff or his deputy and to be brought unto such place or places and the rest of the levies, as the sheriff or his deputy shall appoint. The said places to be appointed as necessary for the inhabitants as possible may be and where there shall be any which shall refuse to make payment of these or any other levies or Court fees that then the sheriff of this county shall have the power to destrain upon any part of their estates for satisfaction thereof

Whereas it appeareth to this Court by bill that WILLM: ffOWLER deceased was indebted unto THO: BULLOCK the quantity of 105 1 Tob stript and smooth It is therefore ordered that ANNE ffOWLER wife of the said WILLM: ffOWLER deceased shall make payment unto the said THOS: BULLOCK of the said debt within 10 days with charges of the Court otherwise execution to be awarded

*f 35a p 72 * Whereas it appeareth to this Court by specialty that JOHN LANCKFIELD is indebted unto WILLM: SHIPP the just some of 9 ℔ 6d. sterling It is therefore ordered that the administrator of the said LANCKFIELDS estate shall satisfy and pay unto the said WILLM: SHIPP the said debt within 10 days according to the acts of Assembly otherwise execution

The deposition of ROBT: HAYES age 46 years or thereabouts sworn & examined sayeth: that beinge to transport 1000 of bricks from Kequotan for MR: BULLOCK the which were due from NICHOLAS WRIGHT the said bricks being demanded by this deponent for the use of MR: BULLOCK but the said NICHOLAS WRIGHT replied that he acknowledged the debt to be one but at the time had no bricks to make payment of the debt but promised this deponent thatat his next return to Kequotan he should have the bricks but before the return of this deponent the said NICHOLAS WRIGHT was dead and further this deponent sayeth not

The deposition of WILLM: EDWARDS age 44 years of thereabouts sworn and examined sayeth: Being at the howse of RICHARD KENNER he heard the said KENNOR (sic) and JOHN MONDS discoursing of some certain reckonings which were between them and the said JOHN MONDS gave the said KENNOR a free discharge but upon the condition that the said KENNOR shall make payment of 40 1 tob at TRESTUM MASSONS but further this deponent sayeth not

The deposition of THOS: CHEELY age 50 years of thereabouts sworn and examined sayeth: that he heard JOHN PAMER demand of GOWINE LANCKESTER grownd for three years and that the said GOWINE did absolutely deny the said PAMER any grownd and also told him he should have none unlesse he would come and live upon it and further this deponent sayeth not

15th MARCH 1640/41 f 36 p 73 btm p 51

The names of such as are indebted unto JOHNATHAN LANGWORTHS estate:

THOMAS BROWNE by booke	137
WILLM: COLEMAN	140
HENRY HAWKINS by booke	100
MR: LOYED by booke	071
JOHN CLARKE by booke	010
ROBERT TAYLOR by booke	005
SIMON PETERS by booke	020
WILL: RAMSHAW by bill	050
WARRON MILLS by bill	120
WILL: EDWARDS by bill	160
MOYSES STONNE by bill	080
THO: DAVIS by bill	100
THO: WRIGHT by bill	200
JOHN WATKINS	120
Total in Tobacco	1213

MR: HARRISON debtor 10 ℔ sterling

The names of those to whom the estate of JOHNATHAN LANGWORTH is indebted in tobacco:

To MR: ffEAKE	793 lbs
To THO: JOYNER	360
To ROBT: LEWIS	300
To THO: HART	150
To JAMES EAVENS	274
To MR: LOYD	

To SIMOND HANCOCK one casse of strong water & 2 pairs of shooes
To JOHN WATKINS one bushel of salt

The names of those to whom the estate is engaged:	℔	S	D
To THOS: TODD	07	00	00
To MR: DIER	03	08	00
To RICHARD WOLMAN	00	12	00
To WILL: SHIPP	02	00	00
To JO: GARDNER	05	00	00
To MATHEW HAYARD	00	06	00
To PETTER SETBOURNE	02	08	00
and 4 barrels of corne			
To PEETER RIGHLESWORTH	01	04	00
and 2 barrels of corne			
Total in money	21	19	00
In corne barrels			06

These accounts delivered upon oath by RICHARD KENNOR

A note of debts received by RICHARD KENNOR being the estate of JOHNATHAN LANGWORTH deceased Imd. by SIMOND HANDCOCK 0066 lbs

By CAPT: SIBSEY	1660
by MR: MASSON	0100
by MR: GAYTER	0300
by ENSIGN THO: LAMBERT	0200

by PEETER PORTER	0052
by ROBT: TAYLOR	0320
by MR: JULIAN	0456
by HENRY HAWKINS	1338
by MR: RAMSHAW	0282
by RICH: OWINE	0820
by MR: SAWER	0887
by MR: WATKINS	0300
by ROBT: GLASCOCK	0400
by WILLM: EDWARDS	0150
by MR: LOYDD	0080
by GEORGE LOCK	1000
At NANSAMUND	0788
by WILLM: DEDFORD (DURFORD?)	0110
by WILLM: NASH	0200
by THOS: SMITH	0100
by JOHN MUNDS	0100
of the cropp	2000

*f 36a
p 74 * Debts discharges and paid by RICHARD KENNOR being due and paid as followeth out of the estate of JOHNATHAN LANGWORTH deceased:

To WILLIAM DEDFORD	1500 1 tob
to CAPT: SIBSEY	0220
Parsons tiths	0080
to WILLM: SHIPP upon bill	0576
to WILLIAM SHIPP by booke	1015
to MR: ROBINSON	1264
to THOS: SMITH	1500
to JOHN MONDS	1500
to MR: LOYDD	0663
Shipt home 7 hogsheads of tobacco containing	2100
Burnt in Lieu of the 7 hogehead	2100

The Burgesses Charges allowed on by this Court:

Find per 4 Hoggs	0080
per 20 pounds of butter	15 1 tob
per 1 hogshead of beere	0060
per beere and diett	0040
per 2 bushels of peas	0010
per 1 case of strong watters	0040
per 1 man to dress the said vittells	0030
per 1 barrel of corne	025
per 2 servants 3 days	0010
per 4 men 7 days	0040
per So much to be abated out of the levies of MR: MEARS for a hogg the which the Burgesses had the last Assembly	0040
	390

12th APRIL 1641 f 37 p 75 btm 52

AT A COURT
HOWLDINGE IN LOWER NORFOLK AT THE HOWSE OF MR: HENRY SEAWELL
Upon the 12th of April Anno. Dom. 1641
PRESENT: CAPT: THO: WILLOUGHBY ESQ.

CAPT: JOHN SIBSEY MR: HENRY SEAWELL
MR: WILLM: JULIAN LEIFT: ffRANCIS MASSON

Whereas it appeareth to this court that THOMAS CODD is indebted unto LANCKESTER LOVETT in the quantity of 5 barrels of corne and 50 l tob he the said CODD being bound with one JOHN WILLIAMS for the said debt and the said WILLIAMS is departed the country without making satisfaction for the same: It is therefore ordered that the said CODD shall make payment of the said debt and provide a boate and hands to transport the said corne from Reffth creek unto the howse of the said LANCASTER LOVETT situated in the Little Creek of Linhaven Parish, the said boate and hands to be provided within eighteen days otherwise execution

Whereas it appeareth to this court by the depositions of several persons that SAVILL GASKINE and ANNE his wife hath scandalously and defamously reported and asserted against ANNE ffOSTER wife unto RICH: ffOSTER concerning her being delivered of a child and that the said child was privately made away the which the said GASKINE nor ANNE his wife can bring any testimony or proof: It is therefore ordered that the said SAVILL shall receive 20 lashes upon the bare back and the said ANNE his wife 10 lashes in the like kind presently to be executed by the sheriff and also that the said SAVILL GASKINE shall make payment of the charges of this court concerning these proceedings in this suit otherwise &c

Whereas it appeareth to this court by a note of particular debts upon oath that JAME WEM (or PEM) is indebted unto JOHN HOLLMES the some of 50 l tob stript and smooth: It is therefore ordered that the said WEM shall by the last of November next ensuing make payment of the said debt with charges of the Court otherwise execucon

These are to certify that SIMOND HANCOCK hath made appear to this court that he hath due to him 50 acres of land by the transportation of ABRAHAM THOMAS into this collony in the Allexander in anno Dom 1637

* Whereas it was ordered by this Court this present 12th of Aprill that SAVILL GASKINE and ANNE his wife for divers scandals reported upon ANNE ffoster wife unto RICH: ffOSTER should undergoe the penalty and censure of this court the said SAVILL was to have 20 lashes on the bare back and the said ANNE his wife to have 10 lashes in like kind but by the entreaty of the said RICH: ffOSTER and his wife The said punishment is remitted and the said order repealed provided and also be it ordered that the said SAVILL and ANNE his wife shall ask the said ANNE ffOSTER public forgiveness here in open Court and also the next sabbath the minister preacheth at their parish church before the congregation there present after the first lesson in morning prayer saying after the minister such worde as he shall deliver unto them and also pay the charges of * f 37a p 76

f 37a p 76 btm 52 12th April 1641

the Court as aforesaid in the former order.

Whereas it appeareth to this Court by Mr. HENRY SEAWELL that he said HENRY, hath received of OLIVER VANHECK in the yeare of our Lord 1638 the sum of 460 lbs of tob.

Whereas CRISTOFER BURROUGH and MARY SOMES are presented to this Court by the Church wardens of Linhaven Parish for committinge of fornication, with absolute testimony of the same it is therefore that the said CRISTOFER and MARY shall accordinge to the statute of England do penance in their parish Church the next sabbath the minister preacheth at the said Church standinge in the middle ally of the said Church upon a stool in a white sheet, and a white wand in their hands all the time of divine service and shall say after the minister such words as he shall deliver unto them before the congregacon there present and also pay the charges of the court.

THOMAS TOOKER and EDY HAIMTINE are to undergo the like penance at their Parish Church according to the tennor of this order and so is SAVILL GASKINS and his wife and to pay the Court charges.

It is ordered per curiam that JOHN GAYTER administrator of the estate of JOHN DRAYTON shall satisfy and pay unto ROBT: BODY Under Sheriffethe fee due to his place for the outcrie of JOHN DRATONS estate otherwise execucon.

the Deposition of JOHN WEBB aged 35 years or thereabouts
Sworn & Examined sayeth:
that he heard THOMAS DAVIS report that SAVILL GASKINE should say that the wife of RICH: FOSTER had a mischance, a child or the like and that the said GASKINE said that he could not endure such base whores and further this deponent sayeth not.

*f 38 *the Deposition of ENSIGN THOS: LAMBERT
p 77 aged 30 years or thereabouts sworn & examined sayeth:
btm that he, this deponent bought of ROBT: PAGE one servant named ANTONY
p53 a Portungall for the sum of 600 lbs tob and urged the said MR: PAGE to let him have the said ANTONY for 4 years but he would not put him off for any longer than 3 years so this said ANTONY being unwilling to live with this deponent the said deponent changed him with CAPT: JOHN SIBSEY for one JAMES MONSERE and further this deponent sayeth not.

the deposition of GEORGE KEMPE aged 28 years or thereabouts
Sworn and examined sayeth:
That TRIESTRAM MASSON about the last of November last sold a piece of land unto THOMAS IVEY the whole bound for the term of six years and the halfe forever whereof it was agreed upon that the said THOMAS IVEY should pay for the said land the sum of £ 8.10s in money prelse as much tobacco as should satisfy the said sum of money. Whereupon the said TRIESTRAM MASSON gave the said THOMAS IVEY order to go upon the said land when he pleased and further this deponent sayeth not.

MATHEWE HOLLMES aged 26 years or thereabouts sworn and Examined delivered the same verbatum.

12th April 1641 f 38 p 77 btm p 53

the Deposition of THOMAS BRITAINE aged 30 years of thereabouts Sworn and Examined sayeth:
That TRIESTRAM MASSON suddenly after he had sold the piece of land to THOS: IVEY he came to the house of the said IVEY and there did relait what he had sold unto the said THOS: IVEY which was a piece of land, with his right and Title thereunto which right he did assure to be the whole for 6 years and the half forever.

These are to certify whome it may concerne that HENRY HAWKINS hath shipped aboard the ffRANCIS 5. hogsheads of tobacco all of this years growth only 40 lbs of ould tob and 150 stripted. The other in blade and stalk - the master of the said ffRANCIS is JOHN HOGGE for this present voyage.

JOHN SIBSEY

*ATT A COURT *f 38a p78

HOWLDINGE IN THE LOWER NORFOLKE the 2nd of MAY 1641

PRESENT:

CAPT: THO: WILLOUGHBY ESQ:

CAPT JOHN SIBSEY LEFT: ffRANCIS MASSON
MR: EDW: WINDHAM MR: HENRY SEAWELL

MR: WILL: JULIAN

Whereas it appeareth to this Court by Condicon that ffRANCIS LAND is indebted unto HUGH WOOD in the sum of Ŀ 6.5s sterlinge for payment whereof he the said ffRANCIS LAND was to ship home one hogshead of tob for England and to stand to the adventure thereof: it is therefore ordered that the said ffRANCIS shall fully perform the said condition bearinge date the 27th Feb 1640 if in case he shall not show sufficient reason to the contrary the next monthly Court otherwise execucon.

Whereas it appeareth to this Court by the oaths of two sufficient men that WILLM: CRUCH hath spoken many irreverent uncomely and unfitting speeches against the Committee of this Court and in a disdainful manner slighted their order granted unto TRIESTRAM MASSON: It is therefire ordered that the said WM: CRUCH shall pay a fine for his misdemeanor the some of 200 lbs tob towards the maintenance of a ferrie here in the county and shall also ask the said Committee forgiveness here in open Court and acknowledge his default otherwise execucon.

The Last Will and Testament of ROBT: HAND proved by the oath of JAMES WARRNER

Whereas it appeareth to this Court by oath of sufficient witnesses that GEORGE WAID (name may be WAIE or WAY *Waid*) deceased was indebted unto WILLM: BURROUGH the sume of 50 shillings sterling and the estate of the said GEORGE WAID being of little value and no man administering upon the estate, it is therefore ordered that the said WILLM: BURROUGH shall have full power to collect together the estate of the said GEORGE WAID wheresoever distributed within the custody of any person or persons within this county unto his own possession and shall in the first place satisfy himself the said 50 shillings with his charges in the collection provided that he put in security unto This Court to be accountable for the estate of the said WAID to any person or persons which hereafter shall have power to call the said estate into question otherwise execucon.

*f 39 p 79 btm 54 *It is ordered by this Court that the estate of (V)ICTOR CRASETT (there is a hole in the paper where the first letter of this name should be) deceased shall be brought by the persons that have it in their possession unto the howse of JOHN STRATTON situated in Linhaven Parish and there the said estate to be sold at an outcry by two men who shall keep an inventory of the said estate so sold with the rate so mentioned and to receive and to be accountable for the same unto this court which said estate according to appointment mey be disposed of for the use of the children of the said CRASSETT deceased. (This name may be CRAFFET)

Whereas there was an order of Court granted by the Governor and Council and directed to the Commander of this County that their Pishe (Parish) Church should be erected and built at MR: SEAWELLS POINT at the cost and charge of the said inhabitants that a chapel of ease should be built in Elizabeth River at the charge of particular families situated in the said river by reason of the remote plantations from the aforesaid pishe Church; It is therefore ordered that at no time after the date hereof there shall be any vestry chosen nor held at the aforesaid Chapell but that the said Chapell shall be accounted a Chapell of ease but no Pishe (Parish) Church and that the vestry shall ever hereafter be chosen and held at the aforesaid Pishe Church provided that their priviledges in the ministration be alike and the charges in the transporting the minister every other Sunday unto the aforesaid Pishe Church be equally levied upon every tithable person inhabiting within the aforesaid Pishe.

Whereas it appeareth to this Court by depositions that certain corne is due from the estate of CAPT: ADAM THORROWGOOD deceased unto CAPT: THOS: WILLOUGHBY the said corne beinge delivered by the servants of the said CAPT: WILLOUGHBY unto CAPT: ADAM THORROWGOODS horses the which this bord (board?) haveing taken into consideracon have therefore ordered that MR: JOHN GOOKIN who intermarried with MRIS SARAH THORROWGOOD late wife to the said CAPT: THORROWGOOD deceased shall satisfy and deliver unto the said CAPT: WILLOUGHBY at his now dwelling house the quantity of 4 barrels of corne within 30 days otherwise execucon.

*f39a p 80

*3rd May 1641

It is ordered that neither RICHARD HORNER nor EDWARD CRADALL should not embezzle or make away any part or parcel of their estate that is bound over unto LANCKASTER LOVETT for their performance according to the terms of a bond made between the aforesaid parties bearing date the 27th of Aug 1640.

MR: HENRY SEAWELL hath entered as security unto this Court for THO: SELLOCK to answer for all debts or obligations which any person or persons shall make appeare to be due before this present date within the Colony of Virginia the said THOMAS SELLOCK hereby being licensed to take shippinge for England.

Whereas LEIFT: ffRANCIS MASSON hath arrested MR: JOHN MEARRES (sic) unto this Court concerning a sume of 400 lbs of regulated tob due unto HUMPHREY HANDMORE the which said sume of 400 lbs tob the said HUMPHREY HANDMORE demanded of the said ffRANCIS MASSON but the said MEARE alleging that he is not provided to answer the suit desireth a reference until the next monthly Court: It is therefore ordered that the said JOHN MEARRE shall put in personal security to discharge him the said ffRANCIS MASSON of all damages which may or shall arise concerning the said sume of 400 lbs tob and also to answer the suit of the said ffRANCIS MASSON according to the premises at the next monthly Court holden in the County.

Whereas it appeareth to this Court that JOHN LANCKFEILD deceased was indebted unto ALEXANDER STONNER(Stonner) in the some of 40 lbs of stripted and smooth tob and the said debt beinge assigned over by the said STONER (Stoner) unto MR: CORNELIUS LOYD: It is therefore ordered that the administration of the said LANCKFIELDS estate shall within ten days satisfie and pay unto the said CORNELIUS LOYD the said debt otherwise execucon.

MR: JOHN GAYTER doth stand bownd with MR: NATHAN STANDESMOR or his security unto this Court for the answering a sute (suit) of one RETHIEN DUDINGE in London concerninge a hogshead of tob was sent home to the said RETHRINE DUDINGE (sic) from Virginia one GEORGE WATTSON by MR: NATHAN STANDSMORE (this name probably should be STAINSMORE) but not delivered.

It is ordered that MR: JOHN GATER (Gater) shall according to former order provide one bed and bolster and rugg and pott for THOMAS HALL his servant according to the tennor of his indenture the said particulars to be delivered unto the said THO: HALL at the next returne of shippinge - Execucon f 40

*Whereas it appeareth to this court by sufficient testimony that p81
WILLM: CRUCH (Cruch) hath made use of one hogshead of tob con- btm
taining 250 nett the which said hogshead of tob was left at the 55
howse of the said CRUCH for the use of MR: ROBT: ffEAKE (ffeake) It is therefore ordered that the said CRUCH shall make present payment of the like sume of 250 lbs tob and caske with Court charges otherwise execucon.

Whereas it appeareth to this Court by specialty that ffRANCIS LAND is indebted unto HUGH WOOD two pairs of shoes It is therefore ordered that the said ffRANCIS LAND shall within ten days make payment of the said debt and court charges otherwise Execucon.

Whereas it appeareth to this Court by a letter under the hand of WILLM: ATTERBURY that he the said ATTERBURY is indebted unto LEIFT: ffRANCIS MASSON in the some of £ 3.14s.7d. It is therefore ordered that ROBT: ffEAKE attorney for the said ATTERBURY (Atterbury) shall give the said ffRANCIS MASSON good security for the payment thereof until such time as there be newes out of England from the said ATTERBURY concerninge the same.

f 40 p 81 btm 55 2nd May 1641

GEORGE WATSON hath produced here in Court a bill of ladginge (sic laden) for one hogshead of tob beinge markt and numbered as in the margen bearinge date the 23 Apr 1639 being shipt aboard the William,CATO GARRISON beinge master (of the) voyage and signed by the hand of MR: ROBT: PAGGE.

The Deposition of WILLIAM TRUMBALL 28 years sayeth that he this deponent havinge order from ROBT:DARBY to carry corne to CAPT: THORROWGOODS horsses (sic) the which this deponent did carrying them a hominy sifter full of corne and further saie that he hath seene divers of CAPT: THORROWGOODS servants carry them corne and at sundry times as namely JOHN WEBB, WILLIAM STEEVENS, JAMES SMITH and JOHN HALLBACK and two of CAPT: WILLOUGHBIES servants namely JOHN SCOTT, JOHN BOULTON and further sayeth not.

The deposition of JOHN WATTFORD 32 sayeth that an agreement produced unto this Court bearinge date the 9th Jan 1639 is a true and absolute agreement maid betweene WILLM: CRUCH and TRESTRUM MASSON and further sayeth not.

*f 40a p 82 The Deposition of ROBT: DARBY 36 sayeth that CAPT: ADAM THORROWGOOD beinge at the howse of CAPT: THO: WILLOUGHBY ESQR: this deponent found occasion to speake unto the said CAPT: THORROWGOOD and told him that CAPT: WILLOUGHBYS servants did grumble that the corne was given unto the said CAPT: THORROWGOODS horses and they being on ellection (sic) to Count whereupon the said CAPT: THORROWGOOD replied that what corne they had eaten he would make satisfaction for to the full and demanded of this deponent what corne he thought the horses had eaten who tould him 3 barrels of corne and the said CAPT THORROWGOOD said that he had 3 barrels of corne at LEIFT: MASSONS the which if he could tell how to gett downe to the said CAPT: WILLOUGHBIES he would make payment thereof in satisfaction of what corne his horses had eaten whereupon this deponent maid answer that being it was so near he would goe and receive it but in a short time after this deponent hearinge that GUILBERT GUY had received the said corne he sought noe further after it and further deposeth that since the last arrival of the said CAPT: THO: WILLOUGHBY into this Collony that there hath been delivered at six several times corne to the said horses, the said corne being delivered in a tray but the quantity this deponent knoweth not and farther saith not.

The Deposition of TRIESTRUM MASSON 22 sayeth: That goweinge (going) to WILL: CRUCH his house to demand of the said CRUCH satisfaction according to the tennor of an order of Court but the said denyeth to make payment and said to the said TRESTRUM that he had the grand order and bid him goe and wipe his arsse with his order and further sayeth not.

The Deposition of MARKES LENNOR (Lennor)aged 24 sayeth: That beinge in the heareinge of certain words spoken between TRESTRUM MASSON and WILLIAM CRUCH he heard the said TRESTRUM demand of the said CRUCH satisfaction accordinge to the tennor of his order of court but the said WILL: CRUCH replied that he had a grand order and he cared not a fart for his order of court and further sayeth not.

The deposition of NATHAN STANDSMOR aged 54 sayeth that in the year of our Lord 1639 this deponent cast up all the accounts debts and recknings that was due betwixt JOHN GATER° and JOHN DRATON and the said accounts beinge balanced the said JOHN DRATTON was indebted unto the said GAYTER° (sic) so much tob as the bill then maid by this deponent doth mention on and this deponent wished the aforesaid parties to draw releases betweene them because theire account was of so longe standinge so this deponent drew theire relesses and they discharged each other but the said DRATTON was remaininge 2000 lbs tob in MR: GAYTERS debt so there was a new bill drawne for the old debte: It was dated after the releasse or else the relese had cut off the specialty and further saith not. (the clerk who wrote this was anything but consistent in his spelling - note the word release and John Gater's name)

*The Deposition of ROBT: ffEAKE aged 37 sayeth: That about the 10th Aug last past this deponent did see CAPT: JOHN SIBSEY deliver unto MR: THO: STAGG three shirts for servants for the which the said THO: SAGG (spelled - Stagg & Sagg by clerk) promised the said CAPT: SIBSEY eather (either) shirts again or else sufficient satisfaction and further sayeth not.

*f 41 p 83 btm 56

17 May 1641

Be it known unto all men by these presents that I, THOMAS MILLES (millrs) of the Lower Norfolke in Virginia planter doth bind myself, my heires executors and assignes in the sum of £ 50 sterlinge mony of England to answer to all such caushons (cautions) and objections which may or shall heereafter arrise against the body or estate of WILLM: BRETT as also to discharge all bills bonds debts reckonings and accounts which shall appeare to be due from the aforesaid WILLM: BRETT unto any person or by attorney or assigne or his or eather of their assignes as aforesaid to the true performance hereof I have set my hand this 17th May Anno Dom 1641

Witnesse: The Mark of
ROBT: ffEAKE THO: MILLRS

(could the name be Miller?) Tho: millrs

The deposition of RICH: LEE aged 32 sayeth: That beinge with WILLM: BURROUGH about July last the said WILLM: BURROUGH sould a boar to GEORGE WADE for 50 shillings sterlinge and bade the said WADE fetch him away at the same price and further sayeth not.

Jurtins Corum me
EDW: WINDHAM

(NOTE: This is still the 2nd May Court. The last entry on f 41 dated 17 May was simply entered on a blank space on the page by Edward Windham and as you will seethere seems to have been no June Court. AGW)

	L. s. d.
MR: HENRY SEAWELL is Creditor 1638 March 12th	
By Cash receaved of MR: RICHARD WAKE	144-12- 9
By cash receaved of MR: WILLM: WEBSTER	173-18- 9
	318-11- 6
Rest to balance this account	003-08- 8

per. me. ROBT: PAGE

More to be accountable to the said MR: SEAWELL ffor Ŀ 130 s. 1 p. 6 adventured in the shipp Allexander as also the profits of the aforesaid monie of the aforesaid shipps voyage to and from Virginia and likewise to accountable to him for Ŀ 40 disburst after the shipps arrival in England for the aforesaid voyage as also to give or his assignes an account of the saile of six hogsheads of tob sent home in the ship Americay (America?) 1638 MR: ROBT: ANDERSON Master of the said shipp. Witness my hand this 12th Mar 1638

per me. ROBT: PAGE -

April the 10th 1639 - Further I ame (aim?) to give the said HENRY SEAWELL or his assigns an account of the saile of two hogsheads of tob I received by MR: WILLMSON: Master of the Janne of London - Lastly I ame to be accountable unto the said HENRY SEAWELL or his assignes for the one halfe of a shallop laydinge (loading or lading) of sasafras roots to be sould in England, share of my fraite for my halfe for the performance of all and of every particulars of these accounts I bind me and my heires executors administrators or assignes unto the said HENRY SEAWELL his Executors or assignes for the true performance - per me. ROBT: PAGE

Wittness: WILLIAM ATTERBURY

(The name Atterbury is in the index as A. Herbury. Atterbury is correct AGW)

f 42 *MR: HENRY SEAWELL is debtor - 1638 -

p 85

btm 57

	L. s. d.
By two quarter cask of wine	011-04-00
By two Shades	000-10-00
By two adz	000-04-00
By two coopers axe	000-03-04
By two perser (?) stocks and four bitts	000-04-00
By one Joynter & form	000-04-00
by one drawinge knife	000-01-04
By 1/2 a peece of silke mooehaire (mohair)	002-14-00
By 10 yards of silver lace	002-05-00
By one caster and band	001-10-00
By one hatt casse	000-04-00
By Coopers nayles	000-06-00
By freight & pettie charges	001-00-00
By one pare of stillyards the last year	001-01-00
By 1/4 part of the charges of the shipp Pellican	260-11-00
By cash disburst for the Alexander	040-00-00
May 12th (1641? or 1638) per MR:ROBT: PAGE	321-19-08

2nd May 1641 f 42 p 85
btm 57

The humble petition of CRISTOFER BURROUGH Showeth that whereas your humble petitioner did at a court houldinge at WILLM: SHIPPS bringe one WILLM: STEEVENS into the Court to have his deposition taken concerninge a difference which than was and is still betwixt your petticoner (petitioner) and CAPT: JOHN SIBSEY concerninge two months service and cloathes and other things which are due from the said CAPT: SIBSEY, now so it is. May it please your worships that he the said CAPT: SIBSEY did without any just cause denie to have the said deposition taken by which meanes your petticoner in regard the said WILLM: STEEVENS liveth not in this County is still kept back from his due contrary to all equity and justice to your petticoners great damage in regards your petticoner in these times of scarsity hath been driven to buy such cloathes as is due from the said CAPT: SIBSEY at greate rates whereof your petticoner desireth that the said CAPT: SIBSEY may be ordered to procure the said WILLM: STEEVENS his personall apparel at the next Court howldinge in the County or else his answere upon oath before a magistrate to such interrogatories as your pet.. shall deliver unto him, the said CAPT: SIBSEY by your pet..

* f 42a
p 86

ATT A COURT
HOWLDINGE AT THE HOWSE OF LIEFT: ffRANCIS MASSON
19 Jul 1641

PRESENT: CAPT: THO: WILLOUGHBY ESQR:
CAPT: JOHN SIBSEY MR. HENRY SEAWELL
MR: EDW: WINDHAM MR: WILLM: JULIAN
LIEFT: ffRANCIE MASSON

Whereas it was ordered by a Court Howldinge in the lower Norfolke the 12 Apr 1641 That SAVILL GASKINE and ANNE his wife should for ffornicacon do pennance in their Pishe Church which being not performed accordingly. It is therefore ordered that the said SAVILL and ANNE his wife shall upon the Second Saboth in August next ensuing do penance in their said pishe church standing upon a stool in the middle alley of the said church in a white sheete and a white wand in theire hands at the time of devine service and shall say after the minister such words as he shall deliver unto them before the congregacon there present and also pay the charges of the court.

THOMAS TOOKER and EDY his wife should undergo the like penance for the like Trespasse committed by them accordinge to a former order havinge date with SAVILL GASKINES order.

These are to certify the right worshipful SIR ffRANCIS WIATT according to the tennor of a warrant bearinge date 7 Jul 1641 that fowre certificates and one order of Court hath been cleared and approved on by the Commiessioners of the Lower Norfolke amounting to the number of 64 hogshead and 560 lbs of tob which said certificates and the said order are returned by HUMPHREY PRICE unto the Secretaries office under the Commissioners hands of the aforesaid county.

Whereas there is a store to be built for the limits of Linhaven extendinge to DANIELL TANNERS Creeke according to an act of assembly and by the requiry of the inhabitants of the aforesaid limitts. CAPT:

THOMAS WILLOUGHBY and JOHN GOOKINS have undertaken to build the said store and to find all necessaries thereunto the said store the said store to be built 60 foote long & 20 foote wide with 8 foote pitch upon the Point of CAPT. WILLOUGHBIE next adjoininge to MR. MASON'S CREEKE. In satisfaction thereof the said CAPT. WILLOUGHBIE and MR. GOOKIN are to have 1200 lb tobacco stript and smooth, to be levied upon inhabitans of the whole county according to the Act of Assembly in that case provided.

It is ordered that the inhabitants of Linhaven shall against the next Monthly Court make choyce of one or two men to answer the objections of MR. SAYER, SHREEFE of the Lower Norfolke accordinge to the tennor of his petticon preferred to this Court and MR. EDW: WINDHAM is hereby required to summone the said inhabitantsto the same effect.

WHEREAS: EDW: CRADALL hath arrested EDW: LILLY unto this Court concerning a peece the which said peece was to be stockt by the said LILLY, the which the said LILLY performed accordinge to a latter agreement, as appeareth by witnesses and was ready to be delivered upon demand; It is therefore ordered that the said EDW: LILLY shall deliver the said peece unto the said CRADALL in as good order as it was delivered to him and the said peece to be sufficiently stockt by the said LILLY and the charges equally to be discharged by them.

WHEREAS: BARTHOLOMEW HOSKINS hath arrested ROBT: HAYES to this Court concerninge a debt of 100 lbs of tobacco the which the said HOSKINS alledgeth to be due to him from the said HAYES but the said ROBT: HAYES makinge it appeare by wittnesses that he hath satisfied the some of 100 lbs of tobacco: It is therefore ordered that the said BARTHOLEMEW HOSKINS shall pay the charges of the Court.

WHEREAS: It was ordered at a Court howldinge in the Lower Norfolke the 2nd May 1641 that if ffRANCIS LAND did not show sufficient proofes to this Court that the condition menchoned in the said order were fully satisfied, that then the said order should stand in force, wherein he having fayled. It is ordered that ffRANCIS LAND accordinge to former order shall make payment unto HUGH WOOD, of the debt mentioned in the said order within 14 dayes, other wise Execution.

WHEREAS: It appeareth to this Court by specialty: that ffRANCIS LAND is indebted unto CAPT: THO: WILLOUGHBY ESQR: the sum of 7 Ŀ Sterlinge due to be paid in England upon 20 dayes sight whereas he havinge fayled: It is therefore ordered that the said ffRANCIS LAND shall, within 20 dayes make payment of the said debt, with forbarance according to the acts of Assembly, with Court Charges, otherwise execution -

It is ordered that SAVILL GASKINS shall pay unto RICH: ffOSTER the quantity of 150 lbs of stript and smooth tobacco, the said some arisinge due unto the said ffOSTER for charges in a sute in Court betweene them, the said SAVILL and RICHARD.

f 43a p 88

*WHEREAS: It appeareth by oath that MARY SOMES was forced by CAPT: JOHN SIBSEY to serve 7 weekes longer in her termof service mentioned in her indenture and hath not given any satisfaction to the said MARY for the same. It is therefore ordered that the said CAPT: SIBSEY shall pay, in sattisfaction of the said 7 weekes service unto the said MARY SOMES the sum of 40 lbs of stript and smooth tobacco with the Court Charges. Otherwise Execution.

WHEREAS: It appeareth unto this Court that GEORGE WAIDE deceased was indebted unto THO: BULLOCK the sum of 2 ₶ . 18s. Sterlinge it is therefore ordered that the said THOMAS BULLOCK shall be satisfied the said debt out of the estate of the said GEORGE WAIDE deceased provided that WILLM: BURROUGH be first sattisfied accordinge to a former order.

WHEREAS THOMAS KEELING is indebted unto WILL BURROUGH the quantity of two pownds of soape It is therefore ordered that the said THOMAS KEELINGE shall meke present payment of the said 2 lbs of soape or else six shillings sterlinge otherwise Execution.

It is ordered that MR: HENRY CATTLINE shall pay unto CAPT: JOHN SIBSEY the sum of 20 lbs of tobacco stript and smoothe the which is due from the said HENRY CATTLINE unto CAPT: SIBSEY for one month's service as by assignment of one MARIE SOMES for three yeares service unto the CAPT: SIBSEY and she the said MARIE makinge it appeare by oath that she had not so longe to serve by one compleate month.

WHEREAS: ELLINE REDER hath petticioned unto this Court against CAPT: JOHN SIBSEY concerning cloathes and corne the which is due unto her but the said CAPT: SIBSEY being unprovided to answere the said ELLINE according to the tennor of her peticion but craveth that her sute may be reffered untill the next Monthly Court; It is therefore ordered that the said CAPT: SIBSEY shall at the next Monthly Court answere to the objections of the said ELLINE according to the tennor of her petticion preferred to this Court.

The Deposition of Leift: ffRANCIS MASSON age 46 years &c Sayeth: That MARIE SOMES, servant of CAPT: JOHN SIBSEY upon her departure out of his service had one greene kertell wastcote the which was whole but the vallew thereof this deponent knoweth not and farther sayeth not.

f 44 p 89 19 July 1641

The deposition of ffRANCIS LAND, age 37 yeares sayeth that he sold unto WILLM: LAYTON one servant, namely GEORGE WAID and for sale of the servant this deponent enjoined the said WILL LAYTON to give him, the said WAID, one pott and bedd to him but not to his assignes and if the said WAID did take up 50 acres of land this deponent was to insure it unto the said WAID and further sayeth not.

The deposition of CORNELIUS LOYD age 33 sayeth That he heard HENRY CATTLINE say divers times that MARIE SOMES came over a servant for fowre years and after she the said MARIE had served one year of thereabouts there was a bargaine betwixt CAPT: SIBSEY and the said HENRY CATTLINE for a parcel of land for 1500 lbs of tobacco for which some of tobacco this deponent hath heard both CAPT: SIBSEY and MR: CATTLINE say that the said CAPT: SIBSEY was to have 500 lbs of tobacco and MARY SOMES for 3 yeares for the 1000 lbs of tobacco and further this deponent sayeth not.

The Humble petition of Xopher Burrough:

Showeth that whereas your petticoner did at a court holden at MR: HENRY SEAWELL's produce a writinge he maid appeare that ffRANCIS LAND was indebted unto him a man servant now, so that it is that he the said ffRANCIS LAND heth since given out divers suspicious speeches concerninge the same, as if your petticoner had forged the writing, whereby he hath raised to your petticoner the infamous name of a forger of deeds and consequently of an impious, impudent perverse person, because your petticoner did then prove the said writing by his owne oath, by which report your petticoner is much defamed and damnified, wherefore your petticoner humbly desireth that, unless he the said ffRANCIS, can prove these, his caluminiative charges, your petticoner may have some reliefe from this court accordinge to equity and justice, and your petticoner shall pray &c.

The earnest petition of CRISTOFER BURROUGH:

Complayninge showeth that your petticoner heveing engaged himself unto ffRANCIS LAND by specialty for 700 lbs of tobacco in part payment for divers goods and servants bought of him the said ffRANCIS, so it is, may it please your worships, that he the said ffRANCIS hath and doth detain and utterly denie your petticoner some part and cuningly concealed other part of the said goods because he knoweth the petticoner cannot have testimony thereof to recover the same by course of common lawe and because he hath found some mistake or neglect in some
* writing then made and passed betwixt the petticoner and
f 44a the said ffRANCIS * contrary to all equity and good
p 90 conscience, whereby your petticoner heth been and still

is much damnified and disabled to sattisfie the said specialty which now he presenteth against your pettioner thereby endeavouring to take away as much as in him lieth, both your petticioners goods and creditt to his greate loss and hindrance, unless your petticioner may have some speedy remedy accordinge to equity and conscience whereof this Court Howld others plea as well as of meere law the premises considered considered your petticioner humbly craveth that he the said ffRANCIS may not proceed against your Petticioner concerning the said specialty, untill he have, accordgine to the custome of the courts of England, made answer in writinge upon oath, to this petticion and to these & other interrogatories which your petticioner shall choose out and your petticioner shall pray &c. viz.

1. Whether he hath delivered unto your petticioner all things whatsoever he sould your petticioner at that time or noe.

2. Whether he or his partner MR: HOWELL, or any other for them or either of them, to his knowledge, hath since that time, either for themselves of either of them or any other, detained, sould, concealed or maid use of any part or parcel of the goods which your petticioner then bought of him, the said ffRANCIS.

3. If anything were not delivered, or, since delivery, to his knowledge made away or any way by them or either of them concealed or kept from your petticioner, what it was and, as near as he can, to deliver particulars.

4. Lastly, that he declare upon oath to the best of his remembrance, what he then sould your petticioner and what he did by word of mouth, except and reserve to himselfe out of his estate which he then sold and whether he sold your petticioner any cask or noe and whether your petticioner were to receive or pay any tobacco and what, and so relate the whole bargaine as it was made in words, having no respect to the imperfect writinge Your petticioner further craveth that all prodeedings herein be kept upon record in the Court Book, and your petticioner shall likewise pray &c.

Be it known unto all men by these presents that we RICHARD HORNER and EDMUND GRADALL of the Lower County of New Norfolke planters, do owe and stand indebted unto LANCKESTER LOVETT of the same County, planter, the full and just some of 1700 lbs of tobacco stript and smooth The tobacco accordinge to the Acts of Assembly made by the Governor and Councell in the year of our lord, 1639, and caske sufficient * to pack the said tobacco in, and *f45
two barrells of good sownd Indian corne which tobacco p91
and corne is to be paid at or upon the 20th day of October which shall be in the yeare of Our Lord 1641. Now know yee that we, the above named RICH: HORNER and EDWARD

f 45 p 91 19 July 1641

GRADALL do bind ourselves or heires or assignes to pay the aforesaid 1700 lbs of tobacco in full quantity as if it weare this yeare to be pair and for the true performance of the same we do jointly and severally bind ourselves our heires Executors administrators or assignes and moreover we do bind over our plantacions and goods for security unto the aforesaid LANCKESTER LOVETT, his heires or assignes and in witness of the truth we the above named RICHARD HORNER and EDMOND GRADALL have hereunto sett our hands and seales this 27th of August 1640.

Signed, SEALED and delivered
in the presents of:
ROBT: EAVES (or Eares) and
JOHN WILLIAMS

RICH HORNER
EDMOND GRADALL
HIS MARK

Be it known unto all men by these presents that we RICH HORNER and EDWARD GRADALL of the Lower Norfolke in Virginia, planters, have condicioned and agreed with LANCKESTER LOVETT of the aforesaid place, planter for the payment of the full and just some and quantity of 1700 lbs of good sweet merchantable stript and smooth tobacco and cask and one barrell and a half of sweet sownd Indian corn, the said some being due from us the aforesaid RICH: HORNER and EDW: GRADALL unto the said LANCKESTER LOVETT as by specialty bearinge date the seventh and twentieth day of August, anno dom. 1640, as under our hands and seals may appear, Nor know ye that we the said RICH: HORNER and EDW: GRADALL accordinge to agreement as aforesaid doth bind ourselves our heires executors administrators and assignes jointly and particularly to pay or cause to be payd unto the above named LANCKESTER LOVETT his heires executors administrators or assignes or to any of them the just and compleate some of 1200 lbs of good sweete merchantable stript and smooth tobacco and casks, and one barrell and a halfe of sownd Indian Corne, due to be paid upon the 10th of October next ensuing the date hereof within the aforesaid Norfolke it being in part of payment of their aforesaid Specialty: Upon true performance whereof, well and truely to be maid and paid we doe bind over unto the aforesaid LANCKESTER LOVETT or to his heires Executors administrators and assignes or to him or either of them our whole estates whatsoever we are * possessed of within the colony of Virginia as howse, plantacion and servants and cattell and hoggs as also all moveables and immoveables to be ours either in our owne possession or elsewhere as also we the aforesaid RICH: and EDWARD do acknowledge that we have delivered into the possession of the said LANCKESTER some part of our estate as his security for the payment of the aforesaid debt of 1700 lbs of tobacco and cask and one barrel and a halfe of corne as also we bind ourselves not to bargain, sell or make away any part of our estates for any use or uses

*f4
p9

whatsoever but for the full and proper use of the said LANCKESTER towards the discharging o the aforesaid debt and in case this condition be not performed of our part accordinge to the tennor hereof that then our specialty to be in force according to the tennor thereof to the true performance whereof and our true intent of the performance of this condicion we have hereunto sett our hands and sealles the 29th of May Anno Dom. 1641.

Signed sealed & delivered in the presents of these witnesses:
ROBT: SMITH ESQ & WILL SMITH

RICHARD HORNER
The Mark of EDW: GRADALL

AT A COURT
Howldinge in the Lower Norfolke the 6 of September 1641 at the howse of MR: JULLIAN ---

Whereas it appeareth unto this Court that MARIE EDWARDS hath sold unto THOMAS SAYER, one servant named PHILLIP LAND and hath assigned all her right and title of the said PHILLIP unto the said THO: SAYER It is therefore ordered that the said THOMAS SAYER shall peacably enjoy the benefit of planting for the said PHILLIP LAND by virtue of this order according to the acts of Assembly in that case provided.

It is ordered that MR: ROBT: HAYES and MR: ROBT: EARES shall praise the whole estate of GEORGE LOCK, deceased, the said estate to be praised (appraised?) in tobacco to the best of theire judgments as they will affearme the same upon oath. * * f46 p 93

Whereas EDY TOOKER was ordered by a court howldinge the 12th of April 1641, for the fowle crime of fornication committed by her, to do penance in theire chappell of ease situated in Elizabeth River accordinge to the full intent and meaninge of the said order and she the said EDY beinge brought to the said Chappell of Ease to perform the said pennance in which time of performance and exhortation delivered unto her by the minister admonishing her to be sorrie for her fowle crime committed, but she the said EDY not regarding the good admonition of the said minister nor obayinge the tennor of the said order did, like a most obstinate and graceless person, cut and mangled the sheete wherein she did penance. It is therefore ordered that the said EDY shall receive at present 20 lashes on the barre back and on Sunday come fortnight do pennance in the aforesaid Chappell of Ease accordinge to the tennor of the said spiritual laws and formes of the Church of England in that case provided. at bot. p 61

Whereas ROBT: SMITH hath petticioned to this court to

be a store keeper for the limits of Linhaven and so to DANIELL TANNER'S creek It is therefore ordered that the said ROBT: SMITH shall supplie the the place of the said storekeeper and to have the bennefit appointed him in the acts of Assembly, provided that he put in Security for the due performance thereof and to be accountable to such persons as shall receave damage in their tobacco after it is safely delivered unto the store in case it be sufficiently proved it was his neglect.

THOMAS TOOKER is to performe the place of storekeeper for the limitts of Elizabeth River, MR: CORNELIUS LLOYD and MR: HENRY CARRLINE haveing pased in Court for his Security that he shall perform as in the former order is inserted.

Whereas there was a some of tobacco received by ROBT: SMITH from the inhabitants of Linhaven River amounting to the some of 1693 lbs of stript and smooth the which said some of tobacco was to have been received by the under shreefe from the aforesaid inhabitants and paid to the captain of the fort it beinge a levie due to him as by virtue of an act of Assembly the which said some of tobacco being fownd to be unmerchantable they, the aforesaid parties are hereby ordered to pay unto MR: THOMAS SAYER High Shreefe for this county the some of 600 lbs of tobacco stript and smooth viz the inhabitants which formerly
* made payment unto ROBT: SMITH of the said some of 1693
f46a lbs of tobacco or any pert thereof which was * not except-
p94 ed. (accepted) on by the said high shreefe shall pay proportionally alike to raise the some of 200 lbs of tobacco and 150 of there abouts to be paid by some particular inhabitants of the aforesaid river which as yett not satisfied their levies and ROBT: SMITH to pay 150 lbs of tobacco and the wife of the said under shreefe namely MARIE EDWARDS shall pay 100 lbs of tobacco the which sums are to be paid unto the said MR: THOMAS SAYER at the store appointed for Lower Norfolke this present yeare and the aforesaid parties as ROBT: SMITH, MARIE EDWARDS and the said inhabitants are by virtue of this order of court freely and fully discharged from the said THOMAS SAYER or his heires, predecessors of assignes or any one of them as touchinge the said levie or any part or parcel thereof.

Whereas it appeareth to this Court upon oath, that JOHN GODFRY hath due to him a debt of 330 lbs of tobacco and cask due from OLI ER VANHECK It is therefore ordered that the said OLIVER VANHECK shall make payment of the said debt within 20 dayes with 8 per cent forbarance together with court charges otherwise execution.

Whereas it appeareth to this court that MARIE EDWARDS

wife of WILLIAM EDWARDS deceased hath sustained damages in a certain some of tobacco received by ROBT: SMITH from the inhabitants of Linhaven by power given him by the said ROBT: SMITH shall pay in full satisfaction of the said damages unto the said MARIE EDWARDS the some of 100 lbs of stript and smooth tobacco it beinge to be paid within 15 dayes if in case he cannot balance his accounts otherwise Execution

It is ordered that CHRISTOPHER BURROUGH and THOMAS BULLOCK shall have power to imposse a levie of 200 lbs of tobacco proportionably amongst thosse inhabitants of Linhaven River which formerly payd a certaine levie unto ROBT: SMITH which would not be excepted on but was adjudged unmerchantable and condemned to the fire and where there is any of the said inhabitants which shall refuse to make payment of their proportion of tobacco It shall be lawfull for the aforesaid THOMAS BULLOCK and CHRISTOPHER BURROUGH to distraine upon any part of theire estates to satisfie the same.

(The Virginia Magazine of History & Biography published these records to this point. Their translation of the records adds commas, periods, and corrected spelling of the Clerk of Court's written account of these records. This book is being as true as possible to the original sans punctuation and using the original spelling by the clerk. AGW)

f 47 p 95 6 Sep 1641
at bot p 62

MR: ROBT: HAYES and OLIVER VANHECK and JOSIAS SMITH his mayte have agreed inthe Court that he the said ROBT: HAYES 330 lbs of tobacco (old debt)and cask unto JOHN GODFREY for OLIVER VANHECK and the said VANHECK and his mat(hole in paper) are to departe and (void space) the plantacion they are now seated on as sonne (?soon?) as theire Cropp is gathered .... off the said plantacion beinge the supposed Land of the said ROBT: HAYES and the said VENHECK was his mate and not to rewenate? nor spoyle the premese nor any priviledges or appurtinances there unto bellonginge.

Whereas it appeareth to this Court that THOMAS CAUSON is indebted unto WILLM: BURROUGH in the quantity of fowre barrells of Corne and he the said THO: CAUSON lledgine that he preferred payment unto the said WILLM: BURROUGH in good sowne Indian Corne The which he could not sufficiently raise It is therefore ordered that the said THOMAS CAUSON shall against the next monthly (Court) prove the same or else shall make payment within 20 dayes of such a some of tobb unto WILLM: BURROUGH as the said quantity of ffowre barrells of Corne hath beene sould for this present yeare otherwise Execution.

CAPT: SIBSEY hath maid appeare to this Court that he hath transported into this collony these 3 persons whose names are here inserted: EDWARD EWONES (Evans?) EDW: GOODAULES and JOHN GOUGH

Whereas It appeareth to this Court by oath that SERG-(torn) WILLM: EDWARDS in his lifetime did accnoledge (sic) that he had receaved all tobb: due unto ROBT: SMITH in Elizabeth river and theireabouts The which tobb: he said ROBT: SMITH hath maid appeare to be the some of 397 lb of stript and smothed tobb: It is therefore ordered that the wife of the said WILLIAM EDWARDS deceased shall make present payment (of) the said debt by discountinge with her otherwise Execution.

f*47a * CAPT: SIBSEY hath maid appeareth to this Court that
p 96 he hath transported into this collony thesse fowre per-
bot. sons whose names are here incerted:
p 62a ANTHONY a portugall in ANNE 1636
transported in the "Geoge"
JOHN ffAWRER in the "Francis" 1639
JOHN CRASSETT in the "Alexander"1639
(see the names below)

Whereas ROBT: SMITH hath petticioned to this Court that he might have free priviledge till Cristmas next for him to procure him a pattent for a parcell of land in the Little Creeke bownded on the Northern part by the land bot p 62a

of CAPT: ADAM THORROWGOOD on the South side by xxedgey marsh and Easterly upon the said Little Creeke and Westerly into the woods the quantity beinge 200 acres beinge Survaied by EDM: SCARBURGH the 20 Aug 1641.

MR: HOSKINS hath transported into this collony JOHN (G?)OODDER in the "Alexander" in 1637.

Whereas it appeareth to this Court that JOHN LANCKFEILD deceased was indebted unto ROBT: HAYES in the some of stript and smothed tobb: It is therefore ordered that the said ROBT: HAYES shall be first sattisfied out of the Estate of the said LANCKFEILD deceased otherwise Exec.

Whereas it appeareth to this Court that CHRISTOFER BURROUGH hath in a most upprobious (uproarous?) manner tax this Court with mistrie and cannot prove the same. It is therefore ordered that the said CHRISTOFER BURROUGH shall for his default pay as ofnine the some of 10 ƀ Sterlinge To be paid in tobb: halfe to the kinge a halfe to Publick uses.

CAPT: JOHN SIBSEY hath assigned unto ROBT: SMITH all his right and title of his certificate for 200 acres of land the which he hath maid appeare to be due to him by the transportinge of ANTHONY a Portugall, JOHN ffARRIOR, JAINE BATTERFELD and JOHN CRASSETT into this Collony. (see these names on page 74)

*f 48p 97 bot 63

* Whereas it appeareth to this Court that CAPT: JOHN SIBSEY is indebted unto ELLINE R-----der the quantity of 2 barrells and a halfe of corne. It is therefore ordered that the said CAPT: SIBSEY shall within 5 dayes make payment of the said corne in full sattisffaction of all demaunds otherwise Execution

Whereas it appeareth by oath that CAPT: SIBSEY sould unto HENRY HAWKINS one necke of land situated in Elizabeth River for the terme of 21 yeares. It is therefore ordered that the said CAPT: SIBSEY shall make the said HENRY HAWKINS a lease for the said land for the treme aforesaid accordinge (to) the forme as the said CAPT: SIBSEY hath maid them to other his tennanta.

Whereas it appeareth to this Court that JOHN STRATTON is indebted unto CAUSON in the quantity of one barrel of Corne It is therefore ordered that the sd JOHN STRATTON shall make present payment unto THOMAS CAUSON otherwise execucon.

MR. THOMAS CAUSSON hath made appeare to this Court that he hath transported into this Collony the persons

f 48 p 97 bot 63 6 Sep 1641

whosse names are as followeth:

HIMSELFE	ROBT: BRINCWELL	MARGRETT RALFE(Rolfe?)
JOHN MORE	GEORGE HARROD	THO: PRICHARD
JOANNE GILBERT	ffrai: SIMONDS	RICHARD LEE
JOHN fford	HENRY GRIDWELL	CLEM THEBOULD
RICH: HORTON	JOHN MORRIS	EDW: LINCH

The deposecon of WILLM: RAMSHAW aged 40 yeares saith that beinge at the howse of CORNELIUS LOYD in came HENRY HAWKINS and CAPT: SIBSEY beinge theire said unto the said HENRY that his oysters made him very ffatt whereupon the said HENRY replied that the oysters weare his owne With that the said CAPT: said unto the said HENRY Good man Rogue though I lett you my land for one & twenty yeares I did not lett you my oysters and farther saith not.

The deposition of ROBT: TAYLOR aged 28 yeares saith that CAPT: SIBSEY sould one parcell of land unto the said HAWKINS and to him this deponent situated in Elizabeth River for the terme of 21 yeares in sattisfaccon whereof this deponent and the said HENRY weare to pay unto the said CAPT: SIBSEY the some of 500 lb tobb -ole?- debt and 2 capons yearely and to discharge the kings rent.

f 48a *

p 98 The deposition of JOHN CRASSETT aged 36 yeares saith
bot that he heard MR^{is}: SIBSEY and ELLINE READERsay that if
p 63athe said MR^{is}: SIBSEY would give her one sute of cloths, two smocks and one pare of shooes and stockins and one sow shott and 3 barrells of Corne it shuld sattisfy her for all that was due unto her for her prentishipp and farther said that the said MRS: SIBSEY delivered unto the said ELINE READER all the aforesaid particulars only the corne which this deponent nowes not whether she receaved it or noe and farther saith not.

Inventory of what goods GEORGE LOCK deceased and HENRY BRAKES his partner were possest of within the collony of Virginia:
Halfe one plantecon and halfe one man servant for 1 1/2 yeares namely WILLM: HALL.
1 fflockbedd & I Boulster with 2 old blankets
1 chest & 1 case with locks & keyes
2 gunnes & 1 Iorne (sic) pott of 3 gals.
3 Pewter platters & 1 payre of potthookes
5 old adds & 3 Iorne hookes
1 old cloath sute & 1 paire of cloath Breeches
1 old waistcoate & 1 shirt & i old paire of shooes
1 paire of sto kins & 1 old sifter & 1 old gridiorne
1 Bible & 1 practis of piety & 3 small bookes
Halfe (of) one Barrowe & halfe (of) 1 sowe in the woods
2 pistolls, 3 trayes, 1 auger & 1 spitt
1 connough (sic?) & 1 paire of tobacco tongues

our cropp of corne & Tobb: growinge
1 Hatchett, 1 skimer & 2 paire of sizers
Debts due to HENRY BRACKES & GEORGE LOCK deseased
(The name above HENRY BRACKES is Brakes for HENRY BRAKES is in the Court Records of Lower Norfolk and this name should not be confused with BROCK AGW)
HENRY RUDKINS by bill 2 cowes & 70 lb tobb:
RICH: HORNER by bill 200 lb tobb:
WILLIAM JOHNSON by bill 90 lb Tobb:
Proved by the oath of HENRY BRAKES

f 49 p 99 bot 64

It is condicione(d) and agreed upon betweene THOMAS HOLLT and JAMES WARDNER of Virginia as followeth That the said partiesare and shall be absolute copartners in and of all goods, lands, chattells, moveables and immoveables for what time the said two parties shall please to live together and if the said partners shall please to part then they shall equally devid(e) theire estates the one to have the one halfe and the other to have the other of what estate that then the said parties shall at theire parting be possest with and it is further agreed upon if it shall please god to call either of the said parties away in the time of theire copartnershipp that then the other shall posses all the said estate left behind giveinge sattisfaction to the creditors. To the true performance of thesse covenants we have hereunto sett our hands the 14 May 1640.

THO: HOLLT
The marke of
JAMES IW WARDNER

Signed and delivered
in the presents of:
RENOLD fLEETE

The deposition of THO: HARRISON Clerkid (?) aged 25 yeares or thereabouts sworne the 14 Nov 1641 saith

That he this deponent beinge present at a Court howldinge in the Lower Norfolke upon the 7th of Sep last past Privetly (privately) wished THOMAS BULLOCK to advise XPOFER BURROUGH not to be forced father to prove it or else to suffer for his fallse accusation. The said THO: replied Lett him alone theire is no cause of feare for we cann and will if occasion shalbe prove at James Towne that this Court hath done Injustice Insstanceing (or Jusstanceinge) in a sute then (in) question betweene ANNE ffOSTER and ANNE GASKIN and farther this deponent saith not.

THOMAS HARRISON

p me
HEN: SEWELL

f 49a p 100 bot. 64a   4 Oct 1641

At a Court howldinge at the howse of CPT: JOHN SIBSEY
upon the 4 Oct 1641
PRESENT: CAPT: THOMAS WILLOUGHBY ESQR:
CAPT: JOHN SIBSEY
MR: HENRY SEWELL   Leift ffRANCIS MASSON

Whereas it appeareth to this Court that JOHN GAYTER hath arrested ROBT: MASTERS to this Court and cannot shewe (show) any just cause for the same. It is therefore ordered that the said JOHN GAYTER shall pay charges of the Court otherwise execucon.

MR: THO: MARSH
JOHN SPENCER   } Sworne Constables
WILLM: SHIPP

THOMAS MARSH hath maid appeare to this court that he hath due to him 150 acres of land for the transportation of himselfe & his wife into this Collony as also one WILLM: SMITH whome he bought of MR: ffLOOD facter to MR: JOHN BEALLE Marchant.

THO: BRITTAYNE hath entred his name to goe for England accordinge to the tennor of an order directed from the Gov[r] and Councell.

Whereas THO: BULLOCK hath arested ffRANCIS LAND TO this Court and XPOFER BURROUGHS atturney of the said THOMAS BULLOCK desieringe a refference to the next monthly Court refuseinge to proceed in the sute. It is therefore ordered that the sd THO: BULLOCK shall make unto the said ffRA: LAND of Court charges and damages otherwise Execucon.

Whereas it appeareth to this Court by condicion that WILLM: BURROUGHS is indebted unto THO: CAUSON in the number of 3 Deare. It is therefore ordered that the said WILLM: BURROUGHS shall within 3 months make payment of the said 3 deare. otherwise Execucon

f 50 Whereas it appeareth to this Court that RICH: HORNER
p101 is indebted unto THO: BULLOCK in the quantity 40 lbs of
bot stript and smoothed tobacco. It is therefore ordered
65 that the said RICH: HORNER shall give the said THO: BULLOCK present security for payment thereof otherwise Exec.

Whereas it appeareth to this Court that JOHN NUTKINE is indebted unto THO: IVEY in the some of 20 lbs tobb stript and smoothed It is therefore ordered that MR: WILLM: JULYAN Atturney of the said NUTKINE shall within 30 dayes make payment of the said debt otherwise Execucon

f 50 p 101 bot 65   4 Oct 1641

Whereas MR: JOHN GOOKINS hath petticioned unto this Court against MR: ROBT: HAYES, WILLM: SMITH & JOHN MORGASON desiering (sic) to have the said parties bownd up to Jamestowne to the next Quarter Court. It is therefore ordered that the sherrife shall take some (security) for their appearance at the next Quarter Court upon the sixth day thereof to answere to the sute of the said JOHN GOOKINS accordinge to the tennor of his peticion pfered here in Court.

The Deposicion of THOMAS CHEELY this deponent saith in April last or theireabouts beinge at THO: CAUSONS, WILLM: BURROUGHS did than demaund his corne of the said CAUSON WHO replied that it was theire in the boate if he would take it. The said WILLM: replied he would take it with allowance and the said CAUSON answered he might take it if he would if he would not he might lett it alone of which corne the said WILLM: told him he would take a barrell and carrie it home to his hoggs farther this deponent saith that the corne pfered by the said CAUSON to the aforesaid BURROWES was good corne only it was wett with salt water and broken off the eares and that the said CAUSON went away without giveinge any other answere to the said BURROWES and came noe more notwithstandinge he stayed theire a greate while and father this deponent saith not.

p me ED: WINDHAM

At a Court howldinge att the howse of MR: HENRY SEAWELL the 15th Nov 1641. LIEFT MASSON beinge absent.

Whereas it was ordered at a Court houldine in the Lower Norfolke the 6 Sep 1641 that ROBT: SMITH shuld put in sufficient security (at?) this Court for his due performance of Storekeeper accordinge to the Tennor of the said order wherein he the said ROBT: SMITH hath proceeded and procured CAPT: JOHN SIBSEY and MR: HENRY SEWELL (sic) for his security who have passed here in Courtthat the sd ROBT: shall pforme accordingly.

MR: THO: TODD hath maid appeare that he hath due to him 50 acres of land for the transportation of JOBE SEAMORE into this collony in the shipp Blessinge in 1637 ROBERT SMITH and THO: TOOKER sworne Storekeepers for the County and in the Injuntions of the Acts of the Last Grande Assembly.

f 50a p102 bot 65a

It is ordered that THO: TODD and ROBT: TAYLOR shall praise the estate of GILBERT GUY deceased in tobacco beinge sworne to that effect to pforme accordinge to the best of their knowledge.

ROBT: TAYLOR hath maid appeare that he hath due to him 200 acres of land by the transportinge of these persons whose names are hereunder (recorded) and hath assigned

f 50a p 102 bot 65a   4 oct 1641

over his right thereof unto JOHN HALLBECK, DANIELL DICKSON (in 1639, ROWLAND RENALLS 1637, ROBT: STEWARD 1639, BEN: GILLMAN 1637.

WHEREAS LANCKESTER LOVETT hath petticioned to this Court to have an order against RICH: HORNER for the paymt of 1350 1 tobb new debt with cask and 1 1/2 barrells of corne beinge 1200 lb theire of and 1 1/2 barrells of corne due by Bond to be paid this cropp and 150 the sd LANCKESTER is ingaged unto JAMES BLISSE for the said HORNER as also that he the said HORNER MAY PUT IN SECURITY into the said LANSKESTER for the payment of 500 lb tobb mor(?) in 1642. It beinge due by as by the aforesaid bond may appeare. It if therefore ordered that the said RICH: HORNER shall make pay(ment) of the said some of 1350 lb tobb and cask and 1 1/2 barrells of corne by the 10 Dec next and also (to) give the said LANCKESTER good security for the payment of the said some (of) 500 lb tobb in 1642 accordinge to the tennor of the aforesaid bond. They these parties haveinge reffered themselfe into this Court with joynt consent (NOTE: right hand side of this page is faded out in some places)

Whereas it appeares to this Court that WILLM: JOHNSON stands indebted unto JOHN HOLLMES in the some of 122 lb tobb stript and smoothed due by bill. It is therefore ordered that the said WILLM: JOHNSON shall by the 10 Dec next make payment of the said debt otherwise execucon.

It is ordered that the sherrife shall bind over Mr: THO: BULLOCK and CRISTOFER BURROWES to James Towne to appeare the 6th day of the next Quarter Court to answere to the objections of CAPT: THOMAS WILLOUGHBY as also to prove theire accusaticons (sic) incerted in theire petticion & pfered at the last Quarter Court against the said CAPT: WILLOUGHBY.

THOMAS BULLOCK, WILLM: BURROUGHS, JO: PHILLIPS & ROBT: BODY have entred (entered) theire names to this Court to goe for England.

ROBT: TAYLOR and LANCKESTER LOVETT have entred theire names to this Court to goe for England.

f51 p 103 - (NOTE: This folio is numbered 50a which is in error)
Bot 66

It is ordered that the shreefe shall bind over to JO: PAINER to appeare at the next Quarter Court at James Towne upon the (6th?) day thereof to answere the sute of WILLM: BLAND accordinge to the tennor of his petticion pferd unto the Court.

It is ordered that those persons liveinge within this County which are indebted unto GILBERT GUY deceased xx xxxx make theire appearance before the next Joyneinge Commissone and theire prove how they have sattisfied theire Ingagements due to the said GILBERT Then they are referred xxxx to pforme att the request of SIMON HANCOCK (&) this not to faile as they will answere the contrary at theire pells (Perils)

Whereas it appeareth to this Court that THOMAS KEELIN(G) did promise payment unto ROBT: (-torn- Name maybe COUCxH) the some of tobb which shuld appeare to be due unto him for (Levixx?) fees from certaine of the inhabitants of Linhaven. THO: KEELINGE beinge ingaged for them the which some appeares to be 207 lb stript and smoothed. It is therefore ordered that the said THOMAS KEELINGE shall by the 10 Dec next make payment of the said with Court Charges otherwise execution.

It is ordered that HENRY BRAKES shall receave the debts due unto himselfe and GEORGE LOCK deceased the which were due to them in theire copartnership provided that he shall be accountable for the same upon demand unto the Court of to any other whome it may concerne.

It is ordered that THO: HUES (HUGHES?) shall within 25 dayes make payment unto THOMAS BULLOCK of the some of 50 lb of tobb stript and smoothed otherwise Execucon.

It is ordered by the request of THOS: CAUSON and WILLM: BURROUGHS that MR: HENRY WOODHOWSE and EDW: HALL, THOMAS BULLOCK, CRISTOFER BURRxxxx (faded) shall end all differences and causes whatsoever dependinge beinge betweene the said THO: and WILLM: in the just and absolute terme of arbitrators cannot come to bringe it to a period. It is reffered to them to make cheyre? of an Xompir? upon whose determinacion the said WILLM: and THOMAS are xx?xxx to the arbiterment upon forfiture of 50 lb tobb to be paid by them who xxxxxx? first refuse to pforme accordinge to the tennor ot the foresaid arbiterment

Whereas it appeareth to this Court ffRANC: LAND is indebted unto ROBT: SMITH in the some of 230 lb of stript and smoothed tobb and past due by bill It is therefore ordered that the said ffRANCIS LAND shall within 20 dayes make payment of the said debt with Court Charges otherwise execucon

MR: THO: BULLOCK hath maid appeare to be due to him the quantity of 50 accres of land by the transportation of REBECCA his wife into this Collony and hath assigned over his right thereof unto THO: TODD in the behalfe of MR: JOHN GOOKINS.

f51a
p104
bot 66a

WHEREAS it was ordered by a Court howldinge in the Lower Norfolke the 19 Jul 1641 that the tithable inhabitants of ye said Norfolk shuld pay proporthonably (sic) for the buildinge of the store at CAPT: THO: WILLOUGHBIE accordinge to the true intent of an act of the last Grand

f51a p104 bot 66a   19 July 1641

assembly. It is therefore ordered that these Inhabitants shall pay in full satisfaction thereof the some of 4 lbs tobb per poll to be collected by the shreefe And it is further ordered that the tithable inhabitants belonging & liveing in the said Norfolke which are injoyned to bringe theire tobb to the said store shall pay proporchonably with the inhabitants of Elizabeth River and those that belonge to the limetts of that store to the full defrayinge of theire charges in hieringe of them a store accordinge to the Acts in that case provided.

Whereas it was ordered at a Court howldinge in the Lower Norfolke the 12 April 1641 that ANNE GASKINE for divers defamations and slanderious speeches raysed upon the wife of RICHARD ffOSTER touchinge her life and not proveing the same shuld aske the said ANNE ffOSTER forivenesse in the pishe Church of Linhaven accordinge to the tennor of the aforesaid order wherein she haveinge fayled sayinge that she would never pforme it as oath doth appeare and beinge arrested to this Court to answere for her contempt wherein she haveinge alsoe failed It is herefore ordered that the shreefe shall take the said ANNE GASKINE into his custody and forthwith conduct her into the howse of CAPT: THO: WILLOUGHBY & theire she shall receave 20 lashes on the bare back & from thence to be conducted to the pishe Church of Elizabeth River & theire to pforme upon the Saboth (Sabbath) next ensuinge thether accordinge to the tennor of the aforesaid order & upon her refusall that then she shall on the Monday then next ensuinge receave 30 lashes as aforesaid to be executed at the howse of MR: HENRY SEAWELL & remaine in the custody of the shreefe untill the insuinge Saboth and upon her refusal as aforesaid then to receave 40 lashes to be excuted at CAPT: SIBSEYS & upon continuance of her contempt to receave every Monday soe insuinge 50 lashes to be executed untill the pformance accordinge to the tennor of the aforesaid order. But upon her pformance thereof to receave a passe from the next commisoners to returne in peace to her habitation.

PHILLIPP LAND (or LANE) aged 35 yeares sworne saith that cominge to MR: GOOKINS his howse and arrestinge ANNE GASKINE she said "Lett CAPT: WILLOUGHBY bringe me from Court & doe what he can he shall neaver make me aske ANNE ffOSTER ('s) forgivenesse. And farther saith not.

f52 Whereas it appeareth by bill that RICH ffOSTER is in-
p105 debted unto M(torn) MARIAN UTIE the now wife to RICH:
bot BENNETT EXQR: in the some of 260 lb tobacco old debt and
67 1 barrel of corne in sattisfac(tion) whereof he is hereby ordered by the 24 Dec next to make payment of the some of 114 lb of tobacco stript and smooth otherwise execuson (Note: Sums do not agree in this record)

(NOTE: It seems that these 1641 orders are either being rehashed or reviewed by the 4 Oct Court. This conclusion is because of the 24 Dec date for Richard Foster on his debt. Thus the return to the 4th of October date of Court. AGW)

It is ordered that THO: CAUSON shall pay unto WILLM: BURROUGHS the some of 30 lbs of tobb stript and smoothed in sattisfaction of a bedd pott due to GEORGE WAIDE deceased from the said CAUSON and now to be paid to the said BURROUGHS by vertue or an order beareinge date in the Lower Norfolke the 2 May 1641

It is ordered that MR: JO: YATES shall by vertue hereof have power to receave and take into his possession the whole estate of GEORGE WATSON who hath been long absentin the woods as also to demand and receave all his debts of tobb or other particulars due within the collony of Virginia and to have power as aforesaid to breake oxen a certaine (Chefly or Chesly or Ohesly?) taking witnesses with him provided that the said JO: YATES shall upon demand deliver a just and true account of the said estate unto this Court or to any other who shall have power to call the same in question and he is further authorized to sell the said -state for tobb at an outcry

Whereas THO: WARD hath acknowledged himselfe to be indebted unto JO: RABLY by bill the some of 120 lb tobb stript and smoothed It is therefore ordered that the said THO: WARD within 15 dayes make payment of the said debt unto ROBERT SMITH attorney of the said RABLIES otherwise execucon.

THO: MARSH aged 26 yeares sworne & examined saith that he heard MR: EDW: WINDHAM demand of the under shreefe his bond wherein he was bownd for ye appearance of ANNE GASKIÑE to this Court who answered that if he would be pleased to move the Court Therewith he shuld have it who answered he had moved the Court concerninge the weoman (sic) whereupon the said under shreefe delivered the said MR: WINDHAM his bond and farther saith not.

CATHERINE SHIPP aged 30 yeares sworne & Examined saith she heard one ANTHONY a Portugall say that if CAPT:SIBSEY would not agree reasonably with him about the releaseinge of a maid servant namely JAYNE BUTTERFEILD That then the said CAPT: SIBSEY shuld keepe the said JAYNE and her child if he would the which she was Bigg with all and farther saith not.

f52ap106

PHILLIPP LAND (or LANE) aged 35 yeares sworne & examined saith that MR: EDW: WINDHAM came unto this deponent and demanded the bond wherein he was bound for ANNE GASKINES appearance who refused to deliver it But the said

f52a p106 bot 67a 4 Oct 1641

MR: WINDHAM said that he had informed the Comander CAPT: THO: WILLOUGHBY that she was on the other side of MR: MASSONS Creeke & could not gett over and that the said CAPT: WILLOUGHBY was satisfied. And thereupon the deponnent delivered him the said bond and farther saith not.

MR: CRISTOFER BURROWGHS aged 29 yeares sworne & examined saith that one RALPH CLARKE and WILLM: BURROUGHS (sic) in his presence did agree that a joynt estate shuld be maid betwixt them upon that plantacion they then lived on of what of what they had provided that whatsoever one had more then the othere shuld be Imployed as he (then?) think fitt to his owne Benifitt only But the plantacion what y[th] theire had to be betwixt them as a joynt estate payinge & bringeinge in and unto it equall proportion both alike & farther saith not

RICHARD HORNER and HENRY BRAKES sworne & examined saith that beinge requiered by RICHARD ffOSTER to vew (view) a parcell of land beinge planted with corne which the hoggs of MR: (GASKIN?) had devouered & spoyled and to the best of our knowledge did vallew it at 30 barrells of corne soffe? (or sosse?) beinge 66 rowes 30 deepe & 57 rowes 60 deepe, 91 rowes 40 deepe, 30 rowes 20 deepe, 58 rowes 12 deepe & farther saith not.

HENRY BRAKES and JAMES BLESSE (BLISS?) sworn & examined saith that beinge requiered to vew (view) the damage done by hoggs in JO: SPENCERS Cornfield they absolute deposse that if the hills of corne that weare remined (remained?) undamnified to the best of theire judgement They might have produced betweene 5 & 6 barrells and farther saith not

Men appointed for Tellinge of plants MR: EDW: WINDHAM, JO: STRATTON & EDWARD HALL
for Little Creek & that side up the river and all thosse places
MR: ROBT: HAYES, THO: KEELINGE & THOS: CAUSON
MR: WILLM: JULIAN from DANIELL TANNERS to the head of the Eastern Branch of Eliz: River and to assist him JO: WATKINS & THO: LAMBERT
for the other side of the River HENRY SEAWELL & THOS: MEARES
for the Westerne Branch LEFT: ffRA: MASSON, ROBT: GLASCOCK and HENRY CATTLINE
from DANIELL TANNERS CREEKE to CAPT: THO: WILLOUGHBIES, CAPT: JOHN SIBSEY, JO: HOLLMES & WILLM: SHIPP

f53 p 107 bot 68

JOHN MORCASON aged 28 yeares Sworne & Examined saith that beinge at the Quarter of MR: JO: GOOKIN when some discou(r)se past betweene JO: WEBB unto JO: GEORGE which to this effect the said JO: WEBB demanded of the said JO: GEORGE wherefore he gave such ill example to come from worke before sunset who replied that if he would he would bee to worke againe said that he needed not to be so eager for he did noe worke at all whereupon the said WEBB tooke an Iorne (iron) and stroake the said GEORGE one stroake over the head there-with Cutt him through the hatt and wounded him in the head so dangerously that his life was to be feared By reason the scull (skull) was much crackt And alsoe struck him another stroake on the arme which cutt him to the bonne and 3 or 4 stroakes more on the shoulders and likewise swore that if he held not his peasse (peace) he would give him such another stroake acrosse that so the said GOERGE stept back and tooke up the pestel But the said WEBB tooke it out of his hands & threw it downe and so they went together by the eares but beinge parted the said WEBB went his way & farther saith not

WILLM: GRANDGER and ARTHUR (?P)RELLSTONE sworne & examined testified the same verbatum with the said MORGASON.

Now xxxx presentes me THO: BULLOCK de Linhaven in County (of) New Norfolke Cyrurgeon in quadraginta libris bone et Legal monete Anghs sotendis: GULIELME (William) SHIPP aut ono certoratxx xeredibus executors vel assignatus sins xx guarn guiden xxx soluronem bone et fideliber et adminis-tratores mexx fermiter & psentes sigilo meo Pigilato dato decimo quin to die novembries anno 1641 (Some of the words of this item are blotted and very hard to decipher besides being in Latin - and the date would now appear to be Nov of 1641)

NOV 1641 or 4 Oct 1641 ?

The condicion of this obligation is such that the above bownden THO: BULLOCK his executors administrators or assignes shall & will well & truly satisfy content and pay or cause to be paid unto the above named WILLM SHIPP or to his certaine atturney his heires & exors administrators or assignes in England the just and futeir: (or Jutier) some of 10 ℔ lawfull mony of England att or before the first day of June next ensuinge the date hereof and in default of payment of the said 10 ℔ in manner aforesaid. If the said THO: BULLOCK shall deliver or cause to be delivered unto the said WILLM: SHIPPS dwelling howse in Virginia at or before the 1 Jan at the first penny in England clearely discharged which shalbe in the yeare of our Lord god 1642 That then this present obligation to be woid and of none ffect or else to be and remaine in full power force vertue and effect

Sealed and delivered in the presence of
MATH: PHILLIPPS
ROBT: BODY

(signed) THO: BULLOCK

f 53a p 108 bot 68a 4 Oct 1641

(NOTE: Please note the dates given in the different items as they would seem to be repeats of former orders in different dates in different years. As this is the first book still extant of the early Lower Norfolk County Records there is no way of checking earlier Court proceedings. AGW)

Know all men by these presents that I CAPT: ADAM THORROWGOOD of Linhaven Esqr: doe give grant & bargain & sell & lawfully posses(s) JOHN GOUGE of one piece or traice(sic) of land situate & lying & beinge betwixt the land of XPOFER BURROUGHS of Linhaven aforesaid on yeone side & a little Indian Creeke on the other side. To have & to hould ye said land to ye said JOHN GOUGE his heires &c -- forever together with all the right title & interest which I heretofore have had of hereafter may or shall have of & to the said land and that the said JOHN GOUGE his heires &c --- shall & may att all time or times hereafter peaceably and Quiettly injoye & possesse the same together with all the benefitt & profitts that may or shall arise of or from it in as full and ample manner as I now doe heretofore have done or hereafter may or shall doe provided that the said JO: GOUGE his heires &c --- doe pay discharge & acquitt the aforesaid CAPT: ADAM THORROWGOOD of and from Kings Rents. In valuable consideration whereof the abovesaid JOHN GOUGE his heires &c --- are to pay or cause to be paid unto the said CAPT: THORROWGOOD his heires &c --- the full & just Quantity of 2000 lb of good merchantable tobacco and the full & whole some of 4£ of good and lawful Englishe mony att two severall payments [vizt] 1000 lb tobbacco & 40 shillings sterlinge att & upon the 10 Nov next ensuinge after the date hereof and 1000 lb of tobb & 40 shillings sterling att & upon the 10 Nov which shalbe in the yeare of our Lord god 1640 which payment beinge well & truly made & pformed that then this bill to remaine firme & irrevocable or else to stand void and of none effect so that it may and shall be lawfull for the aforesaid CAPT: THORROWGOOD his heires &c----------& againe to render upon the said land before mentioned as upon his or their proper inheritance In witness whereof and of every particular of the premises Before resited (recited) we the said CAPT: THORROWGOOD and JO: GOUGE have hereunto interchangeably sett our hands this 7 Nov 1639

Signed and delivered
in the presence of
EDW: WINDHAM

Adam: Thorowgood
John: Gooch

(NOTE: GOUGE in record but GOOCH in signature - could this be the JO: GEORGE of the deposition on f53?)

Receaved of THO: BULLOCK upon this bill in part by me SARA THORROWGOOD ye quantity of 1000 lb tobb & the some of 40 shillings Beinge the one halfe of a debt above specified of 2000 lb tobb & 4£ stelline (Sterling) Wittness my hand this 10 May 1640

Sara: Thorrowgood

5 Oct 1641 f53a p 108 bot 68a

Receaved of THO: BULLOCK accordinge to the Acts of Assembly 40 per centum. The whole remainder of his debt above specified and doe free and acquitt him in full of all debts, bills, bonds and accounts to this day. I say receaved this 28 Mar 1640/41
per me John Gookins

f54 p109 bot 69

Receaved for DAVID WILLIAMS his use 288 lb of tobb of THO: BULLOCK beinge old debt att 40½ per centum
per me John: Gookin

In the name of God amen I JOHN GOOCH of Linhaven pishe in the County of New Norfolke planter beinge sick and weake of body but of perfect memory thanksbe given to God doe make this my last will and testament
1st I bequeath my soule unto the hands of Allmighty god & to my Saviour Jusus Crist my Redeemer next my body to the Earth from whence it receaved it and for such worly (worldly) estate whichit hath God to lend unto me I give and bequeath as followeth: 1st my will and desire is to sett free Danill (Savill?) Gaskine next I give and bequeath all my whole estate unto my loveinge & trusty frend THO: BULLOCK Sirgion & THO: ffRANCIS Gentillman. And of this my last will and testiment I make THOMAS BULLOCK & THOMAS ffRANCIS my whole executors Ane farther I will not.
Witness my hand this 1 Feb 1639/40
Subscribed & delivered as the last will and testament in the presents of us
ROBT: POWIS Clrkxx
and THOMAS CODD
John: Gooch

MR: ROBT: POWIS, Clarke and MR: THO: CODD sworne & Examined saith that this Incerted will is the last will and testament of JOHN GOOCH deceased
Taken before me
THO: WILLOUGHBY

(JOHN GEORGE/GOUGE/GOOCH are they the same man? His signature was apparently written by JOHN GOOKINS?)

Receaved of MR: HENRY WOODHOWSE for payment of 720 lb tobb due to be paid by THOMAS BULLOCK for the use of MR: WOODALL and is in full payment of all debts or bills from the beginninge of the world to this day onely 1 1/2 bushells of Corne Witnesse my hand this 19 dec 1637 J. Conners

I SAMUELL ffosbrooke Agent for MR: JOHN WOODALL discharge THOMAS BULLOCK from all or any service he was bownd to by his indenture to JOHN WOODALL or any other Witnesse my hand this 21 Jan 1635/6 SAMUELL ffOSBROOKE
Samuell ffosbrooke
Sealed and delivered in the presents of us
JOHN ffORSSE
JOHN HOLLOWAY *(NOTE THE DATE 1635/36)*

f54a p 110 bot 69a 31 Jan 1640/1

To all expian (Christian?) people to whome these presents shall come I CRISTOFER BURROUGHS of Linhaven in the in the Lower County of New Norfolke send greetinge whereof I the said CRISTOFER BURROUGHS am possessed of 200 acres of land situate lyinge and beinge upon Linhaven in the county abovesaid the said land beinge bounded Northerly on the land of CAPT: ADAM THOROWGOOD Easterly on the river of Linhaven Sotherly alonge the said River and Westerly into the mayne woods.given and granted unto me by pattent from CAPT: JO: WEST under his hand & seale with the seale of the collony dated the 7 May 1636 as by pattent whereunto relation beinge had more at large it doth & may appeare: Now knowe Ye that I the said CRISTOFER BURROUGH for divers good causes me thereunto moveinge & for & in consideration of a some of tobacco in hand paid and have by these presents for me my heires &c.......give grant assigne sell & sett over forever unto THO: BULLOCK of the same place Sirgion his heires &c.......all that parte of the said 200 acres of land which lieth betwixt the land of the said CAPT: ADAM THORROWGOOD & Salte pond or creeke lyinge next to the now dwellinge howse upon the said land to the Southward from the howse xxxxx to begin upon the land of the said CAPT: THORROWGOOD and thence to run to the said Creeke or pond from any parte of the said pond not going onto the land on the other side thereof to run accordinge as it shall be survaied by the bownds of the said pattent to have and to hold to himselfe his heires &c.....forever with all the howseinge thereon built together with all profitts commodities, priviledges, heridiments & appurtenances whatsoever without molestacion, trobles, hinderances or sutes of Lawe or any Claime or Title from by or under me or by my meanes or procurement & if all the Old field fall not within the same bownds the remainder thereof to be added theireto soe farr as is already shewed. And I the said CRISTOFER doe by these presents for me, my heires &c .....warrant & Avouch & confirme unto him the said THO: BULLOCK his heires &c........the said land as firmly, fully & amply to all intents & purposes in as large & ample maner as in the said pattent is expressed or by consequence may be collected our of the same or otherwise yeilding & passinge unto our Soverigne Lord the Kinge the yearly rent due unto him for the said land beinge lawfully demanded xxxx forevery 50 acres 12 pence per annum In witnesse whereof I have hereunto sett my hand & seale this last day of Jan 1640/1 and in the 16th yeare of the Raigne of our Soveraigne Lord KINGE CHARLES KINGE of England, Scotland, ffrance and Ierland (sic) & defender of the faith &c Xpo: Burrough: [seal]

In presence of us
JAMES SMITH
JOHN MASON

Recorded by me Robt Smith

Date is faint
3? Jan 1641/2? f55 p 111 bot 70

ATT A COURT HOWLDINGE AT THE HOWSE OF LEFT: ffRANCIE MASSON
Date is almost obliterated
CAPT: THOMAS WILLOUGHBY ESQR:
CAPT: JOHN SIBSEY MR: HENRY SEAWELL
LEIFT ffRAN: MASSON

This item is almost obliterated by ink showing through from the back of the page.

MR: THO: MARSH & SIMON HANCOCK sworne to praise the estate of THO: HAUE? or HAND?..........(can't read).....
....

WHEREAS MR. JOHN GOOKIN.............................
councell.........................the 13 Dec last past for the payment of 44 lb of beaver due from JOHNATHAN LANGWORTH deceased as by specialty under the hand of the said JOHNATHAN LANGWORTH appeare the whidh cause beinge refferred unto this Court for the determinacion and end-inge thereof It is therefore ordered that MR: HENRY SEA-WELL Atturney to the said JOHNATHAN LANGWORTH shall make payment out of the said JOHNATHANS estate of the said debt unto the said MR: JOHN GOOKINS in case theire be no test-ifycation out of England this present shippinge. That the said debt is sattisfied otherwise execucon

Whereas RICHARD KENNER standeth indebted unto SIMON HANCOCK in one case of stronge watters Quantity 3 gallons and 2 paire of shooes as by specialty appeareth It is therefore ordered that the said RICH: shall within 20 dayes make payment of the said debt together with Court Charges otherwise execucon to be awarded

Whereas THOMAS HANDS (HAUDS?) standeth indebted unto THO: SABINE in the some of 50 lb of tobb old debt and 2 skins It is therefore ordered that JOHN GILLAM adminis-trator of the said THO: HAUDS (HAUES?) Estate shall make payment unto JOHN HOLBECK atturney to the said SAYBINNE (sic) of the some of 20 lb of tobb stript and smoothed with 2 deare skins provided that the Administrator be first sattisfied otherwise execucon

f55a p112 bot 70a

It is ordered by this Court that JOHN GILLIAM the administrator of the estate of THO: HAND (or HAVE) dec-eased shalbe first sattisfied out of the said estate provided that he make appeare at the next monthly Court what he hath due to him

Whereas JOHN WEBB deceased was indebted unto MR: THO: BULLOCK in the some of 105 lb of Tobb stript and smoothed It is therefore ordered that the said THOMAS BULLOCK shall be sattisfied out of the estate of the said JOHN WEBB otherwise execucon

WHEREAS it appeareth to this court that MR: ROBT: POWIS Clerk was indebted unto JOHN GODFREY in the quantity of 4 barrells of Corne due in 1640 It is therefore ordered that the said ROBT: POWIS shall pay unto the said JOHN GODFREY in sattisfaction of 3 of the barrels of Corne 40lb tobb per barrell and the forth barrell to be paid in kind at the howse of MR: BARTHOLOMEW HOSKINS together with Court Charges otherwise execucon

It is ordered by this Court that in sattisfaction of a debt of 7 ₺ sterlinge due from RICH: KENNOR unto THO: TODD in 1640 that the said RICH: KENNOR shall within 20 dayes make payment unto the said THO: TODD of the some of 160 lb stript tobb together with Court Charges

Whereas GEORGE MEE and JOHN WEBB deceased standeth indebted unto WILLIAM SHIPP in the some of 452 lb of stript tobb It is therefore ordered that the said GEORGE MEE shall within 20 dayes make payment of the said debt with forbearance accordinge to the Acts of Assembly together with Court Charges

Both parties refferinge themselfes unto this.

f56
p113 * Whereas JO: WEBB deceased was indebted unto WILLIAM
Bot SHIPP in the quantityof 320 lb of stript tobb as by spec-
71 ialty appeareth It is therefore ordered that the sais WILLM: SHIPP shalbe satisfied out of the estate of the said of the said JOHN WEBB provided that MR: THOMAS BULLOCK be first sattisfied otherwise execucon of this cause reffered to this Court.

JOHN GEORGE and ISAAC MORGAN have entred their names to goe for England accordinge to the Act in that case provided

Whereas it appeareth to this Court that JOHN WEBB deceased was Overseer unto MR: JOHN GOOKINS and beinge about the affaires of the said MR: GOOKINS struck one JOHN GEORGE servant unto the sd MR: GOOKINS with such an unlawful unlawful instrument that brocke his scull whereby he was inforced to crave the healpe of THOMAS WARD (or WARE) Sirgion who hath cured the same It is therefore ordered that the said MR: GOOKINS shall make payment unto the sd THO: WARD in sattisfaction of the cure of the some of 100 lb of tobb with Court Charges otherwise execucon

Whereas Mr: JOHN GOOKINS is ordered by this Court to pay unto THO: WARD Sirgion the some of 100 lb tobb and Court Charges the withsaid some is paid in the behalfe of one JOHN WEBB deceased & a trespas of battery committed by the said WEBB in his lifetime against one JOHN GORGE servant to the said MR: GOOKINS It is therefore ordered ordered that the sd MR: GOOKINS shalbe sattisfied the like some of tobb with Court Charges out of the estate of the said JOHN WEBB provided that WILLM: SHIPP be first sattisfied 320 lb of stript tobb otherwise execucon.

31 Jan 1641/2 f 56ap114 bot 71a

Whereas it appeareth to this Court that JOHN DIER is indebted unto THOMAS HUES in the Quantity of 200 lb tobb stript and 3 Porringers of shott due by bill It is therefore ordered that the said JOHN DIER shall within 10 dayes make payment of the said debt unto LANCKESTER LOVETT the assigne of the said THOMAS HUES with court charges otherwise execucon

MR: JOHN GAYTER cleared the accounts of JOHN DRATTONS estate and it appeareth to this Court that he is creditor to the said estate 400 lb tobb old debt of the which he hath had report to the Governor and Councell accordinge to order directed to this Court.

Whereas it appeareth to this Court by Specialty that THOMAS CODD as security (for?) EDW: LILLY is indebted unto THOMAS SPARROWE in the some of 293 lb tobb stript and having reffered themselfes unto this Court. It is therefore ordered that the said THOMAS CODD shall within 30 dayes make payment of the said debt otherwise execucon

It is ordered that ffRANCIS LAND security for HUMPHREY PEICE? shall make payment unto DANIELL TANNER of the some of 120 lb of stript and smoothed tobb within 20 dayes otherwise execucon It beinge for charges and damages of a sute dependinge this 2 yeares between the said DANELL and HUMPHREY

Whereas it appeareth to this Court by Specialty that THO: CAUSON standeth indebted unto THO: MARSH in the some of 395 lb tobb stript and smoothed It is therefore ordered that the said THOMAS CAUSON shall make payment of the said debt within 15 dayes with Court Charges otherwise execucon

f57 p115 bot 72

* Whereas it appeareth to this Court by specialty that EDW: LILLY standeth indebted unto WILLM: SHIPP in the some of 4 ₤ sterlinge and 2 cheeres (chairs?) 6 Joyner tooles, and 30 lb of stript tobb. It is therefore ordered that the said EDWARD LILLY shall within 15 dayes make payment unto the said WILLIAM SHIPP such a proportion of tobb as shall produce the said debt of 4 ₤ sterlinge alsoe the 6 Joyners tooles, 2 cheeres, and 30 lb tobb together with court charges

It is ordered by this Court that WILLM: DAVIS shall within 15 dayes make payment unto WILLM: SHIPP of the some of 237 lb of stript tobb The produce whereof is towards the sattisfyinge of (a) debt of 8 ₤ 5/ sterlinge remayninge due to the said WILLM: SHIPP from the said WILLM: DAVIS as by bill may appeare. And alsoe that the said DAVIS shall put in sufficient security that if the said some of 237 lb tobb doth procure the said some of 8 ₤ 5/ sterlinge that then he shall sattisfie the remainer at nextreturne of shippinge with 8 per centum forbarance with Court Charges otherwise execucon

Whereas It appeareth to this Court by bill that WILLM: DAVIS is indebted unto WILLM: SHIPP in the some of 63 lb of stript tobb It is therefore ordered that the said WILLM: DAVIS shall make payment of the said debt with court charges otherwise execucon

Whereas there is a levie for the Cuntry (Country or County?) maid by the grand assembly 1641 as alsoe at this Court for 7 lb tobb per poll for Burdgesses charges to be paid by the inhabitants of this County as alsoe fees due from the said Inhabitants unto the Shreefe and Clarke of this County It is therefore ordered that if any person or persons shall refuse to make payment of the aforesaid levie charges or xxx or to bringe them to such places apoynted by the said Shreefe or his deputy It shallbe Lawfull for the said Shreefe or his deputy to distraine upon theire estates for full sattisfaction of them or any of them And forthwith to make saile thereof or to deliv-er the destress into possession of the Creditor or Credi-tors

f57a p116 bot 72a

* AT A COURT HOLDEN FOR THE COUNTRY? (sic)
OF LOWER NORFFOLK
at
MR: WILLIAM JULIANS HOWSE
26 May 1642

PRESENT: CAPT JOHN SIBSEY MR: WILL JULIAN
LIEUT: ffRANCIS MASON MR: HENRY SEAWELL

Whereas it appeareth unto this Court that THO: IVIE doth owe and standeth indebted unto TRUSTRAM MASON by bill the quantity of 76 lb stript and smoth'd tobb It is therefore ordered that the said THO: IVIE shall pay unto the said TRUSTAM MASON the aforesaid sum of stript and smothed tobb at the dwelling howse of the said MASON within 10 dayes with Court Charges otherwise execucon

Whereas it appeareth to this Court that RICHARD HORNER doth owe unto JOHN MARTEN eleaven dayes worke and 4 lb tobb It is therefore ordered that the said HORNER shall pay unto the said MARTEN 4 dayes worke by the midst of June nest and 7 dayes worke and 4 lb tobb in November following with Court Charges otherwise execucon

The suite betwixt ROBT: EYRES plt and THO: TOD(D) deft. is referred untill the next Court

Whereas it appeareth unto this Court that HENRY HILL doth owe and standeth indebted unto GYLES COLLINS by bill the quantitie of 103 lb of stript and smothes tobb It is therefore ordered that the said HENRY HILL shall within 10 dayes sattisfie the said debt with Court Charges otherwise execucon

26 may 1642 f57a p116 bot 72a

Whereas it appeareth unto this Court that MR. JOHN YATES hath sustayned much losse and hindrance by the neglect of a Mayde Servant by meanes of ROBT: DARBER and RICHARD HARGRAVES It is therefore ordered that the said ROBT: DARBER and RICHARD HARGROOVE shall each of them pay unto MR: JOHN YATES 100 lb tobb in October next and that the said MR: YATES shall pay Court Charges

f58 p117 bot 73

WHEREAS it appeareth to this Court that RICHARD ffOSTER is indebted unto EDW: HOLMES in the quantitie of 12 lb tobb It is therefore ordered that the said ffOSTER shall pay unto the said HOLMES the aforesaid sum of tobb with Court Charges

It is ordered that JANE RIGHTS suite shall cease until JOHH GROVE comes in agayne i- the meanetime that THO: EDWARDS, THO: RIGHT, WILL RAMSHAW shall pay Court Charges

Whereas it appeareth unto this Court that WILL: SHIPP is indebted unto PETER PORTER in the quantitie 62 lb of sufficient Merchantable tobb stript and smothed. It is therefore ordered that the sd WILL SHIPP shall sattisfie and pay unto the said PORTER the aforesaid summe of tobb stript and smothed within 10 dayes and Court Charges otherwise execucon

MR: JOHN WATKINS hath made it appeare unto this Court that he hath due to him 400 acres of Land for the transportation of these persons whose names are here underwritten *(this certificate is not listed in Nugent)*

JEFFIER (or JESTIER) MANCRISAD
MARMADUKE MERRANTON
RICHARD KING
RICHARD KING
NATHANIELL DORCHESTER
EDWARD DEANE
EDWARD TROVELL
EDWARD TROVELL
ELIZABETH SILVESTER
WILLIAM JOHNSON

It is ordered that SYMON HANCOCK who married the relict and administratrix of GILBERT GUYE deceased shall sattisfie and pay himselfe in the first place the quantitie of 88 lb ot tobb our of the estate of the said GILBERT GUYE for the charge of administration and other charges

Whereas it appeareth unto this Court that there is due unto JOHN MARTIN from the estate of GILBERT GUYE deceased [by the acknowledgement of SARA HANCOCK the relict of the said GUYE] 1 barrell of Corne It is therefore ordered that SYMON HANCOCK who m(arried) the relict and administrator of the said GILBERT GUYE shall sattisffie and pay unto the said JOHN MARTIN the said barrell of cor(ne) out of the estate of the said GILBERT GUYE all former orders beinge first satisfied

f58a p118 bot 73a

Whereas it appeareth unto this Court by bill that ffRANCIS LAND doth owe and standeth indebted unto WILL SHIPP in the quantity of 60 lb of sufficient Merchantable f58a p118 bot 73a   26 May 1642

tobb stript and smothed It is therefore ordered that the said ffRANCIS LAND shall within 10 dayes sattiffie and pay unto the said WILL SHIPP the aforesaid quantitie of tobb stript and smothed at the now dwellinge howse of the said SHIPP or at the howse of JOHN HOMES (HOLMES?) with Court Charges otherwise execucon

It is ordered that TRUSTRAM MASON shall make present payment unto MR: THOMAS IVIE of 4/ (shillings) sterlinge and Court Charges to be equally payd between them

JAMES WARNER hath made it appeare unto this Court uppon oath that he hath due to him 250 acres of land for ye transportation of these persons whose names are here under written *(this certificate is not in Nugent)* HUMPHREY BEST (or BELT) CHRISTOPHER PETTYFACE, DARWIN? ffASHALLOR?, STEPHEN BLOCK, JOHN HAMOR

It is ordered that JOHN DYER shall pay unto JAMES WEN? 15 lb tobb for his charge and losse of three dayes worke being subpoenayed to appeare at his suite

p119 bot 74

LOWER NORFOLKE COUNTY RECORDS

From July 1642 till february 1643
(This seems to be just a title page)

f74a p120   This page is blank except for obliterated words

f75 p121

Recordes Anno Dni
1642 1643

for the County of the Lower
Norfolk Court

Page 122 is blank

(page 123 and 124 have a small index which is not very legible. The full index of this publication will take care of this) f76& a p123

Page 125 folio 77 repeats the date:
Records 1642 for the County of Lower Norffolk Court
Page 126 f 77a is blank

To all whome these presents shall come I SIR WILLIAM BERKELEY Govr and CAPT: GENERALL of Virginia send greeting in our Lord God everlasting Whereas for the better ease of the Countrie and quick dispatch of business his Matie is pleased by Instrucons directed to ye Gov^nor and Councell of State to require them to appoynt in places convenient Infirior Courts of Justice and Comis^rs for ye same to determine of suites not exceeding the valew of 10 ₶ or 600 lb of tob^co and for ye punishment of such offenses as ye Govnor an Councell shall thinke fitt to give them power to heare and determine no f# p127 bot 78

Whereupon it was thought fitt and accordingly ordered at a Court holden by ye Govnor and Councell ye 16th day of the present June that Comiss^rs should be appoynted within everie Countye for ye keeping of Monethly Counter offences upon extraordinarie Causes requireing and agreed upon by ye major part of ye Comiss^rs Now Know ye that I ye sd Sr WILLIAM BERKELEY K^t accordinge to ye s^d Orders have assigned you and every of you whose names are inserted to be ye p(re)sent Comiss^rs of and for ye Countye of the Low^r Norffolk (vizt) JOHN GOOKIN ESQ Comander

CAPT: JOHN SIBSEY	MR: HENRY SEAWELL
MR: EDWARD WINDHAM	MR: ffRANCIS MASON
MR: HENRY WOODHOWSE	MR: HENRY CATELING
MR: WILLIAM JULIAN	

(Is THOMAS WILLOUGHBY off on one of his many trips away from the Colony? AGW)

Giveinge and granuting unto or any fower of you whereof ye sd JOHN GOOKIN ESQ or CAPT: JOHN SIBSEY to be always one full power and authoritie to heare and determine all Suites and Controversies betweene ptie and ptie as exceed not the valew of ten pounds sterling or six hundred pounds of tob^o Neyther shall it be lawfull or free for any pson to appeale to ye Court att James Citty in any matter dependinge before ye xxxx torn xxxxxxxxxxxxxxxxxxxxxxxxxx likewise to xxxxtornxxxxx (Note this is continued on p129)

* (page is badly torn at all edges - only the center remains and is faded and probably water damaged) f78a p128

Warrants? for CAPT: WILLOBYE

f 78a p128 16 Jun 1642

JOHN YATE to bee arrestd at his sute an action of debt
xxxxxxxx WILLIAM CAPPS at his sute an action of debt

xxxxxtorn xxxone exicution againste RICHARD OWEN
xxxxxtorn xxxone xxxxtornx against SAVELL GASKINE
" " "one " warrant of debt againste ffRA: LAND
-can't read - an action of debt
-can't read - warant against THO: CASSON
an action of debt
-can't read - one warant againste JO: YATES at the sute of (Robert?) PAGE an accon of debt

signed JOHN SIBSEY

(NOTE: This page is continued from p 127 it is hard to understand why there are two pages in between the Gov. General's item. Following is page 129 AGW)

f79 p129 bot 79 and enroie of you to take deposicons and examinations upon oath for ye clearing of the truth and that you be lawfull for ye Conservation of ye peace and the quiet government and Safetie of the people there residing or beinge and that you keepe and Cause to be kept and observed all orders of Court and Proclamacons directed to you or cominge to your hands from the Governor and Councell and according to the same and as neare as may be accordinge to the lawes of England to inflict punishment upon the offenders and delinquents and to doe and exicute whatever a Justice of Peace or two or more Justices of Peace may doe or execute [such offences onely excepted as Concerne ye takeing away of Life or member] And ffarther you are hereby required from time to time to keepe or Cause ye Clark of the Court to keepe records of all Judgments and matters of Controversie decided and agreed uppon by you or any fower of you as aforsd is pvided. And that you also cause ye Clarke of ye sd Court to bring up a true coppie of all your pceedings at everie Quarter Court unto your Governor and Councell Provided further it is hereby intended that those of his Maties Councell of State in this Colonie are to sett and be of this Comission and to take their places and to have there voyces in judicatury accordinge to their degrees in Councell although they be not pticularly and expressly nominated herein As also that it shall be lawfull for any of the sd Councell uppon any Emergent occasion to call or keepe a Court in the absence of those of the Quorum herein named and Authorized any thinge clause in this Comicon not withstanding And this Comicon is to continue in force untill I by my Comicon under my hand the Seale of the Colonie shall signify the Contrarie. Given att James Citty under my hand and the Seale of the Colonie this 16 June 1642 and in the 18th yeare of the raign of our Sov: Lord CHARLES KINGE of England &c

(Bottom is torn and signature missing)

5 Jul 1642 f79a p130 bot 80 p is blank so f 80 p131 bot 80

AT LINHAVEN

At a Court holden for the County of ye Lower Norffolk at the howse of JOHN GOOKIN ESQ 5 Jul 1642

MR: JOHN GOOKIN COMANDER

MR: EDW: WINDHAM LIEFT: ffRANCIS MASON

MR: HENRY WOODHOWSE MR: HENRY CATTELIN

MR: HENRY SEWELL

Whereas JOHN STRATTEN hath confessed before the Court that he was securitie for GOWIN LANCASTER UNTO ANDREW WARNER in the summe of 100 lb tobb due at all demands It is therefore ordered that the sd STRATTEN shall pay and satisfie unto the aforesd WARNER the somme of 120 lb tobb the 20 Nov next with Court Charges otherwise execucon

THOMAS HAYES SMITH hath engaged himselfe unto this Court to make a --- (hole in page)--- for MR: BARTHO: HOSKINS accordinge (to an?) agreement in writinge betwixt them [within 30 dayes] and to deliver the same unto the said HO(S)KINS or his assigns otherwise to stand to the sen(sure) of this Court

Whereas TIMOTHY IVES arested GEORGE HORNER unto this Court ---(hole)---- not appearing to prosecute the suite It is therefore ordered that the said IVES shall sattisfie unto the said Horner for the losse of (his time?) (by?) his attendance at the Court ----(holes)---------- pownds of tobb the 10 November next

Whereas JOHN BALL did arest WILL CROUCH unto this Court the said BALL shewing noe cause for his accon and suite ----(torn)----- It is therefore ordered that the said BALL SHALL sattisfie unto the said CROUCH for his losse of time the 10 Nov Next 20 lb tobb with Court Charges

(This page is f 1a p 132 p 130 is illegible or has blotted the ink from the following page) f 1a p132 bot 80a

The suit betwixt LIEUT: ffRAN: MASON plt and ELIZABETH MA(xxx hole in page) is referred unto the next Court

Whereas THO: HALL confest before the Court thathe was indebted unto JOHN MARTIN for a suite of clothes 150 lb tobb It is therefore ordered that the said HALL shall sattisfie and pay unto the said MARTIN the said somme of tobb by the 20 Nov next and Court Charges to be equally divided betwixt them

Whereas JOHN DYRE hath carelessly left a Canoe belonging unto THO: WARD Chyrurgeon to his greate ----(smudged) It is therefore ordered that the said DYER shall sattisfie and pay unto the said WARD for the losse of the said Canoe 60 lb tobb the 20 Nov next with Court Charges or else a new Canoe agayne of the length and bigness

Whereas it appeareth to the Court that CHRISTOPHER BURROUGHS standeth indebter by two sever bills unto WM:

SHIPP in ye ---(torn)---of 321 lb stript and smoth'd tobb payable at all demands It is therefore ardered that the said BURROUGHS shall sattisfie unto the said SHIPP the summe of 297 lb tobb the 10 Nov next with Court Charges otherwise execucon

The difference betwixt ffRAN: LA(ND) and (MA)THEW PHILLIPPS is referred untill the next Court

Whereas THO: CAUSON standeth indebted unto (hole-) RO(BT) (DAVIS?) by specialty 38 lb tobb stript and smothed payable at all demands (can't read several words) It is therefore ordered that (the said) CAUSON shall satisfie unto the said DAVIS? the aforesaid sum - (holes0 - of Nov next in the allowance of 25 -torn - hundred and eight -torn- for forbearance and the said Canvas Briches with Court Charges otherwise execucon

f 2
p133 Whereas SYMON HANCOCK who maried the administrator of
bot the estate of GILBERT GUYE deceased (-- badly torn --)
81 (something about ROBT: HAYES & a hhd of tobacco) for the use of LIEUT: MASON to satisfie a debt due from the said GUY'S estate to the said LIEUT: MASON The --?-- ----- appearing to this Court not to be lawfully made It is therefore ordered that the said ROBT: HAYES shall pay the quantitie of 300 lb tobb and a hhd unto LIEUT: MASON for the use of the said GUY'S estate aforesaid otherwise execucon

Whereas THOMAS WARD Chirurgeon hath -(torn)- cure of JOHN DYERS wife It is therefore ordered that the said DYER shall shall sattisfie unto the said WARD 30 lb tobb for the said cure by the 10 Nov next with Court Charges

Whereas SYMON HANCOCK administrator of the Estate of GILBERT GUY deceased hath impleaded ROBT: HAYES administrator of the estate of JOHN LANGFEILD deceased for and concerning a debt of 354 lb of tobb specified in an account of the said GUY'S and the said HAYE'S desiring to demurre upon the said account Tt is therefore ordered that the said HAYES shall (pduce?) Account (to the?) next Court as well of the said 354 lb tobb as also of all such debts as he the said HAYES hath received and disposed of belonging to the Estate of the sd GILBERT GUY deceased according to an account of the said GILBERT GUYES wherewith the said HAYES stands charged ---(smudged)---------

Whereas JOHN WATTFORD was supeonade at ye request of THO: BR----Y (could be BRAMLY?) and the said (BRUMLY?) not appearing It is ordered that the said B---LY shall pay unto the said WATTFORD for his attendance and losse of time 20 lb tobb

Whereas it appeareth unto this Court that GILBERT GUYS Estate is indebted unto BARTH: HOSKINS 200 lb stript and smothed tobb it is therefore ordered that SYMON HANCOCK who maried the Administrator of GILBERT GUY deceased shall satisfie the said some of 200 lb tobb -------(not readable)---- next with allowances of ----(badly smudged -----)with Court Charges all other orders against the said Estate being satisffied otherwise execucon

Whereas it appearet- to this Court that JOHN WELLS deceased is indebted unto BARTHO: HOSKINS 90 lb of stript and smothed tobb --(torn)-- It is therefore ordered that GEORGE (WELLS? (this name looks like --dds) administrator of the said WELLS estate shall satisfie unto the sd HOSKINS the 5 Nov next aforesd some --(torn)-- for forbearance all other orders against the Estate being satis fied Otherwise execucon

JOHN HOMS (HOLMES?) hath made it appeare unto this Court that he hath due unto him for the transportation of theise whose names are here under written 250 acres of land: THO: GELTON (or GOLTON) MARY SMITH, JOHN SMYTH, EDWARD HOMES, NICHOLAS BROWNE (this is not in Nugent)

GEORGE HORNER hath made it appeare unto this Court that he hath due unto him 150 acres of land for the transportation of these whose names are here underwritten GEO: HORNER, HILLINER HORNER, ALICE HORNER(not in Nugent)

WILL CROUCH hath made it appeare unto this Court that he hath due unto him 150 acres of Land for the transportation of these whose names are here under written in the Shipp cald the ffrancis in ffeb last 1641: WILL: CROUCH, MARY CROUCH his wife, JOHN FREEMAN, his man (not in Nugent)

LIEUT: ffRANCIS MASON heth made it appeare unto this Court that there is due unto him 1250 acres of Land for ye transportation of these whose names are underwritten which land is allreadie se(at)ed: ffrancis MASON, MARY MASON his wife, ANNE his daughter, ALICE GANEY, MARGERIE GANEY, THO: WARTERS (WALTERS?), MERRA MILLOW (WILLOW?) MARKE LAYNEERE (LINEER?), ANTHONY RIBBOONE, JOHN JOHNSON, MARKE PROVOOSE, JOHN KINGSBERRIE. NICHOLAS KNOWLS, JAMES RABBISH, ELLIAS HARRIS, RICH: MARTIN, JOHN MIDLETON?, RICH: MAR(torn maybe MORRIS), WODHAM (TUCK?) ALICE JENKINS, HENRY JACKSON, JOHN SHAW, EDW: WHEELER, JOHN ARIS (ARRIS?) ROBT: HILL (see Nugent 134 - 1250 acres last of Aug 1642 bounds of land are given. Names above in parenthesis are as given in NU. This patent is in Pat. Bk #1 Part 2 p 816)

It is agreed by us the Comis^{rs} at this present Court being -(a large hole in page) - 1642 -- of an Act of of Assembly - (large hole) - for planting for Tyable and - (hole)- Commissioners being injoyned to destroy what shall be found more than is allowed as aforsd And for the execution herewith have agreed as is hereafter exprest f 3 p 135 bot 82   5 Jul 1642

CAPT JOHN SIBSEY from CAPT: WILLOUGHBYS howse to DANYELL TANNERS Creeke MR: HENRY SEAWELL and LIEUT: ffRANCIS MASON all ye Easterne and Southern Branch from JOHN WATKINS HOWSE

MR: WILL: JULIAN from DANIELL TANNERS Creeke to MR: WATTKINS howse

MR: HENRY - (hole) -------- all the Western Branche includinge all the - (?)- Norffolk County

MR: HENRY WOODHOUSE Eastern Shore of Linhaven

MR: EDW: WINDHAM all of Little Creek

And MR: JOHN GOOKIN Comdr all the Western Shore of Linhaven -(hole)- for the viewing of -(torn)- Plants

JOHN -(torn)- -OMES (?HOLMES) and WILL: SHIPP to view CAPT: SIBSEYS, COLENE-- SEAWELLS and LIEUT: ffRANCIS MASONS

f3a p136 bot 82a

CORNELIUS LLOYD and HENRY HAWKINS to view Cattel in and MR: WILL JULIANS

MR: EDW: HALL and THO: CAUSON to view MR: HENRY WOODHOUSE his plants

THOS;KEELING and CHRISTOPHER BURROUGHS to view MR: JOHN GOOKIN his plants

WHEREAS CHRISTOPHER BURROUGHS hath made humble suite to this Court for ----?---- of a fine imposed on him at a Court holden at MR: WILL: JULIANS the 6 Sep 1641 for an offence committed against the Court as in the Order of the aforesaid - ? - Court is exprest for which he hath adknowledged himselfe to be hartely sorry. It is therefore ordered that -(the rest of this is almost mpossible to piece together blotted words and holes)

The deposition of HENRY CATTELIN aged 40 yeares or thereabouts taken before the Comander and Commissioners of the Lower Norffolk at the Court holden at linhaven the 5 July 1642 Sayeth that he the deponent with ROBT: HAYES being appointed by order of Court from the Govnor and Councell to praise and devide the estate of CAPT: ADAM THOROWGOOD deceased doth (say?) upon his oath that MR: JOHN GOOKIN and SARA his wife were very carefull to have the Estate equally devided for the children and that he -(torn)- (that there?) hath been greate wronge to ye sd JOHN GOOKINS and his wife by deposicon of his delivered to Mantxxxx CAPT: WILLOUGHBYS accusation against the said MR: GOOKIN and SARA his wife for whereas he sweare theire was old Iron a great quantity being in a store and left our of the Inventorie and a hundred -(hoLe) of sarser Reape? and some -(hole)- Boates This deponent doth declare uppon his oath that he being in the stoare with the aforesd HAYES and MR: GOOKIN did see some bundles of iron.

the quantity whereof was not much and to this deponents remembrance about three or fower bundles and (-hole-) Howse *(the ink has come through from the back of the page and it is impossible to read. Below this there are large holes. This whole page seems to concern CAPT. ADAM THOROWGOOD's inventory AGW)*

(at the bottom of this page there is a large piece torn out)

NOTE: MRS. GOOKIN claimed two small silver boates which she said was a gift to her from her brother in lawe MR. JOHN THOROWGOOD at her marriage --------CAPT: THO: deceased Names of the children are either not given or have been torn out. AGW)

Depositions recorded for EDW: HALL concerning his land *f4a p138 bot 83a*

A deposition of JOHN HOLBECK aged 30 yeares of thereabouts

(same holes as on p 137)

---- land from ye sd ENSIGNE KEELING-----
----
did belonge unto the sd CAPT: THOROWGOOD --------------
that the said EDW: HALL

JOHN HOLBE--
per me ROBT: TYRS Cler:

The deposition of THO: CASSON aged 58 (or 50) yeares or thereabouts taken -----------5 July rnno --------------

(A BIG HOLE TORN OUT)

f5 p139 bot 84

THOMAS KEELINGE for the said Land and that the said CAPT: THOROWGOOD did therein bind himselfe, his heires &c.... that the said ENSIGNE KEELINGE his heires &c..... shuld quietly and peacefully enjoy the said land forever without any hindrance or disturbance of any manner of pson or psons whatsoever And further sayeth not

Teste THO: CASSON
ROBT: TYAS Clk

The deposition of THO: ALLEN aged 28 yeares or thereabouts taken at a monthly Court holden for ye County of Lower Norffolk ye 5 July 1642 deposeth and sayeth as followeth vizt: that about some halfe a yeare of thereabouts before ye death of CAPT: ADAM THOROWGOOD this deponent being wormeing of plates in the ?Iraund? ENSIGNE THO: KEELING called this depont: to come to the howse where CAPT: THOROWGOOD was present and the said CAPT: THOROWGOOD did bid this depont: witnesse that he did then signe and seale a bill of saile and deliver the same as his act and deede unto the sd ENSIGNE THO: KEELINGE for 210 acres of land being on the Eastern Shore Linhaven [and being then f 5 p 139 bot 84a 3 Jul 1642

In the possessionof the said ENSIGNE KEELINGE] to this deponent did reade part of the said Bill of Sayle and accordingly wittnessed the same by his handwriting and farther sayeth not

THOMAS ALLEN
Test ROBT TYAS Clerk

Be it known to all men by theire presents that I THOMAS SAWYER of Virginia doe bind myselfe, my heires &c .... to pay or cause to be paid unto PHILLIPP LAND or his assignes ye just somme of (hole)... 10 ₺ 14/4) sterlinge ... .hole ....in London on ye ..... holes & smudges.... bind me my heires and assignes ... torn......witness my handand seale this 15 April 1642

Witnesse THOMARSH copia THOMAS SAWYER

* f 5a p 140 bot 84a

THOMAS KEELINGE for the said land and that the said CAPT: THOROWGOOD did therein bind himselfe his heires &c...that the said ENSIGNE KEELINGE his heires &c ...... shuld quietly and peacfully enjoy the said land forever without any hindrance of disturbance of any manner of pson or psons whatsoever And further sayeth not

teste THO: CASSON
ROBT: TYAS Clk

The deposition of THO ALLEN aged 28 yeares of thereabouts taken at a monethly court holden for ye County of Lower Norffolk ye 5 July 1642 deposeth and sayeth as followeth izt: that about some halfe yeare or thereabouts before ye death of CAPT: ADAM THOROWGOOD this deponent being warmeing of plates in the (?Iraund?) Ensigne THO: KEELINGE called this depont; to come to the howse where CAPT: THOROWGOOD was present and the said CAPT: THOROWGOOD did bid this depont: witnesse that he did then signe and seale a Bill of saile and deliver the same as his act and deede unto the sd ENSIGNE THO: KEELINGE for 210 acres of land being on the Easterne shore Linhaven [and being then in the possession of the said ENSIGNE KEELINGE] to this deponent did reade part of the Bill of Sayle and accordingly witnessed the same by his hand writing and further sayeth not.

THOMAS ALLEN
teste ROBY: TYAS Clerk

Be it known to all men by these presents that I THOMAS SAWYER of Virginia doe bind myselfe my heires &c...... to pay or cause to be paid unto PHILLIPP LAND or his assignes ye just somme of [HOLE] ....? 10 ₺ 14/4] sterlinge ...... hole......... in London on ye .....holes andsmudges........bind me my heires and assignes....torn ... witness my hand and seale this 15 Apr 1642

Witness: THOMAS MARSH copia THOMAS SAWYER

..........................written of JOHN HOLBECK..... specialities and ....wheresoever due unto me ENSIGNE THOMAS KEELINGE from ye said JOHN HOLBECK from the beginning of the world unto this present day of the date hereof I say received full satisfaction

Witnesse
Edw: EH HALL
the marke of

the marke of
THOMAS Λ KEELING

Recd: of ffRANCIS LAND the 1 May 1639 one bill of JOHN ASHLINS (?) contayning 900 lbs of tobb being for satisfacon for Country Duties Duties and ffees for ye yeare of our Lord 1638

p me THO: LARRYMER

The Jurors

MR: BARTHOLOMEW HOSKINS	ffRANCIS LAND
EDWARD HALL	CHRISTOPHER BURROUGHS
JOHN HOLBECK	THOMAS CAUSON
THOMAS CHEELY	SYMON HANCOCK
THOMAS KEELING	WILLIAM DAVIS
JAMES SMYTH	MATHEW PHILLIPS

Whereas by reference from JAMES E (xxxx?) bearing date 17 Mar 1642 which was...(*there are a lot of holes in this record. AGW)* .... MR. JOHN GOOKIN deft and RICHARD ffOSTER pltf concerning dammage done by hoggs should be heard and determined ....Lower Norfolk by whome it was also thought... that the tryall should be by a ....(hole)....therefore the Jury .....(hole)......examined the evidence on both parts find noe cause therefore any damages

(no folio number is given on this page - should be --- f 6 p141 bot 85

should be allowed for the plaintifs corne which was destroyed the deft having sufficiently proved that he hath kept a sufficient ho....... and sufficient hogge pens accordinge to the acts in that Case made and provided and that the pltf had not fenced his Plants accordinge to the Acts in that Case made and provided Wherefore we give our verdict that the pltf shall pay all Charges of the Lower Court and so the sute to be fully determined

Att a QUARTER COURT holden att JAMES CITTY the 17 Oct last past Whereas a difference depending betwixtRICHARD ffOSTER pltf and MR: JOHN GOOKINS deft was by the sayd Court referred to the Court of Lower Norffolk there to be ended and determined And according to the sd difference was taken into consideration by the sd Court. It was thought fitt by the Commissioners that it should be tryed by a Jurie as the most equitable way. And a jury f 6 p 141 bot 85 3 Jul 1642

of twelve men beinge Impannelled and Sworne for that purpose did find for the deft: as by the sd Jurors verdict doth appeare It is therefore ordered that the sd ffOSTER shall satisfie and pay all charges of the Lower Court occasioned by the sute and this to be a small determination of the sd sute.

Copie of OLIVER VANHICKS letter to MR. SAYER

MR. SAYER my Love remembered thia to give you notice that I have made payment unto ROBT: SMYTH of tje remayner (remainder?) which is due to me in the caske You restraine on the one being 239 lb tobb in Leafe. Therefore pray leave me a note of particulars whiah a discharge & what you receaved that tobacco of me and pay him for the caske.

I rest
Mar 12 1641 Yours to my power
OLIVER VAN HICK

f 6a p 142 bot 85a *(this is marked in book f6p143 should be f 7)*

At a Court held at the Howse of WILL: SHIPP 1642

15 Aug 1642

JOHN GOOKIN ESQ: COMMANDER

CAPT JOHN SIBSEY MR: HENRY SEAWELL
MR: EDW: WINDHAM MR: ffRANCIS MASON
MR: WILL: JULIAN

Whereas it appeareth unto this Court that PETER PORTER hath commenced an action of defamation against CAPT: JOHN SIBSEY ye sd PORTER not being able to prove the same and the said action appeareth by the depositions of MATHEW PHILLIPPS and GEORGE HORNER and many others
bot attestations to be evidently false It is therefore
p86 ordered that the said PETER PORTERshall aske the said CAPT: JOHN SIBSEY forgiveness in the face of the Court and pay all charges expended in the said sute.

Whereas if appeareth unto this court by two? affirmative wittnesses that ELIZABETH MILLS hath farlselyraysed a defamation against ALICE MASON in sayeing that she reported - hole in page - MRS SEAWELL was a noted woman for a thiefe And further Appeareth that the said ELIZABETH MILLS hath scandalized AGNES HOLMES in .... that the said AGNES HOLMES she did say that ALICE MASON was the cause of the death of a young Child) of MR: HENRY SEAWELLS It is therefore ordered that the said ELIZABETH MILLS shall aske the said ALICE MASON and AGNES HOLMES forgivenesse in the face of the Court and receive 10 lashes upon her bare backe for the said .. torn..... *(Note: Next item badly torn what can be read follows . AGW) ... Whereas it appeareth unto(this?) Court by two depositions that xxxx HALL? hath Carrxx xxay a xxxxxxx without any consent xxxxxx the children (of CAPT ADAM THOROWGOOD deceased) the said calfe being xxxxxxxxxxx xxore ordered that xxxx xx Children xxxxxxx of a yeare old within xxxxxxx with Court charges otherwise execucon* p144 bot 86

f 7 p 144 bot 86a

It is ordered that CORNELIUS LLOYD atturnie for COLONELL (T?)RAFFORD .....?..... pay unto JOHN YATES (end of editors note) for himselfe and two men 40 weight of tobb for their charges as wittnesses beinge subpoenard by the said MR: LLOYD in a sute depending betwixt the said COLONELL (?)RAFFORD (Could this be Crafford? the first letter does not look like a C AGW) and THOS: TODD It is therefore ordered that the aforesaid MR: LLOYD shall pay unto ROGER WILLIAMS 20 weight of tobb for his charges and losse of time being likewise subpanayed as a witness in the aforesd sutte

Whereas it appeareth unto this Court that MARCO MILLS did promise to enter into specialty for the payment of 90 lb tobb unto CHRISTOPHER EDWARDS It is therefore ordered that the said MARAO MILLS shall pay the aforesaid sum unto the said EDWARDS by the 10 Nov next with Court Charges otherwise execucon

xxxrt HAYES hath diposed in the face of the Court that he xxx not stand engaged or indebted unto the Estateof GIxx xxxGUY deceased xnything at either in monies xxtornxxxxx It is therefore ordered that xxxx

(Note: 7 lines here are too badly mutilated to read)

xx accordinge to the times and the letters of administration.

f 8 p 145 bot p87

WHEREAS RICHARD POOLE hath made it appeare to this Court that CAPT: ADAM THOROWGOOD deceased did in his lifetime give unto the said POOLE xx hundred acres of land up a Creek called SAM: BENNETTS Creeke ye place where yet(or not) ......?....... ....?...... It is therefore ordered that the said Executor (of) the said CAPT: THOROWGOOD shall deliver unto the said POOLE (two ?) (Indim ers?) soe that the sd POOLE pike (pick?) up a 100 acres of land where he can find it.

Whereas GYLES COLLINSand WILL DAVIS were subpanade at the request of MATHEW PHILLIPPS the sd DAVIS having some ..?.. businesses of his own It is ordered that GYLES

f 8 p 145 bot p 87   15 Aug 1642

COLLINS shall have 40 lb tobb and WM: DAVIS 20 in ye midst of Nov next for their loss of time

The sute betweene ffRANCIS LAND and MATHEW PHILLIPPS is refferred untill the next Court

Whereas SYMON HANCOCK hath demanded of ROBERT HAYES administrator of the estate of JOHN LANCKFEILD the guantitie (sic) of 200 lb tobb old debt Due to the estate of GILBERT GUYE It is consented that the sd HANCOCK shall have an order the next Court for payment he producing proof thereof by the attestation of the Relict of the sd GILBERT GUYE taken at Blunt Point before the Govner and Councel

The sute depending betweene THO: CASON plt and ROBT: DAVIS deft is referred untill the next Court

WHEREAS WILL DAVIS hath mede it appeare unto this Court that ₒₒₒₒₒₒₒ(rest of this is mutilated, about 7 lines see the next page AGW)

f 8a p 146 bot p 87a

xxx holes xxx of ye aforesaid Bills unlesse xxx holes xxx makes his appearance at ye next monthly xxxxx holes answer to ye demand of the said - ? -

WHEREAS ffRANCES DYER ye wife of JOHN DYER hath commited adulterie with HUGH WOOD several times as it appeareth by ₒₒ• hole ₒₒₒₒ as her own confession It is therefore ordered that the ffRANCES DYER and HUGH WOOD shall aske allmighty God forgiveness upon their bare knees in the parish ₒₒₒ?ₒₒₒ ₒₒₒₒ committed and they shall each of them Sunday (Receive?) 15 lashes upon their bare backs

bot p87a WHEREAS IT HATH APPEARED UNTO THIS Court by sufficient pfe (/Proof?) that RICHARD POOLE hath misbehaved himselfe suspiously frequenting ye companie and Societie of ffRANCES - ye wife of JOHN DYER not withstanding divers admonitions to the contrarie and whereas RICH: POOLE hath uttered divers words & xx?xxxx to ye sd person of HUGH WOOD as it heth likewise appeared It is therefore ordered that the sd POOLE shall remayne in the Sherriffes hands untill he enters into recognized ₒₒ?ₒₒfor his sufficient securities for his good behaviour

WHEREAS MATHEW PHILLIPPS was subpanade at the request of PETER PORTER and GEORGE HORNAR by several subpanaes It is ordered that the said PETER PORTER and GEORGE HORNER shall each of them pay unto ye sd PHILLIPPS 20 lb tobb for his attendance at ye Court

It is ₒₒₒₒₒ(hole)ₒₒₒ upon betwixt ye Commissioners and

15 Aug 1642 f8 p143 bot p 87

WILL SHIPP this 16 - (large hole)- a license for ye.... holes ....SHIPP hath engaged ....use his utmost ....ing and accomodation ....entartaynment of.................................County And further further.....on by Commissioners that the Monthly Courts from

(NOTE: The above is most probably a license for Wm: Shipp to keep an ordinary where Courts would be heard AGW)

f 8b p 147 bot p 88

henceforth and meetings shall be twice at WILL: SHIPPS HOWSE and once at Linhaven

Whereas Wee THOMAS GREENE AND MARAO MILLS of ye Lower County of New Norfolk Planters doe stand jointly Indebted unto ROBT: SMYTH of the same place Planter ye just some and Quantity of 825 lb of good sound Merchantable Virginia tobb and one Caske. Now know yee that we the sd THOMAS and MARRA doe absolutely and fully assigne and make over unto ye sd ROBT: SMYTH as his securities for the sd debt of 825 lb tobb and one Caske the which doth appeare to be due to him by specialty. To say all and every our Cropp and Cropps of Tob: and corne wheresoever beinge and belonging unto the sd THO: GREENE and MARRAS Joyntly or severally within ye Collony of Virginia and we doe further Authorize the sd ROBT: his heires or assignes to sattisffie himselfe ye aforsd debt when or wheresoever the said Crop or Cropps shall be hanging or struck. In witness of ye sd promises we ye sd THOMAS GREENE and MARRA MILLS have hereunto sett our hands and seales this 1 Aug 1642

signed sealed and delivered in presents of GILES (G) COLLINS

THOS: (T) GREEN
MARRO (X) MILLS

f 8c p 148 bot p 88a

At a Court Houlden at WILLIAM SHIPPS
15 Sep 1642

PRESENT: JOHN GOOKIN ESQ: COMMANDER

MR: JOHN SIBSEY
MR: MR: EDWARD WINDHAM
MR. WILL JULIAN
MR: HENRY SEAWELL

Whereas WILLIAM JOHNSON and THOMAS HAYES stands indebted unto MR: HENRY CATTLIN in ye sum of 30^{l} due unto him the sd CATTLIN for a Hoggshead of Indian pease bought in ye yeare 1640. It is therefore ordered that the sd JOHNSON and HAYES shall satisffie and pay unto ye sd CATTLIN or his atturney ye full quantitie of 30 lb tobb stript and smothered or allowance for the same forbearance being already satisffied ye said payment to be made by ye 10 Nov f 8c p148 Bot p88c 15 Sep 1642

next with Court Charges otherwise execucon

f 8c p 148 bot p88a
It is ordered that the case depending between CAPT: JOHN SIBSEY and THOMAS MARSH atturney for THO: SAYER late High Sheriff for the County concerning (a) matter of Account for last yeares Burgesses Charges be referred unto ye next Court. And that ye list of such as have payd and such as have not payd now remaininge in the hands of MR: JOHN SIDNEY be then produced and likewise that PHILLIPP LAND undersherriff to the sd SAYER shall then produceall such lists noates or accounts remayning in his hands as doe anyway concerne ye premises. The determination of the sd suite being referred to the opinion of the Court by and with ye Consent of ye sd THO: MARSH

WHEREAS FFRANCES LAND arested MATHEW PHILLIPPS the atturney of DANIELL TANNER to a Court holden at Linhaven ye 4 July last past for and concerning ye detayning of one Bill or Specialty wherein ye sd LAND was bound with HUMFRIE PRICE to the aforesd DANIELL TANNER for the deliverie of one HEIFFER with calfe payable at the feast of St. Michaells ye Arch Angell 1640 And it appearing to
*f9 this Court by*a collaterall bargaine made by and between
p149....hole.....and DANIELL TANNER....(hole)..... 1641 that the sd land should ....(hole)....to ye sd...hole...

(NOTE: The rest of this is water damaged and some holes It seems to be about the delivery of the heiffer and calfe by Christmas last past being not yet delivered . AGW ...LAND to make payment to DANIELL TANNER...............)

Whereas it appeareth that THOMAS TODD hath done certain worke in -(faded) - uppon a Vessel or Boate belonginge to COLONELL ffRANCIS TRAFFORD ye said worke being valued by a sufficient - ? - upon theire oathes to be worth 150 lb It is therefore ordered that the sd COLONEL TRAFFORD shall satisfie and pay unto the sd TODD 150 lb tobb by the 10 Nov next ensueinge.

f 9a p 150 (NOTE: This page if almost impossible to read because of holes and water damage)

.....THOMAS DRIGHT to be paid for a pair of Breeches a cloth suite and a barrel of corne which had been delivered to VICO? (I cannot read the name AGW)

Whereas MARAO MILLS and THO: GREENE stand indebted unto THO: HAES (or HUES) in the full quantitie of 909 lb Tobb by 3 severall specialties doth appeare and the said MARAO MILLS and THO: GREENE being contented for better security of the sd debt (be? served?) the sd THO: HUES or his assignes one Compleate ...(hole)......in case of non-payment of ye aforesaid specialties. It is therefore ordered if the said MARAO MILLS and THO: GREENE or wither of them not pay or cause to be payd unto ye sd THO: HUES ye sd tobb: within one month albeit ye experation of ye sayd specialties ...(hole)....the sd MARAO MILLS and THO: GREENE shall serve the sd (HUES?) ---(smudged)--the full time and terme of one whole yeare apiece.

WILL SHIPP hath made appeare to this Court that there is due to him 100 acres of land for the transportation of two servants at his cost and charges their names being hereincerted LAWRENCE RICHARDS
THOMAS ASHBROOKE (Note: these two servants are given in the 1653 patent to WM: LANGLEYin Nugent 284)

Whereas JOHN HOLBECK deceased standeth indebted unto MR: HENRY CATTLIN in the quantitie of 600 lb of good and merchantable tobb as by specialties appeareatte and likewise seaven paire of sufficient Mens shoes in ye sizes of eleaven (--?--) as by specialtie likewise appeareth It is therefore ordered that the sd MR: CATTLIN shalbe pd out of JOHN HOLBECKS estate. THOMAS CODD being first satisfied

Whereas JOHN HOLBECK deceased standeth indebted unto HUGH HUGH WOOD the quantitie of 68 lb tobb as per a note under yesd HOLBECKS hand appeareth. It is therefore ordered that the sd HUGH WOOD shalbe paid out of the sd HOLBECKS estate. MR: HENRY CATTLIN being first satisfied

Whereas JOHN HOLBECK deceased standeth indebted unto ffRANCIS LAND the quantitie of 800 weight of tobb as by one bill and a note under the sd HOLBECKS hand appeareth It is therefore ordered that the sd LAND shalbe payd out of the sd HOLBECKS estate. HUGH WOOD being first satisfied.
....JOHN HOLBECK deceased......indebted unto THOMAS MARSH 250 lb tobb and 60 lb tobb unto JOHN GATER as by specialtie - - - THO: MARSH being atturney to JOHN GATER to be paid both debts out of HOLBECKS estate
(and)
JOHN HOLBECK deceased indebted unto GEORGE WATTSON by specialtie 220 lb tobb & 3 barrels of corne said debts to be paid unto JOHN YATES for the use of GEORGE WATTSONS Estate out of JOHN HOLBECKS Estate...........other orders being first satisfied

A f 10a p 152 bot p 90a

(NOTE: On the microfilm made by the Church of Latter Day Saints pages 150 & 151 are duplicated AGW) p 152 follows:

Whereas a sute depending betweene CAPT: JOHN GOOKIN plt and THOMAS CASON and JOHN STRATTON defts was reffered by the Governor& Councell to be tryed at this Court by a Jury of twelve able men who were to give in their verdict and f 10a p 152 15 Sep 1642

Judgement to be given thereuppon by ye Court as by ye sd refference bearing date at James Citty the 7 Oct 1642 doth more planely appeare accordinge to which refference a Jury was impanelled sworne who in part gave upp a verdict so farre as the Right of (proprietye?) and (interest?) of the Surveye but could not finish it - ? - and make it absolute in respect of a (vewe?) to be taken of the --?--- Land in question accordinge to the tenor of ye act of Assembly provided for the (reletse?) of ye Deft. It is therefore ordered that the sd Jury consisting of 12 men whose names are incerted under this order shall all and every of them meete ye 14th of ye next month at the Ordinarie at Linhaven then to view the Plantacons in the action and then to give in a full and ....hole.....verdict (accordinge to the sd refference) unto the Court there Holden ye 15 Dec next Whereby the sd Court may proceede to judgment accordinge to ye refference And hereof ye sayd Jury or any of them are not to fayle at their or any of their perills

MR: JOHN HILL foreman	MR: WILL SHIPP	THO: IVIE
MR: THO: LAMBERT	MR: HENRY HAWKINS	JOHN WATTKINS
MR: MATH: PHILLIPPS	MR: MATH: HOWARD	THO: MARSH
MR: JOHN YATES	SYMON HANCOCK	ROBT: GLASCOCK

JOHN HILL hath made it unto this Court upon oath that he hath due to him 100 acres of land for the transportation of ROBT: HUDD and WILL: (LATHBEMECE?)

Whereas it appeareth upon sufficient testimony that ELIZABETH ye wife of MARAO MILLS hath scandalously defamed the wife of MR: HENRY SEWELL in reportinge that she was a noted woman for a thiefe and being utterly unable to prove ye same. It is therefore ordered that the said ELIZ: MILLS shall aske the wife of ye sd MR: SEAWELL forgivenesse here in Court and at ye pish Church at MR: SEAWELLS POYNT uppon Sunday next Come semist^{er}? beinge ye the 27 Nov in ye time of divine Service. In such expressed words as ye Minister shall release unto her and also Satisfie Court Charges

MR: JOHN SIDNEY hath made it appeare unto this Court that he hath due to him 300 acres of Land for transportation of these persons whose names are underwritten:

(Note: Nugent p 155 - 1644 200 acres - which also see.)

JOHN CARRAWAY	THO: WATTKINS	JOHN CLARKE
JONE CARROWAY	ANNE ROBINSON	ELIZA: ffLOWERDAY

f 12 p 153 bot p91

(there is no f 11 & 11a)

Whereas by Act of Assembly bearing date att James Citty ye 3rd of June last It was enacted that the Burgesses

f 12 p 153 bot p 91 3 Jun 1642

(Note this follows the James Citty ——— preceding dated 7 Oct 1642 - The Clerks often found empty spots in the Court Record books and inserted odd datted material AGW)

Charges should be borne by the Inhabitants of ye severall Counties respectively they producing their accts to ye Commis[ers] of ye monethly Courts who are to proportion a Levye for ye same upon all tythable persons And that ye Sherriffe of ye sd severall Counties respectively shall levie and gather upp ye same and uppon refusall or non-payment of anyone to distrayne by vertue of their office.

Whereas MR: EDW: WINDHAM and MR: JOHN HILL late Burgesses for this County have according to the sd act produced their accounts of Charges expended in that service to this Court amounting to ye quantity of 5501 lb of tobb which being proportioned accordinge to the number of ye Tythable persons in ye whole County comes to 17 lb of tobb per poll. It is therefore ordered MR: JOHN SIDNEY, the now Sherriff or his deputie shall by virtue of ye sd Act this order and their Office Levye ye sd 17 lb tobb per poll for ye defraying of ye sd Burgesses charges uppon all tythable persons. And uppon refusall or non payment of any one to distrayne for ye same, And ye sd Sheriff to be accountable to this Court for ye surplus or surplusage being 211 lb tobb.

Wheread CAPT: JOHN SIBSEY hath made appeare to this Court that thereis due to him 1155 lb of Stript tobb for charges expended by him and MR: JOHN HILL at ye Assembly houlden at James Citty in January last being then Burgesses for this County which sd tobb should have been leavied of all ye Tythable persons by seaven pounds of tobb per poll by THOMAS SAWYER ye then Sheriff according to an order of Court bearing date 3 Feb last past. And ye sd SAWYER having utterly neglected and fayled in ye due performance thereof so that ye sd CAPT: SIBSEY is still unsatisfied for his aforesaid Debt to his great damage and prejudice. It is therefore ordered by this Court that MR: JOHN SIDNEY ye now Sherriff or his Deputy shall by vertue of this Order ye Act of Assembly in that case provided and their owne office Demand leavye and reteine of all Tythable persons who cannot make appeare by receipt discharge or otherwise that they have alreadie payd and satisfied ye aforesd levie of 7 lb tobb per poll to the foresd SAWYER or his deputy all such severall quantities of tob as are behind and unpaid with allowance of 25 lb tobb as per cent for not stripping and 8 per cent for forbearance And uppon refusall or nonpayment of anyone to Distreine for ye same ye sd Sherriff being to be accountable to ye sd CAPTAIN SIBSEY for what he receives And in case ye sd Sherriff cannot find so much of tob Due to be levyed as will satisfy ye sd CAPT SIBSEY. It is than Ordered that all such tob as f 12 p 153 bot p 91   3 Jan 1642

shal be found to be behind and unpayd shall (be?) satisfied and payd ye sd CAPT: SIBSEY

A f 12a p 154 bot p 91a

out of the estate of ye aforsd SAWYER for his default for not gathering in ye tob according to order.

Whereas it appeareth unto this Court that there is due unto TRUSTRAM MASON from WILL: CROUCH 557 lb tob for his part of JOHN WATTFORDS wages during the time of their copartnership It is therefore ordered that ye sd WILL CROUCH shall pay unto ye sd MASON ye aforesd summe within 20 dayes And it is further Ordered that if the sd TRUSTRAM MASON shall hereafter prove that JOHN WATTFORD did earne 200 weight of tob due from JOHN GATER then ye sd WM: CROUCH is to be accountable unto ye sd TRUSTRAM MASON who shall have ye one halfe thereof or of any other quantity of tob whatsoever otherwise execucon

ANDREW WARNER and JOHN STRATTEN have both pmised (promised?) this Court to meete at ye next Court at Linhaven to end ye difference twixt them.

91a

To ye Worshipfull JOHN GOOKIN and others his Maties Commissioners. The humble peticon of MATH: PHILLIPPS Humbly sheweth unto this Court that whereas ffRANCIS LAND did impleadye pet^{r} in this Court for deteyning of a Bill and whereas it did appeare to this Court by sufficient testimony that the sd bill was not satisfied and yt your pet^{r} was wrongfully molested. It was ordered yt sd LAND should satisfie all such charges as were expended in ye sd suite by ye sd pet^{rs} as by order of this Court bearing date ye 15 Sep 1642 it doth and may appeare

Wherefore your petio^{r} Desireth this Court to award and order against ye sd LAND for ye sd charges accordinge to ye perticulars under written & your Pet^{r} shall humbly pay

P 3 dayes attendance at a Court houlden at Linhaven 0-6-0
P 4 dayes attendance at 2 Courts houlden at WILL SHIPPS 0-8-0
& 2 voyages over to Kickotan being 4 dayes and hire of boat 1-4-0
P 4 subpoe: and serving 0-8-0
P writing of 4 oathes 0-3-2
P 2 witnesses charges 0-6-0
P 2 witnesses charges 0-4-0
P Coppie of order 0-0-8
P for 3 mens heire that went to receive ye cattle at Little Creeke 0-6-0
P Execution 0-0-12

Summe Total 5-7-2

f 13 p 155 bot p 92   15 Sep 1642

Whereas MATHEW PHILLIPPS Atturney of DANIELL TANNER hath produced a bill of charges amounting to ye quantitie of 572 lb tob expended in a late suite betwixt him ye sd PHILLIPPS and ffRANCIS LAND which said charges were to be borne by ye sd LAND as by an order of Court bearing date 15 Sep last doth appeare. It is therefore ordered that ye Sherriff chall make seasure by vertue of ye sd order of so much of estate of ye sd LAND as shall satisfie the sd charges.

The estate of JOHN WHITE deceased is debitor to WILL CROUCH

P 177 lb left unpaid of his freedome	177
p 200 foote of boards	120
P a Pattent and Countrie Dutyes	120
P a letter Administration	060
P Sherriffs ffees	024
P 2 subpa: & an arest	045
P going to James tty for yr let: of administration	060
Debitor to WM: CROUCH and TRUSTRAM MASON	606
P a Condition for WATFORD time 9 weekes	600
P worke Done P WATTFFORD at MR: SEAWELLS	225
P work done p WATTFFORD at MR: JULIANS	100
P worke done p WATTFORD at MR: LANGWORTHS	100
	1115
	606
JOHN WHITE his estate Amounted a p account	1721
appeareth to ye sum of 1800	1800
Rest to Ballance the Air? 79 lb tob	79
ye which I have payd MR: HENRY SEWELL P order of Court	1721
	1820

This is a true account of the estate of JOHN WHITE deceased given uppon oath by me WILL CROUCH Administrator of ye Estate   Witnesse my hand ye 17 Nov 1642
Teste ROBT: TYAS Cler

Theise may certifie that WILL CROUCH hath given unto this Court a true and perfect Account uppon Oath of ye Estate of JOHN WHITE deceased ye sd CROUCH being Administrator of ye sd Estate.

It is ordered that accordinge to an ---?---of an Act of Accembly that all Counties shall keepe ferries in Convenient places that there shalbe in this County two ferries kept one at DANIELL TANNERS CREEKE and other at Linhaven at the Quarter uppon CAPT: THOROWGOODS heires Land to ye Easterne shore from ye sd Quarter and that for ye payment of ye fferrie man thier shalbe 1600 weight of tob levied out of the whole County And it is referred to CAPT: JOHN SIBSEY and MR: HENRY SEAWELL to agree with ye ferrie man of DANIELL TANNERS CREEKE to CAPT: JOHN GOOKIN to agree with ye other at Linhaven ye next yeare.

A f 13a p 156 BLANK

f 14 p 157 bot p 93   18 Oct? 1642 (hole in paper at Month)

At a Court Holden for ye County of Lower Norfolk
18 hole 1642
CAPT: JOHN GOOKIN

CAPT JOHN SIBSEY   (Lieut ffRANCIS)MASON
MR: EDW: WINDHAM   (MR: HENRY)SEAWELL
MR: HENRY WOODHOUSE

(NOTE: THE CENTER OF THIS PAGE HAS BEEN TORN OUT

No names are left in the first item which is something abot the Sherriff .. return of the writ...............

2nd item: ....JOHN HOLBECK deceased .... something about debts..........

3rd item: ....a condition.........27 Dec 1641 ...... ffERINHAUGH HOWSE........1500.......AND YE SD JOHN MARTIN .... 300 lb tob.............

(the above is all that is left)

f 14a p 158 bot p 93a   15 Oct 1642

(Note: This page is as badly mutilated as p 157 and what is left is as follows AGW)

.....stands indebted unto HENRY BRAKES .....ordered that sd BRAKES shalbe satisffied......estate of sd JOHN?) HOLBECK

Whereas.....BECK deceased stands indebted unto JOHN POWIS ....POWIS shalbe paydye said debt............

............pay unto WILL GRANGER
............subpenade..........
.........a Hogg of MATHEW.........
......appeare upon oath that he hath due to him........ acres of land for the transportstion of................ assigned over to him by CORNELIUS LLOYD
.... BRISON)
.... GILBERT)— JUNE WMDE

........appeare that JOHN CHAMBERS............ quantity of 70 ....an attachment......estate of ye sd........ THO: CODD for securitie of ....

Whereas -hole- STARLINGE was arrested to this Court to answer the - holes- of......and did not appeare either by himselfe or..........Therefore ordered.........shall fayle to make.......at the next Court......Judgement against him

last item......not enough left to make any sense of and no names.

f 15 p 159 bot p 94   15 Oct 1642

(NOTE: ANOTHER BADLY TORN PAGE FULL OF HOLES AGW)

...THO: M(ARSH?) ......(attur)ney of JOHN GATER shall pay unto.....................

...............BONNER.............
Whereas..........
RICH: ffOSTER..............
wise to rec............
.................ffOSTER to pay ......
.... forbearance ....

Whereas it ....to this Court that WILL MIMACK late servant unto HENRY........Covenant and Condition to serve MASTER HENRY CATTLIN ....terme ot 5 yeares in consideration that ye sd CATTLIN SHULD...... ye sd MIMM-- .... yeares service ....he had to serve ....foresd Master HENRY HAWKINS one new man service for his full terme being 4 yeares in Consideration of ye aforesd t-- yeares W..... MIMMACK was bound by indenture to serve ye sd HAWKINS .... therefore thought fit and so ordered that ye sd MIMMACK ....ye sd CATTLIN ye full terme of 4 yeares.......... disbursment of ye aforsd new servant.......and one yeare of ye..............

...............betwixt.....LLOYD and THO: BROWNE is refered to...............

.......Heth made appeare to this Court that there is (due unto him?) 150 acres of Land for the transportation ot... whose names are here underwritten
.......GOOD, ANNE BOSWELL, THO: HARINGTON

(NOTE: this is not in Nugent. an ANNE BOSWELL was a hd rgt in a pattent in 1635 Nugent p 325, to WM: BOTHAM to Westmoreland County AGW)

f 15a p 160 bot p 94a   18 Oct 1642

(Note: only small scraps of this page are left)

.....CORNELIUS (LLOYD?) .....(3000?) acres of land for the ....here underwritten" JOHN GARNETT, NICH: KENT ....SMYTH ....WILL WILSON, PHILLIP WESTON, WILL LEMON, JAMES SMYTH, JOHN MARSHALL, JOHN (G?)ALLBURY, JOHN ___ENT, ffRANCIS BACKER, JOHN BROOKE, THO: BONNER, MR: WA.......KMASTERS, PIGGOTT, ...ILLARD

Whereas.......2 yeares free or neare uppon ANDREW WARDNER ....100 acres of land for ye terme........and in cosideration thereof payd unto ye sd.......(STRATTON?) ...... ye sd STRATEN, ROBT: WEST and WM: WILKINSON...... parcell of Land bought of them by yd sd STRATTON whereas ye (sd) ..... 100 acres is part
(NOTE: I could not find this in Nugent AGW)

f 16 p 161 bot p 95   18 Oct 1642

and now cut off by an Elder graunt if in case ye sd STRATTON shall ever throw ye sd WEST and WILKINSON and recover satisfaction for ye sd land it is further ordered that the sd STRATTON shall pay unto ye sd WARDNER 200 lb of tobb more at all demands otherwise ececucon

(NOTE: There is a large hole in the middle of this page and another at the bottom AGW)

It is ordered that ROBT: HAYES administrator of ye Estate of JOHN LANCKFEILD shall pay unto SYMON HANCOCK who intermarried with ye relict and administrator of GILBERT GUY deceased ye full sume of two hundred and...........due to ye estate of GILBERT GUY...............

Whereas it appeareth (by) Specialty produced in Court by THO: WARREN? A....... of ....WILKINSON that ffRANCIS LAND stands indebted unto ye sd WILKIN(SON?) .... 759 lb tob............at ye great howse at Kickcotan....... therefore ordered that ye sd Land shall make (payment?) ....debt unto ye sd WILKINSON of his assigns.....

howse in Hampton River aforesaid with...........charges otherwise execucon...........Whe..........desire in his Petition forbearance for yd sd debt........(appe)are in Court that ffRANCIS LAND hath taken order with.......... ...eck for ye payment of 200 lb tob for satisfaction of ye sd debt for which consideration ye Court thought not fitt to affix forbearance in regard ye sd HOLBECK was Cast away and did not pforme the payment. Whereby ye sd LAND hath lost his Debt of 200 lb tob

HENRY WATER hath made appeare unto this Court uppon oath that he hath due to him for ye transportation of himselfe and WILL HOLLY 100 acres of land (not in NU)

PHILLIPP LAND hath made appeare unto this Court uppon oath that there he hath due to him 200 acres of land for the transportation of himselfe and three others whose names are here underwritten WALTER(RASH NU182) (OLIVER NU182) HOLLOWAY, ANNE VIROSE (NU182 1648)(PHILLIPP LAND NU 182 and these three hd rgts in 1648 patent to BARTHOLOMEW HOSKINS)

(Next item badly mutilated: ffRANCIS LAND to be payd by WARRIE 50 lb tob

In order to keep page numbers properly on the the right and left margins it has been necessary to insert this blank folio. It was not discovered until the entire book was typed.

Your editors apologies

AGW

f 16a p 162 bot p95a 18 Oct 1642

In ye cause betwixt CAPT JOHN GOOKIN plt and JOHN STRATTON andTHO: CAUSON defts

To the right worsh[ll] SIR WILLIAM BERKLEYKntGov and ye rest of ye Worsh[ll] Councell of of state

The humble petition of JOHN GOOKIN in ye behalfe of CAPT: THOROWGOOD'S children

Humbly sheweth that whereas.......hole...... ye entreaty of some Inhabitants of Linhaven............a parcell of land in 2 dividents ye one 600 acres belonging to ADAM ye heir of CAPT ADAM THOROWGOOD deceased ye other 200 acres belonging to ANNE THOROWGOOD bequeathed to her by will of one ROBT: CAMME deceased. In which survey as appeares by ye platts under ye survaye...... hole...... of JOHN STRATTON and THO: CAUSON were Cutt off ....hole......... having arested ye sd parties for their deinall........... hole............longe owner oftimes ye warrants have not been ....hole..........that in June they both appeared but your petitioner.......hole..............by ye Assembly by reason of ye plot they.........hole......... ---rating of Heires or other mens land. Wherefore ....hole..... ---vis ye benefitt of that act of Assembly ....hole........ Court and to give equity to either as shalbe ....hole.......

And your Petitioner shall pray the Court hath reffered ye Petitioners Cause to be ended and determined at ye next Monethly Court of ye Lower Norffolk to be tryed by a Jury of 12 sufficient men who are to award satisfaction or possession as they shall find cause according to ye Act and ye Court to give Judgement accordingly

Exhibit ---?--- RICHARD Llee CLER COUNCIL

7 Oct 1642

To the Worshipful SIR WILLIAM BERKELRY Knt Gov &c and ye rest of ye WORSH[ll] Councell of State

The humble request of the Commissioners of ye Lower Norffolk Whereas ye last Assembly held at James Citty made an Act ....hole..... ....hole...... that should sett down and build uppon other mens land .....hole.... 12 men should award ye possessor from ye owner ....hole.......ffor building and clearinge and if ye owner should ......hole......-amages awarded by ye Land should be valued .....hole.........We humbly conceive tha ye owner.......hole....... therebeing not expressed in ye Act of Assembly? ....hole....... satisfaction notwith standing his land be(inge?) ....hole ..... worne out by another ....hole..... by the act .....hole..... charges or else to part (with?) ye land a case ....hole....here reffered from you f 17 p 163 bot p 96 Nov 1642

The Land being Orphants we desire to have ye Act explayned wheather or not it may be sould from them

JOHN SIBSEY HENRY WOODHOUSE
EDW: WINDHAM HENRY SEAWELL

Tha answer of the Gover[r] and Councill to ye rest of ye Comm[rs]:

Say that it is ye positive resolution of ye Act that no Orphants Land can be any ways lett, sett or alineated for a longer time than ye Expiracon of their minoritie
3 Nov 1642 RICHARD Llee Cler Council

ENSIGNE THOMAS KEELING aged 34 yeares or thereabouts sworne and examined: The deponent sayeth that at such time as MR: WILKINSON came to viewe his Land chich was in ye yeare 16(hole) this deponent togeather with MR: WILKINSON and MR: WEST and THOMAS (hole) all......... her to view ye convenience of ye sd land wnd then ye sd MR: (hole)son did begin to measure for CAPT: THOROWGOOD at ye poynt of land called Cameo Poynt and from thence measured a mile from ye Creeke side which is now accoumpted ye Second Creeke before hs claimed any Land for himself And this deponent further sayeth that before such time as MR: WILKINSON or WILL LAYTON did seate he this depont and CAPT: THOROWGOOD and WILL: LAYTON did measure ye breadth of ye sd 600 acres and began to measure at ye aforesd poynt called Cames Poynt (Note- your editor belives this is a name of a man CAMS or CAME but it need proving from other records AGW) and further sayeth not
15 Nov 1642 ROBT: TYAS Clk: The Marke of
THO: ↑ KEELING
EDW: WINDHAM

(See Nugent 38 CHRISTOPHER BURROUGHS patent 1636 and ROBERT WEST patent 1636 - both bordering on THOROWGOOD Land AGW)

CHRISTOPHER BURROUGHS aged 30[7]? years or thereabouts sworne and examined: This depont sayth that from tyme to tyme also all before the pattent was granted (us?) after he this depont heard .....hole...... THOROWGOOD divers times talke talke concerning ye 600 acres of Land now in controversie and that at all times ye sd CAPT:THOROWGOOD------ompt ye Poynt called CAMES Poynt ye first beginning ....hole..... that he this depont heard MR: WEST and THO: RUDDER...... hole......THOROWGOOD had by a particular survey of his owne taken .....hole..... and partof their cleere ground from them and that .....hole..... measure at ye sd CAMES Point and further this depont sayeth not
15 Nov 1642 ROBT: TYAS Clk Xop: BURROUGHS

f17a p 164 bot p 96a   15 Nov 1642

EDWARD WINDHAM aged 26 yeares or thereabouts sworn and examined sayeth That to his knowledge CAPT: THOROWGOOD deceased did never lay any clayme to a Creeke in ye Eastern side of Lynnhaven River called by ye name of ye Oyster Creeke as any part or at all belonging to any Patent or Patents by him procured or to him granted and that ye Pattent of 600 acres now in question was always intended to beginne at a Point now called CAMES Poynt to runne up STRATTONS Creeke on one side and ye Mayne River on ye other side. And further this depont sayeth that ye reason why ye sd Pattent was to beginn uppon ye first or second Creeke(was) because it was not then certaynely known which was the Mayne River. And further this depont testifies that CAPT: THOROWGOOD did at severall times measure ye sd Pattent himselfe with a line but did neaver goe on ye other -side?- of ye sd STRATTONS Creeke but did allwayes -begin?- at ye -CAMES?- Poynt and at no other place and further ....hole....sayeth not?-
Nov 1642 ROBTE TYAS Cler: EDW: WINDHAM

HENRY WOODHOWSE aged 35 yeares or thereabouts sworne and examined sayeth: That he neaver heard CAPT: THOROWGOOD make any clayme for his 600 acres of land but beginning at ye second Creeke and that ye reason he claymed ye sd -hole- or Oyster Creeke was to carrie sometimes a dish of Oysters to SIR JOHN HARVIE and that he thought he might have a little more privilege than others in respect he was Comander and further sayth not
15 Nov 1642 ROBT: TYAS Cler: HENRY WOODHOUSE

The Juries Verdict

We whose names are here underwritten being impanelled by vertue -of- a refference bearing date ye 7 Oct 1642 under .....hole ..... Court from ye Gover^{r} and Councell for ye deciding and En(hole-) verdict of a Matter depending in variance betweene CAPT: JOHN GOOKIN plt in the behalfe of the children of CAPT: ADAM THOROWGOOD deceased and THOS: CAUSON and JOHN STRATTON and JOHN STRATTEN defts ....hole. ...survey of 2 dividents of Land situate and beinge ..... hole...... Easterne Shore in ye pish of Linhaven the one divident ....hole..... of ADAM THOROWGOOD sonne and heire of ye sd CAPT: ADAM THOROWGOOD conteyning 600 acres of land the other devident being ye Lands of ANNE THOROWGOOD being to her bequeathed and Devised by ROBERT CAM deceased conteyning 200 Acres of Land. We therefore find by sufficient

(Note: See Nugent 36 - Patent to ROBERT CAVE or CANE - "200 acres 18 Dec 1635 Bounded Wly upon MR: WILKINSON, Nly upon the Creeke and Sly into the Maine land. See also WM: WILKINSON NU 34, & 52 AGW)

f 18 p 165 bot p 97

(continued from above) evidence to be produced that CAPT: ADAM THOROWGOOD did in his lifetime measure ye 600 acres in that Patent menconed beginning his bounds uppon ye

f18 p 165 bot p 97   15 Nov 1642

Second Creeke at a place called CANNS POYNT being ye Second Creek in ye sd Patent menconed. And it appeareth by the platt to us produced that ye survey made by the plt: was bounded uppon ye sd Second Creeke at ye sd CAMS Poynt. Wee therefore doe approve and find the sd survey to be right and duelly surveyed according to ye sd patent Wee also find that ye sd 200 acres due by ROBERT CAMES Patent devised to ye sd ANNE THOROWGOOD to be duly bounded uppon ye 600 acres aforesaid in respect there was for Land found to be due to MR: WILKINSON as by -holes in paper)------tended by ye deft JOHN STRATTEN. And for--holes ------ doth appeare to be elder than ye patent of WILLIAM LAY-----Hole- and by ye deft THOMAS CAUSON. Wee doe approve of ye Survey thereuppon made according to ye aforesaid platt. Now for as much as ye sd --- hole --- doth crave ye benifit of an Act of Assembly for their reliefe ----- hole ------- fins and allow unto ye sd Defts: ye summe of 6500 lb tob towards the charges they have been at in building (and) clearing in manner following Vizt:

Unto ye Deft THOMAS CAUSON YE SUME OF 5000 lb tob and to ye Deft JOHN STRATTEN 1500 lb tob provided that if ye plt (doth) refuse to pay and satisfy unto ye sd Defts ye sd severall lbs tob that then and in that case it may and shall be lawful for ye deft JOHN STRATTEN to have hould and possess as much of ye devidentas in MR: WILKINSONS Patent is menconed as is due to ye sd Plt: by ye aforesd survey for and during ye terme of this two yeares now next ensuing for and towards ye payment of ye sd 1500 lb tob and in case the pltf: refuseth to sattisfy ye deft: THOMAS CAUSON ye sd summe of 5000 lb tob that then and in that case ye pltf: shall assure unto ye Deft: CAUSON ye 20 acres or thereabouts of Cleare ground with the howsing thereuppon standing to him and his heires forever being due to ye sd pltf by ye Survey aforesd. The Deft: paying unto ye pltf ye sume of 400 lb tob for as much also that it appeareth unto us that ye Pltf: had just cause of suite against ye sd Defts we find therefore ye Defts to pay cost and charges unto ye Pltf: which Costs and Charges are to be equally payd by ye sd Defts: All and everie thing herein Conteyned We have agreed uppon and Deliver as our verdict.

JOHN HILL foreman	MATHEW HOWARD	HENRY HAWKINS
JOHN YATES	THOMAS LAMBERT	ROBERT GLASCOCK
MATH: PHILLIPPS	WILLIAM SHIPP	THOMAS MARSH
JOHN WATKINS	SYMON HANCOCK	THOMAS IVIE

f 18a p 166 bot p 97a 15 Nov 1642

Whereas by a Refference of Court from ye Gov[r] and Councell bearing Date at James Citty ye 7 Oct 1642 A cause then depending betweene CAPT: JOHN GOOKIN Pltf: in behalfe of ADAM and ANNE ye children of CAPT ADAM THOROWGOOD deceased and JOHN STRATTEN and THOMAS CAUSON defts: concerning a survey of 200 acres of Land lying uppon Ye Eastern Shore of Linhaven River and was referred down to this Court to to be tryed by a Jury of 12 men and to be ended and determined according ----hole----- which ----hole---- a Jury having been impanelled ----- holes--------- have given in their verdict and found for the Pltf: as in and by ye sd verdict may and doth more fully appeare. It if therefore ordered for a finall determination of ye sd (suite?) according to ye Juries verdict that is Respect ue Pltf: re(fuseth?) to give ye Deft: JOHN STRATTON ye sattisfaction specified that ye sd -----hole----- by ye Sherriff to ye Pltf: in behalfe of ye sd children for Matters of title and propertie the sd land far and dueing ye terme of 2 yeares as is specified in ye verdict (Provided?) that ye sd STRATTEN doe not ---?--- distroy spoyle or lett goe ruyne and howse or howses there on now standing or Gar9dens?) thereto belonging during ye sayd term. And whereas the Pltf: refuseth to give the Deft: THOMAS CAUSON such satisfaction for his charges in building and clearing as in ye verdict is specified It is like wise ordered that ye sd CAUSON shall enjoy all that part of his Cleare ground cutt off by ye Pltf: survey being or thereabouts with the howses thereon standing forever paying unto the Pltf: ye full quantity of 400 lb tob within 15 dayes the Pltf: giving ye sd CAUSON securitie for ye quiett and peaceable possession thereof in Case it be required. And lastly that ye sd STRATTON and CAUSON shall equally detwixt them pay and satisfy unto ye Pltf: 1669 lb tob for his costs and charges occasioned and defended in and by ye sd suite as was ---hole--- made appeare within 15 dayes likewise otherwise execucon

f 19 p 167 bot p 98 16 Dec 1642

WILLIAM VAUGHAN aged 30 yeares or thereabouts sworne and examined this 16 Dec 1642 sayeth that being Goate K(eeper) to MR: JOHN GOOKIN and ye Estate of CAPT: ADAM THOROWGOOD -to yeares now past and at ye time when ye Goate - holes- by MR: HENRY CATLIN and MR: ROBT: HAYES betwixt my now MR[is] and her children since which time theire hath beene lesse -- hole -- Goats and their increase (Vizt?) by ---hole--- and Disease and vermin -------holes --- and further sayeth that ---hole--- increase of female is 12 And that there resteth to this ----hole---- at this present noe more than 100-----hole----- the Childrens Goats Whereof 58 are Breeders

Teste me ROBT: TYAS Clk

f 19 p 167 bot p 98   16 Dec 1642

16 Dec 1642 ROWLAND MORGAN aged 23 yeares or thereabouts sworn and examined Sayeth that he this depont being Cow-keeper to MR[is] and her children and ever since that time having beene employed in the same service of keeping ye cattle belonging to ye estate of CAPT: ADAM THOROWGOOD to this deponts knowledge there hath died of the Childrens Cattle 2 old cows, One 4 yeare old Heifer, 2 that were Cow Calves at ye time when MR: CATLIN and MR: HAYES made ye division which is in all five head of ffemale Catle. And he further sayth that 4 of ye Childrens Cattle have gone barren this yeare last past and that this sd last past yeare ye increase is onely Seaven Cow Calves and further sayeth not

teste: ROBT: TYAS   Cler:

f 19a p 168 Bot p 98a   6 Feb 1642/3

(Note: This is out of place in the original book "A" Probably inserted on the blank back of the preceding page at a later date. AGW)

(This is) Feb 1642/3

SAVILL GASKIN hath this day engaged himselfe or a sufficient man for him before CAPT: JOHN GOOKIN ESQ: Comander, EDW: WINDHAM, MR: HENRY WOODHOUSE, to keep a ferrie beginning from ye 26th of Januarie last past for a Compleate yeare in Linhaven River from ye Quarter untoye Easterne Shore unto ROBT: CAMS Poynt uppon notice given by a HOLLOW or a fire. And likewise from ye affores(aid?) (Qu?)arter unto Trading Poynt uppon notice given aforesd backwards and forwards between both places -----hole------Whereof ye sd GASKIN is to have 800 --hole ---accordinge to Order of Court made ye 15th ---hole----- to be payd to him by ye then Sherriff------hole----SAVILL GASKINS hath subscribed his hand & -------hole----written in ye yeare 1642

The Marke of SAVILL ( ) GASKIN

f 20 p 169 Bot p99 (is continued on next page)

f 20 p 169 Bot p 99 16 Jan 1642/43

At a Court holden at WM: SHIPPS for ye County of Lower Norffolke ye 16 Jan 1642/3

PRESENT: CAPT: JOHN GOOKIN ESQ, COMANDER
CAPT: JOHN SIBSEY MR: HENRY SEAWELL LIEUT ffRANCIS MASON

(Note: This page has been restored, at least what is left of it. AGW)

This may certifie......................HOSKINS being (out?) of this County...................ye General Leavy .....rayse and ....month of October James Citty by ye.....................Sherriff of everie County alotted to............................to severall men appoynted..........................Coming in Gover[r] after this this leavy............particular instructions to free all his Councell................publique Charges CAPT: WILLOUGHBY of this County....in one of the Councell then with SIR ffRANCIS WYATT a................and more in number in his ffamily ye..................per poll the sd HOSKINS fell short in paym..................o[f] the some of 600 lb............................and power brought by SIR ffRANCIS WYATT....................you to take into consideration M............................that you would be pleased............................of this some and that trouble like............thereof......truth and our desire over ye Comisioners of this County have hereunto subscribed our hands this 19 Jan 1642

JOHN GOOKIN
JOHN SIBSEY
ffRAN: MASON
HENRY SEAWELL

The sherriff doth positively asert that MR: POWIS after a sumons presented upon him for his appearance to this Court did Question wheather there was Authority to Comand or request him thither in this County and he hath not ap(torn)ed according to ye tenor of ye Sumon) to answer ye Suite of SYMON HANCOCK in an Action of ....torn....... there shall a warrant issue out for Comanding him to ye next Monethly Court with sufficient Securitie to be taken or his appearance

f 20a p 170 Bot p99a

It is ordered that OLIVER VANHECK for swearing in open Court shall pay to publique uses 20 weight of tob within 4 dayes

These are to certify that JAMES BLISSE and HENRY RUTKINS and (Hole ?) BONNER have according to ye Act set up theire names (& given?) notice of theire intended [God willing] to goe for England this present shipping. (Note: this item is mostly missing AGW) XOP: BURROUGHS to receive payment of debt from THO: BULLOCK

f 20a p 170 Bot p 99a 16 Jan 1642/3

(Note: Only the right side of this page survives. AGW)

OLIVER VANHECK *(evidently lost or owes a grapnel to THO: CAUSON)*

Whereas it appeareth to this Court that ROBT: DAVIS hath fraudently conveyed away certayne things belonging unto the mayde servantof THO: CAUSON. It is therefore ordered that ye sd DAVIS shall pay unto THO: CAUSON 100 weight of tob: for the things soe conveyed away within 20 dayes with Court Charges otherwise execucon and to be fined for Pub-like uses 100 weight of Tob to be payd ye next yeare secretly Dealing and Bargaining with other mens servants

ARTHUR PURNELL of another County having arrested RICHARD ----?--- ye last Court past. The busenesse being referred unto this Court upon ye request of RICH: STARNE --hole--- ye said ARTH: PURNEL not appearing nor any Atturney for him ----- he is non-suited

f 21 p 171 bot p100 16 Jan 1642/3

Whereas it appeareth to this Court that .....torn....... *(BARTHOLOMEW HOSKINS?)* is indebted unto ye estate of WILL: *(Torn. Name may be EDWARDS?)* --- torn --- 50 lb tob. It is therefore ordered------ torn-------- HOSKINS shall make payment of ye sd quantity -----torn---- unto RICHARD OWENS for ye use of -----torn-----------within 15 dayes with Court Charges otherwise ececucon

Whereas THO: DAVIS hath mede it appeare unto this Court that GEORGE EARLE is is indebted unto him the sume of 60/ (shillings) Sterling as by specialty appeareth-----torn-- that an attachment be -----torn-----untill payment be made of ye aforesaid ----torn----

JOHN BALL hath mede it appeare to this Court uppon oath that he hath due to him 50 acres of Land for his owne transportation

CAPT JOHN GOOKIN ESQ: hath made it appeare unto this Court that JOHN LEWIN of Ye Upper Norfolk County deceased was indebted unto him 100 lb tob It is therefore ordered that an attachment be granted agaynst 100 weight of tob in MR: TODDS hand untill such time as ye Administrator of ye sd LEWINS estate shall make payment thereof
(Note: Upper Norfolk County became Nansemond County later)

CAPT: RICHARD PARSONS hath entered a Caveat for 300 acres of Land adjoyningto his Plantation in -------?---Easterne Branch provided he makes the Land to be due unto him

Whereas THO: PRICHARD late servant unto THO: CAUSON humbly complayned to this Court that his sd Master forced him to bind himselfe for two yeares more than he was bound for in his first indenture It appeareth that the Latter act is unlawful and therefore voyd. It is therefore ordered that

f 21 p 171 bot p 101   *16 Jan 1642/3*

ye sd THO: PRICHARD shalbe acquitted of his latter covenant and that ye sd CAUSON shall pay him his Corne and clothes due by indenture according to ye Custome of ye Countrie within 30 dayes with Court Charges otherwise execucon

The Corne and Clothes exprest in this order is 3 barrells of Corne, a Cloth suite, a payre of shoes and stockings and shart (shirt?)

f 22 p 173 bot p 100a   15 Feb 1642/3

At a Court houlden for ye County of Lower Norffolk at the howse of WILL: SHIPP ye 15 Feb 1642/3
PRESENT: CAPT: JOHN GOOKIN ESQ: COMANDER
CAPT: JOHN SIBSEY   MR: WILL:JULIAN
MR: EDW: WINDHAM   LIEUT: ffRANCIS MASON

Whereas SYMON HANCOCK hath made (it) appeare to this Court that WILL: DURFORD is indebted unto him----torn----(5?) hhds of tob shipped home for England by yd sd DURFORD conteyning thi---- six hundred pounds------torn--------- DURFORD---------torn--------- himselfe to be accountable -----torn-------and hath not as yet pformed. It is therefore (ordered?) that ye sd HANCOCK shall have an attachment -------torn------part------torn-------Estate of ye sd DURFORD to ye VA---torn---- sd quantitie of tob untill such time as ye sd -----torn----can give an account of ye sale thereof accordinge to (convicon?)

Whereas MR: ROBT: POWIS Clarke was arrested to this Court and fayled to appeare either by himselfe or his Atturney. EDW: HALL in behalfe of ye sd MR: POWIS did voluntarily engage himselfe that is case ye sd MR: POWIS or his sonne or some other lawful Atturney did not appeare to answer ye suite of SYMON HANCOCK ye next Court then he ye sd EDW: HALL would stand to ye award of ye sd Court. It is therefore ordered that ye sd EDW: HALL shall pforme and stand to what ye Court shall then Order in ye sd suite

It is ordered that HENRY HILL shall have an Attachment agaynst so much of ye Estate of HENRY MICHELL deceased as ye sd HILL shall make appeare to be due unto him ye next Court.

WHEREAS MR: EDW: WINDHAM hath deposed that there is due to him from THO: BULLOCK ye summ of 50/ (shillings) sterling by Bill of Exchange not payd. It is therefore ordered that ye sd WINDHAM shall have an Attachment agaynst so much of ye Estate of ye sd BULLOCK as shall amount to ye value of ye sd debt.

It is ordered that LIEUT: ffRANCIS MASON shall have an attachment agaynst a Heifer and a Calfe pert of ye Estate of WILL: DURFORD being in ye sd MASONS possession untill he be satisfied for a pyre of silke stockins and ye keeping ye

f22 p 173 bot p 101   16 Feb 1642/3

sd cattle so much as by ye Court shalbe thought fitt. *(Note: Wonder how thick they were and if they were knit by hand. AGW)*

f 22 p 174 bot p101a   16 Jan 1642/3 *(Badly mutilated page)*

It is ordered that JAMES WARNER shall have an attachment ....WM: DURFORD for ye Quantitie of 650 lb tob and caske. All former attachments -------of ye sd DURFORDS estate being first satisfied--------------------------

These are to certifie that RICHARD ffOSTER hath according to ye Act of Assembly set up his name to give notice that he intends by Gods Grace to goe for England this present shipping to ye intent that he may have his passe granted for his departure---------

------hole------ CAPT: THOMAS WILLOUGHBY and ffRANCIS LAND is referred to ye next Court

Whereas (it appeareth?) to this Court that JAMES WARNER adminis trator of THO: HOWLT ------hole----- received 105 lb tob being -----torn------belonging WM: WINTERBOTTOM and not to ye Estate of ye sd HOULT not having any warrant for ye same as by severall depositions hath appeared. It is therefore orderedthat ye sd JAMES WARNER shall repay unto ye sd WINTERBOTTOM ye sd Quantitie of tob with 40 lb tob more for charges expended in ye sd suite within 15 dayes otherwise Execucon

A liste of worke done by RICHARD HORNER delivered unto ELLARAS *(or ETTARAS or ELLACAS AGW)* ----------------- *STONARD TO RECEIVE:*

ffor himselfe	℔ 50
ffor JOHN ffITCHET	050
" old BARSOND	015
" STEVEN	030
" CHAPMAN	015
" MRS: OLIVER	030
" DANIELL LIBBY	020
" HICCOLBAUGH	040
By bill of KEMP	200
ffor MR: IRONMONGER	010
	560
More RAPH HARMER	118
	678
	-150
	528
ROBT: JACKSON	030
GEORGE HARRISON	015
	573

f 23 p 175 bot p 102 16 Jan 1642/3

(NOTE: Practically the whole top of this page is missing)

Whereas it
Late of Linhaven
in that SAMI(TH?) of
ROBT: EYRES *(All that is left of this record)*

(However, what follows may belong to the above item)

by ye sd EYRES as by an Order of Court------------------ --granted-------ye sd EYRES to ye sd WILL: SHIPP Doth appeare. And for as much as ye aforsd ALLEXANDER STONAIR did give order --?-- PHILLIPP LAND by (note?) under his hand bearing date ye 13 Dec 1642 to pay unto ye sd RICHARD HORNER ye full Quantitie of 500 lb tob which note being turned by ye sd HORNER unto ye sd ROBT: EYRES in Consider-acon as aforesaid. It is therefore ordered that ye sd ROBT: EYRES shall have an Attachment agaynst 500 lb tob of ye Estate of ye sd Stenar being now in ye hands of ye aforesd PHILLIPP LAND

The Cause betweene HENRY SEAWELL Atturney for ROBT: PAGE Mariner pltf and JAMES WEME Deft is refferred untill ye Court

Whereas JOHN YATES, Churchwarden of ye pish of Elizabeth River hath caused ROBT: MARTIN to be summoned to this Court uppon a presentment for breach of ye Sabbath and having fayled in presenting ye same It is therefore ordered that ye sd MARTIN be acquitted and dismissed ye Court and that ye sd YATES shall satisfie all ye Charges occasoned by ye sd presentment.

Whereas CORNELIUS LOYD did cause EDW: HALL to be arrested to this Court to answer ye suite of PETER KNIGHT Merchant who neither appeared by himselfe or by any other to prose-cute ye sd suite It is therefore ordered that ye sd KNIGHT shalbe non suited and that ye sd LOYD who in ye behalfe of ye sd KNIGHT procured ye sd Arrest shall satisfie and pay unto ye sd HALL 20 lb tob for losse of time and ye Court Charges

f 23a p 176 bot p 102a 16 Jan 1642/3

(NOTE: The top of this page is mutilated)

------------------ *and JANE BUTTERFIELD were presented*
---------------------*BETH PINTER? for Actuall Comitting*
----------------------*tinued in that uncleanesse? along*
--------------------------- *asse and JANE BUTTERFIELD*
----------------------------- *uppon their bare backs*
-----------------------------------*for their offenses*
---------------------------- *they be lawfully married*
--------------------------------------*Oath that uppon*
------------------------------------*1642 in ye time of*
---*JOHN*
--*body and that*

f 23a p 176 bot p 102a 16 Jan 1643/3

----------------- in Concea-------him ---SMYTH whom she -----Declared to be ye right father of her Bastard child --time of her deliverie as was also herd? by several women present att ye time of her deliverie and far as much as many strong and probable arguments have appeared unto ye Court that ye sd SMYTH is not absolutely quilty of ye fact It is therefore ordered that ye sd SMYTH shall pay ye next cropp 150 lb tob for ye building of a payre of stocks ye sd stocks to be built by ye first of May next and 250 weight of tob more the sd next cropp to me HENRY SEWELL Master of ye sd MARY ROUGE in satisfaction for the losse of her time during her lying in. And it is also ordered that ye sd MARY ROUGE shall receive 20 lashes uppon her bare back as a (condignd?) punishment for her heynious offence. The sheriffs and Clarkes fees to be payd by ye sdSMYTH otherwise execucon)(the aforesaid note is the best interpretation your editor could make of this item AGW)

MR: LAND I pray pay unto RICHARD HORNAR 500 lb tob which is for so much Rec: beare witnesse my hand 16 Oct 1642
Wittnesse: ALEXANDER (AS) STONER
THO: CONYA-- Teste: ROBT: TYAS Cler:

f 24 p 177 bot p 103

At a Court houlden in ye Lower Norffolk ye 18 Mar 1642/3 at ye howse of ROBT: GLASCOCK
PRESENT: CAPT: JOHN GOOKIN ESQ: Commander
CAPT: JOHN SIBSEY
MR: WILL: JULIAN MR: HENRY SEAWELL

Whereas DANIELL NEALE and ELINOR NEALE heth confessed before ye Court to be quilty of fornication of ye woman confessing that she hath had two illegitemete Children. The man guilty of one begotten by him upon her body. It is therefore ordered that ye sd DANIELL and ELINOR shall for their sd offence stand in a white sheete ye next Sabbath day in ye pish Church of Elizabeth River and there allmighty God forgivenesse and ye sd DANIELL to put in securitie to pay ye Sherriff such tob as he shall justly make appeare to be his due for charges occasioned by bringing of them both from James Citty. And likewise give securitie that the Child begotten by him be not hereafter chargeable to this County. And it is further ordered that ye sd ELINOR for her second offence shall presently in presence of ye Court receive 10 lashes on her bare back

f24 p177 bot p103   24 Apr 1643

At a Court houlden County of Lower Norffolk at ye howse CAPT: JOHN SIBSEY ye 24 Aprill 1643

CAPT: THOMAS WILLOUGHBY ESQ:
CAPT JOHN SIBSEY
LIEUT: ffRANCIS MASON   MR: HENRY SEAWELL

CAPT: RICHARD PERSONS hath made it appeare to this Court uupon Oath that he hath due to him 300 acres of Land for transportation of himselfe and these servants whose names are here under written

JOHN ye Nagro his wife and Child
BASTEANS a NAGRO
CHRISTOPHER an Indian
ffor his owne transport

(Note: This item is not in Nugent AGW)

f 24a p 178 bot p 103a   *24 Mar 1643*

(Note: Date out of place at the bottom of last page. AGW)

At a Court holden ye 29 Mar 1643
SIR WILLIAM BERKELY Knt GOV: &c
RICH: KEMPE ESQ: CAPT: THO: PETTUS
CAPT: WILL: BROCAS   CAPT: RICHARD TOWNSEND

(This is apparently a Court held in James Citty. The clerks often found blank spaces to insert minutes where they could find spaces. AGW)

This day the GOV[r] elected MR: THO: LAMBERT to be Sherriff for ye Lower Norffolk County for the present yeare with full power to receive..........fees.......(badly blotted).

To ye wors[ll] CAPT: JOHN GOOKIN Commander & JOHN SIBSEY and ye rest of ye Commissioners.

SYMON HANCOCK Church Warden of Linnhaven Parish presenteth into ye (Court?) ye person of JAMES BLISSE of ye same parish for Comitting of a Rape ye maide of MR: LAND upon report from her owne mouth according to his oath taken to the same effect.

It is ordered that CORNELIUS LOYD shall have an Attachment agaynst ye Estate of JOHN TRASSELL for ye quantity of 1200 lb.

f 25 p 179 bot p104   15 May 1643

At a Court holden for ye County of Lower Norffolk at ye Howse of WM: SHIPP on ye 15 May 1643
PRESENT: CAPT: JOHN SIBSEY   LIEUT: ffRANCIS MASON
MR: EDW: WINDHAM   MR: HENRY SEAWELL

JOHN MARTIN hath made it appeare to this Court upon Oath that he hath due unto him by ye assignment of LANCASTER LOVETT 100 acres of Land for ye transport of 2 servants whose names are: WILL COVINGTON
NICH: EARLES

f 25 p179 bot p 104   15 May 1643

This Court taking due cognizance of ye proceedings of ye Jurie Contrarie to ye Act of Assembly !for which it is an especiall rulel doe referre ye same once more to ye care of ye Comiss[rs] of Lower Norffolk who are to take care as well of ye positive bounds of ye Land and ye priority of ye Grant and a Jurie to be impanneled upon ye place togeather with MR: THO: SYMMONS Survayer are to take especall care to ye premises and accordingly to give upp their verdict and ye same to be returned to ye GOV[r] and Council

12 Mar 1643
It is ordered upon ye reference of ye GOV[r] and Councell that theise whose names are here under written be forthwith Impannelled to be upon a Jury for ye surveying of Certeing (certain?) lands in Linhaven who are to give their attendance at ye house of SAVILL GASKIN upon Friday next being ye 19 of this present month. And after ye Administration of ye oath to procede with MR: THO: SYMMONS who is appointed Survayer and soe to give up their verdict to ye next County Court and ------?------ they or any of them are not to fayle upon perill. And it is further ordered that MR: EDW: WINDHAM and MR: HENRY WOODHOWSE shall administer ye Oath unto ye sd Jurie and alsoe goe along with them and take especiall Care that ye Surveyer doth proceede according to ye positive bounds. MR: JOHN SIDNEY foreman MR: THO: BROWNE, MR: HENRY HILL, MR: THO: MEARES, MR: ROBT: HAYES, CEASAR PUGGET, MR: BARTH: HOSKINS, RICHARD WHITEHURST, JOHN HOLMES, MR: ROBT: EYRES: RICH: DAY, HEN: SNAYLE

Whereas it appeareth unto this Court that PHILLIPP LAND is indebted unto RICH: WOOLLMAN ye some and quantities of 338 lb tob and Caske. It is therefore ordered that ye sd LAND shall pay unto ye sd WOOLLMAN ye aforesd debt with Court Charges within 5 dayes otherwise Execucon

f 25a p 180 bot p 104a   15 May 1643

Whereas THOMAS BULLOCK Chyurgion passed a bill of Exchange uppon himselfe to CAPT: THO: WILLOUGHBY for payment of a debt of 7 ₤ 10/ sterling in England ye last yeare and did not prorme accordinge to ye intent and time Limited in ye sd bill. The sd CAPT: WILLOUGHBY therefore presented ye same and produced ye sd protest under the hand of a Notarie Publike and other Authentique parties to testifie that he had not yett received ye sd debt nor any parte thereof. The Court hath therefore ordered that ye sd Debt of 7₤ 10/ Sterling shalbe satisfied and payd to ye sd THO: BULLOCK with 18/ allowance for ye protest and 25 per cent for Damages with Court Charges. All former Ingagements being first satisfied. Otherwide execucon

The cause betwixt SAVILL GASKIN and JOHN MARSHALL is referred untill ye next Court.

f25a p 180 bot p 104a 15 May 1643

Whereas ENSIGNE THOMAS LAMBERT undertook in ye behalfe of ROBT" GLASCOCK to answer ye sute of CAPT: THOMAS WILLOUGHBY for a debt of 10 ℔ sterling and ye sd Debt appearing to be justly due unto him from ye sd GLASCOCK. The Court hath therefore ordered that ye sd ENSIGNE THO: LAMBERT shall pay unto ye sd CAPT: THO: WILLOUGHBY ye aforesd debt of 10 ℔ out of ye estate of ye sd GLASCOCK with Court Charges within 2 moneths otherwise execucon

JOHN WATKINS hath Entered a Caveat for 100 acres of Land lying up ye Broad Creek neere uppon a mile up ye Creeke bounding Nly into ye woods and Ely uppon ye Broad Creeke and for 100 acres more up the same Creeke neere a mile higher or thereabouts Nly into the woods and Sly upon ye sd Creeke.

MR: THOMAS IVIE hath made appeare to this Court uppon Oath that he hath due to him 100 acres of Land for ye transportation of those whose names are underwritten: JOHN COPLAND WILL WOLTS.

MR OLIVER VANHECK hath made it appeare to this Court by Oath that he hath Due to him 300 acres of land for ye transportation or theise whose names are underwritten PETER VANHECK, OLIVER VANHECK, KATHERINE VANHECK WILL: WHISSELLWHITE, JOHN WASE, JOHN TURNER,

(NOTE: See Nugent p 210 RICHARD WOOTON patent 1651 same headrights as above.
Nugent p 220 - OLIVER VAN HICKS Creek toward the head of the Maine Branch of Linhaven River 1651 AGW)

The suite betwixt CAPT: THO: WILLOUGHBY and ROBT: SMYTH is referred untill ye next Court.

f 26 p 181 bot p 105 15 May 1643

Whereas JAMES SYMONS stands bound with ROBT: SMYTH for ye payment of 48 ℔ sterling to CAPT: THOMAS WILLOUGHBY ESQ: and hath petitioned this Court agaynst ROBT: SMYTH for a Counter Bond to save him harmlesse from ye sd CAPT: THO: WILLOUGHBY now for as much as ye sd ROBT: SMYTH is arrested to ye next Quarter Court to answer ye suite of ye sd CAPT: WILLOUGHBY for ye aforesd Debt so that ye sd security hath not beene as yett molested for ye same. It is therefore ordered that ye sd ROBT: SMYTH in Case he be Cast in ye sd suite shall forthwith upon his arrivall home from James Citty give ye sd SYMMONS sufficient securities to save harmlesse from ye sd Bond or any Damage thereby accruing with the Courts charges.

Whereas MR: BARTH: HOSKINS stands indebted unto MR: HENRY WOODHOWSE a good sufficient Cow which should have beene delivered at Kiccoutan and for as much as that Cow is unserviceable which appeares by ye oath of EDW: LILLY who

f 26 p 181 bot p 105a 15 May 1643

expresses a relation of ye Cowkeepers to that effect. It is therefore ordered that ye sd MR: HOSKINS shall pay unto MR: WOODHOWSE a Good Cow that is serviceable for ye pale (pail?) within 12 dayes at ye sd MR: HOSKINS howse with Court Charges otherwise execucon

It is ordered that JOHN GATER shall give a true and just account unto XOP: BURSTON upon Oath ye next Court for 200 weight of tob which he carried for England of ye sd XOP: BIRSTOM. And ye said THO: GATER is to pay him 10 dayes work in Oct next by a sufficient hand with Court Charges otherwise execucon

I HENRY PEARCE doe acknowledge to have received of OLIVER VANHECK a bill of 4 ŧ sterling payable to him from GILBERT NORRIS which after I receive it I doe promise to repay it to whome he shall appoynt in Confirmation whereof I have hereto sett my hand this 28 Mar 1643
Teste: ROBT: HOLTE   HEN: PEARCE

Whereas WILL DAVIS arested THO: HAYES to this Court and hath fayled to prosecute his suite It is therefore ordered that ye sd DAVIS shalbe nonsuited and pay ye charges of ye Court

f 26a p 182 bot p 105a 15 May 1643

Whereas MATHEW PHILLIPPS hath peticoned this Court for 4 barrells of Corne due to him from JOHN RICHARDSON for soe much received of ye sd PHILLIPPS from ROBT: HAYES by way of exchange to be repayed at CAPT: THO: WILLOUGHBYS as by 2 positive depositions appeareth. The Court hath therefore Ordered that ye sd RICHARDSON shall make payment of ye sd corne within 20 dayes with Court Charges otherwise execucon. Provided alwayes that if ye sd RICHARDSON shall produce proofe to ye next Court that ye sd PHILLIPPS hath alreadie received ye sd Corne. Then ye sd PHILLIPPS shall forthwith repay ye sd Corne and Court Charges agayne to ye sd RICHARDSON with damages.

Whereas it appeares that SYMON HANCOCK did lend unto XOP: BURROUGHS 6 yards of yard broade stuffe upwards of 2 yeares past. It is therefore Ordered that ye sd BURROUGHS shall make payment of ye like quantity of stuffe ar a valuable consideration after ye rate of 7 (grates?) per yard ye first pemay? in England at ye Howse of ye sd HANCOCK within 10 dayes after ye arrivall of ye third shipp ye next crop with Court Charges. otherwise execucon.

Whereas it appeares that PHILLIPP LAND is indebted unto JOHN HOMES ye quantity of 180 lb of good and merchantable tob in Leafe. It is ordered that ye sd LAND shall make paymentof ye sd debt at ye sd HOMES HOWSE within 10 dayes with Court Charges.

f 26a p 182 botp 105a 15 May 1643

It is ordered that SAVILL GASKINSS shalbe allowed 20 lb tob by JOHN HOMES for his attendance at Court being subpenayed as a witnesse in his behalfe

Whereas BARTH: HAYNES and JULIAN UNDERWOOD were presented by ye Church Wardens of Elizabeth River for Committing ye Act of Adulterie. It is therefore Ordered that ye BARTH: HAYNES and JULIAN UNDERWOOD shall upon Thursday next stand both in White sheets in ye pish Church at MR: SEAWELLS Poynt and their in ye face of ye Minister and Congregation in ye time of Devine service betweene ye first and second lessons in ye forenoone make a publique acknowledgement of (continued on the next page)

f 27 p 183 bot p 106 15 May 1643

their faule and aske Allmighty God forgiveness in those expresse words menconed in a Schedule here unto annexed

THE SCHEDULE

I B. H. and J. U. doe heare acknowledge and confess in ye presence of the whole congregation that I have greivously sinned and offended agaynst ye Divine Ma[tie] of Allmighty God and all Xtian people in Committing ye ffowle and Detestable sinne of Adultrie and am heartily sorrie and truly penitent for ye same and doe unfaynedly beseech Allmighty God of his Infinite goodnesse to be mercifull ubto me and forgive thia my haynious offence and I doe heartely desire this Congregation and all good people likewise to forgive me and pray for me.

hese may Certifie that MR: CORNELIUS LLOYD and MR: XOP: BURROUGHS being appoynted to view ye account of SARA GUYE Relict and Administratrix of GILBERT GUYE deceased have perused ye same certifyed under their hands at ye foote of ye sd Account that ye sd Executrix hath Alreadie payd and satisfied more than ye sd GUYES Estate doth amount unto as by ye sd account doth appeare which sd account with ye subscription of ye sd MR: LLOYD and MR: BURROUGHS is underwritten.

A list of all such debts as I have payd for GILBERT GUYE 12 Mar 1642/3I IMP:

pd to CAPT: THO: WILLOUGHBY by order of Court 14 ₶ 6/ and 8 lb tob 008
pd unto MR: HEN: SEAWELL per order of Court 1₶10/ and 8 lb tob for ye order 008
pd unto CORKER per order 90 lb tob and 8 for ye order 098
pd unto JOHN WEBB per order 1 barrel of corne and i payre of hoose and 1 payre of shoes and for ye order which comes in all to 108 lb tob 108
pd unto MR: HAYES per order 44 lbs tob stript and for ye order 8 lb which comes with ye allowance to 063
pd unto MR: SAWYER per order 50 lb tob for ye order 8lb058

f 27 p 183 bot p106 15 May 1643

pd unto MR: CORNELIUS LLOYD per order 2 barrels of corne which comes in tob to 120 and for ye order 8 lb	128
pd unto JOHN MARTINE per order 40 lb	040
pd unto CAPT JOHN GOOKIN PER ORDER 3 barrels of corne at 60 lb of tob per barrell and 40 ₶ is money for ye order 8 lb	188
To SYMON HANCOCK for charges as per order	088
	787

f 27a p 184 bot p 106a 16 May 1643

We whose names are here underwritten being requested by ye Court to view ye accompt of SARA HANCOCK ye relict and Administratrix of GILBERT GUY deceased doe find that she hath payd more than ye Estate of ye sd GILBERT GUY amounted unto. Witnesse our hands this 16 May 1643

CORNELIUS LLOYD
XOP BURROUGHS

Whereas MR: XOP: BURROUGHS and MR: EDW WINDHAM by vertue of two attachments to them granted by order of Court agaynst ye Estate of THO: BULLOCK (Vid) to ye sd XOP: BURROUGHS 203 lb tob Unstript and to ye sd EDW: 'INDHAM ye some of 50/ sterling by bill of exchange with 25 per Cent for Damage Did attach a Canoe and Corne so attached shalbe valued by ffower men and as much thereof delivered to XOP: BURROUGHS as shall amount to ye value of ye sd debt and ye remaynder to ye sd MR: EDW: WINDHAM

Tis ordered that LIEUT: ffRANCIS MASON shall have an attachment agaynsy one Cow and a Calfe with ye Encrease which belongs unto MR: WILL: GANEY deceased for whome ye sd ffRAN: MASON stands engaged provided that LIEUT: MASON make ye Engagement appeare to ye next Court and that there be noe former judgments past against ye sd Cattle.

LIEUT: ffRANCIS MASSONN my Love Remembered unto you. This is to intreat you to deliver my heifer and her calfe unto MR: THO: HART and in soe Doeing this my note shalbe your discharge.
Witness my hand this 16th day of Oct 1642
Wittnesse: JOHN STURMAN WILL: DURFORD
(in the margin above is(: Vid ye precedent Note

COSEN ffRANCIS MASON I pray deliver unto SYMON DREW ye Cow and Calfe which this note makes mention of and what is due to you. I will see you satisfied soe with my Love I rest. Your loving Cosen to his power
7 Mar 1642 THO: HART

The suite betwixt JOHN ARIS and WILL: SHIPP is referred untill ye next Court

f 28 p 185 bot p 107   16 May 1643

Whereas it appeareth by ye deposition of SAVILL GASKIN that JOHN HOMES did make an agreement or Composition with OLIVER VANHECK for a debt of 5 £ 10/ sterling due to him ye sd HOMES from ye sd VANECK (Vid) that ye sd VANHECK should pay 2 hhds Conteyning 560 lb neate tob at the howse of CAPT: JOHN GOOKIN in satisfaction of ye sd debt. Now forasmush as ye sd VANHECK hath pformed ye sd agreement within 61 lb tob which ye sd hhds would conteyne. It is therefore ordered that ye sd VANHECK shalbe discharged of his sd monie debt and that ye HOMES shall forthwith deliver up VANHECK his bills he ye sd VANHECK giving specialty for 61 lb of tob to be payd unto ye sd HOMESye next Cropp with forbearance at 8 per cent and likewise satisfie Court Charges

Whereas by Act of Court bearing date 15 Nov 1642 it was ordered that MR: JOHN SIDNEY ye then Sherriff should leavie and receive a 1155 lb tob with 25 per cent for allowance for not stripping and 8 per cent forbearance for ye use of CAPT: JOHN SIBSEY being part of a Leavie of 7 lb tob per poll for Burgesses Charges in ye yeare 1641 (vid) of all such Tythable persons as could not make appeare by receipt discharge or otherwise that they had formerly payd ye same to ye pcedent Sherriff THO: SAWER and that is case their could not be found soe much tob due to be leaved as should satisfie ye sd debt That thenye sd SAWER Estate should stand lyable for satisfaction thereof as more at large in ye sd Order appeareth. Now ye sd JOHN SIDNEY having made appeare to this Court that he hath received but 530 lb tob of ye aforesd debt and that there is still due to ye sd CAPT: JOHN SIBSEY 1029 lb tob which is Avered to have beene formerly received by ye sd SAWER. It is therefore ordered according to ye intent of ye aforesaid Order that Execucon shall forthwith issue out against soe much of ye Estate of ye sd SAWER as shall satisfie ye sd debt with Court Charges
(Note: The name SAWER - could this be SAYER? or SAWYER?)

f 28a p 186 bot p 107a   16 May 1643
In ye other side for want of rome (room?) is entered.

MR: SIDNEYS account to CAPT: SIBSEY concerning ye tob menconed in ye precedent Order

1055 lb tob at 25 per cent	1155
Allowance for not stripping	288
1443 lb tob 8 per cent forbearance	116
	1559
By JOHN SIDNEY received of severall persons	0530
Rest to CAPT: JOHN SIBSEY	1029

JOHN SIDNEY

Mr. THO: TODD hath positively affirmed that in May 1642 or thereabouts he sould unto XOP: NEEDEHAM a Browne Heifer which was once THO: HANDS, next JOHN GILLHAMS and then ye sd TODS which heifer was cropt on both Eares and that he

f 28a p 186 bot p 107a 16 May 1643

did assigne over a Bill of Sale for her to ye sd NEEDHAM being ye same that was given to him

Whereas if appeares ty ye examination of ffRANCIS LAMBERT and ye oath of JOHN MARSHALL that in Aprill last JOHN BALL had pswaded, invegeled and enticed divers of CAPT: JOHN SIBSEYS servants to runne away with him from theire Master fealoniously intending to steale ye sd CAPT: SIBSEYS Shallopp, CAPT: CLAYBORNS Pinnis theire Ridinge at Anchor before the Howse or any other Boate they could lite of(f) to accomodate them in their mischeivious designe contrarie to ye Law in that case provided And for as much as ye sd BALL did not onely intend to have committed ye like a little before and to have stolen powder, shott and other ptovision for that vroage? from PHILLIPP LAND and a boate from MR: CATTLIN but also did actually runne away with a boate not long since and never received any punishment all which ye Court Conceaves to be verie dangerous and bad examples of not timely prevent and have therefore ordered that ye sd BALL shall receive 30 lashes with a whipp of his bare back in presence of ye Court as a deferred punishment for his offences and to deterre others from attempting or acting ye like heereafter

f 29 p 187 bot p 108 17 Jul 1643

At a Court holden at Linhaven ye 17 Jul 1643

PRESENT: CAPT: JOHN SIBSEY MR: HENRY SEAWELL
MR: EDW: WINDHAM LIEUT: ffRAN: MASON
MR: HEN: WOODHOWSE

Whereas LANCHASTER LOVETT hath taken uppon him(self/) in Court to be securitie for ye payment of 2000 Puffe and and Pench (Pinch?) due by specialty to THO: TODD from WILL: CAPPS payable ye last of this moneth. It is ordered that ye sd LANCASTER LOVETT shal satisfie ye sd debt with halfe charges according to ye sd specialty or within 10 dayes after otherwise execucon

CHRISTOPHER NEEDEHAM hath made it appeare to this County uppon Oath that he hath 150 acres of Land due to him for ye transportation of theise three persons into the Collonie (vid JOHN MOLDEN,RICH: LEE(K?)E, THO: ANTHONIE and he hath one child borne within this Collonie called ANNE NEEDHAM (this is not in Nugent)

Whereas WILL: HAWLYE hath in open Court charged THO: WARD with bringing ye desease called ye Country Dutyes into Linhaven it is ordered at ye request of ye sd WARD that ye sd HAWLEYshall forthwith put in securitie for his appearance at ye next Court then and there to answere ye said WARDS suite

Whereas it appeareth to this Court by ye deposition of THO: WARD and other sufficient testimonies that WILL HAWLEY

f 29 p 187 bot p108a 17 Jul 1643

hath spoaken divers words tending to ye disparidgement of CAPT: THO: WILLOUGHBYE. It is therefore ordered that ye sd HAWLEY shall here acknowledge his fault in Open Court uppon his kneese and after at ye pish Church at MR: SEAWELLS POYNT uppon Sunday next Come forth night in ye time of Divine service in theise expresse words - I WILL HAWLEY doe before this Congregation acknowledge that I have spoaken diverse words tending to ye disparagement of CAPT: THOMAS WILLOUGHBY and that being cakt who Counselled me to runne away I should answer I had none but what I had from CAPT: WILLOUGHBY which I acknowledge to be false and am heartily sorrie therefore and doe humbly desire CAPT: WILLOUGHBY to forgive me ye sd offense

f 29a p 188 bot p 108a 17 July 1743

Whereas GEORGE RUTLAND hath unjustly molested ROBT: SMYTH for 13 barrells of corne formerly received and disposed of according to ye sd RUTLANDS appointment appoyntment as appeares by ye Oathes of JOHN POWIS and THO: ADDAMS. It is therefore ordered that ye sd RUTLAND shall pay unto ye sd SMYTH 150 lb tob for charges of Court wittnesses and himselfe by ye last of Oct next otherwise Execucon

Whereas ye Church Wardin and Vestrie of Linhaven have Peticoned this Courtthat GEORGE RUTLAND may be ordered to secure the Parish from keeping his children. It is ordered that if ye sd RUTLAND doe not shew himselfe industrious but appeare negligant soe that there be any likelyhood or probability of his children chargeing ye Parrish then he shall eyther put in securities by ye next Court to save ye sd Parish harmelesse or else be sent from Constables to Constable to ye place where they last lived a whole yeare.

Whereas JOHN GATER is indebted unto XOP: BURSTON ye some of 3 Ŀ Sterling. It is therefore ordered that ye sd JOHN GATER shall make payment of ye sd debt with 71 lb tob for Court Charges by ye last of Oct next otherwise execucon.

JEFFERIE WIGHT hath nade it appeare upon Oath that he hath 50 acres of Land due to him for his owne transportation into this Collonie.

Whereas SAMUELL CHARNICO hath unjustly molested ANDREW WARNER rayther of Malice then otherwise as to us appeares It is therefore ordered that ye sd CHARNICO shall satisfy all charges occasioned by this suite otherwise execucon.

Whereas JACOB BRADSHAW is indebted unto WILL: SHIPP 3 barrells of Corne due by Specialty longe since. It is ordered that ye sd BRADSHAW shall make ½ayment of ye sd corne according to ye tenure of ye specialty with Court charges within 20 dayes otherwise execucon.

f29a p 188 bot p 108a 17 Jul 1643

Whereas SAVILL GASKIN hath made appeare that THO: BULLOCK is indebted unto him 1 Petty Coate and Wast coate a payre of shoes and stockings. It is ordered that ye same shall be payd out of the sd BULLOCKS Estate eyther in kind or ye value value thereof next next to CAPT: THO: WILLOUGHBYES debt otherwise otherwise execucon.

The cause depending betwixt EDW: LILLY Atturney of HENRY ROBINSON and MR: HEN: SEAWELL securitie for MR: JOHN ROFE is referred untill ye next Court then to be fully heard and determined.

f 30 p 189 bot p 109 17 Jul 1643

Whereas EDW: HOLMES arested JAMES SMYTH and hath fayled to declare agaynst him eyther by himselfe or his Atturney It is ordered that ye sd HOLMES shall be non suited and pay all charges occasioned by ye suite with 25 lb tob to ye sd SMITHfor losse of time by ye last of Oct otherwise execucon.

The cause Betwixt ISABELL SAULSBERRIE and JANE WRIGHT is referred untill ye next Court

Whereas it appeares that WILL: EDWARDS deceased was indebted imto CAPT: THO: WILLOUGHBY the some of 10 ₤ Sterling. It is therefore ordered that RICH: OWEN who married MARIE ye relict and Administrator of ye sd EDWARDS shall satisfie ye sd debt by ye 1 Jan next with Court Charges otherwise execucon

Whereas JOHN BALL was punished ye lastCourt for running away once and endevoring ye like a second time himselfe and ffRAN: LAMBERT inticing others to goe with them and now having given just cause of suspicion that they are about the like mischeife and ROGER is agaynefor prevention. Whereof ye Court hath ordered that ys sd Ball shall forthwith put in good Securitie for his Good Behaviour or else to remayne in ye Sherriffs Custodie untill he shall doe so. And that ye sd ffRAN: LAMBERT shall give security to ye Sherriff to forsake and Abandon sd BALLS Ccompanie

Whereas ROBT: SMYTH was subp: at ye request of CAPT: THO: WILLOUGHBY as a Wittnesse of his behalfe. It is ordered that ye sd SMYTH shalbe payd 40 weight for his charge by ye sd CAPT: THO: WILLOUGHBY otherwise execucon

Whereas ffRAN: LAND was arested at ye suite of THO: CEELY for a debt of 1000 lb tob by specialty bearing date ye 14 Apr 1641 part whereof the sd LAND pretends to be allreadie payd and desires res--- and refference to ye next County Court holden at Elizabeth Citty to prove the same at ye request therefore of ye sd LAND the Court hath ordered that ye sd LAND shall put in securities for his personall appearance before ye Commissioners of Elizabeth Cittie

f 29a p 189 bot p 109   17 Jul 1643

at their next Court then and there to answer ye suite of ye sd CEELY.

f 30a p 190 bot p 109a 17 Jul 1643

It is ordered that RICHARD OWEN who maried MARIE ye relict of WILL: EDWARDS deceased shall have an attachment agaynst ye Estate of THO: SAWYER for soe much as shall satisfie a debt of 10Ŀ sterling due from ye sd SAWYER to ye sd MARIE EDWARDS

Whereas ROBT: DARBE hath made appeare that THO: SAWYER is indebted unto him the sume of 3 Ŀ 10/ Sterling. It is ordered that ye sd DARBE shall have an Attachment against the estate of ye sd SAWYER for soe much as shall satisfie ye sd debt

WHEREAS PETER MILLET hath contemptrpusly Disobeyed ye charge of THO: IVY Constable who required his assistance in ye Execution of his Office. It is ordered that ye sd MILLETT shall pay a fine of 100 lb tob to ye County use by ye last of Nov next with 50 weight of tob for charges Otherwise execucon (In the margin of this item); This fine remitted.

LLIEUT: ffRAN: MASON heth made appeare upon Oath that he hath due to him 200 acres of land for ye transportation of JOYCE WYER, THO: WARD, ROBT: PENN & OLIVER CRAFTS *(Note: Nugent 151 - gives this: 200 acres 29 Sep 1643 Record partially destroyed - mentions JNO: HOLMES howse towards GYLES COLLINGS. Trans: of 4 persons: THO: WARD ROBERT PENN? OLIVER CRAFTT, JOYCE WISER - JOYCE WYER is clearly written in Book A, name could be Wier AGW)*

The cause betwixt THO: WARD and HEN: HILL is referred untill ye next Court

It is ordered with ye consent of both parties that all controversies betweene XOP: BURROUGHA, THO: CAUSON and ELIZABETH his wife shalbe finally ended and determined ye next Court -- faded -- they are all to appeare

Whereas HUGH WOOD sould certayne HOGGS to THO: WARD which are all lost excepting one Boore and that by ye neglyence of both parties as to us evidently appears. It is ordered that ye sd WARD shall take the sd Boare that remayneth and pay unto ye sd HUGH WOOD 200 ob tob by ye last of Nov next otherwise Exec: And that ye sd HUGH WOOD shall pay both for ye keeping of ye sd Boare and -------faded----- this to be finall end of all controversies about ye sd hoggs.

The suite betwixt GEO: RUTLAND and THO: WARD is referred untill ye next Court

f 30a p 190 bot p 109a 17 Jul 1643

CAPT: JOHN GOOKIN hath made appeare that there is due to CAPT: THOROWGOODS children 100 acres of land for ye transportation of ELIZABETH TOPLEN, and WILL: SMYTH and hath assigned ye right thereof to RICH: POOLE due to him by vertue of ------ ?------ from CAPT: THOROWGOOD before his decease and since confirmed by order of Court (this isnot in Nugent)

f 31 p 191 bot p110 17 Jul & 5 Jun 1643

Upon complaynt made to this Court that BARTH: HAYNES and JULIAN UNDERWOOD doe usually associate and keepe companie with ye other contrarie to a late order Injoyneinge (sic) Pennance for ye commiyyinge ye foule fact and sinne of Adulterie though not incerted in ye Order.. It is therefore ordered that ye sd HAYNES and JULIAN UNDERWOOD shall upon demand made by ye Sherriff put in Good and sufficient securitie to refraine, forsake and abandon each others company for ye Comittinge of ye like transgression any more may be ye speedier prevented. And in case they or eyther of them shall refuse soe to doe the Sherriff is hereby required & commanded to take them or eyther of them into his custodie and them or eyther of them safely to keepe untill they shall willingly doe ye same. And also to returne his doeing in ye premises to ye next County Court Hereof he may not fayle at his perill

At a Court holden at James Cittie the 5 Jun 1643

Recordatur Present SIR WILLIAM BERKLEY knt. govnor &c

CAPT: JOHN WEST	CAPT: SAML: MATHEWS
CAPT: THO: WILLOUGHBY	CAPT: WM: PEIRCE
RICHARD KEMPE ESQ:	CAPT: THO: PETTIS

Whereas divers psons havinge runnaway servants who when they are taken and returned unto theire maisters theire sd maisters doe neglect to bring them unto the Court where they live or haveing brought them to the Court doe theire interceed for the (remissider?) of theire said punishment with too (inhoslenity?) to psons soe ill affected. And are drawne to those wicked reundles of running awaye imbeasling the goods of theire sd Maisters in hopes (if taken?) of ye like favor shown to them as to others in theire cases. It is therefore thought fitt and ordered that all Maisters who shall have such runnaway servants shall bring them to the next Quarter Courte There to receive such condique? punishment as theire offences shall justly meritt upon the penalty of Coosinge? such servant to be disposed of by the govnor and Councell . And it is Likewise ordered that all such servants or others whoe shall bee consentinge, concealinge or detinge in such running away shall allsoe bee brought to the Quarter Court there to suffer such punishmt as aforesaid. And it is

f 31 p 191 bot p 110   5 Jun 1643 (on bottom of p 191)

allsoe farther ordered that upon Complaint made by any pson or psons to any councellor Commander or next Commissioner shall have power and is hereby authorized to presse boate and men for the psueinge and apprehending of such runnawayes And the charges thereof to be levyed by the owners proporconably once a yeare out of that County and this order to be read at theire severall pish Churches to the intent that publique notice be taken thereof

SAM: ABBOTT Sl:

f 31a p 192 bot p 110a 1 Aug 1643

Recordat
At a Court holden at James Cittie the 1 Aug 1643
SIR WILLIAM BERKELEY Knt, Gov. &c

RICH: KEMPE	CAPT: HEN: BROWNE	GEORGE LUDLOWE)
CAPT: WM: PEIRCE	CAPT: PETTIS ESQR:	THOMAS STEGG (-ESQR:
CAPT: WM: BROCAS	CAPT: HIGGINSON	)

Whereas by reiterated instruccons from his Ma[tie] the excessive scandalous importance of Wynes & Strong Waters into the Colony have beene carefully guided against. And whereas in obedience to those instruccons divers goods, Lawes and orders have been made for the prohibitinge of all excesse which might argse? by want of due execucon of the sd instruccons. But soe it is that experience hath taught us that by the negligence of some and malignity and connvencie of others all preventions hetherto thought of havebeene unequall to the disease. The Court therefore takeing into consideration that the (Interin-ance?) of particulars at a generall standall to the Colonye and tempate? and contynent men as it have ordered that noe debts arysinge from wynes imported strong waters distilled and made in the Countrie shall bee pleadable in any Courts within the Collony 14 dayes after the date of this order And if any account of houlders bee contracted into one generall bill or obligacon soe much as appeares due for wyne or strong Liquors shall bee deducted from the foote of the account allwayes provided that if the Creditor take his oath that noe part greive (or grewe?) due for Wyne his single testimony shall cleare ---- ?----- filling of the debt. And it is further intended by the order that neither ---- ?---- nor others prohibited hereby from selling theire wynes soe they doe it for ready money or commodityes in hand deposited. And it is likewyse ordered that the order together with the order of the last Courte concerning the importacon of wynes and strong waters not exceeding tenne in the hundred in proporcon of other commodityes shall bee affixed to the Masts of all and every the Shipp or Shipps or Pinnances that shall goe out or arrive in this Collonye. And bee likewise read in the severall pish Churches and County Courts. To the intent to take awaye all ptence Ignorance to this order. And it is further provided that this order nor the penalty therein expressed

f 31a p192 bot p110a   1 Aug 1643

shall not extend to the sellers of beere or oyster imported of made within the Collonys or of Wyne made of the grapes groweing within the Collonys or of Sider or Perry? that the planting of Orchards and Vineyards and the soweing of English graine maye bee the better incouraged and rewarded

SAM ABBOTT Cl:

(NOTE: ROBT: TYAS, Clerk of the County Court is hard to decipher, but SAM: ABBOTT's writing for the Quarter Court has been a real test.

The Quarter Court dated 1 Aug is out of place due to some blank space on that page which was utilized to enter the proceedings of the Quarter Court.

f 32 and 32a are missing from the original book.

There was a 15 Sep Court held for it is referred to on p198

Which leads me to believe that the following is the October Court of which it cannot be a positive conclusion AGW)

f 33 p 193? bot p ?   October Court 1643 ?

Whereas THOS: HAYES Hath made appeare that THO: SMYTHERS and JOHN SUTTON are indebted unto him by Bill ye quantity of 395 lb tob and 2½ barrells of Indian Corne which HEN: SNAYLE (in the behalfe of ye sd SMYTHERS and SUTTON) undertooke and paised in Court to see satisfied. The Court hath therefore ordered that ye sd SNAYLE shall satisfie and pay ye sd tob and Corne according to ye tenure of ye bill by ye 10 Nov next with Court Charges Otherwise execucon

Whereas JOHN WATKINS was comitted unto ye Sherriffs custody for being drunke quarrelling and affronting the Court and Charged not to depart and notwithstanding departed and escaped from ye Sherriff without licence. It is therefore ordered that ye Sherriff shall redemand and receive ye sd WATKINS agayne into his Custody and him to deteyne as his prisoner for ye space of 12 howers abd then to release him first takeinge securities for his appearance at ye next Court then and there to answer his contempt

Whereas Certayne goods apperteyning to JOHN CHAMBERS and remayning in ye hands of THO: CODD were accordinge to order Attached by ye Sherriff for ye securitie of a debtof 70 lb tob due by JOHN LAURENCE and for as much as ye sd CHAMBERS as not nor cannot be heard or raysther hath taken any order nor care fore ye satisfaccon of ye sd debt. It is therefore ordered that ye sd goods soe attacht shalbe praysed by 2 sufficient men upon Oath and after valuation by them made sould by ye Sherriff and he to nake payment of ye sd debt with ye charges of ye Court or else to deliver ye sd Goods into ye hands of ye sd LAURANCE for satisfaction.

f 33 p 193?bot p ? Oct 1643 ?

Whereas CORNELIUS LLOYD hath abused and affronted ye Court by divers undervalling? speeches to his Ma-ties Commissioners It is therefore ordered that ye sd LLOYD shall for his offence pay a ffine of 500 weight of tob to be imployed as ye Commissioners shall think fitt and appoynt for ye use of ye County and payment thereof to be made to ye Sherriff by ye 10 Nov next.

f 33a p 194 bot p 111a Oct 1643 & Jan 1643/4

This bill bindeth me OWEN HAYES my heires, Executors or Assigns to pay or cause to be payd unti THOMAS CAUSON his heires &c at or before ye last day of October after ye date hereof ye full and just some of 2000 lb of ye best sort of Virginia Leafe tob and sufficient Caske to put ye sd tob in. And for ye true pformance of ye same I the abovenamed OWEN HAYES doth bind to the named THO: CAUSON all my whole Estate in ye County of Lower Norffolk namely my Plantation and whole Cropp both of Corne and tob and all other goods to me belonging in wittnesse of ye truth I have put my hand and seale this 26 Aug 1643

Wittnesse his
ISAAC WORGAN OWEN (OH) HAYES
Recorded 18 Oct 1643 mark

Jan 1643/4 Whereas GEORGE RUTLAND hath exted divers complaints against several psons inhabiting about Mock Jack Bay (Mobjack?) pyanketanke, Warwick County, Elizabeth City Lower Norfolk, upper Norfolke and the Isle of Wight for breaches of severall of the Acts of Assembly. These are therefore to Authorize the sd GEORGE RUTLAND to doe pforme, prosecute, effect and accomplish by all lawfull wayes & indeavors whatsoever shall bee needfull & expedient in or aboutthe same. To every intent & purpose all Comanders and Commissioners in the severall Courts of Justice are hereby disered to bee ayding and assisting unto the sd GEORGE RUTLAND in the takeing of depositions and examinations for the matters conteyned in the severall informacons or Articles thereupon or in any other or Articles thereupon or in any other matter or thinf whatsoever as to them or other his Ma-ties officers shall seeme fitting Given under my hand the 2 Jan 1643/4
Recorded 16 Feb 1643/4

(Out of place in the book - note the dates.)

f 34 p 195 bot p 112   7 Oct 1643

RECORDAT: Att a Court held at James Cittie 7 Oct 1643
PRESENT: SIR WILLIAM BERKELEY Knt, Gov. &c
CAPT: WEST   CAPT: BROWNE
CAPT: PEIRCE   CAPT; TOWNSEND

Whereas by the importunity of many the Inhavitants of the Collony to the severall ministers of Justice Depositions ofWittnesses and frequently taken in a private manner. And it may bee often ---?--- through ignorance of the Deponts and subtility of the procurers of such Oaths much corruption is used to the great damage and prejudice of the adverse partye. And for asmuch as the takeing of such deposicons before private magistrates is in itselfe illegal otherwise then by Joyned Commission to both partyes. It is therefore ordered that henceforth no deposicons whatsoever shall be effectuall or authentick unles such as shall bee deposed ---- before the adverse partye or otherwyse in the publique Courte of the Collonye

SAM: ABBOTT Cl

f 34a p 196 bot p 112a   16 Nov 1643

At a Court holden for ye County of Lower Norffolk at the howse of WILL: SHIPP 16 Nov 1643
PRESENT: CAPT: THO: WILLOUGHBY ESQ:
CAPT JOHN SIBSEY   MR: HEN: SEAWELL
MR: HEN: WOODHOWSE   LIEUT: ffRAN: MASON

(NOTE: A new Clerk ? for the handwriting changes here)
Whereas it appeareth to this Courte that WILLIAM DAVIES in a high nature Scandalized WILLIAM SMITH in sayeing that he hath committed the fowle act of fornicacon with the wyfe of JOHN DYER and can noe wayes prove the same It is therefore ordered that the said WILLIAM DAVIES shall in satisfaccon of the said scandall aske the said WILLIAM SMITH forgiveness here present in this Court and allsoe in the parish Church of Linhaven the next Sabboath the minister preacheth in tyme of Divine Service repeating such words as shall bee read unto him by the Minister and allso paye all charges expended in the suite

It is ordered that M[ris] SARAH GOOKEN shall have an attachment granted against the estete of CHRISTOPHER NEEDHAM for the satisfyeing of a debt of 857 lb tob which the said MRS: GOOKEN is at the next Countye Court injoyned to make appeare o bee a lawfull dept

Whereas it appeareth to this Court by Specialtyes that WILLIAM JOHNSON standeth indebted unto thomas hayes in the summe of 600 lb tob in leafe and 70 lb of Rolle tob and one paire of shewes and 3½ barrels of Corne . It is therefore ordered that the said WILLIAM JOHNSON shall within 8 dayes next ensueing paye the severall somes of tob, corne and shoes unto the said THOMAS HAYES or his assignes and allsoe paye the charges for one warrant

f34a p 196 bot p 112a 26 Nov 1643

otherwise execucon

Whereas HENRY SNAYLE was indebted unto JOHN HOLMES by bill the some of 1129 ob tob And being arrested to this Court to answere the suite hath not appeared eyther by himselfe or by any lawfull attorney. It is therefore ordered accord-according to an act in that case provided that the said SNAYLES shall satisfie and pay unto the said HOLMES for every 100 lb of tob debt due as aforesaid 20 lb tob per cent that is to saye 226 lb tob present paye. otherwise execucon.

f 35 p 197 bot p 113   16 Nov 1643 *Note the above date*

(Note: There must have been blank space on the preceding page for Nov 26 to precede Nov 16. Most of these errors of Quarter Court dates appearing on pages before earlier dates is due to the Clerk's finding blank space on pages to insert the James Citty actions. AGW)

Whereas it appeareth to this Court that CHRISTOPHER NEEDHAM and ELLIS BROWNE doth by theire Attorney confesse themselves indebted unto ROBERT MORTINE for certaine parcells of goods lost by them our of a boate of the sd MARTINS . It is therefore ordered that the said CHRISTOPHER NEEDHAM or ELLIS BROWNE of both of them according to valuacon of the said parcells of goods ½aye unto the said robert martine the some of 230 lb tob together with Court Charges otherwise execucon

It is ordered that ffRANCIS BRIGHT shall paye unto THOMAS BROWNE 66 lb tob expended in a suite there being noe just cause of molestacon. Otherwise execucon.

Whereas it appeares to the Court that RICHARD OWINS hath in some measure trespassed against a certaine branch of an Act of Assemblie concerning the entertaining of Indians and being thereof lawfully convicted by good sufficient testimony. It is therefore ordered that the said RICHARD OWENS shall for his said offence paye as a ffine unto the Countyes use 100 lb tob and100 lb tob more to GEORGE RUTLAND informer in the case together with charges expended in the suite.

Whereas it appeareth to this Court by sufficiant oath that ROBERT SMITH hath brought of MR; ROBTERT HAYES A Parcell of land conteyning 20 acres situated lying and being within the parish of Lynhaven beginning at a poynt of woods which is included in a Neck commonly called the Richneck which said neck is sytuated in the Little Creeke of the aforesaid Parish. To injoye the said land for 16 yeares next ensueing the Feast of Christmas next in as full and ample manner as he the said ROBERT HAYES his heires or assignes should enjoy the same by vertue of his lease confirmed under the hand of CAPT: JOHN GOOKEN in the

f 35 p 197 bot p 113   16 Nov 1643

behalfe of CAPT: ADAM THOROWGOOD, deceased. It is therefore ordered that the said ROBERT HAYES shall forthwith possesse the said ROBT: SMITH of the said Land pcure sufficient Indented Leases for the absolute and peaceable injoyeing of the said 20 acres of land for the said terme of 16 yeares unto the said ROBERT SMITH his heires and assignes and satisfye the Charges expended in the suite.

The suite depending betweene THOMAS CAUSON deft and JOHN STRATTON at the request of the said CAUSON is referred to the next County Court

The suite depending betweene RICH: KENNOR and SAVILL GASKINS it is ordered that the said KENNOR satisfie the charges expended in the suite.

f 35a p 198 bot p 113a 16 Nov 1643

Whereas THOMAS WARD was for a-certain?- misdemeanor committed at a County Court holden the 15 Sep last past and was bownd to his good behaviour and to make his appearance at this courte which he hath accordingly done. And upon the humble petition of the sd THOMAS WARD unto the board for his release from the tenor abd force of the said bond which accordingly granted. An allsoe ordered that the Sherriffe shall deliver up the said bond unto the said THOMAS WARD with the said WARD satisfying the charges of the Court occasioned by his misdemeanor.

It is acknowledged and confessed in Courts by MR: THOMAS CAUSON that it was the desire of CAPT: JOHN GOOKEN to take satisfaccon for a certaine parcell of Land belonging to the heirs of CAPT: ADAM THOROWGOOD deceased whereby a joynt consent was given both by the plt: and deft: for the sale thereof whereby the Jury Incerted the same in their verdict at the request of the sd plt: and deft:

It appeares to this Court that MR: CESAR PUGGETT hath made appeare per oath that he hath due unto him 50 acres of Land for and by the transportation of one servant named ROBERT TOWNSEND

MR: JOHN GEATER and MR: JOHN SIDNEY having referred themselves unto the courte and bound themselves each to other for to stand to the award of this Court in the sume of 30 ₤ ster. It is therefore ordered that all partyes which are the said suite concerneth doe make their appearance at the next county Courte whereby the said suite depending may be fully ended and determined

Whereas it appeareth to this Court by oath that THOMAS BROMELY hath scandalized MARY OWENS the wyfe of RICH: OWENS accusing her of Adultrye committed with PHILLIPP LAND and can noe wayes prove the same and the Court fynding that the said LAND hath beene the absolute Instrument of the sd Slander it is therefore ordered that the said

f 35a p 198 bot p 113a 16 Nov 1643

THOMAS BROMELY and the said PHILLIPP LAND shall aske the sd MARY OWENS forgiveness in this Courte and further the sd BROMELY shall aske the said MARY OWENS forgiveness in the Chappell of Ease of the Eliz: River the next Sabbath the minister preacheth & that in the tyme of Devine Service before the Congregacon there present repeating which words as shall bee by the minister read or delivered unto him and the sd LAND to paye all such charges as shall bee expended in the suite otherwyse execucon

f 36 p 199 bot p 114 16 Nov 1643

It is ordered that those which are subpeanoed at the suite of RICHARD OWENS shall have foure meales satisfyed for them at the Ordinary by MR: LAND defendent theire names being as followeth p JOHN MUNDS (MAUND?) 4p his wife 4: ANTHONY DELINOS, 4:JOHN BOND, 4: RICHARD OWENS 4:(vizt) ordinaryes a peice *(The 4p & 4: probably 4 Pence ?)*

It is ordered that RICH: KENNOR shall satisfy according to the tenor of an order bearing date with these presents that is to saye that the said KENNOR shall satisfye and paye unto SAVILL GASKINE the summe of 131 lb tob expended in the suite determined by the board otherwise execucon.

It appeareth to this Court by bill that SAMUELL CHORMAGOE is indebted unto THOMAS CODD the summe of 100 lb tob. It is therefore ordered that the said CHARNAGOE shall within 20 dayes make paymt of the sd debt of 100 lb tob together with Court Charges otherwyse execucon

HENRIE RAMM hath made it appeare to this Court that he hath due unto him 50 acres of land for the transportation of his owne pson free into this Collony

(Note: Names in above italics are the best spelling that could be arrived at AGW)

It appeareth to this Court by bill that GEORGE RUTLAND is indebted unto THOMAS CODD the some of 160 lb tob. It is therefore ordered that the said RUTLAND shall within 6 weekes next ensueing make paymt of the sd debt otherwise execucon. But the sd CODD pceeding in suite of lawe without and demand thereof contrary to an Act of Addembly in such cases provided is ordered to pay all charges expended in the suite

ffRANCIS HUNT plt and RICHARD STERLING deft have referred themselves unto MR: LOYD and ENSIGNE LAMBERT absolutely to end & determine of a suite depending betweene them. And in case they shall not agree in their arbitracon MR: WILLIAM JULIAN is likewyse made choice of as an Umpire for fynall determinacon of the sd suite.

It appeareth to this Court that PETER SEXTON hath arrested THOMAS MARSH unto this Court upon an unjust molestation. It is there fore ordered that the said SEXTON shall allowe

f36 p 199 bot p114   16 Nov 1643

and paye unto the said THOMAS MARSH or his assignes the tobacco due for 5 ordinaryes *(is this the charge for a drink or food?)* together with Court Charges otherwise execucon

The suite of informacon (extended?) unto this Court by the request of GEORGE RUTLAND plt and JOHN HOLMES deft it is referred unto a County Court to bee holden in this County the 15 Feb next ensueing provided that the said GEORGE RUTLAND shall procure such order from the Govnor & Councell for the triall of theire said suite depending betweene them to bee fully ended and determined by the Court of this County Court

Whereas it appeareth to this Courte that THOMAS WILLIAMS hath runne awaye from his Maister MR: HENRYE SEAWELL

f 36a p 200 bot p 114a 16 Nov 1643

& hath absented himselfe from the last of January unto the 17 July last past out of the said Maisters service for which tyme his said Maister was at great charges and trouble in seeking of him the sd WILLIAMS. It is therefore ordered that according to the which Act of Assembly in such cases provided he the sd WILLIAMS shall first serve out his tyme and terme of yeares due by Indenture and upon expiracon of the said terme to double the sd 6 moneths which he the sd WILLIAMS hath absented himselfe that is to saye one Compleate yeare And 1/4 of a yeare more which is allotted in satisfaccon of the aforesaid trouble and himdrance in seeking him with Court Charges otherwise execucon

Whereas it appeareth to this Court that JOHN HORNE servant unto MR: HENRY SEAWELL hath absented himselfe of his said Maisters service for the terme of 3 months or thereabouts in which tyme his said Maister hath beene at great charges & trouble in seekinge him. It is therefore ordered that the said JOHN HORME? at the end of his tyme due by Indenture shall according to the 20th Act of Assembly in such cases ½rpvoded serve his said Maister sixe months then imediately ensueinge the end of his service as by indenture And allsoe paye the charges of the Court.

These maye certefy that SAVILL GASKINE hath beene allowed by the Court of this County to keepe an Ordinary for theire entertainment and the Releife of others as other Ordinary Keepers in this Collony ever since December last past are authorized to doe

ROBT: MARTINS account concerning ELLIS BROWNE and CHRISTOPHER NEEDHAM

(see next page)

f 36a p 200 bot p 114a 16 Nov 1643

for 5 yards of sattian	60 lb tob
for a girles smock	24
" an apron	20
" a girles apron	08
" 2 holland Quoises?	20
" 2 quoises	10
" 2 Rotch: Crosse Clothes	10
" a Holland neckcloth	06
" a Holland Crosse Cloth laced	12
" a jead clo(th?)	04
" 3 Scotch cloth neck cloths	12
" a feather boulster	40
" 2 hancks and 3 skeynes of thredd	04

f 37 p 201 bot p 115 16 Nov 1643

Recordat die & anno pding (the day & year preceding) Know all men by these presents that I THOMAS CODD of the Lower Cunty of Norff in the parish of Lynhaven planter doe hereby bynd mee, my heires, executors &c togeather with my whole Estate whatsoever to paye and satisfye all and every debt or debts which WILLM: DAVIES of the same place carpenter die owe or stand indebted unto any pson or psons whatsoever within the Collony of Virginia before the 26 Aug last past. And further I doe hereby bynd mee the sd THO: CODD my heires &c together with my whole estate as aforesaid to save & keepe harmless the aforesaid WILLM: DAVIES his heires &c from all charges and trouble which shall come unto him for or by non paymt of all or any of the sd debts made before the said 26 Aug last past which are by mee to be paid. To the true pformance whereof without fraud or Covin? of the said THOMAS CODD doe bynd myselfe togeather with my whole estate as aforesaid firmely by these presents And doe hereby fully and absolutely Release, discharge and acquitt him the sd WILLIAM DAVIES his heires &c of and from all debts dues and demands, bills, bonds and (any?) writeings whatsoever from the beginning of the world unto this present daye One writing beareing date with these with these presents excepted whereby and wherein the said WILLIAM DAVIES hath sold unto mee the sd THO: CODD his whole estate and fully discharged mee of all demands whatsoever as by the writing whereunto Relacon being had more at large it doth and may appeare. In witness whereof I the said THOMAS CODD have hereunto sett my hand and seale this 23 Sep 1643

Sgned, sealed and Delivered
in the presence of: THOMAS CODD
ROBT: SMITH
WILLIAM SMITH

f37a p 202 bot p 115a 16 Nov 1643

(Item in Latin at top of page) Nowermt universi & psentes me JOHANNOM SIDNEY teneri et firmiter obligari JOHANNI GATHER in trignita libris bone et loyalie nouete Anglie solvend oidem JOHANNI GATHER ant suo certo Attornato theredibie executor &c suit Adquam guiden solucoem bene et fideleter foriends obligo ines prerdes executors &c & presents sigillo indo 6 Nov 1643

the condicon of the abovewritten obligacon is such that if the bounden JOHN SIDNEY shall and will well and truly observe pforme and keepe or cause for him his heire executors, eadministrators or assignes to bee observed pformed fulfilled and kept all such orderor orders of the Court nowe holden this daye make or order betweene the above bounden JOHN SIDNEY and the above named JOHN GATHER as are to bee observed fulfilled and kept on the parte and behalfe of JOHN SIDNEY his exors &c that then this present obligacon to bee voyd & of none effect or else to bee and stand in full power force vertue and effect sealed and delivered in the presence of:

MATHEWE PHILLIPPS JOHN SIDNEY
THO: IVEY

It is conditioned betweene SAVILL GASKINS and RICH: KENNOR that both of them are to meete at the howse of CAPT: THOMAS WILLOUGHBY and there to deliver 2 men upon exchange the one to the other upon the 20 of this present moneth that is to say that SAVILL GASKINE is to deliver his man for the terme of 6 years with one shirte and paire of shoes and one paire of Irish stockins being fownd & in health and the sd RICH: KENNOR is to deliver his servant for the terme of 2 yeares with the consideracon of 300 lb tob & caske and to deliver him in health with one shirt one paire of shewes one paire of Canvas drawers the sd tob to be paid the first of November next ensueinge the date hereof. In witness whereof wee have Interchangeably hereunto sett our hands this present 14 Sep 1643

Wittness RICHARD KENNER
JOHN SIBSEY

f 38 p 203 bot p 116 16 Nov 1643

Recordat 16 Nov 1643
Knowe all men by these presents that I CHRISTOPHER BURROUGHS of Lynnhaven planter doe acknowledge and confesse myself to owe and stand indebted unto JOHN MARTIN of the same place his heires or assignes the full and just some ot 2000 lb of good merchantable tob and caske good and sufficient to hold the said tob being well packed therein to bee paid st the nowe dwelling howse ot CAPT: THOMAS WILLOUGHBY at or before the 10 Dec 164_ to the which paymt well and truly to bee made withour fraud or delaye of the said CHRISTOPHER BURROUGHS doe bynd mee my heires &c together with 3 cowes, 2 heifers, 2 young bulls and my plantation. And I doe hereby

f 38 p 203 bot p 116   16 Nov 1643

further authorish him the said JOHN MARTIN his heires &c upon default of paymt at the tyme and place abovesaid or within a short tyme thereafter within 2 moneths after the first daye to take the Cattle abovesaid with theire increase and the plantacon abovesaid unto his owne custody and the same to sell to the best advantage and first to paye himselfe and then be accountable to mee for the surplus. In witness whereof I have hereunto sett my hand this 23 Sep 1643
Wittness
FRANCIS LAND   Xop: BURROUGH
OWEN (OM) MORGAN
Acknowledged before me ED: WINDHAM

f 38a p 204 bot p 116a 16 Nov 1643

The deposition of ROWLAND MORGAN aged 22 yeares or there abouts sworne and examined the 16 Nov 1643

This depont haveing beene Cowkeeper to CAPT: JOHN GOOKIN deceased and the estate of CAPT: ADAM THOROWGOOD deceased ever since the division of the Cattle betweene MR[is] SARAH GOOKIN and the children of the sd CAPT: THOROWGOOD sayeth that since his last oath taken at Court holden at Lynhaven 16 Dec 1642 there hath dyes of the childrens stock of cattle one old Cowe named ffillpayle And that there were 2 Cowes sold by CAPT: GOOKEN to WILLIAM SHIPP for the Childrens use And that theire remaynes of theire 30 milck whereofthere hath been encrease this yeare noe morethen 8 Cowe calfes and that 3 of them were killed by the woolves at THOMAS CHEELYS. And further this depont saith that to his knowledge there hath noe more of the childrens Cattell Male or female young or old beene at all sold, killed or otherwyse disposed of by the said CAPTAINE GOOKEN or any other by from or under him then the 2 Cowes formerly menconed. And lastly this depont saith that of the whole Stockof Cattle belonging to the foresd children there is nowe remayning at Lynhaven younge and old male and female 63 (vizt)Old Bulls 4, other old steeres 13, Cowes 30, heifers of 2 yeares old 4, yeareling heifers 7, Cowe Calves of the last Fall 5 and further this depont saith not
Teste: ROGTS: TYAS Cler: ROWLAND (mark) MORGAN

The deposition of WILLM: BUDDING aged 18 yeares or thereabouts. The depont haveing beene Goatkeeper to CAPT: JOHN GOOKEN and the estate of CAPTAINE THOROWGOOD

f 39 p 205 bot p 117   16 Nov 1643

and daylie amongst theire goates ever since WILLM: VAUGHAN the last Goat keeper left them. Saith that whereof his oath taken the 16 Dec 1642 there was then 58 breeding Goates of the childrens. Twelve hereof were sold to WILLIAM SHIPP by CAPT: GOOKEN for the childrens use. And 3 more dyed soe there demayned 43 and whereof by that sath there was then 46 weathers? and Ramms there was 13 likewyse of them sold

f 39 p 205 bot p 117   16 Nov 1643

the said WILLIAM SHIPP. And one sold to SAVILL GASKINE for the use of the aforesaid children and 7 more were killed were killed by wolves and other Casualty soe there remaynes Old whethers and Ramms 25 and further this depont saith that the female encrease of the childrens Goates this yeare is 19 at this present tyme, Residue of the female increase being all dead some before they were able to goe abroad. And other some killed by the fall of a howse, woolves and other casualty. And that there remayne noe more of the childrens stock of goats in all at this present then 87 vizt: Old Rams 4, Old weathers 21, Ewe goates 43 Ewe kydds of this last Fall 19, and further this depont saith that to his knowledge there hath not beene anymore of the childrens stock of Goates young or old, male or female eyther sold, killed, or toherwise disposed of by CAPT: GOOKEN or any other by from or under him then the 26 before specified and further this depont saith not

Teste: ROBTE: TYAS CLK: WILLIAM (X) BUDDING

f 39a p 206 bot p 117a 29 Nov 1643

Recordat 29 Nov 1643 The examinacon of THOMAS ANTHONEY aged 25 yeares or thereabouts taken befor MR: EDWARD WYNDHAM one of the Comrs: of the Lower Norff. This exam: sayeth that being at worke at MR: CODDS the 24 Nove last past or thereabouts in the company of WILLIAM CAPPS, MR. CODD, WILLM: HALLY (or HOLLY?) and JACOB BRADSHAWE they the said partyes demanded of this examinant what became of MR: SIDNEYS man that was left in the woods goeing with this examinant to the Eastern Branch and what this Easmt:had done with him. Whereupon this Examt: jestingly replyed he had knockt him on the head, what should he doe with himselfe, not meaning or thinkeing any other thing to jest att them in the same manner as they demanded the question for in truth the examt: sayeth that he did neither harme the said MR: SIDNEYS servant nor ever had any such thought or cause to doe him any much lesse to kill him being a stranger and one he never sawe in his lyfe but twice nor ever had any cause of quarrell against him. And further this Examt: saith that they went togeather till they came into the middle of the greate swampe and there they sate down and pipt? it and when they had done the way being wett the examt: went streight through it but MR: SIDNEYS man tooke his leave and bade this examt farewell and God bee with him and bade him make as much hast(e?) as he would not goe through the water. And with that strooke upon his right hande ubti the Swampe haveing with him 3 doggs and a bundle of beare skynnes upon his back which he had then brought from the examts: Masters howse And since this examts: never sawe or heard of the sd MR: SIDNEYS servant nor knowes not what became of him. And further he confesseth not

Examinat[r] CORAM me   ED: WINDHAM

f40 p 207 bot p 118   29 Nov 1643

WILLIAM CAPPS aged 25 yeares or thereabouts sworne and examined saith that about the 24 Nov last past being at the howse of THOMAS CODD and falling upon certaine urgent discourse concerning a servant of MR: SIDNEYS which THOMAS ANTHONY went out with well into the woods one WILLIAM HOLLY being there present ask the said ANTHONY what he had done with the servant of the sd MR: SIDNEYS whoe replyed that he had knocked him on the head what should he doe with him. And further this depont: sayeth not

WILLIAM CAPPS

Recordat 30 Nov 1643 - Bee it knowne to all men by these presents that I WILLIAM ATTERBURY of london Merchant doe make constitute and appoynt my trusted and well beloved friend THOMAS LAMBERD of ELIZABETH RIVER PLANTER my trusty and lawful attorney for mee and in my name and to my use to aske leavie --- hole --- and receave all and singular debts deeds, goods, tobacco with all other demands whatsoever as are hereafter shall bee due unto mee within the Collony of Virginia by any person or persons whatsoever Authorizing and by these presents giving unto my said trusty and lawfull Attorney all my full power force and lawf-ll authority all or anyone of my debtors for non payment to sue arrest, implead and imprison and out of prison at his pleasure to release and upon paymt to make acquittances or discharges

f 40a p 208 bot p 118a 30 Nov 1643 -

attorney or attorneys one or more under him to make and appoynt and at his pleasure againe to revoke and generally to execute and psecute and doe all and every such Act or Acts, thing or things, in and concerning the premisses as I myselfe maye, cann, might or ought to Doe. If I were there psonally present And whatsoever my said attorny shall doe or cause to bee done in and concerning the premises I stand to allowe of ratefy and confirme as my owne act and deed. In witness whereof I have hereunto sett my hand and seale the 28 Mar 1642

Signed sealed and   WILLIAM ATTERBURY
delivered in the presence of us:
THOMAS SAWYER, MATT: PHILLIPPS

f 41 p 209 bot p 119 15 Dec 1643

At a Court holden for the Lower Norff: at the howse of WILLIAM SHIPP 15 Dec 1643
PRESENT: CAPT: WILLIAM CLAYBOURNE ESQR:
CAPT: THOMAS WILLOUGHBY ESQR:
CAPT: JOHN SIBSEY LIEUT ffRANCIS MASON
MR: EDW: WINDHAM MR: WILLM: JULIAN
MR: HEN: SEAWELL

Whereas it appeareth to this Courte that ANTHONY DELMONS? is indebter unto THOMAS BROMELEY in the summe of 900 lb tob and 2 barrels of Indian Corne it is therefore ordered upon the request of the sd BROMELEY that an attachment shall bee granted against the estate of the said DELMIONS? for security of the said debt of tob and corne. *(Note: This name could possibly be DELIVIONS. AGW)*

CHRISTOPHER NEEDHAM debitor to MRS SARA GOOKEN
12 Nov 1643

p a hogg with allowance & forbearance	135 lb tob
p a bushell of salt	035
p a case of vinegar	030
p bill 403 with forbearance 8^{lb}p cent	435
p bill to JOHN HOLBECKand POOLES 70 with forbearance	82
p 40 lb tob at 3 lb ½ p lb	140
	857

Whereas ut appeareth to this Court that CHRISTOPHER NEEDHAM indebted unto MRS: SARAH GOOKENS the some of 722 lb tob and 135 due one hogg sold unto the said NEEDHAM shall make paymt unto MRS: SARAH GOOKENS of the some of 857 lb tob in case that the sd XPOFER: NEEDHAM doe not make it appeare by the oath of JAMES SMITH that the said 135 lb tob due for the said hogg was not included in any specialty wherein sd NEEDHAM stands bownd for paymt of any some of tob due unto ye said MRS: GOOKENS

f 41a p 210 bot p119a 15 Dec 1643

Whereas MR: JOHN GATER attorney of MR: NATHAN STANDSMORE And MR: JOHN SIDNEY have mutually bound themselves in sufficient bonds to stand to the award of the Courte concerning a debt of 30 powmds due for one plantacon sold unto the said SIDNEY by the said STANDSMORE in the yeare when of? tob should passe at the rate of 12^{d}- per bl for satisfying of money debts due for tha sale of land. It is there fore ordered that the said MR: JOHN SIDNEY shall within 30 dayes nowe next ensueinge make paymt unto the said MR: JOHN GATER the summe of 3000 lb. tob and caske and the charges to bee eaually borne betweene them otherwyse execucon. This being a finall determinacon of the suite and ending of all differences concerning the said Land

It is ordered by the Court that THOMAS ANTHONY shall remaine in the custody of the sherriff of this County untill that

f 41a p 210 bot p 119a 15 Dec 1643

he the said THOMAS ANTHONEY shall bee cleared by just order of Lawe from the suspition of the death of JOHN CLARKE

Memorandi quod die et anno pdict X_ ppferve duo Regi 40 lib sterl solvend fus cond ito ine in fra script

The condicon of this Recognizance is such that if THOMAS ANTHONY the nowe servant of the above bounden CHRISTOPHER NEEDHAM due make his personall appearance at the next Quarter Court holden before the Governor and Councell at James Cittie the 1 Mar there to answere into all such matters as shallbe objected against him on the behalfe of our*Sourvigne Lord the king concerning the death of JOHN CLARKE that then the present Recognizance to bee voyd and of noe effect or else to remaine in full force abd vertue

Test: ROBT: SMITH XPOFER: NEEDHAM
His mark

* f 42 p 211 bot p 120

Whereas it appeareth to the Court that HENRIE HILL is indebted unto ffRANCIS LAND by bill in the some of 350 lb tob and 2000 nayles and 1000 Ruff and Clench?. It is therefore ordered that the said HENRIE HILL shall make present paymt of the sd 350 lb tob and within 20 dayes next ensueing make paymt of the 2000 nayles and 1000 Ruff and Clench otherwise execucon

Whereas it appeareth to this Court that SAVILL GASKIN is indebted unto CAPT: THOMAS WILLOWBY in the sume of 900 lbs of tob and caske. It is therefore ordered that the said SAVILL GASKINE shall within 20 dayes make paymt of the said debt of 900 lb of tob and caske together with Court Charges otherwise execucon

The suite depending between WILLIAM CAPPS and HENRIE HILL is referred unto the next monthly Court

MR: JOHN FORMAHAWKE? hath made it appeare to this Courte that he hath due unto him 50 acres of land for ye transportation of himselfe into this Collony

f 42a p 212 bot p 120a 15 Dec 1643

It is ordered by this Court that all such fees as shall be due to the Clarke of this County Courte shall bee collected by the Sherriffe of this Countye and upon non payment the Sherriff is hereby authorized to destraine for payment upon theire estates of such as shall refuse to satisfye such somes of tob: as will justly appeare to bee due to the said CLARKE of this said Countye

It is ordered by this Courte that the Sherriffe of this County shall collect from every tythable person belonging to the parish of Elizabeth River the just summe of 31 lb tob per polle and one peck of corne which is for the burgesses charges and country dutyes, ferrys, and for killing of wolves and for the like charges due from the Inhabitants of Lynhaven pish to collect the some of 34 lb per poll from every tythable person.

f 42a p 212 bot p 120a 15 Dec 1643

Whereas referrence was granted at a Court holden in this County the 15 July last past concerning a suite depending betweene EDW: LILLIE Attorney for HENRY ROBINSON plt: and HENRIE SEAWELL deft to bee heard the next ensueing County Court. But notwithstanding the sd reference the said LILLIE hath not appeared neyther by himselfe nor any Attorney in his behalfe. It is therefore ordered that the sd EDW: LILLIE shall within 10 dayes make paymt of 500 lb tob for costs and damages sustayned in the suite otherwyse execucon

f 43 p 213 bot p 121 15 Dec 1643

Whereas it appeareth to this Court by oath that HENRY HILL die send for THOMAS WARD Chirurgeon to administer Phisick unto one HENRIE MICHELL. It is therefore ordered that the said HENRIE HILL shall within 14 dayes make paymt of 250 lb tob and caske together with Court Charges otherwise execucon

The suite of defamacon depending betweene THOMAS MILLS and LAWRENCE HUTCHINSON is referred unto the next ounty Court

Knowe all men by these presents that I HENRIE HILL doe constitute and appoynte my well beeloved freind SAVILL GASKINE my lawfull Attorney to answere the suite of THOMAS WARD, ffRANCIS LAND, and WILLIAM CAPPS. And what my lawfull Attorney shall doe. I doe allow of it as done by myselfe. And I the said HENRIE HILL doe by binde mee my heires and assigns to save and keep harmless the said SAVILL GASKINE my lawfull attorney from all troubles or molestacon that shall ensue concerneing the aforesaid suites
Wittness my hand this 12 Dec 1643
Signed and delivered in the presence of: HENRY HILL
THO: TOOKER Recordat 15 Dec 1643

f 43a p 214 bot p 121a 16 Dec 1643
Your humble peticoner HENRY CATELIN sheweth unto your worr^{s} that your said PETE^{r} Bought one nect of ground in the Westerne Branch of Elizabeth River of CAPTAINE JOHN SIBSEY When tob was of value 4^{d} per pownd and that said yeare your peticoner sold unto MR: ROBERT PAGE for 7 pence the pownd upon bills of exchange and nowe as concerning the said land I gave unto the aforesaid CAPTAINE 1500 weight of tob the Land being much about 100 acres of land being thereof small value not unknowne unto your worr^{s}
The humble request of your peticoner is to desire your worr^{s} that CAPT: JOHN SIBSEY would please give to your peticoner a bill of sale for the said Land or that you would give him his oath that he sould your peticoner it by lease or not or suffer your peticoner to take the oath concerning the same.
16 Dec 1643 Teste: RI: CONQUEST HEN: CATELIN

f 44 p 215 bot p 122   16 Dec 1643 Page is Blank

f 44a p 216 Records Anno 1642 and 1643

ELIZABETH TAPLIN and WILLM: SMITH (all that is on page)

f 45 p not numbered - pp217-2221

INDEX

123 ----------------125

Af ? p 222 BLANK and 125 a

(NOTE: A WHOLE YEAR OF COUNTY COURTS IS MISSING HERE AGW)

f 1 p 223 bot p 126   15 Feb 1644/5

At a County Court holden at the howse of ENSIGN THOMAS LAMBERT 15 Feb 1644/45

CAPT: JOHN SIBSEY Commander
MR: WILLIAM JULIAN   MR: HENRY WOODHOWSE)
MR: ffRANCIS MASON   MR: THOMAS LAMBART (- COMRS
MR: MATH: PHILLIPPS)

Whereas MR: JOHN SIDNEY is indebted unto RICHARD KENNAR per bill in the summe of 510 lb tob The Court doth order payment thereof otherwyse execucon

Whereas HENRY WATTERS stands indebted unto JOHN YEATS @ barrells of Indian Corne and acknowledged by the said WATTERS to bee due. Paymt is ordered to bee made of the said Corne within 10 dayes and Court Charges otherwyse execucon

Whereas JACOB BRADSHAWE is indebted unto JOHN HOLMES 370 lb tob per bill produced in Court Payment is ordered to bee made of the tob aforemenconed with Court Charges within 10 dayes otherwyse execucon

f 1a p224 bot p 126a   15 Feb 1644/5

Whereas JESPER HOSKINS is indebted unto THOMAS WRIGHT 510 lb tob upon severall specialtyes produced and acknowledged by the said HOSKINS to bee due. The Court doth order paymt to bee made of the said tob with Court Charges in 10 dayes otherwyse execucon

Whereas OLIVER VANHACK (is?) indebted unto GOWEN? LANCASTER 1172 lb tob and caske remaining due upon a specialty produced in Court. The Court hath ordered paymt to bee made of the said tob and caske according to the specialty aforesaid with Court Charges within lo dayes. Otherwise execucon

Whereas RICHARD WHITEHURST is indebted per bill unto the estate of MRS: SEAWELL deceased 541 pownds of tob. The Court doth order paymt to bee made of the said tob unto MR: MATHEW PHILLIPPS guardian unto the orphants of the

f 1a p 224 bot p 126   15 Feb 1644/5

sd deceased within 10 dayes and the sd WHITEHURST to pay the Court Charges otherwise execucon

Whereas EDWARD SELBY is indebted per bill unto the estate of MRS: SEAWELL deceased 550 lb tob The Court doth order payment to bee made of the sd tob unto MR: MATHEW PHILLIPPS guardian unto the Orphants of the said deceased within 10 dayes with Court Charges otherwyse execucon

Whereas ROBER WILLIAMS is indebted per bill unto the estate of MRS: SEAWELL deceased 767 lb tob Paymt is ordered to bee made thereof unto MR: MATHEW PHILLIPPS guardian unto the orphants of the said deceased within 10 dayes and the said ROGER WILLIAMS to paye the Court Charges otherwyse execucon

f 2 p 225 bot p 127   15 Feb 1644/5

Whereas ffRANCIS LAND is indebted unto MR: MATH: PHILLIPPS (per) bill produced in Court the summe of 900 lb tob and caske and 500 of 6 penny nayles and one powdring Tubb. The Court doth order payment to bee made of the said tob and Nayles and Tubb aforemenconed unto the sd MR: PHILLIPPS with Court Charges within 10 dayes otherwise execucon

Whereas ROBERT HAYES is indebted by specialty 2 Cowes ready to Calve payeable unto MR: BINGHAM on the 1 Jan last past and in default of delivery of the sd 2 Cowes as aforesd the sd HAYES did Covenant to pay 3 Cowes as under the handwryting of the said HAYES appeares The Court doth order paymt to bee made of the 2 Cowes according to the condicon aforesaid within 15 dayes and the Court Charges Otherwyse Execucon to bee granted against 3 Cowes according to Covenant under the hand of the said HAYES. Upon which the Court doth give judgmt accordingly.

Whereas ffRANCIS HUNT is indebted unto RICHARD KENNER Chirurgeon 500 lbs tob and Caske (as) appeares by specialty produced. The Court doth order paymt to bee made thereof within 10 dayes. And the said HUNT (in respect of his Nonresidency) to put in security forthwith before his departure from Court for paymt accordingly with the Court Charges otherwyse execucon.

Whereas the estate of MRS: SEAWELL deceased stands indebted unto MR: WM: CHURCH 300 lb tob as appeares unto the Court by sufficient proofe. The Court, doth order that MR: PHILLIPPS the adm[or] of the deceased pay the 300 lb tob unto the sd CHURCH within 10 dayes and the Court Charges otherwyse execucon

f 2a p 226 bot p 127a 15 Feb 1644/5

Whereas MR: CHURCH is indebtedunto the estate of MRS: SEAWELL deceased 50/ sterl: and 2 paireof shewes due 2 yeares since as appeares by a specialty. The Court hath ordered satisfaccon to bee made unto MR: PHILLIPPS the adm[r] of the said deceased of the said money and shewes within 10 dayes and MR: CHURCH to pay the Court Charges otherwyse execucon

Whereas EDWARD LILLY stands indebted per bill unto ROGER WILLIAMSON 300 lb tob and caske and the bill produced in Court Paymt: is ordered to bee made within 10 dayes of the said tob with Court Charges otherwyse execucon

Whereas THOMAS EDWARDS is indebted unto RICHARD KENNAR Chirurgeon upon accounts 210 lb of tob as appeares unto the Court. The Court with consent of both partyes have ordered that the said EDWARDS shall make paymt of one barrell of Indian Corne and foure score pownds of tob forthwith and 30 lb tob being the remainder of the debt the next yeare and the said EDWARDS to pay Court Charges

Whereas MR: ffERINHAUGH is indebted unto MRS: GOOKIN the summe of 293 lb tob being the remaynder upon a specialty of 700 lb tob produced in Court and confessed by the said ffERINHAUGH. The Court doth order paymt to bee made of the said 293 lb tob in full satisfaccon of the said 700 lb tob within 10 dayes and Court Charges otherwise execucon

An attachment granted unto MR: WM: JULIAN against 2 cowes belonging unto THOMAS HAYES to bee satisfactory for a debt claimed by the said MR: WM: JULYAN and that the Court soe determines thereof

Whereas JAMES SMYTH servant unto MR: CORNELIUS LOYD hath peticoned the Court for his freedome alleaging (that) he hath served 7 years and soe confessed by the said MR: LOYD yet the said SMYTH acknowledging to have an Indenture which he sayeth is in the Custody of his

f 3 p 227 bot p 128 15 Feb 1644/5

father. The Court doth thinke fitt and order that the sayd SMYTH shall contynue still in the service of the said MR: LOYD and send for his indenture. And if it shall appeare thereby that his tyme is already expired Then MR: LOYD us to make satisfaccon for his said service more then is expressed in the sd indenture. And if it shall happen the said Indenture not bee found then the Court hereafter upon further proffe will heare and determine thereof

Whereas JOHN GEATHER is indebted unto RICHARD KENNAR per bill and account produced in Court 490 lb tob. The Court doth order paymt to bee made of the said tob within 10 dayes unto the said KENNAR and Court Charges otherwise execucon

f 3 p 227 bot p 128 15 Feb 1644/5

Memorandum: that MR: THOMAS BROWNE and MR: ARTHUR BROWNE have acknowledged in Court that there is 1300 lb tob due from him the said THOMAS BROWNE unto the said ARTHUR BROWNE and that there is no other debts Reckonings or accounts whatsoever between themthen the 1300 lb tob aforesaid for which there hath beene 2 bills given by the said THOMAS BROWNE but one bill is lost.

Whereas ROBERT HAYES stands indebted unto LEIFETENANT LUDINGTON in the summe of 676 lb tob and Caske due per account as it appeares to the Court. Payment is ordered to bee made of the said tob within 10 dayes and Court Charges otherwise execucon

The difference betweene JACOB BRADSHAWE and WM: DAVYES at the request of ffRANCIS LAND attorney of the said DAVYES is referred to the next County Court and the sd WM: DAVYES is then personally to appeare or else ffRANCIS LAND hath undertaken to abide the censure of the Court

f 3a p 228 bot p 128a 15 Feb 1644/5

Whereas OLIVER VANHECK stands indebted unto WILLIAM SHIPP per specialty and account produced in Court 796 lb tob and allso 4½ barrells of Indian Corne due per bill. The Court doth order payment to bee made of the said tob and corne aforesaid according to the tenor of the said bills with Court Charges otherwise execucon

Whereas MR: JOHN SIDNEY is indebted unto ROBERT SMYTH one Cowe with Calfe and a yearling as it appeares unto the Court. It is ordered that the said MR: SIDNEY shall at Blunt Poynt make paymt and delivery of the said cowe with calfe and yearling aforesaid unto the said ROBERT SMYTH or his assignes within 20 dayes and Court Charges otherwyse execucon

Upon the hearing and long Debating of a sertaine difference depending in this Court between JAMES KNOWW plt and THOMAS BROWNE deft concerning a servant named THOMAS HARWOOD and upon the due perusing of the depositions of MR: JOHN HILL and OWEN SCOTT for the discussing of the busynes. It is the opinion of the Court and they doe therefore accordingly order that the said THOMAS HARRWOOD shall serve the sd MR: KNOTT one whole yeare according to a Condicon and covenant produced under the hand and seale of the said HARWOOD. And is regard the said HARRWOOD hath beene the only occasion of much trouble and difference betweene the sd MR: KNOTT and MR: BROWNE concerning him the sd HARWOOD It is allsoe further ordered that the sd HARWOOD shall satisby unto the sd MR: GNOTT his full charges hereby occationed and allsoe Consideracon for his trouble herein before he depart the service of the said MR: KNOTT

f 4 p 229 bot p 129   15 Feb 1644/5

A difference betweene MRS: SARAH GOOKIN plt and THOMAS CHEELEY deft concerning a debt of 240 lb tob alleaged to bee due from the said CHEELEY per account is referred from to the next County Court to be heard and determined

Whereas OLIVER VANHECK is indebted unto THOMAS ALLEN 178 lb tob per bill and 90 lb tob per account produced in Court. Payment of the sd tob is ordered within 10 dayes and Charges of the Court otherwyse execucon

Whereas PETER PORTER stands indebted unto ARTHUR BROWNE Merchant the summe of 457 lb tob and caske per bill produced in Court. Payment is ordered to bee made of the said tob within 10 dayes and court charges otherwise execucon

Whereas PETER PORTER STANDS INDEBTED UNTO ARTHUR BROWNE Merchant in the summe of 609 lb tob and caske per bill produced in Court. The Court doth order paymt to bee made of the sd tob within tenn dayes unto the said ARTHUR BROWNE and Court Charges otherwise execucon

Whereas WILLIAM EAST is indebted unto RICHARD POOL 400 lb tob and caske per bill produced in Court and acknowledged by the sd EAST. The Court doth order with consent of both partyes that the saud East shall putt in good secutiry for payment of the said tob and caske the next Cropp with lawful forbearance and to paye Court Charges

Whereas ROBERT HAYES is indebted unto PETER PORTER in the summe of 494 lb tob and 1½ barrells of Indian Corne per account duced upon oath of the said PORTER the Court ordered paymt of the sd tob and corne (continued on f4a p 230) aforementioned with Court Charges within 10 dayes unto the said PETER PORTER otherwise execucon

f 4a p 230 bot p 129a   15 Feb 1644/5

An Attachmt granted unto ARTHUR BROWNE merchant against the estate of THOMAS HAYES upon a legall determination to bee satisfactory for a debt of 456 lb tob with caske per bill produced in Court

Whereas JOHN WILLIAMS and ELIZABETH TAPLING are by the Church wardens of Linhaven Pish presented for fornicacon The Court doth upon very good proffe (the said ELIZABETH having had a mischance) order that the said ELIZABETH shall receive 20 good lashes on her bare back in regard it cannot soe plainely appeare that the said WILLIAMS is guilty herein he is to paye the Court Charges otherwyse execucon

Upon the presentment of the Church wardens of Lynhaven Parish of RICHARD POOLE and MARY HILL for fornication upon the generall reports ans causes of suspicion And the Court as yet having noe further proofe notwithstanding doth order that the said POOLE shall give good security

f 4a p 230 bot p 129a 15 Feb 1644/5

by bond or recognizance in the future not to accompany with the said MARY HILL

Whereas JOHN STRATTON is indebted per bill unto MR: ROBERT PAGE in the summe of 1050 lb tob and Caske. And the said STRATTON being arrested to this Crt bormerly by MR: BINGHAM attorney of the said MR: PAGE and yett the said STRATTON not appearing eyther by himselfe of attorney for him. Payment is ordered to be made according to Act of 20 lb for every 100 debt and the said STRATTON not appearing the next Court having notice hereof then the Court further to give Judgmt upon the whole debt as in Case of Nihil Dicit

WHEREAS THOMAS TODD stands indebted per specialty unto ARTHUR BROWNE in the summe of 352

f 5 p 231 bot p 130 15 Feb 1644/5

lb tob and Caske and the said TODD being arested and not appearing eyther by himself of his attornie. The Court doth order the said Todd to paye unto the saidMR: BROWNE 20 lb tob for every 100 debt and in case of non appearance at the next Court then judgment to bee given according to Act as in Case of Nihil dicit for the whole debt

Whereas MR: CORNELIUS LOYD is indebted unto MR: RICHARD NEEDHAM *(Written thusly in original AGW* (Boodham)

900 lb tob and caske and acknowledged bue by the said MR: LOYD. Paymt is ordered to bee made of the said tobacco within 10 dayes and the Court Charges otherwise execucon

Plus asdect? MR: EDW: WINDHAM

Whereas RICHARD BETTS servant unto MR: CORNELIUS LOYD hath peticoned to the board for his freedome according to the Act And the said BETTS havinge at present noe proffe of his age. The Court doth thinke fitt and order BETTS in the service of the said MR: LOYD And if by the nest yeare BETTS DOTH make appeare that he is 21 yeares old when he arrived into this Collony then MR: LOYD to give satisfaccon for his yeares service as the Court shall then thinke fitt and adjudge

Upon a Condicon produced in Court made betweene HENRY HILL and ANDREWE WARNER The Court doth order that the said HILL shall make pformennce of the Covenant herein menconed according to the tenor and true meaning thereof within 30 dayes And the said HILL to paye Court Charges otherwyse execucon.

Whereas WILLIAM DAVYES was arrested to this Court at the suite of JOHN MARTIN And the said DAVYES appearing according to the sd arrest But MARTIN not appearing to psecute his sd suite The Court doth order MARTIN to bee non suited and pay Court Charges f 4a p 230 bot p 130   15 Feb 1644/5

Whereas MR: JULIAN is indebted unto VINSON CURWELL (or CARVELL?) 230 lb tob due for service and worke. The Court doth order paymt thereof within 10 dayes and Court Charges otherwyse execucon

f 5 a p 232 bot p 130a 15 Feb 1644/5
(This is the way the pages are numbered, no f5 AGW)

The Court doth order that MR: EDWARD HALL shall bee first satisfyed out of the estate of THOMAS COOPER deceased what debt he shall make appeare due at the next Court. Orders of JAMES CITTY made by the Govnor and Councell excepted

Whereas ROBERT BOWERS is indebted unto JAMES WARNER for Rent 100 lb tob as appeares unto the Court Paymt at the next cropp is ordered to bee made of the said tob with the Court Charges otherwyse execucon

Whereas THOMAS ALLEN had 2 yeares since a Sword sent him by the wyfe of OLIVER VAN HACK which sword was never delivered to the said ALLEN but the said VAN HACK acknowledged that he received 40/ sterl: in leire thereof from the steward of a shipp as appeares unto the Court by the oath of EDWARD HALL and by other testimonyes. The Court doth order that the said OLIVER VANHACK shall within lo dayes make sattisfaccon of the said 40/ sterl: with Court Charges unto the said ALLEN otherwyse execucon

The difference betweene RICHARD fORSTER plt and THOMAS DAVYES deft concerning 3 barrells of Corne and worke is referred to the next County Court then to be heard and determined

The Court doth order that 563 lb tob bee satisfyed out of the estate of THOMAS COOPER deceased unto LANCASTER LOVETT per bill due and produced in Court MR: EDW: HALL first satisfyed his debt and James Citty orders by the Governor and Council excepted

It is ordered that a ferry bee still kept and maynteyned at DANIELL TANNERS CREEKE for the conveniency & better accomadation of passage for the Inhabitants of this County And WM: LANGLEY having undertaken the keeping hereof at the nex Cropp shall receive 800 lb tob and 6 barrels of --

f 6 p 233 bot p 131

Indian Corne for his paynes to bee taken therein from this tyme till 1 Mar next ensueing this tyme 12th moneth which said tob and Corne aforesaid is to be lavyed and collected and soe the sd WM: LANGLEY to receive payment hereof accordingly from the sherriffe of this County.

Whereas the Estate of MRS: SEAWELL deceased is indebted unto ENSIGNE LAMBERT 216 lb tob per account produced in Court and 25 lbs of Holland Cheese. The Court doth order that paymt bee made of the said tob within 10 dayes and of

f 6 p 233 bot p 131   14 Feb 1644/5

the said cheese /or satisfaccon/ from the said MR: PHILLIPS admor: of the said deceased otherwise execucon

Whereas the estate of MRS: SEAWELL is indebted unto WM: SHIPP 181 lb tob as appeares by an account produced in Court. Paymt is ordered to be made of the said tob unto WM: SHIPP within 10 dayes out of the estate of the deceased by MR: PHILLIPPS the admr: otherwise execucon

Whereas RICHARD CASTLEFORD servant unto MR: HEN: WOODHOWSE hath absented himselfe from the service of his said maister to the great damage and trouble of his said maister. The Court doth order that according to Act of Assembly that the said CASTLEFORD shall receive 30 good lashes on his bare back and at the expiracon of his tyme of service by Covemant serve his Maister 40 dayes and allsoe satisfye all charges hereby occasioned

Whereas a certaine difference depending betweene JOHN MARTIN plt and WILLIAM DAVYES deft was referred unto this Court to be determined. And the sd MARTIN not appearing nor Attorney for him. The Court upon the peticon of the said DAVYES doth order that the said JOHN MARTIN bee non-suited and paye the Court Charges

f 6a p 234 bot p 131a   14 Feb 1644/5

Whereas there was a reference unto this Court of a certaine difference depending betweene MR: PHILLIPPS admr: of the estate of MRS: SEAWELL deceased plt and XPOFER BURROUGHES deft. The court doth order that the said BURROUGHES shall appeare at the next County Court at his perill

The difference betweene JACOB BRADSHAWE deft at the suite of WM: DAVYES for 309 lb tob in referred to the next County Court to bee determined

Whereas ROGER WILLIAMSON hath due unto him 250 ob tob from MR: PAGE for trimming and mending his boat. The Court doth order that MR: BINGHAM the Attorney of the said MR: PAGE shall make paymt of the said tob unto the sd ROGER WILLIAMSON within 10 dayes and Court Charges otherwise execucon

RICHARD POOLE and LANCASTER LOVETT doe acknowledge themselves jointly and severally to bee indebted unto our Soverayne Lord the King the summe of 2000 lb of merchantable tob

The condicon of this Recognizance is such that the if the sd RICHARD POOLE doe not de futuro use of frequent the company of MARY HILL according to the tenor and meaning of an order of this present Court then this Recognizance to bee voyd and of none effect otherwyse to bee in full force vertue and power for the Kinge

f 6a p 234 bot p 131a 14 Feb 1644/5

Whereas ROGER WILLIAMSON was arrested to this Court at the suite of MR: BUSHRODE whoe not appearing nor attorney for Him to prosecute his suite. The Court doth order that the said MR: BUSHRODE bee nonsuited and to paye Court Charges

f 7 p 235 bot p 132 14 Feb 1644/5

Delivered unto WILLIAM SHIPP by LEFTENANT ffRANCIS MASON these papers followeing (VIZT)

A Noat of the ffees belonging unto MR: TYAS
RICHARD KEMP ESQR: his bill for 16‡5pence½penny
MR: ELSINGS letter of attorney
MR: WILLIAM WIGG his letter
MR: ROBERT TYAS his bill of parcells

It is ordered that MR: EDWARD WINGHAM, SAVILL GASKINE, OWEN HAYES, RICHARD POOLE, SAMSON WARING, THOMAS BROOKES HENRY HILL, JOHN HILL, and JOHN ffERINHAUGH doe pay unto ANDREW WARNER 50 lb tob a price in sattisfaccon for the service and imploymt of the said WARNER in the expedicon to the Pomunckey (merck?) otherwise execucon

The dufference betweene ROBERT SMYTH plt and JOHN SIDNEY deft is referred to the next County Courtand MR: SIDNEY to pay Court Charges for non appearance at this Court

The Court doth order THOMAS TOOKER ths present Sherriffe shall by Satterday next give a perfect and absolute account withour any further delaye unto CAPT: SIBSEY with any other 2 of the Conrs: of all the Levyes whatsoever delivered or recommended to this charge of colleccon this present yeare and in default thereof then then the said TOOKER to bee severely fyned or amerced at the discretion of the net session of this Court

The Court doth thinke fitt and order that MR: MATHEW PHILLIPPS the admor: of MRS: SEAWELL deceased should within 10 dayes sattisfy and pay unto MR: THO:

f 7a p 236 bot p132a 14 Feb 1644/5

HARRISON Clarke 1000 lb tob in consideration and satisfaccon for the burial and presching the funerall sermon of MR; SEAWELL and MRS SEAWELL deceased and for breaking grownde in the Channcell for them

Whereas the last Court did grant an Attachment unto CAPT: SIBSEY against the estate of ROBERT LOVEDAYE for to satisfye a debt of 300 lb tob due per bill with Caske. And the sherriffe havinge attached 376 lb tob It is ordered that the Sherriffe shall deliver the sd tob attached unto the said CAPT: SIBSEY in or towards satisfaccon of the sd debt with Charges

f 7a p 236 bot p 132a 15 Feb 1644/5

Recordat 15 Feb 1644

Covenants and agreemts betweene JAMES KNOTT and THOMAS HARROD It is agreed that the said THOMAS HARRODS shall serve the JAMES KNOTT in such service and imployment as he the said JAMES KNOTT or his assignes shall imploy him for one whole yeare. The tyme beginning the 8 Nov next after rhe date hereof. And if the said THOMAS HARROD shall bee sick or lamed during the said yeare that he cannot pforme his labor he is to allowe for it or to make it good but the sd JAMES KNOTT is to keepe him in his sickness or lameness. And I, the said THOMAS HARROD doe bynd myselfe not to bee absent without the consent of the said JAMES KNOTT and I JAMES KNOTT doe bynd myself or assignes to pay unto the said THOMAS 1000 lb tob and caske and 5½ barrells of Corne and to pay the Ministers dutyes and the said THOMAS to lay in two barrels of Corne. In witness whereof wee have Interchangeably sett our hands and seales the 8 Oct 1644

Witness hereunto THOMAS (H) HARROD

JOHN WHINFELL *(There is no signature for JAMES KNOTT)*

f 8 p 237 bot p 133 15 Feb 1644/5

I JOHN MAUINE? doe committ my soule to God that gave it and my body to the earth from whence it came Likewise I will and bequeath to my beloved wyfe ISBELL MAUND all my goods lands and chattles except 1 Red Heifer to my sonne JOHN MAUND and likewise the land I doe nowe possesse when he comes to the age of 21 yeares. Likewise I give to my daughter ELIZABETH MAUND 1 cowe called Tincker and to have her female encrease at her daye of marriage And it is my will that my wyfe have the use of the land and Cattle till my Children comes to age And that is my will that my brotherJOHN ffINCH shall have the overseeing of this my will that it bee pformed And if my said wyfe doe marry in the meantime then the use of the Cattle to come to my brother JOHN ffINCH

WITTNES JOHN (his marke) MAUND

PHILLIP LAND

WM: ( ) SHIPP
his marke

Recordat 11 Mar 1644/5

This bill byndeth mee RICHARD PRESTON of Chuchquotuck *(Chucktuck?)* in the County of Upper Norff: in Virginia my executors or admors: to paye or cause to b, paid to Edward GUNNELL of London Mariner his executors the summe of 12000 lb of good merchantable Virginia tob in leafe and Caske and that upon the 10 of Nov next ensueing after the date hereof In further Cosideration whereof I have firmed to 3 bills for the aforesaid summe beareing date all one date either of which being effect Wittness my hand this 25 Feb 1644 Signed and delivered in the RI: PRESTON
presence of us: ROBERT B(R)BUCKLEY, JOHN SAISON, ARNOLD MASNER

f 8a p 238 bot p 133a   11 Mar 1644/5

Know all men by these presents that I JOHN SIDNEY of Elizabeth River in the lower County of New Norfolk Virginia Gent have sold and delivered unto RICHARD BLUNT of the same place Planter 1 heifar of a browne coulor with the right eare cropt and slitt and cropt and the halfe Moone under the left eare and a white starre upon the forehead white under the belly and the tipp of her tayle white and both the hindar leggs white and the nearefoot before whit and the farre forefoote white on the inside And I the said JOHN SIDNEY doe by these presents for myself my heires &c warrent the said heifar unto the aforesaid RICHARD BLUNT his heires &c that he shall peacefully enjoy the said heifer with all the increase without the molestacon or hindrance of mee the said JOHN SIDNEY my heires &c In witness of the truth I the abovenamed JOHN SIDNEY have hereunto sett my hand this 10 Mar 1644/5
Signed and delivered in the presence of
ROBT: EIRE, WILLIAM (his mark) DYAR   JOHN SIDNEY

Know all men by these presents that I HENRY HILL blacksmyth of Lynhaven have lett and sold unto ANDREW WARNER that Neck of grownd which he injoyes by a lease granted unto him by MRS: GOOKINS with all rights and priviledges that he hath thereto belonging and that the said MR: HILL is to assigne over the lease unto the said WARNER Allsoe the said HILL to repaire the howse and to make partetion 2 Chimnies and to laye the loft 11 which I bynd myselfe my heires &c to pform And to the truth hereof I have sett my hand 7 Sep 164- *(last digit faded out)*
Wittness: JOHN SIDNEY
ROBT: EYRE   HENRY HILL

(Note: There seem to be only 3 items above for the month of March 1644/5 - No March Court?)

f 9 p 239 bot p 134   15 Apr 1645

Att a County Court holden at the howse of MR: WILLIAM JULIAN upon the 15 Aprill 1645
Present: CAPTAINE JOHN SIBSEY COMMANDER
MR: WILLIAM JULIAN
MR: THOMAS LAMBERT   MR: MATHEW PHILLIPS

According to an order from the Right worr: the Governor and Councell EDWARD COOPER hath made appeare that THOMAS MUTTON deceased was indebted unto him for certaine apparrell being due for his tyme of servitude according to the custome of the Countrey

According to order from the Right Worp[ll] the governor and Councell MRS: CHRISTIAN PUBBETT vid(widow) produced upon her oath an Inventory of the estate of CESAR PUBBETT her late husband, deceased

f 9 p 239 bot p 134 15 Apr 1645

ROBERT HAYES is permitted for Conveniencye and better Accomodacon of the inhabitants of this County to keep an Ordinary according to act of Assembly

An attachment is granted unto ARTHUR BROWNE Merchant against soe much of the estate of WILLIAM DAVYS being or remayning in the hands or possession of ffRAUNCIS LAND as upon a legal determination may bee satisfactory for a debt of 535 lb tob due by specialty as appeares to the Court

The suite depending betweene MR: MATH: PHILLIPPS guardian unto the orphants of MRS: SEAWELL deceased plt and XPOFER BURROUGHES deft is referred to the next session of this Court then to bee heard and finally determined

f 9a p 240 bot p 134a 15 Apr 1645

The Court doth fine and amerce THOMAS TOOKER the nowe sherriffe in the summe of 800 lb tob to bee levyed and paydfor the Kings Ma[ties]---- use for the sd TOOKER his great neglect in his office in the not returning the writts and not attendance of the Court being manifested the great prejudice of the Inhabitants Audit The said 800 lb tob to bee levyed or raised by the next Sherriffe upon the estate of the said tooker and to be disposed of as aforesaid

It is ordered that XPOFER BURROUGHS and THOMAS CHEELEY shall pay unto RICHARD ffORSTER halfe a barrell of corne and halfe a barrell of Eares. And that THO: DAVYES shall paye unto the said ffORSTER a barrell of Eares and 20 lb tob and Court Charges to be equally devided betweene the said ffORSTER and DAVYES Otherwyse execucon

MR: MATHEW PHILLIPPS and MR: THOMAS IVEY the Church Wardens of Eliz River parish have exhibited theire presentment against MR: THOMAS HARRISON CLARK, Parson of the said Parish for not reading the booke of Common Prayer and for not administering the sacrament of Baptisme according to the Cannons and order pscribed and for not Catechising on Sunnedayes in the afternoone according to Act of Assembly upon which presentment the Court doth order that the said MR: THOMAS HARRISON shall have notice hereof and bee summoned by the sherriffe to make his psonall appearance at James Citty before the Governor and Councell on the 1st day of the next Quarter Court and then and there to answere to the said presentment

f10 p 241 bot p 135   15 Apr 1645

Recordat 15 Apr 1645

A true and perfect Inventory of the whole Estate of THOMAS MELTON deceased as it was appraised the 12 Mar 1644/5

2 -allow hoggs and i bore	250 lb tob
2 barrells & 4 Bushells of corne	220
in ready tob	254
6 hides, 28 deere skinns & 2 goat skinnes	400
a broken Iron Pott & a pcell of Conners? tooles	150
1 old Rugg	020
	1294
of 1 debt of 1000 lb tob & 5 barrells of Corne due from THOMAS CHEELEY of Linhaven by specialty	1000
The Total is 5 barrells of Corne & if the sd debt bee all recovered & received	2294 lb tob

This estate was appraised the daye and yeare above written by us who heve hereunto sett theire hands to testifye the same

JOHN ( ) STRATTON
XPOFER BURROUGH
THO: CASSON

f 10a p 242 bot p 135a 15 Apr 1645

Recordat 15 Apr 1645

A true and perfect Inventory of the whole estate of Cesar Puggett, Deceased with theJust values thereof according as it was appraised by THOS: CARSON, CHRISTOPHER BURROUGH, JOHN STRATTON, and JAMES CLARKE the twelth day of March Anno D 1644

Impr: eight oxen of 5 or 6 years old	4800
Cesar Puggett p 4	
5 steers one 3 years old and four 2 years old	1500
2 bulls one 5 years old the other 3 years old	0700
15 cows with calve of calfes by their sides	7500
2 cowes which have left their calfes	0800
5 yearling heifers	1200
5 yearling steares	1000
1 old cloth suite with a girdle & drawers	0300
1 other suite of serge with linen drawers	0200
1 other _____ suite & a cloth coat of serge	0250
8 ells of xxxxx 0064	0064
2 yards of xxxxx	0020
2 ells of canvas	0020
7 doz and 4 yards of silk edging cord	0070
a pacell of buttons & silke	0070
1 holland sheete much worn	0040
1 other very old sheete	0010
2 shirts one plaine and 2 xxxx all old	0050
1 paire of silk xxxxxx	0020
1 doz of old napkins & a table cloth	0070

f 10a p 242 bot p 135a 15 Apr 1645

5 course napkins & a tablecloth	0030
1 doz pewter dishes great 7 small	0133
3 iron pots all old and broken	0130

f 11 p 243 bot p 136

1 bed halfe feathers halfe flocks and 1 feather bolster	0250
1 old carpet	0030
2 old trunks	0060
1 old chest, a table, 2 xxxxx and 2 chairs	0230
5 small books	0010
a churner, a barrel, a pair of canhookes? & 8 old milk trayes	0130
a canvas slack bed and a rug &bolster all old	0080
19 deer skins, 3 bears hides & 2 calves skinc	0270
1 server for eight? mouth? with five barrels of corne	0900
a plantation of 200 acres of land with the howseing	2000
more in ready tobacco	0188
a spit, a dripping pan, a brass kettle, 2 small iron kettles, a frying pan, 2 xxxx & a paire of small xxxxx	0200
2 gunnes, an old sword & a cutlass	0500
a crosse saw with xxxx xxxxx	0100
a parcell of carpenters tools & others	0150
a parcell of nails & old iron	0140
	24215

These goods following are claimed by MRS: CHRISTIAN PUGGETT widdowe the relict of the above said CESAR PUGGETT as properly belonging unto herself for furniture or her bed chamber pr vist

f 11a p 244 bot p 136a 15 Apr 1645

Imprs: one feather bed with a bolster, 2 pillows, a paire of blankets and rug and pair of curtaines and vallance two paire sheets and 4 pillow boards valued at	880
3½ yards of serge at	0070
a tablecloth and 6 napkins	0040
6 pewter dishes 6 plates 6 porringers	0109
2 candlesticks, a salt seller, a small flagon, a standish, a bottle, a pair of pinssers	0042
a pair of tongs & a pair of andirons	0100
an iron pot & skillet	0070
a xxxxx, a trunk, a boxe, 2 glasses	0080
a Bible and a psalme booke	0040
	1431
the former is	24215
the total is	25646

Besides this there are 800 acres of land lying remote from plantations & water and hogg which were left in the forrest two years since not accounted of any value they being almost past hope of recovery and being possessed alsoe. certaine debts belonging to the estate which are all or most part of them past hope of recovery vist by specialty due f12 p 245 bot p 137   15 Apr 1645

from JOHN WILLIAMS	2252 tob
from JOHN PRESTON	0600
from PETER CARRINGTON	0500
from JOHN ALLSOP	1000
from THOMAS xxxxx	0160
from THOMAS LEE	0070
	4582
By account due	
from EDWARD HALL 2 pair of shewes, 1200 of nails, 23 of tob	0100
from MR: GRAVE HARDWIN is by this letter 16 t 16 6 8 d so that the whole estate is goods according to the appraisement is	25646
which added to the debts above paid up	30328

The estate of Cesar Puggett was appraised by us who have hereunto sett our hands the day and yeare above mentioned according as it is herein expressed witness our hands:

the marke of JOHN (X) STRATTON
THOMAS CASSON
JAMES CLARKE
CHRISTOPHER BURROUGH

f 12a p 246 bot p 137a 15 May 1645

Att a County Court held at the howse of CAPT THOMAS WILLOUGHBY ESQR:

15 May 1645

CAPT: THOMAS WILLOUGHBY ESQR:

CAPT: EDW: WINDHAM	MR: HEN: WOODHOWSE
MR: ffRAN: MASON	MR: MATH: PHILLIPPS

Mamor: That according to order from the Right Wor: Governor and Councell the oath of a high sherriffe was administered unto JOHN SIBSEY ESQR:

Memor: MR: THOMAS IVEY hath allsoe taken the oath of undersherriff

Att a Court holden at James Citty
10 Apr 1645

Present: RICHARD KEMP ESQ: Governor

CAPT: NATHANIEL LITTLETON	CAPT: THOMAS PETTUS
MR: GEORGE MENIFIE	CAPT: WILLM: BERNARD
MR: RICHARD BENNETT	CAPT: RICH: TOWNSEND

It is ordered that CAPT: JOHN SIBSEY bee the High Sherriffe for the county of Lower Norff: for the yeare. And that he injoye all the Rights power, priveledges, prelieminencyes and authoritye incident to a sherriffe or that any other sherriffe hath had in the Collony. And the Comrs: of the County Court or any two of them, one of the Quorum being one are further required to give the Oath of a high sherriffe unto him and take bond of him with sufficient security to bee responsible and satisfactory for all publique levyes Auditemts: or any other dutyes wheare required to be collected of him ex officio per me SAM: ABBOTT clk:

f 13 p 247 bot p 138   16 Jun 1645

Att a CountyCourtholden at the howse of MR: THOMAS MEARES
16 Jun 1645

CAPT: EDWARD WINDHAM
MR: WILLIAM JULIAN
MR: THO: LAMBARD
MR: EDWARD LOYD
MR: HENRY WOODHOWSE
MR: ffRANCIS MASON
MR: THOMAS MEARES
MR: MATH: PHILLIPPS

It is ordered that JOHN SUTTON make his psonall appearance at the next County Court to answer unto such matters as shall bee objected against him

Whereas THOMAS MARSH is indebted unto WILLM: PARRY the attorney of JOHN REDMAN 300 lb tob and caske per bill produced & due 6 yeares since. The Court doth order paymt thereof with the said 6 yeares forbearance at the rate of 8 lb tob per cent with Court Charges otherwyse execucon

Whereas THOMAS CASON is indebted unto WILLIAM PARRY the attorney of NICH: BROOKES per bill 7Ŀ Sterl: money 5 yeares since. The Court doth order paymt to bee made upon the 10 of Nov next from the said CASON with forbearance at 8 lb per cent unto the said PARRY. And allso that the said CASON shall pay 20 per cent for non-appearance according to an order of Court from Elizabeth Citty and the said CASON to paye Court Charges otherwyse execucon

The Court doth order that RICHARD WORSTER shall detain in his hands soe much soe much of the estate of RICHARD ffORSTER as shall satisfye 1350 lb tob & caske unto LANCASTER LOVETT. And in case the said ffORSTER shall not make retorne of the goods /according to his letters sent unto LANCASTER LOVETT/ by the 1 Feb next Then execution to issue forth for the payment of the aforesaid tob with Court Charges

f 13a p 248 bot p 138a   16 Jun 1645

The Court doth order paymt to bee made unto THOMAS TOOKER of 300 lb tob due for levyes and fees out of the estate of WILLIAM DAVYES otherwise execucon

And attachmt is granted unto MRS: SARAH GOOKIN 290 lb tob due per bill against the estate of WILLIAM DAVYES

An attachmt is granted unto MRS: SARAH GOOKIN for soe much of the estate of WILLM: DURFORD remayning in the hands or Custody of widdow HAWKINS or any other to bee satisfactory upon legall determination for a debt of 5Ŀ Sterl: money due per bill with forbearance thereof and Charges

The suite depending betweene ffRANCIS HUNT and THOMAS WRIGHT is referred to the next Court to be ordered and determined

The Court doth order that ROBERT LOVEDAY shall paye unto THOMAS WRIGHT 3 barrels of corne the 9 Nov Next and for non-paymt of the sorne 200 lb tob with Court Charges otherwyse execucon

f 13a p 248 bot p 138a 16 Jun 1645

The Court doth order that THOMAS WHITE and JOHN MANNING shall paye unto ARTHUR BROWNE, merchant 554 lb tob due per bill by the 10 Oct next with 1 yeares forbearance of the said debt with Court Charges Otherwyse execucon

The Court dpth order that EDWARD LILLY by the 10 Nov next shall paye unto THOMAS CASON 250 lb tob due per bill with lawfull forbearance for 1 yeare & Court Charges otherwise execucon

The Curt doth order that EDWARD LILLY by the 10 Nov next shall paye unto THOMAS CASON 250 lb tob due per bill with lawfull forbearance for 1 yeare & Court Charges otherwyse execucon

The difference concerning Joynary (joinery?0 worke betweene EDWARD LILLY and THOMAS CASON is referred to the next Court to be determined

f 14 p 249 bot p 139   16 Jun 1645

The Court doth referre the difference betweene JACOB BRADSHAWE and RICHARD ABRELL to the next Court to bee determined

An attachmt is granted unto JESPER HOSKINS against the estate of WILLIAM DURFORD for soe much as shall satisfye a debt of 290 lb tob upon a legall determination

The Court doth order that THOMAS CASON Churchw: of Linhaven Parish shall at the next vestrey give and deliver a true account of what tob and corne are received from the inhabitants of the said parish towards the mayntenance of a poore orphant in the custody and charge of THOMAS DAVYES. And the said CASON to make paymt accordingly forthwith unto the said DAVYES otherwyse execucon

The Court doth order that THOMAS DAVYES shall bee satisfyed out of the estate of THOMAS COOPER dec. 1000 lb tob in full satisfaccon for the paynes and arges taken by the said DAVYES and other meanes & provision used for and in the behalfe of the sd COOPER in the tyme of his sickness Otherwyse execucon

The difference betweene THOMAS DAVYES and GEORGE MIE is referred to the next Court to bee heard and determined

The difference betweene MR: JOHN ffERINHAUGH and MRS: SARAH GOOKIN is referred to the next Court to bee heard and deterined

The Court hath taken due Cognizance of the poore estates of ROBERT PORTER and ROBERT JONES being aged and infirme. In consideration thereof have thought fitt and doe order that according to Act of Assembly they the said PORTER and JONES bee exempted from all publique Levyes

The difference betweene MR: PHILLIPPS and CHRISTOPHER BURROUGHS is reffered to the next Court to be heard and determined

f 14a p 250 bot p 139a 16 Jun 1645

It is ordered that MR: CORNELIUS LOYD pay unto THOMAS TOOKER 414 lb tob being due per account for charges and fees and for 14 dayes imprisonment of one JOHN BALL whoe for certaine misdemeanors was committed to the custory of the said TOOKER in the tyme of his sheivalty *(Sheriffy)* the said LOYD having undertakes for the said BALL whoe was thereupon released And the said LOYD is left for remedying the said BALL herein

It is ordered that MR: CORNELIUS LOYD shall satisfy unto MATHEW HOWARD a case of strong waters for takeing up of a boate belonging to one XPIAN: xxxxx a Dutchman the sd MR: LOYD having confessed that he did undertake for satisfaccon in the behalfe of the said XPIAN: otherwyse execucon

The Court doth order that THOMAS DAVYES shall deliver unto THOMAS CASON and EDWARD HALL executors of THOMAS COOPER deceased all clothes and apparrell and other goods whatsoever belonging unto the said deceased blewe cloth suite onely excepted which the said DAVYES is to make appeare he did take off from the deceased corps

It is ordered that JOHN MOORE shall continue in the service of his master JOHN GEATHER according to (xxfadedxx) The said GEATHER having undertaken in Court good usage and sufficient dyett of the sd MOORE during the tyme of his Corennt (Covenant?)

The difference between THOMAS DAVYES deft at the suite of THOMAS WARD is referred to the next Court to bee determined

It is ordered that JOHN MARTIN shall deliver the proporson of Corne belonging unto WM:**SMYTH** of what is left and that WM:**SMYTH** shall possesse the Land and Howseing to sure his Cropp thereupon growing this yeare and that WM: SMYTH shall paye for a moneths provision when the said MARTIN

f 15 p 251 bot p 140 16 Jun 1645

hath delivered it to the said SMYTH And allsoe the said SMYTH to paye the fifth part of what flesh? the said MARTIN can make appeare was spent in his howse since the date of a Covemt: made betweene the said SMYTH and MARTIN till the daye hereof *(It is assumed that the word flesh above may mean the flesh or meat that was consumed)*

Whereas in Jun 1644 this Court did grant an Attachment unto JOHN ROBINSON against the said estate of JONATHAN LANGWORTH deceased remayning in the hands of MR: MATHEW PHILLIPPS for satisfaccon of two terces? of French wyne, 3 dozen of Cards and 3 Combs. And There appearing nowe unpo oath and further prooffe that the said debt is just & due. The Court hath ordered that the said mr. phillipps shall make satisfaccon of the said debt aforemenconde unto the said ROBINSON or his assignes out of what estate he hath in his possession /that/ is belonging unto the said LANGWORTH

f 15 p 251 bot p 140   16 Jun 1645

For the more Conveniencye and further accomodacon of the Inhabitants of this County It is ordered that the next County Court bee kept at ROBERT HAYES HIS HOWSE. And the 2 Courts next after at WM: SHIPPS howse and soe to contynue afterwards vizt: One Court at ROBERT HAYES and two Courts at WM: SHIPPS howse interchangeably

Constables elected for the severall lymitts of the County (vizt:) for the Lower Parish of Elizabeth River: TRISTRAM MASON for the for the upper parish JAMES WARNER for Lynhaven WILLIAM BASNETT for the Easterne branch head RICHARD WORSTER and that the oath of a constable bee administered unto every of them severally as by lawe in such cases is provided.

f 15a p 252 bot p 140a   16 Jun 1645

MEMO: that MR: ROBERT POWIS and MR: THOMAS SAYER doe acknowledge to have given and bequeathed unto SARAH MEARES the daughter of THOMAS MEARES of Elizabeth River a Cowe Calfe one yeare old or hereabouts of colour black and white with a starre in the forehead and cropt on both eares with a peice cutt off under the right eare and a hole in the left eare

MEMO: that MR: THOMAS MEARES doth give and bequeath unto THOMAS WHITE the sonne of THOMAS WHITE a xxxxxx cow calfe of Coulor Redd and white eare marked with a flower deluce and a slitt under the flower deluce (fleur de lis?) on the right eare and cropt with a slitt downe the cropp on the left eare And that the first Cowe Calfe that it shall have to bee converted to the use of ELIZABETH the daughter of the said THOMAS WHITE the elder and if the said THOMAS the younger doe dye during minority the said calfe with the increase to bee Converted to the use of the rest of the Children of the said THOMAS WHITE the elder

MEMO: That MR: BARTHOLOMEW HOSKINS doth give and bequeath unto THOMAS MARSH the sonne of THOMAS MARSH of Elizabeth River. An heifer Calfe aged 18 months or thereabouts of Coulor pyde? black and white and eare marked with a swallow tayle on the left eare which if the said THOMAS the younger shall happen to dye during minority the said heifar with her increase is to bee converted to the use of the rest of the children of the said THOMAS MARSH the elder

f 16 p 253 bot p 141   16 Jun 1645

To the wor[ll] CAPT: EDWARD WINDHAM ESQR: and the rest of his Mc[ties] Comrs:
SIR: The humble peticon of THOMAS TOOKER sheweth whereas JOHN BALL was Committed into your peticoners custody upon suspicion and there remayned for the space of 14 dayes untill MR: CORNELIUS LOYD requested to have him to goe to Jamestown with him your peticoner humbly craveth that he may have an order against MR: CORNELIUS LOYD for the paymt

f 16 p 253 bot p 141   16 Jun 1645

of 480 lb tob due to your peticoner from the said BALL as appeareth per account. And your peticoner as in duty bownd shall ever pray

JOHN BALL debtor

for being Committed into person twice upon suspision	040 lb
for whipping once	020
for 14 dayes imprisionment	420
	480

Whereas THOMAS WRIGHT of the Lower Norff planter stands bownd with mee FR: HUNT od rhe same place planter for 882 lb tob and 2 caske due to THO: TOOKER or his assignes

Knowe all men by these presents that I ffRANCIS HUNT doe bynd over unto THOMAS WRIGHT aforesaid all my goods, chat-tles or cattell moveable or inmoveable every part and par-cell of whatsoever I the said ffR: HUNTam possessed of and shall bee poeessed with all from this present daye untill the said debt of 882 lb tob & 2 caske abovespecifyed shall bee fully satisfyed I fR:HUNT doe likewyse bynd myselfe to live with and not to departe from the said THOMAS WRIGHT untill such tyme as the aforesaid debt shall bee fully satisfyed unles it shall please the Lord of his mercye to take mee our of this transitory lyfe To the true pformance hereof. I have hereunto Interchangeably sett my hand this 1 Mar 1644

ffRAUNCIS (F) HUNT

The words "unto THO: WRIGHT"
were interlyned in the fifth lyne
befor the signing hereof

Signed in the presence of:
THO: TOOKER , ISABELL ([mark]) WELLS

f 16a p 254 bot p 141a   16 Jun 1645

Recordat 16 Jun 1645

Whereas I BARTHOLOMEW HOSKINS in my visitation of sickness did give and bequeath unto BARTHOLOMEW WILLIAMS the sonne of ROGER WILLIAMS to saye one Cowe calfe of about 4 or 5 months old it being a pyde? Calfe and eare markt (faded) the which said calfe I the said BARTHOLOMEW HOSKINS doe acknowledge to have delivered unto the possession of ROGER WILLIAMS father unto the said BARTHOLOMEW WILLIAMS to and for the use of the said BARTHLOMEW sonne of the said ROGER nowe knowe yee that I the said BARTHOLOMEW HOSKINS doe for mee my heires &c freely and Irrevocably confirme the said Cow with all her increase as well Male as female unto and upon the said BARTHOLOMEW WILLIAMS forever: In witness of these presents I have herunto sett my hand and seale this 16 Jun 1645 And further before the signing hereof doe con-firme that if the said child shall dye duringe minority the said with its increase to be converted to the use of the the rest of the children of the said ROGER WILLIAMS

Signed sealed and delivered in presence of:
THO: TOOKER, JOHN ffERINHAUGH   BARTHO: HOSKINS

f 16a p 254 bot p 141a 16 Jun 1645

Know all men by these presents that BARTHO: HOSKINS of Elizabeth River in the Lower County of New Norfolk, Virginia planter gent have sold and delivered unto WILLIAM WILLSON of the same place planter one heifar of Coulor black & white with a Mealie mouth and 2 brown eares, a white starre in the forehead and 4 white leggs and all white underbelly to the throate and a white tayle with black patch upon the rumpe xxxxxfadedxx both eares cropt and a hole in the right and the said BARTHO: HOSKINS doe by these presents for myselfe my heires &c and every of them warrant and assure the said WILLIAM WILLSON his heires exors &c he shall peacefully injoye the said heifar with with all the increase xxxxxxxx faded xxxxxxxxx sett my hand this 10 Jan 1644
Wit: THOMAS TODD, WILLM: CAPPS BARTHO: HOSKINES

f 17 p 255 bot p 142 16 Jun 1645

Recordat 16 Jun 1645
MEMO: that SARAH GOOKIN late wyfe and relict to CAPT: ADAM THOROWGOOD deceased have made Choyse of and doe take for myselfe one Negro woman named MARY being due to mee of my fifth and shares of the Negroes belonging to the said CAPT: THOROWGOODS Estate And this I doe by virtue of his last will and testament. In wittness whereof I have hereunto sett my hand this 1 Jan 1642
Wittness: SARAH GOOKIN
EDW: WINDHAM, JANE SMYTH

MINGO a Negro Cowekeep Lynnhaven

A true and perfect account of the neat cattle belonging to the estate of the children of CAPT: ADAM THOROWGOOD since the last account givenin by ROWLAND MORGAN att a Court Holden at the howse of WILLIAM SHIPP the 15 Nov 1643 intill the 22 Mar 1644

Imp^{ers} there dyed of theires
One old bull called Shabby bull & one other bull 0.0.2
4 old Cowes vizt: Old Tucker, Old Lammas, Pickhorne Lammas, & young Nansie 0.0.4
One cow called Coweslipp strayed awaye and was lost Winter and was never found or heard of since since 0.0.1
Two heifars then 3 yeares old 0.0.2
Total deceased and lost 0.0.9

(continued on next page)

f 17a p 256 bot p 142a 16 Jun 1645

Sold of theires for theire use
One Oxe sold to SAVILL GASKIN 0.0.1
0. 10

The increase of theire Cattle this yeare was 24 Cowe calves whereof 20 are dead all which dyed at home and about the howse with Sicknes and extremity of weather 012

Soe the totall dead sold & lost old & young is 022

Rmayning still of theire stock

x ? x Bulls 2 0.0.2
Oxen 12 0.12
Old Cowes 25 025
Young Cowes of 4 yeares old 002
young Cowes of 3 yeares old 008
Heifars 2 yeares old 5 005
Cowe Calves of the last Fall which are yearlings 12 012
The Totall 066

The stock of cattle at Lynhaven young and old is 66

There hath beene noe more of the Childrens stocke of Cattle beene lost, dead, sold or otherwyse disposed of by MRS: SARAH GOOKIN or any other pson or psons whatsoever then those tenn above expressed including 12 yearlings. And this is a true and just account I doe doe hereby certifye under my hand and seale upon my oathhaveing kept the bookes ever since CAPT: GOOKIN dyed

EDWARD WINDHAM

f 18 p 257 bot p 143 16 Jun 1645

Lyn haven - GEOFREY WIGHT Goatkeeper
A true and perfect account of the goats belonging to the estate of the Children of CAPT ADAM THOROWGOOD since the last account given in by WILLIAM BUDDING at A Court holden at WILLIAM SHIPPS the 15 Nov 1643 untill the 22 Mar 1644

There hath beene killed by the Wolves and other casualty and Dyed
4 old Ramms 004
3 weathers 003
11 old Ewes 011
Young Ewes 15 015
The Totall dead 033

There was sold by MRS: SARAH GOOKIN for theire use fower (vizt) 1 barren Ewe to Savill GASKINE
1 old weather to HENRY HILL
1 weather to THOMAS CHEELY
1 weather to JOHN WACYE? 004

The totall dead & sold is 037

Their Encrease this yeare was 26 ewe kidds whereof There dyed in the hard weather and before they were able to goe abroade 20 020 f18 p 257 bot p 143   16 Jun 1645

Soe there is Nowe Remayninge of theire stock alive	
15 old wethers	015
31 old ewes	031
4 young ewes	004
6 Ewe kidds of the last fall	006
Ye totall nowe living	056

f 18a p 258 bot p 143a 16 Jun 1645

There hath noe more dyed, beene killed, sold or otherwise disposed of by MRS. SARAH GOOKIN or any other pson or psons whatsoever then the 37 above menconed. And that is a true and just account taken from the Goatkeep and to my best knowledge I doe here testifye under my hand and upon Oath having kept the booke ever since CAPT: GOOKIN dyed

EDWARD WINDHAM

One Ewe Kidd falline since	001
Totall	057

Mar 22 1645 A generall & perfect account of horses belonging to the estate of the Children of CAPT: ADAM THOROWGOOD from the division 8 Aug 1641

Impr: 2 browne bay Mares namely Grubb and the young mare haveing then other makes	002
1 Iron Gray Mare	001
1 dark browne stonehorse?	001
2 foales being both mares 1 sorrell and 1 browne	002
1 browne mare a yeare old	001
Totall then young & old was	007

Anno: Dm: 1642

1 browne Mare of 2 yeares old called the blynd foale dyed in the Swamp in the Woods	001
Theire encrease this yeare was nothing	000
Rest	006

f 19 p 259 bot p 144   16 Jun 1645

Anno: Dm: 1643   The Encrease

The Mare grubb brought a browne stone colt	001
The Iron Gray Mare brought an Iron Gray Mare Colt	001
The Young Bay Mare brought a Bay Mare Colt	001
Totall then was	009
There dyed this yeare The young bay mare & her foal	002
Rest	007

Anno Dom: 1644   The encrease was

The Mare Grubb brought a browne stone Colt having then having taken no other marke	001
Totall	008
There dyed this yeare	
One leight bay mare 4 yeares old but never back	001
One browne stone Colt neare 4 yeares old	001
One iron gray Mare & dead 003	004
Now living is EDWARD WINDHAM	005

f 19a p 260 bot p 144a 15 Aug 1645

Att a County Court holden upon the 15 Aug 1645 at the howse of ROBERT HAYES
Present: CAPT: THOMAS WILLOUGHBY ESQ:

CAPT: EDW: WINDHAM | MR: HENRY WOODHOWSE
MR: ffRANCIS MASON | MR: THOMAS LAMBART
MR: THOMAS MEARES | MR: EDWARD LOYD
MR: MATHEW PHILLIPPS

A certificate of Land granted unto MR: MATH: PHILLIPPS in the behalfe of HENRY SEAWELL an orphant sonne and heire of MRS: SEAWELL deceased for the transportation of these persons hereunder named and proved to bee due unto the sd orphant uponoath vizt: THOMAS WILLIAMSON, JOHN SMYTH, MARGARET PORTER,JOHN PARKER, CHRISTOPHER RIVERS, ELIZABETH WOOD, JOHN SCOTT, JOSIAS HATLEDGE, WILLIAM PRYCE, OLIVER SMYTHERS, MARY ROUGE, JOHN HARVEY, JOHN EDWARDS, JOHN NORRWOOD, RICHARD HARTYRAVE, THOMAS SMYTH, ROBERT PAGE, WILLIAM JOHNSON, SIMON PETERS, ROBERT TURNER, ALEXANDER, OWBOUNE*(Could this be Osborne?)*
(Note: The above is not in Nugent - The Patent should have been 1050 acres? AGW)

Upon consideration had of many Inconveinencyesthat may hereafter happen by the marking of cattle by severall men of one certayne marke. Upon the humble request of Robert Hayes the Court doth thinke fitt and order that the said ROBERT HAYES shall after the marke of all those cattle which he has in his custody or possession belonging unto the orphants of JOHN LANCKFEILD deceased being nowe marked thus /vizt/ on the right eare cropt which is the proper marke of CAPT: THOMAS WILLOWGHBY ESQR: And the said HAYES shall forthwith and allwayes hereafter marke the said cattle aforemenconed thus vizt: the right eare cropt as aforesaid with a hole in it and the left eare slitt

f 20 p 261 bot p 145 15 Aug 1645

Upon the request and humble peticon of ARTHUR BROWNE It is ordered that an attachmt bee granted unto the said BROWNE against the estate EDWARD LILLY to bee satisfactory for 488 lb tob and if the Court doe hereafter determine thereof

THE DIFFERENCE DEPENDING BETWEENE ARTHUR BROWNE Plt and THOMAS TOOKER deft concerninge 745 lb tob and caske due per account from the said TOOKER unto the said ARTHUR BROWNE and proved upon oath at the request of the said TOOKERis referred to the next Court to bee determined

An attachmt is granted unto MR: MATH: PHILLIPPS on the behalfe of HENRY SEAWELL orphant of MRS: SEAWELL dec: against the estate of EDWARD LILLY for 376 lb tob and if the Court soe determine thereof to bee lyable for payment of the said summe

The difference betweene CHARLES STEVENS and THO: BROWNE is referred to the next Court to bee determined by the request of both partyes

f20 p 261 bot p 145   15 Aug 1645

Upon the humble petison of THOMAS BROOKE It is ordered that WILLIAM CAPPS shall truely doe and pforme his labor in sawyeing or any other Imploymt: in Carpentary worke according to a condicon made betweene the said BROOKE and CAPPS It beinge alsoe sufficiently proved that the said CAPPS was hired to that purpose And the said CAPPS is to doe & pforme this labor according to the statutes of England - xx ?xx and the said CAPPS to paye the Court Charges

f20a p 262 bot p 145a   15 Aug 1645

An attachmt is granted unto THOMAS SMYTHARS agst the estate of JOHN GUTTERIDGE for 550 lb tob being due unto MR: MATHEW PHILLIPPS from the said GUTTERIDGE And the said SMYTHARS bownd as security for paymt of the said summe

Whereas JOHN COLE was by CAPT: EDWARD WINDHAMappoynted to bee of that number which should sett forth GEORGE RUTLAND the Southward March and is since departed the parish by which meanes the said RUTLAND is dampinfied in his Cropp for want of 2 dayes and a halfes worke which should have beene payd him by the said COLE there being none appoyntedby him to pay it before his departure It is therefore ordered according to the order of the last Councell of Warre that Rutland shall be satisfyed 40 lb tob per day In sattisfaccon of the said worke which amounted to the full quantity of 100 lb tob out of the said COLES estate and allsoe 15 lb tob charges And an attachmt to issue forth against the said COLES estate for the paymt of the aforesaid tob.

Whereas it was ordered at a Court of Warre holden at the howse of RICHARD BENNETT ESQ: the 12 Mar last past that everyone that setts out a man for the Southward March should paye & sattisfye unto him that went worke for his paynes equally and proporconably during the tyme of his absence from home upon the said service And in case any default were in paying the worke at the tyme when it should bee appoynted And by sufficient hands That the party or partyes delinquent should for any such default pay the quantity of 40 lb tob per day Nowe for as much as GEOFRY WEIGHT hath denyed and utterly refused to make paymt of 2 days worke and a halfe to GEORGE RUTLAND being his equall & proporconable share It is therefore ordered that the said GEOFREY WAGHT shall pay and satisfy unto the sd RUTLAND the full quantity of 100 lb tob and allsoe 15 lb tob charges 10 Nov next ensueinge otherwise execucon

f 21 p 263 bot p 146   15 Aug 1645

Whereas CESAR PUGGETT lately deceased did in his lyfetyme imploye GEORGE RUTLAND an attorney for him in divers busy-nesses by which meanes the RUTLAND hath beene at certaine - ? - suite with some trouble and paynes taken in the im-ploymt aforesaid It is therefore ordered that WILLIAM LUCAS whoe marryed the Relict of the said PUGGETT shall satisfy out of the estate of the said PUGGETT unto the sd RUTLAND 600 lb tob & Caske in lewe and full of all his charges and demands whatsoever concerning the Attorneyshipp aforesaid and to bee paid upon the 10 Nov next following otherwise execucon

The Court doth order that THOMAS CASSON shall bee satisfyed out of the estate of THOMAS COOPER deceased 390 lb tob for Charges and trouble taken about the said estate

The Court doth order that ENSIGNE THOMAS KEELING shall bee satisfyed out of the estate of THOMAS COOPER deceased 470 lb tob and caske due per bill all former orders of Court first satisfyed *(Note: The name of COOPER in these records is written COOP with the letters 'er' left off. This Clerk uses the letter p to denote per, pre, por, pro &c AGW)*

The Court doth order that THOMAS WARD chirurgeon shall bee satisfyed out of the estate of JAMES CLARKE lately deceased 530 lb tob due unto the said WARD for Phisick and paynes taken in the tyme of his sicknes of which said 530 lb tob the said WARD is to be satisfyed from the admor of the said CLARKE & if none doth administer by the 15 Oct next then the said WARD may administer in such manner as according to lawe is provided

f 21a p 264 bot p 146a   15 Aug 1645

Whereas it appeares that JOHN HOLMES hath felled fower tymber trees from off the land belonging to the heire of CAPT: ADAM THOROWGOOD to the prejudice and dammage of the said heire It is therefore ordered by this Court that the said JOHN HOLMES in liewe and satisfaccon of the wrong committed and dammage sustained as aforesaid shall satisfy unto MRS: SARAH GOOKINS by the last day of Nov next in the behalfe & for the use of the said heire of CAPT: THOROWGOOD 400 lb tob and allsoe paye Court Charges otherwise execucon

Whereas it appeares that HENRY WESTGATE hath taken up and made use of a grindstone of two foote and halfe were to MRS: GOOKINS It is ordered that the said WESTGATE by or before the last day of Dec next coming shall deliver unto MRS: GOOKINS a grindstone of the like bignes as is afore-specifyed or otherwise pay 150 lb tob in liewe and sattis-faccon hereof with Court Charges otherwyse execucon

The difference in Controversie betweene MRS: GOOKINS plt and LANCASTER LOVETT deft concerning BATHSHEBA the wyfe of the said LANC: LOVETT at the request of MRS: GOOKIN is referred to the next Court to bee heard and determined

f 21a p 264 bot p 146a 15 Aug 1645

for as much as it appeares that BATHSHEBA the wyfe of LANC: LOVETT hath much misdemeaned herself towards NRS: GOOKINS her Mistress and the Court taking due recognizance thereof doe order that the said BATHSHEBA shuld aske the said MRS: GOOKINS forgiveness in open Court upon her knees And if it shall appeare that the said BETHSHEBA shall hereafter misbehave herself in any uncivill or undecent Manner worthy punishmt then she the said BATHSHEBA shall receive twenty lashes on her bare back after she is delivered of her child she nowe goeth withall and pay the Court Charges

f 22 p 265 bot p 147 15 Aug 1645

The difference betweene GEORGE MIE and THOMAS *(the corner of this page is torn off AGW)* xxxxxxxxx by the request of both partyes is referred to the next Court to bee determined

The Court doth order that RICHARD ABRELL shall pay & satisfye unto THOMAS WARD, JOHN DYAR, GYLES COLLINS & WM:CAPPS theire severall charges for one ordinary a peice and 10 lb tob a peice for a dayes tyme All which presons aforenamed were subpened by the procurent of RICHARD ABRELL Otherwyse execucon

Concerning the difference in question betweene CAPT: THO: WILLOUGHBY EXQR: plt against JOHN SUTTON deft for getting a mayd servant of the said CAPT: WILLOUGHBY with child and for dammage and losse of tyme in service thereby sustained It is the opinion of this Court That a former order made by them in their behalfe is full satisfactory = not withstanding upon the request of the said CAPT: THOMAS WILLOUGHBY. This Court doth present the matters in question to the Governor & Councell and doe order that the said SUTTON shall forthwith give bond with security to answere the premises at James Citty upon the first day of October Court next before the hon[ble]--- Gov. & Counsell

It is ordered that LANCASTER LOVETT shall by the 15 Oct next deliver unto JOHN BOULTON in Lynhaven parish according to agreemt proved per oath one heifer & Cowe Calfe remayning at Kecoughtan having a white spott in the flanck the said LANCASTER LOVETT havinge acknowledged to have allready received payment and satisfaccon for the said heifar and calfe from the said BOLTON except a barrell of Eares which the said BOLTON is to paye LANCASTER LOVETT at the next Cropp and LANCASTER LOVETT to paye the Court charges otherwise execucon

f 22a p 266 bot p 147a 15 Aug 1645

An attachmt is granted unto JOHN POWYS against the estate of WILLM: DAVYES to bee satisfactory for 350 lb tob and caske & if the Court soe determine hereof

Whereas the Court hath formerly ordered ROBERT DAVYES to paye 600 lb tob & Caske unto STEPHEN GILLxxx (rest of the name is faded) this Court haveing more seriously considered hereof being for Phisick administered by reason of sicknes occasioned by Pomunkey March last yeare doe suspend the sd order untill the tyme of the publique levyes

This Court doth likewise suspend a former order made agst: PETER SEXTON upon the like occasion and that there issue forth no execucon against RICH: WORSTER concerning that busynes till further order taken by this Court at the tyme of makinge the publique Levyes

The Court doth order JOHN ffINCH to paye unto ROBERT BOWERS by the 10 Nov next 280 lb tob and caske due by bill and one yeares forbearance and the said ffINCH to paye halfe Court Charges and halfe expenses at ordinary otherwyse execucon

Whereas WILLIAM BASNETTS boat & hands were imployed in the fetching of the goods and Corne belonging unto the estete of JOHN MOYE dec: The Court doth order paymt to bee made pf 150 lb tob out of the sd estate unto the said BASNETT in consideracon & full satisfaccon thereof

An attachmt is granted unto MR: MATHEW PHILLIPPS against the estate of JOHN GUTTERIDGE to bee satisfactory for 300 lb tob and Caske upon a legall determination

The Court doth order paymt unto WM: SHIPP of 240 lb tob from the estate of THO: COOP (ER?) dec: per account due upon oath all former orders first being satisfyed

f 23- 267 bot p 148 15 Aug 1645

The Court doth order that JOHN STRATTON by the 10 Nov next doe pay unto ROBERT PAGE his assignes 1050 lb tob and Caske due per bill with 1 yeares lawfell forbearance and the Court Charges And a former order made by this Court for 20 pcent for non appearance is revoked & thereby made voyd by reason it nowe appeareth that JOHN STRATTON was Commanded upon the publique service with a partye in pursuite of Indians at the tyme of the former order granted as aforesaid

The Court doth order paymt to bee made unto WILLM: SHIPP from the estate of WILLIAM EAST dec: of 72 lb tob due per account proved by oath All former orders being first satisfyed

The Court doth order paymt unto WM: SHIPP from the estate of WILLIAM EAST dec: of 72 lb tob due per account proved by oath All former orders being first satisfyed

The Court doth order paymt unto WM: SHIPP of 32 lb tob due per account proved per oath from the estate of JOHN MOYE dec: all former orders beinge first satisfyed

f23 p 267 bot p 148   15 Aug 1645

The Court doth order payment unto JOHN STRATTON of 75 lb tob from the estate of JOHN MOYE dec: all former orders being first satisfyed

Whereas RICHARD KENNAR did arrest WILLIAM JOHNSON to thie Court and JOHNSON not appearing nor any attorney for him The Court doth order JOHNSON to paye 20 per cent according to Act And if the said JOHNSON doth not appeare at the next Court having notice thereof the Court to give Judgmt: for the whole debt appearing due as in Case Nihil dicit

Whereas JACOB BRADSHAWE hath wrongfully arrested RICHARD ABRELL unto this Court concerning the delivery of a cowe The Court doth thereupon order that the said BRADSHAWE shall by rhe 10 Nov next pay unto the sd RICHARD ABRELL 242 lb tob in consideracon of the charges, trouble & losse of tyme hereby occasioned otherwyse execucon

f 23a p 268 bot p 148a 15 Aug 1645

The Court doth order and give liberty unto ROBERT DAVYES and WM: EADY executors of JOHN MOYE deceased to sell at an outcrye the goods and moveables belonging unto the estate of the said deceased /Cattle excepted/ to the benefitt and best advantage of the Creditors and orphants of the said deceased and MR: WOODHOWSE is requested to bee present thereat

The Court doth order that EDWARD LILLY (or Litty?) according to condicon under his hand shall within 2 moneths tyme deliver and satisfy unto THOMAS CASSON one bedstead and a round table long since due by bill and paye Court Charges otherwyse execucon

An attachmt is granted unto ENSIGNE THOMAS LEELING against the estate of EDWARD LILLY to bee lyable to the paymt of 300 lb tob due per bill and the Court hereafter determine

An attachmt is granted unto THOMAS TOOKER agst the estate of EDW: LILLY ro bee satisfactory 191 lb tob claymed by the said TOOKER to bee due for sherriffs fees & if hereafter the ourt doe determine hereof

An attachmt is granted unto ffRANCIS LAND against the estate of EDWARD LILLY upon legall determination to bee responsable for 500 lb tob & one xx?xx due unto the said ffRANCIS LAND per bill

JOHN SUTTON and ffRANCIS LAND doe acknowledge to owe unto our Soveraigne Lord the Kings Ma[tie] 5000 lb of merchantable tob. The sondicon &c That if the said JOHN SUTTON doe appeare at James Citty upon the first daye of October Court next before the governor & Councell to answere the suite of CAPT: THOMAS WILLOUGHBY ESQR: then this recognizance to bee voyd otherwyse to remayne in full force strength and virtue

f 24 p 269 bot p 149   15 Aug 1645

It is ordered by the Court that WILLIAM BASNETT Constable for Linhaven parish shall detaine in his custody HUGH WOOD the said BESSENETT having engaged himselfe unto this Court for the forthcoming of the said WOOD. And if the said HUGH WOOD shall hereafter runne away & haggle abroad as formerly the said BASNETT is to carry the said WOOD before MR: WOODHOWSE or the next Court whoe is requested to see the said WOOD receive 40 good lashes on his bare back as a condigue? punishmt and to take such farther order concerning the said WOOD as he shall fynd Cause

Upon serious perusall of certaine accounts in controversie betweene EDWARD SELBY plt and MR: HENRY CATLIN deft: et e Contra And this Court having discussed the said Matters in difference and long debated the same doe order That the said MR: CATLIN shall by the 10 nov next pay unto EDWARD SELBY 1000 lb tob and Caskein full ballance and satisfaccon of the said accounts and matters now in variance And the said MR: CATLIN to pay all court charges hereby expended Otherwyse execucon

Mamo: An attachmt granted in Dec Court 1644 last past unto MR: HENRY CATLINGagainst the estate of EDWARD SELBYE is by thia Court revoked & utterly made voyd

Memo: That an execucon granted 31 Jan 1643/4 unto MR: MATHEW PHILLIPS against the estate of ffRANCIS LAND for payment of 100 lb tob and Court Charges is by this Court revyued? and to bee in force which sd execucon hath not beene served

WILLIAM MEMOCKS is ordered to give Security for his appearance at the next Court to answere unto such matters as shall bee objected against him on his Masters behalfe

f 24a p 270 bot p 149a   15 Aug 1645

Whereas divers people doexx ? xx customarily and illegally preferre divers and sundry peticons and complaints unto thie Court against severall persons without entry made in the Court Booke by the Clarke or other legall summons causes which Indirect practices do consequently tend to the great disturbance of the Comrs:the retarding of the publique affairs and undoubtedly reputed no small detriment to all those persons whoe are attandant upon the Court concerning such theire busynesses legally commenced depanding and in action This Court upon due consideration had thereof and of divers other inconvenincyes which may happen thereby doth thinke fitt to order and hereby doe publish the same to all the Inhabitants of the Country That they the said Comrs: nor any of them de futuro will not take recognizance or notice at all of any peticon, Complainr, accon, or suite howsoever exerted against any person or persons whatsoever unles the plt:or plts: doe first enter his or theire action in the Court booke and a legall summons caused by the Sheriffe according to Act of Assembly

f 24a p 270 bot p 149a 15 Aug 1645

Delivered to this Court by ROBERT HAYES an account of the estate belonging unto the children of JOHN LANCKFEILD deceased and nowe remayning in the custody and possession of the sais ROBERT HAYES

vizt:

4 Cowes	4	
1 heifar 2 yeares old	1	one old Cowe dyed
1 yearling heifar	1	
1 Cowe calfe	1	
In all	7 head of neat Cattle	

2 Cowes at Kecoughtan which was exchanged for 22 breeding goats & 12 kidds

5 old goats and 3 Ewe kidds which the sd HAYES will bee accountable for unto the estate

Goats in all young and old 42

f 25 p 271 bot p 150 15 Aug 1645

Delivered by THOMAS CASSON an account of what cattle doe belong unto the Orphants of WILLIAM LAYTON deceased and are now remaining in the custody or possession of the sd THO: CASON

16 Milck Cowes	16
2 yeareling heifars	02
7 Cowe calfes	07
Neat cattle in all	25 head

Delivered by JOHN MARTIN an account of what Cattle are belonging unto HENRY WATSON sonne of HENRY WATSON of Eliz: River deceased Vizt:

3 Cowes	3	
1 bull	1	
1 Cowe calfe	1	One Calfe dyed
1 Bull calfe	1	
The totall is	8 heads of Cattle young & old	

Memo: Acknowledged by WILLIAM LUCAS whoe did marry the widdowe and relict of CASAR PUGGETT lately deceased That hthe said CASAR PUGGETT in his lyfetyme die give & bequeath unto OLIVE STRATTON the daughter of JOHN STRATTON one yearling heifar merked thus - vizt: on the right eare slitt and a piece cut out on the upper side of the eare. Which said guift is Confirmed by the aforenamed WILLIAM LUCAS and allsoe by CHRISTIAN /the relict of the sd CASAR PUGGETT deceasedand/ nowe the wyfe of the said WILLIAM LUCAS

f 25a p 272 bot p 150a 15 Aug 1645

Brought in and delivered byROBERT DAVYES and WILLIAM EADY
A true Inventory of the whole estate of JOHN MOYE deceased at Linhaven as it nowe is this 15 Aug 1645
one old feather bedd, 2 old boulsters, warming pan and one old gridiron, a broken paire of tongues, 3 wedges and the handle of a fire shovell 2 Crosse Sawes, one whip sawe, 2 broad axes broken in the head, 2 wimbles, one adds (adz?) one Coopers adds & 2 small playnes2 old chisells, one old hand sawe, 5 small hammers, one drawing knife, 10 pewter dishes, a sawser, one old chamber pott, 2 tynne Candle-sticks, one double salt, one Iron Pott and potthookes, one Brasse skillet without an handle one old brasse kettle full of holes, one Iron pestle, 2 old hatts, one old pewter quart pail, one old Gunne one old Carbine, one paire andirons and 2 small spitts, 3 old truncks sold for 150 lb tob, 275 lb tob of his cropp and a wedding ring of gold

Cattle vizt:

2 milck Cowes	2
1 yeare Halfe old heifar	1
1 bull the same age	1
1 Cowe Calfe 4 months old	1
1 bull Calfe 4 months old	
In all sixe head of cattle	

Debts due to the estate
from WM: JACOBS 200 lb tob
from ROBT: DAVYES one Barrell of corne

3 hoggs in the woods never xxxxx faded out

Debts due from the Estate to severall men

To THO: DAVYES	300 lb tob
To JEFFREY WIGHT	235
To THO: CASSON	082
To JOHN STRATTON	075
To ROBT: DAVYES	100
Totall in debts	792

f 26 p 273 bot p 151 15 Aug 1645

Recordatur: Novermt wrinderso p osents ne Christian PIGGETT de Lynhaven in Cunitat infer: Norff: 30 Jan 1644
(This bond given first in Latin and repeated in English)

The condicon of this obligacon is such that if the above bownden CHRISTIAN PUGGETT her heires exors &c shall deliver or cause to be delivered unto the abovenamed WILLIAM COOLE 2 younge Cowes, 4 yearling heifars, 2 yearlinge steares and 200 acres of Land being part of 800 acres of Land lately taken up by MR: CESAR PUGGETT deceased late Husband of her the said CHRISTIAN PUGGETT and the said Land and Cattle doe convey and confirme unto them by her deed in writig indentedunder her hand and seale at or upon the last day of Apr next ensueing the date hereof or before and further doe deliver or cause to bee delivered one Iron pott and 3 pewter dishes at such tyme as he shall beginne to keep howse himself to bee his owne proper goods and estate then this obligacon to bee voyd and of none effect

f 26 p 273 bot p 151   15 Aug 1645

or else to stand in full force and vertue
Signed, sealed and delivered
the Daye and yeare above   CHRISTIAN (Xn)PUGGETT
written in presence of us: & her seale
XOP: BURROUGH
ROBERT ABRALL

f 26a p 274 bot p 151a 10 Sep 1645

Recordat: 10 Sep 1645 All men shall knowe by these preents that I KATHARINE the late wyfe of OLIVER VANHECK deceased doe by these presents in the tyme of my widdow=hood and befor the daye of my marriage freely give and of my owne accord and good will and in the affection and tender love and care that I owe & beare unto my sonne JOHN VANHECK the sonne of OLIVER VANHECK deceased doe againe freely give and bequesth and in the presence of those whose names are hereunder written doe deliver to the use of my said sonne JOHN 2 Milck Cowes of colour black, one of them a white starre in the forehead. The right eare the upper quarter cutt off and the left eare whole with a hole in it and the other the left Eare cropt To have and to Hold the said 2 black Cowes and the female increase thereof unto the good benefitt and onely use of the aforesaid JOHN VANHECK my sonne and to his heires &c forever. the milke and the male increase of the said Cattle before specified to bee and accrewe untounto the said KATHERINE his mother and her husband GEORGE MIE soe long onely as they shall have the tuition, keeping and bringing up of the said JOHN VANHECK theire sonne. And allsoe the said KATHERINE and GOERGE MIE her husband doe hereby these presents bynd themselves upon any good occasion being thereunto lawfullycalled to bee accountable unto ROBERT POWYES, Clerke or to the Minister and Churchwardens of Lynhaven For the tyme beinge of and concerning the said cattle and the female encrease that shall or may aryse and come of them Yearely and every yeare as occasion may serve during the tyme of his living and keepinge with his said mother or father in lawe soe as the

f 27 p 275 bot p 152   15 Oct 1645

said JOHN VANHECK may receave noe prejudice or dammage in the said Cattle or theire increase during the tyme of his Minority In wittness whereof wee the said KATHARINE and GEORGE MYE have hereunto sett our hands and seales this 15 Maye 1645
Sealed and delivered   KATHERINE VANHECK & her seale
to the use of JOHN VANHECK
in the presence of: the marke of GEORGE MYE & Seale
ROBT: POWYS Clerke
WILLIAM LUCAS
JOHN PRINCE

f 27 p 275 bot p 152   15 Oct 1645

Recordat 15 Oct 1645
Knowe all men by thesepresents that I JAMES PHILLIPPS of Linhaven, planter doe by these presents bynd over unto GEORGE MIE of the same place, planter, 2 heifars one of a yeare old and the other of sixe months old, this security I the said JAMES PHILLIPPS doe bynd over to GEORGE MIE to him and his heires or assignes for security for 500 lb tob due to the said GEORGE MIE from mee the said JAMES PHILLIPPS by specialty. Thia security the said GEORGE MIE is to hold as his owne proper goods untill his debt bee fully satisfyed. In wittness whereof I the said JAMES PHILLIPPS have hereunto sett my hand this 13 Oct 1645

Signed and delivered in the presence of:
WILLIAM LUCAS and JOHN PRINCE   JAMES (^) PHILLIPPS

Bee it knowne unto all men by these presents that I SAVILL GASKINE doe give unto ROBT: GASKINS my lawful sonne as a deed of guift to him and his heires forever one black & white cowe called by the name of Primrose with all female encrease that shall proceed from her. Wittness my hand this 14 Oct 1645

SAVILL GASKINE

In presence of: THOMAS ALLEN

f 27a p 276 bot p 152a   15 Oct 1645
Att a County Court holden the 15 Oct 1645 att the howse of WILLIAM SHIPP
Present:

CAPT: EDWARD WINDHAM	MR: WILLIAM JULIAN
MR: THOMAS MEARES	MR: HENRY WOODHOUSE
MR: MATH: PHILLIPPS	MR: ffRANCIS MASON
MR: EDWARD LOYD	MR: THOMAS LAMBARD

Whereas WILLIAM JOHNSON is indebted unto RICHARD KENNAR 240 lb tob, i fire shovell, one paire of tongues, one gridiron and one paire of Rudder irons as appeares unto this Court and the said JOHNSON being twice arrested to two severall courts and not appearing nor any attorney for him to answer the suite. The Court doth give Judgmt: according to Act of Assembly as in case of nihil dicit. And that the said JOHNSON shall make paymt unto the said KENNAR of the said 240 lb tob debt and Ironwork aforespecified within 15 dayes and 20 for every hundred debt according to a former order of this Court with Court Charges otherwyse exec

A certificate of 50 acres of land granted unto ffRANCIS BAKER for the transportation of himself into this Collony and provedto bee due unto upon oath which right of and to the said 50 acres of land the said BAKER hath assigned over unto THOMAS MYLES *(see Nugent 171)*

Whereas it appeares to this Court that WILLIAM DAVYES was indebted unto JACOB BRADSHAW 300 lb tob And ffRANCIS LAND beinge formerly an attorney for the said DAVYES whoe is now

f 27a p 276 bot p 152a 15 Oct 1645

departed this Collony And the said LAND having in Feb Court last past undertaken in presence of the Court to abyde xx ?xx censure in the behalfe of the said DAVYES. The Court doth nowe thereupon order the said ffRANCIS LAND to make paymt unto the said JACOB BRADSHAWE of the said 300 lb tob due from DAVYES as aforesaid within 16 dayes and Court Charges otherwise execucon

f 28 p 277 bot p 153 15 Oct 1645

A certificate of 50 acres of land granted unto THOMAS MYLES in right and for the transportation of *(the name is blank in the original AGW , see Nu 171 & 174)*

Whereas HENRIK LIGHTHART was arrested to this Court to answere the suite of HENRY SNAYLE And the said HENRICK not appearing nor any attorney for him to answere the said suite. The Court doth order accordinge to Act of Assembly that the said HENRICK shall pay 20 per cent for every 100 debt and such dammages as shall appeare due. And if the said LIGHTHART having notice hereof doth not appeare at the next Court. The Court then to give judgmt in case of nihil dicit against the said HENRICK according to Act afor-said

It is ordered that JOHN WILLIAMS bee forthwith Committed to the safe custody of the sherriffe there to remain till he give good Caution with security for his good abearing towards all his Mat-ies Leige People and especially towards JAMES SMYTH & not to frequent nor come to the howse of MRS: SARAH GOOKIN nor use the company of ELIZABETH TAPLIN. And the said WILLIAMS to appeare at the next sessions of this Court to receive & abyde what further order the Court shall then thinke fitt and adjudge in this Busynes

Whereas JOHN HATTON is indebted unto JOHN PEROTT the summe of 205 lb tob and Caske as appeares unto this Court. The Court doth order the said HATTON to make paymt thereof unto the said PEROTT or his assignes within 16 dayes and one yeares lawfull borbearance with Court Charges otherwyse execucon

Whereas XOPFER RIVARS is indebted unto JOHN PEROTT 200 lb tob & caske. The Court doth order paymt thereof with one yeares forbearance and Court Charges within 16 dayes unto the said PEROTT or his assignes Else execucon

f 28a p 278 bot p 153a 15 Oct 1645

WHEREAS RICHARD WORSTER is indebted unto JOHN PEROTT 450 lb tob and Caske (as) appeares unto this Court. Payment is ordered to be made of the said tobacco with one yeares lawfull forbearance and Court Charges within 16 dayes otherwyse exec:

The difference betweene WILLIAM LANGLEY plt and MR: EDWARD LOYD deft aoncerning a ferry boat which belonged unto the said LANGLEY and was taken away by 2 Runnaways as is alleaged is referred to the next Court to be heard and determined.

A certificate of 50 acres of land granted unto THOMAS MYLES for the transportation of PHILLIP WESTON and proved to be due upon oath *(see NU 171 & 174 also pp 276 & 277 of Book A Nco AGW)*

Whereas it appeares unto this Court that WILLIAM CAPPS is indebted unto RICHARD KENNAR 200 lb tob per bill. The Court doth order paymt thereof within 16 dayes else exec

Whereas it appeares that OLIVER VANHACK deceased was indebted unto THOMAS DAVYES 108 lb tob The Court doth order that GEORGE MIE whoe intermarryed with the relict and widdow of the said VANHACK shall paye the said 108 lb tob unto the said DAVYES within 16 dayes and the Court Charges bee equally divided otherwyse exec

Whereas THOMAS TOOKER is indebted unto ARTHUR BROWNE Merchant 385 lb tob and caske due per account as it doth appeare unto the Court. The Court doth order that the said THOMAS TOOKER make payment of the aforesaid 385 lb tob and caske unto the said ARTHUR BROWNE with Court Charges within 16 dayes otherwyse execucon

f 29 p 279 bot p 154 15 Oct 1645

Whereas JOHN ffINCH per bill stands bownd with PHILLIPP LAND as security unto ARTHUR BROWNE Merchant for the payment of 435 lb tob and caske as appeares unto this Court It is therefore ordered that the said JOHN ffINCH doe make payment of the said 435 lb tob and Caske unto the said BROWNE with Court argesotherwise execucon

Wereas WILLIAM HAWLEY hath wrongfully arrested WILLIAM CAPPS unto this Court upon an unjust allegacon. It is therefore ordered that HAWLEY pay all Charges expended in this suite unto the said CAPPS within 10 dayes Otherwyse exec

Whereas JOHN SUTTON and MAUDLIN PARKER being presented for Incontinendie which said Act plainely appeares soe to bee, MAUDLIN being delivered of a Child. It is therefore ordered by the Court that the said **JOHN SUTTON** doe pennance in a white sheet the next Sabbath daye that divine service is said in the parich Church of Lynhaven by the Minister f29 p 279 bot p 154   15 Oct 1645

there in the face of the whole congregation then assembled and aske allmighty God forgiveness of his said hanious Crime in such manner and using such words as according to the Lawes and Customes are in England provided in such cases and suchOffences committed. And the said MAUDLIN PARKER to receive 20 good lashes on her bare back in presence and atthe next session of this Court for her said fowle offence committed as aforesaid And the said SUTTON to paye all Court Charges

Whereas JOANE RAGGED being presented for being unlawfully delivered of a child which she layeth to JAMES COLLINGS whoe is a servant unto MR: THOMAS BROWNE. The Court doth order that the said JOANE RAGGED shall provide for herself and her said child till this tyme twelve months at which tyme COLLINGS will bee ffree whoe is then to provide for the mayntenance of the Child as the Court shall then further order and determine hereof

f 29a p 280 bot p 154a   15 Oct 1645

It is ordered that JAMES COLLINGS for committing whoredom with JOANE RAGGED shall the next Sabbath daye doe pennace in the Chappell of Ease of Elizabeth River in a white sheete in the face of the whole congregation assembled and aske allmighty God forgiveness for his said hainous fact in such manner and repeating such words to bee delivered by the Minister as according to the Lawe and Customes in England provided in such cases and such offences Committed And the said JOANE RAGGED is to receive 20 good lashes on her bare back in presence of this Court and COLLINGS to paye the Court Charges

Whereas in Maye 1637 there was a Patent for 500 acres of land granted unto THOMAS HOLT lyeing at the head of the Easterne Branch in Elizabeth River which said Patent hath beene since consigned unto SIMON HANCOCK And the said Land in the said Patent specified being lately surveyed by a sworne and authentick survey is nowe fownd to bee but 400 acres as by a Platt thereof produced appears soe as there is 100 acres of Land due unto the said SIMON HANCOCK in right of the said Patent which this Court doth certify accordingly (See Nu 57 *there is no patent to SYMON HANCOCK in Nu)*

Whereas THOMAS WARD Chirurgeon hath administered certaine Phisick and applyed other medicinall Meanes unto the wyfe of JOHN MARTIN And the said WARD having in consideration thereof allready received of the said MARTIN a heifar and 400 lb tob as appeares unto ths Court upon full examination of the differences The Court doth order that the said MARTIN shall within 16 dayes further paye unto the said WARD 300 lb tob more in full satisfaccon of all demands concerning the atters in variance and nowe in question. And the said MARTIN to release WARD of a Covenent? entered into for to save the said MARTIN harmless against RICH: KENNAR concerning a bond of 2000 lb tob for his cure of the said MARTIN his wyfe .

f 29a p 280 bot p 154a   15 Oct 1645

And WARD and MARTIN to paye theire owne Court Charges else exec

f 30 p 281 bot p 155   15 Oct 1645

The Court doth order that THOMAS WARD shall satisfy unto MR: XPOFER BURROUGHS, JEFFRY WEIGHT?, RICHARD ffORSTER, OWEN HAYES, JOHN SUCKER? JAMES STARLING and JOHN RICHARDSON 50 weight of tob per peice for theire severall charges ex½emded in Dyett at the Ordinary and losse of 3 dayes tyme apeice whoe were all subpd: to the Court to testify theire knowledge of the said THOMAS WARD Else exec:

Qhereas MR: WOODHOWSE and MR: HALL were impleaded by THOMAS CASON for a draught bull being accidnetally killed by the doggs of the said MR: WOODHOWSE and MR: HALL as is alleaged. nd itappearing by sufficient proffe and testimony that the said MR: HALL was the Cheife instrmentt therof. The Court doth order that MR: HALL shall within 16 dayes deliver unto the said CASON another bull of the same age and goodnes of the bull that was soe killed and to pay 6 dayes worke of a good sufficient hand for to breake the said bull. And MR: HALL to pay all charges in this suite. else exec:

Whereas this Court did order ffRANCIS LAND to paye unto JACOB BRADSHAWE 300 lb tob for the proper debt of WM: DAVYES whoe is nowe departed this Collony upon the humble peticon of of the said ffR: LAND for his better security. An attachment is granted against the estate of WM: DAVYES to bee satisfactory upon a legall determinacon for the said 300 lb tob unto the said LAND

The Court doth order that THOMAS CASON shall pay unto MR: WOODHOWSE 140 lb tob for the charges of his two men at the Ordinarye and losse of theire tyme being subp: to the Court at the procuremt of the sd THOMAS CASON else exec:

Whereas THOMAS WARD is indebted by bill unto WILLIAP SHIPP 774 lb tob. The Court doth order the said WARD to pay the said tob: unto the said SHIPP within 16 dayes and Court Charges otherwise execucon

f 30a p 282 bot p 155a   15 Oct 1645

The Court doth order MR: CASON to paye unto ELIZABETH HALL 40 lb tob for Charges being subp: to this Court by the meanes and procurement of the said MR: CASON else exec:

The difference depanding betweene WILLIAM LUCAS plt and GEORGE RUTLAND deft concerning a defamacon at the request of the said RUTLAND is referred to the next Court to bee heard and determined.

Whereas JOHN HATTON is indebted per bill 440 lb tob unto MR: ROBERT PAGE as it doth appeare unto the Court Paymt is ordered to bee made thereof unto the said MR: PAGE or to his attorney from the said HATTON within 16 dayes and the Court Charges otherwise exec:

f 30a p 282 bot p 155a 15 Oct 1645

Whereas WILLIAM JOHNSON is indebted unto the estate belonging unto HENRY SEAWELL an orphant the full summe of 400 lb tob and sacke as appeares to the Court . The Court doth order paymt within within 16 dayes to be made of the said 400 lb tob and Caske from the said MR: JOHNSON unto MR: MATHEW PHILLIPPS whoe is guardian unto the said Orphant with Court Charges otherwyse exec

It is ordered that MR: THOMAS CASON shall take a true and perfect Inventory of the estate of JAMES CLARKE deceased and to apprayse the same by appraisers elected to that purpose And the said CASON to detayne in his hands or custody soe much of the said estate as maye satisfy the tythes and levyes of the said deceased and for the residue to bee accountable to the administrators of the deceased estate.

f 31 p 283 bot p 156 15 Oct 1645

Whereas JOHN YEATS did assigne over unto ARTHUR BROWNE merchant a bill of debt of 1000 lb tob and Caske due from CAPT: JOHNSON. And for default of paymt thereof being demanded the said YEATS did undertake to satisfye the said tob unto the said BROWNE as appeares unto the Court under the hand of the said YEATS, It is ordered that the said YEATS by the 10 Nov next shall give good security unto the said BROWNE for paymt of the said 1000 lb tob afore specifyed with Caske by or before Xmas next And hereupon the said BROWNE is to redeliver the bill afore specifyed unto the said YEATS and YEATS to paye Court Charges else exec:

Whereas JOHN YEATS did assigne over unto ARTHUR BROWNE Merchant a bill of debt of 1300 lb tob and Caske due from EDWARD PRINCE And for default of paymt thereof being demanded the said YEATS die promise paymt thereof unto the said BROWNE as it doth appeare unto the Court under the hand wryting of the said YEATS. The Court doth order that YEATS by or before the 10 Nov next shall give good security unto the said BROWNE for payment of the said 1300 lb tob and Caske at or before Xmas next. And thereupon the said BROWNE is to deliver the bill aforemenconed unto the said YEATS and YEATS to pay the Court Charges else exec

WHEREAS GEORGE RUTLAND i indebted unto EDMUND MATHEWE 240 lb tob per bill & 30 lb tob per account and acknowledged by the said GEORGE RUTLAND to bee justly due the Court doth order paymt of the aforesaid tob being in totall 270 lb and Court Charges within 16 dayes else exec

Whereas GEO: RUTLAND is indebted unto MR: JOHN CORKER 466 lb tob and acknowledged by the said RUTLAND TO BEE JUSTLY DUE The Court doth order payment of the said 466 lb tob and Court Charges within 16 dayes else exec

f 31 p 283 bot p 156 15 Oct 1645

An attachmt is granted unto WILLIAM OLIVER against soe much tob as are remayning in the hands of MR: ROBT: EYRE and THOMAS DAVYES and belonging or due unto JAMES TOOKE to bee satisfactory upon legall determination for 250 lb

f 31a p 284 bot p 156a 15 Oct 1645

tob and caske due per bill from the said TOOKE unto the said OLIVER as appeares unto the Court

Whereas RICHARD STERNELL is indebted unto per bill unto MRS: ARTHUR BROWNE 410 lb tob and caske as appeares unto the Court Paymt: is ordered to bee made of the said tob and caske with Court Charges within 16 dayes unto the sd MR: BROWNE else exec

Whereas the estate belonging unto MR: HENRY SEAWELL an Orphant is indebted unto WILLIAM SCOTT 300 lb tob and acknowledged due by MR: PHILLIPPS guardian unto the said Orphant. The Court doth order paymt thereof unto the sd WM: SCOTT or to CHRISTIAN CHRISTIANS asignee of the said SCOTT within 16 dayes from the estate of the sd HENRY SEAWELL Orphant aforenamed otherwyse exec:

An attachmt granted unto RICHARD CONQUEST against the estate of GEORGE RUTLAND to bee satisfactory for 300 lb tob claymed to bee due from the said RUTLAND unto the said CONQUEST for certaine Clerkes fees and for writing divers busynesses for the said RUTLAND when the Court shall further determine the same

The Court doth order that MR: MATHEW PHILLIPPS and MARY ROUGE, SYMON DREW AND MARGARET EVANS?, LAWRENCE RICHARDSON and SARAH KINGE bee all summoned by the sherriffe personally o appeare at the next session of the Court to answere unto such matters of presentment as are exhibited against them by the Churchwardens of Elizabeth River Parish

f 32 p 285 bot p 157 30 Oct 1645

At a meeting of the Councell of Warre for the associated Countyes the 25 Oct 1645

Present: CAPT: THO: WILLOWGHBY	RICHARD BENNETT ESQR:
CAPT JNO: SIBSEY	CAPT: EDWARD WINDHAM
CAPT: THO: DEWE	MR: RICHARD PRESTON
ANTHONY JONES	MR: ffRANCIS HOUGH

These somes of tob hereafter exprest areallowed and approved to bee due from the associated Countyes In the psecucon of the Warre. And appoynted to bee paid as followeth:

	lb
To JNO: MERRIDAY for trimming & mending of boats	0600
To CAPT: THO: WILLOWGHBY for disbursmts per his acct	1644
To MR: MATHEW PHILLIPPS by his acct:	0150
To THO: WARD Chirurgeonfor his paynes & Charge	1000
To HENRICK (LIGHTHART? no last name given) for the hire of his boate	0600
To BARTH: HOSKINS for his boate twice	1400

f 32 p 285 bot p 157   30 Oct 1645

To WM: BASNETT by his acct: 0270
To JOHN GARRETT for cheese 0800
To RICHARD WELLS for cheese 0200
To RICHARD AXAM for ABRAHAMS dyett 0250
To MR: RICHARD PRESTON for worke in the transporting
soldiers and for a Chest lost 0196
To MR: RICHARD BENNETT by his acct 9259
To JOHN SKULL? for a Cutlace lost 0100
To WM: BROOKES for goods lost ye boat being cast away
0200
To NATH: STYLES for goods lost in the said boat 0150
To EVAN WOOLLADS for goods lost in the said boat 0250
To ARTH: JONES for boat hyre provisions, powder
and shott 1308
To MR: JOHN MOORE for a boat lost 0600
To ABRAHAM PITTS for losse of his tyme & Cropp
being wounded in the service 0800

19777

f 32a p 286 bot p 157a   30 Oct 1645

Brought from the other side 19777
To MR: TRISTRAM NASWORTHY for boat hyre &c 1099
To him that was bitten by a snakes towards the
losse of his tyme & cropp 00246
To MR: JAMES KNOTTS for boat hyre &c 00246
To XOPFER ACKELEY Chirurgeon for the voyage 1000 lb
and for cure of Abraham and him
that was hurt by a snake 600 lb
is all 01000
To CAPT: EDW: WINDHAM for mens worke upon the
service 00225
To MR: PHILLIPP BENNETT for hyre of his boate 00700

26781
at 10 per cent is 02678
To WM: (or MR?) BROOKE for a Case broken 00050
To 80 soldiers by order to receive 10 lb tob
per head is 08000
To the Sherriffe for Colleccon of 8050 lb at
10 per cent 00805

In all 38314

It is ordered that for satisfaccon of the abovesaid some of 38314 lb tob there bee levyed of every tythable person within the County of Lower Norrff: 28 lb per polle and uppon every tytheable person in the Countyes of Upper Norff: and the Isle of Wight 31 lb tob per polle In regard these Countyes had and made use of more of those provisions of victualls which are brought into this account then those of the Lower Norff did. And that the sharriffes of the of the aforesaid Countyes respectively shall collect the aforesaid some of 28 lb & 31 lb per polle this present yeare and pay the same as it is appoynted. It is ordered

f 32a p 286 bot p 157a 30 Oct 1645

and forasmuch as those whoe have beene hyred and imployed as scouts doe expect to bb cleared of levyes pretending to bee

f 33 p 287 bot p 158 30 Oct 1645
3 Nov 1645

free by theire imploymt. It is further ordered that neyther they nor any other tytheable person whatsoever shall bee free from paymt excepting such as are exempted by act of Assembly or by order of the County Courts

EDW: WINDHAM	THO: WILLOWGHBY
THO: DEWE	RI: BENNETT
RICH: PRESTON	JOHN SIBSEY
ffRA: HOUGH	ANTH: JONES

Att a County Court holden the 3 Nov 1645
at the howse of WILLIAM SHIPP
CAPT: THOMAS WILLOWGHBY ESQR:

CAPT: EDWARD WINDHAM	MR. THOMAS MEARES
MR: ffRANCIS MASON	MR: THOMAS LAMBERD
MR: EDWARD LOYD	MR: MATH: PHILLIPPS

It is ordered that those 39 men which are allotted with MR: BURROWGHS to sett our a man for the scout doe pay and allowe theire equall share proporconably to HENRY HILL for mending a Chest which MR: BURROWGHS passed for upon acct and to pay 8 lb tob for this order

Whereas it appeares unto this Court that RICHARD CONQUEST hath divers tymes gone to James Towne to copy out the Acts of Assemblys whereby certaine Charges and disbursmts by him beene occasioned. And whereasThe said RICHARD CONQUEST hath allsoe taken paynes xxxx faire wrytings the said and in Collecting them into a booke doth thinke fitt to allowe the said CONQUEST 1000 lb tob and to bee paid in manner followeing vizt 500 lb

f 33a p 288 bot p 158a 3 Nov 1645

to be raysed and Levyed upon the Inhabitants of this County and to bee collected by the sherriffe this present yeare. And 200 lb tob forthwith to nee paid by ENSIGNE LAMBARD out of a fine which the said ENSIGNE LAMBARD hath formerly in the tyme of his shrivalty receaved of RICHARD HALTGRAVE and 300 lb tob more to bee paid to the said CONQUEST out of the nest fine which shall happen to bee made and assessed by the Court for the Countyes use of which 1000 lb tob The Court doth order paymt to bee made to the said CONQUEST accordingly and in such manner as is aforespecified and explained in this order

It is ordered that an attachment bee awarded on the estate of WILLIAM DURFORD for satisfaccon of 500 lb tob due by bill at the suite of THOMAS HOLWELL if the Court doe hereby soe determine hereof

f 33a p 288 bot p 158a 3 Nov 1645

An attachmt is granted on the estate of ffRANCIS HUNT at the suite of MR: EDWARD LOYD the assignee of THOMAS TOOKER for 882 lb tob and 2 Cackes due per bill to bee responsible and for the said debt unto the said MR: LOYD upon legall determinacon

Sn attachmt is granted on the estate of ffRANCIS HUNT at the suite of THOMAS LAMBARD upon determinacon to bee satisfacotry for 640 lb tob per bill unto the said ENSIGNE LAMBARD

It is ordered that ENSIGNE THOMAS LAMBARD and THOMAS TOOKER shall bring in and deliver to the Court at the next session thereof a true and perfect account upon oath of all Clarkes fees which they or eyther of them have received or collected and are anywayes due or appertaining unto the estate of MR: ROBERT TYAS deceased

Whereas by order from the Councell of Warre all persons whatsoever being inhabitants of this County for theire safeguard and defence upon the salvages. *(this should be savages meaning the Indians AGW)* according to the number of people in theire severall famylyes were proporconably allotted to sett our and mayntaine men in manner of a Scout this present yeare last past And whereas divers

f 34 p 289 bot p 159 3 Nov 1645

persons have beene or may bee negligent in the bringing in or alloweance towards theire provisions of powder and shott and other necessaryes and in the paymt of theire tob of corne to such party or soldier by them hyred for the said imploymt And allsoe doe or shall refuse to bring theire severall shares of tob or corne unto one place to bee appoynted by him who hath beene the Cheife undertaker for the sallart to the next party hyred for the said service. All which is contrary to the tenor and true meaning of the said order of the Councell of Warre and allsoe contrary to theire owne contract and agreemt. It is therefore ordered by the Court that the severall Lymitts of precincts respectively bee hereby authorized and by vertue of this order shall have full power to distreyine for full satisfaation upon the estates goods or Chattles of all persons whatsoever which have been or may bee hereafter deliquest in all or any the premises. And the Constable shall receive of or may distrayne upon such delinquents 30 lb per cent for his paynes taken in or about the said distresse

The Court doth order that MR: CORNELIUS LOYD bee paid 100 lb tob out of this present Levye towards the charges of 3 men which the said MR: LOYD payeth forto the Upper Norff: and hath beene charged with in this County.
These severall somes of tobacco followingand hereafter expressed are allowed and approved by this Court to bee due to the particular persons hereunder named and for the publique uses hereafter menconed (Vizt:

f 34a p 290 bot p 159a 3 Nov 1645

Imp: for LIEFT: ROBERT SMYTH's sallary	2000 lb
for 2 ferryes	1600
To THOMAS WORKEMAN for killing 3 wolves	0050
To LANCASTER LOVETT for killing 1 wolfe	0050
To JAMES SMYTH for killing 1 wolfe	0050
To GYLES COLLINGS for killing 1 wolfe	0050
to JOHN CARRAWAY for killing 1 wolfe	0050
To THOMAS DURFORD for killing 2 wolves	0100
To PETER PORTER for killing 1 wolfe	0050
To MR: SIDNEY for killing 1 wolfe	0050
To HENRY th(e?) Negro for killing 1 wolfe	0050
To RICHARD WOOLLMAN for killing 1 wolfe	0050
To SYMON PETERS for killing 1 wolfe	0050
To HENRY HILL for smyth worke done	0060
To RICHARD CONQUESTfor his paynes in often goeing to Jamestown and expences there to copy out the Act of Assembly and for faire wryting them and and collecting them all in one booke *(does this book still exist ? In Lower Norfolk County records? AGW)*	?
To LEIFT: ffRANCIS MASON per his account	0250
To STEPHEN GILL and JOHN BRUSH for phisick administered to and for cure of hurt & sick men upon service	1930
	7040
To MR: MEARES & MR: EDWARD LOYD for expenses and charges at James Towne being Burgesses for Elizabeth River Parish	1454
To THOMAS TOOKER for men hyred to rowe the said burgesses up and downe & for boat hyre	0316
To MR: XPOFER BURROUGH for his charge & expences at James Towne being Burges for Lynhaven Parish	0799
	9609

f 35 p 291 bot p 160 3 Nov 1645

To the sherriffe for Collection & shrinkage at the rate of 5 per cent of the aforesaid 9609 lb tob and for collecting the 420 lb tob of 15 tytheable persons overplus being 28 lb tob prt poll is	500
To me CORNELIUS LOYD per order of Court	100
The totall is	10209

In Lynnhaven parish there is 140 tytheable persons
In Elizabeth River Parish there is 165 tytheable persons
The number of all tytheable persons in the whole County is 305

For satisfaccon of the aforesaid some of 10209 lb tob to the severall persons abovenamed and for the particular uses before specifyed The Court doth order that there be levyed of every tytheable person within thisCounty. That is to sayeFor Lynhaven parish 31 lb tob per polle and for

f 35 p 291 bot p 160   3 Nov 1645

Elizabeth River parish 35 lb tob per polle. In regards those of Elizabeth River Parish were more charged for theire Burgesses then those of Lynhaven were And it is ordered that the Sherriffe shall collect the aforesaid somes of 31 lb & 35 lb tob per polle this present yeare from the inhabitants of this County and soe forthwith make paymt thereof to the severall persons forenamed and in such manner as is appoynted in this order. And for the more speedy Colleccon of the aforesaid tob It is allsoe ordered That at what howse soever there shallhappen to bee and remnant or odd parcels of tob more then will goe in a hogshead. The sherriffe or his deputies shall have hereby full power and authority to comand

f 35a p 292 bot p 160a   3 Nov 1645

one of that family to carry such remnants of odd parcells of tob to the next howse or place where he shall make them up a full hogsheads

The generall Levye made and assented unto by ye Councell of Warre for the associated Countyes for every tytheable person in this whole County is per polle 28 lb tob

Soe the Levye in the totall in the totall for Lynnhaven Parish is 59 lb tob per polle

And the Levy in the totall for Elizabeth River Parish is 63 lb tob per polle

All the tobaccoes Levyed as aforesaid and to bee collected by the sherriffe this present yeare of 305 tytheable persons in thewhole County and as is before exprest amounts in the totall to the summe of 18655 lb

Recordat: 3 Nov 1645

To all Xpian people to whome these these presents shall come &c knowe ye that I BARTHOLOMEW HOSKINS of Elizabeth River in Virginia, planter have bargained, sold, assigned and sett over and doe by these presents bargaine &c unto RICHARD WOOLLMAN of the same place planter one Reddish Browne Cowe aged 8 yeares of thereabouts and commonly called and knowne by the name of Young Nan and marked as followeth vizt: at present cropt on both Eares and a hole cutt through the right eare. To have and to hold the said Cowe with all such increase as shall aryse of her to himself his heires &c forever without the lest trouble, hindrance or molestation of mee the said BARTHOLOMEW HOSKINS my heires, exors &c or any other person or persons whatsoever clayming or pretending any lawfull right or tytle thereunto. And to the pformance herof I bynd myself, my heires &c firmely by these

(continued on next page 293)

f 36 p 293 bot p 161   3 Nov 1645

presents. In witness whereof I have hereunto sett my hand and seale this 21 Oct 1645
Signed sealed and delivered   BARTHO: HOSKINS
in the presence of: & his seale
THO: MARSH, JOHN FFERINHAUGH

Bee it knowne unto all men by these presents that I JOHN BROWNE of Elizabeth River in the County of Lower Norff: planter have given granted bargained and sold unto EDWARD DARSY of the County aforesaid planter 3 head of cattle /vizt/ one Cowe aged about 7 yeares of a brindel Coulor and marked with a Cropp on the right eare and the left eare whole and a steare of Coulor aforesaid aged about 1½ yeares and marked with a cropp on the left eare and the right eare slitt also one heifar calfe brindel as aforesaid aged about 3/4 of a yeare and marked with a cropp on both eares and a slitt in one and doe by these presents give grant bargaine and sell unto the said EDWARD DARSEY his heires &c forever for a valuable consideration pert in hand paid In witness whereof I have hereunto putt my hand and seale this 7 Feb 1642
Sealed and delivered in the   JOHN (+) BROWNE
presence of us: RICHARD WOOLLMAN   and his seale
THOMAS BOUNDER
THOMAS /T/ HORNE

f 36a p 294 bot p 161a 3 Nov 1645

Know all men by these presents that I THOMAS WARD of Lynhaven in the County of Lower Norff: Chirurgeon did by the Command of CAPT: THOMAS WILLOWGHBY serve in an expidition against the Indians to Yawopyin als (alias?) Rawanoake (Roanoke?) as Chirurgeon to the whole company and did divers Cures upon severall men in the said service for which I am to receive sattisfaccon from the associating Countyes of the Isle of Wight, Upper and Lower Norff: Nowe I the said THOMAS WARD for and towards satisfaccon of a debt due from mee to XPOFER: BURROWGHS of Lynhaven aforesaid and for divers other good causes and considerations mee thereunto moveing have given, granted, confirmed, assigned and sett over unto him the said XPOFER: his heires &c fully freely & clearely and absolutely all and every such some or somes of tob as are due unto for my service or cures done in that expedition to have hold receive take and enjoyall and every part and parcell thereof for evermore to his of theire proper use as his or theire owne goods or estate. And I doe hereby authorize him the said XPOFER his heires &c to demand and receive all and every the said some of somes of tobacco due to mee as aforesaid and for default of paymt to take such course against the xxx?xxxx as he the said XPOFER his heires &c shall thinke fitt and upon receipt thereof one or more acquittances discharge or discharges more to make seale and deliver the same and one of more Attorney or Attorneys to substitute and appoynt and againe and againe at his pleasure to revoke

f37 p 295 bot p 162   3 Nov 1645

and further doe whatsoever shall bee needfull and about the premises And lastly I do hereby doe and will ratify confirme and allowe whatsoever be or they shall lawfully doe or cause to bee done in or about the same Irrevocably In witness whereof I have hereunto sett my hand this 20 Sep 1645

In presence of   THOMAS WARD Chirurgeon
JOHN (D) DYAR
JOHN RICHARDSON

Att a County Court holden upon the 15 Dec 1645 at the howse of WM: SHIPP
Present: CAPT: THOMAS WILLOWGHBY ESQR:
CAPT: EDWARD WINDHAM   MR:ffRANCIS MASON
MR: THO: LAMBARD   MR: THOMAS MEARES
MR: EDWARD LOYD   MR: MATHEW PHILLIPPS

he administration of the estate of & belonging unto WM: DURFORD late deceased is granted unto THOMAS MARSH for and in the behalfe of the widdowe and child of the said deceased he putting insecurity to the Court

The administracon of the estate of and belonging unto THOMAS EDWARDS late deceased is granted unto RICHARD OWENS whoe is father-in-lawe to the said deceased & giving security to the Court

Whereas RICHARD KENNAR doth confesse himself to be indebted unto MR: WILLIAM JULIAN the summe of 430 lb tob. The Court doth order paymt thereof within 10 dayes with Court Charges otherwise execucon

f 37a p 296 bot p 162a   15 Dec 1645

Whereas THOMAS CASON is indebted unto the estate belonging to the Orphants of MRS SEAWELL deceased to the summe of 876 lb tob as appears unto the Court per specialty and allsoe acknowledged by the said CASON to bee justly due The Court doth therefore order the said CASON to make payment of the said tob within 10 dayes and Court Charges unto MR: MATH: PHILLIPPS whoe is guardian unto the Orphants aforenamed else exec

According to a former order of Court dated 24 Oct 1644 JOHN STRATTON is forthwith to pay unto THOMAS CASON 400 lb tob with Court Charges else exec:

Whereas JOHN SIDNEY is indebted per bill unto THOMAS BUSHRODE attorney of ROBERT WITHERALL the summe of 330 lb tob as appeares unto the Court and due the last yeare. The Court doth order the said SIDNEY to make paymt of the said tob unto the said BUSHRODE within 10 dayes with allowance pf 8 lb per cent for one yeares forbearance and the Court Charges else exec.

f 37a p 296 bot p 162a 15 Dec 1645

The Court doth order JOHN WILLIAMS before his departure from this Court to give Security by Recognizance for his good behaviour and especially towards JAMES SMYTH and personably to appeare the next Court and not to frequent noe use the company of ELIZABETH TAPLIN servant unto MRS: GOOKINS directly nor indirectly during the tyme of her service with the said MRS: GOOKIN and the said WMS: in not to come within half a mile of the dwelling howse of the said MRS: GOOKINS to have and Intercose (intercourse) with the said ELIZ: TAPLIN eyther by speech or message. And that upon any just proofe made before anyone of the Courts of the said JOHN WILLIAMS his accompanying the said ELIZ: TAPLIN during she is servant unto the said MRS: GOOKIN in any such xxxxxxx as is aforespecified Then

f 38 p 297 bot p 163 15 Dec 1645

the said JOHN WILLIAMS is to receive 20 good lashes on his bare back for his conteinued and non pformance of this order.

The Court doth order JOHN BROWNE and JOHN CLARKE to pay unto MR: MATH: PHILLIPPS Guardian unto the Orphants of MRS: SEAWELL deceased the summe of 270 lb tob and Caske due per bill with Court Charges within 10 dayes otherwise exec:

The difference depending betweene WILLM: LUCAS plt and GEORGE RUTLAND deft is referred to the next Court to bee determined. And the Court doth further order that the said RUTLAND shall enter into bond unto the sherriffe with good security for his personall appearance at the next Court and for his good behaviour in the meantyme otherwyse to remayne in the safe custody of the sheriffe And the sheriffe to have a copy of this order and to see the pformance thereof

WILLIAM CAPPS doth confesse and acknowledge himselfe to be indebted unto MR: MATH: PHILLIPPS the summe of 300 lb tob and Cske due per bill and to pay Court Charges and paymt to bee made of the sd tob within 10 dayes otherwise exec

MR: THOMAS SAYER doth confesse & acknowledge himself to bee indebted unto MRS: SARAH GOOKINS the summe of 815 lb tob due per bill and to bee paid within 10 dayes and the Court Charges otherwyse exec

THOMAS WARD doth confesse & acknowledge himself to bee justly and truely indebted unto THOMAS CASON the summe of 432 lb tob due per bill and to make paymt thereof within 10 dayes with Court Charges otherwyse exec

f38a p 298 bot p 163a 15 Dec 1645

XPOFER: BURROWHS and THOMAS KEELING by order from ROBERT doe confesse & acknowledge that ROBERT HAYES is indebted unto MR: ROBERT PAGE the summe of 1500 lb tob by 2 severall bills And the said HAYES to make paymt thereof within 10 dayes with Court Charges else exec

The Court dogh grant unto ISBELL MAUDS nowe the wife of XPOFER RIVARS a probate of the last will and testament of JOHN MUNDS her late husband deceased

The Court doth order that in Cosiderscon & satusfaccon of the Burgesses theire charges there bee levyed throughout the County 4 lb tob per polle for every tytheable person and to bee collected by the sherriffe this present yeare and to bee paid to those persons hereundernamed

To MR: BURROWGHS for his provisions	700 lb
To " " for men 10 dayes	240
To MR: HALL for his boat 10 dayes	100
To MR: IVEY for his men 25 dayes	200
To the Sherriffe for sallary @ 5 percent	060
Tis in all	1300

Whereas SAVILL GASKINE stands indebted per bill unto HENRY WESTGATE 400 lb tob and ons Caske The Court doth order paymt thereof within 10 dayes and Court Charges else exec

Whereas WILLIAM JOHNSON is in debted per bill unto ffRANCIS WELLS. 200 lb tob and Caske The Court doth order the said JOHNSON to make payment thereof unto the said WELLS within 10 dayes and the Court Charges else exec

Whereas WILLIAM JOHNSON is indebted unto SAVILL GASKINE 554 lb tob ½er bill. The Court doth order the said WILLM: JOHNSON to make payment of the said tob within 10 dayes with Court Charges else exec:

f 39 p 299 bot p 164 15 Dec 1645

Whereas THOMAS DAVYES is indebted unto SAVILL GASKINE 300lb tob and caske and confessed by the said DAVYES to bee due. The Court doth order paymt thereof within 10 dayes and the Court Charges else exec

HENRY WESTGATE doth confesse and acknowledge himself indebted unto MRS: SARAH GOOKIN 300 lb tob and to make paymt thereof within 10 dayes with Court Charges else exec

SAVILL GASKINE doth confesse and acknowledge himself to bee justly and truly indebted unto CAPT: JOHN SIBSEY 300 lb tob per bill and to make paymt thereof within 10 dayes and the Court Charges else exec

The Court doth order THOMAS TODD (OR CODD (Todd) to pay unto EDWARD DARCY and THOMAS HALL 40 lb tob a piece for theire tyme and charge and attendance at the Court 2 dayes they being subpd: to the Court at the request of the said TODD els exec

f 39 p 299 bot p 164   15 Dec 1645

THOMAS MYLES doth confesse and acknowledge himself indebted unto MR: ROBERT PAGE 524 lb tob and a Caske and for further security of the paymt thereof with the forbearance whereof the said MYLES doth promise to assigne convey & sett over his plantation & land thereunto belonging unto MR: MATH: PHILLIPPS for the use of the said MR: PAGE and to pay and to pay the Court Charges als exec

The Court doth order paymt unto WILLM: SMYTH the attorney of XPOFER: NEEDHAM of the summe of 300 lb tob due per bill from WILLIAM CAPPS and the said CAPPT:to paye the said tob within 10 dayes and the Court Charges els execucon

Whereas JAMES STARLING is indebter unto WILLIAM CAPPS 250 lb tob & Caske due per bill The Court doth order the said JAMES STARLING to pay the said tob and Caske unto the

f 39a p 300 bot p 164a 15 Dec 1645

said CAPPS within 10 dayes and STARLING to pay the Court Charges els exec

RICHARD HARTGREAVE doth confess and acknowledge himself indebted unto XPOFER: NEEDHAM 250 lb tob and to make paymt thereof unto WILLIAM SMYTH the attorney of the said NEED-HAM within 10 dayes and the Ct Chg als exec

The Court doth order WM: SMYTH to make appeare at the next Court what tobacco he hath paid or diabursed for the use of XPOFER NEEDHAM to the said SMYTH being attorney of the saidNEEDHAM And to make it appeare by certificate from the Court at Kecoughtan that those debts in question and afore-specifyed were assigned to him for such debts as he the said SMYTH hath paid for NEEDHAM or otherwyse the said SMYTH to satisfy unto THOMAS TOOKER 100 lb tob for fees and levyes due from the said NEEDHAM

JAMES LOPHAM doth confesse and acknowledge himself to be indebted per bill 500 lb tob unto MR: ROBERT PAGE and to make paymt thereof unto unto the said PAGE or his attorney within 10 dayes and the Court Charges And it is ordered that the said LOPHAM doe put in security before his depart-ure from Court To render his body to the sherriffe upon the nonpaymt of the tob within the tyme lymitts as afore-said or otherwise to bee forthwith comitted to the safe custody of the sherriffe till he have satisfd the contents of this order

The Court doth order SAMSON WARING to pay unto JOHN HOLMES 300 lb tob and Caske due per bill as appeares unto the Court And the said WARING to paye the sd tob within 10 dayes and the Ct Chgs unto the said JOHN HOLMES els exec

An attachmt is granted on the estate ofPHILLIPP TAYLOR at the suite of MRS: SARAH GOOKIN for 910 lb tob due to the said MRS: SARAH GOOKIN by 2 severall bills per the assign-ment

f 40 p 301 bot p 165   15 Dec 1645

Of HUGH LEE with consent of the said PHILLIPP TAYLOR as is alleaged and upon a legall determinacon the estate of the said TAYLOR soe attached is to bee satisfactory for the said debt of 910 lb tob aforespecyfied

Concerning the allowance of 6 barrel s of Corne unto WILLIAM LANGLEY from the Inhabitants of Elizabeth River Parish for keeping the ferry and for the more convenycency of paymt thereof. It is ordered that the constables in theire severall libitts respectively shall give notice untill all persons to bring 1½ gallons of Corne per polle by the 10 Jan next unto 2 places vizt: unto MR: PHILLIPPS and MR: JULIANS house being most convenient for the inhabitants & there transportation of the said Corne. And the said constables are hereby authorized to distrayne for 3 gallons of corne upon all delinquents

THOMAS DAVYS and RICHARD POOLE doe confesse and acknowledge themselves justly indebted unto MRS: SARAH GOOKIN the summe of 470 lb tob and to make paymt thereof unto the said MRS: GOOKINS within 10 dayes and Ct Chgs else exec

Whereas it appeares to the Court that JOHN MARTIN is indebted per bill and account 323 lb tob 323 lb tob unto CAPT: THOMAS WILLOUGHBY The Court doth order paymt thereof within 10 dayes and MARTIN to pay the Ct Chgs else exec

Whereas JAMES WARNER stands indebted unto MR: ARTHUR BROWNE 276 lb tob due per bill and being the remaynder of a greater summe wherein the said WARNER stands bownd with ROBERT BOWERS for the paymt thereof as appeares unto the Court It is ordered that paymt bee made of the said 276 lb tob from the said JAMES WARNER unto the said MR: BROWNE with the Ct. Chgs within 10 dayes else exec

An attachmmt is granted unto JAMES WARNER on the estate of ROBERT BOWERS upon legall determination to satisfy 276 lb tob and Ct. Chgs granted unto ARTHUR BROWNE by order of this Court being the proper debt of the said ROBERT BOWERS as appears unto the Court

Whereas the estate of MRS: SEAWELLS deceased is indebted unto EDWARD HOLMES 1144 lb tob as appeares unto the Court. And the sd EDWARD HOLMES being indebted per acct unto the estate of the said deceased 552 lb tob In ballancing of which accs: according to Act of Assembly. The Court doth order that MR: MATH: PHILLIPPS guardian unto the Orphants of the sd deceased shall pay unto the said EDWARD HOLMES 592 lb tob our of the said deceaseds estate within 10 dayes else exec

Whereas John ARIS (HARRIS) is indebted per bill 400 lb tob and caske assigned unto ARTHUR BROWNE and the said MR: BROWNE being indebted 12 lb tob unto the said ARIS as appeares unto this Court In ballancing of which accts according to Act of Accembly the Court doth order the said

f 40a p 302 bot p 165a 15 Dec 1645

ARIS to pay unto the said MR: BROWNE 388 lb tob and Caske with the Ct Chgs within 10 dayes else exec

The difference depending betweene ARTHUR BROWNE attorney of HUGH LEE plt against JOHN ARIS deft concerning a debt of 600 lbtob and Caske due per bill and payeable the 27 Nov 1644 upon the allegacon of the said ARIS that there was a collaterall agreemt made by the said HUGH LEE and him the sd ARIS since the said bill entred into is refered to the next Court to be heard and determined. And the said ARIS in the meanetyme is ordered forthwith to give security unto the sherriffe to stand to the tenure and abyde the censure of the Court in Case

f 41 p 303 bot p 166 15 Dec 1645 he doth not prove that there was a Collaterall agreemt as is aforespecifyed

Whereas JOHN WILLIAMS is indebted unto ARTHUR BROWNE 494 lb tob and caske per bill assigned. And it appearing to the Court upon oath of the said WMS: that 375 lb tob was for wyne. It is ordered according to Act of Assembly that the said WMS: shall paye 241 lb tob and Caske xxx?xxx being part of the 494 lb tob aforesaid with Court Chgs within 10 dayes and residue of the said tob the next yeare according to Act of Assembly And not to depart the sherriffes Custody till he give security for payment thereof as aforesaid

An attachmt is granted unto RICHARD KENNAR CHIRURGEON for the summe of 430 lb tob on the estate of JOHN NORRWOOD remayning in the hands of MR: WILLIAM JULIAN to bee satisfactory for the said debt upon a legall determination

The Court doth order that WILLIAM JOHNSON shall paye unto EDWARD CHISSELL 400 lb tob and Caske due per bill as appeares unto this Court paymt to bee made of the said tob within 10 dayes & the Ct Chgs else exec

Whereas ROBERT LOVEDAY stands indebted unto THOMAS WELLS the assignee of FRANCIS HUNT in the summe of 378 lb tob and 2 Caske dueper bill as appeares unto the Court. It is ordered that the said LOVEDAY shall make paymt of the said 378 lb tob as aforesaid and the 2 Caskes unto the said THOMAS WELLS with the CT Chgs within 10 dayes else exec

The Court doth order that JOHN BOLTON shall pay unto ENSIGNE KEELING 40 lb tob for his charges and tyme in attendance the Court being subpd: for a wittnes at the request of the said BOLTON in a cause hereto fore depending between the said BOLTON AND LANCASTER LOVETT defendants else exec

f 41a p 304 bot p 166a 15 Dec 1645

Whereas THOMAS WARD is indebted unto THOMAS TOOKER for levyes and fees 582 lb tob due the last yeare as appeares unto the Court. The Court doth thereupon thinke fitt and accordingly order that THOMAS TOOKER shall discount the said 582 lb tob with the said WARD out of the 600 lb tob which is awarded out of the levyes by the last Assembly to bee paid the said WARD for his paynes being Chirurgeon at the Chickohommie March else exec

Whereas RICHARD CONQUEST hath exhibited unto the Court an account of certaine Clarkes fees with charges & other expences amounting to the summe of 976 lb tob & claymed to be due unto the said CONQUEST from JOHN YEATS who being arrested unto this Court and not appearing Nevertheless the Court upon perusall of the said account doe fynd that some of the fees menconed in the account did aryse at his Maties suite and the expenses were occasioned thereby and some part of the fees did accrewe for the said YEATS his owne particular. Whereupon the Court doth concerne that the fees which are claymed at his Maties suite according to the Act of Assembly are to bee pformed ex officio but for the charges occasioned and those fees which concerne the said YEATS his owne pticular ought to be paid and satisfyed by the said YEATS And therefore the Court in consideracon of the said account of 976 lb tob aforespeci-fyed doe order the said YEATS to paye unto the said RICHARD CONQUEST within 10 dayes 600 lb tob in full of the said account aforemenconed else exec

Whereas SIMON DREW and MARGARET EVANS were presented unto the Court for Incontciency And the Act plainly appearing soe to bee by the open confession of the said partyes accused It is therefore ordered by the Court that the said SYMON DREW doe pennance in a white sheete the next

f 42 p 305 bot p 167 15 Dec 1645

next sabboath daye that the minister preacheth in the parish Church of Elizabeth River in the face of the whole congregation then assembled and aske allmighty God for-giveness for his hanious act in such manner and using such words as according to the Lawes and customes are provided in such cases such offences being committed. And the said MARGARET EVANS shall receive 19 good lashes on her bare back in presence of an at the next Court which shall happen to bee after her delivery of the child she nowe goeth withall

Whereas it appeares unto the Court that MR: MATHEW PHILLIPPS hath gotten with child MARY ROWGE (or ROUGE) whoe is deliv=ered thereof and being a servant unto the Orphants of MRS: SEAWELL deceased the said Orphants are dampinfyed thereby in their estate. In consideration thereof It is ordered that the said MR: PHILLIPPS according to Act of Assembly shall pay or satisfy unto the estate of the said orphants

f 42 p 305 bot p 167   15 Dec 1645

600 lb tob for the dammages thereby occasioned in sort as aforesaid and it is further ordered that the said MR: PHILLIPPS shal give good caution with sufficient security bot to mayntaine the Child and to discharge the parish thereof

The Court doth order that MR: MATH: PHILLIPPS shall pay 1000 lb tob for a fine for his act of Incontinency with MARY ROUGE and the said MR: PHILLIPPS is to 300 lb tob thereof unto RICHARD CONQUEST according to a former order made at the last session of this Court and the other 700 lb tob MR: PHILLIPPS is to pay unto the Sherrife whoe is hereby ordered to collect the same and the paymt to bee made by the 15 Jan next And the 700 lb tob residue of the said fine is to be disposed of for the use of the parish of Elizabeth River and in such manner as the Court shall hereafter thinke fitt to dispose thereof

f 42a p 306 bot p 167a 15 Dec 1645

The Court doth order that MARY ROUGE shall forthwith and in presence of the Court receive 39 good lashes on her bare back and at or before Mooneday next to depart the howse where she nowe liveth and ever after the said MARY ROUGE shall not frequent nor come to the howse belonging to the Orphants of MRS: SEAWELL deceased upon payne of such punishmt as the Court shall thinke fitt further to inflict upon her the said MARY ROUGE upon any just proofe of her misdemeanor thereof and Contempt of this order

(Note: Is the reason for the large fine and excessive punishment of MARY because MATHEW PHILLIPPS is a Commissioner? AGW)

Whereas LAWRENCE RICHARDSON and SARAH KING were presented unto the Court for Incontinency and the act plainely appearing soe to bee by the open confession of the said partyes accused It is therefore ordered by the Court that the said LAWRENCE RICHARDSON doe pennance in a white sheete the next Sabbath daye that the Minister preacheth in the Parish Church of Elizabeth River in the face of the whole congregacon than assembled and aske allmighty God forgiveness for his hanious act in such manner and using such words as according to the Lawes and Customes are provided in such cases such offences being Committed and the said SARA KINGE shall receive 19 good lashes on her bare back in presence of and at the next session of this Court

Whereas it appeares by a specialty produced under the hand of THOMAS TOOKER and by him alsoe confessed that the said TOOKER is indebted unto HUGH LEE 144 lb tob which is assigned unto ARTHUR BROWNE by the said HUGH LEE. It is ordered that the said TOOKER shall not be released out of the Custody of the Sherriffe till he make paymt thereof unto the said BROWNE with the charges   else execucon

f43 p 307 bot p 168   15 Dec 1645

Whereas by order of this Court bearing date the 15 Feb 1643/4 by the acknowledgmt of ROBERT HAYES that he stood indebted unto MR: CORNELIUS LOYD 400 lb tob Paymt was ordered to bee made of the said tob upon demand otherwise exec: which said order is revived by this Court and to bee in force as formerly to all intents and purposes whatsoever

This bill byndeth mee ROBERT LOVEDAY my heires & c to pay or cause to bee paid unto WILLIAM SHIPP or his assignes the full and just summe of 255 lb of good sownd merchantable tob in leafe with sufficient caske to bee paid in Elizabeth River at or upon the 10 Oct next after the date hereof And for better security I the said ROBERT LOVEDAY doe bynd over one Bull of 4 yeares old which is nowe in the Custody of PARSON WILKISON at Kecoughtan marked thus vizt with the Swallowtayle on the right eare and a hole underneath and its colour black and to the true pformance hereof I have hereunto sett my hand this Dec 1645
Signed and delivered in
the presence of us
JOHN FFINCH   ROBERT LOVEDAY
THOMAS (TV) WATTERS

This bill bindeth mee SAVILL GASKINE my heires or assignes to paye or cause to bee paid unto WILLIAM SHIPP his heires orassignes the full and just quantity of 1118 lb of good sownd. merchantable tob in leafe and Caske due to bee paid without fraud or deceit at or upon the 10 Oct next ensueing the date hereof and for

f 43a p 308 bot p 168a 16 Dec 1645

better security I said GASKINE doe bynd and sett over unto the said WILLIAM SHIPP one bobtayle Cowe commonly knowne by the name of Nansey and 2 yearling steares cropy and slitt in the left Eare the said Cowe and steares are at the nowe dwelling howse of the said GASKINE In witness hereof I have hereunto sett my hand thia 16 Dec 1645
Signed in presence of
THOMAS WARD   SAVILL GASKINE
THOMAS TUCKER

This byll bindeth mee THOMAS MYLES MY HEIRES & c to paye or cause to bee paid unto WILLIAM SHIPP or his assignes the full and just quantity of 830 lb tob with good sefficient Caske to bee paid without fraud or deceit to bee paid in Elizabeth River at or upon the 10 Oct next after the date hereof and for the better security thereof I THOMAS MYLES doe bynd over 2 Cowes one called by the name of Cherry the other by the name of Jewell marked thus That is to saye Cropt on the left eare and slitt on the Right Eare the one being about 3 years old the other being at the howse of the said THOMAS MYLES in wittness my hand this 16 Dec 1645

f 43a p 308 bot p 168a 16 Dec 1645

Signed and delivered in presence of
JOHN ffINCH   THOMAS (X) MYLES
WM: OLIVER

Recordat 15 Dec 1645 *(Note date items above dated 16 Dec)*
A noat of the goods of JOHN MOY deceased sould at an Outcry MR: HENRY WOODHOWSE being present thereat
Sold to MARTIN COLE 2 old broad Axes 2 Agers, 2 Adses, 2 plaines, 2 Chissells, 1 hand sawe for 82 lb tob

(Continued--

f 44 p 309 bot p 169   16 Dec 1645

Sould to ROBERT DAVYES 2 crosse Sawes, 3 Iron Wedges, 1 drawing knife, 1 frowe?, 1 hammer,1 old Axe, 1 Iron ring for 290 lb tob
Sould to WILLIAM EADY 1 whipsawe and 1 gunne for 152 lb tob,
Sould to SAMUELL CHARNIKOE 1 old Chest, 1 smoothing Iron, 1 flintstone, 1 tray, 1 payle and some other olf Lumber for 154 lb tob
Sould PETER GRINTO 2 hatts, for 142 lb tob
Sould to RICHARD HILL 2 Andirons, 2 Iron spitts for 150 lb tob

Sould to WILLIAM JOHNSON Some old Iron and Brasse for 36 lb tob
Sould to ROBERT DAVYES 1 wedding Ring for 231 lb tob
Sould to ROBERT DAVYES 1 Gunne for 231 lb tob
Sold SAMUELL CHARNIKO 4 Pewter dishes and a skillett for 136lb tob

Sold to WILLIAM JOHNSON 3 pewter disher, 6 old Porringers, 2 salt sellars for 134 lb tob
Sold to SAMUELL CHARNIKO 1 Iron pott andpestell & 1 frying
f44a p 310 bot p169a   1 frying pann for 270 lb tob
Sold to ROBERT DAVYES 4 Pewter dishes 1 pewter quart pott for 202 lb tob

Sold to WILLIAM JOHNSON 1 fetherbedd and a bolster for 410 lb tob
Sold to MR: HENRY WOODHOWSE 1 warming pann for 66 lb tob

Att a County Court holden at the howse of ROBERT HAYES
16 Feb 1645/6

Present: CAPT THOMAS WILLOUGHBY ESQR:

CAPT: EDWARD W DHAM	MR: HENRY WOODHOWSE
MR: ffRANCIS MASON	MR: THOMAS MEARES
MR: THOMAS LAMBART	MR: MATH: PHILLIPPS
MR: EDWARD LOYD	

The Court doth order that an administration bee granted unto ELIZABETH ffEILDGATE on the estate of PHILLIPP ffEILDGATE her late husband deceased she entring into bond with good security for the safety of the Court & to pforme the act

Whereas RICHARD HARTGRAVE stands indebted unto the estate of or belonging to the Orphants of MRS: SEAWELL deceased 220 lb tob due by bill. The court doth order present payment thereof to bee made unto MR: MATH: PHILLIPPS whoe is guardian unto the said Orphants with Court Chgs else exec f 44a p 310 bot p 169a

Whereas certaine matters of difference concerning accounts were debated of betweene JOHN MARTIN and THOMAS WARD

f 45 p 311 bot p 170   16 Feb 1645/6

In full balancing thereof It is ordered that the said WARD shall presently pay unto the said MARTIN 57 lb tob and the Ct Chgs And generall discharge to bee forthwith drawne between them the said WARD and MARTIN for all matters whatsoever else exec

The Court doth grant unto JOHN GEATHER and administration on the estate of HENRY WALTERS late deceased the said GEATHER entring into bond with security for the saving harmlesse of the Court and to pforme the Act

The Court doth order that MRS: GOOKINS shall discharge THOMAS DAVYES from FLORENTYNE PAYNE soncerning a debt due by bill for 110 lb tob stript and smoothed And the said MRS: GOOKINS is further ordered to pay 27 lb tob unto the said DAVYES with the Court Charges else exec

Upon the humble request of JOHN WILLIAMS by the assent and in presence of JAMES SMYTH The Court doth discharge and Remitt the said WILLIAMS of and concerning his bond or Recognizance formerly taken by order of this Court for the peace and good behavior of him the said WILLIAMS towards and concerning the said JAMES SMYTH And williams to pay the Ct Chgs else exec

Whereas RICHARD ffORSTER residing out of this Collony according to letters imported hath not sent nor made any retorne of goods unto LANCASTER LOVETT in leiwe of 1350 lb tob with Caske by the said ffOSTER formerly receaved from ye

f 45a p 312 bot p 170a 16 Feb 1645/6

said LANCASTER LOVETT as hath sufficiently appeared unto this Court by former testimony. It is nowe ordered according to the true intent or meaning of a former order of this Court that RICHARD WORSTER being the attorney of the said ffOSTER shall forthwith satisfy and pay unto the said LANCASTER LOVETT out of the estate of the said RICHARD ffOSTER 1500 lb tob and Caske with the CourtCarges in full satisfacon of the said 1350 lb tob and Caske aforespecifyed and the forbearance thereof else exec to yssue forth against the said ffORSTERS estate remayning in the Custody or possession of the said RICHARD WORSTER for the said 1500 lb tob & Caske & Ct Chgs else exec

The difference betweene THOMAS WARD attorney of RICHARD PINNER and FRANCIS LAND is referred to the next session of the Court to bee heard and determined

The presentmt of EDWARD HALL and JOHN MARTIN Churchwardens of Lynhaven Parish for thia present yeare 1645

f 45a p 312 bot p 170a 16 Feb 1645/6

They and eyther of them present CLEMENT THEOBALD of Lynhaven Singleman and ELIZABETH HALL his woman servant for living and continency in apparent fornication soe as a bastard Sonne was lately borne of her, and as wee are informed she hath charged JOHN POWYS the sonne of MR: ROBERT POWYS to bee the father of ye same. In witness whereo whereof wee have hereunto sett our hands this 16 Feb 1645
ROBT: POWYS Clicus EDWARD HALL his mark
JOHN MARTIN

f 46 p 313 bot p 171 16 Feb 1645/6

Allsoe they and eyther of them further say and present one JOHN NORRIS servant to THOMAS CASON. That the said NORRIS was taken lyeing with the said ELIZABETH HALL as by farther testimony it may hereafter appeare
ROBERT POWYS CLK
EDW: (X) HALL
JOHN MARTIN

The Court doth order that CLEMENT THEOBALDS and ELIZABETH HALL and JOHN POWYS and JOHN NORRIS doe make theire personall appearance at the next Court to answer unto such misdemeanors and matters of presentmt: as are and shall bee objected to against them. And the sherriffe to take security for theire appearance accordingly

The Matters in question betweene WM: LUCAS Plt and GEORGE RUTLAND deft is referred to the next session of this Court to bee heard and determined

Whereas MAUDLIN PARKER the servant of CAPT: THOMAS WILL_ OWGHBY was ordered to receive punishmt by Whipping for beinge delivered of a child unlawfully gotten by JOHN SUTTON It is ordered upon the hearty contricon of the said MAUDLIN that the punishment of whipping bee wholly remitted And that the said MAUDLIN and SUTTON shall both doe pennance in a white sheete the next Sabbath day in the Parish Church of Elizabeth River in such manner as is provided and accustomed in such cases

THOMAS CASON doth asknowledge a Judgemt presently to posse against his whole estate for satisfaccon of 753 lb tob due unto MR: ROBERT

f 46a p 314 bot p 171a 16 Feb 1645/6

PAGE per two severall bills And the said CASON to pay the Ct Chgs else exec

Whereas GEORGE KEMP hath beene taxed for killing of hoggs and the Court finding some cause of suspicion thereof doe order that the said GEORGE KEMP shall not hunt with doggs in the woods nor shoote of any gunne but in his owne defence if occasion happen or in the plantation where he liveth. And this order by bee in force during the Courts pleasures

f46a p 314 bot p 171a 16 Feb 1645/6

Whereas ROGER WILLIAMS and RICHARD WORSTER did assigne over unto ARTHUR BROWNE on bill of 500 lb tob and caske due from ffRANCIS LAND which said bill of debt was formerly assigned over by ROBT: SMYTH late deceased unto the said WILLIAMS and WORSTER This Court upon due examination doe fynd that ffRANCIS LAND according to a tre sent him under the handwryting of ROBERT SMYTH being the first Creditor did satisfy the debt of 500 lb tob and Caske aforespecifyed unto JACOB BRADSHAWE before any assignment made as aforesd of the bill in question

Whereas WILLIAM SMYTH is indebted unto JOHN MARTIN per account as appeareth unto the Court the summe of 181 lb tob The Court doth order the said SMYTH to make present paymt of the aforesaid debt unto the said JOHN MARTIN with the Court Chg else exec

f 47 p 315 bot p 172 16 Feb 1645/6

The differences depending betweene THOMAS DAVYES plt against JOHN BAKER deft et e contra are referred to the next sitting of the Court to bee heard and determined And ye said BAKER to putt in security before his departure from Court for his departure from Court for his appearance accordingly

Whereas it appeares unto ths Court that ROBERT LOVEDAY is indebted 300 lb tob and caske per bill unto JOHN BAKER present payment is ordered to bee made of the said tobacco and the Ct Chgs unto the said BAKER FROM ROBERT LOVEDAY aforenamed else exec

Whereas WILLIAM EADY is indebted unto JOHN BAKER 200 lb tob as appeares unto the Court. Paymt is ordered to be made thereof with the Ct Chgs else exec

An attachmt is granted on the estate of JOHN GODFREY at the suite of RICHARD CONQUEST for a debt of 1068 lb tob and caske and for soe much os the said GODFREYS estate as may bee esponsible and satisfactory for the said debt with damages and charges it the Court hereafter doe soe determine

Whereas it appeares unto this Court that THOMAS TOOKER is indebted unto RICHARD CONQUEST 500 lb tob per bill and 190 lb tob per account acknowledged to bee

f 47a p 316 bot p 172a 15 Feb 1645/6

justly due unto the said CONQUEST The Court doth accordingly order the said TOOKER to make present payment of the tobacco before menconed being 690 lb in all with Court Charges els exec

Whereas WILLIAM EAST late deceased in his life tyme was ordered to pay unto RICHARD POOLE 400 lb tob and caske with certaine charges menconed in a former order of this Court. It is nowe therefore ordered that JOHN STRATTON whoe is administrator with the said EAST deceased doe satisfy the said the said 400 lb tob with the Charges aforemenconed unto

f 47a p 316 bot p 172a 15 Feb 1645/6

the said RICHARD POOLE with other Court Charges since expended out of the daid deceaseds estate else exec

Whereas WILLIAM EAST deceased in his lyfetyme stood indebted unto LANCASTER LOVETT 235 lb tob as appeares unto the Court Paymt is ordered to bee made of the said tob out of the deceaseds estate by JOHN STRATTON adm: thereof else exec

WILLIAM EADY one of the administrators of the estate of JOHN MOY deceased and one of the guardians of the Orphants pf the said deceased in the behalfe of the said Orphants doth asknowledge a Judgmt against the estate of or belonging to the said Orphants to satisfy a debt of 230 lb tob due per bill unto ROBERT HAYES whoe is the lawfull asignee of JEFFREY WRIGHT else exec

f 48 p 317 bot p 173 15 Feb 1645/6

Whereas BARTHOLOMEW HOSKINS is indebted unto RICHARD KENNAR 2000 lb tob per bill and there appearing a collaterall agreement made by the said KENNAR and MARTIN since the said Bill entred into the Court doth accordingly order by consent of both partyes that MARTIN shall paye and satisfy 600 lb tob present and 600 lb tob the next cropp unto the said RICHARD KENNAR in full of the said 2000 lb tob debt with Court Charges else exec

Whereas MR: HENRY SEAWELL deceased in his lyfetyme did promise to deliver unto JOHN HOLMES one double Rugg which as yet is not delivered as appeares unto the Court. MR: MATT: PHILLIPPS being guardian unto the orphants of the said deceased is hereby ordered to make present satisfaccon for the said Rugg aforementioned unto the said JOHN HOLMES out of the said orphants estate else exec

Whereas it appeares to the Court that HENRICK LIGHTHART is indebted per account unto THOMAS CHEELY 274 lb tob It is therefore ordered that the said HENRICK LIGHTHART doe make present payment of the said 274 lb tob with Court Charges unto the said CHEELY else exec

f 48a p 318 bot p 173a 15 Feb 1645/6

According to an Act of Assembly The Court doth grant Judgmt against the sherriffe for to pay 320 lb tob and Court Charges appearing due per bill unto MR: THOMAS MARSH from DEBORAH GLASCOCK the relict and administrator of ROBERT GLASCOCK late deceased

According to an act of Assembly the Court doth grant unto the Sherriffe an attachment agaist the body or estate of DEBORAH GLASCOCK widdow for 320 lb tob with the Court Charges and the estate or body soe attached to bee responsable for the aforesaid tob as the Court shall then determine thereof

f 48a p 318 bot p 173a 15 Feb 1645/6

Whereas SAMSON WARING is indebted unto GYLES COLLINGS 426 lb tob & Caske as appeares unto the Court ordered that present paymt bee made of the aforesaid tob with court charges from the said WARING unto the said COLLINGS else exec

Whereas JOHN RIGG hath complayned against DEBORAH GLASCOCK his late Mrs (Mistress?) for certaine apparrel due to him for his servitude according to the Custome of the Country. The said matter in question is referred to MR: EDWARD LOYD to consider thereof and I heare and determine the same

Upon due proffe made that HENRICK LIGHTHART hath transported JOHN GUTTERRIDGE out of this Collony into Mariland contrary to Act of Assembly. It is accordingly ordered that the said LIGHTHART shall forthwith enter into bond with security for payment of 803 lb tob at the next cropp unto HENRY SNAYLE whoe is

f 49 p 319 bot p 174 15 Feb 1645/6

the just Creditor of the said GUTTERFIDGE for soe much as appeares unto the Court

Upon due and legall proofe made That HENR: LIGHTHART hath transported JOHN GUTTERGIDGE out of this Collony into Mariland contrary to Act of Assembly. It is accordingly ordered that the said LIGHTHART shall forthwith enter into bond with security to paye 795 lb tob and caske at the next cropp Unto HENRY BRAKES whoe is the next Creditor of the said GUTTERIDGE for soe much as appeares unto the board

Upon acknowledgmt of ENSIGNE LAMBART to bee justly in debted 830 lb tob with caske unto the orphants of MRS: SEAWELL deceased. The Court doth order that the said ENSIGNE LAMBARD shall forthwith make payment thereof with Court Charges unto MR: PHILLIPPS who is guardian unto the said Orphants else execucon

The Court doth order that JOHN MERRIDAY shall pay unto MR: PHILLIPPS guardian unto the orphans of MRS: SEAWELL deceased 69 lb tob for the use of the said orphants being the proper debt of ROBERT SMITH deceased with whome the said MERRIDAY was Copartner as appeares to the Court

Whereas by a former order of this Court the sherriffe hath attached the proper estate of JOHN GUTTERIDGE (vizt) 9 barrells of Indian Corne in the hands of HENRY SNAYLE and allsoe a specialty of 550 lb tob and caske due from CHRISTOPHER BURROUGHS for the use of MR: PHILLIPPS towards satisfactiicon of a certaine debt of

f 49a p 320 bot p 174a 15 Feb 1645/6

300 lb tob due from the said GUTTERIDGE as appeares unto the Court It is ordered that the said 9 barrells of Corne bee appraised by the sherriffe according to act and delivered

f 49a p 320 bot p 174a 15 Feb 1645/6

to the said MR: PHILLIPPS for and towards the satisfaccon of the said debt aforemenconed and Ct Chgs and that the said BURROUGHS bee impleaded by the said MR: PHILLIPPS at the next court for the said 550 lb tob and caske aforemenconed and towards the Remaynder of what shall be left unsatisfyed and if any overplus then to bee disposed of according to further order

Whereas WILLIAM CAPPS stands indebted unto WM: SHIPP 423 lb tob being the remaynder of a specialty of 623 lb tob Payment is ordered to bee maed of the said 423 lb tob and Court Charges unto the said WILLIAM SHIPP else exec

Whereas it appeares unto the Court that THOMAS MARSH being the attorney of THOMAS SAYER hath disbursed out of his owne estate 1130 lb tob 2 yeares since for the proper use and behalfe of the said MR: THOMAS SAYER in the discharge of an execucon It is thereup ordered that the said SAYER shall forthwith pay or satisfy the said 1130 lb tob with 2 yeares forbearance at 8 lb per cent & Court Charges unto the said THOMAS MARSH otherwyse exec

f 50 p 321 bot p 175 15 Feb 1645/6

EDWARD HALL administrator of the estate of THOMAS COWPER deceased according to Act hath exhibited his account xx ?xxx the said deceaseds estate which by serious perusall and due examinacon thereof. The Court doth fynd the said EDWARD HALL to have paid beyond Assets

Whereas the sherriffe by order hath amongst divers papers and wrytings attached for a debt of 300 lb tob due unto ffRANCIS LAND from WILLIAM DAVYES whoe is departed this Collony 2 bills of debt due to the said DAVYES vizt one from WILLIAM SMYTH of 120 lb tob and the other due from WILLIAM EAST deceased of 70 lb tob. The Court doth give lycence unto the said ffRANCES LAND to demand and receive or else legally implead the said bills or specialtyes aforemenconed in or towards satisfaccon of his debt of 300 lb tob aforesaid

The Court doth grant unto JOHN MERRIDAY the copartner of ROBERT SMYTH late deceased an administration of the estate pf the said deceased provided he put in Security to discharge the Court and pforme the Act

It is ordered that JOHN MERRIDAY after an administration of the estate of ROBERT SMYTH late deceased and exemplified according to Act shall by sufficient deed or other conveyance in the lawe release and extinguish all his right and tytle unto WILLIAM SMYTH brother of the said deceased of such certainecattle which properly and particularly belonged unto the said ROBERT SMYTH and exempted from copartnershipp And that the said WILLIAM SMYTH doe discharge certaine Cattle at Blunt Poynt which were in Copartnershipp betweene the said ROBERT SMYTH and MERRIDAY from all

f 50a p 322 bot p 175a 15 Feb 1645/6

Charges and arrears not exceeding 300 lb tob or 3 barrells of Corne besides the keeping of the said Cattle

The Court doth order ENSIGNE LAMBARD to pay unto MR: CORNELIUS LOYD 300 lb tob which ENSIGNE LAMBARD detaynes in his hands being justly due to the said MR: LOYD appeares to the Court else exec

Whereas an execucon was lately granted and executed on the body of EDWARD HALL at the suite of THOMAS CASON for certaine charges menconed by an order of this Court And the said CASON having demanded 140 lb tob more then was due or really intended by the said order The Court doth require and command that deduction bee and an abatement made of the said 140 lb tobaforesaid by the said CASON else exec

Whereas THOMAS WARD attached 5 barrells of Corne belonging unto MR: WOODHOWSE and prosecuted his suite. It is ordered that the sd MR: WOODHOWSE shall by 2 sufficient men veiwe the said corne by measuring the same and certify unto the Court what dammage of shrinkeadge the said Corne hath Sustayned

Whereas CAPT: JOHN SIBSEY, MR: THOMAS IVEY and RICHARD CONQUEST have beene presented to the Court by an Inquest; Upon request made by the parties aforenamed Respite is granted until the next Court to traverse the said presentmts or otherwise to stand to the Censure of the Board

f 51 p 323 bot p 176 15 Feb 1645/6

Whereas MARY ROUGE was ordered to receive punishmt by whipping for being delivered of a child unlawfully begott as by a former order of this Court may appeare. Nowe upon the hearty contrition and sorrow of the said MARY ROUGE for her said offence The court doth alter the said punishmt into a ffyne and order the said MARY ROUGE to pay to the use of the County 500 lb tob for redemption of her said punishment els exec

An attachmt is granted unto ENSIGNE LAMBART on the estate which was formerly belonginge unto THOMAS HOLT DECEASED TO SATISFY a flock bedd or the value thereof upon legall determination of the Court

An attachmt is granted unto HENRICK LIGHTHART on the estate of or anywayes belonging unto JOHN GUTTERIDGE to bee responsable and satisfactory for such paymts or debts as the said HENRICK LIGHTHART is lyable to and as the Court shall further determine thereof

The Court doth order that MR: CORNELIUS LOYD shall pay unto JOHN GODFREY 25 lb tob per daye for his work done upon MRS: GOOKINS pinnace

f 52 p 323 bot p 176   15 Feb 1645/6

Recordat: 16 Feb 1645/6
An Inventory of the estate of THOMAS COWPER deceased.

Imprs:	1 bedd and Rugg an Auger, an axe, 2 suite of clothes	150
Imprs:	a Cowe and Calfe	750
"	a Cowe	650
"	a bull	500
"	a heifar Calfe & steere yearling	500

(continued on next page)

f 51a p 324 bot p 176a   15 Feb 1645/6

Imprs:	4000 nayles, 2 paire of shoes, a servants wastcoat, a Monmouth capp	300
"	a gunne, carpenters tooles & 2 bare skinnes	200
"	1 steare 3 yeares old & the vantage	500
"	400 acres of land in 2 Patents	800
		4350

(Note: see NU 168-200 acs to EDW HALL adm of THOS: COOPER 1646, 10 Jun)

JOHN (/X/)STRATTON
ffRANCIS LAND

Receaved of WALTER PRESSAR		050 1
"	tob due from EDW: HALL	040
	The Totall is	4440

Paid per me EDW: HALL out of the estate of THOMAS COOP(ER) deceased

Imprs:	to ffRANCIS LAND p order	700 lb
"	to ENSIGNE THO: KEELING porder	503
"	to LANCASTER LOVETT p order	561
"	to THOMAS DAVYES p order	1008
"	to THOMAS CASON p order	350
	Debtor to EDW: HALL	3162
	to CAPT: THO: WILLOWGHBY with caske	900
	ffor carrying out the same tob	020
	ffor one goat at the ffunerall	150
	ffor receiving of a Patent	050

f 52 p 325 bot p 177   16 Feb 1645/6

Imprs	for a letter of administracon	060
"	for a peticon for the estate	008
"	for the Copye of an order	008
"	for expenses & charges to myselfe	100
		1296
	The Totall	4458

Coopers estate is debtor to EDWARD HALL Executor thereof per a probate of the will	0050
	4508

f 52 p 325 bot p 177   16 Feb 1645/6

Recordat: 16 Feb 1645
This bill byndeth mee HENRY NEEDHAM of Linhaven byndeth mee HENRY NEEDHAM of Linhaven, planter my heires &c to pay or cause to bee paid unto ENS: THOMAS KEELING of the same place his heires &c the full and just summe of 800 lb tob of good sownd merchantable tob and caske together with one Cowe which goeth by the name Woodward marked with a Cropp on the right eare and slitt in the Cropp and underheeled and slitt on the right eare and one pyde? heifar white of the back and white -nder the belly marked with a swallowe thart? on the left eare and slitt and and underheeled on the right eare to the true pformance hereof & bynd mee my heires &c to pay the said debt at or before the 10 Oct next after the date hereof wittness my hand this 20 Oct 1645
In presence of us: HENRY NEEDHAM
THOMAS ALLEN, EDWARD CANNON

f 52a p 326 bot p 177a   16 Feb 1645/6

Rocorded: in Court 16 Feb 1645/6
To all to whome this present writing shall concerne knowe ye that I ENSIGNE THOMAS KEELING of the Parish of Lynhaven in the County of Lower Norff planter doe by these presents turne over unto, as a deed of guift, ADAM KEELING my true and lawfull sonne One cowe which goeth by the name of white Foote marked with swallow whart of both eares with small piece cutt under the right eare with all the female encrease which cowe I the said THO: KEELING HAVE endeavoured to procure out of an Ewe Goate and her encrease given by CAPT: ADAM THOROWGOOD deceased and hath beene carefully looked after for him the said ADAM KEELINGS benefitt. To the true meaning of this truth I bynd myself my heires &c and have hereunto sett my hand and seale this 24 Apr 1645
Signed, sealed and delivered
in presence of us   THOMAS (X) KEELING
JOHN MARYE (or Wacye),   AND SEALE
THOMAS ALLEN, JEFFREY (X) WYGHT

Whereas I THOMAS WARD have assigned unto xpofer BURROWGHS all such pay or wages as were due me for my service to Yawopan als Rowanoke and whereas 1000 lb tob is appoynted to bee paid mee for the said service I doe hereby acknowledge Judgmt against the said 1000 lb tob to the said XPOFER BURROWGHS in part payment of a debt of 3000 lb tob due to the said XPOFER from mee witness my hand
THOMAS WARD

f53 p 327 bot p 178   16 Feb 1645/6

Recordat 16 Feb 1645/6 Memo: I SAMUELL CHARNIKOE doe give from mee my heires &c to OLIVE STRATTON daughter to JOHN STRATTON one Cowe Calfe marked on the right Eare slitt and a peice cutt out under the Eare and a peice cutt out on the upper side of the eare as witness my hand this 15 Feb 1645/6

Wittness at present   SAM (ſſ) CHARNIKE
THOMAS ALLEN

Recordat 16 Feb 1645/6 Memo: That whereas I THOMAS SAWYER did receive of THOMAS MARSH at my last goeing for England a bond for certaine moneyes due from MR: THOMAS RINGALL to the wyfe of the said THOMAS MARSH. I doe hereby bynd myselfe to bee responsable for the same as witness my hand this 19 Jan 1645/6

Know all men by these presents that I WM: DURFORD of elizabeth Ruver Shipwright for divers Causes mee herewith moveing have bargained and sold and doe by these presents bargaine, sell and deliver unto Xpofer BUSTIAN one black Coulored Cowe cropt on both eares a slitt into and two pieces taken from underneath, one yearling Cowe Calfe pyde collored of the aforesaid marke one black bull yearling Cropt on both eares a slitt in the neare eare to have hold and injoy the aforesaid Cattle with theire encrease to him and his heires, exors &c and to his

f 53a p 328 bot p 178a   16 Feb 1645/6

or theire owne proper use and benefitt Without the lett hinderance or disturbance of him ye said WILLIAM DURFORD his heires &c forever. In wittness whereof I have hereunto sett my hand this 30 Sep 1645

Signed & delivered in presence of   WILL DURFORD
EDD: LOYD, THOMAS TOOKER

16 Feb 1645/6 Knowe all men that I ARTHUR BROWNE of London merchant doe hereby release, discharge, exonerate and acquitt PETER PORTER of Elizabeth River blacksmyth fully, freely and absolutely of and from all debts, dues & demands, bills, bonds, wrytings and accounts, suits, actions, cause of action and Judgmts whatsoever from the beginning of the World to this present daye first above written Wittness whereof I have hereunto sett my hand

In presence of   p mee ARTHUR BROWNE
XPOFER BURROUGH
HENRY CATELIN

Receaved by mee RICHARD DOLEMAN for the use of JOHN JEWITT Comander of the ship "Sevill Merchant" of THOMAS BROMBLE for the use of ARTHUR BROWNE merchant the some of 680 lb

f 54 p 329 bot p 179   16 Feb 1645/6

tob hereby discharging and acquitting ye sd ARTHUR BROWNE concerning his bill

f 54 p 329 bot p 179   16 Feb 1645/6

for the said debts wittness my hand
from aboard the Shipp   JOHN JEWITT 1645
Sevill merchant

Recordat 17 Feb 1645/6 London the 5 Jan 1642/3
MR: CESAR PUGGETT these are to certify you that nowe I have receaved according to two former bills of exchange and your letters the money of my LORD MORLEY though with some trouble and am sorry that I had it not sooner are soe many that I am glad I have it nowe though I cannot send the returne this tyme, it shall bee made good to you by the first the next yeare or if any goe away from hence this yeare after these that are gone and did Intend to have sent some other things to you but wee have had and have such hard and miserable tymes and our Land being all in (Armes?) one against another that wee know not what to doe but I hope hereafter it will bee better and then I hope to accommodate your request and expectation MR: STAINSMORE informs mee that you have given him tobacco for satisfaccon for transporting your sonne but it is such a base Commodity

f 54a p 330 bot p 179a 17 Feb 1645/6

will not pay halfe of my Charge Soe with my best respects to you. your good wyfe and the rest
I rest and remayne
Your loving friend to use

HARDWINE

Indorsatur:

To his very good ffreind
MR: CASAR PUGGET in Virginia
this deliver

(NOTE: The signature above is hard to decide. I looks like it might be GRACE to your editor or Edward, however the first letter doesn't seem to be either G or E AGW)

Receaved of MR: CESAR PUGGETT the 24 Mar 1641 2 hhds tob weighing neat 555 lb tob in full of all demands concerning WILLIAM COLES passage and all other thinges belonging to him by mee NATHAN STAINSMORE In witness whereof I have hereunto sett my hand
NATHAN STAINSMORE

Recordat 20 Feb 1645/6 Dat. in Virginia 22 Jun 1643
Within 20 dayes sight of this my second bill of exchange my first and third not being paid. I pray pay unto CAPT: JOHN GOOKIN or his assignes the full some of 8 £ sterl: which is for soe much received here. pray fayle not to make good paymt and putt it to account as per advice

To my loving father
SUTTONSTAM
in Amsterdam

Your loving sonne
DIRCK SUTTENSTAM

f 55 p 331 bot p 180   29 Mar 1646

RECORDED 29 MAR 1646
Att a Quarter Court holden at James Citty
13 Mar 1645/6

PRESENT SIR WILLIAM BERKELEY knt, gov &c

- ? - RICHARD KEMP	ESQRS	CAPT: HEN: BROWNE	ESQRS
CAPT: SAMUEL MATHEWS		CAPT: THO: WILLOWGHBY	
CAPT WILL: BROCAS		GEORGE LUDLOWE	

Upon certificate from the howse of Commons that CAPT: JOHN SIBSEY high sherruff if Lower Norff County hath produced his accounts and presented the same and made paymt and colleccon according to the Trust of his office. It is therefore ordered that he bee hereby discharged from the said office. And this order to be his Quietus
Exhibit Examined
SAM: ABBOTT Chirc

Att a Quarter Court holden at James Citty the 17 Mar 1645/46
Present SIR: WM: BERKELEY knt gov &c
CAPT SAM: MATHEWS   CAPT THOS: WILLOWGHBY
COLLONELL NATHA: LITTLETON   CAPT: HUMER: HIGGINSON
MAJOR RICH: MORRISON
(A big hole is torn out of left hand side of this xxxx the Governor hath elected, xxxxxxxxxxxxxxand the Court xxxxxxxxxCAPT: EDWARD WINDHAM high sherriffe of xxxxxxxx Norfolke County with all rights, powersxxxxxxxxxxxxxxxxxx authorityes, profittsxxxxxxxxxxxxxx the said officexxxxxx xxxxxxxxxxxxxx   SAM ABBOTT This is all that can be salvaged from this item AGW)

f 55a p 33? bot p 180a   7 Apr 1646

Recordat 7 Apr 1646
Att a Court at MR: WILLIAM JULIANS
present MR: WM: JULIAN   MR: THO: LAMBARD
MR: ED: LOYD   MR: THO: MEARES

CAPT: EDWARD WINDHAM was sworne high sheriffe for the County of Lower Norff according to the within menconed order. And is to give security at the next Court. Likewyse THOMAS TOOKER was sworne undersheriffe
WILLM: JULIAN

Att the howse of WILLIAM SHIPP
15 Apr 1646
Present: CAPT: JOHN SIBSEY COMMANDER
MR: MATHEW PHILLIPPS

In respect that severall persons having accons depending in this Court and some doe not appeare, and some doe not attend to present the same. The Court is therefore xxx xxxtorn xxxxx till the 15th MAY next att such tyme and place aforesaid All persons whatsoever being arrested or summoned are hereby required to appeare and such proceedings to bee then as at present should have beene

f55a p 332 bot p 180 15 Apr ;646

by CAPT: THO: WILLOWGHBY EXQR:
CAPT: J .N sic SIBxxx (hole in paper)
15 May (hole in paper)
(This item is badly mutilated) ICHARD ? SAMPSON? xxxxx NORWOOD xxxxxxxx GRIMES

f f 56 p 333 bot p 181 15 May 1646

Att a County Court holden 15 May 1646 at the howse of WM: SHIPP CAPT: JOHN SIBSEY COMMANDER
MR: ffRANCIS MASON MR: THOMAS LAMBARD
MR: EDWARD LOYD MR: MATH: PHILLIPPS

The Court doth order that an administration bee granted unto ELLEN LIGHTHART widdowe on the estate of HENRICK LIGHTHART her late husband deceased she entring into bond with good security to save harmless the Court and to pforme the Act

An attachmt is granted unto SAMUELL CHARNIKO on the estate of GEORGE RUTLAND whoe is -(smeared)- the County for satis-faccon of 1000 lb tob and 8 barrells of Indian Corne Clay-med due to to the said CHARNIKO from the said RUTLAND. And the estate aoe attached to bee satisfactory for the said debt of tob and corne aforemenconed upon legall determinacon

The difference depending betweene RICHARD POOLE deft at the suite of JACOB BRADSHAWE plt being referred to the Court Is referred to the next Court to be heard and determined

The Court doth order ffRANCIS LAND to peye unto THOMAS WARD Attorney of RICHARD

f 56a p 334 bot p 181a 15 May 1646

PINNER the assignee of JOHN ROBINSON for 420 lb tob at the next cropp with 3 yeares forbearance at 8 per cent and to pay Court Charges else exec

Whereas WILLIAM NASH stands indebted unto MRS: SARAH GOOKINS 5 Ł 5 Ł sterling due and payable five years since, before the Act as appeares unto the Court. It is ordered that the said WILLIAM NASH shall forth give security for payment of the said 5 Ł sterling with 4 yeares lawfull forbearance at 8 per sent and Court Charges unto the said MRS: GOOKIN else exec

Whereas is appeares to this Court and allsoe confessed by THOMAS WARD the attorney of SAVILL GASKINE that he the said GASKINE is indebted unto MRS: SARAH GOOKIN in the some of 2046 lb tob and caske. The Court doth order that the said GASKINS shall pay or give full satisfaccon unto the said MRS: GOOKIN for the saud 2046 lb tob and caske within 20 dayes else exec

GEORGE HORNER hath made appeare upon Oath unto the Court that he hath due unto him 50 acres of land for the transpor-tation of one man servant named RICHARD GEFFERYES into this Collony (not in NU)

f 57 p 335 bot p 182   15 May 1646

Whereas THOMAS DAVYES stands indebted unto GEORGE BEACH 7 barrells of Indian Corne due last yeare. The Court doth order that the said THOMAS DAVYES shall pay the said 7 barrels of Corne within 20 dayes and allsoe pay one barrell of corne for the forbearance and to acquitt the sd BEACH of 14 lb tob which he oweth the said DAVYES and pay the court charges else exec

The Court doth order that Xpian: LUCAS, KATHERINE MYE, ANNE KEELINGE, JANE LAND, ANNE GASKINE, MARY SMYTH, ISBELL HAYES & THOMAS WARD, shall severally enter into bond with good security for theire appearance at James Citty on the first day of the next Quarter Court before the Governor & Councell to declare theire full knowledge concerning ELIZABETH TAPLIN servant unto MRS: GOOKIN and nowe prisoner and accused for being lately delivered of a child and for making away thereof. And the sherr (sherriff?) is hereby injoyned and required to see the due pformance of this order whoe is allsoe further authorized to take into his custody all and every the persons aforenamed that shell refuse to give bond with security as aforesaid

It is ordered that the sherriffe shall detaine in his custody MARY PERRE and RICHARD RAGGED til they fynd security for theire appearance at James Citty before the Governor & Councell on the first day of the next Quarter Court to give full evidence concerning ELIZABETH TAPLIN on his Mats behalfe

f 57a p 336 bot p 182a   16 May 1646

Whereas JOHN STRATTON is indebted unto GEORGE BEACK remaynder per bill 600 lb tob and caske due and payable the 10 ct 1644 as appeares unto the Court. It is ordered that the said JOHN STRATTON make payment thereof forthwith with lawfull forbearance at 8 per cent and Court Charges unto the said GEORGE BEACH?
(This name could be BEACK, BEACH Beach BEARK ? BECK?)
or BEARK ? BERK, BECK?)

It is ordered that HENRY SNAYLE doe give security before he depart the Court for the delivery of 9 barrells of corne upon demand formerly attached by the sherriffe and awarded by the Court for satisfaccon of a debt of 300 lb tob and charges proved due unto MR: MATH: PHILLIPPS and the said Corne is to bee appraysed according to former order made and provided else exec

It is ordered that CLEMENT THEOBALDS and JOHN POWIS forthwith enter into bond with good security for theire appearance at the next Court to answere unto such matters of presentment as are exhibited against them.

The Court doth order ELIZABETH HALL in presence of the Court to receive 20 good lashes on her bare back for divers misdemeanore apparent whoredome she being a xx?xx and delivered of a child as by presentmt and other testimony appeares to the Court

f 58 p 337 bot p 183 16 May 1646

The matters depending in variance betweene THOMAS DAVYES plt and JOHN BAKER deft *(Note: the ink is blotted and coming through from the other side of the page making it almost making it almost impossible to read - the case is referred to the next Court AGW)*

RICHARD WHITEHURST is elected and by the Court confirmed to bee Constable for the Easterne Branch and that the oath of Constable bee administered unto him by the next Court

LANCASTER LOVETT elected and by the Court confirmed to bee Constable for Lynhaven and the oath to bee administere to him by the next Court

GEORGE KEMP and JOHN NORRWOODS are elected constables for Elizabeth River Parish xxxxxxxxxxxxxxxxxxxxxxxxxxxxxx in theire severall precincts where they doe inhabite respectively and the oath of Constable to bee administered unto them by the next Court

THOMAS TOOKER doth confesse himselfe to bee indebted unto xxx?xxx 1100 lb tob and caske xxxxxxxxxx(the rest of this page is full of holes)

f 58a p 338 bot p 183a 16 May 1646

Whereas THOMAS IVEY did borrowe a boat of JOHN HOLMES which said boat was never as yet redelivered as appeares to this Court. It is therefore ordered that the said THOMAS IVEY shall pay at the next cropp unto the said JOHN HOLMES 250 lb tob in full satisfaccon for the said boat being judged the full value thereof. And MR: IVEY to pay Court Charges else esec

Whereas ffRANCIS LAND was arrested to this Court for debt at the suite of THOMAS PLATT who is the attorney of CAPT: WILLM DOUGLAS And the said PLATT nor any for him appearing to prosecute his said accon. The Court doth order PLATT to bee non suited and allsoe to pay 100 lb tob unto the said LAND for disturbance and losse of tyme and to pay the Court Charges else exec

Upon the complaint of ffRANCIE LAND unto this board that there is a bill at Lynhaven remayning and is much prejudicall to the Inhabitants there in theire fenced grownds & amongst theire Cattle. It is therefore ordered that MR: SAYER whoe made xxxxx?xxxxx of the said Bull fower yeares since have notice hereby to fetch away the said Bull (rest of this item is full of holes)

f 59 p 339 bot p 184   16 May 1646

It is ordered that RICHARD CASTLEFORD servant unto JOHN HOLMES being charged with foggery and with other fellonious acts and misdemeanors bee safely kept in custody of the sherriffe and to bee layd in irons and soe remaine untill he bee (henceforth?0 delivered by the due order of his Ma-ties---- lawes

Whereas ELIZABETH TAPLIN single woman and servant unto MRS: SARAH GOOKIN hath been accused for the murdering of her child which she was lately delivered of as appeares to the Court or the xxxxxx?xxxx away thereafter the Court doth order that the sherriffe according to former order given him shall safely keep in his custody the body of the said ELIZABETH TAPLIN and to putt her into Irons and the said ELIZABETH soe to remayne untill such tyme as she bee from thence delivered by order of (the Court?)

(the next itemis almost impossible to read - the ink is coming through from the other side of the page and there are holes, small & large)

xxxxxxxxxthere issue forth warrants
xxxxxxxxxxx the Sherriffe xxxxxxxxxfor the
xxxxxxxxof JOHN BALTON?, HENRY BRAKES, ARTHUR ENGxxxxxxx
NICHOLAS MASON and MARYxxxxxxxxxxxxxxxxxxof misdemeanors
xxxxxxxxxxxxxhis Ma-ties----   behalfe
shall bee xxxxxxxxxxxxBy the informacon
of RICHARD CASTLEFORD servant unto JOHN (HOLMES?) at a Court
to be holden on Wednesday next
xxxxxxxxxxxxxxxxxxxxxxxxxxxxxxxxxxxxxQuarter Court
xxxxxxxxxxxxxxxxxx

f 59a p 340 bot p 184a 18 May 1646

Recordat 18 May 1646 (page is mutilated and badly blotted & iI suspect water damaged as the past few pages have been)

Be it knownxxxxxxxxxxxxxxxxxxxthat I EDWARD LILLY have bargained and sold xxxx unto ADAM HAYES sonne to ROBERT HAYES his heirer &c forever one heifer markedxxxxxxxxxxx xxxxxxxxxxxxxwith all my right and titlexxxxxxxxxxsaid heifer and her increasexxxxxxxxxxxxxxx sett my hand the 17 Feb 1645/6

Wittnes: EDWARD LILLE
JOHN PRINCE
JACOB BRADSHAWE

Recordat: 18 May 1646 Whereas I XOPFER BERG (BOYCE? SEE NEXT PAGE)of the County of Warrick River in Virginia Planter have sold unto THOMAS WRIGHT of the County of Lower Norff: in Virginia planter as aforesaid vizt: two xxxxxholexxxxxxabout the age of 4 yearesxxxxxxxxxxsaid Cowes being all black (rest of this is mutilated)

f 60 p 341 bot p 185   18 May 1646

being xxxxxxxxxxxxholesxxxxxxxxxxxxxxxxxxxxxxxxxxxxxxxxx That I the said XPOFER BOYCE for mee my heires &c deliver the said Cowes into the possession of JANIE WRIGHT the wyfe of and assignee of the said THOMAS WRIGHT To have and injoy them with theire encrease forever xxxxxxxxxxxxxxxxxxxxxxxxxxxxxxxxxxxxxxxxxxxxxxxxxxxxxxx

xxxxxxxxxxxxxxxxxxxxxxxxxxxxxxxxby vertue of a bill of sale affirmed under the hand of the asignee of My LADY DAILE xxxxxxxxxxxxxxxxxxxxxxxxxxI have hereunto sett my hand this 20 Jan 1643

Witnessed: CHRISTOPHER (B) BOYCE
ROBT: SMYTH and seale
PHILLIPP LAND

f 60a p 342 bot p 185a   18 May 1646

(this page is worse than the last one)

Court at the Howse of WILLIAM SHIPP xxxxx May 1646
Present: CAPT: JOHN SIBSEY COMANDER
MR: WILLIAM JULIAN MR: HENRY WOODHOUSE
MR: ffRANCIS MASON MR: THOMAS LAMBARD
MR: THOMAS MEARES MR: MATH: PHILLIPPS
MR: EDWARD LOYD

The Court doth order that JOHN HOLMES and AGNES his wyfe HENRY BRAKES, ARTHUR EAGLESTON, NICHOLAS MASON, JOHN BOLTON & MARY SMYTH shall enter bond with good security for theire personal appearance at the next Quarter Court holden at James Citty xxxxxxxxxxx to answere the fellonious killings of certaine Tame hoggs xxxxxxxxxxx they or any of them stand charges withall by the afirmation of RICHARD CASTLE-FORD or THOMAS LEACH

The Court doth order that GYLES COLLINGS and HENRY SNAYLE shall forthwith enter into bond severally to prosecute at the next Quarter Court holden at James Citty before the Governor & Councell by endictmt according to due order of Lawe, JOHN HOLMES and AGNES his wyfe HENRY BRAKES, ARTHUR EAGLESTON, NICHOLAS MASON, JOHN BOLTON and MARY SMYTH and every of them for fellonious killing of certainxxxxxxxxxx

f 61 p 343 bot p 186   18 May 1646

tame hoggs being the proper xx?xx him the said GYLES COLLINGS xxxxxxxxxxxxxxx xxxxxxxxunto this Court

The Court doth request CAPT: THOMAS WILLOWGHBYESQR: /as much as concerneth him/ that the cause JOHN HOLMES AND AGNES his wife, HENRY BRAKES, ARTHUR EAGLESTON, NICHOLAS JOHN BOLTON, and MARY SMYTH to bee presented by endictmt according to due order of his Mat---[ies] Lawes for the fellonious killing of certaine tame hoggs being the proper goods of him the said CAPT: THOMAS WILLOWGHBY as appeares unto

f 61 p 343 bot p 186 18 May 1646

the Court and the sherriffe is hereby requested immediately to give the said CAPT: WILLOUGHBY notice hereof

The Court doth order that THOMAS LEACH now servant unto MR: HENRY WOODHOWSE shall bee forthwith bownd with security personally to appeare at the next Quarter Court holden at James Citty before the Governor & Courcell to give such evidence as he knows against JOHN HOLMES and AGNES his wyfe HENRY BRAKES, ARTHUR EAGLESTON, NICHOLAS MASON and JOHN BOLTON and MARY SMITH or any of them concerning the fellonious killing of certaine tame hoggs

The Court doth order that I JOHN HOLMES and AGNES his wife, HENRY BRAKES, ARTHUR EAGLESTON, NICH: MASON, and JOHN BOLTON shall all of them enter into bond with good security personally to appeare at the next Quarter Court holden at James Citty before the Governor & Councell to answere the felonious killing of (rest of this is mutilatedxxxxxxxxxxxxxxxx

f 61a p 344 bot p 186a 18 May 1646

The Court doth order that MR: MATHEW PHILLIPPS shall give bond to presecute at the next Quarter Court holden at James Citty before the Governor & Councell by endictmt according to due order of his Mat[ies]--- Lawes JOHN HOLMES and AGNES his WYFE, HENRY BRAKES, ARTHUR EAGLESTON, NICHOLAS MASON and JOHN BOLTON and all and every of them for the fellonious killing of certaine tame steare of or belonging unto him the said MR: MATH: PHILLIPPS as doth appeare to the Court

MR: HENRY WOODHOWSE is requested by the Court to take the depositions of EDWARD (GRADELL?) upon oath concerning his delivering a message to RICHARD ABRELL on Sunneday last And the deposition soe by him taken to bee transmitted to the Clarke of the Court And allsoe MR: WOODHOWSE is requested to take the deposition of ROBERT HAYES And as MR: WOODHOWSE shall see cause further to order this matter in xxxxxx?xxxxxxxx

Whereas all matters of faith accons, & difference by Act of Assembly are referred for tryall to the severall County Courts respectively. And for as much as by a former order of this board the Courts for this County were sometymes kept at the howse of ROBERT HAYES at little Creeke in Lynnhaven parish and sometymes at the howse of WILLIAM SHIPP in Elizabeth River Parish. Inter: Vicem: as by the said order may appeare Nowe for the remotness of the saidplace at Little Creeke aforemenconed and the Insueing xxxxxxxxx?xxx thereof. And for the better xxxxxxx ? xxxxxxxx and more ease of all persons whatsoever xxxxxxxx this Court (rest of this is too mytilated to read xxxxxxxxx

f 62 p 345 bot p 187   18 May 1646

(mutilated) xxxxxxxxxxxordered that all Court xxxxxxxxx for this County bee constantly and duely kept xxxxxx at the nowe dwelling howse of WILLIAM SHIPP xxxxxxxxxxxxxx xxxxxxxxxxxxxxxxxxxxxxxxxxxxxxxxxxxxxxxxxxxxxxxxxxxx Whereas by 54th Act Act of the 2 Mar 1642/3 The Comrs: of the severall Countyes xxxxxxxxxxxxxxxximpossible to readxxxxxhath hitherto been neglected in this County to the great detriment thereof xxxxxxxxxxxxaccording to the said date aforespecified order that s sufficient prison bee forthwith erected at the howse of WILLIAM SHIPP xxxxxxxxxxabd that all xxxxxxxxxCare beexxxxxxxxx taken xxxxxxxxxxxxxxxxxxxxxworkmen and take the immediate building thereof said workmen are to bee agreed with by the Comrs: or the major part of them. And the said Prison to be built at the generall Charge of this County

Recordat: 13 Jun 1646
Knowe all men by these presents that I WILLIAM GOLDSMYTH of the Easterne Branch of Elizabeth River planter doe xxxxxxxxxxxxxxxxxxstand indebted unto JOHN SMYTH, Cooper belonging to the Shipp Mary of xxxxxxx1800 lb tob xxxxxx

f 62a p 346 bot p 187a 13 Jun 1646

xxxxxxx(this is continued from p 345) xxxx (and it is a bill or bond from WILLIAM GOLDSMYTH binding over his plantacon unto JOHN SMYTH)
6 Apr 1646
wittness   WILLIAM GOLDSMYTH
JOHN SIDNEY, HENRY NICHOLAS

f 63 p 347 bot p 188   15 Jun 1646

Att a Court holden 15 Jun 1646 at the howse of WILLIAM SHIPP
WILLIAM SHIPP
Present: CAPT: JOHN SIBSEY Comander
MR: THOMAS LAMBARD   MR: THOMAS MEARES
MR: EDWARD LOYD   MR: MATH: HILLIPPS

Concerning the difference in question betweene THOMAS MARSH & XPOFER BUSTIAN. It is ordered that the said THOMAS HARSH shall pay unto the said BUSTIAN 5 dayes worke of a sufficient hand and the Court Charges else exec

Whereas ffRANCIS LAND stands indebted unto WILLIAM DOUGLAS merchant 13 £ Sterl: money due by specialty and was payable in 1643 as appeares unto the Court. It is ordered that the said ffRANCIS LAND shall pay the aforesaid 13 £ Sterl:money unto THOMAS (PLATT?) the attorney of the said DOUGLAS with the forbearance at 8 per cent. And the said ffRANCIS LAND to pay the Court Charges else exec

The Court doth order JACOB BRADSHAWE to pay 200 lb tob unto RICHARD POOLE for unjust molestacon and charges expended in this suite concerning the demanding of a debt of 600 lb tob and caske due by bill which xxxxx rest is mutilated xxxxxxx

f 63a p 348 bot p 188a 15 Jun 1646

It is ordered that JACOB BRADSHAWE and RICHARD SMYTH shall pay at the Cropp 100 lb tob a peice to the publique use of the county for theire unlawful gaining at Cards. And the fine to bee collected as aforesaid disposed of according to further order else exec

Whereas it appeares unt the Court that MRS: SEAWELLS estate stands indebted unto WM: SHIPP 2 barrells of Indian Corne. It is thereupon by consent ordered that MR: MATHEW PHILLIPPS whoe is guardian unto the orphants of the decedent shall satisfy out of the said estate 200 lb tob unto the said SHIPP in liewe and full satisfaction of the said corne else exec

CLEMENT THEOBALDS, JOHN POWYS, and ELIZABETH HALL are required to appeare at the next Court to answer unto certaine matters of presecution and the sherriffe is hereby injoyned to take security for theire appearance and the matters in question to bee fully heard and determined

An Attachmt is granted unto ffRANCIS LAND on the estate of GEORGE RUTLAND being departed this Collony for satisfaccon of 225 lb of tob when the Court shall further determine thereof

MR: THOMAS Mxxxxx, JOHN WATKINS, PETER PORTER, and xxxxxx holesxxxxxxxxrequested bythe Court to apprayse the estate of x

f 64 p 349 bot p 189 15 Jun 1646

HENRY WATERS xxxholexxxx JOHN GEATHER being administrator thereof

The Court doth order that the estate of WM: DURFORD remayning in the hands of THOMAS MARSH whoe is administrator thereof bee sold at an outcry to the benefit of payeing the decedents debts

Whereas of late it hath beene frequently still is given out and reported by sundry Credible persons that DEBORAH GLASCOCK /the reputed relict of ROBERT GLASCOCK late deceased/ was sometyme heretofore married in England to her husband which is yet living. The said DEBORAH having likewyse aftooned (often?) confessed soe much whoe allsoe lately reported that she had sent for him, her said husband xxxx holexxxxin hither out of England nevertheless the said DEBORAH being intended to Intermarry with one JOHN ffERINHAUGH and the and the Court takingdue notice of such disorderly xxxurses which then conceive to bee apparent adultery and forbidden by the lawes both divine & humane and therefore in noe sort to bee permitted. In regard whereof as allsoe to (pre)vent the horrid crymes. The Court hath thought fitt to & hereby doth prohibite matrimony to bee had or solemnized by the said DEBORAH aforenamed with the said ffERINHAUGH or with any other person whatsoever upon penalty

f 64 p 349 bot p 189   15 Jun 1646

of such(strict?) Courses to bee taken xxmutilatedxx as according to lawe is provided in these cases and that

f 64a p 350 bot p 189a 15 Jun 1646

this (bee) published to the intent that Ministers and other people may have notice hereof.

15 Jun 1646 It is this day ordered by a Vestrey that MR: MATHEW PHILLIPPS lately Church Warden shall bee satisfyed by the next Churchwarden 130 lb tob having disbursed soe much for the use of Elizabeth River Parish which xxxxxxx appearesxxxxxxxxxthe tobacco to be levyed in the pish of theire inhabitants pporconably to bee collected as aforesaid

10 Jul 1646 Recordatur: Whereas wee OSMOND COLCHESTER Cite(z)? Citizen? & Merchantaylor of London And WALT: MITCHELL Citizen and Apothecary of London stand lawfully seized in fee simple and our (are?) heires of and in a Certaine plantation and lands thereunto belonging late in the tenure or occupacon of JONATHEN LANGWORTH Chirurgeon deceased lyeing and being in Lower Norffolke in Virginia and of and in all woods, tymber trees, commodityes and other the appurtenances thereunto belonging as by the Conveyances and assurances in that behalfe more plainely may appeare. Nowe knowe all men by these presents that wee the said OSMOND COLCHESTER & WALTER MITCHELL for divers good causes & conderacons hereunto especially moveinge have

f 65 p 351 bot p 190   10 Jul 1646

authorized, constituted and appointed xxxxxxxxx our well beloved friend MR: MATHEW PHILLIPPS of Lower Norfolke in Virginia aforesaid agent xxxxxxxxxxtrue & lawful Atturney xxxxxxxxxfor and in our names to enter into and upon the foresaid plantation or upon some part thereof in ye xxxx ?xxxx of the whole and after such entry made then for us and in our names to take possession thereof And after such possession thereof had and taken to sell & Convey the same with the lands and appurtenances thereunto belonging to and with such person and persons and for such prize & somes of money as our said Attorney shall thinke reasonable and fittinge or otherwyse to dispose of the same as wee by any wryting under our hands shall order and appoynt. And wee give and by these presents grant unto our said ATTORNEY his substitutes and assigns all our full power and authoritye in and concerning the premises to doe and pforme such Act & Acts thinge and thinges devise and xxx?xxx for the Conveying or assuring of the aforesaid Conveying or assuring of the aforsaid plantation as to Lxxxx shall appertayne and according to the use and Custome of Virginia And one Attorney or more attorneys under him to make xxxx xxxxxxxx to pforme execute and further whatsoever f 65a p 352 bot p 190a 15 Jul **1646**

shall bee needfull, necessary or xxxxxxxxxxxxxxxxxxxxxxx xxxxxxxxxxIn witness whereof wee have hereunto putt our hands ands and seales xxxxx17 Sep 1645xxxxxxxxxxx

Signed sealed and delivered
by the above WALTER MITCHELL
in the presence of:
MATHEW LOCK (or LARK)Notary publique
GEO: TOWNCOW Sec:

WALTER MITCHELL
OSMOND COULCHESTER
EDWD: GUNNELL

JOHN ROBINSON
WILLIAM DAY

THOMAS JAQUES

WILLIAM HAWKINS

(see LANGWORTH patent NU 78,81,92,99)

Recordat 15 Jul 1646
To all Xtian people to whome this present shall come I ROBERT HAYES of Lynhaven in the Lower County

f 66 p 353 bot p 191 15 Jul 1646

of New Norff: planter send greetings &c Whereas by Pattent bearing date the 9 Aug 1637 and in the 13th yeare of the Raigne of our soveraign Lord King Charles there was granted unto HENRY POOLE 160 akers of land lyeing up Lynnhaven by the Governor of Virginia under his hand and sealed with the seale of the Collony. To have, hold and injoye to him and his heires forever whereunto relation being had more atlarge it doth & may appeare. And whereas he the said HENRY POOLE hath by assignmt under his hand for himself, his heires and assignes fully & absolutely assigned, sould and sett over the said Pattent with the land therein contayned togeather with all profitts, commodityes, priviledges & hereditmts thereunto belonging unto mee the said ROBERT HAYES my heires, executors adms: and assigns as fully & absolutely as by the said pattent it was granted unto him the said HENRY POOLE his heires &c without exception as by the said assignmt is hereunto relation being had more at large it doth appeare Nowe knowe yee that I the said ROBERT HAYES for and in consideration of a some of tobacco allready in hand by mee received have and by these presents doe for myself, my heires &c fully, cleerely & absolutely grant bargaine, sell, assigne and sett over forever unto OWEN HAYES of the said Lynhaven, planter.

f 66a p 354 bot p 191a 15 Jul 1646

his heires &c a parcell of Land being part of the said Land in the said pattent specified vizt: beginning at a markt tree standing in the Southwest side of the Land now in the tenure of DAVID WILLIAMS and from thence to Stretch Southwest unto the Land of THOMAS CHEELEY and Norwest? towards the water and Southwest into the mayne woods. The whole breadth which is or shall bee found to bee betweene the said

f 66a p 354 bot p 191a 15 Jul 1646

marked tree and the land which belongeth unto the said THOMAS CHEELEY by vertue of a pattent of 100 acres of land which I the said ROBERT HAYES have sould unto the said THOMAS CHEELEY which breadth is supposed to bee betweene 60 & 70 poles. The said land with all the priviledges, profitts &c To have hold, occupy and peaceably enjoy forever xxxxxxxxxxxxxxxxxxx*(Note: the rest of this is badly smudged and seems to be a repetition of what usually appeares in all deeds AGW)*

f 67 p 355 bot p 192 15 Jul 1646

xxxx release and quite Clayme unto him the said OWEN HAYES . In his full and peaceablt possession thereof being being and to his heires &c all the estate ryght, tytle, Interest, Clayme, benefitt of condicon and power of redemption use possession, reversion, clayme & demand which the said ROBERT HAYES have or anyway might or ought to have or by any meanes eyther by the said Pattent or otherwyse or which I may hereafter may have by Pattent or any other meanes whatsoever. In witness whereof I have hereunto sett my hand and seale this 17 Nov 1640 xxxxxxxxxxxxxx

Signed sealed & delivered ROBERT HEYES
in the presence of us & his seale
XOPFER: BURROUGHS
JOHN SPENCER

Indorsatur:

To all to whome this present writing shall come knowe yee that I OWEN HAYES of Lynhaven, Planter doe by these presents firmely and freely resigne all the right and tytle of ½ of the grownd which is specified in this bill of sale to WALTER PRESSAR of the same place, planter for him his heires executors &c forever with all the priviledges and

f 67a p 356 bot p 192a 15 Jul 1646

rights and &c xxxxxxxxxxxxxxxx(not legible)xxxxxxxxxxxAnd further I doe resigne to the said WALTER PRESSAR ½ of the Neck of Grownd joyning to the said plantation Whereunto I the said OWEN have hereunto sett my hand this 15 Jun 1643

Signed & delivered
in presence of OWEN (O H) HAYES
THOMAS (T) MELTON
THOMAS ALLEN

plus Indorsat

Know all men by these presents that I OWEN HAYES doe for mee my heires &c have sold unto EDWARD LILLY the plantation where I live and all the land appertayning to it as is herein menconed in this bill of sale for and in consideration of 3500 lb tob to mee in hand paid doe sell and have sold to the sd EDW: LILLY to him his heires &c forever and likewise the Neck of Land that the sd OWEN HAYES did buy of ROBERT HAYES last. In wittness the truth I have sett my hand this 27 Feb 1643 OWEN (H) HAYES

f 67a p 356 bot p 192a 15 Jul 1646

Teste: the words three thousand and five hundred was interlyned before the delivery CEASAR PUGGETT

NOTE: In book A pages 352 - 356
The following notes are what is in Nugent's Cavaliers and Pioneers relating to the almost obliterated facts and hard to read items between these pages.

NU 62 - HENRY POOLE Gent: 150 acs LNco 9 Aug 1637 within the territorye of Lynhaven Nly upon land lately belonging to HENRY SOUTHERNE now in possession of LT: RICHARD POPE-LEY Wly upon the river, Ely into the Maine woods & Sly upon the river.

NU 61 - LT: RICH: POPELEY 700 acs LNco 14 Jul 1637 upon the Chesopian Shore within the territory of Lynhaven Nly upon land of WM: LAYTON Wly upon the river Ely into the woods Sly up the river Due in right of marriage with ELIZABETH SOUTHELL the relict of HENRY SOUTHELL.

See also: HENRY SOUTHELL 25 Nov 1636 Nu 51 same bounds as this. (above)

NU 34 THOS: KEELING 100 acs Eliz: City Co 18 Nov 1635 Nly upon land of HENRY SOUTHWELL Ely upon the back river Sly upon land of WM: MORGAN Wly on the Maine Land

Your editor hopes that the above will help clarify some of the items so badly damaged,
Alice G. Walter

f 68 p 357 bot p 193   4 Aug 1646

Recordat 4 Aug 1646 Knowe all men that I JOHN MARTIN of Lynhaven planter doe acknowledge to have delivered to JOHN WORKEMAN of the same place as really brought & sold one heifar calfe of 3 months old coulored browne cropt & slitt on the right eare and a hole in the left eare. And further I doe enjoyne myself that the said JOHN WORKEMAN shall peaceably injoy the said calfe without any molestacon by any that may or should in any way lay clayme to the said Calfe and do hereby advich? the true, honest, just and lawfull sale made by mee In witness hereof I have hereunto sett my hand this 1 May 1643

Wittness: JOHN MARTIN

ROBERT CLARKESONN

Att a County Court holden upon the 15 Aug 1646

present: CAPT JOHN SIBSEY COMANDER

MR: WILLIAM JULIAN   MR: ffRANCIS MASON

MR: EDWARD LOYD   MR: MATH: PHILLIPPS

Lieft: ffRANCIS MASON hath declared upon his corporall Oath that he did at noe tyme receive any satisfaccon of any person of persons whatsoever for or concerning a Gunne which he the said LEIFT: MASON did formerly sell unto HUMFREY (HAMNAR?) deceased

f 68a p 358 bot p 193a 15 Aug 1646

Whereas BARTHOLOMEW HOSKINS stands bownd with ALEXANDER STONER for the payment of 1000 lb tob and Caske unto WILLIAM BARKER the administrator of STEPHEN PENNELL payeable 10 yeares since as appears unto the Court. It is thereupon ordered that the said HOSKINS shall make paymt of the aforesaid 1000 lb tob and Caske with the forbearance at 8 per cent for the time since it became due as aforesaid unto the sd WILLIAM BARKER with theCourt Charges else exec

An attachmt is granted unto EDWARD CANNON against the estate of GEORGE RUTLAND beeing departed this Collony for to satisfy a debt of 256 lb tob due by bill when the Court shall have further determination thereof

A certificate of 50 acres of Land is granted unto JOHN YEATS for his right in the transportation of ANNE WYNNE into this Collony being made appeare to be due as aforesaid upon oath of the said YEATS
(see NU 270 - renewed 1652 to JOANE YATES)

Whereas ROGER WILLIAMS is justly indebted unto THOMAS BUSHRODE 948 lb tob and Caske as appeares unto the Court and allsoe acknowledged due by the sd WILLIAMS. The Court doth order present payment of the sd 948 lb tob and caske with Court Charges unto the said THOMAS RUSHRODE else exec

Whereas GEORGE PARRINGTON, EDWARD SELBY, ROBERT JONES and ROBERT BOWERS are severally presented unto the Court by JOHN NORRWOOD constable of Elizabeth River Parish for theire not

f68a p 358 bot p 193a 15 Aug 1646

planting and not tending of Corne according to act of assembly It is ordered that the aforsd

f 69 p 359 bot p 194 15 Aug 1646

partyes aforenamed bee summoned to appeare psonally at the next sessions of this Court to make answers unto the said presentment as they will answere the Contrary at theire perill

Whereas JOHN CARRAWAY and others of his family are presented unto the boardby RICHARD WHITEHURST Constable of the Eastern Branch in Lynhaven Parish for not planting or Corne according to the Act of Assembly It is ordered that the aforesaid CARRAWAY bee summoned to appeare psonally at the next session of this Court to make answere to the contrary at his perill

All matters of difference concerning presentmts or otherwise betweene JOHN POWYS and CLEM: THEOBALD are once more referred to the next Court to bee fully heard and finally determined

Whereas sundry matters in variance pending in this Court betweene THOMAS DAVYES plt: and JOHN BAKER deft: (etic contra?) at the humble petition of both parties were referred o a Jury of 12 able men which said Jurors being sworne for ye tryall of theire Causes have by theire verdicts fownd for the plt: THOMAS DAVYES 20 lb tob more to bee paid him by the said BAKER upon both which said JOHN BAKER doth crave an appeale to the Governor and Councell which this Court doth grant accordingly the said BAKER putting in good security to pursue his said actions on the first day of the next Quarter Court and to pay double dammages in Case he be cast? in the saud suits according to Act of Assembly in this behalfe xxxxx?xxxxx provided

f 69a p 360 bot p 194a 15 Aug 1646

The busynesses and matters depending in this Court concerning her and MR: WILLIAM JULIAN concerning her the sd ELIZABETH YELLOWE being delivered of a dead child are referred to the next session of this Court then to bee fully heard and finally determined And that in the interrim summons doe issue forth for the personall appearance of RICHARD RUSSELL Chyrurgeon to give further evidence such as he knoweth unto the Court therein

The Court doth order THOMAS IVEY to pay 30 lb tob unto SAVILL GASKINE for losse of tyme and Charges being summoned for a wittness

Whereas XPOFER: ROWLES (or RAWLES) singleman hath gotten with child ELIZABETH YELLOW singlewoman servant unto MR: WILLIAM JULIAN. The Court doth order the said ROWLES to pay at the Cropp 500 lb tob unto the said MR: JULIAN in consideration of the damage sustayned by the meanes & occasion of the said ROWLES in getting his said woman servant with child as aforesaid and ROWLES to pay Court Charges else ex exec f f 69a p 360 bot p 194a 15 Aug 1646

Whereas it evidently appeares to the Court that XPOFER: ROWLES singleman hath committed the fowle offence of fornication with ELIZABETH YELLOWE singlewoman a servant unto MR: WILLIAM JULIAN It is therefore ordered that the said ROWLES shall on Sunneday tomorrowe come forth right after the first Chapter read doe pennance in a white sheet according to Custome used in like Cases in the Parish Church of Elizabeth River and Mr: And MR: MARSH according to his owne proffer is to fynd or then bring with him a white sheet for that purpose and to put it on And ROWLES is ordered to pay the Court Charges

Whereas JOHN HARVYE servant unto MR: MATHEWE PHILLIPPS as guardian unto the orphants of MRS: SEAWELL deceased hath in a pemptory and unfitting

f 70 p 361 bot p 195 15 Aug 1646

manner made divers complaynts at severall tymes against the said MR: PHILLIPPS unto the Court without any just Cause. And hathlost thereby much tyme in service besides said causes, trouble & expenses arysing. It is thereupon ordered that the said HARVYE shall forthwith receive 20 good lashes on his bare back for his said misdemeanors and pay for two ordinaryes and Court Charges unto the said MR: PHILLIPPS else exec

The matters in difference upon account betweene MR: CORNELIUS LOYD plt against MR: WILLIAM WHITBY the attorney of CAPT: DOUGLAS THOMAS DEACON & COMPANY defts are referred by consent of both partyes to the next sessions of this Court being on the 1 Sep next and then to bee fully heard and finally determined

Whereas it appeares unto the Court that CORNELIUS LOYD stands indebted unto CAPT: WILLIAM DOUGLAS 400 lb cropt tob due by bill and 50 ₤ sterl: money due upon account /before the Act/ It is ordered that the said CORNELIUS LOYD shall make present paymt unto THOMAS PLATT attorney of the said CAPT: DOUGLAS of the said 400 lb tob with an allowance of 35 per cent for stripping and 8 per cent for 5 yeares forbearance and allsoe to pay the said 15 ₤ sterling money with two yeares forbearance /being not due xx?xxx before/ after the rate of 8 per cent and the said CORNELIUS LOYD to pay Court Charges else exec

Whereas NICHOLAS BRIDGES deceased by bill stands indebted unto JOHN HOLMES the lawfull assignee of HENRY SNAYLE 700 lb tob payable the last day of Jun 1645 as

f 70a p 362 bot p 195a 15 Aug 1646

appearance unto the Court. And for as much as allsoe it doth apparently appeare unto the Court by the deposicons of WILLIAM PARRY & DANYELL TANNER that MATHEW BASSETT hath intermeddled in the estate belonging unto the sd BRIDGES deceased by selling a boat thereunto belonging unto the sd BRIDGES deceased by sellinge a boat thereunto belonging without any order or administration taken our or granted The Court doth order that the said MATHEW BASSETT shall make present payment of the aforesaid summe of 700 lb tob unto the said HOLMES he the said BASSETT being executor in his owne wrong else exec

The Court is (adjourned) till the 1 Sep next and all suits or causes of accons now depending on then yo (be?) proved as they nowe should have done And all partyes arrested or summoned to appeare this present day whose busynesses are not determined are required to appearance then; as they will answere the contrary at their perill

Ordered to bee recorded Whereas there is a difference depending betweene MR: THOMAS MEARES and THOMAS SAYER concerning a percell of land in controversie betweene them Nowe knowe all men by these presents that wee the said MEARES and SAYER for the full and finall ending and determination of all desputes and controversies in and about the said the said Land in question have voluntarily and mutually elected and chosen RICHARD BENNETT, PHILLIP BENNETT, TRISTRAM NORSWORTHY and EDWARD LOYD as arbitrators and in Case the said 4 persons doe not agree that then they choose an Umpire. And wee the abovesaid THOMAS MEARES and THOMAS SAYER doe bynd ourselves our

f 72 (should be 71) p 363 bot p 196 15 Aug 1646

heires exors: &c in the summe or quantity of 10,000 lb good tobacco to ward? to and abyde the Award and Arbitrament of the abovesaid Arbitreators or the Umpireadge of and personthey shall choose the aforesaid tobacco to become due and payable by and from him that shall make defacto herein within 30 dayes after the said Arbitreatores have agreed and drawne up their agreement award and Umpireadge concerning the premises in wryting under theire hands and seales. In witness whereof wee the abovesaid THOMAS MEARES and THOMAS SAYER have hereunto putt our hands and seales Dated 13 Jul 1646

Sealed, subscribed and delivered in the presence of THO: HARRISON
EPAPHRODITUS LAWSON

THOMAS MEARES & his seale
THOMAS SAYER & his seale

Wee whose names are here unto subscribed being elected and authorized by MR: THOMAS MEARES and MR: THOMAS SAYER as Arbitrators to Compromyse and Compose a difference of land as by e wryting under theire hands and seales bearing date with these presents doth appeare And wee the sd Arbitrators

f 72 p 363 bot p 196   15 Aug 1646

having mett accordingly and weighed & considered the severall allegacions and proofes of eyther side as well by Pattent and the surveighoers plat as by the Attestacons and deposicons of such as were knoweing of the land in dispute between them Doe hereby determine award and Conclude that an old marked Pyne standing upon a poynt to the Westward of MR: MEARES his howse /which Pyne is nowe new marked on the other side/ shall bee the bownd betweene theire lands That is to say MR: SAYERS Land to runne from the said Pyne Westerly unto POWDE -

f 72a p 364 bot p 196a   15 Aug 1646

Poynt. MR: MEARES his land from the said marked Pyne Easterly to Boteweights Creeke. And from the aforesaid Pyne standing by the River to Runne South into the woods along by a great marked oake lately deeded And wee doe farther agree and owned that MR: THOMAS MEARES shall pay 250 lb tob unto MR: SAYER towards his Charges in Surveighinge of the aforsd Land. In wittness whereof wee have hereunto sett our hands and seales the 13 Jul 1646

RI: BENNETT & his seale
PHIL: BENNETT & his seale
EDD: LOYD & hia seale
TRIS: NORSWORTHY & his seale

(see NU 269 THOS: SAWYER for bounds - Nehuntas Cr. & Billingsgate Cr. & NU 171 THO: MILES on Nehuntas Cr)

see also NU 84 THOMAS SAWYER, NU 57 Thomas Sawyer
NU 57 " "
NU 65 THOMAS TODD

Att a Court houlden at Eliz: Citty 20 Jun 1646
Present: CAPT: WILLIAM CLAYBORNE
MR: SYMON PURCHY or PURSIFY   MR: PETER STEVERTON
MR: THOMAS CELLY   CAPT: NATHANIEL OLDES

It is ordered by this Court that RICHARD HILL shall according to a former order of the 29 Dec 1643 sattisfy and paye unto CAPT: LEONARD YEO 22½ barrells of Corne with Court Charges or else exec Extrah: p: mee HENR: POOLE Cler Cur

Att a County Court holden 1 Sep 1646
Present CAPT: JOHN SIBSEY COMANDER
MR: WILLIAM JULIAN   MR: ffRANCIE MASON
MR: THOMAS LAMBARD   MR: MATH PHILLIPPS

Upon diligent and serious perusall of the accounts of CAPT: JOHN SIBSEY high sheriffe for this County last yeare concerning his collecons and paymts of the levye unto severall men according to order and to the trust imposed on him. It doth manifestly appeare unto the Court by receipts, discharges, acknowledgmts and other sufficient proof that the said CAPT: SIBSEY hath duely satisfyed and made payment /in the totall / to severall men the summe of

f 73 p 365 bot p 197   1 Sep 1646

which the Court upon request of the said CAPTAINE SIBSEY doth certify accordingly

Ordered to be recorded

MATHEW PHILLIPPS gent aged 45 yeares or thereabouts sworne and examined sayeth that MR: RICHARD WAKE and this deponent being togeather about the 15 day of Jul 1646 at the howse of CAPT: THOMAS WILLOWGHBY did aske the said RICHARD WAKE what course he the said WAKE would take for payment of that money which he the said WAKE did owe him. Whereupon the said WAKE confessed that he did owe the said CAPT: WILLOWGHBY 150 ₤ Sterl: besides the forbearance. Whereupon the said CAPT: WILLOUGHBY said that

f 73a p 366 bot p 197a 1 Sep 1646

it was due these 4 yeares since MR: WAKE answered that it would bee 4 yeares in September next And that he was very willing to take any course that CAPT: WILLOWGHBY thought fitt for sattisfaccon of the said debt with the forbearance and further sayeth not

p me MATH: PHILLIPPS

The Court doth order that a Commission of administration on the estate of MR: RICHARD WAKE deceased bee granted unto CAPT: THOMAS WILLOWGHBY ESQR: who hath apparantly made appeare by proffe upon oath and other sufficient testimony that he is creditor to the said estate 198 ₤ Sterling Money. The said CAPT: WILLOWGHBY entring into bond with securitye to save harmlesse ye Court

The Court doth order that a Commission of administration on the estate of WILLIAM SALISBURY late deceased bee granted unto MR: MATHEW PHILLIPPS having intermarried the widdowe & Relict of the sd decedent. He the sd MR: PHILLIPPS entring into bond with security to save harmless the Court

Whereas RICHARD WAKE late deceased was indebted unto MR: JAMES STONE and Company 13 ₤ 8/3pence sterl: money for the transportation of himself and sonne & other goods into the Collony & was never satisfyed as appeares unto the Court It is ordered that MR: CORNELIUS LOYD the attorney of the sd STONE and Company shall bee satisfyed the sd 13/8/3 sterl: out of

f 74 p 367 bot p 198   1 Sep 1646

the decedents estate provided CAPT: THOMAS WILLOWGHBY ESQR: bee first satisfyed his debt of 198 ₤ sterl: out of the estate of the said deceased

The Court having perused the accounts of all payments of the Levyes concerningXPOFER BURROUGHS his owne particular and ordered to bee paid him by CAPT: SIBSEY high sherriffe last yeare doe fynd that there is nowe remayning in the hands of the sd CAPT: SIBSEY 158 lb tob & noe more which

f 74 p 367 bot p 198   1 Sep 1646

they order to bee paid unto the sd BURROWGHS by the 10 Dec next with forbearance at 8 per cent else exec

The Court having duely perused and examined the accounts of the paymt of 1000 lb tob due unto THOMAS WARD Chirurgeon per order of the Councell of Warre and to bee paid by CAPT: SIBSEY late High Sherriff doe fynd that there is due unto the said WARD in ballance of the aforesd accounts 108 lb tob which the Court doth order CAPT: SIBSEY to pay unto XPOFER BURROWGHS the attorney of the sd WARD with forbearance at 8 per cent upon the 10 Dec next else exec

The matters in difference between MRS: SARAH GOOKIN plt and JOHN WILLIAMS deft: are referred to the next Court to be heard and determined and eyther party is then to appeare at their perill

f 74a p 368 bot p 198a 1 Sep 1646

The Court doth orderthat a warrant doe forthwith issue forth against RICHARD RUSSELL Chirurgeon for his appearance next Court to answere the contempt wherewith he stands charged

The busynesses in Court about DEBORAH GLASCOCKE & JOHN ffERINHAUGH concerning theire Contract of Matrimony referred to Thursday next come sevenight And ffRANCIS BRIGHT is hereby ordered then to appeare and to produce what testimony he can or knoweth of concerning the premises

Whereas the matters in variance depending in this Court between THOMAS IVEY plt: and XPOFER BURROWGHSdeft: concerning a boat taken away and dampinfyed at the request of the said BURROWGHS were referred to s Jury of 12 able men impannelled and sworne for tryall of the said Cause which Jurors fownd for the plt: THOMAS IVEY upon which verdict the Court duely taking the premises into consideration with costs of the suite and all Court Charges order thereupon that the said BURROWGHS shall pay unto the said THOMAS IVEY 520 lb tob for the said boat by the 10 Dec next the said THOMAS IVEY having expended and paid soe much else exec

An attachment is granted unto MR: CORNELIUS LOYD for 11Ŀ Sterl: money against soe much of the estate belonging or appertayning unto CAPT: WILLIAM DOUGLAS & being in his owne hands or Custody untill the said CAPT: DOUGLASS or his attorney doe retorne a bill which the said MR: LOYD did formerly deliver the said DOUGLAS

f 75 p 369 bot p 199   1 Sep 1646

and alsoe MR: SAMUELL CHANDLER his oath that he hath not at that tyme paid CAPT: DOUGLAS the money with an assignment upon the back of the bill by reason it is in CAPT: DOUGLAS his (- torn -) and untill the Court doe further consider thereupon

f 75 p 369 bot p 199   1 Sep 1646

WHEREAS THOMAS DAVYES is indebted unto per bill unto THOMAS TOOKER 240 lb tob as appeares unto the Court. It is ordered that the said THOMAS DAVYES give security to make payment thereof with Court Charges and one yearer forbearance before he depart the Court or to remaine in the Sherriffs custody

The difference between THOMAS TOOKER plaintiffe and JAMES LOPHAM deft: is referred to the next Court. JOHN HOLMES having in presence of the Court undertaken for the psonall appearance of LOPHAM

The cause depending betweene MR: CORNELIUS LOYD plt and THOMAS SAYER deft: by consent of both partyes is referred to the next County Court

Whereas HENRY NEEDHAM hath assigned over unto XPOFER: BURROWGHS in consideration of 450 lb tob & caske, one browne heifarand 2 black cowes and one black steare calfe and one old grisled boare as appeares to the Courts. And the said HENRY NEEDHAM being since departed the County

An attachment is granted unto the said BURROWGHS against the goods aforespecified to bee responsible unto the said BURROWGHS in such manner as

f 76 p 370 bot p 199a 1 Sep 1646

as the Court shall hereafter further determine thereupon

Whereas PETER PORTER being impanneled a Juror and hath not attended the Court. It is ordered that the said PETER PORTER shall pay 200 lb tob as a fyne to the use of the County for the Building of a prison

It is ordered that THOMAS BROWNE & RICHARD OWENS shall diligently veiwe the Cropps of Corne of EDWARD SELBY and to make report thereof the next County Court

MATHEW HOWARD and LAWRENCE PHILLIPPS are appoynted by the Court to view the cropps of Corne of ROBERT JONES and ROBERT BOWERS and to report thereof to the next County Court

WILLIAM SHIPP and WILLIAM CROUCH are elected and appoynted by the Court to view the Cropps of Corne of TRISTRAM MASON and to make report thereof to the next County Court

MR: JOHN SIDNEY and MR: RICHARD WORSTER are hereby ordered to view the Cropps of Corne of JOHN CARRAWAY & his Company and to make report thereof to the next County Court

MR: GEORGE (PUTTERGBON?) is ordered to appeare personally at the next Court and to bee xxxxx?xxxx to appearance and to answer contempt

The matters concerning WILLIAM JULIAN and ELIZABETH YELLOWE his servant her being delivered of a dead child are referred to the next Court to be fully heard and determined xxxxxx olexxxxaforenamed to bee present

END OF BOOK A

INDEX

The original Court Records give the Folio number, a page number - usually at the bottom of the page. The page numbers given in this index are the page numbers of this manuscript given at the bottom of each page. It is hoped that this will help the reader to refer to the original records if desired.

R

WARING Samson 164,205,216

PLACE

SHIPS

BOOK "B" LOWER NORFOLK COUNTY, VIRGINIA
2 NOVEMBER 1646 - 15 JANUARY 1651/2

TABLE OF CONTENTS

FOREWORD

The priceless 17th century records of Lower Norfolk County, Virginia, have been restored rebound and are kept in a humidity-controlled vault so that they may be preserved for future generations.

While readily available for the use of serious researchers, there are several factors which limit the full utilization of these volumes. 17th century handwriting, at its best, is difficult enough for 20th century readers to decipher without the further complications of unfamiliar abbreviations, poor spelling and the inevitable tears, rips, stains and smudges common to old documents. The old index leaves much to be desired.

It was for the laudable purpose of making these old records more usable that this transcription was made. Book "B" of Lower Norfolk County records, covering the period from 2 Nov. 1641 to 15 Jan. 1651/2, has been beautifully transcribed and completely indexed by Alice Granbery Walter. I hope that you will enjoy the benefits of using this transcription as much as I.

Alice Granbery Walter is well equipped to tackle a task such as this. Her experience in reading 17th century records and her background as a genealogist and historian have been of inestimable value in producing this transcription.

Mrs. Walter is a descendant of many of the Lower Norfolk County and Princess Anne County early Colonial Families. Among those are Nash, Herbert, Hoggard, Nimmo, Cornick, Keeling, Boush, Attwood, Carraway, Cartwright, Etheridge, Ivy, Mason, Thelaball, Land, Langley, Lovett, McCoy, Martin, Nicholson, Tatem, Whiddon, Woodhouse, et als. Her most recent ancestor from Cheshire, England, was Dr. Joseph Harding who came from Cheshire, England, in the late 18th century.

She has published 5 books of the records of the Courts and Land Patents, and the Granbery Genealogy, and has also published 13 Genealogical Charts of various Norfolk County and Princess Anne County families.

Mrs. Walter is now working on a transcription of Book "A" of Lower Norfolk County Records. I, for one, am looking forward with eager anticipation to the publication of this next work.

Charles B. Cross, Jr.

Charles B. Cross, Jr., Clerk

Circuit Court of the City of Chesapeake,

formerly Norfolk County

PREFACE

This transcription of Book "B" of the Lower Norfolk County Seventeenth CenturyRecords gives all the information contained therein which is eligible. There are many pages torn, faded, water damaged and some parts missing. The repetition in deeds and other records has been eliminated in order to reduce the number of pages required to publish this book.

It should be noted that the Eastern Shore referred to in many of these records does not always mean the same place. Your editor always thought that the Eastern Shore meant the Eastern Shore of Lynnhaven River, as it does indeed, but have since realized that there are Eastern Shores of Back Bay, Linkhorn Bay and other areas. The Upper Precinct of Lynnhaven River refers, more often than not, to the Back Bay section of what was Princess Anne County from 1691 until 1963 when it became part of the city of Virginia Beach. "Down to Capt: Willoughby's" is in reality North, down the Elizabeth River toward the mouth where Willoughby Spit is today. The same applies to all of the waterways down meaning towards the mouth of the river and up meaning from the mouth to the head.

All folio numbers of the original record are noted in the margins. An asterisk,(*), denotes the beginning of the following folio. This method is used to facilitate the ordering of copies of records from the Virginia State Library or the Chesapeake Circuit Court House. These institutions will appreciate receiving the folio number and book number when you request copies as it will save their staff a lot of time and effort.

Where there is a doubt some of the words and names are reproduced as written in the original record. There are examples of the script all through the book. Most signatures are written by the Clerk of the Court and are not to be taken as the signature of the person whose name is signed to documents. More important, the clerks wrote what they "Heard" which is the reason for so many different spellings of the same name. The name Etheridge has been found spelled Evrg in some records, and Evearg in others.

The arithmatic leaves something to be desired, the addition is often wrong. Any name beginning with an H should be looked up under F as well for it is sometimes impossible to decide which letter the Clerke meant. Any name beginning with L could look like an H.

There are missing pieces and damaged pages which are listed below:
10 - The beginning of this folio has no connection with folio 9a.
45a - 46 - 47 - no names appears on these folios.
75 - some of this is too faint to read
74 to 76 - is impossible to read in spots, faded and probably water stains.
78 - parts cannot be read
93a to 101a are missing from the original book and are not on the microfilm, however, they were obtained from the Virginia State Library and the information in them is in this book.
102 - this folio starts in the middle of an entry on the microfilm, but is complete with folio 101a.

112a on is very hard to read - the handwriting is very small and fancy with flourishes which obliterate the line underneath. This must be a new clerks handwriting. Did Thomas Tooker die or is he just absent?

143 - the top of this folio is almost completely gone.
143a - most of this is torn
144a - top is torn and faded, it is a deed but no names are eligible.
146 - top of folio torn and some of it is missing
147 - ditto
148 - torn and parts missing. It seems to start by naming the processioners or collectors of tythes
148a - top torn
153a - top torn and parts missing
161 - badly torn at the top, sides and a strip out of the middle.
164a - top cannot be read
170 - almost completely missing
181 - large pieces missing
181a - ditto
182 - only one word can be read on the top half - "Present;" - which probably means a Court date is missing.
182a - most of this is missing
182a - parts missing
183 - only two small scraps are left
183a - almost entirely missing, only pieces of names are left
184 - top is missing and some holes, writing smudged
200 - The jump in folio numbers from 190a to 200 is a mistake for 200 is a continuation of 190a. Your editor does not think any folios are missing.
205 - this folio is numbered 206 but is really 205.

For a continuation of these records see Virginia Colonial Abstracts volume 31, Lower Norfolk County 1651-1654 abstracted by Beverley Fleet. This is the first 84 pages of Book "C". See also The Virginia Genealogist Magazine volume 15 Number 1, January-March 1971 where corrections appear of Mr. Fleet's abstracts by your editor. There are 300 more pages in Book "C" which I hope to publish someday.

In the meantime work progresses on Book "A" which I hope to publish at a future date if the response to this publication merits another publication.

Alice Granbery Walter

RECORDED: 2 November 1646 By the Governor & Captain Generall of Virginia

... JOHN MUNDS late of this Colony deceased did by his last will & testament nominate & appoint ISBELL his wife his executrix.............said ISBELL did at a County Court holden for Lower Norfolk County upon the 15 Nov 1645 make humble suit to the board that a Probate of the said will might be graunted unto her.............full power is hereby given and granted unto her ....given at James Citty.........this 10 Mar 1645/6 Munds f1

/s/ WILLIAM BERKELEY

By the Governor and Captain General of Virginia:

..........Whereas THO: EDWARDS late of this Collony, deceased dyeing Intestate leaving an estate in divers goods, rights and debts whereof RICHARD OWENS hath made humble suit......administration might be granted unto -torn xxxxxxxxxxxxxx - * RICHARD OWENS to bring in a true and just account of the remaynder of the said estate ...... 10 Mar 1645/6 *f1a

Edwards Owens /s/ WILLIAM BERKELEY

By the Governor &c -

..........whereas WILLIAM DURFORD late of this Collony deceased dyeing intestate and leaving an estate.......and on the behalfe of the widdow and orphants of the said deceased THOMAS MARSH hath made humble suite to the County Court of Lower Norfolk that a -(faded)- administration might bee graunted unto xxxxxxxxx xxxxx decedents estate............ on behalfe of the widdowe & orphants of the said deceased according to order of the said County Bearing date the 5 December.........Doe give and grant unto the said xxxx NARSH (sic) the administration of -(torn)- xxxxxxxxxxxxxxxx that he xx xx THOMAS NARSH (sic) shall present unto the Comrs of xxxxxxxxxxxxxxx lawfully appraised - (torn xxxxxxxxxxxxxx) - * satisfye and pay all such debts ....the said THOMAS NARSH (sic) ....given at James Citty 10 Jun 1646. f2

Marsh Marsh Marsh /s/ WILLIAM BERKELEY Rowe

By the Governor &c -

............Whereas PHILLIPP ffEILDGATE, Gent: late of this Collony deceased dyeing intestate and leaving an estate.............hereof... ..... ELIZA: ffEILDGATE the widdowe and Relict........hath made humble suite ....that a Commission of Administration might be graunted unto her.......according to an order of the said Court bearing date 16 Feb 1645/6 doe give and graunt unto said ELIZABETH the administration (Note: bottom of this page is torn) * ....satisfye and pay all just debts .....given at James Citty 10 Mar 1645/6 f2a

/s/ WILLIAM BERKELEY

(Note:- From this point on the phrase "By the Governor and Captaine General of Virginia will be eliminated as the signature will show that William Berkeley graunted the various items.) AGW

2a continued - March 1645/6

................Whereas HENRY WATE late of this Collony deceased dyeing intestate and leaving an estate..........whereof JOHN GEATHER (sic) hath made humble suite...........that a Commission of Administration be graunted unto him of his said estate as Brother in law to the said deceased. Nowe know ye .... according to an order of the County Court of Lower Norfolk.....16 Feb 1645 doe give..........unto the said JOHN GEATHER the Administration of all and singular....................
3 *................Given at James Citty this 10 Jun 1646.

/s/ WILLIAM BERKELEY

................Whereas HENRICK LIGHTHART late of this Collony deceased dyeing intestate and leaving an estate.........ELLEN LIGHTHART widdowe the relict of the deceased hath made humble suite.........that a commission of Administration might be granted unto her...........to an order
3a of the said County Court.........15 May 1646*doe give and graunt unto the said ELLEN LIGHTHART the administration.......Given at James Citty ....4 Oct 1646.

/s/ WILLIAM BERKELEY

5 Nov 1646 - ordered to be recorded: An accoumpt of the estate belonging to the Orphants of HENRY HAWKINS deceased in January 1642/3:

Bequeathed unto SAMUELL HAWKINS as Doth appeare in the will two Cowes and one heifer.

One Cow calfe killed per wolves 1643
One Calf dead at MR: LOYDS 1644
One yearling Cowe calfe killed in the woods this Spring 1646
Two Cowes of the principle stock dead this spring 1646

Remayning

One black cowe cropt on both eares and a piece taken from underneath each eare.

One yearling Cowe Calfe Cropt on both Eares with a hole in the right ear.

Left unto HENRY HAWKINS two Cowes & one Steare
One of the two Cowes dyed ye same yeare 1642:
The other Cowe dyed this Spring 1646 without any female encrease.
Three bull calves are all the male encrease hitherto.

Remayning

One two yeare old heifar given him in exchange of the Steare.
p me EDWARD LOYD this 15 Aug 1646 (end of 3a)

4 * 5 Nov 1646 - ordered to be recorded.................... I JOHN NUTKINS of Virginia, Planter have assigned..........my well beloved friend WILLIAM JULIAN of Elizabeth River, Gentleman in the County of Newe Norfolke my true and lawfull deputy and attorney.........Sealed with my seale..........30 Jun 1640.......By mee JOHN NUTKINE.
wittness hereof:
GEORGE KEMPE, BARTHOLOMEW HAYNES

The 1 Oct 1642 (or 1648? - date is written 1642) from OKINGHAM Loving and Christian freind and Maister having any opportunity to returne such thankes as your former kindnesses may Justly vindicate. I willingly imbrace notwithstanding the distance of place between us desire to bee myndfull of you and yours and though I shall not nor Indeed cannot make a sufficient (Eqquiball requit ?) for xx a deserved favour yet I am not nor I here never* shall forgett them. I must 4a further engage myself to you and intreating you to sell of my Plantation for money if you can or else for tobacco but that is worth little.

I have sent many letters to you and a token of my Love but I never heard of you receiving any one onely one letter which doth not a little grieve mee. The first year I could not compasse to send those things which I promised onely a Small token I sent to my loving Mistres a pare of Cordwanx gloves. The Second yeare I received a letter which put me in mynd of those former promises and ingagements the which the ten shillings due to the Parson I payd to MR: WATE (or Wake?) and a Calfes Claw-d? I left at MR: WAKES to bee sent and I would have payd that money which was due to you for the tobacco which you payd for mee to THOMAS BRITTAINE.

Here is but little news thats good in ENGLAND all in a Combuscon which I doubt not but you are fully acquainted with. I desire to bee remembered to all my friends and likewyse to heare from you.

And this with my kynd love to yourselfe and to my Sweet Mistress I committ you to the proteccon of the Allmighty to whome my desire for you is that he would blesse you with all spirituall blessings aboundantly in Christ Jesus and together with you all the whole plantation and Rest.

Yours to commaund
JOHN NUTKINE

for my plantation if you shall think fitt because RICHARD KEMP desires the forsaking of mee I shall bee willing if he will give as much as another. I am content I expect from him the which if you receive it I would entreat you to satisfy your selfe and send mee the Remaynder.

I have heard of xxxxxx THOMAS BRITTAN coming into ENGLAND but never heard from him by ROBERT TAYLOR he is well and desires to bee remembered to you and his Attorney MR: LAMBETH.

And for my heifar you may keep it and make sale of it whichever you please and likewyse I desire to have it spe(e)dally done because I heard of your coming home which I should bee very Joyfull once more to see yoy for us. I would entreat you to send by MR: PRICE my good friend.

INDORSAT:

To his much respected freind MR: WILLIAM JULIAN dwelling in ELIZABETH RIVER give these I pray.

* 5

........Whereas RICHARD WAKE late of this Collony deceased dyeing intestate.......leaving an estate......in care whereof CAPT: THOMAS WILLOWGHBY hath made suite to the Commissioners of Lower Norfolk County for a Commission of Administration might bee graunted unto him of his said estate as Creditor thereunto (the) summe of 198 pownds Sterl: money........according to order of the said County Court....1 Sep 1646 do give and graunt unto the said THOMAS WILLOWGHBY ESQR the administration.... given at James Citty the 4 Oct 1646 /s/ WM: BERKELEY

5a 5 Nov 1646

Recorded 5 November 1646 by the Governor & Captaine General of Virginia

.....Whereas WILLIAM SALISBURY late of this Collony deceased dyeing Intestate and leaving an estate...........in Care whereof MATHEW PHILLIPPS haveing intermarried with the widdowe and Relict of the decedent hath made humble suite to the County Court of Lower Norfolk that a Commission of Administration might be graunted unto him............. according to an order of the said Court .... 1 Sep 1646.......graunt unto the said MATHEW PHILLIPPS the Administration &c................. Given at James Citty.......4 Oct 1646 /s/ WILLIAM BERKELEY

6 Ordered to be recorded the 1 Nov 1646

Att a Quarter Court holden att James Citty 10 Oct 1646

Present: Sr WILLIAM BERKELEY knt Governor &c
MR: RICHARD KEMP) CAPT: HENRY BROWNE)
CAPT: WM: BROCAS) MR: GEO: LUDLOWE) Esquires
SGT: MAIOR RICH: MORISON

Upon the peticon of MR: WILLIAM JULIAN to bee eased of and from his MA^ts (Majesties) service by and in his attendance upon the County Court of Lower Norfolke alleaging therein his great age and inability of body occasioned thereby The Court therefore in consideracon aforesaid have according to the desire of the petitioner released him of his said attendance and outed him from the said Commission In whose stead the Court doth likewyse authorize CORNELIUS LOYD to take place in the said and dignty of Office as the said MR: JULIAN did and theire next County Court to bee admitted into the same.

Examined pp me JOHEM MEAD

Mr. CORNELIUS LOYD did upon the 6 Nov 1646 take the Oathes of Supremacy and Allegiance with the oath of a Com^r in the presence of CAPT: JOHN SIBSEY, MR: EDWARD LOYD & MR: MATH: PHILLIPS and was admitted as abovesaid.

Recorded by order the day and yeare abovesaid. (1 Nov 1646) Whereas by the late Act of Assembly ordayning all causes of what value soever to be tryed at County Courts, And all letters of Administration to bee from the said County Courts graunted most of the ffees and proffitts belonging to the place of Secretary are come and devolved to the Clarkes of the xxxxx County Courts.

Now know yee therefore that I SIR WILLIAM BERKELEY knt, Governor doe graunt unto RICHARD KEMP Secretary the said Clarkes places and to place and displace what Clarkes he shall think fitt in the said severall Courts respectively and to make what Composition he shall think fitt with the said Clarkes in lieu of such profitts which doe accrew to them by the said Act and were due to the Secretary his office. Given under
6a my hand (*) and the seale of the Collony 10 Sep 1646.
Teste: SAM: ABBOTT CCur /s/ WILLIAM BERKELEY

To all to whome to whome these presents shall come I RICHARD KEMP Esqr: Secretary of State of Virginia send greet(ings)in our Lord God

Everlasting. Whereas SIR: WILLIAM BERKELEY knt Governor &c by deed under his hand and seale of the Collony bearing date the 10 Sep 1646 for the causes and reasons herein exprest hath given and graunted unto me all the Clarkes places of the Severall County Courts within the Collony with full power to place & displace what Clarkes I should thinke fitt in the said several County Courts respectively as by the said Deed relacon thereunto had doth more at large appeare. Nowe knowe yee that I the said RICHARD KEMP Esqr: for certaine considerations mee hereunto moveing have and doe by these presents accordingly appoint ordayne place and Invest RICHARD CONQUEST, Gent: in the Clarkes place and office of the County Court of Lower Norf: Giving and Graunting.........all fees &c above the value of 1600 pownds of tobacco or ₤ 10 Ster:................. Given at James Citty....4 Oct 1646 /s/ RICH: KEMPE & his Seale 6a

* ATT A COUNTY COURT HOLDEN UPON 6 NOV 1646 7

PRESENT:

CAPT: JOHN SIBSEY) MR: EDWARD LOYD
MR: CORNELIUS LOYD) MR: MATH: PHILLIPPS

These summes of tobacco hereafter exprest are allowed of and approved by the Court to bee due from the Inhabitants of this County and appoynted to bee payd to the particular persons hereunder named and are as followeth (vizt):

To XTOFER (Christopher) BURROWGHS in full of his accomt being for goods loste and dampinfyed & tob: expended in 1645. —0507:

* To CAPT: WINDHAM in full of his accopt for fees and other charges concerning ELIZABETH TAPPEN his Mat^s prisoner —1200: 7a

To RICHARD FORSTER (FOSTER) for killing one wolfe 0050:
To MRS. GASKINS her negro for " " " 0050:
To JOHN HOLTON for " " " 0050:
To RICHARD ABRELL for " " " 0050:
To RICHARD ACTON for " " " 0050:
To MR: PHILLIPPS for " " " 0050:
To TRUSTRAM MASON for " " " 0050:
To CAPT: WINDHAM for Iron Bolts and chaynes for prisoners 0300:
To WM: OLIVER for 31 dayes attendance on the burgesses at Jamestowne 1645 0310:
To MR: IVEY for three mens roweing up and downe the burgesses in all 23 days at 10^l tob^o per day 0230:
To MR: CORNELIUS LOYD per his accpt for his Charges being Burgesse 1645 2570:
To MR: CORNELIUS LOYD per order of Assembly 0220:
To MR: EDWARD LOYD and MR: ROBERT EYRES for charges at the ordinary at James Citty & expenses theire bill past for so much 2715:
To MR: EDWARD LOYD for more charges 0373:
To MR: THOMAS MEARES for more charge 0373:
To MR: ROBERT EYRES fore more Charge 0373:
To GYLES for howse Roome for ye Burgesses 0325:
To WILLIAM SHIPP for Candles 0020:
To CAPT: WILLOWGHBY for 10 gall of Sack at 25^l tob^o per gall 0250:
To ROWLAND for 22 days service on Burgesses at James Citty 10 p day0320:

To the widdow LIGHTHART for her boat 9 dayes to carry up the burgesses 0080:

8 *To MR: THOMAS MEARES for his boat to fetch downe the burgesses 0050:
To fower Men ten dayes at 10^{l} tob^{o} per day to rowe up the Burgesses 0400:
To MR: MEARES for a hogg & bread to ye Men 0450:
To WILLIAM SHIPP for dyett and lodging for the men that went up with the burgesses 0336:
To WILLIAM SHIPP for a Roome for a prison till Aprill next 2325:
To RICHARD CONQUEST for Clarkes ffees and for wryting /as per accopt/ concerning ELIZ: TAPPEN 0400:

Is in the totall 11410:

To the sherriffe for sallary at 5 per cent 00580:

11990:

ffor satisfacon of the abovesaid summe of 11,990 pownds of tobacco. It is ordered that there bee levyed by the sherriffe proporconally according to the rates prescribed in the Acts of Assembly and in manner following vizt:

ffor 329 persons at 25^{l} tob^{o} per polle	8225:
ffor 490 Cowes at 5^{l} tob^{o} per cowe	2450:
ffor 163 Goates at 2^{l} tob^{o} ½ per Goat	0407:
ffor 2 horses at 40^{l} tob^{o} per horse	0080:
ffor 38000 Acres of Land at 5^{l} tob^{o} per Cent	1900:
The Sherriffe to Collect in all	13062:

Out of Which said Summe of 13,062 pownds of tob^{o} and one halfe pownd being levyed by the sherriffe as aforesaid /and occasion bee by distresse/. It is ordered that he make such payments to such persons and for such uses as are above specified and appoynted by the Court and for the surplusage and remaynder the Sherriffe to make payments according to further order; or to bee accomptable for the same unto the Court.... for the use of the County.

8a * It is ordered according to the Real intent and mean(ing) of the Act of Assembly That all those persons whatsoever which have sett out a soldier for or concerning the Mar(ch?) in taking OPPO CHAUCKONOUGH shall be satisfyed.....the sherriff out of their Levyes by deduction........pownds of tob^{o} per .....with allowance allsoe for theire powder and shott. (This page is water damaged)

AT A COUNTY COURT HOLDEN UPON THE 16 Nov 1646

PRESENT: CAPT: THOMAS WILLOWGHBY, Esqr
CAPT: JOHN SIBSEY) MR: CORNELIUS LOYD)
MR: ffRANCIS MASON) MR: HENRY WOODHOWSE)
MR: THOMAS LAMBART) MR: THOMAS MEARES) COMRS:
MR: EDWARD LOYD) MR: MATH: PHILLIPPS)

Whereas PETER PORTER being warned to attend xxxx last Court upon a Jury and was amerced? for his default 200 pownds of tobacco upon the humble peticon of the said PORTER therein alleaging he was Wind bownd at NANSIMUN. The Court in consideracon thereof doth mitigate the said fine and order the said PORTER to pay 50 pownds of tobacco to the use of the County with the Court cost otherwyse execucon.

Whereas GEORGE HORNER did implead DEBORAH GLASCOCK widdowe for 500 pownds of tob^{o} due for worke upon the request of JOHN ffERINHAUGH The attorney of the said DEBORAH the matter of debt in question is referr-ed to the next court and if the said DEBORAH GLASCOCK doth not make it then appeare that she hath paid or satisfyed the said debt for HORNERS use, then the said DEBORAH GLASCOCK is to pay the said 500 pownds of tobacco with such costs and dammages as the Court shall thinke fitt.

An administration is ordered to bee graunted unto MATHEW HOWARD and ROBERT BOW(ERS?) on the estate of

(Note: The above is the way this page ends and there is no page 9 or 9a)

(Note: Folio 10 begins as follows which seems to have no connection to the preceding page 8a:) *10

Court doth order payment thereof in 15 dayes & the Court Charges.

The Court doth order that HENRY HILL, WILLIAM JOHNSON, WILLIAM SMYTH, SAMUELL CHARNIKOE? Samuell Charnikoe and JOHN POWYS shall personally appeare at the next Court to answere unto the present-ment of LANCASTER LOVETT for note planting of Corne as is specified in the presentment and the parties aforesaid to bee sumoned by the Sheriffe.

It is ordered that JOHN WILLIAMS doe receive twenty good lashes on his bare back in presence of this Court for two frequenting the Company of ELIZABETH TAPPEN late servant unto MRS: GOOKIN contrary to the tenor of a former order of this Court dated the 15 Dec 1645 and made soe appeare by sufficient proofe upon oath and the said WILLIAMS to pay the Court charges.

In the difference between WILLIAM LUCAS & THOMAS DAVYES concerning a lost cowe that was hyred by DAVYES, each to beare his own charges.

17 Nov 1646
Present vt Antea

Whereas it appeares to the Court that HENRY SNAYLE is indebted in bal-lance upon accoumpts unto RICHARD CONQUEST 159 pownds of tobacco due the last yeare. The Court doth order payment thereof....and SNAYLE to pay the Court charges within 15 dayes.....

Whereas it appears unto the Court that ffRANCIS BAKER and JAMES SYMONS are indebted unto WILLIAM SHIPP 2330 pownds of tobacco and 6 barrels of corne. Payment is ordered to be made......and the Court Charges within fifteene dayes.

Whereas JOHN SIDNEY is indebted unto ROBERT GRIFFITH by 350 pownds of tobacco as xxxxxxxxxxpayment is ordered to be made.

end of folio 10

10a 17 Nov 1646

The matter in difference betweene THOMAS DAVYES plantiffe and THOMAS CHEELEY defendt at the request of the said DAVYES is referred to the next Court to be heard and determined.

The difference depending betweene CHRISTOPHER BOY(CE) plaintiffe and JOHN SIDNEY is referred to the next Court.....

CAPT: EDWARD WINDHAM hath voluntarily undertaken to satisfy unto JAMES WARNER on the behalfe of THOMAS BUSHRODE and for his use a case of sack with a lock and key within 15 dayes....(sack is a wine)

Upon the petition of THOMAS CARTWRIGHT against ELLIS BROWNE concerning a parcell of hoggs in the xxxxx thereof. It is ordered that the said hoggs bee equally divided betwixt them and to bee so shared by xxxxxx in different men /theire neighbors/ and the said ELLIS BROWNE to pay Court Charges als execucon.

The difference between THOMAS CASON plaintiffe and THOMAS TODD defendt at the request of the said CASON is referred to the next Court........

Whereas HENRY SNAYLE and THOMAS SMYTHIARS are indebted unto JOHN HOLMES 1100 pownds of tobacco and caske doe by bill. Payment is ordered to be made..............

An attachment is graunted unto RICHARD HARTGRAVE on the estate of JOHN NUDGHATT (or Nudghoff?) for certain Commodityes to the value of 2 and 20 shillings fowre pownds Ster: at the first penny with a paire of shoes due by condicon produced in Court......to bee satisfactory for the said debt unto the said HARTGRAVE.

Whereas it appeareth to the Court that RICHARD GARDNER servant unto
11 RICHARD OWENS hath very much absented (*) himself out of his said masters service by often running away to the great preiudice (prejudice) of the said RICHARD OWENS and negleck of his affaires. It is ordered thereupon that the said RICHARD GARDNER from this day forward shall serve the said RICHARD OWENS 18 compleate moneths according to Act of Assembly in satisfaccon of his service lost in running away as aforesaid and if the said GARDNER shall hereafter runne away then to bee lyable to further satisfaccon as is above menconed.

Whereas RICHARD WORSTER is indebted unto JAMES WARNER 247 pownds of tobacco.....payment ordered to be made...... (Note: the name Worster, although spelling is with a W is almost certainly FOSTER. There are many items in other records which spell the name both ways. AGW)

The Court doth order JONATHAN NEALE to pay 3 and 20 days worke unto JOHN CARRAWAY and to pay all Court Charges.............

JOHN RICHARDSON is indebted unto JOHN MARTIN 300 pownds of tob^{o}....... ordered that payment be made..........

JACOB BRADSHAWE was pressed to goe to RAPPAHANNOCK the MARCH 1644 in the roome of WALTER PRESSAR. It is ordered that those persons at Lynhaven that were then to sett out said PRESSAR shall proporconably amongst them pay unto the said BRADSHAWE what worke is remaining due to the said BRADSHAWE and allsoe 200 pownds of tobacco in lieu of his provision in goeing out the said MARSH als Execucon (The word Marsh or March could mean a march in Rappahannock?)

The estate of WILLIAM DURFORD deceased is indebted unto SIMON HANCOCK 17 shillings 8 pence Ster: money as appeares unto the Court.......... ordered that THOMAS NARSH (MARSH?) administrator out of the said decedents estate. WILLIAM DURFORD deceased did owe unto MR: CORNELIUS LYD (LOYD) 910 pownds of (*) tobacco as appeares....by accoumpts 11a
of the said LOYD......ordered that THOMAS MARSH (or NARSH) being administrator shall satisfy the said debt out of the decedents estate.......

THOMAS MARSH made appeare unto the Court that WILLIAM DURFORD deceased was justly indebted unto him 1757 pownds of tobacco.

The Court doth order that JESPER HOSKINS bee satisfyed out of the estate of WILLIAM DURFORD deceased (blurred) hundred and 90 pownds of tob°..... THOMAS MARSH.....to make payment......

The Court doth order that WILLIAM SHIPP bee satisfyed out of the estate of WILLIAM DURFORD deceased 56 pownds of tobacco.......THOMAS MARSH admr to make payment......

....order that THOMAS MARSH admr of WILLIAM DURFORD doe satisfy out of the decedents estate due for 3 months dyett of the deceased........... 300 pownds of tobacco unto MR. CORNELIUS LOYD........................

....order that THOMAS MARSH admr of WILLIAM DURFORD doe satisfy out of the decedents estate 50 pownds of tobacco unto MR. EDWARD LOYD and made appeare to be justly due from the decedent.

ELLEN LIGHTHART widdowe ordered to receive out of the Levye this present year 50 pownds of tobacco more then the 80 pownds already allowed for the use of her boat to carry up the Burgesses in respect she hath made appeare that the Grapnell belonging to her said boat was broken.

end of folio 11a

*12

Upon a former reference to this Court It is nowe ordered that ELIZABETH YELLOWE singlewoman and servant unto MR: WILLIAM JULIAN doe immediately receive 20 good lashes on her bare back for her Incontinency with XPOFER (Christopher) ROWLES (or Rawles) and thereupon being delivered of a bastard child and this Court doth order MR: WILLIAM JULIAN to pay all the Court charges for which the said ELIZABETH YELLOWE shall make satisfaccon unto the said MR: JULIAN at the expiracon of her Indenture or before she depart her service.

THOMAS SAYER is indebted unto WILLIAM COARD, Marriner the summe of 4960 pownds of tobacco & caske being the remainder of a debt due upon bond for 9200 pownds of tobacco & caske provided in Court and acknowledged by the said SAYER.....ordered that payment be made......one years forbearance......

JAMES SMITH attorney of HENRY HILL doth acknowledge a Judgment for 300 pownds of tobacco due by bill unto JAMES LOPHAM with one years forbearance..........

JOHN STRATTON was arrested to this Court to answere the suite of GEORGE HAWKINS whoe not xsecuting his suite.....ordered that HAWKINS bee therefore non-suited and pay 40 pownds of tob^{o} for charges to the said STRATTON.

XPOFER ROWLES (Rawles?) is discharged of his Recognizance (appearance in Court) taken to appeare this Court and is ordered to doe penance by standing in a white sheet in the Chappel of ELIZABETH RIVER in the face of the Congregacon on the next Sabbath day that any publique meeting is had according to the Intent of a former order for his incontinency with ELIZABETH YELLOW & to pay Court Charges.

12a *

LANCASTER LOVETT is ordered to bee paid out of the present levy....50 pownds of tobacco for killing a wolfe.

THOMAS DAVYES - ditto

WILLIAM PELL - ditto

THOMAS WILLIAMS IS ORDERED TO PAY 100 pownds of tob^{o} for a ffyne to the use of the County for being drunk upon a Lord's day as appeares by his owne confession.......

Whereas EDWARD SELBY, JOHN CARRAWAY, ROBERT BOWERS, TRUSTRUM MASON, GEORGE PARRINGTON and others were presented to this Court for not planting of Corne.....the parties aforesaid having traversed theire presentments are discharged every man payeing his owne Court Charges.

...the difference between CLEMENT THEOBALDE and JOHN POWYES concerning ELIZABETH HALL /now the wyfe of the said THEOBALDE/ her being delivered of a bastard Child and the fathering thereof were re(fered?) to the session of this Court to bee fully determined and upon long debate thereof and it appearing by the deposicons of many credible persons that CLEMENT THEOBALDE is the father of the said bastard child. It is ordered that the sd THEOBALDE doe aske forgiveness in the face of the Court and in the Parish Church of Lynhaven on the next Sabbath day devine service is said and the congregation present by acknowledging his wishfull accusacon of the said JOHN POWYS in the matters aforesaid and allsoe pay all charges expended or occasioned in the Suite which the Court is to assesse at their nest session by bill of costs to bee presented unto them by the sd JOHN POWYS.

It is ordered that JOHN POWYS doe pay unto JANIE LAND the wyfe of FRANCIS LAND 120 pownds of tobacco for charges of her xxxxxxxxxxx her man being often Subpenoed to the Court by the said JOHN POWYS * 13

JOHN HOLMES hath undertaken for the psonall appearance of AGNES his wife at the next Court to answer the suite of CAPT: THOMAS WILLOUGHBY other-wyse the said JOHN HOLMES to bee lyable to the award of the Court.

Execucon (written in margin)
Whereas it appeares unto the Court by several accopts &c that THOMAS SAYER is indebted unto MR: CORNELIUS LOYD 2921 pownds of tob^o^. The Court with consent of the said MR: LOYD doth order payment thereof with in Sixe weekes and the Court Charges otherwyse execucon.

18 Nov 1646
Present vt Antea

Ordered to be recorded (vizt):
Whereas by Act of Court bearing date at JAMES CITTY the 22 Apr 1645 It was ordered that an Attachment bee awarded at the suite of CORNE-LIUS LOYD against soe much of the estate of ROBERT PAGE as will be suf-ficient security for 237 pownds 17 shillings and 2 pence Ster: money and 2000 pownds of Tobacco claymed by the said LOYD from the said PAGE. as will be sufficient security for satisfaccon of the aforesaid debt and it to detayne in your custody or otherwyse soe to provide as that it may bee lyable and responsible for the said debt. Hereof fayle not or you will answere the Contrary at your pitt (peril). Given at JAMES CITTY under my hand this 22 Mar 1645/6. /s/ WILLIAM BERKELEY

To the Sheriff of Lower Norff: his dep^tie^ or dep^ties^:

The Court doth order that the estate of MR: ROBERT PAGE attached in the hands of MR: MATHEW PHILLIPPS and others at the suit of MR: CORNELIUS LOYD 237 pownds 17 shillings 2 pence Sterl: money and 2000 pownds of tobacco shall bee and remayne in the Custody and possession of the (*) said 13a MR: PHILLIPPS till the 20 Dec 1647. And if the said MR: ROBERT PAGE shall not by that tyme come or send to make answers unto the Clayme and demands of the said MR: CORNELIUS LOYD then the aforesaid estate to bee lyable to satisfaccon for the aforementioned de debts upon the legall determination of the Court. MR: PHILLIPPS haveing undertaken that the said estate in his hands shall bee forthcoming to bee answerable as aforesaid.

An attachment is granted unto MR: CORNELIUS LOYD the administrator of JOHN WEBB deceased against whatsoever estate of PHILLIPP KERAWICH, merchant deceased it remayning in the hands of WILLIAM SHIPP and to bee satisfactory unto the said MR: CORNELIUS LOYD for what debt or debts shall bee made appeare to bee due and oweing from the said KERAWICH deceased unto the said WEBB deceased upon legal determination.

Whereas the Grand Assembly Anno D^m^ 1642 out of theire Christian care and tender commiseration of the fatherles did ordayne and enact that all guardians and overseers should nowe every yeare deliver exa(ct?) accoumpts of orphants estates and of theire improv(ment?).

And the Commissioners allsoe thereby injoyned to be very carefull and circumspect not only in ye provisions of such orphants but allsoe in the Godly education of them and preservacon of theire estates, as by the said Act more at large appeares. And MRS: SARAH GOOKIN having as yet given noe such accoumpt of the estates of the children and Orphants of CAPTAIN ADAM THORROWGOOD long since deceased as by the Act aforementioned she ought to have done though very often requested there unto.

It is thereupon ordered that the said MRS: GOOKIN shall exhibit unto this board at the next Court (being upon the 15 Dec next) a true and perfect accoumpt upon oath oath of all and singular the estate belonging to the Orphants of the said CAPT: ADAM THORROWGOOD of what nature quality or condition soever it is and of the imp(ro)vement thereof since the division And the Sheriffe is forthwith required to give the said MRS: GOOKIN expresse notice of this order.

14 *

All matters of suite in difference betweene CAPT: THOMAS WILLOWGHBY ESQ: the administrator of MR: RICHARD WATE deceased and CAPT: JOHN SIBSEY concerning the accoumpts and Copartnership of the decedent with the said JOHN SIBSEY after much p(er)usall of the said accoumpts and long debating thereof by the Court at the request of the said CAPT: WILLOWGHBY alleaging the accoumpts of CAPT: SIBSEY to bee imp(er)fect and insufficient are transmitted to the consideration of the Governor and Counsells upon the fifth day of the next Quarter Court /being the 25 day of this instant November/ the said CAPT: WILLOWGHBY forthwith entering into bond for his appearence as aforesaid and to pay double damages according to Act of Assembly is provided in Cases ofAppeals.

In due obedience to the eighth Act of the last Grand Assembly for the taking of just and true Lists of all tytheable persons, lands, horses, Mares, Geldings, Cowes, Sheep and Goats within this County wherein it was concerned there is a great defect to the injury of the publique. And the Court confiding in the Care, Integrity and Circumspection of these persons herein named doe accordingly order and appoynt them and every of them respectively in theire severall Lymitts hereby specify to take true and perfect lists of all the tytheable persons lande, heifers, Mares, Geldings, Sowes, of three years old and of all breeding sheep and goats in like manner /vizt/:

EDWARD HALL and WILLIAM LUCAS for Lynnhaven
JOHN HOLMES for the Little Creek
SIMON HANCOCK for the Eastern Branch
THOMAS BROWNE for the Western Branch
JOHN ffERINHAUGH from Daniell Tanners Creeke upwards to Broad Creek including the Southern Branch
& THOMAS IVEY from the said Daniell Tanners Creeke Downewards (North not South as it would seem -GW) to CAPT: WILLOUGHBY and all and every the persons aforenamed are strictly required in theire several precincts as is afore expressed to take special care to use theire best endeavors &c.............

Ordered to be Recorded: An Accoumpt of the Cattle of ROBERT ffITT? (HITT?) Hitt deceased delivered the 18 Nov **1646** by MR: THOMAS SAYER upon Oath /vizt/ Old Brown, Coale, Chitt, these three went fallow. Wenn, Genteel, Pye, Young Browne,one heifer, one Cowe Calfe, 9 ffemales in all and 3 bull calfes. /s/ THO: SAYER
(Note: This name is probably HILL, but note how it is written. AGW)

THOMAS HOWELL aged xxvy (26) yeares or thereabouts sworne in Court sayth that he the deponent heard MR: JULIANS man NICHOLAS WYATT say that after HENRY MERRITT was free that the said NICHOLAS had 3 yeares to serve and more this depont: sayeth not. /s/ THOMAS HOWELL

........I JOHN WEST Esquire, Governor and Captaine General of Virginia send Greeting......WHEREAS: by letters bearing date the 22 Jun 1634 from the right hon^{ble} the Lords of his Maties (Majesties) hon^{ble} privie Counsell. Theire Lo^{ps} (Lordships) did authorize the Governor and Counsell of Virginia to dispose of such proporcons of Land to all planters being free men as had power to doe before the yeare **1625** when according to divers orders and constitutions in that case...........and appoynted all dividents of land any wayes due or belonging to any adventurer or planters of what condicon soever were to bee layed out and assigned to them according to the severall conditions in the same mentioned. Nowe knowe yee that I the said CAPT: JOHN WEST ESQR: doe with the consent of the Counsell and State Give and graunt unto CAPT: WILLIAM TUCKER e(sqr?) and one of the Counsell of state 200 acres of land scytuate Lyeing and being upon the North side of the Westermost Branch of Elizabeth River beginning fo(r) measure at a Creek called Allington, his Creeke and bownding South South West upon the said Creeke North North East upon a branch of the said River called Warw(ick?) branch West North West into the Woods and East South East up -(the bottom of this page is torn off and all that remains is of no value)- the said WILLIAM TUCKER * by and 15
for the transportation at his owne proper costs and Charges of fower persons into this Collony whose names are with the records menconed under his patent. To have and to hold ....given under my hand this 14 Jul 1635............ /s/ JOHN WEST John West

xxiy (22?) Nov 1646
I CORNELIUS LOYD GENT: doe assigne over this pattent......unto RICHARD JONES his heires &c........-(bottom of page torn)- this day of November...................... /s/ xxxxxxxx LOYD

end of folio 15
* 15a

AT A COUNTY COURT HOLDEN UPON THE 15 DEC 1646 PRESENT:

CAPT: THOMAS WILLOUGHBY ESQR:

CAPT: JOHN SIBSEY	MR: CORNELIUS LOYD
MR: ffRANCIS MASON	MR: THOMAS MEARES — COM^{rs}
MR: THOMAS LAMBART	MR: MATH: PHILLIPS
MR: EDWARD LOYD	

WHEREAS: AGNES the wyfe of JOHN HOLMES hath spoken certaine thunderous words tending to the great disparragement of CAPT: THOMAS WILLOWGHBY, Esqr: as appeares by the deposicon (of) HENRY SNAYLE and THOMAS SMYTHAIRS. It is ordered thereupon that the said AGNES HOLMES shall receive in presence of this Court fivete(en)e good lashes on her bare back and allsoe weare a pa(per?) upon her head with these words written in Capital letters /vizt/ for slaundering CAPT: WILLOWGHBY sayeing "I would put him by his oath for a fr-d (fraud? or Freak? this word is so badly faded that only the fr can be read, however it seems to be a five letter word, not a four letter one!) that I know and allsoe to weare the said paper on the Lords day at the Parish Church at Linh(aven) and on a Lords day at the publique meeting xxxxxx Elizabeth River one howre (hour) in each place and the Sheriffe to see the pformance hereof be(tween?) this and the next Court. And the said AGNES HOLMES to pay all the Court Charges or Execucon.
(Note: Today, 1970, they get by with bombings and worse - but such drastic punishment for calling someone a fraud, or whatever the word is. AGW) - (Should we take heed and punish our criminals?)

An Attachment is graunted unto MR: ROBERT EYRE against the estate of PETER GARNIBOOTE? being in the hands of the said MR: EYRE for satisfaccon of a debt of 200 pownds of tobacco and caske..................

The difference between GEORGE HORNER plaintiffe and DEBORAH GLASCOCK defendt: xxxxxxxxx 500 xxxxxxx xxxx consen(t?) of both parties xxxxxx xxxx xxfered to the next Cxxxx bee hxxxx -(rest of the page, the right hand corner missing - probably contained not more than two or three words at most)

16 *

A judgment of this Court dated 15 Oct 1645 graunted unto RICHARD KENNAR against WILLIAM JOHNSON is revived and execucon to issue forth xx upon the said former order.

A Certificate for 1050 acres of Land is graunted unto DEBORAH GLASCOCK, widdowe made appeare to bee due upon her oath for the transportation of those persons into this Collony here undernamed /vizt/

ROBERT GLASCOCK and DEBORAH GLASCOCK

ELIZABETH BRAY	JOHN BRADWELL	
ROBERT BIRD	JOHN HEBDEN	
ffRANCIS BRIGHT	WILLIAM BURGESS	These 7 are assigned unto RICHARD WHITEHURST
THOMAS SHEPARD	JOSEPH MILLER	
WILLIAM COLEMAN	RICHARD TINDLEY	
JOHN RIGG	ROBERT TINDLEY	
JOHN WILKINSON	DEBORAH CROSWELL	
MATHEW READ	ROBERT BOWERS	
AMYE EDGAR	PETER RIGGLESWORTH	
HENRY GARDNER		

WHEREAS: it appears unto the Court that THOMAS SMYTHAIRS is indebted unto the estate belonging unto the orphants of MRS: ALICE SEAWELL decd: the summe of 550 pownds of tobacco and Caske due by bill. The Court doth order payment thereof with the Court Charges unto MR: MATHEW PHILLIPPS guardian unto the orphants ....within ten days.

THOMAS SMYTHAIRS is indebted unto the estate of HENRICK LIGHTHART decd: 264 pownds of tob° and Caske...........ordered that the said SMYTHIARS doe (pay) the said debt with Court charges xxxxxxxx LIGHTHART the de( ) administraxxx xxxxx said decedent within xxxxxxxxxxxxxxxxxxxx xxxxxxxxxxxxxxxxxxxxxxxxxxxxxxxxxxxxxxxxxxxxxxx that DEBORAH xxxxxxxxxxxxxxxxxxxxxxxxxxxxxxxxxxxxxxxxxxxxxxxxxxxxxxxxx SIMON OVERZEE (These last two lines are probably a different record from the above - see what follows on next page.) *16a
merchaunt upon accoumpt the summe of 770 pownds of tob° and caske. It is ordered that payment thereof bee made within tenn dayes............

It is ordered that SIMON PETERS doe pay unto GEORGE HORNER one barrell of Indian Corne...........

WHEREAS: JOHN ARIS (Harris) is indebted unto CAPT: JOHN CHESMAN 600 pownds of tobacco and Caske......ordered that payment bee made........

WHEREAS: ROBERT SMYTH deceased.....was indebted unto MR. ROBERT PAGE 440 pownds of tobacco.......It is ordered that JOHN MERRIDAY being Copartner with the said decedent and JOHN ARIS now bee Copartner with the said MERRIDAY doe pay said debt...............................

WHEREAS: JOHN MERRIDAY and JOHN ARIS are indebted unto JOHN LASH 340 pownds of tob° and Caske per bill.....It is ordered that payment bee made..........

WHEREAS: the difference depending in this Court betweene THOMAS SMYTHAIRS plantiffe and ELLEN LIGHTHART administratrix of HENRICK LIGHTHART deceased defendt: concerning the xxxxxxxxacon of JOHN GUTTERIDG out of this Co(llony?) xxxxxxxxx -(rest of page is torn off)-xxxxxxxxx

*17

....sworne by theire verdict have fownd for the defendt ELLEN LIGHTHART The Court doth give Judgement thereupon and further order the said SMYTHIARS to paye 50 pownds of tob° unto the said ELLEN LIGHTHART for costs of the suite als execucon.

Upon the peticon of MR: EDWARD LOYD unto the board for satisfaccon for the care an(d) trouble in lookeing after and keeping certaine neat cattle formerly belonging unto JONATHAN LANGWORTH deceased and now appertayning unto WALTER MICHELL and OSMOND COLCHESTER the assignees of the said LANGWORTH as is alleaged. The Court doth order MR: EDWARD LOYD to receive satisfaccon therefore out of the estate of the said MICHELL and COLCHESTER as followeth: /vizt:/ 20 pownds of tobacco a piece yearely for nyne Cowes till the said Cowes come to the age of three yeares and 20 pownds of tobacco a piece yearely for all such other Cattle which shall bee delivered by the said MR: EDWARD LOYD unto MR: MATHEW PHILLIPPS the Attorney of the said MICHELL & COLCHESTER for theire use and MR: EDWARD LOYD to give a generall discharge for keeping the said cattle and MR: PHILLIPPS to receive the said cattle and to acquitt the said MR: EDWARD LOYD therefrom.

MORE PRESENT MR: HENRY WOODHOUSE

The suit commenced in this Court on the behalf of ANNIE ONELY and JOHN DAVENPORT by JOHN CARTER by way of accon sur 'le Case against WILLIAM LUCAS having Intermarried the Relict and administratrix of CESAR PUGGETT deceased for a pretended debt of ₤ 57/13/5 Ster: money and surmysed to bee due form the said decedent xxxxxxxxxxxxxxxxxxxxxxxxxxx (last line has been torn off of the page) xxxxxxxxxxxxxxxxxx at the
17a * instant desire of the said JOHN CARTER being the Attorney of the said ANNE ONELY and JOHN DAVENPORT is transmitted to the Governor and Counsell for the 10th day of the Quarter Court. The said CARTER immediately giving bond with security & then and there to (be) presente with effect (sic) the aforesaid suit or accon against the said WILLIAM LUCAS allsoe to pay double daminges as according to Acts of Assembly is pvided in Cases of Appeal.

WHEREAS: JOHN ARIS (or AVIS?) Avis and JOHN MERRIDAY are indebted unto MR: MATHEW PHILLIPPS per accoumpt the sum of 540 pownds of Tob^{o} and Caske......ordered that payment thereof be made..................

All matters of difference upon bills, debts and accoumpts between MR: ROBERT POWYS and THOMAS CASON are referred by consent of partyes to the arbitration and award of HENRY WOODHOWSE and MR: EDWARD HALL.

It is ordered that JOHN MARTIN shall appeare at the next Court to answere the suit of LAND (most probably Francis Land)for a debt of 150 pownds of tob^{o} and 4 barrells of Corne claymed by the said LAND and MARTIN for expresse notice thereof by a Copy of this order.

An attachment is graunted unto ANDREW WARNER against soe much of the estate of NATH: BASSETT (this name is Mathew, see later) as upon legal Determination may bee satisfactory for a Debt of 1000 pownds of tobacco claymed by the said WARNER to bee due per bill from the said MATHEW BASSETT.

It is ordered that THOMAS BROOKE bee nonsuited and doe satisfy unto WILLIAM LUCAS 30 pownds of tobacco for charge & for molestacon.

(last two lines on this page are mutilated)

that THOMAS
of ROBERT

end of folio 17a

15 Dec 1646 18

* JOHNS, deceased the summe of 1504 pownds of tob^{o}. The Court doth order payment thereof unto EDWARD BUDDEN attorney of JOHN JOHNS administrator of the said decedent within 30 days and the said TODD to pay the Court Charges. (Note - last page Thomas (Todd?) Budden 18

The Court doth order in ballance of accoumpts that MR: HENRY WOODHOWSE doe pay unto MR: THOMAS CASON 120 pownds of tob^{o} provided the said CASON shall make it appeare at the next Court by sufficient testimony that the said MR: WOODHOWSE was to stand to all casualtyes in the keeping of two turkeys.

Upon a bill exhibited unto this board by JOHN POWYS according to the tenor of a farmer order the last session of this Court. It is ordered that CLEMENT THEOBALDE shall satisfy and pay unto the said JOHN POWYS on the 20 Nov next yeare the summe of 895 pownds of tob^{o} and within 20 dayes the said THEOBALDE is to give bond with sufficient security for paymant thereof at the tyme aforesaid. Otherwyse execucon

It is ordered that THOMAS BROOKE bee nonsuited and pay unto WILLIAM BASNETT 30 pownds of tobacco for charges and for Molestation.

16 Dec 1646
present vt Antea

MR: JOHN SIDNEY doth promise to appeare at the next Court to answere the suite of CAPT: JOHN WEST ESQR: in an accon of debt and to abyde by award of the Court therein.

WHEREAS: Emergent occasions of many busynesses have at present Interveyned. It is thereupon thought fitt and ordered that a Court bee holden for this County xxxxxxxxxxxxxxxxxxxxxxxxxxxxxxxxth day of *
Jan next and all psons required to take notice thereof............ 18a
ordered to be recorded.

NOVEMBER 9 1646: Article betwixt LEIFTENAUNT ffRANCIS MASON and WILLIAM DOWNMAN concluded and agreed upon as followeth /vizt/:

IMPRIMUS: the said WILLIAM DOWNMAN hath himself his heires &c bargained and sold unto the said ffRANCIS MASON his heires &c 100 acres of Land for which Land is nowe in the possession of the Leift: And the said DOWNMAN is to confirme said land before a Judge of the Court.

ITEM: in consideration whereof the said LEIFT: MASON is to deliver for the use of WILLIAM DOWNMAN one servant for the terme of yeares to bee betwixt 5 and 10 years and the right of 100 acres of Land 3 barrells of -(faded)- the worth of 1000 pownds of Tob^{o} to to be paid in Linnen, woolen, shews (shoes) and stockings -(faded)- say part in hand the residue of the goods and corne upon the confirmation of the land, the serv(ant) to bee paid the next yeare for the preformance hereof wee the abovenamed doe bynd ourselves the assumpsit (sic) of 4000 pownds of Tob^{o} per each to the other. Witness our hands....... ffRA: MASON
Wit: JOHN CHISMAN, THOMAS BRIDGES, EDWARD L..... WILLIAM DOWNMAN

Received 14 Mar 1642 of MR: CESAR PUGGETT in full payment of a bonde of 2000 pownds of tobacco with said bond CAPT: PIERCE hath yet in his custody the summe of 2000 pownds of merchantable tobacco. I say received in full of all dues debts & demands for the use of CAPT: WILLIAM PEIRCE
Wittness: JOHN WALKER per me WILLIAM SHEERES

.... I JOHN MARTIN of Lynhaven doe deliver one cowe for the use of HENRY WATSON in lieu of one Cowe which MR: BARTHOLOMEW HOSKINS gave unto the said HENRY which cowe was killed with a tree and further the said Cowe being now delivered before MR: BARTHOLOMEW HOSKINS and MR: SIMON HANCOCK being marked and having such markes as followeth: that is to say cropped and slitt in the cropp on the left eare and a slitt under the right eare coulored browne and all white under the belly and a white ridge along the back and mealy mouthed which cowe with all the female increase is to goe for the use of the said HENRY WATTSON.
Wittness my hand 12 Oct 1646 /s/ JOHN MARTIN
Wit:
THOMAS ($^{T}_{D}$) DAVYES & ANDREW (AB) BODNAM

16 Dec 1646

Ordered by the Court to be recorded vizt:

The accoumpt of tobacco which hath beene payd by order and bill for the use of JOHN MOYE deceased as follows:

	tob°
October Court 1644 paid by order to THOMAS DAVYES	300
August Court 1645 paid by order to WILLIAM SHIPP	032
January Court 1645 paid by order to MR: CASON	070
AUGUST Court 1645 paid by order to WM: BASNETT	150
More by bill to JEFFREY WRIGHT	200
19a * Paid by order to JACOB BRADSHAWE for Rappahannock March	010
Paid by order to ffRANCIS LANG for a payle (sic)	030
Paid to RICHARD ffORSTER fforster for the boyes keeping	100
due to mee from the estate of JOHN MOYE which) I produce oath of upon the Inventory)	100
Summe is	1022
	and Caske

The amount of Clerkes fees paid for the use of JOHN MOYE deceased (vizt):

August 1645 for copy of an order to sell goods	008
More for recording the goods sold	012
for the copy thereof attested	012
October Court 1646 per oath vzt WM: JOHNSON	004
for the Recording of the Inventory	020
for the Copy thereof attested	020
Summe is	076

Paid for the use of JOHN MOYES Children this present yeare 1646 for the Levy	
for 300 acres of land	060
for 2 cowes	040
for the Kings Rent for 300 acres of Land paid in partof (seaventy?) [illegible]))	029
Summe is	129

Continued on page 19

The accoumpt of Goods bought for the use of the sonne of JOHN MOYE deceased vizt:

		Tob°
Judp 83	2 ells of Canvis	024
"	for one ell of Callicoe	009
"	for Cloth to make him cloathes	050
"	for making his clothes and 2 shirts) - fynding buttons and thredd)	050
"	for mending an old gunne	030
"	for one ell of Canvis	010
"	for 1½ yards of Lynnen	012
"	for one payre of showes (shoes)	015
"	for a quarter of a pownd of thredd	006
"	for 3/4 of an ell of Canvis	010
"	for 2 ells of Canvis	020* 20
* "	for one yard of cotton	010
"	for 2 yards of cloath	005
"	for one barrell of Eares (corn) Layd in for his dyett. More for a hatt	025
"	for a yard and a quarter of Ribbin	003
"	for 3 yards and halfe of Lynnen 14[1] per yard and Caske	053
"	for 2½ yards of Searge at 18 per yard and Caske	048
"	more for a shirt	027
	Summe is	473

ffor expences two days being summoned)
to the Court at Mr: HAYES in August 1645) (blank)
ffor expences two dayes being summoned)
to the Court at WILLIAM SHIPPS in October 1645)

The Cropp of JOHN MOYE deceased in 1644 in tobacco was	275
ffor his Corne it was disposed of for the use of his children	
More three turkeys sold for	150
ffor WILLIAM EADYES Eadyes these was deducted of the cropp	120
More allowed for the badnes of his tobacco	050

The accoumpt of tobacco receaved for goods sold at an Outcry vizt:	
Receaved of MARTIN COLE for goods sold him	032
Receaved of SAM CHARNIKE (Cornick? or Charnicoe ?) for goods sold him	500
Receaved of MR: WOODHOWSE for goods sold him	060
Receaved of MR: CASON for a pewter chamber pott by order before MR: WOODHOWSE	020
Receaved of THOMAS KEELING 350 fower penny nayles for a debt of five penny nayles which he owed to JOHN MOYE deceased	
*	20a
More receaved of WILLIAM JOHNSON for goods sold him	036
Receaved of WILLIAM JOHNSON for goods sold him	344
Receaved of WILLIAM JACOB by bill for the use of JOHN MORE deceased	200
Receaved of WILLIAM JOHNSON for goods sold	200
Summe is	1508

Continued on page 20.

The accoumpt of the Cattle belonging to the estate of JOHN MOYE dec'd.

IMPRIMUS two Cowes
" one bull of one yeare and three quarters old or thereabouts
" One heifer of the same age
" One bull and one heifer of two yeares three quarters old or thereabouts
" One Steare Calfe and one Cowe Calfe of Nyne moneths old &c

This accoumpt was delivered into Court by ROBERT DAVYES and WILLIAM EADY being overseers of the aforesaid estate.

AT A COUNTY COURT HOLDEN UPON THE 20 Jan 1646

PSENT: CAPT: THOMAS WILLOWGHBY ESQ:
CAPT: JOHN SIBSEY) _(MR: THOMAS MEARES
MR: CORNELIUS LOYD)- COMRS: (MR: EDWARD LOYD
MR: MATH: PHILLIPPS)

A former Order of this Court bearing date the 20 Feb 1644 graunted unto ROBERT SMYTH deceased against MR: JOHN SIDNEY for the delivery of a Cowe with Calfe and a yearling at Blunt Point; Upon the peticon of WILLIAM SMYTH brother of the decedent is revived and execucon to issue forth as according to the said former order.
(Note: Blunt Poynt was in Warwick County)(AGW)

21 *

The difference in suite betweene MR: MATH: PHILLIPPS plaintiffe against ROGER WILLIAMSON and RICHARD WORSTER defend[ts] by consent is referred to the next Court to bee heard and determined.
(Note: Even though the name is written Worster this name is undoubtedly Richard Foster. A matter of the double f (ff) creeping into the records as W. AGW) Worster

The matters in suite depending in this Court by way of accon sur le case betweene CAPT: THOMAS WILLOWGHBY ESQR: Complaynaunt against SAMPSON WARING and THOMAS BROOKE defend[t] at the request of the said CAPT: WILLOWGHBY are transmitted to the consideration of the Governor and Counsell upon the 10th day of the next Quarter Court the said CAPT: WILLOWGHBY entering into bond &c.......................................

Whereas RICHARD SMYTH is indebted unto SIMON HANCOCK 300 pownds of tobo & Caske .... ordered that payment thereof be made within ten dayes ....

WHEREAS: it appeares unto the Court that REINORD CORNELISON ffOXE is indebted unto EDWARD HALL Chyurgeon the summe of 700 pownds of tob[o] and caske for playsters (sic) &c administered unto the said REINORD by the said HALL in his voyadg (voyage) to Virginia and paynes taking. The Court doth order payment thereof within 10 dayes and Court Charges.....

WHEREAS: SAMPSON WARING is indebted unto ARTHUR BROWNE Merchaunt 520 pownds of tob[o] due p(er) bill as appeares unto the Court. It is ordered that payment be made within ten dayes..............

The difference in suite betweene ELLEN LIGHTHART [illegible] (widow?) p[lt] and CAPT: THOMAS WILLOWGHBY ESQR: def[t] for a debt of sixe hundred pownds of tob[o] and Caske is referred to the next Court to be determined.

* 21a

An administration is ordered to bee graunted unto WILLIAM CAPPS on the estate of JAMES SMYTH deceased being kinsman to the decedent the said CAPPS putting in good security according to Course for the dischargement of the Court.

WHEREAS: the sherriffe hath attached one Grizell *Grizzell* Cowe, one red and white cowe & two grizell shotes p(ro)perly belonging unto JOHN MUDGETT whoe is iustly (justly) indebted unto RICHARD HARTGRAVE certayne goods and commodityes to the valew of twenty shillings fower pence ster: money at the first pennys with a paire of shewes (shoes) as appeares unto the Court. It is ordered thereupon that the said Hoggs bee apprased or values by fower sufficient men to be appointed by the sherriffe and the said HARTGRAVE to bee satisfyed his said debt with Court Charges.

The difference in this Court depending betweens CAPT: WILLIAM ATTERBURY Comp[tt] agst MR: WILLIAM JULYAN ([illegible]) deft concerning a debt of £ 9/5/6 Ster: p(er) specialtye at the request of the said MR: JULYAN is referred to the next Court to bee heard and determined.
(Note: The name Atterbury is in the indexes at Chesapeake Court House as WILLIAM A. HERBURY. Name is written thusly: *Atterbury* AGW)

JAMES SMYTH late deceased did a little before his death give over /as alleaged/ for the paymt: of one hhd of tob unto THOMAS WARD Chyrurgeon which was received by WARD accordingly but nowe detayned. It is ordered that said hhd of tob[o] remayne where it is and to bee disposed of according to further order of the Court.

WHEREAS: CHRISTOPHER BURROWGH being impleaded by RICHARD CONQUEST for certaine Clerkes fees occasioned at his Ma[tes]: suit which said ffees the Court according to their construccon * of the Acts of Assembly do 22
conceive Justly due apertayning unto the said CONQUEST by vertue of his office and dayly attendance therein Notwithstanding the said BURROWGHS doth desire to appeale from heare to the Governor and Counsell which is accordingly graunted BURROWGHS entering into bond with security his appearance upon the 6th day of the next Quarter Court &c.............

Attachment graunted unto GEORGE WHITE CLARKE upon the estate of EDMOND THORROWGOOD for £ 13 sterling money claymed by the said GEORGE WHITE and to bee satisfactory for the same upon a legall determination.

WHEREAS: THOMAS BONNER indebted unto DEBORAH GLASCOCK widdowe administratrix of ROBERT GLASCOCK deceased 45 shillings Ster: money due by bill Ordered by consent of DEBORAH and JAMES WARNER ye attorney of the said BONNER that present payment bee made with Court Charges...............
(Note: Deborah *Glascocke* and in the same record Robert *Glascocke* AGW)

WHEREAS: JOHN MACEY is indebted unto WILLIAM SMYTH 121 *l*l of Tob[o].... ordered that payment bee made.......................... *Macey*

22 continued 20 Jan 1646/7

(NOTE: From this point on the Whereases and other superfluous wording will be eliminated to some extent. AGW)

WILLIAM SHIPP agst ROBERT HAYES deft: concerning a debt of 1450 l tob° at the request of said CAPT: WILLOWGHBY in the behalfe of the said HAYES is referred to the next Court............

CERTIFICATE is granted unto RICHARD KENNAR that according to Act of Assembly hath sett up his name at the Court House dore (door) to give publique notice (of his) intended voyage to England this present shipping.

22a *
THOMAS WARD indebted unto JOHN HOLMES p(er) bill 1462 l tob° & Caske.. ....payment is ordered to bee made within 10 dayes...................

......by former order the sherriffe hath attached one heifar of the proper estate of GEORGE RUTLAND who being indebted unto EDWARD CANNON 255 l tob° p bill......ordered that heifar bee appraysed by fower sufficient men......and delivered unto CANNON.......towards the debt.....

Attachmt: graunted THOMAS WARD Chyrurgeon agst: Estate of WILLIAM BASNETT for 500 l tob° & caske..

Ordered that THOMAS SAYER be non suited and pay unto JAMES SYMONS 20 l tob° for molestacon.

THOMAS OWEN is non suited & ordered to pay unto THOMAS HUGHES for molestacon.

JOHN HILL to pay unto CAPT: WILLIAM ATTERBURY ₤ 6 sterling money /due by act/ within 10 dayes..........

23 The difference depending in this Court betweene RICHARD CONQUEST * and ROBERT HAYES in accon of debt for 922 l tob° at the request of CAPT: WILLOWGHBY in HAYES behalfe........to the next Court.......

RICHARD CONQUEST plt: agst THOMAS IVEY deft: concerning divers debts reckonings and accoumpts nowe in controversie are referred to the next Court......IVEY then to prove upon oath what is due unto him from the said CONQUEST since the 22 Jun 1646 last past..........

JOHN BASON, Marrener plt and RENIORD CORNELISON FOX deft: concerning the Good Shipp called the BLACK ffOXE nowe ryding at anckor in Elizabeth River are referred to the next Court to bee heard and determined. And one or both partyes in the Interim to pcure an Interpreter and allsoe to procure the Charter Partye made between them to bee translated out of Dutch into English.

Ordered 21 Jul 1646 by MR: HENRY WOODHOWSE that JOHN MARTIN should pay unto ffRANCIS LAND 162 l tob° within 10 dayes then next following.....
Ordered 21 Jul 1646 by MR: HENRY WOODHOWSE that JOHN MARTIN should pay

unto ffRANCIS LAND 140 1 tob^o within 10 dayes.........................

Recordat die et Anno p dicbe

ffRANCIS LAND aged about 35 yeares sworne sayeth that about the 1 Apr 1644 he being at the howse of MR: GEORGE WHITE before his marriage with MRS: SYBILLA CODD She desiring the $depon^t$ to speake unto MR: WHITE concerning her daughter SUSANNA CODD to have of her husband CODDS Estate; which the deponent went * to MR: WHITE and moved the question to him 23a
according to her desire he graunted to give her daughter one heifar & one of her bedds more certainly this depont: sayeth not. Further this depont: sayth that the said heifar was not out of the mothers estate but MR: WHITES

ffRANCIS LAND

(NOTE: I cannot blame Mr. Beverley Fleet for wondering whether this name was Land or Laud. It is Francis Land as the records prove but is written: Another question is whether this Susanna Codd could have been Todd? The name is clearly written Codd - & AGW)

DEPOSICON of MR: CORNELIUS LOYD aged 39 yeares or thereabouts taken 1 Sep 1646 Sayeth that MR: WILLSON, Maister of the Shipp HAPPY RETURNE did often tell this depont: that he would give that little black negro boy which tended on him in the Rownd Howse unto THOMAS SIBSEY the sonne of JOHN SIBSEY sayeing that he tooke great affeccon to the child when he carried his mother (xxxx?) him to ST. CHRISTOPHERS. And further that he (the depont) being one tyme aboard the aforesaid shipp the said MR: WILLSON sent the negro /which negro is black Jackwhich is at CAPT: SIBSEYS/ downe to CAPT: SIBSEY by -faded- deponent and wished this depont: to tel(l) CAPT: SIBSEY and his wife that he sent the Negroe boy as a guift to his son THOMAS SIBSEY and further sayeth not.

CORNELIUS LLOYD

.... I ROBERT PAGE do acknowledge to have received of CAPT: JOHN SIBSEY 2 hhd of tob^o aboard the Shipp Pleiades conteyning neat in Virginia 583 pownds of tob^o which I bynd myselfe to make sale of /God sending mee safe to my desired Port/ and sale being made I am to pay unto MR: WILLIAM ATTERBURY the summe of ₤12 sterlinge and to bee accoumptable to the said CAPT: SIBSEY for the surplus /and in case it produce more/ and if the tob^o doth not make the sume of*₤12 ster:* CAPT: SIBSEY to be account- 24
able to ATTERBURY for so much as shall bee wanting..........9 Apr 1643

Wit: CORNELIUS LOYD p mee ROBT: PAGE

Receaved the 7 Apr 1646 of
414 CAPT: THOMAS WILLOWGHBY 5 hhds of tob^o weighing grosse for the which
418 I am to bringe
416 in such goodes as he doth write for by mee and to be accoumptable to
428 him for it he payinge ffreight and charges and to stand to all dangers
413 of the sea.

by mee ROB: ROUES/or/ RENES ?

(Note: What the numbers in the margin above mean I know not. AGW)

30 Jan 1646/7 Recorded by the Governor & Capt Generall of Virginia .....I SIR WILLIAM BERKELEY Gov&c.................................... Whereof ROBERT JONES late of this Collony deceased dying intestate and leaving an estate......in care of MATHEW HOWARD and ROBERT BOWERS..... according to order of Lower Norfolke County Court bearing date 16 Nov 1646 I doe give and graunt unto ye sd HOWARD and BOWERS administracon on the estate of the decedent.....& they to bring in an Inventory to
24a*the next County Court &c...... given at James Citty 30 Jan 1646/7
/s/ WILLIAM BERKELEY

By the Governor and Captain Generall of Virginia

WILLIAM BERKELEY knt Gov &c......granting administracon unto WILLIAM CAPPS on the estate of JAMES SMYTH late of this Collony deceased who dyed intestate and left an Estate in care of WILLIAM CAPPS being kinsman to the deceased /according to an order of Lower Norfolk County
25 *Court 12 Jan 1646/7/ 30 Jan 1646/7 WILLIAM BERKELEY

ATT A COUNTY COURT HELD FOR NANSEMOND 29 Dec 1646
PRESENT:
MR: OLIVER SPRYE)
MR: PHILL: BENNETT)- MR: EPA: LAWSON
MR: RICH: PRESTON)

WHEREAS: JOHN MANSELL Mansell servant to GEORGE TAYLOR hath peticoned the Court for his freedome and it appeares that he came into this Country with RICHARD EPHAM by Indenture for 3 years the which he hath served and entered into a new covenant with the said GEORGE TAYLOR for fower yeares. The which the Court conceives to ve of noe force And hath ordered that the said MANSELL bee free and TAYLOR to pay him his corne and clothes. And whereas said MANSELL hath in his service with the said TAYLOR gotten certain tob^{o} and other things by his trade. Court orders that he shall give an accoumpt thereof and deliver the same to TAYLOR or make him satisfaccon for the same.

Teste TOBY SMYTH Cler Cur

ATT A COUNTY COURT HOLDEN UPON THE 15 Feb 1646/7
PRESENT: CAPT: THOMAS WILLOWGHBY ESQ:

MR: CORNELIUS LOYD) MR: ffRANCIS MASON)
MR: THOMAS LAMBART)-- MR: THOMAS MEARES)- COMRS:
MR: EDWARD LOYD) MR: MATH: PHILLIPPS)

25a
*It appeares to the Court that MR: CORNELIUS LOYD per bill became boend with JAMES STONE Merchant for the delivery of a servant with a bedd and 2 suites of clothes unto LAURENCE PHILLIPPS at or before the last day of Dec last past......Ordered that MR: CORNELIUS LOYD shall....in liewe & satisfaccon of the said servant with clothes and bedding pay unto LAWRENCE PHILLIPPS 2000 l tob^{o} & Caske & Court Charges within 10 dayes.

Attachmt: graunted PETER GARINTOOTE Carenfoote agst the estate of WILLIAM BASNETT for a debt of 320 l tob^{o} & Caske with one yeares forbearance & Court Charges.

A certificate is graunted unto JOHN MARSHALL for 100 acres of land made appeare due upon oath for the transportation of WILLIAM BAXTER & ELIZABETH COLLINGS into this Collony.

.....ordered upon balance of accoumpts betweene JOHN ARIS (or Avis?) and JOHN MERRIDAY defts: at the suite of EDWARD STONE Comp^{t}: that ARIS and MERRIDAY shall pay unto STONE one Clothe suit and 3 barrels of corne with Court Charges. (ARIS, AVIS - Harris? - written Aris/Avis)

ROBERT BOWERS acknowledged a debt of 195 l tob^{o} and one hhd, the remainder of a specialty, unto JAMES WARNER to be justly due.....Paymt: is ordered.

Attachmt: graunted unto SAVILL GASKINE agst Estate of THOMAS BREWER... .... for a debt of 350 l tob^{o} and Caske unto GASKINE when the Court shall further determine thereof.

WILLIAM SMYTH ordered to make paymt: of 260 l tob^{o} within tenn dayes unto JOHN MARTIN.

* 26

* ATTCHMT: graunted unto THOMAS [illegible] nd SAMPSON WARING agst Estate of WILLIAM BASNETT for 382 l tob^{o}......

Attachmt: graunted unto ffrancis LAND agst Estate of WILLIAM BASNETT Corne a debt of 2 barrells of Indian Corne and 175 l tob^{o} when the Court shall have determined the same.

CHRISTOPHER BURROWGHS is indebted per bill 1452 l tob^{o} & Caske and acknowledged justly due by RICHARD SMYTH attorney of BURROWGHS. Payment is ordered to be made unto the said HOLMES.

.....I CHRISTOPHER BURROWGHS doe hereby nominate &c ....RICHARD SMYTH my lawfull attorney to answere the suite of JOHN HOLMES 13 Feb 1646/7
Xop BURROWGH

It appeares upon the oath of GEORGE HORNER that DEBORAH GLASCOCK is indebted unto said HORNER 560 l tob^{o} out of which summe there is 150 l tob^{o} and noe more to be deducted upon accoumpt for goods which sd GEORGE HORNER took up and received of JOHN BASON by the procuremt of sd DEBORAH.....it is thereupon ordered that the said DEBORAH shall pay 410 l tob^{o}....remaynder of the debt with Court Charges within 10 dayes unto the said HORNER....

It is the opinion of the board /having maturely discussed the same/ that CAPT: WILLIAM LUCK the lawfull attorney of JAMES ABRATHAT Merchant * to sue and implead ROGER ffLETCHER Merchant for a debt of £ 41/5 ster: 26a due by bond unto the said ABRATHAT.

It appeares to the Court that ROGER ffLETCHER Merchant is indebted per the copy of a bond pduced under a Publique Notaries hand unto JAMES ABRATHAT Merchant the 20 Oct 1645 and was for goods and merchandizes imported into the Collony as is alleaged.....Ordered that whatsoever

26a continued 15 Feb 1646/7

estate of or belonging unto said ROGER ffLETCHER is remayning in the hands or custody of ENSIGNE LAMBERT or THOMAS BRIDGE or eyther of them to the value of said £ 41/5 sterl: shall remayne in deposite with the said LAMBERT and BRIDGE and they forthwith to give bond.......said CAPT: LUCK forthwith to give bond with security to prove the said debt.......

QUINTAN GRAVES hath sett up his name at the Court Howse dore to give notice of his Intended voyage for England this present shipping.

JACOB BRADSHAWE ordered to pay unto ARTHUR BROWNE Marchant 260 l tob^{o} in full remaynder of all debts and accoumpts.

27 Memorandum: that I JACOB BRADSHAWE doe * appoynt my friend WILLIAM CAPPS to bee my lawfull Attorney &c.....and to sue JOHN DYER..........
11 Feb 1646/7 JACOB BRADSHAWE
Wittnes present CLEMENT THEOBALD

JAMES SYMONS ordered to pay unto THOMAS SAYER 500 l tob^{o} & caske with 3 yeares forbearance & Court Charges within 10 dayes.
(Note: this is a good example of the Court Script·)
being used entirely differently in the same record.)
& in the record below, still another form of S. AGW)

ROBERT HAYES ordered to pay unto WILLIAM SHIPP 1450 l tob^{o} and one barrell of Indian corne & Court Charges within 10 dayes.

RICHARD WORSTER ordered to pay unto ARTHUR BROWNE Merchaunt 347 l Tob^{o} & Caske.

Upon the peticon of MR: WILLIAM JULIAN the Court doth thinke fitt and orders that CAPT: WILLOWGHBY being admr: of MR. RICHARD WAKE deceased doe forth with deliver unto said MR: JULIAN such writings as doe concern MR: JULIAN onely debts or ingagmts belonging to the decedent from the said MR: JULIAN onely excepted.

ANDREW WARNER was bownd for the psonal appearance of EDWARD LILLY at this Court to answer the suite of THOMAS BROOKE and SAMPSON WARING in
27a an accon of debt and sd LILLY not appearing * It is ordered that ANDREW WARNER shall bee lyable to satisfy the Award of the Court if he does not bring forth the body or sufficient goods of EDWARD LILLY to satisfy the debt in question at the next Court.

WILLIAM CAPPS adminitrator of the estate of JAMES SMYTH deceased ordered to pay THOMAS WARD Chyurgeon 300 l tob^{o}...

UPON a former Reference of this Court It is now ordered that ROBERT HAYES shall pay 922 l tob^{o} unto RICHARD CONQUEST per bill.......

An Attachmt graunted unto WALTER PRESSAR upon the estate of WILLIAM BASNETT for a debt of 145 l tob^{o}.

WHEREAS the Sheriffe at the suite of GEORGE WHITE by a former order of

Court hath attached in (his?) owne hands 2500 l tob° of the p(ro)per estate of EDMUND THORROWGOOD. It is nowe ordered that MR: ROBERT POWYS Clerke the attorney of said THORROWGOOD........shall upon notice to him given appeare at the next Court to answer the demaunds of GEORGE WHITE /or some other attorney for THORROWGOOD/ or otherwyse the board will give Judgemt: for the paymt: of the said 2500 l tob° unto the said GEORGE WHITE. White

* The Court doth thinke fitt and accordingly orders that OWEN POWELL 28
Merchaunt as an Interpreter shall truly explaine to the board out of Dutch into English and out of English into Dutch betweene WILLIAM WRIGHT Merchaunt and JOHN BASON Marriner Comptts and REINORD CORNELIUS ffOX defendt concerning the matters in question and nowe in controversie about the Shipp called the FOXE Foxe of Aucusion? Auncusion for the true and faithfull pformance whereof the said OWEN POWELL hath taken his corporall oath by the appoyntment and Jurisdiction of the Court.

Upon long hearing and much debating of the matters in controversie betweene WILLIAM WRIGHT Merchaunt and JOHN BASON Marriner Complaynaunts against REINORD CORNELIUS ffOXE Foxe defendant concerninge the Shipp called the FOXE of Ancusion? in " " ' Foxe in her voyage from thence to the Port of Virginia. And whereas it appeares by a Charter Party made betwixt them produced in Court and faithfully translated out of the Dutch into English that the said RENIORD CORNELIUS FOXE did amongst other things ingage and oblige himselfe unto the said WRIGHT and BASON that the said Shipp was well caulkt and fight (fit?) and should bee sufficiently provided with all needfull necessaryes whatsoever. And whereas it appeares by sundry testimonyes and many deposicons of able workemen and carpenters taken upon oath whoe have viewed searched and have beene employed about the said Shipp and allsoe by the testimonyes and deposicons of all the Seamen both Dutch and English belonging to the said Shipp and taken upon Oath that the said Ship is very badd insufficient and unserviceable and not fitting for her voyadge intended by the Charter pty: aforementioned. And whereas it appeares likewyse by testimonyes taken upon oath that by the ill estate and sadd condicon of the said shipp the FOXE being contrary to the undertakings & Ingagemt of the said RENIARD CORNELIUS ffOXE Foxe in the Charter Ptye the said Comptts WRIGHT and BASON and all other * 28a
ffraighters ffreighters of the said Shipp dare not hazard theire persons nor will adventure theire goods therein by reason whereof the the said Comptts WRIGHT and BASON have not onely all together left theire voyage but are very much dampinsyed Dampnifyed as sufficiently appeares unto the Court; and as is afore declared. Upon due and serious consideracon of all which It is ordered that the said CORNELIUS ffOXE shall pay of Satisfy unto the said WILLIAM WRIGHT and JOHN BASON and to the other hyrers or ffraighters of the said Shipp being (one pty?) these two words are faded) in the said Charter party the summe of 400 pownds Ster: money within 5 dayes -(faded)- Court doth conceive and adindy? Adindy to bee but a reasonable satisfaccon for soe great an hindrance & such damage sustayned by the said Comptts: WRIGHT and BASON and the other ffreight rs of the said Shipp by xxxxx great insuficiency thereof in her Intended voyage specified in the said Charter pty. And

it is allsoe further ordered that RENIARD CORNELIUS ffOXE paye and satisfy all Court charges als^{o} execucon.

a test MR: THOMAS MEARES

(NOTE: Aucusion or Aucasion or Ancusion or Ancasion in Holland: The name of this place is written: Aurusion Aurusion

See also folios 30 to 32a where there are more records on this same suit, and further research into the place name) AGW.

Upon the petition of THOMAS CHEELEY the Court doth order that THOMAS DAVYES be non suited & pay 30 l tob^{o} unto the said CHEELEY for charxxx and molestacon.

16 Feb 1646/7

Whereas upon a former reference to this Court nowe appeares that THOMAS IVEY is iustly (justly) indebted unto RICHARD CONQUEST 311 l of tob^{o}. It is ordered that the said THOMAS IVEY shall pay or satisfy the aforesaid 311 l of tob^{o} unto the said RICHARD CONQUEST with Court Charges within tenn dayes ......

The Court doth order that the estate of MR: ROBERT PAGE formerly attached shall according to a former order of the Court remayne to satisfy the award of the Court and to bee responsable unto the demaunds of MR: CORNELIUS LOYD upon further determinacon.

29 * An attachment is graunted unto MR: MATHEW PHILLIPPS attorney of RALFE SERACOLL, Merchaunt against the estate of MR: MORE FANTLEROY to bee satisfactory for a debt of 1200 pownds of tob^{o} due to the said SERACOLL upon legall determinacon of the Court.
(The names are written: Seraroll/Seraroll & Fantleroy)

The difference depending in this Court between CAPT: WILLIAM ATTERBURY against WILLIAM SHIPP deft: in an accon of debt concerning 55 pownds 11 shillings 11 pence upon accoumpt, at the request of the said WILLIAM SHIPP is referred to the next Court to bee heard and determined.
(NOTE: name is written dHerbury but in the index as A. Herbury)

It is certifyed that VINSON CURVELL Curvell hath sett up his name at the Court howse dore according to Act of Assembly to give publique notice of his intended voyage to HAMBORROWGH Hamborrowgh this present shipping.

Whereas it appeares to the Court that THOMAS IVY is justly indebted unto RICHARD CONQUEST for Clerkes fees and for wryting of many busynesses of concernmt: for the use and behoofe of the said IVY the summe of 500 pownds of tob: which the Court have computed to be reasonable upon pusall (perusal) of the accopts produced by the said CONQUEST. It is thereupon ordered that the said THOMAS IVEY shall within tenn dayes make payment of the said 500 pownds of tob^{o} & sherriffs fees..........

MR: ROBERT EYRE hath sett up his name at the Court Howse dore to give publique notice of his intended voyage to England this present shipping.

Ordered to be recorded:

Noverint universi per presentes me Rogerum ffletcher de London Mercatorem teneri et firmiter obligari Jacobo Abrathat de Civitate London Mercatori in Quadraginta libris bone et legalis monete Anglie solvend eidem Jacobo Abrathat aut suo certo Attornato executor vel administrator suis Ad quam quidem solucionem bene et fideliter faciend Obligo me heredes executores et administrator

....

(Note: There is more of this Latin record, however the following is directly below:) *

*Condicon of the obligacon is such that if the abovesaid ROGER ffLETCHER his heires &c shall well and truly pay or cause to be payd unto the above named JAMES ABRATHAT his executors administrators or assignes £ 41/5 lawfull money of England on 20 Oct next ensueing the date above written at or in the nowe dwelling howse of the same JAMES ABRATHAT scituate in Marke Laine? Lane , London that then this obligacon to bee voyd or else itt to stand and remayne in full force and virtue Rogen ffletxxx Sigillat deliberat in presentia mei 29a

Dudley Lovell

Ista Copia concordat cum Originali obligacone sup sigillo dni Rogen ffletcher facta Examinacone mei Chr (xx above (Chas?)) Townsend No Pu Et Johis Byrt eius Servi

....I JAMES ABRATHAT of London Merchaunt have assigned &c.............
WILLIAM LUCK, London Marriner my true and lawful attorney for mee and in my name to sue for recover and receive of ROGER ffLETCHER of London Merchaunt £ 43 of lawfull money of England to mee due by one obligacon dated 18 May 1645.......................................* 30
(this is a longwinded power of attorney).............................
In wittness whereof I have hereunto sett my hand and seale dated the 16 Sep 1646........................... JAMES ABRATHAT
Sealed and delivered in the presence of mee RICHARD BEST, JOHIS BYRT servi CHR: TOWNSEND Scrx

Ordered to be recorded
In the Name of God Amen: A Charter partye made the fouth day of September 1646 and an agreement made by mee ABRAHAM PYLL a publique Scrivenor allowed and admitted of by the Lords of Holland dwelling

in Aucusion in the presence of the following partyes namely WILLIAM
WRIGHT, ROWLAND MARSTONE and JOHN BASON togeather all (and) everyone
as all /in solidum/ all English Merchants and ffraighters to REINARD
CORNELIUS the ffOXE husband and Maister of the Shipp next under God
named the ffOXE being of burthen about twoe hundred sixty tunnes, and
being mounted with sixe good iron gunnes, and all other Ammunition for
Warre accordingly made in manner and form as followeth, /vizt/ that
the aforesaid husband is obliged with the shipp to bee ready with the
first, to deliver her fight (fit) and well Cauklt, and allsoe to bee
pvided with Anchors, Cables, Sayles, Ropes, and in all other needfull
necessaryes to bee sufficiently provided. The which being thus made
30a ready, then shall the officers and Marriners be * taken care for by
ffraighters /vizt/ theire wages and Victualls; thus done then shall
the Maister sett sayle and runne with the first convenient wynd and
weather, right through the seas to Virginia and there having delivered
and traded her goods, then to lade her againe with such goods and wares
as the ffraighters please and then the said Shipp being laded, the
Maister and officers with the aforesaid Shipp, /with the next faire
wynd and weather which God shall bee pleased to send/ sett sayle back
again for the Tassell and then to the porte where he is to deliver All
which in forme and manner before written being accomplished the aforesaid ffraighters shall first and not before bee injoyed and obliged
to give unto the said husband or his owners for his deserved ffreight,
that is to say for each moneth that the voyage shall last /to reckon
a Running Moneth according to the Almanack/ the summe of five hundred
gilders per month, togeather with xxxx Averige and Pylotage according
to the manner and custom of the Pears (Peers?); which voyadge shall
begin when the said shipp shall bee without the last boye (bouy?) in
the Tassell. And then the said shipp being arrived at the desired port;
and at Anchor then shall the ffraighters bee ingaged for seaven months
certaine(ly?) all though the voyage could bee performed in a shorter
tyme; but in case it doth contynue longer then to pay as is before
menconed; vizt: every moneth five hundred gilders; And it is allso
agreed that the ffraighters in theire Returne may putt into Rochell (La
Rochelle, France) to seek convoye, but fynding there none for the Tassell the fraighters may then arrive in the Mase there being arrived the
ffraight shall then bee due and the shipp out of pay. Allsoe it is a-
greed that if the said shipp doe arrive in the Mase that the ffraighters shall pay the halfe of the Charges to bring her to the Tassell or
31 otherwyse to agree thereupon; Moreover it is * conditioned that the
shipp shall not bee carried into any unfree place to trade in any manner. Allsoe wee are on both sides agreed that the shipp shall bee ready
to sett sayle in the space of one and 20 days without further delay or
any neglect of eyether side, beginning upon the Nynth of this instant
moneth; ffurther the ffraighters shall pay for such powder as they
shall unnecessarily shoote away or deliver other powder in the place;
Allsoe it is condiconed that the ffraighters shall give to the shipp
one Jack and fflag. Allsoe it is condiconed that the said husband
shall eat and drinke and sleepe in the Cabbin at the ffraighters charges; but his wages to bee payd him by the rest of his owners; It is
allsoe condiconed that the said husband shall have privelidge to lay
into the shipp soe much goods as may produce fower hogsheads of tobo

without payeing ffraight for; and it is agreed the shipp shall bee delivered at Aucusion; Whereunto we bynd our selves each to other for the performance of what is aforesaid menconed both in our plans and estates; and especially the ffraighters the goods shipped aboard; And the husband, his said shipp, ffraight and all belonging to her to bee under submission unto all Courts and Justice to this being uprightly done within Aucasion in the presence of PETER HOOKE and HERRICK TOPPIAS as witness hereunto with mee x x Notarie Publique

At sea the seaven and twentieth of November 1646. A Testification
of all the Seamen belonging to the shipp called the ffOXE of Aucasion
in Holland concerning the insufficiency of the said shipp being bownd
for Virginia to loade merchaunts goods: having found amisse in her in
the first place her laste? * knee being broken; secondly her 31a
plancks workinge afore and after in the hould: thirdly her plancks
and knees betwixt decks workeing and boults broken and Trunnells:
fourthly in her sterne wee found a great Leake; fifthly All her seams
afore and after above water without board and within was all very leak-
ey soe that wee had no place to keepe any goods drye in the shipp nor
drye place for any man to sleep in. Sixthly her sides workeing both
from the deck. Seaventhly her mayne m st was cract soe that in extrem
of weather wee were forced to fish the Mast. Eightly, wee had not one
spare boult nor Rope block in the Shipp, nor scarce ane (any) good running Rope in the shipp. Nynthly there is severall bea(mes?) broken,
and severall knees come from the side. Tenthly: at sea wee were forced to strike our Gunnes into the hould to ease her sides that they die
not one fall from the other. Eleaventhly that being not enough wee were
forced to strike her Anchors from her bowes and Cables and (put?) them
into the hould. A second tyme our Mayne Mast crackt and wee stayd him
and fisht him and in staying of him wee halled up beams and deck and all.
Unto all which the said seamen both Dutch and English and Chyrurgeon belong to the said Shipp have deposed and upon their Oathes doe affirme
the same to be truth in Court before the Com^{rs} aforesaid; the fifteenth
day of February Anno Dm 1646/7, and allsoe have hereunto subscribed
theire names.

JOSIAS SMYTH
the marke of + DERECK POWELL
the marke of X AMBROSE COOKE
GERRITT GERRITTS
THOMAS MICHELL
the marke of B NATHANIELL HARRAWAY
ARYS ffOOPZOON
*

the marke of X ARION MICHELL
the marke of M WILLIAM CHAPMAN
DOEDE DOEDES
the marke of X WILLIAM CLASON
JOHN LUKE
TYS YAROP (or Yacop?)
EDWARD HALL Chyrurgeon

32

* The deposition of OWEN POWELL Merchaunt aged 35 yeares or thereabouts sworne sayth that being about two hundred leagues up from the Tassell to the best of this deponents knowledge, about twelve of the Clock at night or thereabouts hearing and preceving the insufficiency of the shipp this deponent caused ye Carpenter to goe and viewe the shipp in severall places and demaunded of the carpenter, whether he knew any help or remedy for the strengthening of the said shipp; the Carpenter replyed that he knewe none; thereupon there were two lights

hung out, one before, and one behynd to give notice /as this depon[t] did conceive/ to the other shipps for to Releive them; Whereupon the other shipps stayed that night: The next morning WILLIAM WRIGHT and REINARD CORNELIUS the ffOXE and this deponent went aboard the PETER SMYTH to seeke some releife (or realease) and were (or nere) paryes? to supply the want of the said shipp and finding there very little Releife this deponent remayned aboard the said Peter Smyth two dayes and two nights, in regard that he was feareful1 to adventure himselfe in the said shipp but after this depon[t] considering that his goods and merchandize were aboard the said shipp FOXE he the depon[t] went aboard againe and there contynued with much discontent, and greatly discomforted, seeing the shipp workeing her sides from the deck and allsow boweing lengthwyse one of her fore beames being Rotten; and fell: insoemuch that this depon[t] tooke peines (pains) -or- (pine) wherefrom with his hand. Her mayne mast crackt in two severall places, and some certaine Stantialls sett betweene decks, to hold the deck, and to strengthen the shipp, soe farre as the Company could conveniently doe; likewyse the said shipp was bownd about with three hawsers quite under
32a * the keele and they had not one place /to the best of this deponents knowledge/ but was defective both for lodging and otherwyse; And further this deponent sayth not.

EDWARD HALL Chirurgeon of the shipp called the FOXE sworne sayth that the said shipp being in company with Peter Smyth; and being in a most desperate condition, the deponent and the whold Company of the said shipp the ffOXE, were very willing and desirous to have transported themselves with ye said Peter Smyth but he not willing to entertayne them, the deponent and the said shipps company were inforced to committ themselves to the mercy of God: and soe to would the said shipp with hawsers; And further sayth not.

THOMAS TODD shipp carpenter aged 36 yeares or thereabouts sworne sayth That this deponent being hired to come to work aboard the shipp called the ffOXE did fynd the said shipp very unfitting for the transportation of any merchaunts goods without dammage nor fitting to adventure to sea without great casualty and Dannger to the best of the deponents Judgement. And further sayeth not.

JOHN YEATS Shipcarpenter aged fifty one yeares or thereabouts sworne sayeth; that he this deponent being hyred to come to work aboard the shipp called the ffOXE did fynd the said shipp not fitting for the transportation of any merchaunts goods without dammage nor fitting to adventure to sea without great casualty and Danger to the best of the deponents Judgement. And further he sayth not. Recorded 18 Mar 1646

ATT A COURT HOLDEN at the HOWSE OF
ROBERT PARTIN in the COUNTY of the ISLE OF WIGHT
10 August 164_ (the 6 is missing)

33 * PRESENT: CAPT: WILLIAM BERNARD ESQR:

Recorded MR: ROBERT PITT MR: JAMES TOOKE MR: GEORGE ffAWDEN
MR: PETER HULL MR: SILL: COLTON MR: ROBT: WATTSON
MR: JNO: GEORGE MR: JAMES WILLIAMSON

A NOTE ABOUT THE VOYAGE OF THE FOXE

The name of the ship is the FOXE as can be seen by examining the Court Script for the letter x as it appears in the word sixthly and for the capital F which is written with the lower case double ff as is usually found in these early records.

Anyone reading the script without this examination of the letters would read the name as HOPE, and so it seemed to your editor until the realization that there was no other letter H formed the same way in this Clerk's handwriting.

A letter was written to Holland inquiring about the place names in this record: Aucusion/Aucasion/Ancusion &c, The Mase, The Tassell, Rochell, and their various spellings. The reply from Holland, confirmed my feeling that Rochell was La Rochelle in France; The Tassell was the Texelstroom in Holland; and the Mase was the River Maas passing Rotterdam. The authority in Holland could find no town or place named Aucusion or anything like it. (see their letter on the next page)

AGW

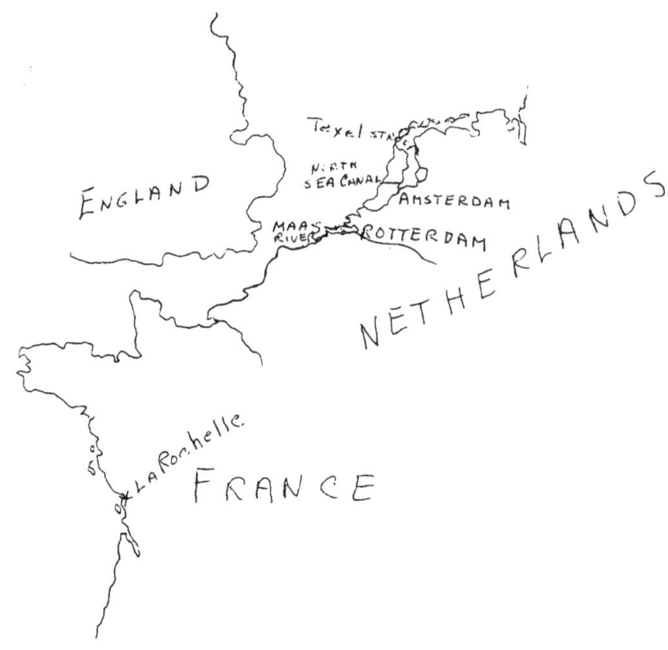

ALGEMEEN RIJKSARCHIEF

EERSTE AFDELING (CENTRALE REGERINGSARCHIEVEN VOOR 1795)

Telefoon 180196 (4 lijnen)
Postgiro 507588

's-Gravenhage, 29th January 1969.
Bleijenburg 7.

Bericht op schrijven van: 8th January 1969

No. C 14/VR.H.

Onderwerp:

Mrs.A.Granbery Walter
455, East Fifty-first Street
New York
New York 10022
U.S.A.

Dear Miss Granbery Walter,

in reply to your above mentioned letter I beg to inform you that also on our maps no town of the name Aucusion, or something like that, was found.

Indeed, the meaning of the "Tassell" is the Texel-stroom (stroom=stream) and "Rochell" is the french harbour-town La Rochelle.

The "Mase" is the river Maas, passing Rotterdam and in the 17th century debouching in the neighbourhood of Briel(l)e. (in lat.52°)

For the second part of your letter I suggest to address to the Centraal Bureau voor Genealogie, Nassaulaan 18, Den Haag.

The keeper of the first section,

(Mrs.Dr.M.A.P.Meilink-Roelofs.)

Algemeen Rijksarchief
Bleyenburg 7
Den Haag
HOLLAND

Exer: ffor as much as JOSEPH ORDWAY became bownd with WILLIAM STOCKLEY and GEORGE HIGHAM for theire appearance at WARRWICK COUNTY COURT, being arrested at the suite of JOHN SEAWARD for 757 pownds of tob^o And forasmuch as neyther the said HIGHAM nor STOCKLEY appeared to the accon soe that Judgement proceeded against the said JOSEPH ORDWAY as there (their?) security. The Court hath ordered that the said HIGHAM shall within 20 dayes give sufficient security for the payment of the said debt and charges unto the said JOSEPH ORDWAY or his assignes at or before the 10 Nov next and Court Charges otherwyse execucon.

THO: WOMBRELL Clr Cur

ATT A COURT HOLDEN UPON THE 22 MARCH 1647

PRESENT:

CAPT: JOHN SIBSEY)	MR: CORNELIUS LOYD)	
MR: ffRANCIS MASON)_	MR: THOM: MEARES)-	COM^rs
MR: THOM: LAMBART)	MR: MATH: PHILLIPPS)	
MR: EDWARD LOYD)		

The Court to be holden upon the 15 Apr for this County upon divers emergent occasions is adjourned till the 26 daye of the said moneth: and all psons arrested or summoned th[illegible] are required to take Notice thereof and to make theire appearance accordingly as they will answere the Contrary at theire perill.

* ATT A COURT HOLDEN AT ELIZ: CITTY 27 Aug 1646 33a

PRESENT: CAPT: WILLIAM CALIBORNE

CAPT: LEONARD YEO)_	CAPT: NATH: OLDIS)_
MR: THOMAS CELY (Ceeley?))	MR: JOHN CHAUNDLER)

It appeareth to this Court by confession that THOMAS DAVYES doth owe unto HENRY POOLE 350 l tob^o. It is therefore ordered that said THOMAS DAVYES shall the 10 Nov next satisfy unto the said HENRY POOLE or his assignes with one yeares forbearance and Court Charges else execucon.

Extr: p(er) mee HENR: POOLE Clr Cur

ATT A COURT HOLDEN UPON 26 day of Aprill 1647

PRESENT:

CAPT: THOMAS WILLOWGHBY ESQR:

CAPT: JOHN SIBSEY)	MR: THOMAS MEARES)	
MR: ffRANCIS MASON)-	MR: CORNELIUS LOYD)-	COM^rs
MR: MATH: PHILLIPPS)	MR: THOMAS LAMBART)	

......WILLIAM SHIPP ordered to pay forthwith unto CAPT: WILLIAM ATTERBURY £ 25 ster: money with fforbearance at 8 pownds p(er) cent for 5 yeares & the Court Charges.

Upon the peticon of MRS: SARAH GOOKIN administratrix of the estate of CAPT: ADAM THORROWGOOD deceased It is ordered that THOMAS HUGHES doe henceforth desist from falling any tymber trees upon the land belonging unto the heire of the decedent . And the Court doth further order and appoint MR: BARTHOLOMEW HOSKINS with GYLES COLLINGS to inquire and viewe what tymber trees HUGHES hath allready gelled or other damage done upon the said land and to make report thereof unto this board at the next Court.

34 *

The difference depending in the Court betweene CAPT: ffRANCIS YARDLEY Complaynaunt agst JOSIAS SMYTH deft: or an account SMYTH hath received of CAPT: YARDLEY upon the request of MR: THOMAS LAMBART in the behalfe of SMYTH is referred to the next Court.

Estate of ROBERT JONES late deceased is indebted unto MR: CORNELIUS LOYD 80 pownds of tobacco as appears unto the Court. Present payment is ordered thereof out of the estate.

Adms: of the Estate of ROBERT JONES to make present payment of halfe a barrell of Indian Corne unto THOMAS TOOKER.

LEONARD GUNNIS *Gunnis* to give security for the payment on 20 Oct nest unto ffRANCIS LAND 458 l tob° per bill.

PHILLIPP LAND ORDered by the consent of HENRY CATLIN his attorney to pay unto ROBERT EYRES 900 l tob° upon the 20 Oct next.

MR: CORNELIUS LOYD was bownd for the personall appearance of WILLIAM WR(ight?) to answere the suite of THOMAS (name missing from page) and the said WILLIAM WR(ight?) xxxx appearing It is ordered according
34a to xxx xx Assembly that the said MR: CORNELIUS LOY(d) * satisfy the award of this Court if he doth not bring forth the body or sufficient goods of said WILLIAM WRIGHT to satisfy the debt at the next Court.

JOHN BROWNE - a certificate of 100 acres of land for the trans: of PATIENCE BOWERS & GEORGE COLVEY. (This is not in Nugent)

EDWARD HALL Chirurgeon ordered to pay unto WILLIAM SHIPP 392 l tobO due by bill.......

Administrators (not named) of the Estate of ROBERT JONES deceased ordered to pay unto SIMON PETERS 2 barrells of Indian Corne out of the estate............

THOMAS MARSH (or NARSH?) was bownd for appearance of JOHN BASON to answer suit of WILLIAM SHIPP in an accon of debt BASON not appearing said MARSH ordered to pay or bring forth the body or sufficient goods of JOHN BASON to the next Court. (NOTE: Thomas Marsh later left Norfolk County and went to Maryland where he became quite prominent. See Maryland records. However, with the broad a pronounciation in these records this could possibly be - Nash pronounced Narsh? - that is - if the two men were in the records of this same book - see the way the M is written: *Marsh* *Marsh* your editor leaves the decision open)

GEORGE WHITE Cl:? agst JACOB BRADSHAWE ordered upon equall ballancing of accoumpts on eyther part that BRADSHAWE shall deliver...a bill or debt for 250 l tob° unto MR: WHITE to bee cancelled and both partyes to pay theire owne Court charges.

It appeares by confession that SAVILL GASKINE is indebted unto JOHN SUTTON 3½ barrells of Indian Corne. Ordered that present paymt be made.

CAPT: THOMAS WILLOWGHBY ESQUIRE ordered to make paymt forthwith of 600 l tob° & caske & Court Charges unto ELLEN LIGHTHART widdowe..........

ANDREW WARNER being bownd for appearance of EDWARD LILLY at suit of THOMAS BROOKE and SAMPSON WARING in an accon of debt. It was ordered at the last Court that WARNER should satisfy the debt, if he should not at this Court bring forth the body or sufficient goods of EDWARD LILLY and ANDREW WARNER having fayled.....now ordered that said WARNER Shall forthwith pay 636 l tob° & Caske unto the said BROOKE and WARING......

CAPT: WILLOWGHBY administrator of RICHARD WAKE deceased ordered to pay 100 l tob° unto SAMPSON WARING for a Coffin for the buryall of the decedent.

MR: WILLIAM JULIAN ordered to pay on 1 Nov next ₤ 9/5/6 Ster: money with 6 yeares forbearance at 8 per cent and Court Charges unto CAPT: WILLIAM ATTERBURY.

SAMPSON WARING ordered to pay unto CAPT: WILLOWGHBY 6ι0 l tob° & Caske

* 35a

* SAMPSON WARING ordered to pay unto JAMES LOVE 1467 l tob° & caske due by bill.

JOHN MARTIN plt: agst ffRANCIS LAND deft: referred to the next Court.

JOHN ffERINHAUGH who married the administrator and Relict of ROBERT GLASCOCK deceased ordered at or before Nov next to shipp for the use of MR: ROBT: PAGE assignee of ISACK GILLBANCK 2000 l tob° & caske to satisfy the remainder of a debt of ₤ 20 sterl: money the decedent had and received.....and that if the 2000 l tob° shall more than satisfy the sd debt the said GILLBANCK to bee accomplished to the said ffERINHAUGH the overplus and if the 2000 l tob° doe not pay nor satisfy the said debt of ₤ 20 ster: then the said ffERINHAUGH according to condicon of decedent to be lyable further to shipp aboard such considerable quantities of tob° to satisfy ₤ 20 ster:

JOHN ffERINHAUGH who married the Relict and adm: of ROBERT GLASCOCK deceased ordered to pay unto MR: ROBERT PAGE 40 shillings ster: money with 4 yeares forbearance at or before 10 Nov next for a debt of the decedent unless ffERINHAUGH shall not in the Interim prove the said debt allready satisfied.

EDWARD MAJOR ordered to pay unto JOHN GROVE atty of MR. ROBERT PAGE xxxx (rest of this page is torn off)

* To be Recorded: To the Worr: the Comrs: of Lower Norfolk County 36
The peticon of CAPT: THOMAS WILLOWGHBY ESQR: the administrator of MR: RICHARD WAKE deceased and CAPT: JOHN SIBSEY with the consent of the widdowe and Relict of the decedent:

Whereas there have been and still are divers suits betweene your pet^{s}:
concerning certaine articles of Copartnershipp ......entered into by
CAPT: JOHN SIBSEY and the decedent (Richard Wake) ....and concerning divers reckonings &c made by vertue of the said Copartnershipp.
The peticoners do desire the Court to order that all such matters of
difference in the Copartnershipp may bee putt to the perusall and
auditing of fower men, indifferently to bee elected ......the peticoners are both ready to enter into bond of 100,000 l tob^{o} with good
security each to other

THOMAS WILLOWGHBY
JOHN SIBSEY

According to the peticon and desire of CAPT: THOMAS WILLOWGHBY ESQR:
the administrator of MR: RICHARD WAKE deceased, and CAPT: JOHN SIBSEY
with the consent of the widdowe and Relict of the decedent. It is
ordered that all matters of Difference betweene the peticoners con-
36a cerning certaine Articles of * copartnershipp made and entered into by
the said CAPT: JOHN SIBSEY with the decedent which have relation to
xxxxxxxxx the said Copartnershipp bee committed to the perusall and
auditing of fower able men...
to make report to this Court........and CAPT: WILLOWGHBY and CAPT:
JOHN SIBSEY according to their volumtary desire & request doe enter
100,000 l tob^{o} bond in security each to other to stand, abide &c......
whatsoever order, doome &c.........this Court shall make upon such report.....................

MR: CORNELIUS LOYD agst RICHARD KENNAR deft: in an accon sue le Case
Before Judgmt: doth appeale to the Governor and Counsell which granted
and appoynted for the 5th daye of the next Quarter Court provided MR:
LOYD will immediately enter into bond with security..................

WILLIAM LUCAS and ffRANCIS LAND appointed Churchwardens for the parish
Of Lynhaven and ROGER WILLIAMSON to bee Churchwarden for the Easterne
Branch and the oath.......to be administered to them.

SAVILL GASKINE appointed Constable for Lynnhaven
THOMAS HAYES appointed Constable for Little Creek
JOHN CARRAWAY appointed Constable for the Easterne Branch
THOMAS SPARROWE & WILLIAM LANGLEY appointed Constables for Elizabeth
River Parish
and the oath to be administered to them.
37 *
An attachmt graunted unto WILLIAM SHIPP agst the estate of WILLIAM
WRIGHT for 951 l tob^{o}..

Ordered to be recorded
ATT A QUARTER COURT HOLDEN AT JAMES CITTY the 5th of March 1646/7
PRESENT: SIR WILLIAM BERKELEY knt Governor &c
CAPT: JOHN WEST) CAPT HEN: BROWNE CAPT: WILLM: BERNARD)
RICHARD KEMP) CAPT: THOMAS WILLOWGHBY CAPT: HUMP: HIGGINSON) - ESQR^{s}
GEORGE LUDLOWE CAPT: THO: PETTUS)

This day the Governor with the consent of Counsell elected MR: ffRANCIS MASON High Sheriffe of the Lower Norfolke County to be admitted and sworne at theire next Court..
p mee SAM: ABBOTT C1C

According to order from the Governor and Counsell MR: ffRANCIS MASON is admitted High Sheriffe and hath taken the oath of High Sheriffe for this County /with the oaths of Supremacye & allegiance, according to Course/ and allsoe given bond with security for due execucon of his place.

THOMAS IVYE is sworne Under Sherriffe.

An attachment is graunted unto OWEN POWELL agst the estate of WILLIAM WRIGHT for a debt of 1200 l tob^{o} & Caske /claymed by POWELL/ upon further determination of the Court.

MRS: SARAH GOOKIN and MR: MATHEWE PHILLIPPS ordered to bring in and give a full and pfect accoumpt at the next Court of such Estates belonging unto the Children and Orphants, in theire Custody and proteccon.

37a

* 31 April 1647? (date is written xxxy) or (xxxi th - 29th?) or (26th?)
(Your editor believes this date is meant to be the 26th)

PRESENT: CAPT: JOHN SIBSEY CAPT: EDWARD WINDHAM
MR: CORNELIUS LOYD MR: THOMAS LAMBART

An attachmt is graunted unto MRS: SARAH GOOKIN agst the estate of JAMES SMYTH deceased for a debt of 850 l tob^{o} and other ingagemts due from the decedent and claymed by MRS: GOOKIN.

.......I ROBERT BOGGIS of Nancemund in Virginia, Planter, for divers causes &c and in consideracon of the love of MR: GEORGE WHITE cleric towards mee and my wyfe in our extreme sicknes, doe give, graunt &c... ....this Deed of Gift to JOHN WHITE the sonne of said GEORGE WHITE, one heifar calfe of halfe a year old marked .... to him and his heires &c.............

1 Mar 1644/5 Teste GEO: WHITE
ROBERT BOGGIS
ELIZ: xxxx ffITTLE her marke

38

* ....I WILLIAM ATTERBURY of London, Merchant, for divers good causes &c.......and in consideracon of ....the sume of tobacco herein specifyed /vizt/ one hhd of tob conteyning 260 l of neat tobacco in hande payd the summe and quantity of 800 l tob^{o} & Caske to me payd att or upon 1 Nov next ensueing.........have given &c.....and sold unto JOHN MONNS? Monns his executors &c forever one neck of land lyeing in the Western Branch of Elizabeth River betweene two creekes the one boending on the lands of CAPT: JOHN SIBSEY, the other on land of HENRY CATLIN conteyning by estimacon 100 acres or thereabouts

.....and running from the water side one angle into the woods.........
3 Mar 1641/2 WILLIAM ATTERBURY Atterbury
Wit: THOMAS MARSH, THOM: MEARES, MATH: PHILLIPPS

(Note: There are no pattents in Nugent for William Atterbury or the name William A. Herbury as this name is indexed in the Lower Norfolk County records. AGW)

38a * These presents doe further wittness that I CAPT: JOHN SIBSEY of Lower New Norfolke County doe satisfy and confirme unto the above-named CHRISTOPHER RIVERS his heires &c.....the 100 acres of land mentioned in the bill of sale abovewritten and doe alsoe by myselfe, my heires &c........... by these presents to save and keepe harmless him and them from the molestacon of any person.......................
20 Jan 1646/7 JOHN SIBSEY and seale
Wit: CORNELIUS LOYD & MATH: PHILLIPPS
(Note: There seems a missing record. There is no mention of "the above named Christopher Rivers" above this last item. How did Capt. John Sibsey come into possession of the land? - AGW)

Acknowledged in Court by JOHN GODFREY and ordered to bee recorded this 27 April 1647.........I JOHN GODFREY of Elizabeth River in the County of Lower Norfolke and in the consideracon of 1216 l tob^{o} and Caske to mee in hand payd have.........sold............unto RICHARD CONQUEST of the place aforesaid, Gent: 2 black Cowes.......& their increase......
39 witness.......*I have hereunto sett my hand this 25 Jan 1646/7.
Wit: RICHARD WOOLLMAN JOHN GODFREY
ROBERT LUSBIE Lusbie his marke
WM: OLIVER
Cowes were delivered in the presence of the witnesses 25 Jan 1646/7.

29 May 1647 Recordatur

Adyn 16th March 1645/6 IN VIRGINIA:
Att three (since?) pay this my first bill of Exchange, my second not being payd unto MR: WILLIAM WEBSTER or his assignes in Middell: (Middelbourgh, Hol?) the summe of Ŀ 212/12/4 flemish in Banko the valew heere in myselfe and place it to accoumpt adio
Yo^{r} loving freind
Wit: RICHARD WAKE ROGER ffLETCHER
Accepted for ARTHUR BROWNE
1 May 1646 : pay the Contents unto MR: ISAAC GILLBANCK or his order
Yo^{rs}, WILL: WEBSTER
Received the full Contents of this bill by mee ISAAC GILLBANCKE: Actum Middll: the 11 Aug 1646
& Indorsatur
To MR: ARTHUR BROWNE, Merchaunt in Middelbourgh Middelbourgh

(Note: There is a Middlesbrough in Yorkshire, England, but also a Middelburg in the Netherlands and because the money mentioned is "flemish" and the spelling this must be in Holland)

ATT A COUNTY COURT HOLDEN - 15 Jun 1647

PRESENT: CAPT: THOMAS WILLOWGHBY ESQR:
CAPT: JOHN SIBSEY) MR: CORNELIUS LOYD)
MR: HEN: WOODHOWSE)- MR: THOMAS LAMBART)- COM^{rs}:
MR: MATH: PHILLIPPS) MR: EDWARD LOYD)

Administracon is ordered to bee graunted unto ROBERT DAVYES on the estate of JACOB BRADSHAWE late deceased, DAVYES first entring into bond with security to bring in an inventory of the decedents estate at the next County Court.

JOHN MARTIN ordered to pay unto ROWLAND MORGAN 150 l tob^{o} at the Cropp for unjust molestacon.

It was ordered in Court in July 164X (figure gone from page) that ROBERT HAYES administrator of JOHN LANCKFEILD should pay 854 l tob^{o} unto SIMON HANCOCK and as yet remains unsatisfied.......now ordered that HAYES make payment unto HANCOCK out of the decedents estate at the next cropp. And thereuppon sd: HANCOCK hath voluntarily undertaken and doth promise (to) beeresponsible and to pay 454 l tob^{o} thereof unto any man the Court shall thinke fitt and appoynt to bee imployed for the use of the Orphants of the said LANCKLFIELD..

Ordered that ROWLAND MORGAN doe pay unto FRANCIS LAND in consideracon of his servant ROBERT PAGE his charges and losse of tyme /being summoned to this Court on behalfe of MORGAN/ 30 l tob^{o}.

THOMAS TOOKER deft: agst JOHN HOLMES Comp^{t}: is referred to the next Court.

40

* In due obedience to the 15th Act of Assembly of the 19 Nov 1645.... ....it was enected that by the 25 June a list should bee yearely taken by some psons appoynted for that purpose by the County Courts in each County of all Tytheable psons, of all Cowes, above 3 yeares old, of all horses, Mares, Geldings of 3 yeares old and upwards and of all breeding sheep and goats in like manner...............................

THOMAS CASON for the Eastern Shore of Lynhaven
ffRANCIS LAND for the Westerne Shore at Lynhaven
ROBERT HAYES for the Little Creek)_ in Lynhaven
JOHN CHAUNDLER for the Easterne Branch)
THOMAS MARSH from Danyell Tanners Creeke upwards to Broad Creek, including the Southern Branch of Elizabeth River
RICHARD OWENS for the Westerne Branch in Eliza: River
WILLIAM CROUCH from Danyell Tanners Creeke downewards (North) to Capt: Willowghby's in Elizabeth River Parish.

Upon examinacon of Accoumpts produced by JOHN GEATHER the administrator of HENRY WATERS late deceased. It appeares unto the Court that GEATHER hath payd beyond Assetts which is hereby certifyed to the Secretaryes Office. (Therefore?) Quietus est may be graunted him accordingly.

40a 15 Jun 1647

THOMAS MARSH being bownd for the psonal appearance of JOHN BASON at the last Court at the Suite of WILLIAM SHIPP in an accon of debt and BASON not appearing.......Ordered that MARSH forthwith pay 951 l tob^o unto SHIPP.

ATT A COUNTY COURT HOLDEN - 15 Jun 1647 (sic)

PRESENT: CAPT: WILLIAM CLAIBORNE
SGT: MAJOR RICH: MORISON
MR: CORNELIUS LOYD MR: THOMAS LAMBART
MR: HENRY WOODHOWSE MR: MATH: PHILLIPPS
MR: EDWARD LOYD

In the cause depending betweene CAPT: WILLOWGHBY administrator of MR: RICHARD WAKE deceased and CAPT: JOHN SIBSEY concerning accoumpts of Copartnership between the decedent and CAPT: SIBSEY..........ordered that all partyes on eyther pt^e shall upon oath make answer unto such Interragatoryes or questions as they or any of them shall bee examined upon concerning the matters in question as aforesaid. And allsoe that they doe freely communicate and interchangeably oaths each to the other true and pfect copyes all letters pappers, accoumpts or
41 wrytings............which doe properly concern * the copartnership... in the presence of MR: CORNELIUS LOYD, MR: THOMAS LAMBART, MR: EDWARD LOYD & MR: MATH: PHILLIPPS or any two of them........to meete at the howse of MR: WILLIAM SHIPP...

Ordered that by this day moneth MRS: SARAH GOOKIN & MR: MATH: PHILLIPPS shall produce and bring unto the Com^rs: a full and present accoumpt of whatsoever estate is in their hands or possession belonging unto the children or Orphans in theire custody.

Ordered to be recorded /vizt/ 12 Jun 1647

A Coroners inquest to viewe the body of PERREGRINE BLAND who departed this lyfe the 11 Jun 1647......having duely viewed the Corps(e) and the place where it was foend dead, and made deligent inquiry concerning circumstances ....which passed immediately before his death....... doe testify to the best of our knowledge.......that neyther any act of his owne nor anything done to him MR: PEREGRINE BLAND by any other hath beene the cause or occasion of his soe strange and sudayne (sudden) death but rather doe conceive that he dyed a naturall death having finished the course which God had appoynted him in this lyfe. And that he was not sensible of Death when it came upon him but determined his lyfe in his sleepe . And we are the rather induced to this opinion because
41a that as * he was seene sleeping soe he was fownd dead with his eyes and mouth closed and his armes and other parts of his body lyeing after the same manner as they were when he was sleeping.......wee have delivered our verdict fully and freely..
XOP: BURROWGH, JOB CHAUNDLER, THOMAS CASON, THO: KEELING his marke, WILLIAM LUCAS, HENERY NEEDHAM, JOHN DYAR his marke, HENRY HILL, RICH: RP POOLE his marke, RICH: LEE his marke, JOHN MERRIDAY, SIMON ROBINSON his marke.

ffRANCIS YARDLEY deposed 12 Jun 1647 before CAPT: EDWARD WINDHAM testifyed: On 11 Jun 1647 MR: PEREGRINE BLAND, being at the howse of MRS: SARAH GOOKIN in Lynhaven, broke his fast at the table in company with mee and others and fedd hartily and passed away his tyme healthfully and cheerefully and after breakfast, past sometime with the companye in Divers Discourses drinking in the Interim moderately a dramm and a cupp of sack, till his occasions calling him to goe with MR: EYRES and MR: HALL Chyrurgeon to the Easterne Branch, he went to the Gate with mee the sd: depont: in serious discourse when being at the gate I requested him to go againe till the heate of the day was over but could not psuade him and he p(re)ferred to sitt downe at the Gate till MR: EYRES came: but rose suddenly up again and againe and went on the waye whereupon I returned in to call MR: EYRES whoe went forthwith out after him desiring a man to direct them to Little Creek myselfe remayning within sent a negro to them. The next tydings I heard was that he was turned aside unto the barne fort and fallen asleepe, some three howers
after MR: * WINDHAM and MR: EYRES brought mee sadd tyding of his 42
death in the Barne forte Barne forte I went to see him and fownd him lyeing on his right side, his Arme under his head dead and purging at the mouth frothy blood.

Jurat^r coram p me FRAN: YARDLEY
EDW: WINDHAM

The deposicon of ROBERT EYRE aged 38 yeares or thereabouts 12 Jun 1647 ....being at the howse of MRS: SARAH GOOKIN upon Fryday 11 Jun 1647 MR: PEREGRINE BLAND being there he was intended to goe to the Easterne Branch with this depont: and EDWARD HALL Chyrurgeon but MR: BLAND went forth with CAPT: YARDLEY before this depont, whereupon this depont: did desire CAPT: WINDHAM that he would be pleased to sett us in the right path to the Little Creek which CAPT: WINDHAM did goe along with the Doctor and this depont:, and missing of MR: BLAND wee chanced to look into the Barne yard and there wee see him asleepe. Then CAPT: WINDHAM and this depont: and the Doctor went in to wake him and would have had him eyther to goe into the howse or to go forward of our Journey but he desired that wee would lett him rest a little and he would goe along with this depont: whereupon wee got him to lye in a shedd in the shade and went our wayes and afterwards this depont: came to see him againe fownd him awake and did desire him that he would walke into the howse or otherwyse that wee might bee goeinge and did desire mee in these words Good Cousin lett mee alone a little and I will goe by and by so this depont: went and lay downe and fell asleepe and about halfe an houre after CAPT: WINDHAM came to look for him and fownd him dead and came presently and told this depont: whereupon this depont: went with
the Capt: and fownd that he was dead. * indeed and further sayeth not. 42a

Wit: EDW: WINDHAM ROBERT EYRE

.....deposicon of EDWARD HALL, Chirurgeon aged 25 yeares or thereabouts taken 12 Jun 1647.......being at the howse of MRS: SARAH GOOKIN at Lynnhaven upon 11 Jun 1647 with MR:ROBERT EYRES and fynding there MR: PEREGRINE BLAND who was cousin to MR: ROBERT EYRES were very joyfull of their meeting and concluded the next day to goe to the Easterne Branch Soe on the morrowe following we broke fast togeather being all well and in health soe within a short space after he the said BLAND being urgent to bee gone went forthwith CAPT: YARDLEY sayeing he would goe a little before, soe this depont: having some occasions to (?) him a little space ROBERT EYRES stayed with him this depont: dep(ar)ted the howse with CAPT: WINDHAM and MR: EYRES whoe seeking for MR: BLAND did fynd him in a little howse after the end of the barne asleepe, soe waking him desired him to goe, otherwyse to return to the howse to sleepe but they could not p(er)suade him soe they came away to the howse againe and about an hour after this depont: went forth to see how he did and fownd MR: BLAND and MR: EYRES lyeing feet to feete and hearing him talke as though he were in a dreame this deponent departed soe about one hower after CAPT: WINDHAM went out and fownd him dead and further he sayeth not.

Wit: EDW: WINDHAM EDW: HALL Chyrurg:

JACOB BRADSHAWE ordered to pay 157 1 tob[o] unto THOMAS CHEELEY within tenn dayes given under my hand 4 Jan 1646/7.........................

HEN: WOODHOWSE

43 * 15 Jun 1647 INVENTORY of HENRY WALTERS late deceased taken 10 Dec 1646. Exhibited in Court by MR: GEATHER and appraysed by PETER PORTER, GEORGE HORNER, JOHN BROWNE and THOMAS TOOKER.

One Bible	040
1 old silke gartyr and a halfe	010
5 old bands, two old Neckecloths and one old capp	002
two old locks and keyes	005
6 yards of silletting (fileting?)	001
i small iron pott and potthookes weighing 15 lbs	030
1 pewter dish weighing 3 lbs	016
One Iron pestell weighing 13 lbs	026
2 Iron hookes, 3 old hoes, 1 old hatchett, 1 drawing knife, 1 hammer	010
1 old sifting tray, 1 old knife, 2 aules, 1 old shoemakers knife, 1 payre of tobacco tongs, 1 small gynlett, 1 packett Inkhorne, & 20 sheets of pap(er)	020
1½ lb of powder	015
1 lb shott	002
1 bushell of pease	025
6½ barrells of Corne	195
1 tufted Holland suite	175
1 chest	100
1 old Rugg, Pillowe and bolster	070
one Cowe	500
The totall	1242

A true and just accoumpt of JOHN GEATHER adm: of the estate of HENRY WALTERS deceased, this 15 June 1647.

	Imprimus: Payd to MR: BROWNE	216
43a	Payd to MR: MATHEW PHILLIPPS	150
*	Payd to MR: CONQUEST for ffees	165
	Payd to MR: HARRISON 1 barrell of Eares and more	020
	to the taylor for work	025
	2 dayes worke to CAPT: WILLOWGHBY	(amounts not given)

2 dayes worke and charges goeing to the Court at Little Creek	Amt.
4 days worke fetching up the Corne & carrying it to the howse	not
for a wynding sheet and buryall and losse of tyme	given
for the trouble in tyme of his sickness	"
for tyme spent and Charges in coming to this Court	"
for the abovementioned worke, Charges and other things I doe require	40
for tobacco due to myselfe upon account	04
for 2 yeares dyett and washing	40
The total summe is	141

Recorded 15 Jun 1647

.... ffRANCIS WIATT knt Gov &c of Virginia ....
* graunting unto THOMAS SPARROWE 300 acres of Land scytuate lyeing 44
and being in the County of Lower Norfolke upon the Western Branch of Elizabeth River being over against a Creeke called Brownes Baye & beginning at a small Oake which standeth at the side of a small Gutt or Creeke running for length Southeast & by South to a white oake standing on the side of a Mayne Poquoson and for breadth from the aforementioned tree South West and by South 150 pole by the Maine Branch side to a marked Oake and againe for Length South & by South over a small Creeke to a marked white oak which said 300 acres of land is to bee augmented and doubled when he or his assignes shall have sufficiently peopled and planted the same...........The said 300 acres of Land being due in right of his owne psonall adventure and for the transportation of 5 psons ....all whose names are in the Records menconed under this
Patent * ....Given at James Citty 10 Dec 1640. 44a
ROGER WINGATE Trer FRANCIS WIATT (see Nu 120)

Recorded 15 Jun 1647
.....I WILLIAM BASNETT of Lynhaven, Planter do sell and sett over &c unto GEORGE SPENLOE .....100 acres of land nowe seated by mee WILLIAM BASNETT and one Shallopp of 22 foote by the keele nowe lyeing at my landing place........and doe give him the sd SPENLOE as full possession as I myselfe have or had in them. And in case the said WILLIAM BASNETT doe well and truely make paymt of 1900 lbs of good sownd tob^{o} and 3 hhds unto the said SPLENLOE and 400 l tob^{o} unto MR: HENRY WOODHOWSE to be paid the 10 Dec then the said land & Shallop to
bee delivered back unto BASNETT and in case this above specified * 45
tobacco bee not payd then......to remayne in the possession of GEORGE SPENLOE..........have hereunto sett my hand
7 Jun 1647 the marke of WILLIAM BASNETT
Wit: WILLIAM CAPPS, WILLIAM EADYE (0) his marke

Recorded 15 Jun 1647
......I HUMPHREY SAYER of the Little Creek, Planter for the better security of the debt which I am bownd by this specialty to pay unto JOHN HOLMES.......it being 835 l tob^{o} doe bynd over unto him my whole cropp of tobacco which I am nowe Injoyed withall or shall bee this yeare....
8 May 1647 HUMPHREY SAYER
In presence of HENRY H BRAKES his marke

Recorded 15 Jun 1647
INVENTORY of ROBERT GLASCOCK late deceased taken 25 Sep 1646 and apprased by MR: CORNELIUS LOYD, MR: EDWARD LOYD, JOHN NORRWOOD and THOMAS TOOKER. VIZT: in tobacco

IN THE HALL

2 feather bedds, 1 coverlidd, 1 boulster, 2 pillows -(torn)- bedstead with curtains and vallans 1200
45a * 1 Table & frame with a forme 0045
Ticking for a boulster 0040
2 Couches 0120
1 great wooden chayre & tobacco dryer 0040
2 chests and 2 gunnes 0245
4 payre of old sheets 0200
1 old shirt 0030
2 old suites of Cloathes & 1 Coate 0250
halfe a dozen of falling bands 0250
2 payre stockins 3335
2 payre of pillow beares 0030
1 Bible and a Sermon Booke 0020
1 hanging Earthen Candlestick 0015
2 table Cloathes & 1 doz: Napkins 0150

IN THE BUTTERY

4 Pewter dyshes a bason & salt sellar 0090
1/2 dozen of porringers (some of these amounts) 0---
1 dozen Pewter spoones (are badly faded) ----
1 flagon & a drinking Cupp & 2 dramme cupps ----
2 chamber potts ----
1 Quart pott and 2 small saucers ----
1/2 dozen paynted butter dishes ----
1 dozen wooden milke dishes 004-
1 churne and 2 butter tubbs 0060
2 Creame Potts 1/2 dozen dishes 0050
4 old boxes & other Lumber 0040

IN THE MAYDS CHAMBER

46 *1 flock bedd and boulster, 1 rugg & 1 old bedstead 0060

IN THE KITCHEN

2 iron potts & 2 payre of pott hookes 0180
1 iron skellett & 1 iron spitt 0025
1 iron dripping pann & Iron pestell 0010
1 little old table & forme 0010

IN THE LOFT OVER THE KITCHEN

2 old flock bedds & boulsters, 1 old rugg & coverlidd & 1 old ticking filled with huskes 0030
1 powdering tubb, a milk payle, 3 oll bucketts & other old tubbs 0080
a trammell & other hookes to hang potts with 0015
3 awgurs, 1 pickaxe, 9 old howes, a broad axe, a small sawe, 3 narrow axes, a Chissell, a Rest for a sawe, an old iron wedge & 2 wooden shovells 0080

continued on next page:-

IN THE LITTLE CHAMBER

fether bedd & boulsters & 2 pillowes, 1 rugg and striped curtains and vallans	1200
3 payre of sheets & 2 payre pillow beares	0220
A paire of tongs, a warming panne & a broken looking glasse & a small chaire & a small trunck	0110

SERVANTS

2 men servants havinge 2 yeares a piece to serve	2000
2 servant Mayds having 3 yeares to serve	2000
a boy to serve 6 yeares	1250
a small boy for eleaven yeares	0800

OF THE CROPP

20 hhds of tobacco cont?	6000
39 barrels of corne at 25 l tob^{o} p barrel	0975
a boate at	0850
The Plantation and Howsing	3500
Severall debts due to the estate	2243

* NEAT CATTLE &c 46a

10 Cowes	5500
1 old bull and 2 bulls of 2 yeares old	0900
2 Oxen, 2 steares of 3 yeares old, ? steares of 2 yeares old	2900
3 heifar calves & two steare calves	0600
1 bull calfe & 1 cow calfe	0150
2 sowes, one bore & 6 shoats 1/2 yeare old	0600
3 old turkeys & 6 young ones	0250
fifty poultrey young and old	0200?
The totall summe is	35850?

₺ 2/5 in money sterl:

Recorded 15 Jun 1647 - An Inventory of the goods and chattels of PHILLIPP ffELLGATE, Gent: late deceased taken 15 Sep 1646 and appraysed by MR: EDWARD LOYD and MR: MATHEW PHILLIPPS. VIZT: in tob^{o}

1 black cloth suit with a cloke	500	
2 old stuffe suits	200	
a buff doublet with a paire of cloth breeches with a gold lace	200	
2 old sadd coulored cloth suits with a Cloke	180	
1 old short cloth coat	050	
Lyning for a short coat of Squirrell skyns	030	
3 old dowlas shirts, a new halfe shirt, an old halfe shirt, 3 night capps and halfe a dozen paire of bands and cuffes	236	
a small Gold ring	070	
* 5 paire of boot hose topps ?	050	47
2 old paire of silke stockings, 2 paire woosted stockings and a paire of silke stirrupp hose	080	
a paire of black silke garters	030	
a paire of old boots, 2 paire of new shewes & 3 payre of old shewes	075	
one old beaver hatt, 1 old gray felt, 1 old Mountero Capp & a silver hattband	095	
a gold hatcht Sword	080	
an old Crossebowe and an old Citron, a suite of Black Armour, an headpiece of white armour, a playne Muskett & Rest & a suite of bandileerees	200	

47 continued 15 Jun 1647

two bedsteads	050
2 fether bedds & 1 boulster, 1 flock boulster, 1 old suite of curtaynes and vallans of thynne stryped stuffe & 1 blew Rugg, & a very old greene rugg & 2 old white blankets	540
1 Cedar Chest and boxe	100
5 old windowe curtaynes and an old Chimney Cloth	060
2 old payre of sheets & 2 old payre of pillow beares & an old course sheet & halfe a dozen of course hand towells, 3 small table cloths & halfe a dozen of Napkins	230
Halfe a dozen of old greene cloth chayres	080
an old payre of broken Andyrons & a shovell and tongs	025
2 fowling peices and one birding peice? & a carbyne without a lock	310
His Coat of Armes and 2 old pictures and escutcheon	030
47a * 5 barrells of powder cont: 10 l & 5 barrels of shott conteyning C 1 pownd weight?	465
Nyne payre of shoes	135
2 payles, 2 broad howes, 2 narrow howes & 2 felling axes & 2 Ammunition Swords	110
2000 of sixe penny nayles, & 2000 4 penny nayles & 500 ten penny nayles & 250 of twenty penny nayles	119
6 knives, sixe lockram? shirts & 2 shirts for a boy	144
3 dozen and one pownd of Candles & 2 pownd of thredd needles, 8 paire of Irish stockings, 2 paire of canvas drawers, & 2 Jacketts (amt. faded)	XXX
3 Monmouth capps, 3 cotton wastcoats & halfe a firkin of soxe (firkin is about 1/4 of a barrel), & 28 pownds of Match(e)s & a bushell and a halfe of white salt and three gallons and a quart of vinacre? (vinegar?)	248
s Servant boy and a Servant Mayd	2600
2 sacks and 3 syves	0054
a parcell of bookes	0080
The totall summe is	6713

Recorded the 15 Jun 1647

I THOMAS HA<u>RIS</u>ON of London, Mariner doe acknowledgeto have received of WILLIAM PRESLY of Elizabeth Citty County in Virginia one bill of Lading for 6 hhds of tobacco. Dated the 27 Mar 1643 and marked WP and
48 affirmed * by EDWARD GUNNELL and consigned to JOHN HOGGINS as also a note under the hand of the said HOGGINS for the payment of the produce of the said tob[o] to WILLIAM ALLEN of London, Merchant, the which said note beareth date 27 Mar 1643 answerable to the bill of Lading. In wittness of the abovesaid I have hereunto subscribed this 3 Apr 1643.
Teste: ROW: BURNHAM, NICHOLAS BROWNE THO: HARRISON

ATT A COUNTY COURT HOLDEN 13 Jul 1647

PRESENT: CAPT: WILLIAM CLAIBORNE, ESQ:
MR: CORNELIUS LOYD) MR: THOMAS LAMBART) COM[rs]:
MR: EDWARD LOYD) MR: MATH: PHILLIPPS)

In the cause depending betweene CAPT: THOMAS WILLOWGHBY Esqr: administrator of MR: RICHARD WAKE deceased Complaynant and CAPT: JOHN SIBSEY

concerning matters of accoumpts Copartnershipp betweene the Defendent
and the Decedent. It is ordered /by both the said partyes consent/
that all busynesses aforemenconed /notwithstanding any bonds heretofore entered into, or orders of Court formerly made on eyther part/
bee from hence referred to bee heard and determined by the Governor
and Counsell on the Seveanth day of October Court next.

MORE PRESENT: CAPT: THOMAS WILLOWGHBY ESQR: & CAPT: JOHN SIBSEY

Whereas MRS: SARAH GOOKIN hath beene oftentymes by severall orders of
this Court formerly and alsoe at this present summoned to give in an
account according to Act of Assembly of all the estate belonging to the
children of CAPT: ADAM THORROWGOOD deceased in her custody and possession which MRS: GOOKIN utterly refuseth as by a lre (letter) under her
hand appeareth. Ordered upon her said contempt that the Sheriffe shall
within tenn dayes by vertue of this order levy by distresse on the pper
(proper) estate of the said MRS: * GOOKIN the full value of 500 l 48a
tob^{o} to bee disposed of as shall hereafter shall bee thought fitt. And
if the said MRS: GOOKIN shall not at the next Court give an accoumpt of
the said Childrens estate Then this Court to sett a further xxxxxx or
punishmt on the said MRS: GOOKIN as they shall thinke fitt.

Read in Court the 13 Jul 1647 and ordered to be recorded.
Sr: Yo^{r} letter received with the Copy of an order of last Court, please
to take for answere that my resolutions are from this inferior Court to
appeale to the Grand Court of the Governor and Counsell at James Citty
there to give up such accoumpts as shall bee required or are requisite
in case the lawe may compell (the?) executrix and mother of her children left likewyse by will sole guardian to theire full age to give xxx
(faded) accoumpts to any but her children and of this xxx desire if it
bee not just to see a president at any tyme eyther xxxx Realme of England or in these parts when and xxxx an executrix in my condicon was
ever called to (accom^{pt}?) before the full age of their children, or by
any xxxxx but theires; the difference in the premise as suxxx xxx
betweene MR: PHILLIPPS and myselfe, that adxxxx not of any parity he
beeing an overseer only and likewise admitted by consent of this Court,
and fully lyable to the power thereof, but myselfe all free from such
brief commands and with that resolution remayne confident that none but
my children may call mee to accoumpt; nor they till full age untill
when I desire not to be molestes, or at least feel I have president,
whereupon I am ready to deliver as Just an accoumpt as any other. I
much wonder that myselfe, of all others should bee marked out to bee
troubled in this kynd. I being able to shewe many presidents to confirme these my resolucons lastly please to understand that I lye not
solely under the power of this Court, the greater part of the estate
reamyning under the Jurisdiction of another togeather with some accoumpts as yet restant in * England, and I conceive I should doe 49
wrong to that Court to Register any accoumpts here: Soe rest.

SARA: GOOKIN

My respects to your selfe ********** and wyfe most kyndly remembered
to whome I have sent a small basket of apples p the bearer. Superscrib-
ed To MR: THOMAS IVY high Sheriffe of Lower Norfolke.

49 continued 13 Jul 1647

(Note: Your editor wonders how the Lower Norfolk County Court liked being called "inferior", a lower Court of course, but? Some of the Commissioners were on the Council. There is a little buttering up going on here, on Sara's part. Thomas Ivy was the "Under" Sheriff, not the High Sheriff, and she must have known it. AGW)

The Com[rs]: doe appoynt at theire next session to pose and examine the accoumpts at this present produced and exhibited by MR: MATHEW PHILLIPS concerning the estate of the orphants of MRS: ALICE SEAWELL deceased in his custody or protection.

Recordatur duodermio die August 1647

To all Christian people &c......I ROBERT HAYES of the Little Creek in the parish of Lynhaven in the County of Lower Norfolk, Planter........ am lawfully possessed of a parcell of land scytuate lyeing and being in and upon the Easterne side of Lynhaven River parte whereof was by mee bought from LIEFTENAUNT RICHARD POPELEY and parte from MR: HENRY POOLE. ....for and in consideration of a valuable summe of tobacco to mee in hand payd and for divers good causes............. have given, granted, bargained, sold and assigned &c........... unto EDWARD COOPER of Lynhaven, Planter all that parte of the saidLand which lyeth betweene the land formerly by mee sould unto OWEN HAYES nowe in the tenure of EDWARD LILLY and the land by mee sould unto THOMAS DAVYES which said land by mee nowe sould unto EDWARD COOPER is thus bownded /vizt/ be a marked Gum tree which standeth upon the uttermost Northeast edge of EDWARD LILLY his land and by a direct lyne stretching itselfe due Northwest from the said Gumme tree to Lynhaven Riverside and Southeast to the uttermost extent of the myle from the said River side into the
49a woods and from that place where the said lyne shall come to the * water of the river directly to a Creeke called the Indian Cabbin Creeke and soe Southeast alongst the said creeke to the uttermost head of the Mayne Branch thereof and thence to the end of the myle and thence to the end of the first direct line running Southeast from the aforesaid marked Gumme tree To have and to hold...............................
50 in witness whereof I have sett my hand and seal 4 Aug 1647 ROBERT HAYES
Wit: XOP: BURROWGH acknowledged before me EDW: WINDHAM
RI: CONQUEST

ATT A COUNTY COURT HOLDEN 16 Aug 1647

PRESENT: CAPT: THOMAS WILLOWGHBY ESQR:

CAPT: JOHN SIBSEY) MR: HENRY WOODHOUSE)
MR: THOMAS LAMBART)- MR: EDWARD LOYD)- COM[rs]
MR: MATH: PHILLIPPS)

A certificate of 100 acres of Land to THOMAS MARSH proved due upon oath for the transportacon of JACOB ATTWACK and NATHAN KINGSLAND.
(See Nugent 179 John Clarke for the same headrights and also Nugent pp 57, 67, 122, 174, 179, 445 & 497 for Thomas Marsh) Name is written Thomas Marsh also Attwack the headright.

A certificate for 100 acres of land to CAPT: ffRANCIS YARDLEY for transportation of SIMON a Turke and John a negro.

A certificate is granted unto JOHN SIDNEY *Sidsey* for 250 acres of land proved due upon the oath of CAPT: JOHN SIBSEY for the transportation of DANYELL MALY (or NALY), THOMAS DUNTON, MARY PEIRCE, SARAH KING, and MARGERY BROUGH. (the Msare written: *Maly - Mary-Margery*
and *Capt John Sibsey*

MORE PRESENT: MR: CORNELIUS LOYD

Upon the peticon of BARTHOLOMEW HOSKINS: It is ordered that he bee exempted and cleered of the publique Levye and allsoe from all publique service /touching his pticular pson/ in the County in respect the said HOSKINS is aged and infirme and allsoe did belong unto the Collony in SIR THOMAS DALE's tyme.

Exhibited in Court by ROBERT DAVYES the administrator of JACOB BRADSHAWE deceased /vizt/:
An Inventory of the estate of JACOB BRADSHAWE deceased taken the 3rd day of July 1647 according to ye appraisment mede thereof by XPOFER: BURROWGHS, FRANCIS LAND, WILLIAM LUCAS and THOMAS CHEELEY sworne to prayse the said estate before MR: HENRY WOODHOWSE one of his Mats Comr for this County * 50a

a Bull of three or fower yeares old	300
a Psalm booke & a testament	015
one shirte	020
one old suite of Clothes	050
one Wolfeskin and one Deere skin	020
one knife & one neckcloth	003
a parcell of Lumber	040
one small old unfixed gunne	050

THESE GOODS FOLLOWING ARE IN COPARTNERSHIPP
BETWEENE JACOB BRADSHAWE & WILLIAM EADY vizt:

Three small Pewter dishes & 2 porringers	036 ye halfe	018
2 old payles	020	005
a bedd and a blankett	100	050
an Iron Pott & 3 Iron hookes made of hoopes	040	020
2 old sifters	008	004
3 old turkeys & 2 younger	100	050
fowerteene poultry old & young	030	015
6 hogg shewts (shoats?)	200	100
	524 ye halfe	262

More of JACOBs pticular a barrell of Eares which was his pvison 050
more one man hyred betweene them to make a Cropp which is not yet finished nor praysed.
Appraysed as abovesayd by us XOPER BURROWGH, FRANCIS LAND, WILLIAM LUCAS, THOMAS CHEELEY his marke.
A list of bylles and noates whereby certayne debts (are) due to the estate of JACOB BRADSHAWE deceased.

50a continued 16 Aug 1647

	Tob°
A bill from JOHN HASNETT Hasnett & HUGH WOOD Hugh due in the yeare of our Lord 1648	1200 l
A bill from ARTHUR LEHAY Lehay	0200
51 *A bill from JOHN DYAR	0270
A Bill from RICHARD ABRELL assigned from THO: CHEELEY	0140
A Bill from WILLIAM BASNETT	0770
A Bill from WILLIAM CAPPS for & Caske	0500
A noat from THOMAS DAVYES to GEORGE MIGH to pay	0108
A noat from THOMAS DAVYES to EDW LILLY to pay	0150
A noate from JOHN MARTIN to WM: LUCAS to pay	0030
	3608

More: an old shott bagg & Powder horne
A Cannoe which was betweene JACOB BRADSHAWE & WILLIAM EADY

The Enquest concerning the death of JACOB BRADSHAWE deceased 11 Apr 1647

The opinion of these men underwritten is that JACOB BRADSHAWE lyeing upon a Cheste did receive his death at the hands of God by lightning and thunder from heaven as he was Reading in a booke, having thereby received a bruise in his head and the hayre of some parte of his head being burned and likewyse upon his shoulder. Witness our hands this 12 Apr 1647:
JOHN STRATTON, WILLM: WB BASNETT, RICHARD W ffORSTER, WILLM: CAPPS, WALTER PRESSAR, JOHN WOODWARD, THOMAS ALLEN.

The Court doth order that ROBERT DAVYES administrator of JACOB BRADSHAWE deceased shall pay unto MR: HENRY WOODHOWSE Woodhowse 360 l tobacco made appeare by sufficient proofe to bee due from the decedent.

51a *
ROBERT BRADSHAWE administrator of JACOB BRADSHAWE deceased ordered to pay unto THOMAS TOOKER 144 l tobacco by accoumpt from the decedent.

Attachment granted unto RICHARD CONQUEST for 109 l tobacco due from EDWARD STONE p bill & accoumpt pduced for Clerkes ffees agst the estate of said STONE in the hands of JOHN MERRIDAY.

It is ordered that RICHARD ffORSTER, OWEN HAYES & ISBELL his wife, JOHN WACEY Warcey (MACEY?), and EDMOND LINDSEY als yeoman doe personally appeare at the next Court to answere unto such matters as they bee demaunded.

Ordered that RICHARD ABRELL, JOHN SUC(KETTE?), SIMON HANCOCK be satisfyed by EDWARD HALL 20 l tobacco a piece having been summoned for witnesses in HALLs behalfe.

A certaine Difference betweene MRS: SARAH GOOKIN Comp[tt] and WILLIAM CAPPS administrator of JAMES SMYTH deceased referred to a Jury of 12 (men) whoe doe fynd that the controversie was a trespasse, and not being sued for in the decedents lyfetyme therefore the estate of the decedent is not lyable to make satisfaccon for the said trespasse dyeth with him.

Whereas the Sherriffe by former order from this board hath attached in the hands of MRS: SARSH GOOKIN 2 cowes, 2 steares & a yearling heifar of the proper estate of JAMES SMYTH deceased and ordered that MRS: GOOKIN bee satisfyed 1060 l tobacco out of the said Cattle being apprysed by EDWARD HALL, THOMAS ALLEN, WILLIAM LUCAS, and SAVILL GASKINE upon oath the said 1060 l tobacco being made appeare due from ye decedent................

52

* 17 Aug 1647

PRESENT: CAPT: JOHN SIBSEY) MR: CORNELIUS LOYD)
MR: THOMAS LAMBART)-)- COM^rs
MR: MATH: PHILLIPPS) MR: EDWARD LOYD)

Ordered that WILLIAM LUCAS, ffRANCIS LAND, ROBERT HAYES, JOHN CHAUNDLER, THOMAS MARSH, WILLM: CROUCH & RICHARD OWENS doe in theire severall lymitts respectively according to former order given them carefully take exact lists of all lands holden in this County and deliver the same to the Sheriff by this day moneth.

Ordered that THOMAS CONYERS bee nonsuited and pay 30 l tobacco unto JOHN CARRAWAY for molestacon.

Attachment graunted unto RICHARD CONQUEST for 108 l tobacco in the hands of JOHN STRATTON of the proper estate GEORGE BEACH for ffees due from the said BEACH and to bee satisfactory for the same upon further determination.

A Certificate of 250 acres of Land unto ANDREW NICHOLLS for transportacon of himselfe, ELIZABETH his wife, & his 3 children vizt: ANDREW, ELIZABETH & WILLIAM. (Note: In Nugent p 179 : RICHARD WHITEHURST Patent for 250 acres - 20 Oct 1648 - on Gaythers Creek of the So. Br. of Eliz. Riv. for transportation of the same headrights as in the above certificate.)

The Court doth amerce MR: ffRANCIS MASON High Sherriffe 200 l tobacco to bee payd for his Ma^t: use because of his neglect in the Levying a distresse on the proper estate of MRS: SARAH GOOKIN for 500 l tobacco according to the tenor of a former order and if the said Sherriffe shall not levye the said 500 l tobacco as aforesaid within 10 dayes nowe next coming then this Court to sett a further Malctxx? or fyne on the said sherriffe and as they shall thinke fitt. (Note: Sarah must have had the men in her spell, or they were afraid of her. AGW)

* 52a

MORE PRESENT: CAPT: WILLIAM CLAIBORNE ESQR:

The Court doth thinke fitt againe to give MRS: SARAH GOOKIN respite till the next Court to bring in an accopt and Inventory of the Estate of the Orphans of CAPT: ADAM THORROWGOOD and if (she) shall not by that tyme deliver in an accopy and Inventory then this Court doe order that the Sherr: immediately after next Court to levy by distresse on the proper estate of MRS: GOOKIN the sume of 1000 l tobacco more to bee disposed as hereafter shall bee thought fitt and alsoe further course to bee taken with the said MRS: SARAH GOOKIN concerning the premises.

The Court to be held upon 15 (Oct?) 1647 in respect of the Grand Assembly is advanced to the 9 Nov following.................................

Absent: CAPT: WILLIAM CLAIBORNE ESQR: Present: CAPT: EDWARD WINDHAM

Ordered that BLANCH ARMESTRONG shall aske CAPT: SIBSEY forgiveness in Court for abusing him in unjust language and she is to receive 10 stripes on the bare back for her abuse to MRS: SIBSEY.................

Upon the said BLANCH her acknowledgmt in Court for submission the punishment is remitted upon her good behavior.

The Clerke to receive pay for all warrants &c issued.

53 * 6 Oct 1647 in Recorded

ATT A COURT HELD AT THE DEEP CREEKE on 22 Apr 1647

PRESENT:

CAPT: THOMAS BERNARD)	MR: WILLM: RABNETT
MR: ZACK: CRIPS)-	MR: THOMAS DAVIES
MR: WILLM: WHITBY)	MR: THOMAS TAYLOR

THOMAS CASON ordered to make payment unto THOMAS CEELIE for 2200 l tob & caske within 10 dayes.

Teste: ROBERT PYLANDE ClCur

These are to certifye that this order was verbally copied out of the records. p mee: ROBERT PYLANDE ClCur

ATT A COUNTY COURT HOLDEN 14 Oct 1647

PRESENT: CAPT: JOHN SIBSEY

MR: THOMAS LAMBERT	MR: CORNELIUS LOYD
MR: MATH: PHILLIPPS	MR: THOMAS MEARES

Court to be adjourned because of late Adjournment of the Assembly to 1 Nov the Comr: being Burgesses until the 15 Dec following.

53a * RECORDED THE 10 Dec 1647 vizt: the 10 Nov 1647

PRESENT: SR: WILLIAM BERKELEY Knt: Governor &c

CAPT: JNO: WEST)	CAPT: THO: PETTUS)	
RICHARD KEMP ESQ:)_	MR: RICHARD BENNETT)_	ESQR:
CAPT: SAM: MATHEWES)	CAPT: HUMF: HIGGINSON)	
CAPT: HEN: BROWNE)	CAPT: WILM: BERNARD)	

WILLIAM LUCAS doth confesse a judgement for the (faded) of 500 pownds of tob^{o} and Caske upon (faded) tenth day of November next unto MR: WILLM: WHITE or to his assignes.....als Execucon.

15 Dec 1647 53a

Upon the petition of CAPT: ffRANCIS YARDLEY who hath lately intermarried
with MRS: SARAH GOOKIN it is ordered that the ffyne of 500 pownds of
tob° levyed upon the estate of the said * MRS: GOOKIN by former order 54
of the Court bee wholly remitted and that the said CAPT: YARDLEY according to his owne premisse and undertaking shall by the 15 day of Apr
next coming exhibit a faire and justifyable accoumpt unto this Court of
all the estate belonging to the orphanes of CAPT: ADAM THOROWGOOD ESQ:
long since deceased with the improvement of theire said estates since
the division.

JOHN WATTKINS doth acknowledge that he hath graunted bargayned and sold
unto RICHARD CONQUEST his heires &c forever 250 acres of Land scytuate
and being on the South side of the River over against Kecoughtan and a-
butting North East upon a Creeke which parteth it from the Land of CAPT:
WILLIAM TUCKER extending itselfe South West along the branch of the
said River 125 pole at 16 foote and an halfe the pole unto the land of
LIEUTENANT JOHN CHEESMAN and contynuing South East upon the Mayne Land
and North West upon the Mayne River: to which said 250 acres of land
was granted by pattent under the Great Seale of the Collony bearing
date at JAMES CITTY 2 Sep 1624 by SIR FRANCIS WYATT Knt then Governor
of Virginia unto JOHN SIBSEY of KECOUGHTAN Yeoman his heires and assignes forever and afterwards vizt: upon the 16 Jan 1630 for a valuable
consideration by the said JOHN SIBSEY bargained sold & Conveyed unto
THOMAS WILLOUGHBY his heires and assigns forever and afterwards Vizt:
upon the 18 Dec 1635 for a valuable consideracon by the said CAPT:
WILLOUGHBY bargained sold and conveyed unto the said JOHN WATTKINS his
heires & assignes forever and afterwards vizt: upon the 23 Sep 1647 * 54a
for 1500 l tob° in hand payd.........being a valuable consideracon by
the said JOHN WATTKINS bargained & sold unto RICHARD CONQUEST his
heires &c............

JOHN (+) WATTKINS
Acknowledged in Court 15 Dec 1647 CORNELIUS LOYD
ATTESTOR: RIC: CONQUEST ClCur

THOMAS HARRISON Clerke ordered to pay an accoumpt of £ 7/17/4 unto
CAPT: WILLIAM ATTERBURY within 10 dayes..............................

WHEREAS: WILLIAM CAPPS Adm. of JAMES SMYTH decd hath impleaded MRS:
SARAH GOOKIN now the wife of CAPT: ffRANCIS YARDLEY for 600 l Tob° and
the Pduce of 3000 Plants and for satisfaccon for covering part of a
howse and for finishing the Malt Howse and for other imployment alleaged
due to the decedent. Ordered that MRS: YARDLEY cleare the same upon her
oath or by other proofe or otherwyse to bee lyable to the award and censure of the Court.

JOHN ffINCH ordered to pay 540 l tob° unto RICHARD HALL within 10 dayes.

* ROBERT JONES ESTATE DEBTOR: 55

To MATHEW HOWARD per accoumpt	811 l tob°
To ROBERT BOWERS per accoumpt	523
To Severall Men per accoumpt	195
	1529

Creditor per Contra

By Appraisement of the Cropp		1652 l tob^{o}
" tob received of LOVEDAY		0180
" tob received of LOVEDAY		0440
" tob from ANDREW NICHOLLS not received		0500
		2372
By ANDREW NICHOLLS bill		
Tob to MR: IVEY & others	deduct	1529
	Rest	0843

It appeares to the Court that MATH: HOWARD & ROBERT BOWERS joynt adms: of ROBERT JONES decd have payd beyond assetts........Quietus est may be granted unto them.

ROBERT EYRE ordered to be payd 200 l tob out of the Estate of JACOB BRADSHAWE decd for a debt.

THOMAS WRIGHT ordered to pay unto SIMON DREW 300 l tob within 10 days

JOHN JOHNSON ordered to pay unto MR: ffRANCIS MASON 329 l tob & Caske within 10 dayes.

JOHN MARTIN ordered to be paid 150 l tob out of the Estate of JACOB BRADSHAWE decd, all former orders first satisfyed.

55a Whereas: JOHN CORNELISON is indebted unto LANCASTER LOVETT 364 pownds of tobacco with bill as appeares to the Court. Payment is ordered to bee made of the said tob^{o} within 4 dayes and the Court Charges als Execucon.

16 Dec 1647 PRESENT et Antea

And more present MR: HENRY WOODHOUSE

These summes of tobacco followeing are allowed of and ordered to bee payd by the severall Collectors to the partyes hereafter named (Vizt)

	tob^{o}
To ANDREW NICHOLLS for killing one wolfe	0100
To WILLIAM BASNETT for one wolfe	0100
To EDWARD COOPER for one wolfe	0100
To JOHN PORTER for one wolfe	0100
To MR: SIDNEY for 2 hoggs and 4 dayes worke to come to Mr:MEARES	044X
To MR: MEARES for provision for himselfe & other his fellow Burgesses	121X
To WILLIAM PELL for one wolfe killed	0100
To CAPT: SIBSEY for a wolfe killed by his Negroe	0100
To MR: WOODHOUSE for provision for himselfe and other his fellow Burgesses	222X
To CAPT: WILLOUGHBY for a wolfe killed by his servant	0100
To XPOFER BURROUGH for a boat & 2 hands 2 dayes to transport MR: WOODHOUSE	0050
To JEFFREY WRIGHT for 52 dayes service upon the Burgesses	0520
To CAPT: EDWARD WINDHAM for the hyre of a Sloope and hands to carry up the Burgesses	0540

To MR. CORNELIUS LOYD for howse roome at JAMES CITTY & for provision for himselfe 0900

To MR: IVY for men to rowe up the Burgesses 0910
To MR: MASON for boat hyre &c 0250
To CAPT: WINDHAM for a Case of Drinke 0080
7832

To the Collectors for Sallary at 10^{l} per St is 0788
Totall summe is -------------------- 8620

*For satisfaccon of the aforesaid summe of 8620 l tob............ 56
ordered that there bee levyed upon the Inhabitants of this County.....

	l tob
For 360 Tytheable psons: @ 15 p polle	5400
" 546 Cowes @ 3^{l} p Cowe	1638
" 121 Goates @ $1\frac{1}{2}^{l}$ p Goate	0181
" 5 horses & mares @ 24 p horse	0120
" 36560 Acs: Land @ 3^{l} p Cent: (per 100 acres)	1097
ffrom CAPT: WINDHAM by an overplus of the last yeares Levye	0400
The Total is	8836

MR: CORNELIUS LLOYD Collector is debtor

By 70 tytheable persons @ 55^{l} p head	3850
145 cowes @ 11^{l} per Cowe	1595
49 Goates @ $5\frac{1}{2}^{l}$ per Goate	$269\frac{1}{2}$
1 Horse @ 88^{l} p horse	088
2660 acs @ 11^{l} p Cent (per 100 acres)	0286
	6089

Per Contra Creditor

To himselfe by the assignment of CAPT: ffLEET	0600
" p provision	0800
" for MR: VAUS	0330
" for STEVEN GILL	0800
" for County Levyes	0900
To MR: RICHARD BENNETT in part	1299
ffor Sallary of 6089^{l} at 10^{l} p cent	0610
	5339
To JOHN WATTKINS	0750
Summe Total	6089

* MR: EDWARD LLOYD is debtor l tob 56a

70 psons tytheables p polle @ 55^{l}	3850
71 Cowes @ 11^{l} p Cowe is	781
6150 Acs of Land @ 11^{l} p Cent	$671\frac{1}{2}$
	$5302\frac{1}{2}$

Per Contra Creditor

By his sallary at 10^{l} p Cent for $5302\frac{1}{2}^{l}$	0530
To RICHARD BENNETT	$4772\frac{1}{2}$
Summe Total	$5302\frac{1}{2}$

56a 16 Dec 1647

MR: THOMAS LAMBART Collector is debtor	
23 Tytheables persons @ 55^{l} per polle	1265
36 Cowes @ 11^{l} p Cowe is (The amounts are faded)	03XX
20 Goates @ $5\frac{1}{2}^{l}$ p Goate	0XXX
1550 acres of Land at 11^{l}	0XX5½
	1938½
MR: THOMAS LAMBART p Contra Creditor	
To RICHARD CONQUEST	17XX½
To Himselfe for sallary $1936\frac{1}{2}^{l}$ @ 10^{l} p Cent	019X½
Summe Total	1938½

CAPT: JOHN SIBSEY Collector is debtor	
46 Tytheable persons @ 55^{l} per polle	2530
84 Cowes @ 11^{l} p Cowe	0924
15 Goates @ $5\frac{1}{2}^{l}$ per Goate	0082½
6750 Acres of Land @ 11^{l} p Cent	0737½
By Bill of CAPT: WINDHAM	0268
	4542
Per Contra Creditor	
To MR: RICHARD BENNETT in ffull	1929
To RICHARD CONQUEST	0755½
To CAPT: WILLOUGHBY	0100
To himselfe	0100
To JAMES KNOTT	0100
57 * To MICHAELL BATT	0724½
To himselfe for sallary @ 4542^{l} @ 10^{l} p Cent	0454
Totall is	4542

MR: MATHEW PHILLIPS Collector is debtor	
24 Tytheable persons @ 55^{l} p polle	5170
128 Cowes @ 11^{l} p Cowe	1408
37 Goates @ $5\frac{1}{2}^{l}$ per Goate is	0203½
4 Mares & horses @ 88^{l} p horse	0352
8835 Acres of Land @ 11^{l} p Cent	0968
By Bill & accoumpts of CAPT: WINDHAM	0812
	8913½
Per Contra Creditor	
To Michaell Batt in full	0097½
To MR: SIDNEY for 2 hoggs & 4 dayes work	0440
To JOHN PORTER for a wolfe	0100
To himselfe for MR: WOODHOUSE	1310
To MR: THOMAS MEARES	1015
To CAPT: WINDHAM	0620
To MR: IVY	0910
To MR: ffRANCIS MASON	0250
To ANDREW WARNER	0100
To WILLIAM PELL	0100
To Xpofer Burroughs	0050
To MR: CHYLES	0640
To MR: BLAND	1787
To SIR WILLIAM BERKELEY	0604
To himselfe for sallary of $8913\frac{1}{2}^{l}$ @ 10^{l} p cent	0890
Summe Total	8913½

MR: HENRY WOODHOUSE Collector is debtor

By bills of CAPT: WINDHAM received	2066	
58 persons @ 55^{l} p polle is	3190	
74 Cowes @ 11^{l} p Cowe is	0814	
* 5200 Acres of Land @ 11^{l} p Cent	0572	57a
Due to him which MR: PHILLIPPS is to pay	0402	
	7104	

Per Contra Creditor

To SIR WILLIAM BERKELEY	4803
To WILLIAM BASNETT	01X0
To EDWARD COOPER	0100
To himselfe	0917
To JEFFREY WRIGHT	0520
To himselfe for sallary of 6642^{l} @ 10 p Cent	0664
The Totall is	7104

Judgement given this (15?) day of October 1637 that JOHN PENRICE should pay unto MR: CORNELIUS LLOYD 800^{l} tob.....ordered that MR: PENRICE is to pay .. unto sd MR: LLOYD with Court charges ....

Ordered the 16 Jun 1645 that THOMAS CASON upon the (faded) November next following should pay WILLIAM PARRY Atty of NICHOLAS BROOKE £ XXXX Sterling being then 5 years due with forbearance at 8 p Cent and allsoe that CASON according to order of the Court from ELIZABETH CITTY should pay 20 p Cent for Non appearance........which judgemt: this Court doth revive.

Absent MR: HENRY WOODHOWSE

The Inventory of JAMES SMYTH decd & appraysed by EDWARD HALL, SAVILL GASKIN, (WALTER?) PRESSAR & THOS: ALLEN vizt:

	l tob	
* one old band, one horne combe 1000 of pinns, one ell of ribbon	0020	58
one Cowe & one Cowe Calfe	0600	
one old Cowe & one Bull Calfe	0400	
one yearling heifer at	0250	
one yearling Steere at	0200	
one Steere at fower yeares old at	0400	
	1870	

EDWARD (H) HALL his marke
SAVILL GASKINE WALTER PRESSAR
THOMAS ALLEN

ITEM: one bill of SAVILL GASKINE for	0370
ITEM: one bill of EDWARD HOLMES for	0050
Totall summe is	2290

p me WILLIAM CAPPS

ROBERT DAVYES Adm: of JACOB BRADSHAWE decd ordered to pay out of the decedents estate 140 l tob due by remaynder of a bill unto THOMAS NEEDHAM former orders being first satisfyed.

The Court upon 16 Feb 1645/6 upon (faded) grownd and sufficient proof that HENRICK LIGHTHART had transported JOHN GUTTERIDGE out of the Colony........did give judgmt: that HENRICK LIGHTHART since deceased should give security for 803 l tob at the next Crop....unto HENRY SNAYLE being the just creditor of JOHN GUTTERIDGE.....NOWE ORDERED THAT IF

ELLEN LIGHTHART the widdow & relict do not bring sd GUTTERIDGE into the Collony before the last day of ffebruary next......then she is to pay the 803 l tob unto HENRY SNAYLE.

58a * JOHN CORNELISON (sic) ordered to pay 224 l tob unto SAVILL GASKINE.

JOHN CARRAWAY ordered to pay unto WILLIAM SHIPP assignee of THOMAS CONYERS 1½ barrells of Indian Corne......

Difference depending betweene THOMAS CONYERS plt: & JOHN CARRAWAY deft: concerning certayne tymber.......upon request of CARRAWAY is referred to the next Court.

It appeares by sufficient proof (that) EDMUND LINDSEY als YEOMAN hath spoken divers scandalous words & infamous speeches concerninge LUCY the wife of EDWARD HALL. LINDSEY als YEOMAN to receive 20 lashes on his bare back and shall stand 3 Sabbath dayes at the Parish Church of Lynnhaven.......with a paper upon his head with these words following in Capitall letters (vizt) I, EDMUND LINCLEY als YEOMAN doe stand here to acknowledge the great wrong I have (faded) in the slandering of MRIS: HALL with my tongue ....sd LINDSEY als YEOMAN shall pay the Court charges als execucon and the Churchwardens of Lynhaven Parish to see that the above order is performed.......................................

MR: THOMAS CEELY is justly indebted unto NATHAN STAINSMORE ₤ 10 Ster: money due tenne yeares sithence (sic) and sd CEELY being arrested to this Court by the presentment of MR: EDWARD LOYD the attorney of *
59 STAINSMORE, and the sd CEELEY not appearing it is ordered that the Sheriffe having taken noe security for his appearance shall pay the debt with 10 yeares forbearance with the Court Charges unto the sd MR: EDWARD LLOYD for the use of the sd STAINSMORE if he the said Sheriffe do not bring in the body or sufficient goods of the sd CEELEY to the next Court.

Upon peticon of LAWRENCE PHILLIPPS the Court doth grant him license to keepe an Ordinary in the nowe dwelling howse of WILLIAM SHIPP in such manner as the said WILLIAM SHIPP did as well for the accomodacon of the Courts in the keeping of theire Courts as for provision & dyett for Strangers and for the Inhabitants of this County.
(NOTE: It is easy to understand why the Courts were held at WILLIAM SHIPPS - the Commissioners could imbibe while holding Court.)

RICHARD ffORSTER doth promise to deliver upon demaund unto MR: COR: LLOYD GENT: .....one cowe ...being at Lynhaven at the PLANTATION of EDWARD HALL.

Certificate for 50 acres of Land unto THOMAS MYLES for trans: of SARAH REINOLDS.

CAPT: EDWARD WINDHAM and JOHN HILL ordered to pay a debt of 3246 l tob unto RICHARD BENNETT.

MARKES LEONARD was impleaded by THOMAS CONYERS upon a certain condicon or covenant for service entered into two yeares since and it appearing by profe that LEONARD was for a consideracon fully acquitted from the covenant, Ordered that CONYERS be non suited & pay 50 l tob dammages for unjust molestation .

* THOMAS HUGHES arrested HENRY SNAYLE to the Court and HUGHES not pro- 59a
secuting his suite it is ordered that he be non suited and pay 30 l tob
unto SNAYLE for lelestacon & 40 l tob for 2 witnesses.

THOMAS DAVYES ordered to pay 250 l tob p accoumpt unto CAPT: EDWARD WINDHAM.

HENRY HILL ordered to pay 1552 l tob & Caske p bill unto SIMON OVERZEE, Merchant.

It appears by proofe that JOHN CORNELISON bought a Servant of HENRY SNAYLE.....which SNAYLE afterwards sold unto HENRY BRAKES and refuseth to deliver the servant to CORNELISON.......ordered that SNAYLE pay 100 l tob and BRAKES doe pay 100 l tob more for dammages for detaining the servant from CORNELISON.

JOHN CORNELISON acknowledges Judgment for 800 l tob unto HENRY SNAYLE.

HENRY SNAYLE acknowledges Judgment for 800 l tob unto HENRY BRAKES.

WILLIAM JOHNSON acknowledges Judgment for 400 l tob unto HENRY HULL.

JOHN ASNETTE acknowledges Judgment for 270 l tob unto ffRANCIS LAND

Absent MR: MEARES

RICHARD KENNAR is indebted unto the estate of JOHN WEBB decd 3300 l tob.
* and Caske per bill which amongst other wrytings was burnt in the tyme 60
of the Massacre by the Indians in the howse of the said WEBB as is alleaged by MR: CORNELIUS LLOYD the Administrator of the said WEBB. The
Court doth order paymt of the said tobaccos and Caske unto the said
MR: CORNELIUS LLOYD with lawfull forbearance and Court Charges within
ten dayes otherwyse execucon.

Whereas GEORGE HAWKINS stands indebted unto RICHARD STERNELL 420 pownds of tobacco as appeares unto the Court, Payment is ordered to bee made thereof within tenn dayes and Court Charges otherwyse execucon.

It is ordered that MR: HENRY WOODHOWSE having notice hereof shall at the next Court produce an accoumpt of the Crops and Corne and any other estate which did formerly belong unto THOMAS BREWER and was attached by the said MR: HENRY WOODHOWSE and the overplus if any shall bee fownd to bee delivered unto MR: THOMAS LAMBART in lieu of a debt dew (due) from the said BREWER unto the said MR: LAMBART.

Upon the Humble Petition of THOMAS IVY the Court doth grant him licence to keepe an ordinary for the accommodation of dyett (diet) for Strangers and the Inhabitants of the County and to have the like privileges as any other ORDINARY KEEPER hath or victualler useth provided it be according to the Lawes of the Countrey.

A Certificate of 250 acres of land are graunted unto MR: CORNELIUS LLOYD for the transportation of THOMAS WRIGHT, JAMES STRINGER, THOMAS GARRETT, THOMAS GODBY & THOMAS RADFORD into this Colony and proved due upon oath.

A Certificate of 250 acres of Land are graunted unto THOMAS WRIGHT for the transportation of PETER DEGOE, GEORGE BUSTAIN, WILLIAM STARLING, ROBERT LANGLEY, URSULA BAYLIE into this Collony proved due upon oath.

ffor certayne urgent Busynesses and necessary occasions apparent; it is thought fitt and ordered that there bee a Court holden upon the 18 Jan next and that the inhabitants of the County and all other persons whome it may concerne doe take notice thereof accordingly./

60a * GEORGE HAWKINS, Cowper (Cooper?) ordered to pay the next year unto RICHARD STARNELL for certaine worke 300 l tob.

ROBERT DAVYES adm: of JACOB BRADSHAWE decd ordered to pay unto RICHARD CONQUEST 100 l tob for recording the Jurys enquest concerning BRADSHAWES death.

THOMAS TOOKER is admitted & Sworne Clerke of this Court being deputed by RICHARD CONQUEST.

THOMAS TOOKER atty of WILLIAM ROBERTS Compl^{tt} (Complainant) agst PETER RIGGLESWORTH deft: by consent of both partyes is referred to the hearing of MR: CORNELIUS LLOYD, MR: THOMAS LAMBART, MR: EDWARD LLOYD & MR: JOHN HILL......to meet at the house of MR: CORNELIUS LLOYD before the 18 Jan next ....to be finally determined by them.

Judgmt: given 15 Feb 1645 that ROBERT HAYES should pay unto LEIFTENANT LUDDINGTON 626 l tob & Caske with Court Charges, HAYES haveing fayled in paymt: Judgmt: revived.

Recorded 16 Dec 1647

To the Worsh^{ll}: CAPT: THOMAS WILLOUGHBY ESQR: and the rest of his Ma^{tes}: (Majesty's) Comrs: Peticon of WILLIAM CAPPS adm: of the estate of JAMES SMYTH sheweth that MRS. SARAH GOOKIN stands indebted unto the
61 decedents estate * 600 l tob the product of 3000 plants and for covering part of her howse and for finishing the Mault Howse and for certaine (work) SMYTH was employed in in the Winter tyme. Yr: Peticoner desires order for the payment of same. The peticoners cause was referred to this court at the request of CAPT: ffRANCIS YARDLEY.

16 Aug 1647 Teste: RI: CONQUEST Cl Cur

16 Dec 1647 is Recorded

MEMORANDUM: That EDWARD LILLY doth release & discharge HENRY ROBINSON of and from all debts &c..........of the estate of sd: ROBINSON which was formerly in the custody of mee sd: EDWARD LILLY..... 6 Dec 1647.
Wit: THOMAS ALLEN, THO: REDBY

Recorded 16 Dec 1647 61

ROGER ffLETCHER of Boston in New England, Merchant appointing "my loving freind" (sic) THOMAS BRIDGE, Merchaunt my true and lawful attorney..........* in any part of place within the Collony of Virginia 61a
In Boston in New England 7 Oct (164(7) ROGER ffLETCHER.
Witt: ROBERT CHILD, DAN: GOOKIN

ATT A COURT HOULDEN 20 Jan 1647/8

PRESENT: MR. JOHN SIBSEY, MR. CORNELIUS LOYD, MR. EDWARD LOYD, MR: HENRY WOODHOUSE, MR: MATH: PHILLIPPS

ATTACHMT: graunted unto MR: WILLIAM JULIAN agst estate of RICHARD KENNAR for ₤ 3 sterl: money.

These are to certifie that MR: JOHN HILL declared himselfe to bee betweene 50 & 60 yeares of age and hath continued in this Collony of Virginia 25 yeares and upwards......to have formerly lived in the University of Oxford of the trade of a Bookebinder and is the sonne of STEPHEN HILL of Oxford aforesaid ffletcher (sic). And JOHN HILL is well at present and in good health as appeares to the Court and in liklihood of life/ (Why the reference to ffletcher?)

Difference betweene MRIS: YARDLEY deft: at the suite of WILLIAM CAPPS adm: of JAMES SMYTH decd is referred to the determination of CAPT: EDWARD WINDHAM and MR: HENRY WOODHOUSE to meete at the house of SAVILL GASKIN before the next Court.

62

* CAPT: ffRANCIS YARDLEY ordered to pay unto THOMAS TODD 300 l tob for worke of himselfe and man in haulling in a Pinnace formerly belonging to CAPT: JOHN GOOKIN.

MR: JOHN ffERINHAUGH ordered to pay unto JOHN HARVYE adm: of WILLIAM HEATH decd 380 l tob..........

CAPT: WILLIAM ATTERBURY acknowledges full satisfaction of MR: WILLIAM JULIAN for a debt of ₤ 9/5/5 Sterl: Money............................

Attachmt: graunted MR: JOHN fferinhaugh agst Estate of JOHN BASON for soe much as ffERINHAUGH hath payd unto GEORGE HORNER concerning accts: of the sd BASON.

Upon peticon of CAPT: ffRANCIS YARDLEY - ordered that JOHN HOLMES & EDWARD HALL, Chirurgeon doe view the bodyes of RICHARD RAGGED and a Maid Servant & a negroeman being servants to CAPT: YARDLEY & to make report before the next Court & of theire present estates and condicon occasioned by THOMAS WARDE, Chyrurgeon as is alleadged...............

ROBERT HAYES atty of HENRY BATTS ordered to pay 120 l tob unto ffRANCIS LAND.

PRESENT MORE: MR: THOMAS LAMBARD

SAVILL GASKIN ordered to pay 40 l tob unto WILLIAM CAPPS adm: of JAMES SMITH decd.................

HENRY MERRITT was Master? and copartner with WILLIAM HEATH decd....... Ordered that MERRITT bee possed: and enjoy the full halfe part of the last yeares proffitt of their trade & 530 l tob which MERRITT hath payd for HEATH decd from RICHARD SMITH Atty of JOHN SAVAGE ye adm of ye decedent.

62a * MR: EDWARD LOYD atty of NATHAN STAINSMORE comp[tt]: agst MR: THOMAS CEELY for a debt of ₤ 10/ sterl: and 10 yeares forbearance is referred to next Court. JOHN SIBSEY security for MR: CEELY.

GEORGE ASHALL is non-suited & to pay unto HENRY MERRITT 40 l tob for unjust molestacon.

ANDREWE WARNER ordered to paye unto OWEN HAYES 60 l tob for 2 appearances at Court.

THOMAS TOOKER Atty: for WILLIAM ROBERTS plt: agst PETER RIGGLESWORTH deft: is againe referred to the hearing of MR: CORNELIUS LLOYD & MR: EDWARD LLOYD, MR: THOMAS LAMBARD and MR: JOHN HILL...................

WILLIAM OLIVER & JOHN DAWBER & WILLIAM SHIPP hath sett up their names at the Court House doore to give notice of theire intended voyage for England.

These are to certify that WILLIAM LUCAS in the true and Lawfull Adm: of CAESAR PUGGETT decd.

OWEN HAYES gives security of 5 heade of neate cattell for 300 l tob & caske to be payd at the next Cropp unto MR: CORNELIUS LOYD.

63 * Recorded unestimo die Jan 1647
DEPOSITION: of ARTHUR BROWNE aged 58 yeares or thereabouts sworne sayeth "I did /the last year/ give & deliver unto CAPT: JOHN SIBSEY one boy servant called THOMAS DUDSTONE for his full terme of yeares for his taking in of my tob and some further agreements.

ARTHUR BROWNE

I, JOHN SIDNEY of Elizabeth River in Lower County of New Norfolke, Gent. have sould unto RICHARD WOLLMAN of the same place Planter a blacke heifar & a redd heifar calfe........ JOHN SIDNEY
Wit: THOMAS TABB, WILLIAM (+) WILSON

Deposition of RICHARD ABRELL aged 23 yeares or thereabouts sworne sayeth "....at the arrivall of MR: PAGE........by virtue of a letter of Creditt from the then MRS: SARAH GOOKIN given to this depont: together with WALTER IRBY did buy of JOHN MURREY 2 servants, a man & a woman for the use of MRIS: SARAH for 4000 l tob & Caske and MURREY did come to Lynnehaven and did there marke the number of 10 hhds of tob but before he departed the woman servant complayned that she was diseased whereupon

MURREY compound in the presence of ARGOLL YEARDLEY ESQ: with CAPT: ffRANCIS YARDLEY to pay for her cure and did himselfe declare....that he had sould him an unsound wenche ....Afterwards in the absence of CAPT: YARDLEY the wenche did relate that MURREY had undone her for by him shee had gott that disease, which is the poxe (NOTE: this goes on and on) .... this deponent did paye * 2000 l tob for the man 63a
and 500 l tob for the menche? ....

RICHARD (R) ABRELL
Overseer to CAPT: YARDLEY

Deposition of SAMPSON WARINGE aged 30 yeares or thereabouts....sworne sayeth..... (this repeats what the above deposition says).............

19 May 1645 - Before mee JOSHUA MAINET Notary publique dwelling in London Sworne.....the witnesses after named personally appeared MR: NATHAN STAINSMORE of London, Merchant......appointing EDWARD LLOYD of Elizabeth River in Virginia, Planter,*his attorney.................... 64

WILL: CHURCH — NATHAN STAINSMORE
JOSHUA NOSTOCK — JOSHUA MAINET Not: Pub:

* 64a

Recorded 21 ffeb 1647/8

Received 26 Oct 1646 of CAPT: GEORGE HEIGHAM in full of his bill in Virginia ₤ 4 of lawful money in England.

Wit: WILL ffELGATE — ELINOR BABB
ROBERT HOY (?)
ffRANCIS HOY (?) (NOTE: the H in Hoy is made in the same way as the H in Heigham. AGW)

Recorded 18 Nov 1647

I, RICHARD KEMPE ESQR: doe release & discharge RICHARD CONQUEST of & from the payment of a bill of debt for 350 l tob & caske paybale 1646 and delivered by mee to MR: WILLIAM HAREGRAVE, Maister of the shipp Globe /but the tob & caske has been received by mee/ 18 Nov 1647

RICH: KEMP

ATT A COUNTY COURT HOLDEN 15 Feb 1647/8

PRESENT: CAPT: JOHN SIBSEY — MR: HENRY WOODHOUSE
MR: MATH: PHILLIPPS — MR: EDWARD LLOYD

Whereas such stormy & tempestuous weather at present happening hath deteyned the other Comrs: from coming to keepe Court and divers people also...........Court to be held 23 Feb 1647/8

Certificate of 100 acres is granted to THOMAS GODBYE for trans: of ANN GODBYE and ROBERT PORTER.

* The Court on 1 Sep 1646 did order that MR: WILLIAM WHITBY should pay 65
unto MR: CORNELIUS LLOYD 4500 l tob with Court Charges & alsoe for surveying of 1500 acres of Land what shall appeare to be justly due... said Judgmt: is revived..

Recorded 15 Feb 1647.8

WILLIAM BASNETT ordered to pay 160 l tob unto ffRANCIS LAND.

65 Recorded 15 Feb 1647/8

WILLIAM BASNETT ordered to pay 170 l tob unto ffRANCIS LAND 7 Jun 16
1647 HEN: WOODHOUSE

Recorded 16 Feb 1647/8

I, CHRISTOPHER BURROUGHS of Lynhaven, Planter, being lawfully possessed of 200 acres of land lyeing and being in Lynhaven bownded Easterly upon the West side of Lynhaven River Southerly on a Creeke of the said River beginning at an Old Pine within the said Creeke running Northwesterly into the woods as be a Pattent graunted unto me by SIR JOHN HARVEY knt. Gov. dated 21 Feb 1638/9............in consideracon of a some of tob to me in hand payd.......bargaine, sell and sett over unto JOHN MORE and
65a ANDREW BODNAM.............. * JOHN MORE and ANDREW BODNAM to give BURROUGHS first refusal on any future sale of this land.
20 Mar 1642 XOP: BURROWGHS
Wit: WALTER PRESSER & EDMUND (X) LYNSY

Wee the within named JOHN WARE and ANDREW BODNAM do assigne & sett over this Bill of Sale and all our right and title to the Land unto WILLIAM SM(YTH?) of Lynhavem, Planter.
Last day of Mar 1645 JOHN WARE
Wit: XOP: BURROWGHS & WALTER PRESSER ANDREW (B) BODNAM

Received by mee MATHEW PHILLIPPS of WILLIAM SHIPP those bills & accoumpts hereafter specified:

	LAWRENCE PHILLIPPS bill	5438
	ffRANCIS BAKER & JAMES SIMONS bill	2290
	THOMAS TOOKERS bill	2000
	RICHARD STERNELLS bill	1453
66	* THOMAS ALLENS bill	1200
	JOHN ffINCH bill	1000
	JOHN MANNING bill	0503
	JOHN CARRAWAY bill	0314
	TICHARD WOSTERS (FOSTER?) bill	0600
	MR: JOHN ffERINHAUGH bill	0650
	JOHN PARKER bill	0417
	JASPER HOPKINS bill	0300
	HENRY MERRITT bill	0253
	ROWLAND MORGAN bill	0343
	GEORGE HEIGHAM bill	0239
	JAMES REINES bill	0420
	JOHN MERRIDAY & JOHN ARIS (HARRIS) bill	0321
	EDWARD GILLIES bill	0375
	MR: THOMAS SAYERS bill	0329
	JOHN MARSHALLS bill	0256
	RICHARD CONQUESTS bill	0322
	MARKE LEONARDS bill	0124
	RICHARD STARNELL bill	0040
	CAPT: JOHN SIBSEY bill	0400
	RICHARD ACTON bill	0800
	ffRANCIS LAND bill	0700
	RICHARD ABRELL bill	0410
	RICHARD SMITH bill	0147

THOMAS WATKINS bill	0090
ROBERT EMENS (EWENS?) bill	0374
RICHARD HALL bill	0030
THOMAS DADFORD bill	0200
JOHN WILLIAMS bill	0090
JOHN POWIS bill	0733
CHRISTOPHER BURROWGHS bill	0112
CAPT: ffRANCIS YARDLEY bill	0316
LAWRENCE PHILLIPPS bill	3100
JOHN MERRIDAY & JOHN ARIS bill	1350
THOMAS WHIRE bill	0410
JOHN HAYMON bill	0170
RICHARD WOOTTEN (or MOOTTEN) bill	0370
SAMSON WARING bill	0206
WILLIAM RAMSHAWE bill	0274
*JOHN SPENCERS bill	0145 66a
HENRY SNAYLE & THOMAS SMITHERS bill	0283
THOMAS TODD note	0040
WILLIAM ATTERSLIE BILL	))@)
THOMAS SIBSEY bill	0594
JOHN CORNELIUS bill	0685
JOHN HOLMES bill	0250
JOHN ROGERS & PARRIES bill	0750
THOMAS HUGHS bill	0320
THEOPHILUS HONES (could this be JONES?) bill	0200
GILES SEXTON bill	0058
WILLIAM PORTER bill	0250
THOMAS CONNERS bill	1313
ROBERT STAFFORD bill	0200
CHARLES STEWARDS bill	0030
GEORGE RUTLAND bill	0400
ROBERT HAYES accoumpt	0100
ENSIGNE KEELING accoumpt	0030
JOHN DIER accoumpt	00xx
THOMAS WARDE, Chyrurgeon accoumpt	0xxx
JAMES STARLING accoumpt	0070
WILLIAM HAWLEYS accoumpt	0030
ROBERT GRIMES accoumpt	0079
PETER RIGGLESWORTH accoumpt	0050
CHRISTOPHER RIVERS accoumpt	0080
CAPT: BURBAGE accoumpt	0234
MR: CORNELIUS LLOYD accoumpt	0250
ROBERT BOWERS accoumpt	0030
RICHARD WOSTERS accoumpt (this name is Foster)	0060
ELLIS BROWNE accoumpt	0089
JOHN MERRIDAY accoumpt	0206
WILLIAM WILLSON accoumpt	0019
GEORGE BEACHES accoumpt	0060
WILLIAM EDWARDS accoumpt	0024
ANTHONY HOSKINS accoumpt	0027
ROBERT TAYLORS accoumpt	0038
TOTALL	35993

JOHN HOLMES note for tob for payment of ₤ 20 ster:
67* ffRANCIS BAKER & JAMES SYMONS bill for 6 barrells of corne
JOHN ARIS bill for 6 dozen pipes & one payre of shoes
GEORGE ASHALL bill for 7 payse of shoes
THOMAS WATTS. accoumpt for 200 foote of planke
JOHN MERRIDAY & JOHN ARIS condicon for a boate
LAWRENCE PHILLIPPS Indenture and Bond
One Pattent for 200 acres of land
Three Servants Indentures
A Certificate for 100 acres of Land
JOHN WATKINS - condicon
MR: BROWNES accoumpt 190 l tob
All which foresaid bills, accoumpts & other writings, I MATHEW PHILLIPS doe hereby binde mee my heires &c to deliver or bee accoumptable for them /the danger of fire and water excepted/ unto WILLIAM SHIPP his heires &c when I shall bee there unto desired.
Wit: ARTHUR BROWNE & THOMAS LEE P Mee MATH: PHILLIPPS

An advise for MR: MATH: PHILLIPPS concerning such other business as is left to him by WILLIAM SHIPP.

DANIELL NEALE To look after DANIELL NEALES bill of 2151 l tob
To take in MR: SIDNEYS bill for 6 cutts of timber & 621 l tob MR:EIRES
To take 2 hhds of tob cont: 821 grosse
To looke after tenn head of neate cattle being in these places vizt:
3 cows 2 yearlings at home
1 bull at CHRISTOPHER RIVERS
2 steares at Linhaven
1 heifar & 1 yearling heifar at GEO: KEMPES
1 Pattent from MR: ABBOTT
4 barrells of corne from BARTHOLOMEW HOSKINS
1 barrel from RICH: WOSTER (FOSTER) next yeare
To accoumpt with MR: MARSH & what are not allowed by MR: MARSH to take in
Which said bills, accoumpts, Cattell & all other things herein specified
I MATHE: PHILLIPPS doe bind myselfe my heires &c to be accountable to
67a WILLIAM SHIPP..........* 21 Feb 1647/8
Recorded 22 Feb 1647/8 MATH: PHILLIPPS
Wit: ARTHUR BROWNE & THOMAS LEE

MEMORANDUM: that this daye JOHN CORNELISON came before me (and) acknowledged himselfe to be justly indebted unto CAPT: ffRANCIS YARDLEY the quantity of 350 l tob & caske the full satisfaction & payment thereof within tenn dayes........................ EDW: WINDHAM
Wit: JAN: CORNELEN?

ATT A COUNTY COURT HOLDEN 20 Feb 1647/8

PRESENT: CAPT: JOHN SIBSEY
MR: CORNELIUS LLOYD MR: MATH: PHILLIPPS
MR: THOMAS LAMBART MR: EDWARD LLOYD

Attachment granted to THOMAS SMYTHIARS agst Estate of JOHN GUTTERIDGE for 550 l tob by order 15 Aug 1645 said attachment revived.

CAPT: JOHN SIBSEY agst CAPT: THOMAS WILLOUGHBY adm: of RICHARD WAKE, Merchaunt decd. Reffered to the next Court.

* * 68

An Attachment graunted unto MR: THOMAS LAMBART agst the estate of WILLIAM HEATH decd for 300 l tob due unto THOMAS MITCHELL from the decedent uppon acct: .... the said 300 l tob assigned over to LAMBART by MITCHELL

By order of the Court 20 Jan 1647/8 an attachment graunted unto MR: THOMAS LAMBART agst the estate of WILLIAM HEATH decd for 300 l tob due unto THOMAS MITCHELL from the decedent uppon accoumpt....the said 300 l tob assigned over to LAMBART by MITCHELL.

20 Jan 1647/8 an Attachment issued forth agst the Estate of RICHARD KENNAR Chyrurgeon at the suite of MR: WILLM: JULIAN for £ 3 sterl: money claymed to be due for rent. Sherrife has attached 2 cowes of the estate of RICHARD KENNAR. sd attachment to be suspended until Xmas next and if KENNAR can not by that time bring certificate under hand of MR: ROBERT PAGE that said debt was formerly payd by KENNAR unto MR: PAGE for the use of MR: JULIAN then KENNAR to pay the debt. MR: THOMAS LAMBART security for KENNAR.

MORE PRESENT CAPT: EDWARD WINDHAM

CAPT: WILLIAM ATTERBURY agst CAPT: ffRANCIS YARDLEY referred to next Court.

16 Feb 1645/6 This Court did give judgement against HENRICK LIGHTHART for 803 l tob unto HENRY SNAYLE AT THE NEXT............(can't read).. of a debt due upon accoumpt unto the sd SNAYLE from JOHN GUTTERIDGE whome sd LIGHTHART had transported out of this Colony & he now dec'd. ELLEN LIGHTHART, widow, ordered to pay 15 Dec 1647 * if she did not 68a bring GUTTERIDGE back into the Colony on or before the last day of Feb instant. SNAYLE received cloth valued at 303 l tob in part of the 803 l tob. ELLEN now ordered to pay 500 l tob within 10 days.

Whereas MR: CORNELIUS LLOYD was bownd with JAMES STONExxxxxx late decd unto LAWRENCE PHILLIPPS for delivery of a servant by 31 Dec 1646. MR: LLOYD ordered to deliver unto LAWRENCE PHILLIPPS a servant....upon the arrivall of the first & second Shipp the next returne shipping.

Difference betweene ELLEN LIGHTHART agst THOMAS TOOKER defendt: in accon of debt to the next court.

23 Feb 1647/8 WILLIAM EADY ordered to pay debt of 300 l tob to THOMAS IVEY.

23 Feb 1647/8 THOMAS ALLEN hath given Publique notice of his intended voyage for Holland the present shipping.

The Court did give judgment 16 Feb 1645/6 that MRS: SARAH GOOKIN now the wyfe of CAPT: YARDLEY should pay THOS: DAVYES 24 l tob and Court Charges The Court now orders that CAPT: YARDLEY pay the debt and Court Charges.

69 20 Feb 1647/8

THOMAS MARSH on behalfe of CAPT: WILLIAM LUCK Atty: of JAMES ABRATHAT of LONDON, Merchant hath caused MR: THOMAS LAMBART & THOMAS BRIDGE Attys: of ROGER ffLETCHER Merchant to be arrested in an accon of debt. THOMAS MARSH fayling in execucon is non-suited.

WILLIAM SHIPP haveing arrested MR: ROBERT POWIS, Clerke but neglecting to take bayle for appearance it is therefore ordered that if the Sheriff shall not bring forth the body or goods of MR: POWIS at the next Court then the Sheriff to be lyable for payment of the 730 lb tob unto MR. SHIPP.

RICHARD STARNELL did for the use of himselfe and others take up certaine goods of THOMAS LEE valued at 1207 l tob. STARNELL made payment of unmerchantable & rotten tobacco. Ordered to pay 1039 l of good tobacco within ten dayes.

CAPT: JOHN SIBSEY, Planter agst JOHN MERRIDAY deft: for 467 l tob referred to next court.

The sheriffe hath arrested ffRANCIS LAND at the suit of THO: DAVYES for 3 barrels of corne & 56 l tob and not taking bayle the Sheriffe shall bring forth the body or goods of said LAND at the next Court or otherwise pay the debt to DAVYES.

To RICHARD STARNELL 23 Feb 1647/8 a Certificate for 250 acres of land due for the transportation of: GEORGE GUEST, ELIZABETH MALAM, EDWARD WEBB, JOHN JILL (HILL?) & JOHN HILTON.

69a 18 Nov 1646 The estate of MR. ROBERT PAGE in the hands of MR: MATHEW PHILLIPS and others. A debt not paid as per court order 20 Dec 1646. MR. PAGE was gone to sea and did not receive the order. If MR. PAGE does not arrive the 1st or 2nd ship from London or send by some Atty: then the Court to proceed to Judgment in favor of MR: CORNELIUS LLOYD.

MR THOMAS CEELEY indebted, Ŀ 10 Sterling, to NATHAN STAINSMORE 17 Aug 1638 with tenn yeares forbearance. Court of 23 Feb 1647/8 ordered payment by 21 dec. EDWARD LLOYD Atty: of STAINSMORE.

CAPT: JOHN SIBSEY (this item is faded and hard to read) hath made it appear by severall (papers?) under MR: WAKES hand & xxxxx by his booke xxxxx SIBSEY was co-partner with WAKE in
70 the shipps JOHN & BARBARY, AMERICAN & ffraighter of the SHIPP PELLICANS BLESSING and for so much as their co-partnership is now depending in law in this Country of Virginia. .... Desired by the co-owners that you the other parte owners of the said shipps ....give accoumpts of Profitt & Losse of the shipps or eyther of them for every voyage .....unto MR: WILLIAM ATTERBURY and MR: ARTHUR BROWNE or eyther of them.

At a Quarter Court holden at James Citty
3 Mar 1647/8

PRESENT: SIR WILLIAM BERKELEY knt Gov: RICHARD KEMPE, THO: STEGG, CAPT: WM: BERNARD ESQ:, RICH: BENNET, GEO: LUDLOWE.

3 Mar 1647/8 70

MR: RICHD: CONQUEST elected High Sheriff of Lower Norfolk County. SAM: ABBOTT Tests

6 Mar 1647/8: RICHARD CONQUEST sworne High Sheriffe by CAPT: JOHN SIBSEY, MR: CORNELIUS LLOYD & MR: THOMAS LAMBERT.

Recorded: 1 Apr 1648

ATT A COURT HELD AT THE HOWSE OF MR: PETER TALBOT 21 Dec 1647
PRESENT: MR: ZACH: CRIPS MR: HENRY FILMER MR: WM: RABNET
MR: JNO: HARLOW MR: THO: DAVIES MR: WM: WHITBY
A judgement confessed by MR: JNO: SIDNEY for 866 l tob & caske due from him to MR: THO: BUSHRODE to be paid within tenn days
ROBERTU RYLAND CL: CUR:
(NOTE: This is probably WARWICK COUNTY COURT as names in this item owned land there. AGW)

Recorded 7 Apr 1648 70a

EDWARD LILLY of ELIZA: CITTY COUNTY selling to THOS: ALLEN & EDWARD CANNON one necke or tracte of land situate & lying &c ....on the Eastern Shore of Lynhaven River in Lower Norfolk County being the land the sd LYLLY (sic) did buy from OWEN HAYES of Lower Norfolk County. Dated 4 Apr 1648.
WITNESSES: JOHN (X) GILES, ED: LILLEY & STEVEN (X) BROWNE

ATT A COUNTY COURT HOLDEN 15 Apr 1648
PRESENT: CAPT: JOHN SIBSEY, MR: CORNELIUS LLOYD, MR: THOMAS MEARES & MR: EDWARD LLOYD, MR: THOMAS LAMBERT.

Upon peticon of WILLIAM LUCAS the Court orders that the Estate of JOHN MOYE decd. bee equally divided between the two children of sd MOYE the land only excepted......1/2 parte to be delivered unto WILLIAM LUCAS for use of that childe in his custody & tuition [Hee giving security]. Estate to be devided by MR: HENRY WOODHOUSE & MR: EDWARD HALL.

MORE PRESENT: CAPT: EDWARD WINDHAM, MR: HENRY WOODHOUSE,
MR: MATH: PHILLIPPS.

LEIFT MASON late High Sheriffe by his deputy by virtue of an execution under the hand of the Governor made sezure? upon a maide servant of CAPT: THOMAS WILLOUGHBY ESQR: for satisfaction of 1000 l tob due to CAPT: JOHN SIBSEY [by Judgement of the Governor & Court] from CAPT: WILLOUGHBY and the maide servant deteyned by CAPT: WILLOUGHBY. Ordered that Lieut: MASON shall bring forth the maide servant to satisfy the deft: or else to pay the aforesd debt.

JOHN HATTON pltf: agst: ROBERT PORTER deft: referred unto the 71
hearing and determination of MR: EDWARD LLOYD.

71 15 Apr 1648

THOMAS OWEN plt: agst: WM: BASSNETT referred to next Court.

Judgement confessed by NICHOLAS CROUCH for payment of byll unto MR: ffRANCIS MASON with forbearance at 8 l tob per cent and the Court Charges.

NICHOLAS CROUCH deft: ordered to pay 250 l tob due by byll unto MARKES LEONARD.

Certificate for 400 acres of land to MR: THOMAS MEARES due for transportation of: RICHARD DORANCE?, JOHN HOSKINS, JOHN HARRIS, JOHN CARLIERE, JOHN WOODCOTT, ANN ASKUE & one negro. (NOTE: see Cavaliers & Pioneers - Nugent p 182)

CAPT: JOHN SIBSEYS suite against CAPT: THOS: WILLOUGHBY ESQ: administrator of MR: RICHARD WAKE decd. by way of accon sur le case for costs of suite for causeles(sic) molestacon as is pretended by the petitioner in a former suite where in the sd: CAPT: was complaynant against the said CAPT: SIBSEY ....from hence referred by consent of both partyes to -faded- determined by the Governor & Counsell and is not -faded- determined according to their order. It is the opinion of this Court that if the said CAPT: SIBSEY hath cause accon against the said CAPT: WILLOUGHBY as is alleaged hee ought to sue for remedy herein before the Governor and Counsel.

JAMES CROCKETT Creditor of JOSEPH -FADED- granted administration on his estate.

ffRANCIS LAND [upon the full balance of all accoumpts] to pay THOMAS DAVIES 30 l tob & 1 barrell, 3 bushels & a peck of Indian Corne.

71a CAPT ffRANCIS YARDLEY deft: to deliver unto PETER FREDERICKSON his Chest and all tooles which hee deteynes from him. Case referred to the next Court.

JESPER HOSKINS appointed Constable for the Eastern side of Elizabeth River beginning at CAPT: THOMAS WILLOUGHBYS ESQ: and so upwards (South) on that side of the River as far as MR: HOSKINS including MR: HOSKINS house.

XOP: (CHRISTOPHER) RIVERS appointed Constable for the other parte of Elizabeth River beginning at the house of MR: DAINES and soe upwards (South) on both sides of the Westerneand Southern Branches & on that side of the Easterne Branch including RICHARD BLUNTS plantation als ROBERT MARTINS & the other plantacons backward.

HENRY NICHXXX (end of name missing) appointed Constable for the head of the Easterne Branch beginning at EDWARD DORSEYS and soe upwards on both sides of said river including RICHARD WOOLMANS Plantation.

HENRY SNAYLE appointed Constable for the Lymitts of the Little Creek..... on both sides of the said creeke including all the branches of the saide Creeke where any plantation is seated.

WILLIAM EADY appointed Constable for the lymitts of Lynnhaven River beginning at CAPT: ffRANCIS YARDLEY and soe upwards on both sides of the sd: river including all the Creeks and Branches where any plantation is seated.

WHEREAS: it is credably given out that ROGER ffLETCHER xxxx 72
faded xxxxxx is cast away through the casualty of the Sea coming from New England he xxxxxx and haveing an Estate in debt xxxxxxxxAdministration on the estate granted to THOMAS BRIDGE on the sd: Decedents estate on the behalfe of the orphans of the said decedent.

SAM[LL]: CHARNOE Pltf: agst: JOSEPH BURCH to the next Court.

Attachmt: granted unto JOHN HOLMES agst: the Estate of THOMAS HUSE (HUGHES?) for 140 1 tob.

The Comrs: have appointed 14 Jun 1648 for an Orphans Court.

Attachment served upon the estate of JOHN GUTTERIDGE remayning in the hands of HNERY SNAYLE. SNAYLE to pay THOMAS SMYTHAIRS 300 1 tob.

MR: HOSKINS, MR: HAYES, JOHN HOLMES and GYLLES to view the land in difference betweene JOSEPH BURCH Pltf: & HENRY SNAYLE before the next Court.

THOMAS CASSON Pltf: agst: JOHN STRATTON to the next Court.

MR: CORNELIUS LOYD pltf: agst THOMAS CASSON deft: to the next Court. CASSON giviing security for his appearance.

THOMAS GODBY, aged 30 years or thereabouts, sworne sayeth: that being at the house of RICHARD STARNELL did see sd: STARNELL packing and repacking 2 or 3 hhds of tob taking out of one & putting in to another the same night that MR: THO: LEE Merchant came to receive his tob & further sayeth not.
signed: THOMAS (X) GODBY

ANN GODBY aged 20 yeares or thereabouts sworne sayeth that 72a
being at the house of RICHARD STARNELL, RICHARD JONES came in and asked STARNELL how he did and he replyed the worse for the sd: JONES & JONES asked why & STARNELL sayde because I received bad tob of you & told JONES that one of the hhds of tob was as he expected, the other was very bad & now forced to pay it to WILL: SHIPP for tob he owed SHIPP for the next years pay & further sayeth not. Signed: ANN (e) GODBY

These are in his Majesties name to will and require you that upon sight hereof you goe & enter the house of WILL: CAPPS and there to make search for a certaine parcell of tob (sellomoushie?) taken away from WALTER PRESSER and secure the same being found hereof stayle not as you will answer the contrary at your perill. Given under my hand 29 Jan 1647/8
HENRY WOODHOUSE

To the Constable of Lynnhaven River.

72a 15 Apr 1648

ROBERT HAYES selling a cowe to NATHANIEL HAYES.
Witness: ROBT: DARBIE

ANDREW NICKHOLES, Seaman, of the Eastern Branch of Elizabeth
River selling 300 acres of land to RICHARD ACTON. One half
of a parcell of land which formerly belonged to JNO: GODFREY
by him sold to THOMAS CASSON by him sold to ANDREW NICHOLS
(sic)... the land being in the head of the Eastern Branch
lyeing on the Southward side of the said branch and beginning
73 * at a marked white oak standing uppon a point on the Maine
Branch side and running for length SSW 320 poles adjoyning
on the land of RICHARD WHITEHURST to a marked gumm and soe
West 152 poles by the mayne poynts unto a marked red oake soe
NNE 320 pole adjoyning on the land of HENRY NICKHOLAS unto a
marked Pine standing on a Poynt on the Eastward sideof the
mouth of a Little Creek and soe - xxxx - East 156 pole by or
nyeup the Mayne Branch side to the first station. 18 Oct 1647
WIT: BARTHO: HOSKINS & ROBERT EYXXX (name is faded)
signed: ANDREW NICKHOLES

Dated 14 Jan 1647 Recorded 1 May 1648: UMPHRY BEST of
Elizabeth River, Planter, selling to ABRAHAM THOMAS of Elizabeth River, Planter, 1/2 of a parcell of land which now
- faded - being 150 acres formerly belonging to HENRY NICKOLLS
& purchased by me ....lyeing on the Southward side of ye Eastern Branch of Elizabeth River & beginning at a marked pine
standing on the Mayne Branch Side & running for length SSW
320 pole to a marked Red Oak and soe SE 75 pole unto a marked
Red Oake & soe NNE 320 pole unto a marked Pyne standing on a
poynt on the East side of the mouth of a Little Creek and
adjoining on the land of JNO: GODFREY and so WNW 75 pole to
the mouth of the said Creeke unto the first station. Said
land belonging to HENRY NICKHOLES as the pattent doth XXXXX
73a which land I the said BEST warrant& insure.
signed: ABRAHAM THOMAS
WIT: ROBERT EYRE & SYMON (SH) HANCOCK

1 May 1648

DEBORAH GLASCOCK widow selling unto RICHARD CONQUEST for a
valuable consideracon one yearling Cowe Calfe & one -faded-
Bull Calfe nowe being amongst the neate cattle of ENSIGNE
LAMBARD. 20 Sep 1646 signed: DEBORAH (+) GLASCOCK
WIT: JOHN ffERINHAUGH & WILLIAM (M) HEATH

DEBORAH GLASCOCK, late widow and relict of ROBERT GLASCOCK
late decd, in the time of her widowhood for a valuable consideracon did sell RICHARD CONQUEST * one yearling cowe calfe
& one Bull Calfe, Deed dated 20 Sep 1646. Nowe know ye that
I JOHN ffERINHAUGH hath intermarried with the said DEBORAH
.... doe hereby confirme unto RICHARD CONQUEST ....
30 Nov 1647. signed: JOHN ffERINHAUGH
WIT: THOMAS BRIDGE & RICH: STARNELL

(NOTE: folios 74 to 76 are faded and water stained. Only parts of these pages are legible. AGW)

INDENTURE: 11 daye of XXX XXXX betweene EDWARD STANDLEY & ARTHUR LUDFORD. STANDLY granting unto LUDFORD xxxxxxxxxxxx (NOTE: There is not enough of this legible to determine whether this is the Indenture of LUDFORD or the sale of land or something else. AGW)* EDWARD STANDLEY came into *74a
this Country in the WILLIAM & JOHN. MR: GREYE (or IVEYE) being Master. 20 Nov 1647. WIT: SAMUEL HUTCHINSON

Recorded: 29 May 1648

WILLIAM DURAND, A MEMORANDUM that upon the 27 May 16xx [being the Sabbath day] wee whose names are hereunder -faded- being requested by RICHARD CONQUEST GENT:, High Sheriff of Lower Norfolk County for his aide and assistance giving publique notice to the inhabitants of Elizabeth Riverin the said County to forbear & desist from -neire? faded- meetings and usuall assemblies themselves together continueing the lawes & government of the Collony.....thereupon assisting the High Sheriff .....did fynd one named WILLIAM DURAND, much people, men, women & children assembled & together in the Church or Chappell of Elizabeth River aforsd in the forenoon of the sd day & did see the sd WILLIAM DURAND goe into and,xxxxxxx the Deske or Reading Place of the sd church and also in the Pulpitt he hath customarily by space of these three months last past uppon several Sabbath dayes preached to the said people xxxxxxxxxxxxxthat the High Sheriff did xxxxxxxxxxxx and those xxxxxxxxxxxxxhath not xxxxxxxxxxxxxxxxxxxxxxxxx 75
(NOTE: Your Editor assumes that this must refer to Quaker Meetings, however, this record must have been water soaked. Several words can be read in scattered places but make no sense without the missing parts. AGW)

WILLIAM BERKELEY Gov. granting administration unto THOMAS BRIDGE atty of ROGER ffLETCHER decd. ROGER ffLETCHER having been cast away through the casualty of the sea (coming from?) New England hither & dyed intestate. Administration granted on the behalfe of the Orphans. Dated 4 Jun 1648

6 Jun 1648

xxxxxxxx appointing the Commissioners for Lower Norfolk 76
County: CAPT: JOHN SIBSEY, MR: EDW: LLOYD, MR: JOHN HILL, MR: ffRANCIS MASON, MR: THO: LAMBART, MR: THOMAS BROWNE, MR: EDW: WINDHAM, MR: MATH: PHILLIPPS, MR: HEN: WOODHOUSE, MR: THOMAS MEARES.

ATT A COUNTY COURT HELD 15 Jun 1648 76a
PRESENT: CAPT: THOMAS WILLOUGHBY ESQ:
CAPT: JOHN SIBSEY MR: MATTH: PHILLIPPS
MR: THO: LAMBARD MR: THO: MEARES

Court is adjourned until the 15 Jul 1648.

76a 15 Jun 1648

Certificate to THOMAS IVY for 100 acres of land for the transportation of WILLIAM BUTLER & JOANE BUTLER.

THOMAS LAMBARD hath made it appeare there is due unto him for transportation of 4 persons 200 acres of land: THOMAS COCKS, ANN CHETER, HEN: CORAWAY & SUSANN HARTLEY. Written in the margin: Assigned on to ED: HALL, Chirurgeon. (see Nu 260)

Certificate to MR: THOMAS LAMBARD for 600 acres of land due for the transportation of 12 persons: SAMUEL ROBERTS, JAMES ROBERTS, MATH: HOLMES, HULDY CHAPxxx, ROBERT LUSNY?, WILL: NICHOLSON, JOHN TAYLOR, ELIZABETH COLLINS, JOSEPH BORO (Nu gives BOWE), ELLEN GALLEPP (Nu gives Allen), ELIZABETH HEUES, THO: ABBOTT. In the Margin is written: To CARTWRIGHT and SAMUELL ROBERTS & JAMES ROBERTS assigned on to JOHN MORTON. (See Nu 269 SAVILL GASKINS)

ATT A COUNTY COURT HELD 15 Jul 1648
PRESENT; CAPT: THOMAS WILLOUGHBY ESQ:, CAPT: JOHN SIBSEY
MR: MATH: PHILLIPPS, MR: ffRANCIS MASON,
MR: THO: LAMBARD, MR: JOHN HILL, MR: THOMAS BROWNE

To CAPT: ffRANCIS YARDLEY 950 acres due for the transportation of 19 persons: ELIZABETH GARLAND, MARY (PARR?), WILLIAM SMITH, THOS: WHITTBY, WILLIAM JOHNSON, NICHOLAS NICLAYSEN, HANNABALL SPICER?, HARMAN MAYER, CORNELIUS JOHNS, PAUL REYNERS, PETER LOVALL, WILLIAM COOKE, EDMUND STANLEY, EDWARD ABBOTT, JOHN
77 ARNELL, MARY ELLIS, ANN STAGG, JOHN WELLS, HENRY SELBY.

Certificate to ROBERT HAYES for 50 acres of land due for the transportation of ELLNOR JOANES.

The next two items are illegible. An Attachment to someone agst RICHARD STARNELL is carried over to the next Court.

CLEMENT THEOBALL ordered to pay 400 and (some?) 1 tob unto MR: HENRY WOODHOUSE with forbearance.

WILLM: JOHNSON pltf: agst HENRY HILL deft: to the next Court.

77a MR: MATHEW PHILLIPPS hath made it appeare that he hath payd unto CAPT: JOHN SIBSEY by earnest request of WILL: JOHNSON -?- for the use of sd JOHNSON 225 1 tob. JOHNSON now ordered to pay MR: MATHEW PHILLIPPS.

EDWARD CANNON to pay 544 1 tob unto -faded- SAYER att the next Cropp.

CAPT: THOMAS WILLOUGHBY agst CAPT: JOHN SIBSEY to next Court.

Certificate to ffRANCIS LAND for 250 acres for trans: of 5 persons: JANE DRIVER, JANE RUDDEFORD, EDWARD LONG, JOHN JOHNSON, ALCE YOUNG

WILL: BASNETT deft: agst THO: OWEN pltf: to next Court.

ANN GODBYE to receive 15 lashes upon her bare back and aske MRS: ELIZABETH LLOYD forgivenesse in the face of this present Court for most grosely defaming of the sd MRS: LLOYD. And ANN GODBYES husband THOMAS GODBYE to pay the Court Charges.

RICHARD ffOSTER att his goeing for England being ffive years
or thereabouts did give and bequeath unto SARAH WILLIAMSON
daughter of ROGER WILLIAMSON one Cowe Calfe.... RICHARD
WORSTER Atty of ffOSTER ordered to givethe cowe calfe & her
increase to the child for her use......

JOSEPH BURTCH the -faded- of MARY STEVENS ordered to pay unto
SAM[LL]: CHARNI(COE?) xxxxxxxxxxxx the clothes due to the said
STEVENS by the Custom of the Country for her service ended
xxxxxx(most of this is too faded to read)

The Court hath once more thought fitt xxxxx MRS: YARDLEY to
make her appearance and -faded- her accoumpts upon the 1 Aug
1648 xxxxxx the Court may take the xxxxxxxx faded xxxxxxxxx
and MR: HENRY CATLIN & MR: ROBERT HAYES xxxxxx desired to be
present to xxxxxxx the devision of the said estate

CAPT: THO: WILLOUGHBY ESQ: agst BARTHOLOMEW HOSKINS to the
nest court.

JANE XXXXXXXX agst ANN GODBYE to the next Court.

WILLIAM BERKELEY Gov. granting * unto JOHN WATTKINS 200 acres 78a
of land on the Eastward side of Elizabeth River and the Northward side of the mouth of the Easterne Branch of the said
river and beginning at a marked pine upon a pynt (sic) called
FOWRE FARTHING POYNT and running by the said Eastward Branch
side ESE 232 pole unto a marked pyne standing on a poynt ye
Westerne side of the mouth of a Creeke named Dun of the Mire
and running upp the side of the said Creeke over -faded-
poynts NNE 14 pole unto a marked gum standing in a gutt or
branchside & soe WNW 232 pole crossing unto a marked pine and
soe SSW 148 pole crossing small gutts or poynts & butting
toward the Maine River to the first menconed marked tree. The
said 200 acres of land being due unto JOHN WATKINS by assignment from CAPT: THO: WILLOUGHBY ESQ: p a patent bearing date
18 Feb 1636 * Given at James Citty 1 Apr 1644. Acknowledged 79
in Court 15 Jun 1648. (This is not in Nugent)

I, JOHN WATKINS, for the some of 3000 l tob & Caske........
to me in hand paid have sold unto RICHARD CONQUEST GENT: and
THOMAS BRIDGE Merchant the 200 acres of land in this pattent
menconed or intended. Dated 7 Apr 1648.
WIT: MATH: PHILLIPPS signed: JOHN (+) WATKINS

I, JOHN HARVIE Knt. Capt. General of Virginia, by a writing 79a
under his hand ..... bearing date at James Citty 6 Dec 1638
.... did give and graunt unto JONATHAN LANGWORTH 600 acres
of land in Lower Norfolk County on the Westerne Branch of
Elizabeth River on the East to the River (?) and NE towards
the woods with a Creeke on either side of the said 600 acres
being due for the reasons in the said writing. These presents
also further wittnesseth that JONATHAN LANGWORTH by a deed
under his hand dated 3 Oct 1640 ...... for the consideracon
therein expressed did graunt unto OSMOND COLCHESTER and WALTER
MICHELL * (NOTE: Rest of this is illegible on folio 80) 80*

80a 15 Jun 1648

(NOTE: MATHEW PHILLIPPS may have bought this 600 acres for the end of this record, dated 1 nov 1646, JOHN WATTKINS is buying the land from MATH: PHILLIPPS and he signed the deed) WIT: JOHN HILL & THOMAS MEARES

Pattent from JOHN HARVEY Knt. late Gov. & Capt Gen. of Virginia to CORNELIUS LLOYD dated last of Nov 1640 (or 1641) 400 acres of land .... Westerne Branch of Elizabeth River on the South side of the said river bounding Easterly upon xx faded xx commonly called the Choice Tree, Westerly up the river, Southerly into the woods, Northerly upon the
81* River. * CORNELIUS LLOYD sells to JOHN PIPER, ROBERT BOWERS
81a & WALTER GRYMES, all Planters of Elizabeth River. 16 Jul 1648
WIT: THOS: TOOKER CL: CUR: signed: CORNELIUS LLOYD

82 The names of the Vestrymen for Elizabeth River Parish who mett together 1 Aug 1648: CAPT JOHN SIBSEY, MR: HEN: CATLIN, MR: COR: LLOYD, MR: THOMAS LAMBARD, MR: ffRANCIS MASON, MR: THO: SAYER, MR: JOHN HILL. In respect that some of the Vestry are lately deceased and others who are living doe absent themselves and refuse to bee of this Vestry .... the Above named doe nominate the following in the roome of those exempted: MR: MATH: PHILLIPPS, MR: THO: BROWN, MR: JOHN ffERINHAUGH, MR: THOMAS IVY. All Vestrymen to meet at the now dwelling house of LAWRENCE PHILLIPPS the 1 Oct 1648.

JOHN NORWOOD to appeare before the Vestry to render an accoumpt proffitts of the Glebe Land ever since PARSON HARRISON hath desented his Ministeriall office and denyed to administer ye Sacraments &c to us and the inhabitants .... Attested: RI: CONQUEST Sherr:

JOHN NORWOOD to appear before the Vestry of Elizabeth River Parish 10 Oct 1648.

82a ATT A COUNTY COURT HELD 15 Aug 1648
PRESENT: MR: ffRANCIS MASON, MR: JOHN HILL
MR: MATH: PHILLIPPS, MR: THO: BROWNE

CAPT: THOMAS WILLOUGHBY ESQR: Pltf: agst: CAPT: JOHN SIBSEY to the next Court.

MORE PRESENT: CAPT: THOMAS WILLOUGHBY ESQ:, CAPT: JOHN SIBSEY,
MR: THOMAS LAMBARD.

Administration of the estate of JOHN KEMP decd. granted unto RICHD: CONQUEST he being the greatest creditor.

Administration granted JOANE YATES widow on the estate of her late husband JOHN YATES.

Case of BARTHOLOMEW HOSKINS & CAPT: THOS: WILLOUGHBY referred
83 to the next Grand Assembly. This concerns 2100 l tob.

WILLIAM BASNETT deft: to pay debt of 1068 l tob to MR: THOMAS OWEN with 6 years forbearance only deducting 300 l of tob to the said BASNETT for a cabynett.

By an order of the Quarter Court at James Citty dated 3 Apr 1648 a judgement agst JOHN KEMP decd for 1450 l tob to be paid to THOMAS NEWHOUSE by RICH: CONQUEST administrator of JOHN KEMP decd.

The debt of JOHN KEMP decd. to THOS: NEWHOUSE assigned over to CARBERY RIGAN.

JOHN KEMP decd in his lifetime confessed a judgement at a County Court at James Citty dated 27 Apr 1747 for 1200 l tob and costs of Court to be voyd to JOHN BROACH to be paid out of estate. 83a

Attachment granted unto ROBT: EYRE against the tob and the Chest remayning in the hands of EYRE and belonging to JAMES (PENES?)

THOMAS MARSH agst: JOHN ffERINHAUGH & his wife DEBORAH referred to the next Court.

PETER ffREDERICKSON agst: CAPT: ffRANCIS YARDLEY deft: to the next Court.

CAPT: WILLIAM CLAYBORNE ESQ: Planter, Atty: of ARTHUR ELLIOTT agst JOHN ASKUE pltf: to pay ASKUE 20 l tob for non-appearance als a non suite.

MR: MOORE FANTLEROY Pltf: to pay unto MATH: PHILLIPPS 20 l tob for non-appearance als non suite. 84

THOMAS ADDAMS to take an inventory of every part & parcell of the estate belonging to BLANCH ARMSTRONG decd. and soe to take possession thereof, itt being given to said ADDAMS by the said ARMSTRONG upon her death bed which hee the said ADDAMS is to make appeare at the next court and further order to bee taken.

JOHN DYER TO Pay 20 l tob to CAPT: ffRANCIS YARDLEY deft: towards his charges for needlesse molestation.

JOSEPH BURCH Pltf: agst: SAMLL: CHARNICOE Deft: referred to the next Court.

JOHN CORNELIUS Pltf: agst ROBERT DAVYS to the next Court.

ANDREW NICHOLLS to pay debt of 210 l tob unto RICHARD ACKON (ACTON?)

JOHN ARIS (HARRIS?) Pltf: agst: ffRANCIS LAND to next Court.

WILLIAM CAPPS Pltf: agst ROBTE: DAVYS to next Court. 84a

SAMLL: CHARNICOE Pltf: agst: WM: POWELL Deft: to next Court.

MR. EDWARD HALL, ENSIGNE THOMAS KEELING, LANCASTER LOVETT & HENRY WESTGATE are requested by the Court to view the Land in difference between CAPT: ffRANCIS YARDLEY & WILLIAM

84a 15 Aug 1648

ffANN Deft: and report to the next Court.

CAPT: ffRANCIS YARDLEY Pltf: referred to the next Court.

Attachment granted unto RICHARD CONQUEST for 271 1 tob in the hands of (THOS:? faded) WRIGHT belonging to GEORGE WHITE the deft:

ATT A QUARTER COURT AT JAMES CITTY 3 Apr 1648 (or 1645?)
PRESENT: RICH: KEMPE ESQ: Gov. &c.
CAPT: JOHN WEST CAPT: HENRY BROWNE CAPT: THOMAS PETTUS
CAPT: SAMLL: MATHEWES CAPT: NATHL: LITTLETON

85 JOHN KEMP Pltf: to pay 1450 1 tob to THOMAS NEWHOUSE.

THOMAS NEWHOUSE Deft: assigning the above debt over unto (name is not legible) 2 May 1645?.)

ATT A COUNTY COURT HELD AT JAMES CITTY 27 Apr 1648
PRESENT: CAPT: ROBT: HUTCHINSON
MR: WM: BUTLER MR: ROBT: HOLT MR: WM: BARRETT
vera copia - ROBT: MIGH CL: CUR:

JOHN KEMP to pay JOHN BROACH 1200 1 tob & Costs

ATT A COUNTY COURT HELD UPON 28 Feb 1647/8 (Out of place in these records, but at the bottom of the page with the only item occuping most of the following page.)
PRESENT: CAPT: JOHN SIBSEY MR: THOMAS LAMBARD
CAPT: EDWARD WINDHAM MR: EDWARD LLOYD
MR: CORNELIUS LLOYD MR: MATHEW PHILLIPPS

85a Whereas the Court upon the 16 Feb 1645*did give Judgement agst: HENDRICK LIGHTHART for paymt: of 803 1 tob unto HENRY SNAYLE at the next Cropp then following in lieu of a debt due upon accoumptunto said SNAYLE from JOHN GUTTERIDGE whom said LIGHTHART had transported out of this Collony contrary to Act of Assembly.......said LIGHTHART being since deceased upon peticon of HENRY SNAYLE the Court ordered 15 Dec 1647 that ELLEN LIGHTHART widow & executrix of the decedent should pay the 803 1 tob unto said SNAYLE upon a full rehearing of the case. It now appeares that said SNAYLE received cloth to the value of 303 1 tob in part of the said debt. It is therefore ordered that said ELLEN LIGHTHART shall onely pay 500 1 tob. THO: TOOKER CL: CUR:

....I, HENRY SNAYLE doe assigne the within specified (order) of Court unto CAPT: ffrancis YARDLEY. 5 Aug 1648
86 TESTE: EDW: WINDHAM signed: HENRY (HS) SNAYLE

24 Aug 1648

JOHN HARVIE Fov. &c granting unto THOMAS DAVIS 300 acres of land being in the xxxxxxxx New Norfolke upon the South side of the Eastern Branch of Elizabeth River oposite to the land of THOMAS SAWYER 5 or 6 miles up the river Easterlyto the head of the river upon a Creeke Northerly upon the Mayne River and a Marsh, Westerly downe the river and Southerly into the
86a woods. * Given at James City 22 May 1637. (see Nu 57)

I, LAWRENCE PETTERS doe hereby assigne and make over the whole divident of land within the patent unto RICHARD WHITEHURST. 7 Oct 1639. signed: LAWRENCE PEETERS (NOTE: The above is all the information contained in this item in Book B, however, Nugent gives (p188) "Granted to THOMAS DAVIS by patent 22 May 1637, by whom it was assigned to LAWRENCE PETERS & purchased by sd. WHITEHURST of PETERS." This is the 15 Mar 1649/50 patent to RICHARD WHITEHURST.AGW)

ATT A QUARTER COURT HOLDEN 1 Sep 1648 87

SIR WILLIAM BERKELEY Gov &c.
MR: RICHARD KEMP RICH: BENNETT CAPT: THO: WILLOUGHBY
CAPT: SAMLL MATHEWS CAPT: THO: PETTUS GEO: LUDLOWE
CAPT: HEN: BROWNE CAPT: WM: BROCAS THO: STEGG
CAPT: WM: BARNARD CAPT: HUMP: HIGGINS

RICHARD CONQUEST to deliver the inventory of the estate of JOHN - faded - to the next County Court. 31 Aug 1648.

JNO: ffERINHAUGH Pltf: agst; THOMAS MARSH Deft: is referred to the 4th day of the Court n

Recordat 6 Oct 1648 87a
WM: BERKELEY Gov &c granting administration on the estate of JOHN YATES, who died intestate, unto JOANE YATES the widdow & relict according to order of Lower Norfolk County Court dated 20 Aug 1648. Given at James Citty 31 Aug 1648. yabob

ATT A MEETING OF A VESTRY UPON 2 Oct 1648 for PARISH of ELIZABETH RIVER. 88
PRESENT: CAPT: JOHN SIBSEY MR: COR: LLOYD MR: JOHN HILL
MR: MATHEW PHILLIPS MR: THO: BROWNE MR: HEN: CATLIN
MR: JOHN ffERINHAUGH MR: (THO:?)SAYER MR: THOMAS -?-

MORE PRESENT: MR: RICHARD CONQUEST

MR: ROBERT POWIS for performing his Ministerial duties with no satisfacon these 4 yeares past is to be paid 1 yeares full tyths in tob & corne of all the Inhabitants of this Parish.

Ordered by the Vestrythat JOHN NORWOOD shall pay unto the Church Wardens 300 l tob for the Rent of the Glebe Land this present yeare last past. 88a

MR: JOHN HILL & WILLIAM CROUCH are elected Church Wardens for the Parish of Elizabeth River & Oath to be administered at the next Court.

ATT A COURT HELD 2 Oct 1648. Recorded as before.
PRESENT: CAPT: JOHN SIBSEY, MR: JOHN HILL, MR: MATH: PHILLIPPS
MR: THO: BROWNE
Court to be held 15 Oct 1648 because of both a Quarter Court on 12 Oct and an Assembly about to begin.

88a 6 Oct 1648

ATT A COUNTY COURT HELD 6 Oct 1648

PRESENT: CAPT: JOHN SIBSEY

MR: THOMAS LAMBARD MR: JOHN HILL

MR: MATH: PHILLIPPS MR: THO: BROWNE

Ordered that Mr: HENRY CATLIN, THO: HAYES, ROBERT EYRE, GEORGE KEMPE, TRUSTRAM MASON, JOHN HOLMES, JOHN MARTIN, & WILLIAM LUCAS take exact lists of all the tytheables, cowes, goates, horses & mares & land and deliver the same to MR: MATHEW PHILLIPPS upon Wednesday 11 Oct 1648.

89 Recorded 30 Oct 1648

ROBT: MARTIN of Elizabeth River, Planter, selling to RICHARD BLUNT of the same place a tract of land containing 250 acres onely - a neck of land to bee excepted out of ye aforesaid 250 acres which was formerly sold THOMAS MYLES & now in the tennor and ocupacon of said MYLES which neck of land doth lye up ye Indian Creek & beginneth at ye first branch & so runns to ye miles end which land is thus bounded as per ye Pattent doth appear vizt: Westerly upon a Creeke called ye Indian Creek Northerly upon the River, Easterly upon ye Reedy Swamp & Southerly into the woods.....running North & South for length & East & West for bredth.

WIT: WILLIAM PELL, THOMAS H HALL Signed: ROBERT RM MARTIN

89a ATT A COUNTY COURT HELD 3 Nov 1648

PRESENT: CAPT: JOHN SIBSEY

MR: THO: LAMBARD MR JOHN HILL

MR: MATH: PHILLIPPS MR: THO: BROWNE

Recorded 6 Nov 1648

Dated 5 Nov 1648 - NATHANIELL KINGSLAND late servant of THOMAS MARSH being in a boat with ROBERT PIERSON 1 Oct 1648 the wind caused the sayle of the boate to turn and thereupon the boate turned over and the said NATHANIELL drowned, came to his death Upon view of the corps found and appearing to the cassak? which is known to bee the Cassak? that the said NATHANIEL did weare by the testimony of ye said -faded- And that the said boate is Attached in regard it was the cause of his death and is apprayсed to ye value of 100 l tob and remaynes in Custody of the said Sheriffe. SIGNED: JOHN NORWOOD

90 WM: CROUCH

GEO: KEMPE

WIT: RI: CONQUEST High Sheriff JOHN MERRIDAY

15 Nov 1648

Petition of ALICE MASON,widdow & relict of MR: ffRANCIS MASON decd, & LEMUEL MASON for a Commission of Administration on the estate of the said MASON decd. to be granted to them both.

15 Nov 1648

Probate of the will of RICHARD HALL is granted to MATHEW HOWAR

Certificate for 250 acres of land granted to SYMON HANCOCKE due for the transportation of: PETER WELDINE, BRIGITT (ELIMS?) SYMON ROBINSON, JOHN COOPER & GEORGE HUDSON

15 Nov 1648 90

Certificate to JOB CHANDLER for 300 acres of land due for the transportation of MARY ffRANCIS, ROBT: BAYLY, JOHN MARTIALL, MARY ALLEN, EADY CRANDELL & THO: LAYTON. 90a

CHRISTOPHER COPELAND Pltf: agst: ffRANCIS LAND deft referred to the next Court.

Certificate to CAPT: ffRANCIS YARDLEY for 400 acres of land for transportation of WILLIAM ELLIS, ELIZABETH ffOUCKS & six negroes.

The Sheriff hath attached one cedar chest and 160 l tob part of the estate of JAMES FARIS? in the hands of MR: ROBT: EYRE. The Court has appointed SYMON HANCOCKE & RICHARD WHITEHURST to appraise the Chest and return to EYRE as parte satisfacon of his debt. (Faris)

The Sheriff hath attached one byll in the hands of RICHARD ACTON of 200 l tob due to HENRY TREESELL. RICHARD ACTON ordered to pay the said tob unto ANDREW NICHOLLS - ? - payment of 600 l tob & Charges due to NICHOLLS from TREESELL.

ROWLAND MORGAN to answer for misdemeanor at the next Court.

1200 l tob due to MR: BURROUGHS for funeral expenses in burying JOHN KEMP decd.

RICHARD CONQUEST administrator of JOHN KEMP decd.

The estate of JOHN KEMP decd. to * be sold at an outcry on 8 Dec 1648. 91

1800 l tob to be paid to CARBAY RIGAN from the estate of JOHN KEMP decd. the Adm: & XOP: BURROUGHS being first satisfyed.

GEO: SPENLEY to be satisfied 300 l tob out of the estate of JOHN KEMP decd.

16 Nov 1648
PRESENT ut antea

CARBRY RIGAN - of his remote residence from this County the Court allows ROBERT DAVYES to be his lawfull Atty:

The order passed by MR: HENRY WOODHOUSE betweene WILL: BASNETT & ROBT: DAVYES BEE authentique & said DAVYES to deliver BASNETT his bill.

JOHN CORNELISON is non suited & ordered to pay ROBT: DAVYES 40 l tob towards his charges & his attendance 2 Courts.

WILL: BASNETT to bee satisfyed out of the estate of JOHN KEMP decd. 250 l tob.

MR: BARTH: HOSKINS, MR: ROBT: HAYES, JOHN HOLMES & GYLES COLLINS to view land in difference betweene JOSEPH BURCH Pltf: & HENRY SNAYLE deft: before the next Court. 91a

The oath of Churchwarden is respited to be administered to JOHN HILL & WILL: CROUCH untill an Authentique Copy bee produced under the hand of the Clarke of the Assembly.

91a 15 Nov 1648

MATH: PHILLIPPS agst: JOHN ffERINHAUGH deft: The cowe in difference between them to be delivered unto MR: PHILLIPPS with her encrease for the use of OSMOND CHOLCHESTER - ? - by the said ffERINHAUGH from JOHN SMITH where said Cowe is deteyned......ffERINHAUGH to pay the charges.

Dated 18 Oct 1648 - CAPT: THO: WILLOUGHBY ESQ: is ordered to deliver an accoumpt of the whole estate of MR: RICHARD WAKE decd. 18 Oct last past: Peticon of CAPT: JOHN SIBSEY the Commissioners doe certify that WILLOUGHBY hath not performed the order from the Govenor and Councell.

Attachment granted THOMAS CASSON agst the estate of JOHN BASON or WILL: WRIGHT for 1500 l tob & Caske due to the said CASSON.

THOMAS TOOKER & JANE WRIGHT Pltfs: agst: MR: CORNELIUS LLOYD & ELIZABETH his wife Defts: referred to the next Court.

MR: RICHARD CONQUEST, High Sheriff, hath attached the estate
*92 of MR: WILL: DURAND for * the payment of 5600 l tob being charges expended by the said sheriffe in his Mat^{ies}: suite agst: said DURAND. Now ordered that..put in security until debt is proved.........-

THOMAS CASSON in Aug 1645 obteyned an order against EDWARD LILLY for the delivery of Certayne Joynery Ware.....and the said CASSON under oath that he hath not recd: the Joynery Ware.... the former order to be revived.

ROBERT PEIRSON to remain in Sheriffs Custody until he putt in Security for appearance at James City at the next Quarter Court....concerning the death of NATH: KINGLAND late servant to THO: MARSH. MR: RICHARD CONQUEST High Sheriff to preferre a byll of Indictment agst: PEIRSON.

CORNELIUS LLOYD hath very much abused his Ma^{ts}: Com^{rs}: in words as alsoe in not obeying theire command upon his committment to make personal appearances at next Court & to give security.

92a The particulars of ye accoumpts & payments for this present yeare [Vizt] 100 l tob for each wolfes head: RICHARD WOOLMAN for two heads, THO: DADFORD for one, SYMON PETERS, THO: ETHERIDGE, GILES COLLINS, RICH: NICHOLLS, HEN: NEEDHAM, RICH: ACTON, JOHN CARRAWAY & JOHN PORTERone wolfes head each. RICH: CONQUEST Sherr: for MR: ABBOTT for receiving fees about the Countyes Busyness 1001 l tob. Due to MR: HENRY WOODHOUSE shortage in last yeares levyes. 462 l tob. To MR: RICHARD CONQUEST Sherr: for a prison for ye County for a whole year 900 l tob. To the collectors for their collections -faded-

MR: RICHARD CONQUEST High Sheriffe for mens hyre & dyett at James Citty concerning carrying up of Lynnhaven Burgesses & bringing them down. 0322 l tob

MR: RICHARD CONQUEST High Sheriffe to be paid out of the County Levy for mens hyre, dyett & provision concerning MR: COR: LLOYD his goeing up to bee Burgesse 0483 1 tob

MR: ROBT: EYRE as p his acct: concerning himselfe & MR: HOSKINS being Burgesses theire charges. 2436 1 tob

MR: RICHARD CONQUEST High Sheriffe for mens hyre concerning MR: THO: LAMBARD his going up to bee Burgess & for mens hyre for bringing him downe. -faded-

MR: ffERINHAUGH for 3 men to fetch up MR: LAMBARD & for pvision ye imployment in full of his acct: -faded-

MT: THO: LAMBARD concerning his charge being Burgess. In full of his acct: -faded-

TOTAL 8517 1 tob

Ordered that there bee collected of every tythable pson in the County, being in number 334. 25 1/2 1 tob per pole the aforesaid 8517 1 tob. 93

MR: HENRY WOODHOUSE is appointed Collector for the Eastern Shore of Lynnhaven River.

MATT: PHILLIPPS is appointed Collector for the Western Shore of Lynnhaven & for the Little Creeke. The said MR: WOODHOUSE & MR: PHILLIPPS both of them to collect of 131 persons in both theire lymitts at 54 1/2 1 tob per pole.

THE TOTAL 7139 1 tob

The said MR: WOODHOUSE & MR: PHILLIPPS are to pay unto MRS: MORRISON in part of her Summe allowed her by ye assembly 6028

To soe much of last yeares Levye being due unto MR: WOODHOUSE 0462

To themselves for Sallary thereof 0649

THE TOTAL 7139

MR: THO: LAMBARD is appointed to Collectfrom 39 tythable persons in ye Easterne Branch in Lynnhaven Parish 54 1/2 1 tob per pole which amounts to 2144

And MR: LAMBARD to pay unto MR: ROBT: EYRE in part of his acct: 1950

and to himselfe for sallary 0195

TOTALL 2145

Allsoe MR: THOMAS LAMBARD is appoynted to collect the whole levyes as aforesaid from DANIELL TANNERS CREEKE up the Easterne & Southerne branches including MR: ffERINHAUGHS & MR: THOMAS MEARES is appoynted to collect the whole levyes up the Westerne Branch including MR: DAYNES. 93a

And the said MR: LAMBARD or MR: MEARES to collect of every tythable person in theire lymitts 54 1/2 1 tob which should amount to 6693 1/2

And they are to make payment to MRS: MORRISON more of her payment 1415

To MR: RICH: CONQUEST in full 2904

To MR: EYRE in full	0456
To MR: COR: LLOYD assigned him by CAPT: WOOD	0400
To MR: THO: LAMBARD in full	0690
To RICHARD WOOLMAN for two wolves heads	0200
To theire sallary for Collecting	0608 1/2
TOTALL	6693 1/2

CAPT: JOHN SIBSEY is appointed to collect 54 1/2 1 tob of every tythable person from DANIELL TANNERS CREEKE downwards to CAPT: WILLOUGHBYES which should amount to - faded -
And he to make payments to:

MRS: MORRISON in full		0968
MR: fferinhaugh in full		-xx-
THO: DADFORD for a wolves head		100
SYMON PETERS	"	100
THO: ETHERIDGE	"	100
GYLES COLLINS	"	100
EICH: NICHOLLS	"	100
HENRY NEEDHAM	"	100
RICHARD ACTON	"	100
JOHN CARRAWAY	"	100
JOHN PORTER	"	100
To himselfe for Sallary		XXXX
TOTAL - (can't read)		

Collectors to give accoumpt each to other of tobacco they receive & theire paymts:.......all of which is to bee performed by the collectors when the Court shall require them thereof.

94 Exhibited in Court by JOANE YATES. An Inventory of the goods and Chattell & Cattell of JOHN YATES late deceased taken the 13 Nov 1648 and apprysed by THO: SAYER, RICH: SMITH, JAMES WARNER & JOHN ffINCH vizt in Tobacco:

IN THE HALL

Impes one bedsted, one feather bedd, one pillowe one Rugg, two blanketts, two sheets, Curtaynes & vallance	1 tob 1200
Item one ould table, one forme	0120
Item two ould Chayres	0060
Item two ould settells	0030
Item two ould Small Chests	0050
Item one ould Trunke	0020
Item three old Small Gunns	0200
Item one Small pistoll	0030
Item two looking glasses	0050
Item twenty small Lysborne dishes	0070
Item three small Iron potts	0120
Item one bigger Iron pott	0050
Item one old brasse kettell	0060
Item one brasse Skillett	0025
Item one large frying pann	0020
Item two small frying panns	0020
Item one pott rack	0015
Item one payre of tongues	0010

Item one small Lamp	0003
Item one Chimney Cloth	0080
Item two payre of Small Stillyards	0080
Item one small silver sack Cupp & one silver Dramm Cupp	0100
	2353

IN THE BUTTERY

IMP: one Trundle bedsted, one flock bedd one pillowe two Blanketts	0160	
Item one parcell of powder	0040	
Item one Small Chest	0020	
Item one sute of Clothes	0200	
Item one parcell of old Clothes	0100	
Item one Case & bottells	0015	
Item 12 small peeces of pewter	0120	
Item 4 pewter porringers, 2 pewter Candelsticks, one pewter salt, i Aquevite bottle, one drinking Cupp, one quart pott, one pint pott	0070	94a
Item tenn Lysborne Dishes	00xx	
Item two old spades	00xx	
Item two shirts worne	00xx	
Item one payre of holland sheets one pillow beare	00xx	
Item three course Sheets	00xx	
Item one teble Cloth, 12 napkins & one towell	00xx	
Item six old napkins	00xx	
Item one old table Cloth, 12 napkins & one towell	00xx	
Item six old napkins	00xx	
Item one old table Cloth	00xx	
	10xx	

(The edge of the page is torn off from top to bottom.)

IN THE CHAMBER

Imp: one old feather bedd, one boulster two Course Sheets, one old blankett & one old Rugg	03xx
Item one old Couch, one Couch bedd, 1 blankett and one pilloew	00xx
Item two Bibles & other old Bookes	02xx
	06xx

IN THE CLAUSETT

IMP: 23 peeces of earthen ware	00xx
Item two old powdring tubbs two small rundletts & one double Anchor	00xx
	00xx

IN THE QUARTRING HOUSE

IMP: one old flock bedd one boulster & one blankett	01xx
Item one boy servant	12xx
Item one other servant	0500
	18xx

IMP: paid to GEORGE HORNER	03xx

94a 15 Nov 1648

DEBTS DUE IN BILLS

IMP:	one bill of JOHN NORWOODS		03xx
Item	one bill of WM: WHITBY	Caske	06xx
Item	one bill of JOHN WINBURY (or WMBURY)		12xx
Item	one bill of THO: EDMUNDS	Caske	04xx
Item	one bill of MATH: BASSETT	Caske	04xx
Item	one bill of GEORGE LOBB	Caske	04xx
Item	one bill of THO: ETHERIDGE	Caske	03xx
Item	one bill of WM: JOANES	Caske	04xx
Item	one bill of RALPH SPRAGGIN		03xx
Item	one bill of JOHN HAMUND	Caske	03xx
Item	one bill of MR: BRUSTER	Caske	03xx
Item	one bill of THEOPHILUS HONE		04xx
Item	one bill of THO: DAVIS		01xx
Item	by notes MR: MARSH hath to receive		11xx
			91xx

95

IN THE WORKHOUSE

IMP: a parcell of Boatwrights old tooles	0350
Item a parcell of TARRE	0140
Item one grindstone y^t (that) is Crackt	0020
Item a parcell of old Iron	0030
Item one pestell	0040
Item 2100 of Ruff & Clench	0150
Item 3000 Roughs	0045
Item 500 double tenns	0030
Item 360 halfe Crowne nayles	0040
Item old lumber	0040
	0915

IN THE YARD

IMP: one old shallopp	0150
Item one old wherry (a light rowboat)& one old sayle	0200
Item one old Cannoe	0020
Item six old oares	0090
	0460

IN THE COWPENN

IMP: ffive Cowes at 400 l tob p Cowe	2000
Item two heifers at two yeares old at 260^l p $heif^r$	0520
Item one steere at two yeares old	0200
Item one Bull at one yeare old	0100
Item one steere at a yeare old	0100
Item two weanling Calves	0140
Item one Bull of six yeares old	0300
	3360

IN THE HOGGPENN

IMP: ffive Sowes	0600
Item two Barrowes (a male hog castrated before maturity)	160
Item two Sowes	0160
Item two barrowes	0160
Item six shotes	0240

Item two Boores (Boars) 0200
Item one pigg 0010
1630
THE TOTALL SUMME IS 1 tob 19751

(NOTE: this is the end of JOHN YATES Inventory which began on page 94)

95a

In the name of God Amen: I RICHARD HALL of Virginia being weake in body but in perfect memory [thankes bee to God] doe make this my last will and testament: ffirst I bequeath my soule to Jesus Christ my Mediator & Redeemer and my body to the earth; and for my worldly goods w[ch] the Lord hath given mee; after my debts are payd & my funerall expenses discharged I bequeath as followeth: ffirst I bequeath unto MATHEW HOWARD the elder one yeareling steere Calfe. I bequeath unto ANN HOWARD a Cowe calfe & a barrowe shote. I bequeath unto ELIZABETH HOWARD my two Cowes with all theire encrease after the date hereof, alsoe I bequeath unto ye said ELIZABETH HOWARD my Sow with all encreaseexcepting three shotes, I give one Sow shote of a twelve moneth old to MATHEW HOWARD the younger, I give one Sow pigg to CORNELX (end of this name is torn off) HOWARD and my hatt; I give one Sow pigg to JOHN HOWARD and my workclothes & my handkercheife; I give unto MATH: HOWARD the elder my best payre of breeches; I give unto SAMUELL HOWARD all the tob[o] that is oweing unto mee after my debts are payd; I give unto THO: HILL my bedd, boulster, & blankett & my chest, & my old suite w[ch] I now have on, & two payre of shoes & stockens: I desire MATHEW HOWARD (the) elder my sole executo[r] of this my last will & testament. Wittness hereof I have hereunto sett my hand this 21 Aug 1645. Signed: TICHARD HALL
Signed & delivered in the presence of CORNELIUS LLOYD.
The mrke of THO: HILL.

BY THE GOVERNO[r] & CAPT GENERALL OF VIRGINIA

To all to whome these presents shall come I S[r] W[m] BERKELEY knt Governor & Cap[t] Generall of Virginia send greeting in our Lord God everlasting WHEREAS RICH: HALL late of this Collony deceased did by his last will & testament nominate and appoint MATHEW HOWARD the elder hsi executor And the said MATHEW did at a County Court holder for Lower Norfolke upon the 15 day of Nov 164x make humble suite to the board that a probate of the said will might bee graunted unto him, for w[ch] cause fuxx power and lawfull authority is hereby given & graunted unto him the said MATHEW HOWARD to dispose of all and singular the goods rights & Creditts of the said decedent according to the true intent & meaning of the said will & testament expressed: Given at James Citty under my hand and seale of the Collony this 15 Nov 1648.
signed: WILLIAM BERKELEY

ESTATE OF JOHN KEMP IS DEBT 1 tob

IMP: ffor halfe a barrel of Corne 050
ffor a Cowe shote 050
ffor drawing a Lyst of writings & making his will 300
ffor Charge of his buriall 450
ffor one to attend him & accomodacon in his sicknesse 200
ffor tyme spent in & about the estate taking the Inventory & makeing ye appraysmt & looking to itt 450

1500

An Inventory of the estate of JOHN KEMP deceased with the appraysmt thereof made by MR: THO: CASON, MR: EDWARD HALL, WILLIAM BASNETT & EDWARD CANNON the 22 July 1645.

IMP: A Chirurgicall Chest with medacm^{ts}, Instrum^{ts}) & other small appurtenances thereunto belonging) 0400
Item Seaven books of Chirurgerye vigo his workes,) the Surgions Mate; two of Barrowes method of phisick) pte of the Regm^{t} of health, Aristotles problems) 0200
Item sixe Divinity bookes vizt: a small bible, Mr.) Caluins Institutions ye practice of piety ye true) watch, Christs Combate with Satan, the other) effectual Calling) 0250
Item Some small bookes of small valew 0050
Bastalls abridgm^{t} of ye statutes & pt of ye Court) Baron & Leeb?) 0200

Item 2 peeces of scarlett embroydered with gold & silke 0150
Item a yard & halfe quarter of Duch broad cloth 0060
Item a pound of blacke & browne thred 0020
Iten an Indian basskett with silk & thred & other) small things) 0100
Item a yard & a halfe of Stuff 030
Item a small bedd, boulster, pillow, blankett, matt) beddsted * bedcord) 0700
Item a black suite & Cloke 0400
Item a long Cloth Cloke 0100
Item an old Chest with lock & key 0040
Item some peeces belonging to a buff Coate 0020
Item a Rapier & part of a belt 0050
Item one other Sword 0020
Item an old Sword & Dagger 0025
Item a Combe brush & Looking glasse 0030
Item three gunns & a small pitternell with a lock 0300
Item two potts , a brass kettell, a smale skellett) & a frying pann) 0100
Item an old paire of Creeps, a paire of tongues) pott hookes & hangers) 0030
96a Item a tobaccoe knife 0010
Item a parcell of old pewter & brass 0040
Item a pewter standish & pewter pott 0030
Item fower smale vices 0150
Item a wheele to twist silke 0050

Item a parcell of old smiths tooles, & hamers files, a scruplate & tapps an old gouge & chisells & lumber & a peece of plate to tagg poynts	170
Item two payre of taylors sheeres a pressing Iron & thimble	0030
Item a pcell of old Carpenters tooles	0100
Item two old empty rundletts & fish hookes 2 sifters & trayes & a tob wheele	0080
Item a peece of raw hyde & a peece of tanned leather	0020
Item a payre of wafer irons	0005
Item an old stock of a gunn, a pestell, grindstone, 3 small shott	0046
Item a plate of a sawe & a stone morter	0020
Item a payre of braysiers sheeres	0020
Item three henns	0015
Item a Cowe & bull calfe	0500
Item another Bull calfe three moneths old	100
Item an old sowe with piggs	150
Item a sowe shote	060
Item a boat with old Canvas for a sayle, ropes & a broken grapnell	800
Item two hhds of tob defective	400
Item a steere hurt praysed	400
surat in Cur XOP: BURROUGH The total is	6060

BY THE GOV & CAPT GENERALL OF VIRGINIA

To all to whome these p^{r}sents shall come I WILLIAM BERKELEY knt Gov & Capt Generall of Virginia send greeting in our Lord God everlasting. Whereas MR: ffRANCIS MASON late of this Collony deceased, dyeing Intestate and leaving an estate in divers goods, rights, Creditts: In Care whereof ALICE MASON widdow the Relict of the said deceased & LEMUELL MASON her sonne have made humble suite to the County Court of Lower Norff: that a Comission of Administration might bee graunted unto them of ye said decedents estate Now know yee that I the said Sir WILLIAM BERKELEY knt for the better ordering & securing of the said estate according to an order of ye said County Court bearing date the 15 Nov 1648 doe give & graunt unto ALICE MASON & LEMUELL her sonne the Administration of all and singular the goods, rights & Creditts
of the said * decedents estate of what nature, quality or *97
condicon soever they bee, or in whose Custodye soever they bee or remayne within the Collony of Virginia: And doe by these p^{r}sents further order and appoynt that the said ALICE MASON & LEMUELL her sonne shall p^{r}sent unto the Com^{rs} of the said Lower Norff: at theire next County Court a true and perfect Inventory of the said estate being lawfully appraysed by fower sufficient men upon oath: And further that they satisfye and pay all such debts as remayne due and oweing from the said estate to any person or persons within the Collony soe farre as the estate will affoard. And after such debts are payd, then they the said ALICE & LEMUELL to

give a true and Just accoumpt of the surplusage and remaynder of the said estate, when they shall bee thereunto lawfully called, and deliver the same to the Com[rs] of the said Lower Norff County, for the use of such person or persons unto whome it shall more lawfully or of right belong or appertayne Given at James Citty under my hand and the seale of the Collony this 22 Nov 1648. signed: WILLIAM BERKELEY

RECORDAT 2 Dec 1648

March 4th 1647/48

Delivered by mee JOHN ffERINHAUGH to MR ffRANCIS HOUGH [by Fods pvidence bound for England] these severall writings as followeth: (In the margin) Cop:sit HOUGH.
MR ROBT PAGE his obligacon for seaven hhds of tob & twenty & seaven shillings & sixe pence sterl:
One bill of ladeing under MR: PAGE his hand for 5 hhds of tob
One bill of ladeing under MR: GOODWINES hand for 4 hhds of tob
One note under the hand of JO: ROBINSON Chy[r] for 2 hhds of tob
One note under the hand of ROBT FFEAKE Marriner for 60[l] tob and a Rugg or Coverlett
A Letter of Advice concerning the said writings
A letter of Attorney to the said MR: HOUGH from mee the said JOHN ffERINHAUGH.
A Bill of Ladeing for 5 hhds of tob now shipped aboard MR WHARTON for MR PAGE.
97a Which said Writings I the said ffRANCIS HOUGH Merchant doe asknowledge to have Recd; as witness my hand the day and yeare above written: signed: ffRA: HOUGH

13 Dec 1648

An Inventory of the goods & Chattells of MR RICHARD WAKE deceased taken the day and yeare above written and appraysed by WILLIAM SHIPP: JOHN HOLMES: LEMUEL MASON and JAMES THELABALL: as followeth:

	l tob
Imp: Three ffeather Bedds, three Boulsters, one payre of Blanketts, two Ruggs, three pillowes & one quilt Matris	2300
Itm: ffifteene dishes of pewter, three pewter Basons one pewter Cullender, thirteene pewter plates, eighteene sarcers, foure porringers, sixe candlesticks, foure littell pewter potts, three Chamber potts, three pye plates, two flagons	0450
Item Three fyer shovells, three payre of tongues, one payre of brass Andirons, two payre of Cobyrons one grydiron & two payre of potts hooks	0220
Itm Three kettells, foure Iron potts, threeskilletts on Trivett & one brass skimmer	0560
Itm: Two old Ladells & foure pye peeles	0020
Itm: One spinning wheele	0003
Itm: One warming pann	0015
Itm: Two empty cases of bottells	0010

Itm: one appell roster & one forke for a toste	0014	
Item: one hamper & a flaskett wth old writings and Lumber	0020	
Itm: ffive small drinking glasses sixe gally potts and seaven bottells	0030	
Itm: one Cheny dish, one bason, three littell stone potts, one glasse Jack?, one payre of scailes, one mincing knife, one cleaver, eight basketts & a dripping pann	0150	
Item: one Bagg of Lumber	(Blank)	
Itm: one bread grater & a stone Morter	0050	
Itm: one Brasse pestell & Morter & one pippkin	0025	
*Itm: one Cypress box, three pictures	0080	98
Itm: one rich purce	003x	
Itm: one Corall for a Child (a playpen?)	0100	
Itm: two bodkins	0060	
Itm: one diamon ring wth two stones	0200	
Itm: two gold rings	0150	
Itm:one silver thimble	0012	
Itm: three small pearles	0025	
Itm: two other purses	0003	
Itm: one watch out of kelter	0300	
Itm: one amber bracelett, one Corall bracelett, one Cornelion bracelett	0050	
Itm: one small silke flower and some small remnants of Ribbon	0030	
Itm: three black silke laces some black silke braide & some old gold Lace	0040	
Itm: one payre of Koses? & garters some needles, thredd tape and pinns	0055	
Item: one Cherry Dramm cupp some thredd Laces, two payre of gloves	0035	
Itm: one yard of yallow sarcenett?	0030	
Itm: three Looking glasses, one brass tob box	0100	
Itm: one silver porringer	0060	
Itm: one silver maudlin cupp three silver spoones one dram cupp tipt with silver	0200	
Itm: one muff, one scarfe, one thinn hood, two Maskes & other old hoods	0110	
Item: two stick stones, two smoothing Irons	0050	
Itm: two cullered silke & gold Crosse Clothes & quoines	100	
Itm: tenn neck handkercheifes two gorgetts, tenn payre of Cuffs	0330	
Itm: three holland hoods, six headclothes, seaven neckclothes thirteene quoines & Crosse Clothes three capps, three handKercheifes five payre of gloves, two payre of socks, six smocks, twelve aprons, two lynnen wastecoats	0700	
Item two pinn pellowes, one payre of shooes & stockens, one black sattin capp, some old bands, Cuffs and bloves	0070	

98a 13 Dec 1648

Itm: some phisicall druggs 0005
Itm: some small peices of linnen 0100
Itm: some small quantity of Coullored silke and)_
Cruell (Crewell?), white browne & black thread) 0060
Itm: two brushes, one Combe & brush, one payre of)_
sycers, some parcell of old bone lace) 0050
Itm: one trunke full of raggs 0060
Itm: ffoure locks and keyes 0080
Itm: two roles for gownes, one head role, two hayre)
laces and fille::ts)-0030
Itm: twenty six canvace napkins, three Canvace)_
sheets, three flaxon sheets, six course towells) 0250
Item two payre of flaxon pillow beers, foure course)
table clothes, one payre of course sheets, three)
payre of ordinary sheets, three fine sheets, one)- 0350
head sheet.)
Itm: five payre of pillow beeres, five course table)
clothes, one payre of course sheets, one payre of)
course pillowbeers, foure dozen of ordinary nap-)_0350
kins five ordinary towells, two payre of pillow-)
beers nine course towells, twelve napkins)
Itm: one sute of damaske & one sute of dyaper 0500
Itm: three dozen of trenchers one old knife)_
one Chafing dish) 0080
Itm: two Clokes, one Coate three doubletts and one)_
payre of breeches) 0400
Itm: two bird cages 0040
Itm: eleaven old stooles and Chayres 0300
Itm: one Iron back for a Chimney, one Iron Jack)_
to turne the spitt) 0150
Item: two littel tables, one bedsteed, and one)_
trundle bedsteed) 0130
Itm: one old watch, some old Iron 0020
Itm: one small box of phisicks 0020
Itm: one standish 0020
Itm: one payre of rich gloves, one hatt, one payre)
of roses and garters, two gold girdells, one)- 0320
leather purse, one leather belt)
Itm: five yards of English Mohayre 0075
99 Itm: three redd velvett Cusheon Cases old velvett 0450
& Plush
Itm: two tob boxes, one payre of boots, two tynn)_
funnells & extinguishers) 0080
Itm: one dozen of freng, one Crimson quilt of sarcenett350
Itm: one sute of Crimson taffety Curtaines and)
vallance, with a head of ye same, one Crimson)- 1000
serge teaster & foure gilded knobbs)
Itm: foure stoole cases & one Chayre Case of redd)
Cloth, one Case of Irish stich, three greene)- 0450
carpett Clothes)
Itm: one Crimson taffety mantle, two of scarlett)_
bayes, & two other mantles) 0250
Itm: one payre of Crimson velvett slippers 0010

Item	Amount
Itm: one dimity cloke, foure small downe pillowes six suits of Lynnen for a young Child, one roler?, thirty peeces of Lynnen for Children, and some other odd things for Children	0320
Itm: one payre of brass snuffers, three bibles	0155
Itm: two payre of striped Curtaines and valance with heads to them	0420
Itm: one Irish stich Carpett, one striped Carpett and Cupboard cloth	0450
Itm: three remnants of hollands	0090
Itm: thirteene Cusheons	0500
Itm: thirteene Cusheons	0500
Itm: one petticoat & wastcoat of tabee, one petticoate & wastcoat of ducape?, one skie couller taffety petticoat	0900
Itm: one stich taffety petticoat, one wrought petticoat, one greene stuff petticoat, one scarlett bayse petticoat, one quilted wastcoate	0500
Itm: one goune and petticoat of black stuff, one redd baysecoat, one bayse wastcoat, two cloth Cases for stooles	0400
Itm: two old beaver hatts, two [illegible] twenty small bookes, one writing box with drawers	0230
*Itm: two pound and a quarter of sugar, two pack needles, one marking Iron, some quantity of starch & spice, two small Cases of Soape	005x *99a
Itm: one spice grater, one stone bottle, three trunks, three boxes & three Chests	047x
Itm: one boxe of writings, two surrenders, and two glister pipes & a small parcell of Lyne	0020
Itm: one old payre of fine sheets and three pillowbeers	0150
Itm: one muskett, a bolt & bandeleers, a pistol a frame for a bason, a stoe, a sword, a bible, a flannel blankett, eleaven yards of dimity, a payre of goldscailes & two ffanns	0460
The totall summe amts to	17882

ffound written in two small bookes as followeth:

Delivered unto MR IVY the 17 Jan (1645/6), the summe of three gallons wanting a pinte of vinegar rests unpayd for.

Delivered unto MR IVY at severall tymes three quart juggs of vinegar and rests unpayd.

Sould unto MR STAMPE this 22 Jan 1645/6 five pound of Castell soape at 6 1tob p pound wch is to bee recd of MR ffLETCHER.

Sould unto WILL ADAMS this 23 Jan 1645 seaven pound of Castell soape and rests unpayd at 6 1tob p pound.

Sould unto MR HOLMES and MRS SHIPP the 27 Jan 1645 five pound of reasons for wch recd 2s 6d.

99a 13 Dec 1648

Sould unto MRS SIBSEY this 28 Jan 1645 twelve pound of reasons, rests unpayd.

Sould unto WILL ADAMS this 28 Jan 1645: sixe gallons of vinegar at 15^{1}tob p gallon & rests unpayd.

Delivered unto CAPT SIBSEY the 25 Jan 1645; one hundred weight of swann & goose shott; and a rundlett of vinegar conteyning three gallons and a halfe.

100 Sould unto WILL ADAMS the 14 Feb 1645: one poundof peper, tenn pounds of soape: WILL ADAMS foure knives

Sould to MR: FLETCHER sixe pound of Castell soape

Sould to MR IVY sixteene pounds of reasons and his wife a knife and one knife more.

Sould unto WILL ADAMS and MR BRIDGES foure pound of reasons.

May 29 WILL SHIPP halfe a gallon of vinegar.

Delivered unto the house at severall tymes sixteene quart Juggs of vinegar.

100a Delivered unto MR WILLOUGHBY one bottle of vinegar ffor washing of our Clothes three Cases of soape.

MR ffLETCHER two pound of reasons.

CAPT WINDHAM two pound of reasons.

WILL SHIPP a !eice of dymity.

Delivered unto CAPT JOHN SIBSEY the 28 Jan twelve pound of reasons, the 25 Jan 1645/6; delivered one hundred weight of shott swann & goose, sixteene pounds of powder, two rundletts of vinegar, and at other severall tymes in bottles 19 gallons 25.
twelve payre of stockens, sixe shirts, two pound of black & browne thredd. six dozen of hooks & eyes, halfe a thousand of pinns, a quarter of a pound of white thredd, two yards and three quarters of brode Cloth, silke and buttons, twelve pound of reasons, one hundred weight of shott swann & goose, sixteene pound of pouder, nineteene gallons of vinegar, five and twenty pounds of soape, one pound of peper, one pound of ginger, fifteene gallons of sack, twelve pound of Candles, the quarter parte of a reame of paper, one lanthorne?, halfe a pound of wormefeed, penns and Ink, a parcell ofsmall nay les:

two pounds of black and browne thredd: halfe a gross of hooks and eyes, twelve payre of stockens, sixe shirts, halfe a thousandof pinns, sixe knives, halfe a pound of wormefeed: (or wormeseed?)

SIMON PETER a Combe.

May 13 sould to EDWARD HOLMES a peice of dimity 100^{1}tob/

The 19 JOHN ARIS a peice of dimity: 100^{1}tob.

The 15 MRS LAMBART a petticoate 200^{l}tob.
ffoure Combes 008:

The 16 THO: DAVYS a peice of dimity: 100^{l}tob & six pound of soape: 20^{l}tob, a quart of vinegar x^{l}tob 1^{l} of wormeseed 5^{l}tob

WILL ADAMS a peice of dimity 100^{l}tob & foure douzen of buttons twelve pounds of tob.

My selfe a peice of dimity & foure douzen of buttons.

MR CONQUEST a peice of dimity 80.

LEMUELL MASON a knife.
*My sonne a peice of dimity & foure douzen of buttons. *101

WILL ADAMS two pound of soape; ffoureteene.

THO: PLOTT a peice of dimity: ninety ffoure dozen of buttons twenty foure.

In the other Booke

1645 Jan: Cured MARY her thumb, more a hurt of her back & legg. a medicine for ye wormes, a Cordial.

JOHN the neger a Cordiall.

DANIELL two Cordialls one for to cause him to sweate, a water for his throte and mouth.

1646 Aug 3: MRS SIBSEY a Cooling Julip: gave her a Cordiall

THOMAS SIBSEY his hand: Mingo his Legg.

1645 ffeb ye 27 JOHN WILLIAMS a bottle of water for his throte, a Cordiall. May a sore throte.

May ye 15th JOSIAS, MR PHILLIPPS man a sore eye.

16th THO: DAVEYS the taylor a vomite.

MRS SALSBURY a purge.

Aprill the 20 1646 JOHN ARIS an innard medicine for a bruise, and a searecloth & an oyntmt for his back.

Aprill 28th 1646 EDWARD HOLMES a Julip.

May the 13th CHRISTOPHER a sore mouth.

1646: LEIFTENANT MASON his daughter Cured of the Emrods May
July the 2nd HENRY WAKE lett blood.
3^{d} My Partner SIBSEY lett blood: 4th GOODY BAKER lett blood.

5th MR PHILLIPPS his maid Margarett lett blood.
Aug 2^{d} JOHN HOLMES his wife a medicine for her spleene.

1646 July ye 23th (sic) WILL SHIPP a purge 24th went to lett him blood.

Aug ye 3^{d} THO: SIBSEY lett blood; the maid Mary lett blood.

101 13 Dec 1648

1645 MR ffLETCHER 2 doz of pill Cocke (or Coche?): water for his eyes, a purge; more water for his eyes, Seané? & Coleander seed 10^{l}tob.

ffeb ye 4th a purge: May the 17th a purge: more Seane; and Coleander seed 10^{l}tob & Carraway seed.

101a Delivered to MR PUDDINGTON a lotion for his throte.

May the 29th MR BRIDGE a purge of Ruberb.

MRffLETCHER a searecloth, and oyntment. Ap^{ll} ye 2^{d} for his hand.

MR BRIDGE for Curing his hand.

MR ffLETCHER 2 forecticks to Cause sweat; a purging dyett drink. two drying dyett drinks; 2 small drying dyett drinks.

Debts due formerly to the estate

ffrom DOCTOR WALDRON:	4400
ffrom MR ROBINS	1200
ffrom MR THO: WARDE	1100
	6700

Debts recd

of DOCTOR WALDRON	4400
of MR ROBINS	1200
of EDW: HOLMES	0100
of MR HARRISON for certayne spices & other goods	0300
of MR THO: WARDE	1100
	7100

THO: WILLOUGHBY:

CAPT THO: WILLOUGHBY ESQ: hath deposed this to bee a true Inventory of MR RICH: WAKE dec: before MR: THO: LAMBARD & MR MATHEW: PHILLIPPS: the 13 December 1648.
Jurat die et anno supradicto Coram.
THO: LAMBARD et MATH: PHILLIPPS.

The totall summe is as appeares by the severall pages amts to	17882
By debts due in tob	06700
By tob due from MR HARRISON for goodsbought of MR WAKE	00300
More due from EDWARD HOLMES	00100
By money 4^{l}:05^{d} ster:	24982

As for the Chest wch is at CAPT SIBSEYS itt could not bee appraysed in respect it was not present, and as for pticulars of certaine goods sould by MR WAKE in his lifetime; as appeares by certaine papers a Copy whereof being inserted in this Inventory and noe value sett upon the goods; could not bee apprayed by us in respect they were loose papers; wee whose names are here under written being sworne to apprayse the pticulars menconed in this Inventory have to the best of our Judgments apprayed them to the summe of seaventeene thousand * eight hundred eighty two 1 tob & ₺ 4/5 in ready money as appeareth by the sd Inventory. As witness our hands the day & yeare aforemenconed: WILL: SHIPP, JOHN HOLMES, LEMUELL MASON, JAMES THELABALL, All these appraysers have been sworne by us. THO: LAMBARD, MATT: PHILLIPPS.

RICHARD CONQUEST aged 28 yeares Sworne sayth that about May last was twelve month MR WAKE [noe deceased] being at the house of CAPT WILLOUGHBY and being in conference in the presence of this deponent CAPT: WILLOUGHBY desired this deponent to tell CAPT SIBSEY That is he the sd CAPT SIBSEY would utterly relinquish the 1000 1 tob for which the sd CAPT: SIBSEY had gotten on order of Court then hee the said CAPT WILLOUGHBY was contented to putt the busenesses concerning the Copartnershipp of MR WAKE & CAPT SIBSEY to the hearing of fowre men and soe to bee determined by the Court upon theire report, or the said CAPT WILLOUGHBY used words to that same effect, and accordingly this deponent did speake to CAPT SIBSEY and afterwards drew a discharge for ye said 1000 1 tob This deponent sayeth that after the Arbitrators had made theire report to the County Court of Lower Norff: CAPT WILLOUGHBY and CAPT SIBSEY being in earnest dispute and contending in words CAPT WILLOUGHBY in presence of the Com[rs]: that were then present did preffer to Have the bussynesse ended by the said Court and the said CAPT WILLOUGHBY seemed to bee very earnest with CAPT SIBSEY to have the same determined, and the said CAPT WILLOUGHBY sayd if soe bee you will not have the busynesse here determined or heard, referr itt to Jamestowne [or words to that effect] and soe at the same time afterwards they both [vizt:[CAPT WILLOUGHBY and CAPT: SIBSEY did consent and agree to referr itt to the Governor and Counsell. This deponent sayth CAPT WILLOUGHBY did goe two severall tymes last Winter about Xmas to meet the Arbitrators at CAPT SIBSEYS house & at theire last meeting CAPT WILLOUGHBY was very ill and full of payne[as hee a good while had complayned of] and in the Phisitians hands, and in the Judgmt of the deponent could not meet; and this deponent sayth that CAPT WILLOUGHBY [till then] desired & endeavored [as farr as hee could preceive] to have an end of the busynesses and further sayth not.

16 Aug 1648 RI: CONQUEST

WIT: ffRANCIS MASON & MATH: PHILLIPPS

The words [till then[are left out in a coppy hereof delivered unto CAPT: WILLOUGHBY.

ATT A COUNTY COURT HELD 15 Dec 1648 102a

PRESENT: CAPT: JOHN SIBSEY MR: JOHN HILL
MR: MATH: PHILLIPPS MR: THO: BROWNE

JOHN DYER pltf: agst: CAPT: ffRANCIS YARDLEY & SARAH his wife defts: referred to the nextCourt.

102a 15 Dec 1648

WILLIAM COLE Pltf: agst: THO: WARDE Chyrurgeon Deft: referred to next Court and to give Security for his appearance......and the Court doth also give MR: MATH: PHILLIPPS authority to take the oath of MARGRETT SMITH on behalfe of WILLIAM COLE Pltf:

CAPT: EDWARD WINDHAM is non-suited and ordered to pay 20 l tob unto MRS: ALICE MASON and LEMUEL MASON her sonne, Administrators of MR: ffRANCIS MASON deceased towards & theire (sic) Charges for attendance at Court in respect the said CAPT: WINDHAM did not appeare nor anyone for him to prosecute the said Administrators.

ROBERT HAYES to pay 3600 l tob and Caske & forbearance according to Specialty under his hand unto JOB CHANDLER atty of SUSANNA SMOOT.

EDWARD COOPER acknowledged debt of 320 l tob due in 1645 with 8 l tob forbearance to THO: CASSON.

Attachmt: granted unto JOHN WATFORD agst: Estate of RICHARD MORGAN for 170 l tob due by byll xxxxxx in Court as alsoe for County Levyes, Ministers Dutyes & Court Charges.

MORE PRESENT: MR: HEN: WOODHOUSE & MR: THO: LAMBARD

103 THO: WARDE Chyr, Pltf: agst: JOHN HOLMES deft: referred to the next Court.

The Gov: & Councill upon pusall of the acct^s exhibited unto them by RICH: CONQUEST High Sheriffe concerning WILL DURAND have ordered sd CONQUEST payment of 5569 l tob out of ye Estate of sd DURAND marked: and Whereas THO: MARSH stands bound unto the sd High Sherr: in the penalty of 12000 l tob that the estate attached should be forthcoming....unto sd CONQUEST: But sd DURAND hath since conveyed the same out of the County xxxxxx therefore ordered, with the consent of MARSH, as of ye sd CONQUEST that MARSH immediately after 1 Feb next (1648/9) shall pay the 5669 l tob unto CONQUEST if ye sd DURAND doe not make paymt:

Attachmt: granted EDWARD COOPER agst Estate of EDWARD LILLY for 320 l tob due from sd COOPER and LILLY unto THO: CASSON in 1645 ......The sd COOPER hath confessed a judgmt: agst himselfe of the sd debt.

These are to certify whome it may concerne that we THO: LAMBART, MR: MATH: PHILLIPPS, MR: RICHD: CONQUEST & MR: THO: IVY doe well remember that when CAPT: THOMAS WILLOUGHBY, Esqr: petetioned to this Court for letters of administracon on the Estate of MR: RICHD: WAKE decd. CAPT JOHN SIBSEY was willing to lett CAPT: WILLOUGHBY adm: on the estate soe that hee might be first satisfyed, and the said CAPT: WILLOUGHBY sayd yea yea or words to that effect.

THO: TOOKER to pay 2000 l tob & caske due by specialty unto WILLIAM SHIPP.

Administration of the Estate of STEPHEN HICKS decd [on behalfe of the Mother of ye said decd] granted to THOMAS SAYER.

THOMAS CASSON to pay a bill of 779 l tob unto CAPT JOHN SIBSEY the Atty: of ARTHUR BROWNE, Merchant.

Certificate to MR: XOP: BURROUGHSfor 150 acres of land due for the transportation of: JOHN HUNGXXXXX (Nu gives this name as HUNGERTON p 221), ffARDIN ffANTRES, RICHARD CASTELFORD. (see also Nu 180)

Certificate to WILL: COLE for 50 acres of land due for transportation of SARAH MELFORD.

In regard the sessions of the Grand Assembly xxxxxxxx 10 Feb next this County Court to be held the 15th day of xxx is prociourned? to the 1st day of Feb.

RECORDED 16 Dec 1648

WILL: CAPPS to pay 200 l tob unto THOMAS TOOKER the last of Oct next. Given under my hand 8 Sep 1647.
HEN: WOODHOUSE

Indorsat: 22 Sep 1647 THOS: TOOKER assigning the 200 l tob to RICHARD CONQUEST. signed: THOS: TOOKER

RECORDED 17 Dec 1648
The Cattle Mark of Moses Lynton.

ATT A COUNTY COURT HELD 1 Feb 1648/9 104

PRESENT: CAPT: JOHN SIBSEY, MR: THO: MEARES, MR: THO: LAMBARD, MR: JOHN HILL, MR: MATT: PHILLIPPS, MR: THO: BROWNE

Judgmt: acknowledged by JOHN MANNING for 503 l tob unto WILL: SHIPP by Specialty.

RICHARD MORGAN to pay 242 l tob unto WILL: DAYNES

Whereas SYMON PETERS hath impleaded THO: LEE, Merchant of 800 l tob for his paynes & service done bof sd LEE ...... 185 l tob has been paid to sd PETERS towards satisfacon... LEE ordered to pay PETERS 20 l tob more in full satisfacon. (NOTE: amounts of tob. Looks like someone is out 595 l tob?)

Whereas BARTHO: HOSKINS impleaded THO: TODD upon 2 specialtys doe 3645 l tob & Caske......2412 l tob have been paid in part ....ordered that sd TODD pay BARTHO: HOSKINS 1258 l tob in full satisfacon.

MR: CORNELIUS LLOYD & ELIZABETH his wife defts: agst: THO: TOOKER and JANE BRIGHT pltffs: referred to the next Court.

JOHN DYER to remain on land he now liveth on untill the last of Dec next without any molestacon of CAPT: ffRANCIS YARDLEY or any in his stead & DYER shall not suffer xxxxxx part of the housing now standing upon the said Land. To bee xxxx but shall at the expiracon of the aforesaid tyme leave all the housing tennantable; And alsoe that MR: ROBERT POWIS

shall dwell and live in y^t house y^t was built for him
104a without any molestacon from said DYER * during the said DYERS aboud upon the said grounds as aforesaif and the charges to be payd by the said DYER.

Ordered that ROWLAND MORGAN for comitting of the great & lothsome sinn of drunkenness shall by 1 May next cause a payre of stocks to be built and placed before the Court Doore & that hee doe publiquely before the face of this Court asknowledge that hee hath greatly abused CAPT: ffRANCIS YARDLEY in words and that hee is hartily sorry for it and alsoe to pay the Court Charges.

WILL: COLE Pltf: agst: THO: WARDE Chry: left to the next Court.

ROWLAND MORGAN has most rudely behaved himselfe towards CAPT: EDWARD WINDHAM. MORGAN ordered to apologize in Court.

RICHARD STARNELL ordered to deliver a man servant to ZACHARY TAYLOR.

JOHN ffINCH acknowledges a debt of 1000 l tob unto WILL:SHIPP

THOS: MARSH Pltf: agst Estate of PETER GRINTOE for 600 l tob & Caske with 3 yeares forbearance.

ROBERT EYRE GENT: according to Act of Assembly hath set up his name at the Court Dore of his intended voyage for England this present shipping.

COURT TO BE HELD UPON THE 20th DAY OF THE PRESENT MONTH. (Feb)

Ordered to be recorded 1 Feb 1648/9
105 The Jury haveing seriously considered upon the cause in difference betweene MR: THO: IVY pltf: and TRUSTRAM MASON deft: according to evidence pduced doe find the deft: ought to give assurance of the said Land according to Covenant, and lay itt out where he hath putt him in possession.

Deposition of WILLIAM MORE aged 32 yeares of thereabouts sayeth: That he, last Summer haveing surveyed a parcell of land for MR: IVY, MR: IVY desired this depont: to goe with him to CAPT: SIBSEY and hee would see whether the CAPT: would let him survey a pcell of Land [50 acres as this depont: remembreth] which IVY said hee bought whereuppon CAPT: SIBSEY made a demurre, but after sayd, it should bee laid out for there were divers shares in the land and every man must have his share and they would conclude of a tyme to have a survey & further sayeth nott. WILL: MORE

Deposition of WILL: BUTLER aged 26 years or thereabouts sworne sayeth: That last Summer this depont: living with MR: IVY, the sd MR: IVY demauned his right in certayne ground he had bought of TRUSTRAM MASON and TRUSTRAM had him bring a Surveyor and he would give him his right, and when MR: IVY had brought a Surveyor the sd TRUSTRAM would not sett him to worke, nor shew him where to begin to survey when ye sd MR: IVY did tender ye Surveyor at his own charge and further sayeth not.

ATT A COUNTY COURT HELD 15 Feb 1648/9
PRESENT: CAPT: JOHN SIBSEY MR: THO: MEARES
MR: MATT: PHILLIPPS MR: JOHN HILL MR: THO: BROWNE

Attachment granted unto MR: RICHARD CONQUEST upon 271 l tob attached in the hands of THO: WRIGHT of the estate of GEO: WHITE XX, being due for fees. CONQUEST to be payd by WRIGHT.

SAM[ll]: LEE, Maister of the shipp Providence ordered to del- 105a
iver unto TRUSTRAM BENNET his chest that hee deteyned at the house of CAPT: JOHN SIBSEY or MRS: SARAH JULIAN when sd shipp cometh downe & BENNETT to pay the Court Charges.

Ltre: of administration granted JOHN KENNAR, son & heir on the estate of his father RICH: KENNAR decd. MR: RICH: CONQUEST to be guardian unto JOHN KENNAR during his minority.

MRS: ALICE MASON administrator with LEMUELL MASON of MR: ffRANCIS MASON decd. to pay 370 l tob unto CAPT: EDWARD WINDHAM proved by oath of THO: TOOKER.

MR: THO: LAMBART doth confess judgment unto MR: CORNELIUS LLOYD of 2670 l tob & Caske in full satisfaction of a bill of 4700 l tob & Caske

LAWRENCE PHILLIPPS ordered to pay unto PETER PORTER for the use of SUSANN PORTER the summe of 400 l tob & Caske in full satisfaction for a yeares service accomplished by JOHN LEEto and with the said PHILLIPPS.

JAMES THELABALL is nonsuited & ordered to pay unto JOHN MERRIDAY 20 l tob & Court charges for non appearance.

JOHN DYER is non suited & ordered to pay unto CAPT: EDWARD WINDHAM 20 l tob for non appearance.

THO: CHEELY pltf: agst: HEN: ROBINSON deft: to next Court.

EDWARD CANNON fined 500 l tob for not appearing according 106
to a summons executed on him by the under sheriffe and pcured at the request of THO: CHEELY pltf: agst: HEN: ROBINSON deft:

RICHD: WORSTER to pay WILL: SHIPP 500 l tob with allowance for Caske........due by Specialty.

JOHN ffERINHAUGH shall pay unto RICH: BECK the corne and clothes due to ELIZABETH, his wife for her service done & pformed with the said ffERINHAUGH and his wife. And the said ELIZABETH shall make appeare upon oath before one of the Comrs: what clothes she hath allready received....... ffERINHAUGH to pay Court Charges.

In the difference depending betweene THOMAS TODD pltf: & BARTHO: HOSKINS concerning land bought by TODD of BARTHO: HOSKINS. TODD having appealed to the Gov. & Council for determination.....TODD to put in security for appearance before Gov. & Council upon 5 Mar next.

WILL: COLE Pltf: & THO: WARDE Chy[r]: Deft: Concerning the curing of a thumb of the wife of the said COLE undertaken by the sd WARDE Chy[r]: and WARDE having allready received 300 l tob for his paynes according to agreement. It is the opinion of this Court [in respect ye saide WARDE hath not made a cure of the thumb] that hee, WARDE shall repay unto WILL: COLE 150 l tob and the charges to be equally divided between the Pltf: and Deft: and the witnesses to bee allowed 20 l tob a piece for their attendance each Court.

106a RICH: WORSTER Atty: of RICH: ffOSTER to deliver unto JOHN CARAWAY who hath intermarried with the relict of ROGER WILLIAMSON decd: for the use of SARAH WILLIAMSON the Cowe and all her increase which was bequeathed unto SARAH by RICHD: the god-father of SARAH, when he went for England. The said JOHN CARAWAY putting in security for same.

JOHN POLLARD Pltf: agst: ROBERT DAVYES Deft: referred to the next Court.

Certificate to CAPT: JOHN SIBSEY for 350 acres of land due for the transportation of 7 persons: JOHN PEATE, AXXX WATSON, THO: SHERRIFFE, ANDREW WOLSON, JAMES MILLACHA, MARY EVANS & BARBARY CARTER.

RICH: DEVERS Servant unto MR: THO: MEARES for Committing fornicacon with SARAH REINOLDS, shall, according to Act of Assembly at expiracon of his time specified by Indenture serve said _aster one whole yeare and that both the said DEVERS and REINOLDS shall during the time of divine service stand in white sheets the next Sabbath in the Chappell of Eliza: River, that MR: POWYS shall preach.

GEO: WAKEFIELD & URSULA BAYLY, WILL WATTS & MARY, MR: LLOYDS nexxxx for their severall appearances at the next Court to answer charges agst: them.

THOS: TOOKER & JANE WRIGHT Pltfs: agst: CORNELIUS LLOYD & ELIZABETH his wife referred to the next Court.

107 JAMES SYMONS was commanded not to depart from the Court until he answered the Complaint of CAPT: JOHN SIBSEY .... he did depart and It is therefore ordered that the Sherriffe take SYMONS into his custody......and to answer his contempt the next Court.

JOHN BIGGS hath set up his name at the Court doore to give notice of his intended voyage for England this present shipping.

PRESENT vt antea

It appeares that JOHN ffERINHAUGH stands bound to ye peace & his good behavior in the sume of 10,000 l tob & that he hath forfeited his recognizance if he bee not cleered thereof & he shall appeare the next Court to answer the premises .... Ordered to be recorded.

I, ffRANCIS WELLS of London in the County of Middlesex revoking & recalling a Pow[r]: of Attorney made by me unto PETER PORTER of Elizabeth River in the County of Lower Norff: in Virginia............I do hereby constitute, ordeine & appoynt,in his stead, my well beloved friend THOMAS DADFORD of Elizabeth River and the County aforesaid my true * and lawfull Attorney............................ 107a
Dated 22 Aug 1648 ye signe of ffRANCIS WELLS
Wit: WM: SHIPP, WM: OLIVER

MR: GEO: WHITE DC

Feb 1645/6	
P Sub: p[r]sts MR: COR: LLOYD	xx
P Sub: " JACOB BRADSHAW	xx
P Deposicon MR: COR: LLOYD	xx
P " JAC: BRADSHAWE	xx
Jan 1646/7	
P Subp: p[r]sts ffR: LAND	xx
P his deposicon	xx
P recording thereof P yo[r]: order	xx
P Cop: depos: MR: COR: LLOYD	25
P " " of JAC: BRADSHAWE	25
P Peticon p[r]sts THOROWGOOD	20
P Order " "	15
P Attachmt: to the Sheriffe	30
P entr: p[r]sts JAC: BRADSHAW	04
Feb 1646/7	
P peticon de THOROWGOOD	20
P " p[r]sts BRADSHAW	10
P a long ler: to MR: BENNETT	20
P cop: order de THOROWGOOD	15
P order p[r]sts BRADSHAW Apr 1647	08
P recording a deed of guift	15
Totall is	271

15 Feb 1648/9
This acct: was pved & allowed by the Court

Teste: THO: TAKER CL CUR

108

CAPT: JOHN WEST Gov: granting a patent of 100 acres of land to PETER PORTER upon the East side of Elizabeth River, North upon a Creek running up between this Land and DANIELL TANNER. outh into the woods, West upon a Bay of the River and East upon a branch of the aforesaid Creeke, the said 100 acres of land being due unto him as followeth: 50 acres for his own personal adventure and 50 acres for 1 servant named THO: MAN. * PETER PORTER assigns over unto JESPER HOSKINS 108a*
the above patent 15 Feb 1648/9. PETER PORTER
Wit: RICH: HARROW Teste: THO: TOOKER CL CUR:

108a 17 Feb 1648/9

I WILLIAM BERKELEY Gov. & Capt General of Virginia .... send greeting........Whereas STEPHEN HICKS decd dying intestate leaving an estate ...... whereof THO: SAYER hath made humble suite.....that a Commission of Administration might be granted him.....in behalfe of ye Mother of ye said decedent.....Administration granted to THO: SAYER.............

109 Gov: WILLIAM BERKELEY

RICH: KENMAR late of this Collony deceased dyeing intestate & leaving an estate ...... JOHN KENMAR sonne & heir of the
109a decedent graunted administration of his father's estate.

20 Mar 1648/9

PRESENT: CAPT: JOHN SIBSEY MR: THO: LAMBART MR: MATT: PHILLIPS

Ordered to be Recorded

Invoyce of goods wth MR: THOMAS MARSH of MR: JOSEPH BEAMANS ffeb the 14th 1647.

IN VIRG[a]:

In the margin: [mark] Tob: for the pceeds of these goods to be marked with this mark.

52 yards of broad Cloth
2 peeces of kerseys
a pcell of Irish Stockens 3 doz for men 6 doz for boys &c
(This is a list of various items)
Goods brought by mee to MR: MARSH his house of MR: BEAMANS
(Another list of stockens &c)
The some of ye other side amounts to 21.01.09

110 (Another list of nayles, bootes, &c)

Goods which came in MR: VARNELL 69.03.00

Some is 99.19.09

110a Invoyce of Goods left with MR: THO: MARSH of MR: ABRETHATTS

(In the margin): [mark] Tob for the pceeds of these goods to bee marked with this marke

(Another list of various items) Some is 72.00.00

These pcells mentioned on the other side and written, I, THO: MARSH doe acknowledge to have received of CAPT: WILLIAM LUCK & doe binde myselfe, mine heires, Executors &c.....to be accoumptableunto the above said WILLIAM LUCK or to his assignes for ye pceeds of the said goods or to deliver them .... 15 Feb THO: MARSH
Wit: JOSEPH MAYONE

Invoyce of goods left with MR: THO: MARSH for my pp account 15 Feb 1647/8.

(Another list of gunns, powder, knives and other things)

Some is 07.03.XX

BILLS LEFT WITH MR: MARSH

QUINTON GRAVES his bill for 900 1 tob & caske
MR: JOHN ATTERTON his bill for 2670 1 tob
JOHN VALENTINE & THO: WATERS bill for 1905 1 tob
GILES WEBB his bill for 2063
NICHOLAS BENNETT his bill for 0424 1 tob
ROBERT BIRD his bill for 2300 1 tob
MR: EPAPHRODITUS LAWSON his bill for 0394 1 tob
9657
This bill of 900 1 tob belongeth to the Shipp 900
Totall 10557

Three Indentures made over to MR: PUDDINGTON as alsoe a bond under the hand of GEORGE PUDDINGTON I have taken with mee. 15 Feb 1647/8 THO: MARSH

An Acct: of MR: CORNELIUS LLOYD for 1237 1 tob & Caske
One bill I sent ashoare by JOHN BREWER of MR: IVERSONS for 426 1 tob 14 large looking glasses &c..............
rec: THOMAS MARSH

Whereas there was a Condicon made last yeare by mee GEORGE PUDDINGTON of Lower Norffolke in ye River of Nancemum, Planter, to ship aboarde the Sarah of London, MR: WILLIAM LUCKE, 30 hhds tob within 50 dayes after the arrival of the sd shipp in Virg^{a}: xxx(can't read the next line)xxxxxxxxxx GEORGE PUDDINGTON finding tob to fall shortt have assigned
19 hhds of tob unto MR: ROBT: BOND of London, Merchant,*to 111a*
make sale of them for the best advantage of PUDDINGTON towards paymt of £ 60 sterling unto ye abovesd WILLIAM LUCKE and if ROBT: BOND should nott paye WM: LUCKE... PUDDINGTON binds over unto LUCKE for the paymt of £ 60 Sterling. My three servants & my cropp which please God to send me next yeare. 8 Feb 1647/8 GEORGE PUDDINGTON
Teste: THO: TOOKER CL CUR:

These writings next before recorded concerning CAPT: WILLIAM LUCK & MR: THOMAS MARSH et als pduced & delivered in Court by EDWARD CANNON 20 Mar 1648/9 being taken upp & saved from the wreck of CAPT: LUCKS Ship.

In regard to the unseasonableness of the weather it is thought fitt ye Court bee progned: untill 15 Apr 1649.

Deed of WILLIAM JACOB to WILLIAM BASNETT for 100 acres of land Dated 17 Oct 1644 & Recorded 6 Apr 1649. .... with all rights & privileges as are expressed in the Grand Patent. The aforesaid 100 acres bounding poynt blanck with
his first bounds upon a small fresh runn neare unto the 112
wading place of MR: HENRY WOODHOUSE and soe running for length along the fresh runn and soe by a fresh water pond, the breadth extending from the said wading place Southerly upon the Baye to have and to hold &c....... 17 Oct 1644
Wit: HEN: JORDEN, RICH: HILL

112 9 Apr 1649

ATT A COURT HOLDEN ATT JAMES CITTY 9 pr 1649
PRESENT: SIR WILLIAM BERKELEY Knt. Gov. &c
MR: RICHARD KEMPE CAPT: SAM^{ll}: MATHEWS THO: STEGG)
CAPT: HUMPHREY HIGGINSON GEO: LUDLOWE) ESQRS:

MR: HENRY WOODHOUSE & MR: JOHN HILL shall bee of the Quorum in the Commission of Lower Norfolk County.

112a The Sherr: . . may make his deputy for his under sherr: whoe in matters concerning his minestriall office may wholly execute ye peace in right of ye High Sherr:

They are the Kings Deputyes within theire County and theire Charge is to keepe the Kings peace within theire said County and to suppresse and punish Malefactors there. The Sherr: may not bee abridged of anything xxxx or belonging to his office. SAM: ABBOTT CLR:

(NOTE: THE HANDWRITING CHANGES HERE Probably a new Clerk? It is very hard to read as it is small and full of flourishes which obliterates the lines below. AGW)

ATT A COUNTY COURT HELD 16 Apr 1649
PRESENT: CAPT: JNO: SIBSEY MR: MATH: PHILLIPPS MR: JNO: HILL
MR: THO: LAMBART MR: THOMAS MEARES MR: THOMAS BROWNE

There is an item about the Commissioners or a Commissioner and MR: MATH: PHILLIPPS name is in the item. It is hard to read.

The matter in difference betweene THO: CHOOL? and HEN: ROBINSON is againe referred to the next Court. Chool

Upon the petition of THO: IVY upon the verdict of a Jury concerning a difference depending betweene ye said IVY & TRUST^{m}: MASON about xxxxx Land the Court doth give Judgement thereupon but xxxxxx TRIST^{m}: MASON shall have time till xxxx next to xxxx verdect? and to pay the Court charges.

113 CAPT: JOHN SIBSEY hath impleaded WM: DAINES for detayning a pcell: of the xxxxx land the sd WM: DAINES doth xxxxxxxxx xxxxxxxxxxxxxxxx both parties to appeare upon the 6th day of the next Quarter Court.

THOMAS WRIGHT & LAURENCE PHILLIPPS are Securities for the appearance at Court of WM: DAINES.

LEMUEL MASON ahth made it appear upon oath that there is due unto him 400 acres of land for the transportation: MARGARET CLITHERBY? (Nu gives MARY EITHERBY), DOROTHY WINCKFORD (or WAYNE FORD), ROBT: RUSSELL, THO: WARDS, SARAH WALKER, MARGARET EVEFINES?, THO: REINOLDS & ROBT: WINTER. (Nu 187 - gives Pat. to HEN: BRAKES for 250 acres 13 Mar 1649 with the first 5 head rights listed in this certificate. Nothing in Nu on LEMUELL MASON for this certificate. AGW)

Certificate to THO: ADAMS for 100 acres of land due for the transportation of HEN: HINSON & OLIVER CROSTS.

The difference between CAPT: THO: BURBAGE plt: & CAPT: ffRANCIS YARDLEY deft: upon the peticon of sd YARDLEY is referred to the next Court.

Certificate to WM: DAINES for 200 acres of land for the transportation of four persons: ALEXANDER ASH, ALEXANDER ROGERS, JAMES SCOTT & SARAH MINTORNE.

Attachment against the estate of JOHN ffERINHAUGH for 10,000 l tob and a bond for the peace & his good behavior ....no execution shall issue forth until after the next Quarter Court.

113a

GEO: WAKEFIELD & URSULA BAYLEY servants of THO: WRIGHT were psented by ye Churchwardens of Elizabeth River for Committing of fornicacon....sd parties to do penance in the Chappell of Elizabeth River by wearing a white sheet and a white rod in their hands upon the next Sabbath day.

ffRANCIS LAND was arrested to the Court by JAMES THELABALL but appeareth not. It is ordered that the Sheriff bring security for his appearance to the next Court.

JNO: ROBINS hath impleaded JNO: MERRIDETH for not building of four boates according to articles of agreemt. Merrideth to pforme the sd articles by Xmas next & in the meantime to give security for the pformance.

JNO: POLLARD is non suited & ordered to pay ROBT: DAVIS? 20 l tob for non appearance.

WM: WATTS & MARY [MR: CORNELIUS LLOYDS negro woman] to do penance by standing in a white sheete with a white Rodd in their hands in the Chappel of Elizabeth River in the face of the Congregation.

CON: LLOYD pltf: agst. THO: IVY deft: referred to the next Court.

tho; wright to pay 20 l tob to ffRANCIS HUNT for unjust molestation.

JAMES WARNER granted ltres: of administration on the Estate of BEN: ffOSTER decd.

114

THO: TOOKER Pltf: and JANE WRIGHT Pltf: agst: COR: LLOYD & ELIZA his wife referred to the next Court & the Sheriffe is authorized to summon ANN GODBY to the next Court.

The 19th of April 1649
AT LINHAVEN AT THE HOUSE OF SAVILL GASKIN

PRESENT: MR: HENRY WOODHOUSE MR: MATH: PHILLIPPS
MR: JNO: HILL MR: WM: WHITBY

Ltres: of administration on the Estate of CAPT: WM: LUCK decd. on behalfe of MRIS: -(blank)- LUCK widdow granted unto MR: WM: WHITTBY & MR: RICHARD CONQUEST.

INVENTORY of THOMAS EDWARDS deceased.

	1 tob
1 flock bed & an old Rugg	80
1 old Chest wth Locks & Key	100
1 Pestle and weeding hoe	50
1 frying panne	25
1 hamer, one xxxx	11
3 yards & 1/2 of Linnen @ 6 1 p yard	21
2 grindstones	100
6 barrels of Corne @ 40 1 tob p barrell	240
1 sowe 3 sould for	100
his croppe of tob° the yeare of his decease	420
1 xxxxx	10
1 heifer killed by the wolves & 1 xxxxx shote	...
Appraysed 19 Mar 1648/9 Total	1415

by EDWARD SELBY & RICHARD (X) JENNINGS
Presented in Court & sworn unto by RICHARD OWENS 16 Apr 1649

INVENTORY of STEPHEN HICKS deceased Appraysed by THO: RINGOLD, JAMES WARNER, JNO: BROWNE & THO: HARRINGTON 16 Feb 1648/9. Amounts to 3811 1 tob besides ye cropp which amounts to 1428 1/2 k tob. TOTAL 5249
114a Presented in Court 16 Apr 1649 and sworne to by THOMAS RINGOLD, THO: SAWYERS & JAS: (W) WARREN.

I TRUSTRAM MASON for divers & good causes hath sold unto MR: THOMAS IVY the 1/2 of his devident of Land which sd TRUSTRAM MASON doth now posess, the 1/2 of the cleared land to bee MR: THOMAS IVYS and the 1/2 of the uncleared land likewise. The houses excepted and for ye sd land MR: IVY is to give MR: MASON one sufficient cowe bigge with calfe betweene this & Christmas next. 2 Nov 1644
Teste: JOHN ffINCH Signed: THOMAS IVY TRUSTRAM (M) MASON

I ffRANCIS WELLS of London, co. Middlesex doe recall a letter of attorney made by me unto PETER PORTER of Elizabeth River in Norfolk County Virginia ....and in his stead & place now appoint my well beloved friend THO: XXXXXXX of Elizabeth River this 22 Aug 1648 Signed: ffRA: (X) WELLS
Wit: WM: SHIPP & WM: OLLIVER (name above may be DADFORD?)

26 Feb 1648/9 - ELIZABETH BECK hath today accordinge to a Court Order brought upon oath all such clothing as shee brought with her from her MRS: MRS: JNO: ffERINHAUGH all which appeares to be little enough to satisfye for one working day suite. Whearefore ye said MRS: ffERINHAUGH is to deliver tunto ELIZABETH BECK more: one new petticoate & waiscoate, one new smock, one new paire hose & Apron with headcloth & some head cloaths & 3 barrels of
115 corne. Ordered by us JNO: HILL & THOMAS BROWNE

BENJAMIN ffOSTER decd: late of this Collony died intestate & leaving an estate ....JAMES WARNER being the greatest creditor is granted administration of the estate. 13 May 1649

THE NAMES OF THE VESTRYMEN:

JNO: HILL	MR: CORNELIUS LLOYD
MR: THO: LAMBERT	MR: RICHARD CONQUEST
MR: MATH: PHILLIPPS	MR: THOMAS SAWYER
MR: THO: BROWNE	MR: THOMAS IVY

Att a Meeting of the Vestry upon 14 May 1649 for Elizabeth River Parish. MR: SAMPSON CALVERT nominated & elected & 115a
made choice of by the Vestry to bee theire Minister.
JAMES WARNER elected Churchwarden.
WM: CROUCH for divers reasons well weighed to bee & continue Churchwarden till Easter next xxxxxxx(faded)xxxxxxxxxxxxxxxx
MR: LEMUELL MASON & MR: WM: SHIPP are nominated & elected and are to bee of this xxxxxxx (can't read last word)

Recorded 14 May 1649: I, NELLKIN? LIGHTHART widow of HENRICK LIGHTHART ..... appoint CAPT: ffRANCIS YARDLEY GENT: my attorney. JOHN CLASEN of North Holland, Marriner (he is mentioned in this power of attorney but what it says is not legible. AGW) 14 Aug 1648.
Wit: EDWARD WINDHAM & JON OWNELYS
(This is signed NELLKIN or WELLKIN LIGHTHART her mark)

DANIELL PEIRCE of ye Island of Barbadoes & ye shipp Swallowe now riding at anchor in Virginia ..... discharging & acquiting CAPT: ffRANCIS YARDLEY from all & every bargain accoumpts &c......... 22 Feb 1647/8 116

I DANIELL PEIRCE of ye Island of Barbadoes & of ye shipp Swallowe, Merchant selling to CAPT: FRA: YARDLEY of Linhaven three men & one woman namely Francisco, Emanuell, Antonio -(faded)- and Maria. 22 Feb 1647

Wit: EDW: WINDHAM & JOHN HEALLY Signed: DANIELL PEIRCE

NATHANIELL POWNDALL of ye Citty of Bristoll, England selling negroes to CAPT: ffRANCIS YARDLEY for the use of CAPT: NICOLAS PHILLIPPS of London, Marriner & Comander of ye Merchant friggott. 20 Apr 1649.

116a

Recorded 28 May 1649

SARA THOROWGOOD appointing "my loving brother" JOBE CHANDLER to be my attorney concerning Cowes in the last will & testament "of my father, CAPT: ADAM THOROWGOOD decd."
Wit: EDW: WINDHAM & THOMAS BRIDGE Signed: SARA (S) THOROWGOOD.

Appraisers appointed by RHICHARD CONQUEST High Sheriffe to value a small boat which formerly belonged to JNO: ffERINHAUGH, he being in the boat with some others, the boat turned over and the sd ffERINHAUGH drowned. (The rest of this is faded) Appraisers: THOMAS BRIDGES & TIMOTHY IVES

117

ROBERT PAGE, Marriner of ye Shipp Pliades...xxxxxxxxxxxxxx (This is faded and hard to read)xxxxxx RICHARD KENMAR & His wife are mentioned xxxxxx 6 Apr 1642
Wit: JOHN SIBSEY Signed: ROBT PAGE

117 28 May 1649

ATT A COUNTY COURT HELD 15 Jun 1649

PRESENT: CAPT: THOMAS WILLOUGHBY ESQ:

CAPT: JNO: SIBSEY	MR: MATH: PHILLIPPS
MR: JOHN HILL	MR: THOMAS MEARES
MR: THO: LAMBART	MR: THOMAS BROWNE

This day THO: BRIDGES was admitted & sworne Clerke of ye Court. (Is is hoped that the script will now be easier to read with a new Clerk. AGW)

MR: RICH: CONQUEST plt: agst: CAPT: THO: WILLOUGHBY referred to the next Court.

Probate is granted unto DEBORAH ffERINHAUGH widow of the last Will & Testament of JNO: ffERINHAUGH her husband deceased.

JNO: WILLIAMS to deliver up a bill xxxxx faded xxxxxxxxxxx LEMUEL MASON stands indebted unto ye sd WILLIAMS before ye next Court.

15 Jun 1649

CAPT: ffRA: YARDLEY hath caused CAPT: JNO: CLAUSON to bee arrested in an accon (action) of defamation & having made appear no ground or cause since. It is ordered y^t ye sd CAPT: YARDLEY bee non suited & pay 20 l tob for unjust molestacon.......... (see also Clayson and Clasen)

Whereas CAPT: FRA: YARDLEY as atty of ELLEN LIGHTHART widd: hath impleaded CAPT: JNO: CLAUSON upon no just cause of suite but upon unnessesory & xx faded xxx It is therefore ordered that xxxxxxx YARDLEY to pay CLAUSON 150 l tob for charges for wrongful molestacon.

117a Probate of the will of EDWARD HODGE, Merchant decd. granted to MR: CORNELIUS LLOYD according to ye tenor of ye will.

THO: TOOKER to pay charges for non-appearance unto CAPT: THO: WILLOUGHBY

Upon ye oaths of MR: HENRY CATELEN? and ROBT: KETT it appears to ye Court that MR: EDW: LLOYD was made ye lawfull attorney of THO: LEE & by reason the house of ye sd LLOYD with all his writings was by disaster burnt as he sayeth.. .....LLOYD to be reimbursed with ye same power as he had when his letters of atturney was Extant.

A cow formerly belonging to MR: RICHARD KENMAR decd was sett upon & xx faded xxx in ye ground of MRS: JULIAN now ye wife of WM: SHIPP. MRS: JULIAN wife of WM: SHIPP ordered to pay MR: RICH: CONQUEST guardian unto JNO: KENMAR ye administrator of ye decedent RICH: KENMAR.

THO: TOOKER & JANE? WRIGHT plts: agst: MR: CORNELIUS LLOYD & ELIZA: his wife to the next Court.

THO: MARSH pltf: agst: DEBORAH ffERINHAUGH widd: concerning a boy servant which frequently doth runne away & as is generally xxxxxxx xxxxxxxx & want of apparel. It is ordered that ye sd boy servant shall remain with MR: LAMBARD till

DEBORAH doe send clothing for him.........................

We do present THOS: TOOKER for misbehavior toward the wife of JASPER HOSKINS. Signed: JOHN HILL & WM: CROUCH

LAURENCE PHILLIPPS appointed Constable for Elizabeth River 118

THOS: WRIGHT appointed Constable for Western Branch

ABRAHAM THO: (sic) appointed CONSTABLE for Eastern Branch

RICH: FOSTER appointed Constable for the Eastern Shore at Linhaven.

JOSEPH CURCH (CHURCH?) appointed Constalbe for Little Creek

WM: NOTT pltf: agst: WM: DAINES deft: to next Court.

Corne & Tobacco for MR: ROBT: POWIS tythes to be brought in to MR: THO: LAMBARD

150 acres of land due unto TIMOTHY IVES by ye gift of MR: WILLIAM CHURCH decd. due ye sd CHURCH for his severall transportations into this Colony.

A Patent dated 16 Jul 1636 for 200 acres granted unto MR: ffRANCIS TOWERS. It is the opinion & Judgement of ye Comr^{s}: who well know ye sd land that CORNELIUS LLOYD who now injoyes the same is to have his breadth upon ye Western Branch of Elizabeth River & so to Runne a myle backwards to wards ye maine River being James River and that Elizabeth is Cxxxxxxxx or deemed to begine at a point called Cranney Point.

CAPT: ROBERT PAGE aged about 42 yeares sayeth that he did pay ..... unto ye wife of RICH: KENMAR the full product of 2 hhds of tob which he received of ye sd RICH: KENMAR in 1642...............................ROBT: PAGE
Teste: THOMAS BRIDGES (His script is no better than before)

I JNO: ffERINHAUGH of Elizabeth River Planter.............
Will dated 7 Jun 1648 Will probated 12 Jul 1649 118a
He left "all he possessed" to his wife DEBORAH and appointed her his executrix.
Wit: ED: HALL Chirurgeon & GEO: HEIGHAM. Both witnesses proved the will.

SIR: WM: BERKELEY knt: Gov: granting probate of the will of JOHN ffERINHAUGH's will to his wife DEBORAH. 31 Jul 1649

EDWARD HODGE of Virginia Merchant
Will dated 20 (or 10) Jun 1649 Will probated 15 Jun 1649
......loving friend MR: CORNELIUS LLOYD doe receive all such goods & servants as shall be consigned to mee this next shipping out of England & that the said LLOYD be accountable for ye sd goods & servants to my loving Brother MR: SAMUEL HODGE, Merchant in Broad (Hurst?) & that ye sd LLOYD doe make (returnes?) of ye same according to order to him from my sd brother......unto WM: ROBINSON (Cowy?) all my wearing

Apparell & all other things thereunto belonging which I have
119* now att JNO: MARTINS in Linhaven.........*unto my loveing frend CORNELIUS LLOYD my plantation in Linehaven which I bought of CAPT: ffRANCIS YARDLEY, also all debts due unto me and all other of my estate in Virginia.

CORNELIUS LLOYD Executor; (will is not signed)
Proved to be the last will of EDWARD HODGE
Witnesses: Teste: THOS: BRIDGE CL CUR:
MATHEW HOWARD, GEORGE RIDLEY

ATT A COUNTY COURT HELD 16 Nov 1648 (sic)

PRESENT:	CAPT: JNO: SIBSEY	MR: THO: MEARES
	MR: THO: LAMBARD	MR: JOHN HILL
	MR: MATH: PHILLIPPS	MR: THO: BROWNE

Land in Controversy betweene JOSEPH BIRCH & HENRY SNAILE & we hould our opinion that GOODMAN BIRCH is to have three whole necks to the (merch?) that is next to SNAILES soe along to the grand paten of CAPTAIN ADAM THOROWGOOD wheare unto wee have set our heads 13 Apr 1649 and soe from ye Black (Humpe?) his breadth according to ye grand patent BARTHO: HOSKINS, ROBERT HAYES, GYLES COLLINS, JNO: HOLMES

119a HENRY SNAILE of ye Little Creek in Lynhaven Parish Deed dated 12 Feb 1648/9 to HENRY WESTGATE .....one neck of land being some of the devident of land granted by pattent unto ROBERT HAYES by HON: WM: BERKELEY Knt. Gov. & by HAYES sould unto mee (HENRY SNAILE) the wch land is by survey found to contain 110 acres & bounded: Beginning at an ould former xxxxxxxxxx tree by ye water Damms side so running 266 poles up a long ye ould marked trees WSW to a quarter marked tree in ye oaken swampe from thence running XXX poles SSE to another mked tree from thence ENE with mked trees over a beaver dam down to ye dams side.......from thence to ye first station. Bounded with ye dams aforesaid 110 acres & likewise one pcell of land next adjoining to the former menconed xxxxxxx lieing betweene ye former tract xxxxxxxx & ye beaver dams & marked trees along ye Path that crosseth xxxxxxx REINOLDS his necks xxxxx 12 Feb 1648/9
Wit: WM: MORE & THOMAS WARDE Signed: HENRY H S SNAILE

13 May 1649 - SARAH JULIAN widd: of Lower Norfolk County Deed of Gift unto SARAH KEMPE the daughter of GEORGE KEMPE of ye same County, Planter 2 Cow Calves...................
Teste: THO: BRIDGE CL CUR: Signed: SARAH HS SNAILE

120 The deposition of JOSIAS MULDERS aged 23 yeares of thereabouts sworne sayeth that DEBORAH ffERINHAUGH his Mistress did beate her Mayde Servant in the quartering house before the xxxxxxx more like a dogge than a Christian and that at a Certaine time I felt her head which was beaten so soft as a springe in our xxxxx and thatthere was a wording shee complayned and said her backbone as shee thought was

Broken which beating and that I did see the mayds arms naked which was full of black & blue bruises & pinches & her necke likewise & afterwards I told my MRis: of it & sayd that 2 or 3 blows could not make her in such a case....... (there is more to this but is very hard to read)

MICHAELE MCKAYE aged 22 yeares or thereabouts, his depo= sition - He swore to the deposition of JOSIAS MULDERS. Teste: THOMAS BRIDGE CL CUR:

Upon the depositions of JOSIAS MULDERS & MICHAELL MCKAYE of ye misusages of CHARATIE DOLLEN by her Mris: DEBORAH ffERINHAUGH & by many other often complaints by others sufficient testimonies & although the sd DEBORAH hath had advertisemt thereof from ye Court & has persisted in ye very Ill usadges of her sd servant.........It is therefore ordered that ye sd CHARATIE shall no longer remain in the house or service of her Mris: but is to be continued at ye house of MR: THOMAS LAMBARD until such time as DEBORAH ffER-INHAUGH dye or otherwise dispose of her sd servant

120a

ATT A COUNTY COURT HELD 15 Aug 1649
PRESENT: CAPT: JNO: SIBSEY MR: MATH: PHILLIPPS
MR: JNO: HILL, MR: THO: LAMBARD, MR: THO: BROWNE

Whereas MR: EDWARD LLOYD, & MR: THO: MEARES COMRS:, EDWARD SELBY, RICHARD DAY, RICHARD OWENS, THO: MARSH, GEORGE KEMPE, JNO: NORWOOD were presented to the board by the High Sher-iff for not repairing to theire Parish Church and refusing to heare Comon Prayer which is contrary to sevll (sic) statutes ordered that these psons: shall have Liberty till ye 1 Oct next xxxfadedxxxxx & to confirm thesselves & to make personall appearance upon ye 1 Oct for such action as shall be thought fitt.

MR: RICH: CONQUEST Pltf: not appearing is non suited & ordered to pay CAPT: THOS: WILLOUGHBY 155 1 tob in full of all Charges.

Mris: MASON supenoed to August Court in case of RICH: CONQUEST & CAPT: THO: WILLOUGHBY

CAPT: ROBT: PAGE atty of HUGH MIDDLETON to deliver to THO: BEST a bond of ₤ 60 sterling where ye sd BEST stands in-debted to ROBT: BEST decd whose wife ye sd MIDDLETON marr-ied & ROBT: PAGE to pay 200 1 tob for Court charges.

121

To the Worrshipfull CAPT: JNO: SIBSEY with the rest of the Comrs: ffor Lower Norfolk County. (This is a long full page record about everyone over 16 years of age being required to go to Church. So much of it is faded......... the punishment decided on, for those accused on f 120a for non attendance cannot be read with.

Signed: RICHARD CONQUEST
High Sheriff

121a 15 Aug 1649

Certificate to BARTHOLOMEW HOSKINS for 50 acres of land due for the transportation of THOMAS CAKEBREAD?

CAPT: ROBT: PAGE to pay MR: EDW: MAJOR -amount is faded - CAPT: SIBSEY is the security for MR: PAGE.

THO: BRIDGE administrator for the children of ROGER ffLETCHER decd. pltf: & CAPT: THO: WILLOUGHBY ESQ: administrator of RICH: WAKE decd. deft: referred to the next Court.

MR: RICHARD CONQUEST pltf: assignee of THOS: TOOKER agst: CAPT: THO: WILLOUGHBY ESQ: to the next Court.

WM: DAINES to pay account of 400 l tob to WM: NOTT

Attachmt: graunted agst: the Estate of OWEN MORGANE being departed out of this Collony for 730 l tob at the sute of THO: DAVIS..............

122 CAPT: ffRANCIS YARDLEY to pay 3497 l tob & Caske to CAPT: THO: BURBAGE

JAMES THE LA BALL pltf: agst: LEMUELL MASON deft: that GEORGE HORNER shall agst: the next Court, make, appraise, upon oath, what quantity of planke hee received of the sd MASON for the use of sd THE LA BALL & what shal bee wanting of 2000 foote, the sd MASON is to make good as soone as hee can podce: (produce) planck to bee sawed wth ye first Conveniency and ye sd MASON is to signe a deed of halfe HOGGS ISLAND when the sd THE LA BALL shall demand the same

MR: THO: LAMBARD granted administration on the estate of PATRICK EGERTON decd.

WM: CROUCH & JAMES WARNER Churchwardens of Elizabeth River Parish have exhibited their presentmts: unto the board agst: RICHARD STARNELL, CAPT: THO: WILLOUGHBY ESQ:, MR: RICH: CONQUEST Sherr: MICHAELL LAURENCE, WM: JOHNSON and his wife, MARY, SIMON PETER & his wife ALOE, CHRISTOPHER WICKSTED & his wife MARGERY, EDWARD WINDET & his wife MARY........... It is ordered that warrants doe issue forth all the sd psons: for their personall appearance at the next Court to make answer to ye sd psentmts:

ABRAHAM THOMAS Constable of ye Eastern Branch of Elizabeth River (this item is badly faded) a warrant for GEORGE HIGHAMS appearance at the next Court.

122a It is ordered that RICHARD ffOSTER, JOSEPH BURCH, ABRAHAM THOMAS, THOMAS WRIGHT & LAWRENCE PHILLIPPS Constables shall take a list of tytheable psons within theire limitts & exhibit the same unto the Court to bee holden on the first of Oct next.

This Court to be proreged? untill ye first of Oct next & all business now depending then to bee heard & determined
....

PATRICK EGERTON decd: & dieing intestate, administration of his estate is granted unto THOMAS LAMBARD as creditor. 23 Aug 1649 Recorded 31 Aug 1649 WILLIAM BERKELEY 123

20 Jan 1648 - Recorded 31 Aug 1649 GEORGE HEIGHAM to pay unto SIMON OVERZEE Merchant & THO: LAMBARD GENT: or either of them 602 l tob upon 10 Oct next for the whole 100 acres of land that I GEO: HEIGHAM doe now enjoy.
Teste: THO: TOOKER CL CUR: Signed: GEO: HEIGHAM

ATT A COURT HELD 1 Oct 1649
PRESENT: CAPT: JOHN SIBSEY
MR: JNO: HILL MR: MATH: PHILLIPPS
MR: THO: LAMBARD MR: THO: BROWNE

Certificate to JOANE YEATES widdow for 150 acres of land for ye transportation of: JONATHAN BARTRAM, ANNE WINN, & WALTER CANSINGTON.

Certificate to HENRY NICHOLS for 100 acres of land due for the transportation of himselfe & ANNE HARDING his wife.

Certificate to HUMPHREY BELT for 50 acres of land due for the transportation of MARGERY CRAGGES, his wife.(see Nu289)

TO APPEARE AT JAMES CITTY: 123a

MR: EDWARD LLOYD Comr: for not attending Church & for obstinately refusing to heare Common prayer.
MR: THOMAS MEARES Comr: for not coming to Church
EDW: SELBY for not coming to Church
RICH: DAY for not coming to Church
RICHARD OWENS for not coming to Church
THO: MARSH for not coming to Church
GEORGE KEMPE for not coming to Church
JNO: NORWOOD for not coming to Church

WM: POWELL, non appearance at Court to answer the sute of RICH: SMITH atty: of SAMUELL MATHEWES to the next Court.

NICOLAS WYETT found guilty of crimes & misdemeanors its ordered that he be clappt up in Irons and deliver him to the Sherrif of James Citty to answer before the Governor & Counsel

RICHARD STARNELL to pay 1820 l tob & Caske to ENSIGNE THO: LAMBART GENT:

It is the jdgmt: of this Court that JOANE YEATES now the wife of RICH: YEATES is now x[r]t (xrt) of BENJAMIN ffOSTERS Estate and that it doth appeare to the Court that 124
the sd JOANE was a free woman when the sd YEATES married her. (This is the complete item. It is confusing for the xrt may mean executtrix, but at first it looked like "noe prt. The first letter is most likely an x as it does not match the letter p in this clerk's script. AGW)

124 1 Oct 1649

SUSAN RIVERS of Ratcliffe Parish of Stepney in co. Midd: widdow appoints my trusty friend CAPT: THOMAS WILLOUGHBY of Virginia my atturney to review (all things) due unto me as wife unto ROBERT RIVERS decd: due to me in Virginia. Mr atturney to receive of MR: MICHAELL (Pxxxxxx?) of Virginia or THOMAS KERBIE all such monies as may be due unto me. 10 Jul 1647 SUSAN RIVERS
Wit: SAMUELL WADE & THOMAS SMART
(NOTE: This name may not be RIVERS. It could be ROEVRES which makes one wonder if the name is ROUVIERE? The name is badly faded in each place it has been written. Both RIVERS & ROUVIERE were familiar names in the area.)

124a

ATT A COURT HELD AT THE HOUSE OF THOMAS IVIES
31 Oct 1649

PRESENT: CAPT: JNO: SIBSEY
MR: JNO: HILL MR: MATH: PHILLIPPS
MR: THO: LAMBARD MR: THO: BROWNE

CAPT: THO: WILLOUGHBY administrator of RICH: WAKE decd to pay 1000 l tob & Caske unto THOMAS BRIDGE administrator of ROGER ffLETCHER decd:

CAPT: THOS: WILLOUGHBY ESQ: to pay unto RICHARD CONQUEST Assignee of THO: TOOKER -xxxx- hundred & 87 l tob for fees

EDWARD HODGE decd: was indebted to JNO: MARTIN for balance of account 423 l tob for diett. CORNELIUS LLOYD executor to HODGES shall pay MARTIN.

CORNELIUS LLOYD Executor of EDW: HODGE ordered to pay: unto WM: SHIPP by bill 700 l tob & Caske; unto BARTHO: HOSKINS 700 l tob.

At the request of MR: EDWARD LLOYD order obtained by LLOYD agst: MR: THO: CEELY on behalf of NATHANIEL STAINSMORE dated 23 Feb 1647/8.....faded.......revived?..............

Debt to SAMUELL MATHEWS to be paid by WM: POWELL unto RICH: SMITH atty: of MATHEWS.

125 THOS: CAUSON did tender to the Sherr: towards redemtion of his body certaine land lying in Linhaven which sd land xxxxfadedxxxx by former patents & otherxxxxxxxxxxxxxxxxxx incombered as is alleged to the Court. Therefore ordered that CAUSON shall produce sufficient security to ye Comrs: at ye next Court for ye Condicons peaceable xxxxxxx Injoying of ye sd land in such manner as by condicon under xxxxxxxx appeareth and as the Court shall approve it.

JASPER HOSKINS agst the estate of ROBT: WOODY for 690 l tob & 3 barrels of Corne with a paire of bloves which Corne & tob in ye hands of sd HOSKINS & to be liable for satisfaction at further determination of the Court.

Judgment acknowledged by JASPER HOSKINS for 210 l tob & caske unto GEORGE KEMPE.

THO: KEMPE to pay debt to JOSEPH BURCH 1 tonne of caske and 337 l tob.

BARTH°: HOSKINS did acknowledge that he tooke up 800 acres pf land according to the contents of a Pattent sould to MR: THO: TODD dated 1 Jan 1645.

WM: POWELL stands indebted to SAMUELL CHARMORE by account 495 l tob. Ordered that paymt: be made.

An Attachmt: granted unto SAMUELL CHARMORE agst: the estate of BART°: RENOK for 200 l tob & 1 barrel of Indian Corne.

Certificate to JOHN MARTIN for 200 acres of land due for the transportation of FA: STUART, ELIZABETH BROOKES, JOHN BOWERING & THO: BAXFORD. 125a

An order dated 15 Aug 1649 for 3497 l tob obtained agst: CAPT: ffRANCIS YARDLEY by CAPT: THOS: BURBAGE............ all proceedings to stop and both to make appearance.

A judgmt: is acknowledged by MICHAELL LAURENCE for 1050 l tob & Caske unto MR: MATH: PHILLIPPS.

WM: MARGARETT to appear at the next Court or his Securities to stand xxxxxxxxxxxxxxx

JOSEPH BURCH ordered to furnish ye wife of SAMUELL CHARMOORE with clothing.

COMMISSIONERS TO MEET AT THE HOUSE OF CAPT: JNO: SIBSEY ON 10 Nov 1649

31 Oct 1649 - Matters of sute depending agst: LAURENCE PHILLIPPS & ANNE his wife to the next Court.

Certificate to JNO: CUBBIGH for 50 acres of land due for the transportation of JOANE WELCHE.

31 Oct 1649 - Probate of JNO: WATTKINS decd: granted to ffRANCIS, wife of ye decedent.

Certificate to THO: TOD(D) for 50 acres of land due for the transportation of ELIZ: BARNARD.

Ordered that Warrants doe issue forth for ye personall appearance of all those psons: herein named [VIZT:]

* ARTHUR EGLESTONE & MARY his wife 126
JA: THE LA BALLE & ELIZ: his wife
MR: SAMPSON CALVERT, Clerke
LAU: PHILLIPPS & ANNE his wife
MR: CORNELIUS LLOYD
DEBORAH ffERINHAUGH now ye wife of GEO: HIGHAM
JNO: SMITH

LAURENCE PHILLIPPS formerly licensed to keepe an ordinary & to retaile brew, wine & strong waters and now the sd LAURENCE & his wife having misdemeanered themselves in a high manner & suffered many disorders in their house. It is therefore ordered that the sd LAURENCE PHILLIPPS shall not from hence forward keepe any now ord^{ry} nor sell any brew, wines or strong waters........until they have answered misdemeanors to ye satisfaction of the Court.

COURT TO BE HELD AT THE HOUSE OF THO: IVY THE LAST DAY OF NOVEMBER 1649

INVENTORY of EDW: HODGE decd. taken 19 Sep 1649. Appraysed by CAPT: EDWARD WINDHAM & JNO: MARTIN.

	1 tob
2 cloth clokes	300
1 parcel of Copper headbands	60
1 ould Dublett & 1 ould breeches	20
5 yards xxxxx & holland	30
1 Citterne	20
1 case of pistols	60
2 books	50
1/2 xx of cards	10
1 prospective glass	3
1 old paire of tables	30
1 old boate 2 oares 1 sayle Rudder & Tiller	300
1 old xxxxx 2 old gunns	150
	1133

126a INVENTORY OF EDWARD HODG taken 5 Oct 1649 Praysed by RICHARD STARNELL & JOHN ffINCH.

1 overworn suitt & coat	40
1 old hatt & 1 pr of ould shooes & stockings) 1 ould pr: stirrop stockings)	20

Sworne to by CORNELIUS LLOYD 31 Oct 1649

Teste: THOMAS BRIDGE CL CUR:

19 Oct 164? Recorded 31 Oct 1649 - WILLIAM JULIAN selling 200 acres of land to ROBERT TAYLOR of Elizabeth River, Planter, which is part of a pattent of 500 acres being a neck of land upon the south turning of ye said River. East upon a Creeke & South upon a Creeke & North into ye woods as is bounded in the patent bearing date 22 Jul 1634. (see Nu 48)
Wit: ABRAHAM WEEKES, WILL: HANCOCK
ROBERT TAYLOR sells this 200 acres to EDWARD DORSEY 20 Oct 1649.

127 WM: BERKELEY Knt & Gov. &c granting a Patent of 800 acres in Lower Norfolk County unto MR: BARTH^{o}: HOSKINS on ye Northward side of ye Easterne Branch of Elizabeth River & beginning at a marked tree standing on a point by ye Maine Branch side and runningfor length by East 476 poles unto a marked white oak & so East by South 400 pole unto a marked Maple tree & so West by North 149 pole unto a marked pine standing by ye head of a creeke called HOSKINS

Creeke & so running down by or nye on ye Westward side of
sd creeke unto a marked pine standing on a point at ye mouth
of ye sd creeke & from ye sd pine running down by or by or 127a
nye on ye Maine Branch side unto the first mentioned marked
tree. Due for transportation of 16 persons.
Dated 1 Jan 1645 signed: WM: BERKELEY
Recorded 31 Oct 1649
HOSKINS assigns his right over to THO: TODD 31 Oct 1649.
Teste: THO: BRIDGES

JOHN WATKINS will dated 20 Feb 1648 Will Pro: 31 Oct 1649
..... my plantation whereon I now live unto my beloved wife
ffRANCIS WATKINS untill my sonne JOHN WATKINS come fully to
the age of 16 years & then hee to have -(faded)- acres of
cleare & plantable ground to occupy & manner to his own
personal use & benefitt & when hee my sonne is at age of
21 yeares then to have the 1/2 of the full devident [the
dwelling houses excepted] & after ye decease of my wife
he shall enjoy the whole devident and in case my son JOHN
shall die before 21 yeares then the plantation to be
divided into equall parts & shares according to my moveable
goods. 2 The rest of my whole estate......to my wife...... 128
during her widowhood & if she marry estate to be divided
......betwixt so many of my Children as shall then be
living & unmarried.......well beloved friends MR: PHILLIPP
BENNETT & MR: EDW: LLOYD to be overseers. JOHN (+) WATKINS
Wit: RICHARD OWENS, THO: MASH (M) & MATHEW READ
Will was proved by RICHARD OWENS & MATHEW READ
Teste: THO: BRIDGE CL CUR:

13 Nov 1649

COUNTY LEVIES TO BE PAID:
RICH: CONQUEST Hi: Sheriff paid 500 l tob for a prison
out of the County Levies for this present year
paid 1050 for boate hire & mens wages
paid 1099 for charges concerning MR: DURAND
MR: RICH: BENNETT ESQR: paid in full of an order of Court
dated 15 Nov 1647 3246 l tob
MR: BART^{o}: HOSKINS pait 3246 l tob as per acct: being Burgess
MR: THOS: LAMBARD paid 2250 l tob per account being Burgess
ROBERT EYRES paid 240 l tob as being Burgess
MR: JOB CHANDLER his account as being Burgess 400 l tob
LANCASTER LOVETT paid for 4 wolfes heads 400 l tob
GYLES ROLLINS paid for 1 wolfes head 100 l tob
SIMON BARROWS paid for 1 wolfes head 100 l tob
MYLES LINTON paid for 3 wolves heads 300 l tob
RICHARD KING paid for 1 wolfes head 100 l tob
RICHARD WOOLMAN paid for 1 wolfes head 100 l tob
GEORGE KEMPE paid for 1 wolfes head 100 l tob
PEETER HILL paid for 2 wolves heads 200 l tob
ffRANCIS ffLEETWOOD paid for a wolfes head 100 l tob
RICHARD JENNINGS paid for a wolfes head 100 l tob
JNO: WILLIAMS paid for a wolfes head 100 l tob

128

WM: LUCAS paid for a wolfes head 100 l tob
ANDREW WARNER paid for a wolfes head 100 l tob
EDWARD COOPER paid for a wolfes head 100 l tob
SIMON PETERS paid for a for a wolfes head 100 l tob

128a

HENRY WOODHOUSE to collect tythes for Eastern Shore of
Lynhaven River for 72 tytheables and to pay as followeth:
WILLIAM LUCAS to be paid 100 l tob for a wolfes head
JOHN WILLIAMS to be paid 100 l tob for a wolfes head
ANDREW WARNER to be paid 100 l tob for a wolfes head
EDWARD COOPER to be paid 100 l tob for a wolfes head
MR: JOB CHANDLER to be paid for beeing Burgess
MR: RICH: BENNETT ESQ: in prt:
MR: JNO: CORKER
To himselfe for Sallery (figures are faded)

CAPT: JOHN SIBSEY is appointed to collect tythes from
Daniell Tanners Creek downewards to CAPT: WILLOUGHBYS.
40 tytheables & to pay as followeth:
SIMON PETTERS to be paid for a wolfes head 100 l tob
MR: RICHARD BENNETT in full 1655
To himself for Sallery

MR: JOHN HILL is appointed to collect tythes for the
Western Branch including MR: WM: DAINES for 69 tytheables
and to pay as followeth:
129 PEETER HILL to be paid for 2 wolves heads 200 l tob
ffRANCIS ffLEETEWOOD to be paid for a wolfes head 100 l tob
RICHARD JENNINGS to be paid for a wolfes head 100 l tob
MR: RICHARD CONQUEST Sherr: in part 2627 1/4 l tob
To himselfe for sallery 302 l tob
MR: THOMAS LAMBARD is appointed to collect tythes for
ye Easterne & Southern Branches including MR: GEORGE
HEIGHAM for 84 tytheables and to pay as followeth:
MYLES LINTON to be paid for 3 wolves heads 300 l tob
RICHARD KING to be paid for 1 wolfes head 100 l tob
RICHARD WOOLMAN to be paid for 1 wolfes head 100 l tob
GEORGE KEMPE to be paid for 1 wolfes head 100 l tob
To himselfe being Burgess 2288 l tob
MR: ROBERT EYRES to be paid remainder for being Burgess 240
MR: JNO: CORKER in part 557
To himselfe for Sallery 360 l tob
Total 4053

MR: MATHEW PHILLIPPS is appointed to collect tytheables in
Little Creek & the Western Shore of Lynnhaven River for
115 tytheables and to pay as follows:
LAN: LOVETT to be paid for 4 wolves heads 400 l tob
GYLES COLLYNS to be paid for 1 wolfes head 100 l tob
SIMON BARROES to be paid for 1 wolfes head 100 l tob
MR: BART^{o}: HOSKINS for being Burgess 978 l tob
MR: RICH: CONQUEST in full 525 3/4 l tob
MR: JNO: CORKER in full 2841 l tob
To himselfe for Sallery 504 l tob Totall 5548 3/4

ATT A COURT HELD 20 NOV 1649 AT MR: IVIES

PRESENT: CAPT: JNO: SIBSEY
MR: HENRY WOODHOUSE MR: JNO: JILL
MR: THOMAS LAMBARD MR: THO: BROWNE

MR: SAMPSON CALVERT Minister of Elizabeth River Parish hath acknowledgd to have Committed ye grevious sinne of adultry with ANNE ye wife of LAURENCE PHILLIPPS: Now upon ye hearty *contrition of ye sd MR: CALVERT concerning his sd fowle 129a*
offence presented to ye Court in writing under his owne hand. It is therefore ordered that hee do make the same confession in both Churches by reading ye sd writing to ye people two severall Sundays vizt: Sunday next come Senight at ye Parish Church & ye Sabbath day following at ye Chappell.

Whereas LAURENCE PHILLIPPS & ANNE his wife used most undecent & ungodly talke & Communicacon & thereby have slandered & greatly defamed many severall persons of good and known reputation Vizt: MR: THO: LAMBARD, MR: MATH: PHILLIPPS CAPT: THO: BURBAGE, MR: RICHARD CONQUEST, MR: CORNELIUS LLOYD, MR: THOMAS MARSH & THOMAS BRIDGE, MRIS: ELIZ: SIBSEY, MRIS: ELIZ: LLOYD & DIVERS OTHERS as appears by ye testimony of ye sd MR: CALVERT upon oath. It is thereupon ordered that ye sd LAURENCE PHILLIPPS & ANNE his wife............ for 2 severall Sundays......stand at ye great door........ with a paper on their heads with names of all those they have defamed & ......pay Court Charges & also refrain from keeping an ordinary.

MORE PRESENT: MR: MATH: PHILLIPPS

GEORGE HEIGHAM now ye husband of DEBORAH ffERINHAUGH to pay debt of 2703 l tob to THOMAS MARSH.

ATT A COURT HELD 30 Nov 1649 130

PRESENT: CAPT: JNO: SIBSEY MR: THO: LAMBARD
MR: JOHN HILL MR: THO: BROWNE

.... ye Sheriff, on Monday next, to put ye sd MR: WM: MOSELEY in possession of ye houses & plantation which hee hired of agreement proved by several testimonies upon oath GEORGE HEIGHAM to pay all Court Charges.

PEETER CALLOWHILL was bound servant to WM: DAINES for the terme of 7 yeares & the sd DAINES pretending that ye sd CALLOWHILL hath not served his full time of service ye Court hath therefore granted an attachment against the estate of the sd CALLOWHILL in ye custody of the sd DAINES upon further determination of the Court.

Upon petition of MR: THOMAS LAMBARD an attachment is granted against so much of the estate of HENRY MERRITT as will make satisfaction for 403 3/4 l tob due by bill.

THOMAS WRIGHT shall pay unto GEO: WAKEFIELD corne & clothes due to him for service according to the Custom of the County.

CORNELIUS LLOYD granted an attachment agst: JOHN STRATTON for 10,000 l tob & Caske.

COURT ADJOURNED because the unseasonableness of the weather.

130a ATT A COURT HELD 19 DEC 1649 ATT MR: IVIES
PRESENT: CAPT: JNO: SIBSEY MR: THO: LAMBART
MR: JNO: HILL MR: THO: BROWNE

An attachment is granted BARTHO: HOSKINS agst: JNO: BAYLY for 508 l tob.

WM: SHIPP pltf: agst: FRA: LAND deft: for 768 l tob & Caske. LAND ordered to make payment.

An attachment granted RICH: SMITH agst:HENRY MERRITT for 1064 l tob & Caske.

Upon ye confession of JNO: COOKE y[t] he owed EDWARD HODGE decd: 140 l tob & Caske. It is ordered y[t] ye sd COOKE shall pay unto MR: CORNELIUS LLOYD executor of sd HODGE decd ye aforesd ls tob & Caske within 10 dayes......

Upon mutual consent of RICH: WORSTER plt: & JOHN CARRAWAY deft: certifyed to ye Court by MR: THO: LAMBART & THO: TOOKER....case depending to the next Court.

CAPT: ffRA: YARDLEY to pay CORNELIUS LLOYD assignee of ROBT: HOLT 3420 l tob & Caske.

SIMON HANCOCKE to gather ROBT: POWIS tythes in ye Easterne Branch & to call a Vestry on Easter next.

Ordered that GEORGE HEIGHAM pay JOAN YEATES 40 l tob for all her former troubles in coming to Court.

Upon request of MR: CORNELIUS LLOYD it is ordered y[t] ye Sherr: shall place testimonie in a Case depending betweene ye sd LLOYD plt: & CAPT: ROBT: PAGE deft: about his returning ye writte executed & agreed by tomorrow morning
131* by Eyght of ye Clock & if in Case of non appearance*the sd LLOYD to xxxxx according to his petition.

MICHAEL LAURENCE & FRANCES ye wife of WM: JOHNSON presented by the Churchwardens for committing fornicacon. It is ordered that ye sd LAURENCE shall pay halfe the charges towards ye building of a bridge over ye Creeke betweene CAPT: SIBSIES & MR: CONQUEST plantation and that ye sd ffRANCIS to have 15 lashes on ye bare back after she is delivered of ye child which is conceived she now goeth with all. (This is the way this ends)

CAPT: THO: WILLOUGHBY, MR: RICH: CONQUEST, JNO: WILLIAMS & MARY his wife, SIMON PEETER & ALOE his wife, CHRISTO: WICKSTED & MARGERY his wife, GEO: HEIGHAM & DEBORAH his wife, JAMES THE LA BALLE & ELIZ: his wife, ARTHUR EGLESTONE & MARY his wife, LAURENCE PHILLIPPS & ANNE his wife, RICHARD HARNELL, MR: CORNELIUS LLOYD were presented by WM: CROUCH

& JA: WARNER Churchwardens. It is ordered that every of the foresaid pties: shall pay theire severall Charges.

JAMES THE LA BALL deft: to pay 29 l tob to WM: MERRITT plt:

JA: THE LA BALL deft: agst: WM: MERRITT pltf:. MERRITT to pay 2400 l tob & Court Charges.

THOMAS WRIGHT is indebted unto GEORGE WAKEFIELD his service some clothing according to the custom of the County....... to pay WAKEFIELD Clothing, corne &c.......

It is ordered that JANE ye wife of THO: WRIGHT shall prove to ye next Court two depositions that GEO: WAKEFIELD should have said that if MR: HILL & MR: BROWNE had not counselled ye sd WAKEFIELD that hee ye sd WAKEFIELD had served a yeare longer & if in Case they do not prove it to undergoe ye sensur (censure?) of ye Court.

EDWARD WILDER deft: arrested to ye Court by MR: LEMUEL MASON & appeareth not....to the next Court........

MR: ROBT: POWIS to pay unto MR: WM: SHIPP 408 l tob.

Upon peticon of THOMAS BROWNE an attachmt is granted agst: the estate of WM: BESSE? for 520 l tob. 131a

HEN: SNAILE pltf: and NELKIN ye wife of JNO: CORNELISON deft: ......& sd SNAILE, THO: SMITHERS & SD NELKIN to make appearance at ye next Court.

Upon peticon of JNO: CORNELISON..... an Order of Court 16 Dec 1647 agst HEN: SNAILE to bee revived.

Warrants agst: WM: MARGARRET & a summons agst: JOB CHANDLER for theire personal appearance at ye next Court.

Upon peticon of WM: SHIPP......Sherr: to give notice to FRANCIS LAND that he appeare at ye next Court....and ENSIGNE LAMBART or MR: WOOD(HOUSE?) are requested to take WM: SMITHS deposition..............

Case between THO: BRIDGES & GEO: HEIGHAM referred to the next Court.

Ordered that the Constables attach ye body of EDW: HALL Chirurgeon & him forthwith to bring before CAPT: JNO: SIBSEY to answer to all such matters as shall bee objected agst: him at his Mat[s] sute.

WM: CROUCH & WM: SHIPP were bound for ye good behavior of LAURENCE PHILLIPPS & ANNE his wife & ye sd PHILLIPPS having forfeited theire recogniseness by theire misdemeanors. It is therefore ordered that ye sd PHILLIPPS & his wife doe forthwith enter into bond with sufficient security for theire good behavior & psonall appearance at ye next Court.

JNO: COOKE hath sett up his name at ye Court doore to give notice of his intended voyadge for England this present shipping.

An execution was heretofore served on THO: CAUSON for 2200 l tob & Caske & Court Charges at the suite of MR: THO: CEELY which sd execucon grounded upon an order of a County Court held at Deepe Creeke in COM. WARWICK & ye sd CAUSON having thereupon tendered a parcell of land in redemption of his body which is alledged to ye Court to bee xxxxxxxx & whereas it appears that sd CAUSON was bound by bill obligatory as also by promise to ye Court before ye time to produce to ye Court sufficient security for ye sd CEELY his peacable enjoying ye sd land & ye sd CAUSON having failed thereon notwithstanding divers orders of ye Court.. ....therefore ordered that execution ......agst: ye sd CAUSON for paymt: of aforesaid tob:.......an execucon was formerly served on ye body of THO: CAUSON for ℔ 7 ster: money for non appearance with ye Court Charges at ye suite of WM: PARRY first grounded upon an order of a Court held at Eliza: Citty & afterwards vizt: 5 Dec 1647 Received & confirmed by Judgmt: of this Court & ye sd CAUSON [not delivering the land to WM: PARRY] CAUSON to pay ye sd money.

MORE PRESENT: MR: MATH: PHILLIPPS at his house layeing on ye bed.

At the peticon of MR: THOMAS LAMBART a judgmt: is granted agst: the estate of FRA: LAND for 1443 l tob & caske & Court charges.

Ordered a warrant doe issue agst: MARY ye wife of THO: HORNE for her appearance at ye next Court to answer to what shall bee objected agst: her on ye behalfe of y Vestry

JAMES WARNER administrator of BENJAMIN ffOSTER pltff: & MR: THOMAS LAMBART deft: in an accon of Chancery.......... ye Court thought fitt.......(This gives LAMBART until the next Court to answer the complaint.)

132a In the case depending betweene MR: CORNELIUS LLOYD plt: & CAPT: ROBT: PAGE deft: & upon an order of ye present day (part?) agst: MR: RICHARD CONQUEST Sherr: ye sdCONQUEST hath appealed to James Citty......& CONQUEST to have theire Judgmt whether ye xxxxx be liableto pur? by witnesses ye Class? in the returns of ye writte both parties agreed & ye writte executed.

Upon the request of MR: CORNELIUS LLOYD ye Comrs: have authorized MR: JOHN HILL & MR: THO: BROWNE to examine wittnesses on ye behalfe of ye sd LLOYD plt: agst: CAPT: ROBT: PAGE deft: the Clerke of Court to be then present.

MEMORANDUM: Upon 27 Jul 1649 accts were weighed between RICHARD STARNELL & RICHARD BECK & ye sd RICH: BECK doth acknowledge indebtedness to RICH: STARNELL the sum of 643 l tob to pay debt...........

Dated 9 Jan Recorded 30 Jan 1649/50 (This is not in proper order datewise, but is in the middle of the page) In regard of ye late death of MR: MATHEW PHILLIPPS [one of ye collectors for ye pish of Lynhaven] we doe hereby appoint JNO: HOLMES in ye room & or place of ye sd MR: PHILLIPPS, and for his precincts or limitts to collect all Levies & with as great powers.................
Wit: HEN: WOODHOUSE, JOHN SIBSEY, THO: LAMBART & JNO: HILL

12 Jan 1649/50

ATT A COURT HELD AT YE HOUSE OF MRIS: ANNE PHILLIPPS widdow
PRESENT: CAPT: JNO: SIBSEY MR: HEN: WOODHOUSE
MR: JNO: HILL MR: THO: LAMBERT

MATHEW PHILLIPPS decd dieing Intestate & without a will, a letter of administration is granted unto ANNE his widdow 133
on her sd husbands estate by WM: BERKELEY Knt: Gov &c. Dated 18 Jan 1649/50 Recorded 30 Jan 1649/50.

Wm: BERKELEY Knt: Gov: &c on her 31 Oct 1649 petition granting probate to ffRANCIS, wife & Executrix of JNO: WATKINS decd. will.

133a

Recorded 15 Feb 1649/50

THO: TOD(D) of Elizabeth River sould in the yeare 1640 unto ALEXANDER HALL & ABRAHAM PATRECK a parcell of land 250 acres situate in ye County of New Norff: upon the South side of the Easterne Branch of Elizabeth River beginning at a Creeke the land being a necke & the Creeke being on ye West side of ye necke bounded up the River East Northerly down the river West Southerly into ye woods South Easterly & being distant from ye mouth or entrance into the River about 6 miles......ALEXANDER HALL afterward sould unto (JAMES?) called his part of ye sd land which part ye foresd: ABRA: PATRECK bought & afterward sould unto the whole unto RICH: WOLLMAN and deceasing before he had any bill of sale from MR: THOS: XXXXXX adm: of ye sd PATRECK require mee in theire behalf to give the sd WOLLMAN a bill of sale & now ye sd WOLLMAN having sould the sd land unto WM: WILSON requireth likewise I should confirme ye sd land unto ye sd WILSON... ...(he confirms to WILSON) 10 Dec 1649
Wit: EDWARD (ED)DORSEY & RISH: WOLLMAN Signed: THOMAS TOD

JNO: CARRAWAY hath given unto JOHN CARTWRIGHT Eldest sonne unto THO: CARTWRIGHT of Lower Norfolk County one heifer of two yeares old.... Recorded 15 Feb 1649/50

INVENTORY of the estate of ROGER ffLETCHER, Marchant decd. 134
BILLS DUE THE ESTATE:

	l tob
MR: RICH: WAKED decd due ye 13 Nov 1646	1000
MR: PEETER KNIGHT	1200
MR: JOHN SIDNEY oweth	110
MR: RICH: KENNER	114
MR: THO: BROWNE	24
MR: THOMAS IVY oweth by remainder of a bill	10

134

MR: GEORGE CHINING	1000
MR: RICHARD CONQUEST	1200
MR: EDWARD MOORE & MR: JOSIAS SMITH	936
HENRY BRADLEY	570
JNO: MEREDITH	1517
CAPT: JNO: SIBSEY	100
CAPT: THO: BURBAGE	236
SAMPSON WARRING	328
WILLIAM ADAMS	125
MR MR: THOS: LAMBARD	400
Presented in Court by THOMAS BRIDGES & sworn to by JOHN SIBSEY, JOHN HILL & THOS: BROWNE	1600
Total	10090

ATT A COUNTY COURT HELD 15 Feb 1649/50

PRESENT: ATT LAU: PHILLIPPS

JNO: SIBSEY MR: THO: LAMBART

MR: JNO: HILL MR: THO: BROWNE

The difference depending between RICH: WORSTER & JNO: CARRAWAY is referred to ye next Court & ye sd WORSTER in ye (interum?) shall procure MR: JNO: MEARES his oath that ye sd MEARES had never had any dealings with ye sd WORSTER but onely 6 hhds of tob that was paid MR: MARSH for him at plunt point. (This might refer to Blunt Point on the South side of the James River in Warwick County?)

The difference between HEN: SNAILE plt: & NELKIN ye wife of JOHN CORNELISON to the next Court. A warrant to be issured for sd SMITHERS appearance.

134a MR: JNO: HILL & MR: THO: BROWNE pltfs: agst JANE ye wife of THO: WRIGHT referred to the next Court.

Two accons entered at ye sute of WM: SMITH plt: agst: OWEN HAYES deft: by reason of sd HAYES his not being well are referred to ye next Court.

Upon ye peticon of ALEXANDER WOOBORNE it is ordered that MR: JNO: HILL beeing one of ye Collectors for MR: SAMPSON CALVERT, Clerick, his tythes shall pay unto ye sd WOOBORNE 160 l tob being for making ye sd CALVERT clothing.

Upon the peticon of JNO: WORKMAN...... ordered that RICH: ffOSTER, Constable, shall deliver unto ye sd WORKMAN such clothing & other things as hee hath of his having been brought to him by an Indian man......

All persons who have obtained Probates, letters of Administration, Inventories, bonds, & orphants estates to make theire personal appearance in Court 25 March next.

Certificate delivered to ye Court by ye High Sherr: that MR: XXXXX JOHNSON a New England man hath refused to take ye oath of allegiance.......Warrant to be issued for his appearance on Monday ..xxxrest is fadedxxxxx

It is the Judgmt: of the Court that JNO: BAKER is a freeman & that hee may dispose of himselfe & chuse his guardian.

Attachmt: granted RICHARD OWEN agst ROBERT PORTER depted (departed?) out of ye County for 1000 1 tob & Caske due by bill.

Ordered that JNO: COOKE shall have full power & authority to take his boat, sails, Rigging & ye owers (sic) that weare lately taken away by an Indian man when ye sd COOKE can find them.

ROBERT KETT gives notice of his intended voyadge for Holland this present shipping.

135

ATT A COURT HELD 25 Feb 1649/50
at LAU: PHILLIPS

PRESENT: CAPT: JOHN SIBSEY
MR: HEN: WOODHOUSE MR: JOHN HALL
MR: THO: LAMBART MR: THO: BROWNE

Upon the request of WM: BUTLER for his wife, the matter in difference betweene JNO: WILLIAMS plt: & JOAN BUTLER is referred to the next Court.

ROBT: DAVIS acknowledges judgmt: for paymt: of 1984 1 tob to MR: RICH: CONQUEST adm: of JNO: KEMPE dec'd: at demand.

An attachmt: is granted unto GEO: BRAND agst: RICH: ABRELL due by acct .... for 453 1 tob .... ye sd ABRELL BEING depted: out of this County.

Upon peticon of ABDOLA MARTIN..... it is ordered that hee shall have possession of ye estate of HAMET MARSELLON decd: a Countryman of his, conceiving the estate to be but of a small value.

WM: SMITH plt: agst: OWEN HAYES deft: In a sute of salt (sic) & batterie HAYES shall be dismist & pay Cort chgs: Ye sd SMITH to be non-suited & pay unto HAYES 10 1 tob and to take his cow when he can find her.

CERTIFICATE to THO: TODD for 350 acres for the transportation of: JOB SEEMERS?, SIMON PARRETT, CHARLES SEBEYLY, WM: DUNBARRE, JNO: PINNE?, KATHERINE HUYTTE and EDM: SHEAREMAN.

It appeares to ye Court that MR: OWEN POWELL tooke wrongfully in Holland a hh of tob weighing neare 355 1 tob from THO: ALLEN........ therefore ordered that ye estate of ye sd POWELL in the custody of MRIS: ANNE PHILLIPPS, widdow shall make satisfaccon for 800 1 tob & Caske to bee forthwith paid unto ye sd ALLEN with Court Charges.

ANNE HAYES widdow & relict of ROBT: HAYES decd: is granted adminis- 135a
tration on his estate.

WM: BASNETT acknowledges judgment for paymt: of 364 1 tob unto MR: RICH: CONQUEST adm: of JNO: KEMPE decd.

EDWARD CANNON hath confessed judgmt: for ye paymt: of 263 1 tob unro MR: RICH: CONQUEST adm: of JNO: KEMPE decd.

JNO: DIERS hath confest judgemt: for ye paymt: of 263 l tob to MR: RICH: CONQUEST adm: of JNO: KEMPE decd.

Ordered that THO: TOD shall pay unto ye sd BARTHO: HOSKINS 1608 l tob & Caske with court charges within 10 dayes.

The estate of JNO: BAYLY is attached by BARTHO: HOSKINS for 508 l tob & Caske.

THO: LEWIS to serve CORNELIUS LLOYD, his master, one year more to make up ye eight yeares promised.

Ordered that ye estate of MR: OWEN POWELL in custody of MRIS: ANNE PHILLIPPS shall be accountable unto CAPT: JNO: SIBSEY 255 l tob & Caske & half an Ankor of (Irons?) -xx?xx- payd by ye sd CAPT: SIBSEY to MR: MATH: PHILLIPPS decd & THOS: LEE which tobacco be-longed to ye acct: of ye sd POWELL.

Judgemt: is confest by THO: BUTTEIRS for ye paymt: of 778 l tob unto CAPT: THO: WILLOUGHBY with Court Charges.

CAPT: ffRAN" YARDLEY confest judgemt: for ye paymt: of 400 l tob to WM: ODEON.

136 In sute between CAPT: THO: WILLOUGHBY plt: & CAPT ffRANCIS YARDLEY deft: ...... on the request of sd YARDLEY is referred to ye next Court.

THOMAS ALLEN & EDWD: CANNON, or either of them, shall pay CAPT: YARDLEY 760 l tob & caske.

THO: WRIGHT to give bond for ye good behavior of JANE, his wife, that she shall not abuse any of his Majesties peoples or theire owne servants & ye sd JANE hath acknowledged her offence to MR: THO: BROWNE in open Court

Attachmt: granted JOB CHANDLER on Estate of RICH: ABREEL being departed out of this County for 482 l tob with Court Chgs:

JOB CHANDLER to pay HEN: BRAKES 330 l tob.

A special warrent to issue forth for ye personall appearance of ROWLAND MORGAN at ye next Court at ye sute of HENRY BRAKES & the Sherriffe to take him into his Custody untill he give security.

Ordered that GEORGE MEE shall bee authorized to sell all the Estate of PHILLIPP JONES decd at an outcry & MR: HEN: WOODHOUSE is requested to bee then present & ANDREW WARNER is ordered to bee first satisfyed 266 l tob & 2 barrells of Corne it beeing for his diett & funeral Charges & then the sd MEE to satisfye himselfe as farre as the Estate will goe, his debt being 849 l tob with Caske.

HEN: SNAILE plt: ags: NELKIN ye wife of JNO: CORNELISON .... ordered that THO: SMITHERS shall make paymt unto HEN: SNAILE 600 l tob & each partie to beare theire own charges.

136a An attachmt: is granted unto RICH: CHAPMAN agst: the estate of GEORGE COBB for 1600 l tob.

Ordered that MR: CORNELIUS LLOYD shall pay THO: RINGOLD 1300 l tob with Court chgs:

CAPT: JNO: SIBSEY atturney of ARTHUR BROWNE.....judgemt: is acknowledged by ffRA: LAND for ye paymt: of 370 l tob with caske & forbearance & Court Charges unto ye sd SIBSEY.

Upon peticon of ffRA: LAND a judgmt: is acknowledged by LAURENCE PHILLIPPS for ye paymt: of 668 l tob.

WM: SMITH to pay unto THO: LAMBART 348 l tob & Caske.

JOB CHANDLER plt: agst: (WM: ?) MARGARRET deft: ....upon his sub=mitting in open Court ye sd CHANDLER it is ordered that the sd MARGARRET shall pay Court Charges and bee quits. (This name may be MacGARRET?)

JOHN MOORE shall pay unto WM: COLLE 400 l tob & Caske.

An attachmt: is granted unto MR: THO: LAMBART agst: the Estate of JNO: CLAUSON for 1120 l tob & Caske.

Ordered that HEN: MERRITT shall pay unto RICH: SMITH 810 l tob & Caske.

GEO: HEIGHAM acknowledges judgemt: for ye paymt: of 1700 l tob unto THO: BRIDGES or his assigns.

THO: LAMBART assignee of CAPT: WM. CLAIBORNE ESQ: .... An attachmt: is graunted agst ye estate of JNO: CORKER unto ye sd LAMBART for ye paymt: of 800 l tob.

THO: SMITHERS is granted an attachmt: agst the estate of JNO: 137
GUTTERIDGE who is long since depted: this collony for the payment of 550 l tob & Caske & Court Charges.

It appeareth by ye deposicon of FRANCIS LAND & WM: SMITH that ye two bills menconed in a writing under ye hand of WM: DAVIS bearing date 8 Aug 1648 and not due to be voyd by ye sd LAND. It is the opinion of the board that ye sd LAND is cleare of them.

It appeareth by deposicon of OWEN HAYES that 3 barrels of corne specified in a small note dated 8 Aug 1648 was not due for him to pay ....sd HAYES not liable to make satisfaccon.

It is ordered that MR: JNO: HILL shall pay unto MRIS: ANNE PHILLIPPS 243 l tob for ye use of MR: SAMPSON CALVERT Clerke unto sd MR: HILL beeing out of the beeing out of the returns of ye sd CALVERTS his tythes.

Attachmt: granted unto LAU: PHILLIPPS agst the Estate of JNO: PIGOTT for 915 l tob due for diet & lodging for himselfe & his people.

By reason of the often Runing away & pilfering of URSULA BAYLY it is ordered that LAU: PHILLIPPS shall forthwith bring ye sd URSULA servant Mayd to GEO: HEIGHAM to CAPT: SIBSEY his house & there cause her to bee given 30 lashes on ye bare backe & afterwards conveye her to her Master.....& her sd Master shall provide meals, drinks, & clothing for her & farther Cure of her legge that heareafter no more Complaints bee made by her ye sd Mayd not none of his Sarvants & ..... GEO: HEIGHAM to pay all Court Charges besides other Charges & ye sd URSULA is to make him satisfacon in service.

Ordered that LAU: PHILLIPPS & his wife be released of theire bonds wherein they are bound to theire good behavior .... & to take in theire sd bonds & to pay all Court Charges.

THO: WRIGHT preferred a peticon agst GEO: WAKEFIELD who had beene his sarvant for matters already determined .... It is therefore ordered that ye sd WAKEFIELD is clear of those matters & the sd WRIGHT to pay all Court Charges for wrongful molestacon.

137a CAPT: JNO: SIBSEY hath made it appear this 26 Feb 1649/50 to mee that FRA: LAND stands indebted unto CAPT: WM: ATTERBURY by remainder of a specialty the sum of 184 1 tob. I doe order that sd LAND shall remaine in ye Sherr: Custody untill hee make satisfaccon thereof with Charges. signed: JOHN HILL

LandLord HANDCOCKE - The case stands with me thus, that I must see this man cured of his leggs. I pray agree with ye Doctor as Cheape as you can, Here is one servant I hoope hee will not exact upon mee, I would intreat you to put of the boy as soone as you can, I was told WILSON would have him & the man too at what rate you thinke good, I am a trouble unto you but, shall endevor to make you amends for all in the Interim. I shall rest.

Your friend to command JOHN PIGOTT John Pigott

26 Feb 1649

I pray send the gun to MR: TAYLOR by these men.

(The above is a letter to SIMON HANDCOCKE SHExx (Sherr?)

ATT AN ORPHANTS COURT HELD 27 Feb 1649/50
ATT YE HOUSE OF MRIS: ANN PHILLIPPS

PRESENT:	CAPT: WM: CLAIBORNE ESQR:	CAPT: JNO: SIBSEY
	MR: HEN: WOODHOUSE	MR: JNO: HILL
	MR: THO: BROWNE	MR: THO: LAMBART

This day being mett concerning the Estate of HEN: SEWELL decd by the opinion of the Court & Consent of JNO: HOLMES, Overseer, and MR: LEMUEL MASON who hath intermarried with ANN the daughter of the sd SEWELL. it was agreed as foll: That ye estate of MR: MATH: PHILLIPPS late decd shall bee responsible & give security to make good the estate of ye sd HEN: SEWELL either in kind or vallew as it was left at the decease of ALOE ye wife of ye sd HEN: SEWELL by Inventory & if any difference arrise in ye - xxxxxxxxx - of any of ye goods which shall bee undelivered xxxx It shall bee determined by ye Court & for any of ye goods wanting or disposed of by ye sd MR: PHILLIPPS. The valew of them shall bee praysed & stated by fower Indeffrent men chosen by & on behalf of ye Orphants of ye sd LEMUELL (this should read HENRY) & MRIS: ANNE PHILLIPPS aforesd administratrix of the sd MR: MATH: PHILLIPPS No money to bee given or brought for ye Education of the sd SEWELL orphants or for any other xxxxxx or quitence whatsoever.

PRESENT: CAPT: JOHN SIBSEY, MR: HEN: WOODHOUSE, MR: JOHN HILL, MR: THO: BROWNE

...Ordered that 3 hh of good sound tob be provided to bee sent for Holland with MR: THO: LEE to bee sould there for the best advantage of HEN: SEWELL who is to goe for Holland with the sd MR: LEE & comitted to his trust in the disposing of him ye sd HENRY, the sd MR: LEE being his kindsman & seeming to bee very desirous to have the yough (young?) man with him & ye sd MR: LEE to give an acct: to ye Court the next yeare of ye pduce of the sd 3 hh of tob It is also ordered that MR: JNO: HILL, MR: THO: LAMBARD, JNO: HOLMES & THO: IVY who are by ye mutual consent of MR: LEMUELL MASON who married ANNE ye daughter of ye sd HEN: SEWELL and MRIS: ANNE PHILLIPPS aforesd are to meete & arbitrate ye buysiness bee held on the 25 Mar next & on the 26 Day beeing the next day following. A Court to bee held for ye County the 27th day beeing the next day following Is appointed for an Outcry for ye Sale of the Goods belonging unto ye foresd HENERY orphant of HEN: SEWELL decd. Also ordered that MR: THO: LEE shall give good security for the return of ye sd HENRY SEWELL to the Court when required according to his nowe proposition. CAPT: JNO: SIBSEY & LEMUELL MASON to take the security in the name of the Court.

PRESENT: CAPT: JNO: SIBSEY MR: JNO: HILL)
MR: HEN: WOODHOUSE MR: THO: LAMBARD)- COMRS:
MR: THO: BROWNE)

Upon the willingness & good satisfaction WM: LUCAS hath given the Court in the keeping JNO: MOYE'S decd youngest child it is ordered that MR: JOHN GOODWIN who hath made appeare the order the Grand father of the sd child, gave him, to demand & to carry the sd young boy named RICHARD MOYE for London in England to his sd Grand Father's shall pay unto ye sd WM: LUCAS 1200 1 tob in goods as English goods are sould for keeping the child fower years last past. ROBART DAVIS having given in Court a satisfactory acct: concerning JNO: MOYES estate decd: It is therefore ordered that ye sd DAVIS shall have ye keeping of JNO: MOYE sonne of JNO: MOYE decd and that ye said DAVIS shall have all the male increases that shall procede from the cattles now belonging unto ye sd JNO: MOYE from this instant * & forward as long as hee ye sd DAVIS shall have ye keep= 138a*
ing of ye (calfe?) and in regard all ye cowes have calves already it is thought fitt and ordered that ye sd DAVIS shalbee allowed a reasonable consideration the next year for keeping the sd boye for ye first yeare & that what cost of charges the sd DAVIS shall bee at in causing ye sd boye to bee brought up in learning. I, JOHN GOODWIN, Mariner in ye behalfe of MR: RICHARD WHEELER ye childs Grandfather hath undertaken to give him ye sd DAVIS sattisfaccon

CAPT: THO: WILLOUGHBY ESQ: did heretofore deliver unto (JERY?) HOSKINS, EMMA WAKE a fatherles & motherles child & that ye sd HOSKINS hath voluntarily at his owne (faded) charge kept & maintayned ye sd orphant 10 months & -(faded)- to keepe & provide for it. Now upon ye voluntary motion during -(faded)- and undertakings of MR: RICH: CONQUEST unto ye Court to have ye sd child in his tuition & to mayntaine & educate her as his owne /the inability of ye sd HOSKINS & other reasons well weighed & considered it is thereupon thought fitt and ordered that ye sd HOSKINS -(faded)- with deliver ye sd orphant unto ye sd MR: CONQUEST to bee mayntained & brought up according to promises aforesd and ye sd MR: CONQUEST is to pay at ye next cropp unto ye sd HOSKINS 300 l tob with caske in lieu & satisfaction of 10 months diett & maintenence of ye sd child.

Recorded 27 Feb 1649/50 - On the 1 Oct 1649 before mee MR: JOSHUA MAYNETT Notary & Tabellion Publick admitted & sworne dwelling in London in presence of the wittnesses hereafter named personally appeared RICHARD WHEELER, Cittizen & (Inholden?) of London, the which appeares made ordayned & by these presents in his stead & place doth put & constitute JOHN GOODWIN of Ratcliffe in ye County of Midd: Marryner his trusty & lawfull Attorney giving & granting his Atty: full power &c ..../as Grandfather of ye sons of
139 the late JOHN MOYE in Virginia deceased, who was killed by the last massacre of the Indians/ To aske, demand & take out of the hands of ...... whatsoever person or persons in Virginia aforesaid his said two grandchildren, sonns of ye sd JOHN MOYE deceased. The elder of which called by ye name of (blank in the record) MOYE to settle in Virginia aforesd & to recover for the said Jxxx MOYE of whatsoever person or persons theire heirs &c.......for goods
*139a effects rights accts: creditts & plantations whatsoever * shall be found all which, goods, cattle &c .... of ye sd JOHN MOYE decd ....to take into .... custody ...... of ye sd GOODWIN & ye same with him to bring for England .... (This goes on and on) ....This done passed in the City of London in ye presence of JOHN PIGOTT, RICHARD CLAY & JAMES MARSHALL.
JOSHUA MAYNETT, Notary Pub. Signed: Richard Wheeler and his seale

An acct: of so much of the Estate belonging to the Orphants of JOHN MOYE deceased as came to ye hands of ROBT: DAVIS.

The Estate is Debtor to ROBERT DAVIS		1571
Tobacco payd JNO: STRATTON	75	
" " RICH: ffOSTER for diett	160	
Total debits amount to	3804	

CREDITS: By a bull sould MR: WOODHOUSE
A sowe paid to JOHN STRATTON of JOHN MOYES for a debt
140 (This inventory takes a whole page. The amounts in Credit Column are too faded to read)
WM: EEDY is to give an accoumpt of 564 l tob belonging to this Estate

Estate of JOHN MOYE: Cattle increased since 1648.
Total credits 1633
300 acres of land due to JNO: MOYE sonne to JNO: MOYE decd.
Sworne to in Court 26 Feb 1649 Teste: THO: BRIDGES CL CUR
Tho Bridgs

ATT A COURT HELD 26 Mar 1650

PRESENT: CAPT: JOHN SIBSEY
MR: HEN: WOODHOUSE MR: THO: LAMBART
MR: HOHN HILL MR: THO: BROWNE

A probate of ye last will and testament of MRIS: ANN HAYES decd late administratrix of MR: ROBART HAYES decd is granted unto NATHANIELL HAYES and THOS: WORKMAN Executors of the aforesaid last will........

ATT A QUARTER COURT HELD ATT JAMES CITTY 16 Mar 1649/50

PRESENT: THE HON: SIR WILLIAM BERKELEY Knt. Gov.

CAPT: SAMLL: MATHEWS	CAPT: THO: PETTUS	ESQR:
CAPT: WM: CLAIBORNE	MR: GEO: LUDLOW	
CAPT: HEN: BROWNE	CAPT: RALPH WORMLY	
CAPT: WM: BERNARD	CAPT: BRIDGES FREEMAN	

It is ordered that ye Comrs: of Lower Norff: shall have theire request in theire petition granted MR: WM: MOSELEY, MR: RICH: CONQUEST and MR: LEMUELL MASON are adjoyned in Commission with ye rest of ye Comrs: of Lower Norfolk.

Teste: MR: THO: CROSBY CL CUR: Tho Crosbys

This day MR: LEMUELL MASON hath taken ye oath of supremacy & allegiance according to ye tenor of this order a few mentioned - (the page ends this way)

MORE PRESENT: MR: LEMUELL MASON 140a

WHEREAS: THOMAS TODD hath made it appeare upon (oath) that CAPT: ffRANCIS YARDLEY stands indebted to him the (sum) of 600 1 tob & caske for trimming of a scoope & promised to make paymt: thereof unto MR: BARTHO: HOSKINS, the sd YARDLEY having failed in ye paymt: thereof according to his promise...........Ordered that ye sd CAPT: YARDLEY shall make paymt: unto THO: TODD or his assigns with Court Charges.

.... atachmt: that issued forth the last Court agst the Estate of RICH: ABRELL towards parmt: of 553 1 tob & Caske due to GEO: BRAND. The Sherr: hath attached 2 sowes & 3 shotes in the hands of SAVILL GASKINS being part of ye estate.........now ordered that execucon doe issue forth according to -(faded0- the attachmt: & the goods attached to bee delivered into ye possession of ye sd GEO: BRAND.

Petition of MR: THO: MEARES concerning ye difference betweene him and ROBERT BOWERS .... ordered that ye sd BOWERS -(faded)- ... a specialty for ye paymt: of 3000 1 tob & Caske at ye next cropp according to agreement and that WATFORD shall have 4 acres of cleare ground for -(faded)- yeare hee paying rent for it, also MR: MEARES is to have -(faded)- doore & all ye sawed planck or boards on ye plantation except stairs and that ye sd BOWERS shall make present paymt (to) MR: MEARES of the sum of 500 & odd 1 tob with Court Charges.

SARA REINOLDS Sarvent Mayd to MR: THO: MEARES for scandalizing her sd Master in saying & reporting hee had had ye use of her body & that shee was with child by him who beeing searched found to ye contrary. It is therefore ordered that ye said SARA REINOLDS shall have 35 lashes on ye bare back & bee quitte shee paying all ye Court Charges.

CERTIFICATE to JNO: WILLIAMS for 50 acres for the transportation of: MARY WRIGHT into ye Collony proved due by me RICH: CONQUEST & assigned over unto ye sd WMS:

CERTIFICATE to JNO: DIERS for 100 acres for ye transportation of ffRANCES ELDRIDGE & ELLIN HODGE his wife.

141 An attachmt granted JNO: DIER agst the Estate of RICH: ABRELL /as DIER shall find/ for 400 l tob and Court Charges.

This day MR: WM: MOSELEY hath taken the oath of supremacy and allegiance.

MORE PRESENT: MR: WILLIAM MOSELEY

.... at ye last Court a reference was graunted upon ye request of CAPT: ffFRANCIS YARDLEY plt: in a case depending between (him) and CAPT: THO: WILLOUGHBY deft: ....referred to the next Court.

Case betweene JNO: WILLIAMS plt: & JOANE ye wife of WM: BUTLER deft: .....Ordered that ye sd JOANE BUTLER appeare at ye house of MRIS ANN PHILLIPPS & acknowledge that shee hath wronged ye sd WILLIAMS and pay 20 l tob towards his Court Charges.

It is ordered that a Certificate be issued unto RICH: NICHOLS to certifie his frends in England that hee is here living and in liklihood of life and ye certificate to be signed by the Comrs:

CERTIFICATE to WM: MOSELEY for 550 acres for transportation of himselfe & SUSANNA his wife, WM: & ARTHUR his sonnes, SUSAN ROBINSON alias CORKER, ELIZ: WEST, ANNE LAMBERT, EDW: FREEMAN, HENRY LAMBERT, JOST? WILLIAMS & THO: HARRINGTON.

CERTIFICATE to THO: MARSH for 50 acres for transportation of ROBT: ffISHER.

141a Upon ye request of CAPT: THO: WILLOUGHBY by his sonne attachmt is granted agst so much of ye estate of SAMPSON CALVERT Clereke /where he shall find it/ as shall make satisfaccon for 800 l tob & Caske with Court Charges.

27 Mar 1650

Whereas JNO: HOLMES hath made it appeare that JNO: BOLTON in his lifetime passed unto him a bill under his hand for the sum of 685 l tob & Caske to (payd?) the ensuing cropp........Ordered that ye Sherr: doe seiqe the estate of ye sd BOLTON decd now in ye custody of WM: JOHNSON who hath intermarried with ANN ye wife of ye sd BOLTON decd...............until adm: doe issue forth uppon ye aforesd estate.

MR: HILL & MR: LAMBERT NOT PRESENT

Whereas at a Court hearing dated 27 Feb last past MR: JNO HILL, MR: THO: LAMBART, JNO: HOLLAND & THO: JUY (IVY) by ye Mutual Consent of MR: LEMUELL MASON who intermarried with ANN ye daughter of MRIS ALOE SEWELL decd & MRIS ANN PHILLIPPS adm: of MR: MATH: PHILLIPPS decd were appointed to be arbitrators to value that part of the Estate of ye aforesaid ALOE SEWELL decd which could not be delivered in kind by ye sd (ANN) PHILLIPPS according to Inventory.....if any difference should arrise concerning the decaye & Impairing of such goods (should) be undelivered in kind that they should make report thereof which order they have preformed. (ALOE is given as ALICE in some of these records)

In the difference between MRIS ANN PHILLIPPS & MR: LEMUEL MASON concerning a wench named KATHERINE -(faded)- belonging to CAPT: WM: DUGLAS as by Inventory of MRIS: ALICE SEWELL decd. appeareth, the busyness is referred to ye next Court. (ALICE is called ALOE in earlier records)

An attachmt is graunted MR: CORNELIUS LLOYD agst JNO: STRATTON for 6300 l tob & Caske & 2 hh of tob & Caske with Court Charges.

(The beginning of this record is torn)............................ 142
goods weare ....taken away from MR: THO: WILLOUGHBY by MANUELL ye Portugesse .... ordered that ye goods so found be returned unto ye sd WILLOUGHBY & that ye sd MANUELL shall not come to or neare the house of ye sd WILLOUGHBYS by a mile or have any communicacon with ANN WATKINS his Mayd without ye consent of ye sd WILLOUGHBY & if he shall bee found.......to receive 20 laskes on ye bare back ....(the rest of this has most of the key words missing)

.......ordered in the difference about MR: LEMUEL MASON, his wedding, concerning charges expended by MR: MATH: PHILLIPPS decd that ye sd MR: MASON shall allowe MRIS ANNE PHILLIPPS adm: of ye sd PHILLIPPS decd toward the charges of said one fatt hogge of 2 years old and a fatt goate and ye sd MRIS PHILLIPPS to bee discharged of a silver spoon which was left at the said wedding.

MR: LEMUELL MASON stands charged by MR: MATH: PHILLIPPS decd in Jul 1648 ... 379 l tob at 14 l for a knife with Cash....to the next Court.

ATT A QUARTER COURT HELD ATT JAMES CITTY 13 Mar 1649/50
PRESENT: THE HON: WM: BERKELEY Knt. Gov.
SIR THO: LUNSFORD Knt. Barronett
CAPT: HENRY BROWNE CAPT: WM: BARNETT)
CAPT: THO: PETTUS CAPT: RALPH WORMLY) ESQ:

It is ordered that MR: THO: BROWNE bee High Sherriffe of Lower Norfolk County & oath administered-

Order graunted at the last Court unto CAPT: JNO: SIBSEY agst est: of OWEN POWELL in the hands of MRIS: ANNE PHILLIPPS for ye sattisfaccon of 255 l tob & caske and an halfe anker of drams with Court Charges. CAPT: SIBSEY received full satisfaccon & promising to keep ye sd ANN PHILLIPPS harmless.

Top of this page is torn 142a
(one line is missing)

ATT AN ORPHANTS COURT HELD 28 Mar 1650
PRESENT: CAPT: JNO: SIBSEY
MR: HEN: WOODHOUSE MR: JNO: HILL)
MR: THO: LAMBART MR: WM: MOSELEY) COMRS:

Delivered these following plats to MR: LEMUEL MASON & MRIS: ANNE PHILLIPPS with ye consent of ye Court for ye use of HENRY SEWELL, sonne of HENRY SEWELL decd... Gold ring -(missing word)- one Silver Tankard Mrkd: $_H{}^S{}_A$, one Grimell? ring with a (missing word) a Great silver beer bowle, one gimel ring.. A Silver Wine Cuppe mrkd $_H{}^S{}_A$, one side ring with a xxxxxx, one Great Silver Salt Mrkd I-S-I , one ring with a gard... ffive Silver Spoones marked the same, one gold ring....One silver dram cuppe without; one small ring with thxxxxxx a Mrke xxxxxxx Let? ye present my goods xxxxxxxx a Silver Whistle & Chaine with 3 bells without a currexxxxxxx. It is ordered that MR: LEMUELL MASON aforesd doe give with security that ye plate & rings bee forthcoming or Court shall demand them.

It was agreed that MRIS: ANNE PHILLIPPS shall have and Injoy the plantation & houses with -(faded)- man named MANUELL?,/the thickett excepted/ belonging unto HENRY SEWELL where shee now liveth, with all ye preveleges thereunto belonging untill Christmas next ensuing -(faded)- for satisfaccon for ye negroes & Rent of ye houses & land shee ye sd MRIS: PHILLIPPS is then to pay unto ye Comrs: 1200 1 tob.

By reason ye 15 June next beeing ye Court day fallin on a Saterday which is inconvenient for an Outcry to bee the next day beeing the Saboath Day it is therefore ordered that the next Court be reserved for the 18 June next & that ye next day bee held an Outcry for ye sale of divers goods belonging unto HENRY SEWELL sonne of HENRY SEWELL decd.

143 The top of this page is almost completely gone.

(Following is what may be letters of Administration the top of the record is missing) ..... decedents estate xxxxxx order and appoint ye sd ANN HAYES shall present a perfect Inventory of ye sd estate... 20 Mar 1649 Recorded 28 Mar 1649 Signed: WM: BERKELEY

RICHARD NICHOLS aged betweene 30 & 32 years or thereabouts having continued in ye Collony about this 14 yeares last past & declaring himselfe to bee of Oxenbury in Huntingtonshire, a Taylor & sonne of HEN: NICHOLS of ye same place (In?) hold living at ye sign of ye (?) White House is this day -(torn)- & likelyhood of Life & hath Certificate thereof of ye Court which it grants.
27 Mar 1650 in Virginia. Witnesses are torn off.

143a xxxxxxxxSTARLING xxxxxxxxxxxThe words, now her heirs xxxxx signed & delivered in presence of THO: TOOKER, JNO: MERREDITH. (NOTE:It is hard to tell whether this is a will or not, but it doesn't seem to be a STARLING will if it is one.)

THOS: MEARES of Virginia, Planter hath sealed an obligation of 74 1 tob for ye paying of xxx 7 ℔ xx shill 9 pence unto ROBERT PAGE & ye use of ye Company of ye good shipp called PLEIADES xxxxxxshipp -(parts of this are missing)- Whatever tob shall bee shipped by ye sd MR: THO: MEARES xxxxxxxxxx 2 Dec 164_.

144 ROBERT BOWERS of Eliza: River, Planter buying a pattent of 400 acres xxxxxxxxx -(the signature and most of this deed is torn and blurred)-

144a (NOTE: The top of this page is torn and faded. It is a Deed, but no names are legible)

THO: MEARES selling 400 acres of land lyingxxxxxxxx most br. of Eliza: River. (most of this is torn) Signed THO: MEARES

CODICILE to will of ANNE HAYES will dated (missing) pvd. 26 Mar 1650 ... to ELLEN HAYES my daughter in law ....my late deceased husband ....NATHANIELL HAYES my sonne ....ADAM HAYES..... third parte to be equally divided between ye sd NATHANIELL & ADAM HAYES & THO: WORKMAN and JNO: WORKMAN my sonnes....... that JNO: WORKEMAN & ADDAM HAYES my sonnes......give & bequeath unto JANE NEEDHAM my kinswoman. NATHANIEL HAYES & THO: WORKEMAN Executors..............
Wit: JNO: HOLMES, JNO: MARTIN & WILL: JERMY Signed: Anne Hayes
(this will is torn)

145a

This may be something about the probate of ANNE HAYES codicile or will on the preceding page, but it is torn and parts are missing and your editor cannot be sure just what it is.

Peticon of ffRANCIS YARDLEY to the Worshipfull Comrs: of Lower Norfolk.

Humbly Sheweth: That your petitioner sums: 2 years since at request of CAPT: THOMAS WILLOUGHBY did lend the said CAPT: WILLOUGHBY a mare, to xxxxxxx vs a ffatt calfe from Lynhaven to his house which mare ye sd CAPT: WILLOUGHBY promised lawfully & expeditionatly to be returned but contrarily his owne turne being served did not pform his sd promise for ye sd mare was kept at his house so long xxx xxxx xxx fille about 3 months old was starved for want of ye xxxxx & the mare in ye like Condicon for want of food & had xxxx xxxx xxxx xxxx fetch the sd mare, shee had xxxxxx died further CAPT: WILLOUGHBY is indebted for ye sd ffat Calfe to your petitioner to this day xxxxxxx ordered that CAPT: WILLOUGHBY repay a Heifer of such age, the Calfe had now beene at or else another Cow Calfe fully as fatt as that was your petitioner sent him xxxxx with his damages and charges.

146

SAMUEL MATHEWS - (a badly torn record which seems to be a letter to the Commissioners) xxxxxxxTHO: WILLOUGHBY by his xxxx will & testament xxxxxxx WILLOUGHBY of xxxxxx will with xxxx that he ye xxxxxxxx pose of any manxxr of importance with my aprobacon xxxxxxxxxx or ye sonne attaines to full age of twenty xxx xxxxxxxxx sonne shall act concerning his fathers xxxtion xxxxxxxxxxxxx and valid untill his power bee xxxxxx xxxxxx xxxxxxx very loving friend
ENDORSED: SAM MATHEWES
To His very loving frends the Comrs: of Lower Norfolke those present.

ATT A COURT HELD 18 Jun 1650
No Commissioners names given as being present.

CERTIFICATS to WM: SHIPP & SARA his wife for 800 acres for transportation of his 2 sonnes, ffRAN: & MATHEW SHIPP, CATHERINE LEE, JA: SHERLES, MARGARET FAYE (or DAYE), D-RCA JOHSON, MATT: YOUNGER, JNO: GILLET, BRIAN SCOTT, AN- STEVENSON, PEETER PATTEN, EDW: CLABORNE. BARTHO: HAYNES, RICH: GOODE, MARGARET HARINGTON & NICOLAS WYETT.

CERTIFICATE to JNO: STRATTON for 150 acres for transportation of: JNO: ffRANKLIN, MARGARET HEATH & PATIENCE TOMELIN.

CERTIFICATE to GEORGE KEMPE for 100 acres for transportation of himselfe & MARY HUTCHINSON, his wife.

CERTIFICATE to WM: WATTS for 100 acres proved due to him by WM: SHIPP for the transportation of HENRY MERRITT & MARY ROGERS.

146a LAURENCE PHILLIPPS - This item is torn and missing. There is not enough left to decipher.

-(torn & missing)- unto ROBT: HAYES decd 2 barrels xxxxxxxxxxxxxxxxx sd KEMPE xxxxxxxxTHO: xxxxxxxxxxxxxxNATH: HAYES exors of ANNE Hxxxxx

In the case betweene RICH: OWENS plt & xxxxx PORTER deft a reference granted to sd PORTER as (request) of MR: THO: LAMBART Atty of ye sd PORTER xxxxxxxxto pay a colletterall agreemt made betweene xxxxxxxx OWENS & THO: EDMUNDSxxxxxxxxxxxxxxxxxxxxxxxxxxxxx

MR: RICH: CONQUEST hath taken ye oath of allegiance & is joyned to the Commissioners of ye County..........

MORE PRESENT: MR: RICH: CONQUEST

Case betweene THO: SMITHERS plt & EDWARD WILDER deft in scandalizing ye sd SMITHERS /in saying hee saw ye sd SMITHERS a swiming of HEN: SNAILES, his wife/ as by ye oath of WM: JOHNSON & ANNE his wife & his owne confession it is therefore ordered that ye sd WILDER shall aske ye sd SMITHERS forgivenes for this his offence in open Court & next Sabbath day that MR: POWIS holds service at Lynhaven pish Church ye sd WILDER shall stand with a peper on his hat confessing xxxxxxxx & to pay Court Charges.

The petition of LAURENCE PHILLIPPS concerning MR: HEIGHAMS Mayd SARA her diet one m^{o}: & for correcting of her according to an order of Court ....ordered that ye sd HEIGHAM shall pay PHILLIPPS 100 1 tob with Court Charges.

147 The top of this page is torn and some of it is missing.

Inventory of RICH: KENNER decd to be produced by MR: THO: LAMBART & MR: RICH: CONQUEST.

MR: ROBT: EIRES hath sold unto OLLIVER SPRYE 350 acres of land lieing in Rappahannock as on the patent doth appeare which land ye sd SPRYE hath since sould unto JAMES BAGNALL.

RICH: STARNELL ordered to pay HEN: MERRITT 300 1 tob & Caske & 50 1 tob toward Court Charges.

Whereas MICHAELL LAURENCE for conveying ROSE, MRIS: PHILLIPPS Mayd servant to Lynhaven with an intent to have married her & for detein-ing her two dayes & nights out of her sd MRIS: service her MRIS: being absent. It is therefore ordered that ye sd LAURENCE shall satisfye & pay unto ye sd MRIS: PHILLIPPS 500 1 tob at ye next cropp & also .....shall make (gone?) ye other halfe of a sufficient bridge ....over a Creeke xxxxxxxxxxxxx Chapel. JNO: SIBSEY & RICH: CON-QUESTthere being a former order that ye sd LAURENCE was to pay halfe ye charges towards ye sd Bridge and to make satisfaction for what goods were found missing during MRIS: PHILLIPPS absence.

CAPT: THO: WILLOUGHBY did formerly arrest CAPT: ffRANCIS YARDLEY.... and he not appearing ...... ye sd YARDLEY shall pay unto ye sd WILL-OUGHBY 1020 1 tob & Caske at the next Crop with Court Charges.

(This page starts with missing pieces) - xxxxxxxSTEGGE, ESQ: xxxxxxx ESQR: SEMOR? xxxxxxxTHO: xxxxxxxxagent of CAPT: xxxx STEGGE ESQR SEMOR? (Senior?) was arrested to this Court at ye sute of MRIS ANNE PHILLIPPS adm: of MR: MATH: PHILLIPPS her husband decd and not appearing xxxxxxxx ordered that Judgement be awarded agst CAPT: JNO: SIBSEY his security for 4 servants with all damages & Court Chgs.

DANIELL MOLY sarvant to CAPT: JNO: SIBSEY ffor conveying ROSE, MRIS: PHILLIPPS mayd sarvant to MICHAELL LAURENCE at an unseasonable time of night that at ye experacon of his time serve CAPT: JNO: SIBSEY 2 months & MRIS: PHILLIPPS 2 months more for ye fault & pay Court Charges.

In difference between DANIELL MOLY -(faded)- CAPT: JNO: SIBSEY deft: .... ordered that ye sd MOLY shall serve CAPT: SIBSEY untill ye 28 May next.......also give bond with security that if MRIS: PHILLIPPS hath lost any goods in or at ye time ROSE was absent that -(faded)- satisfaccon for them.

CAPT: ffRANCIS YARDLEY arrested CAPT: THO: WILLOUGHBY & not appearing himselfe ......that ye sd YARDLEY be non suited & pay Court Chgs.

A probate is graunted unto DOROTHY HATTON widdow & relict of JNO: HATTON decd & to JNO: HATTON her sonne of the last will & testament of the aforsd JNO: HATTON decd.

ANN WATKINS Mayd Sarvant to CAPT: THO: WILLOUGHBY ESQR: being delivered of a child & will not confess ye father of it. It is ordered that ye Sherr: cause 30 lashes to bee given her on ye bare back forthwith except shee confesseth who gott the child.

Top of the page is torn and parts are missing...................... 148
It seems to start by naming the processioners or collectors of tythes and the only readable part is:

...HENRY BRAKES for ye Little Creek & ye Western Shore of Lynnhaven & WM: CAPPS for ye Easterne Shore of Lynnhaven.

JNO: MARTIN plt agst WM: JOHNSON deft to next Court

RICH: JENNINGS Atty of HENRY CASKER hath impleaded ROBT: PORTER for 800 1 tob due upon acct. MR: THO: LAMBART Atty of sd PORTER hath promised before ye Court that CASKER at ye returne of ye shippe shall take his oath that there is soe much due to him from PORTER as is specified in ye acct that hee ye sd MR: LAMBART will make paymt hereof unto ye sd CASKER.

Ordered that paymt be made unto WM: CAPPS of 230 1 tob out of the Estate of PHILLIPP JONES.

Whereas MR: THO: MARSH hath transported divers psons out of this Collony that were indebted certaine sums of tob for officers fees unto MR: RICH: CONQUEST & other psons in this County, which CONQUEST by virtue of his office to collect ... ordered that MR: MARSH make payment to MR: CONQUEST.

Ordered that the following take lists of the tytheables:
ROBT: POWIS JUNIOR in ye Little Creek & ye Western Vranch of Lynhaven
THO: ALLEN for ye Western Shoare of Lynhaven
GEO: HEIGHAM for psons in ye head of ye Easterne Branch including GEO: KEMPE
WM: SHIPP for the Easterne Branch including MR: HOSKINS and for the Southern Branch and then down to Daniel Tanners Creek
CHRISTO: RIVERS in the Western Branch including MR: DAVIS
MR: THO: IVY from Daniell Tanners Creek to CAPT: THO: WILLOUGHBYES

148a The top of this page is torn.

xxxxxxxxxxxxxxxxxxATKINS (WATKINS?) Sarvant xxxxxxxxx doe make her appearance at ye next Court xxxxxxxxxxxxxxx good lashes upon her bare back lest shee dxxxxx xxxxxxxx who is the father of the child. (Is this ANNE WATKINS?)

JOHN BOLTON
wd 17 Feb 1649/50 wp Jun 1650 by THO: WARD & HENRY BRAKES
Wit: THO: WARD, WILL: (COOX?), HENRY [H] BRAKES?
.....being sick and weak.. unto ye daughter of JOHN SUTTON decd the next cow calfe that falles this year..... unto ANN WESTGATE ye daughter of HENRY WESTGATE the next cow calfe that falleth after............unto JOHN SPENCER a cloth sute...........unto my wife all my cattle beeing in all 7 hedd with all the rest of my goods........to her owne proper use to dispose of as shee pleaseth. (No executor named)
Teste: THO: BRIDGES CL CUR: Signed: JOHN [mark] BOULTON

JOHN HATTON in Elizabeth River
wd 7 Jan 1649/50 w. recorded 18 Jun 1650 wp 18 Jun 1650 by both witnesses: JOHN HILL & THO: BROWNE
......being sick & weake in body .... unto DOROTHY HATTON my loving wife all my land & houses buring her natural life & one cow which
149 I had of MR: THO: BROWNE, on & besides her pte of the rest of my estate whom also with my sonne I make joint executor .... all of my estate, goods, cattell & chattells /my debts being payd/ shall bee equally divided among my wife and all my children only all my land & houses I give unto JNO: HATTON my eldest sonne after ye decease of my wife, his mother, who also with my sd wife I make joint executors.
Teste: THO: BRIDGES CL CUR: Signed: JOHN [mark] HATTON

INVENTORY of the Estate of JOHN HATTON who deceased 19 Jan 1649/50 This list consists of the usual beds, iron pots &c... no value is given to the Estate. Recorded Jun 1650

Recorded 19 Jun 1650

149a The humble peticon of THO: WILLOUGHBY JUNIOR in ye behalfe of his father sheweth that whereas MARGRAT the sarvant of MR: CONQUEST hath xxxxxxxxxx broken up ye doores of the house and stolen certain goods of the sd CAPT: THO: WILLOUGHBY & -(faded)- all that was found before confessed it, that all the things -(faded)- hee had, shee gave him, and shee -(faded)- found with a gould ring, which ring was amongst the goods that was stolen which your peticoner is ready to make to appeare xxxxxxxxxxMaid to be triedxxxxxxxxxxxxxxx

INDENTURE: Made in Virginia 15 Jul 1649 betweene THOMAS SAYER of Elizabeth River Lower Norfolk County of the one part & THOMAS MEARES, GENT: of the other part.... for and in consideration of 300 acres of land bought by SAYER of MEARES as by indenture under his hand and seale bearing date (20th?) these presents. SAYER for his heirs exors &c doth agree to pay MEARES the full summe of 6000 l of good sound tobacco ...... in three payments ... 1 Dec 1650, 25 Dec 1651 and 25 Dec 1652 as also pay yearely all such Quitt Rents ..... and for the true pformance of the 6000 l tob & Caske as aforesaid SAYER for himselfe, his heirs &c doth * assign & sett over unto 150*
MEARES his heires &c all that tract of land that hee (SAYER) bought of MEARES .... as also all that tract or divident of land hee, SAYER, doth now occupy, possess & injoy/being 150 acres of land commonly known to bee the land of WILL: RAMSHAW/ with all the houses &c .... also more over these presents doth further testifie that THOS: SAYER doth declare himselfe to bee the true & rightfull owner of the aforesaid 150 acres 150a
Wit: RICH DAUE, THO: RINGOLD, JOHN BIGGS Signed: THO: SAYER & Seale

An INVENTORY made this 23 Mar 1649/50 (year is faded) of all the goods and chattells of ANNE HAYES widd late decd by us whose names are hereunder described. IMPRIMUS: in Snailes Roome

one feather bedd & bolster, one blew Rugge, one Broad cloth xxxx
one posted bedstead wth valence, one matr: & bed cord, one fraxxxxxx and forme, one chair, one Sidye? Cubbeard xxxxxxxxxxxxxxxxxxxxxx

FROM IN THE BUTTERY IN SNAILES ROOME

3 Earthen potts, one wooden platter & a tray, one flesh xxxxxx, small cupps, one marsh tubb, one grindstone

FROM IN THE NEW BUTTERY

3 iron potts, one fryinge pan, one spitt, two barrels, 2 towells, 2 xxxxx 1 small earthen platter, 1 choppinge xxxxxxxx 1 Iron stirringe stick, 1 paire of pott hooks, 1 xxxx sifter, 2 small rundletts, 1 other rundlett
1 pair xxxxxxxxx pound weight, 1 sifting tray, i old chest without a cover xxxxxxx baggs

FROM IN THE OULD BUTTERY

3 anchor Caskes, 3 earthern potts, 2 Farrs?, 1 doxxxxxx locks and key
2 small Farrs?, i trimming iron, one small sifter, 1 xxxxx, 1 small copper kettle

ITEM IN THE MIDDLE ROOMS

1 canvas ticking fild with feathers, one feather boulster, one xxxxx
1 cotton blankett 1 xxxxx xxxxx, 1 twill blocke bedd & xxxx boulster
1 white Rugg, 1 xxxxxx

FROM IN THE SMALL LODGING ROOME

1 cattails bedd & Boulster, 1 broad cloth blankett, a small boate saile

150a 19 Jun 1650

IN THE HALL

8 greate pewter dishes, 2 more pewter dishes, 2 small butter dishes, 1 chamber pott, 2 candlesticks, 1 pewter salt seller, 2 pewter quart potts
2 pint pewter potts, one xxxx xxxxx 2 small pewter cupps, 1 other
151* small pewter cupp, 2 dram cupps, 1 small Samover * 1 pint pewter xxxx (blurred and hard to read) xxxxx xxx pails, irons, hatchetts &c xxxxxxxxxxxxxxxxxxxxxxxxxxxxxxxxxxxxxxxxxxxxxxxx
Indian baskett xxxxxxxxxxxxxxxxxxxxxxxxxxxxxxxxxxxxxxxxxxxxx

IN ONE OTHER SMALL LODGING ROOME

1 rugg, 3 old feather pillows, 1 flock boulster, 2 old blanketts, 1 warming pan, 1 sithe , 1 sedar box, 1 anchor, 1 stone jugg, 1 greate chest, 3 paire of canvas sheetes, 1 tablecloth, xxxxxx xxxxxxxxxxxx (sheetes &c ?) xxxxxxxxxxxxxxxxxxxxxxxxxxxxxxxxxxxxx
(there follows a list of yards of various materials)
Bodkin, stockins, apron, drawers, napkins, beds, &c

151a FROM WITHOUT DOORES *

xxxx cowes xxxxxxxxxxxxxxxxxxxxxxxxxxxxxx
6 barrells of corne xxxxxxxxxxxxxxxxxxx

ROBERT DARBY
HENRY WRIGHT

AT A COURT HELD 19 Jul 1650

PRESENT: CAPT JNO: SIBSEY MR: JNO: HILL
MR: LEMUELL MASON MR: RICH: CONQUEST

CERTIFICATE to JNO: MARTIN for 100 acres for transportation of THO: MOORE & LUKE LEVERMAN. (This is in Nugent)

WHEREAS: JOHN CUBBIGH, CAPT: THO: WILLOUGHBIES (faded) and AMY WHITE servant mayd to the sd CAPT: WILLOUGHBY xxx faded xxx appeared according to ENXXX (Ensign?) THO: LAMBARTS Letter (faded) Complaint of ye sd AMY the business is referred to ye next Court ..... also ANN WATKINS mayd sarvant to CAPT: WILLOUGHBY is then personally to appeare for further proof at AMY WHITES request.

WM: JERMY this day admitted Clerke of ye County Court and hath taken the oath.

A bill binding PEETER HILL to pay EDW: LLOYD 942 lbs tob with caske to be payd in Eliza: River at or before 15 Nov next ensuing and for security .. pass over one black cow .... formerly bought of LLOYD
Dated 18 May 1650 PEETER HILL
Wit: WILLIAM BURGES, RICHARD OWENS

152 ATT A COUNTY COURT HELD 15 AUG 1650

PRESENT: JOHN SIBSEY THOMAS LAMBERT WILLIAM MOSELEY, GENT
JOHN HILL GENT. RICHARD CONQUEST GENT LEMUELL MASON GENT.

CAPT: ffRANCIS YARDLEY agst THOMAS WILLOUGHBY GENT: to the next Court

EMANUELL DOLVEERE plt: agst THOMAS WILLOUGHBY deft: to the next Court

JOHN ffERINHAUGH in his lifetime was in debted unto STEPHEN WARREN for 1185 lbs tob & Caske ....ordered that GEORGE HEIGHAM who intermarried the relict of JOHN ffERINHAUGH to pay the debt and Court Charges

Complaint of GEORGE HEIGHAM against URSULA BAYLY, his servant, for her often with drawinge herselfe out of the sd HEIGHAMS (service?) to his xxxxxx and hindrance xxxxxxx ordered that URSULA serve HEIGHAM for one whole yeare after experacon of her terme in sattisfacon of her offence

THOMAS BRIDGE to bringe in account of the estate of (JOHN?) FLETCHER to the next Court and the difference between BRIDGE and ROBT: EYRE be then determined.

NOTE: This next is faded and some of it cannot be read. The name may be CROKE but your editor cannot be sure. The first letter is, however, a capital C. AGW
ROBTE GRIMES arrested to the Court by HENERY CROKE? xxxxxxxxxxxx GRIMES together with his mate had taken 6 bedds of plants xxxxxxxxxx 300 or 400 plants xxxxxxxxxxxxxxxxx which were given by said (CROWE?) to one MR: DAYNES for wante xxxxxxxxxxxxxxxxxxxxx

WILLIAM JOHNSON was arrested to the Court at suite of JOHN MARTINE, THOMAS WARDE being his security xxxxxxxx to the next Court. 152a

HENERY MERRITT was arrested to this Court at the sute of ffRANCIS BRIGHT xxxxx IVY being the security to the Sheriffe xxxxxxxxxxxx to the next Court.

HENERY MERRITT was arrested to the Court by THOMAS WANESWORTH, MR: IVY being his security to the next Court.

ANNE WHITE hath unjustly made severall complaints agst JOHN CUBBIDGE .....ordered that ANNE acknowledge in Court that shee hath done CUBBIDGE wrong and if any other complaints shee is to bee punished.

JOHN CUBBIDGE hath heretofore spake scandalous and abusive words agst CAPT: JNO: SIBSEY one of the Comrs: ....CUBBIDGE to acknow-ledge his fault in Open Court ....and to be severely punished if repeated agst any of the Comrs: in the meantime to pay Court Charges. Complaint of THOMAS SAWYER for and concerninge damage done by oxen .... (this is blurred and faded)

MR: LAMBERT & MR: CONQUEST to meete at the house of MR: LAMBERT uppon 4 Sep next to take the INVENTORY of the Estate of RICHARD (K?)ENNER deceased to be appraised by MR: IVY, MR: SHIPP?, JOHN MERRIDITH and JASPER HOSKINS.

THOMAS LAMBERT GENT: stands indebted to JOHN MERRIDITH for 150 lbs tob for the repayinge and amending of a Xeyne Boate at the request of MR: THOMAS LAMBART xxx being not yet unpaid xx ordered that LAMBART pay 153

NOTE: the following is all that is legible of the record: WHEREAS: there is a difference betweene xxxxxxxxxxxxxxxxxx MR. LEMUELL MASON xxxxxx PHILLIPPS concerning certain goods which were MRS. ALICE xxxx

xxxx said LEMUELL MASON having accepted both Governor and Counsell xxxxxxxxx xxxxxxxx it is therefore ordered the sd LEMUELL MASON shall put in security according to Act of Assembly and make his appearance before the Governor and Council and xxxxxxxx the first xxxx October Court next.

Difference betweene ANNE PHILLIPPS widd adm: of MATHEW PHILLIPPS decd and LEMUELL MASON GENT: concerninge xxxxxxxxxxxxx in the possession of MRS. SEWELL, the said ANNE PHILLIPPS having appealed to the Governor and Counsell xxxxxxxxto give Security and to make appearance the Sixt (sic) Oct next.

CORNELIUS LLOYD plt: agst STEPHEN KEY referred to next Court.

Attachment heretofore granted agst the estate of OWEN POWELL in the hands of MRIS: ANNE PHILLIPPS widd: at the sute of THOMAS ALLEN. The Sheriffe hath executed same by attachinge 19 paire of Wadmall stockings, 4 paire of blacke bootes, 6 lampes, 33 paire of yarn stockings, most of them motheaten xxxxxxxx they should be appraised and then delivered to THOMAS ALLEN towards satisfaccon of his debt.

CERTIFICATE: to RICHARD OWENS for 300 acres for transportation of: himselfe, MARY his wife, and four servants vitz: (Milka?) HUFFEY, NICHOLAS XXffeway, HENERY HILLS and THOMAS ROPER.

CERTIFICATE: to THOMAS WHITE for 100 acres for transportation of two servants JOHN BIGGS and GEORGE GOODMAN.

CERTIFICATE: to THOMAS SAWYER for 550 acres for transportation of eleven persons: himselfe, ffRANCES SAWYER, ffRANCIS SAWYER, ROBTE: ffITT (or HITT?), MARGARET YELLOW, ELIZABETH YELLOWE, WILLIAM HEATH, MARGARET CARTER, JOHN BORINGE, ANNE SAWYER and ffRANCIS ELLYOTT.

CERTIFICATE: to LEWIS ffARMALL for 150 acres for transportation of: himselfe, ELIZABETH ffARMALL his wife, and EDMUND CREEKEMAN.

153a NOTE: The top of this page is torn and parts are missing. The first item is something about 300 or 400 plants. See Robert Grimes on f 152, page 143.

JOHN NORWOOD of Elizabeth City, Planter, selling for 4000 lbs tob unto PETER MICHOLSON with the rest of the owners of the shipp called the HUISSON NASSAU belonging to OLSSINGEN in Zeeland 200 acres of land being on this first entrance of the Eastern Branch? of Elizabeth River bounded or limited accordinge to a Patent granted unto me by SIR WM: BERKELEY bearing date the last of Apr 16(44?) John Norwood
Dated 27 Feb 1649 Recorded 15 Aug 1650
Wit: ROBTE: HELMS, HENRY JULLUS
WM: JERMY/CL: CUR:

154

AT A COUNTY COURT HELD 15 OCTOBER 1650

PRESENT: CAPT: JOHN SIBSEY, MR: JOHN HILL, MR. THOMAS LAMBERT, MR. RICHARD CONQUEST, MR. LEMUEL MASON

There were no cases because the Assembly started meeting the 10 Oct. Court to be held 1 Nov 1650.

AT A COUNTY COURT HELD 1 NOV 1650

PRESENT:	CAPT JOHN SIBSEY	MR. HENRY WOODHOUSE
	MR. RICHARD CONQUEST	MR. JOHN HILL
	MR. THOMAS LAMBERT	MR. LEMUELL MASON

WILLIAM JOHNSON indebted unto JOHN MARTIN 700 lbs of tob with caske and certaine Smithers worke. JOHNSON to pay balance due on this account, deliver Smithes worke and court charges.

CHRISTOPHER NEEDEHAM longetime stood indebted unto ROBTE: HAYES late deceased for 1400 lbs tob. NEEDEHAM makinge it appeare that the debt is fully paid ..... the said bill shall be canceled.

WILLIAM JOHNSON INDEBTED unto THOMAS ADDAMS for 200 lbs tob .... to pay this debt in 10 days.

154a

Upon peticon of ROBTE DAVYES it is ordered that ye one WHEELER send into this Country suffaccon (sic) unto the said DAVYES for the bringing up of JOHN MAY an orphant now in the custody of the sd DAVYES betweene this and Christmas next, that then soe much of the orphans Estate sall be appraised by JOB CHANDLER, JOHN STRATON, EDWARD HALL, and THOMAS DILLON as shall make satisfaccon unto the sd ROBTE DAVYES for the bringing up of the said orphan.

Administration granted unto ROGER CROSSE on the estate of WILLIAM HOBSON deceased, giving bond with good security for the safety of the Court, And the said CROSSE -(faded)- ffRANCIS BRIGHT & MATHEWE READE from all damages that may arise to them by reason of the Estate of WM: HOBSON

THOMAS LAMBERT GENT: engageth himselfe to the Comrs: of this Court in the some (sum) of 20,000 lbs tob that ROGER CROSSE shall at the next Court bring in a true inventory of WILLIAM HOBSON.

ROBTE: DAVYES shall pay unto JOHN MOORE -(faded)- & halfe of Indian corne xxxxxxxxxx for worke done for DAVYES.

It is further ordered by this Court that if any man hereafter shall hyer or take -xxxx- the foresaid JOHN MOORE that they shall allowe ye sd MOORE competent wages for his hire and if MOORE after such engagmt shall without sufficient cause withdraw himselfe out of such service and neglect the same, that then MOORE shalbe taken to ye Constable and carried to the next Justice of Peace and to receive 20 or 30 lashes uppon the bare back and then to return to service again.

THOMAS IVEY atty: of HENERY MERRITT acknowledges judgmt for 620 lbs tob & caske unto ffRANCIS BRIGHT to be paid upon demand.

SAMUELL CHARINCOE standeth indebted unto RICHARD CONQUEST as Administrator of JOHN KEMPE deceased for 864 lb tob. CHARINCOE to make paymt in 20 days.

EDWARD WINDHAM standeth indebted unto JOHN DYER, assignee of PEETER ffREDERICKE in ye some of 370 lbs of tob by bill. WINDHAM to pay debt and Court Charges.

WILLIAM CLEAVER standeth indebted unto JOHN DYER -x torn x- 300 lb tob CLEAVER to pay in 10 days and Court Charges.

WILLIAM JOHNSON indebted unto THOMAS SMITHERS 240 lb tob. JOHNSON to pay in tenne days and Court Charges.

THOMAS GODBY & his wife agst RICHARD BECKE & his wife upon full hearing ordered that RICHARD BECKE & his wife, in open Court, shall aske GODBYE & his wife forgiveness and if hereafter BECKE's wife abuses GODBY's wife she shall be severely punished.

THOMAS CONYERS hath arrested THOMAS WORKEMAN to appeare & CONYERS not appearing to be non suited and pay Court Charges.

CERTIFICATE: to JOANNE YATES for 50 acres for transportation of one maide servant MARY SYARLOCKE. (name is hard to read and Nugent also gives this spelling p 270)

CERTIFICATE: to BARTHOLOMEW HOSKINS for 50 acres for transportation of one man servant WALTER DENHAM.

CERTIFICATE: to RICHARD ffOSTER for 250 acres for transportation of himselfe, DORCAS ffOSTER his wife, DORCAS ffOSTER his daughter, RICHARD STREETE and HENRY WILLIAMS.

RICHARD CONQUEST agst SAMUEL CHARNICOE to next Court.

SAMUELL MATHEWES ESQR: agst GEORGE ASHALL to next Court.

THOMAS BRIDGE agst ffRANCIS YARDLEY to next Court.

THOMAS ALLEN agst CAPT: ffRANCIS YARDLEY to next Court.

155a CAPT: ffRANCIS YARDLEY agst JAMES LOPHAM to next Court.

CAPT: ffRANCIS YARDLEY agst JAMES LOPHAM in an accon of defamaccon is referred to the next Court. (this is the second case recorded)

THOMAS ALLEN agst CAPT: ffRANCIS YARDLEY to the next Court.

CAPT: ffRANCIS YARDLEY agst EDWARD HALL to next Court.

LAWRENCE PHILLIPPS and TRISTROM MASON to the next Court.

THOMAS DAVYES agst WILLIAM (JERMY?) to next Court.

ROBTE: EWENS (EVENS?) agst GEORGE HEIGHAM to next Court.

SIMOND CORNIX agst ROBT: POWES JUNR: to next Court.

SIMOND CORNIX agst JOHN DYER & ROBT: POWES JUNR: to next Court.

RICHARD CONQUEST guardian of JOHN KENMAR and administrator of RICHARD deceased agst GEORGE HEIGHAM to the next Court.

ffRANCIS BRIGHT agst WILLIAM DAVENALL & MARY his wife to next Court.

ROBTE: EYRE agst THOMAS BRIDGE to next Court.

156 CAPT: ffRANCIS YARDLEY agst THOMAS WILLOBY JUNR: to next Court.

EMANUELL DOHEERE? agst THOMAS WILLOUGHBY to next Court.

INTERREGATORYE: Exhibited in Court by THOMAS ALLEN and sworne to by RICHARD LEE. FIRST: Whether you doe knowe a Cow of heifer belongeing to CAPT: YARDLEY his Penn which goeth by the name of JAMES SMITHERS his cor of heifer. Whether you doe knowe the marke of JAMES SMITHERS cattle or not . What cowe that was which you said to ANNE GASKIN had another Cowe Calve. Whether you doe not knowe a steare which was JAMES SMITHERS belonging to CAPT: YARDLEY his Penn. The said RICHARD LEE answereth negatively to owne on interregation.

WILLIAM QUINTAN Recorded 10 Oct 1650 Dated 1 Jul 1650. We whose names are here underwritten beinge unpannelled and sworne to viewe the body of QUINTAN (missing) who was found dead uppon the Lower Point of the mouth of the Creeke called Clarkes Creeke in the Westerne Branch of Elizabeth River uppon the day and yeare abovewritten And to enquire by whatmeans he came to his death and having viewed the said boddy wee find as followeth: That the said WM: QUINTAN goinge into theiver to washe himselfe and going beyond his Reach was carried off with the tide And soe was drowned without cause of any other.
Signed: THOMAS WRIGHT, PETER RIGGLESWORTH, JOHN HATTON, RICHARD STARNELL the Jury.
Sworne to before me THOMAS BROWNE, High Sheriffe. 156a

WILLIAM SAMSON Recorded 10 Oct 1649 (must mean 1650)Dated 1 Jul 1650 Jury sworne to review the boddy of WILLIAM SAMPSON who was found dead uppon the flatts of a Creeke called BROWNE's Bay in the Western Branch of Elizabeth River on 1 July 1650 ....WILLIAM SAMPSON going into the river to wash himselfe and seeinge another boy which was likewise drowned at the same time, in Danger, seekinge to help him was himselfe drowned without any cause of any other witness.
Jurors: RICHARD OWENS, RICHARD (MARK) JENNINGS, WILLIAM (MARK) DAVENALL, JOHN HARRIS, THOMAS (MARK) HOLLOWAY, MATHEW (MARK) READ, THOMAS (MARK) PARKER and five other names of jurors which are faded.
Sworne before me THOMAS BROWNE, High Sheriff.

ATT A COUNTY COURT HELD 15 NOV 1650

PRESENT:	CAPT: JOHN SIBSEY	MR. THOMAS LAMBERT
	MR. RICHARD CONQUEST	MR. JOHN HILL
	MR. WILLIAM MOSELEY	MR. LEMUELL MASON

LANCASTER LOVETT, Churchwarden of Linhaven Parish concerning a debte of 750 lb tob and caske due from Executors of ANNE HAYES widd decd who was administrator of ROBTE: HAYES her husband who stoode indebted to the aforesd parish and being long since due. Executors of ANNE HAYES to pay the debt and Court charges.

On order from the Governor the Court has appointed MR: WOODHOUSE & MR: CONQUEST or either of them to demand and receive .... all such debts as are due from any pson or psons within this Collony concerninge the wrecke of CAPT: LUCK's Shipp and to give an account unto the Court 15 Feb next. All who fayle to pay to be arrested to the Court.

Probate of the last will and testament of GEORGE HORNER granted unto ELLEN HORNER late wife of the sd GEORGE HORNER and sole executrix named in the will. 157

ANNE PHILLIPPS widd to be satisfied out of the Estate of JOHN CLAUSON decd 1034 lb tob and Caske.

157 15 Nov 1650

ffRANCIS LAND to be satisfied out of the estate of JOHN RICHARDSON being dpted out of this Collony for 370 lb tob leafe and Court Charges. (dpted meand departed)

ROBTE EYRES atty of RICHARD CLARKE Wine (cooper?) of London agst the estate of ROGER ffLETCHER decd now in the hands of THOMAS BRIDGE. (No amount given)

CAPT: JOHN SIBSEY shall be satisfied out of the estate of ROGER ffLETCHER to the next Court.

THOMAS BRIDGE to bring in a full and perfect inventory of the Estate of ROGER ffLETCHER, decd to the next Court.

ffRANCIS LAND has in his possession one cowe belonging to MARGY RUTHERFORD and ANNE RUTHERFORD orphans which hath - xxxxxx - tymes like to have been mired and lost - xxxxxx - ordered LAND shall kill the Cowe and make what proffitt he can of her and give an account to the Court in behalfe of the orphans.

SYMOND CORNIX presented to the Court by LANCASTER LOVETT, Church Warden of Linhaven Prish for a (sermon?) and abroad and for a most impudent and shamefull carriage and behaviour found a widdowe woman being his servant. It is therefore ordered that a warrant issue forth agst the said CORNIX for his psonall appearance at the next Court to make answere to the psentment.

Peticon of HENRY SNAYLE as alsoe uppon the informacon of the Vestry of Lynhaven Prish that he is an aged man decreped and havinge a great chardge of children. It is by this Court thought fitt and ordered that the said HENRY SNAYLE shall from henceforward be free from all taxacons and Publique Levyes Excepting Church duties.

157a Peticon of RICHARD CONQUEST administrator of JOHN KEMPE decd that whereas GEORGE SPENLEY dyed intestate with a sufficient estate whereby to satisfy his debts and beinge indebted unto the decedent (John Kempe) and a little before the death of SPENDLEY........... the people where he lived have possessed themselves of SPENDLEYS ESTATE without order. It is therefore ordered by this Court desired that MR. WOODHOUSE by order from this Court authorized should make inquiry either xxxxxxxxxxx Examincon of witnesses and to call before him whome he shall think fitt to learne whoe hath possessed themselves of SPENDLEYS Estate and to make a report to the Court.

HENRY WOODHOUSE to investigate an estate.

CERTIFICATE: to ffRANCIS LAND for 200 acres for transportation of: DARBY BROWNE, THOMAS WILSON, WILLIAM SISSELL and ANNE GRATICKE. (NOTE: Nugent gives this name as GATICKE)

CERTIFICATE: to NICHOLAS SEABORNE for 100 acres assigned on by MR: RICHARD CONQUEST for transportation of two servants: JOHN ARRUNDLE and MARY GREENE.

CERTIFICATE: to RICHARD WHITEHURST for 300 acres for transportation of: ARGHILL CAMMERON (Nugent gives Camoron) DAVID MURROWES, THOMAS SANDERSON, WILLIAM CASTLE, BARTHOLOMEW WARD, MATHEW MATHAIS & ANNE LOVELL.

15 Nov 1650

CERTIFICATE: to WILLIAM MORTON for 100 acres assigned on by THOMAS LAMBERT agent for transportation of two servants, ANNE PATES, SAMUELL ROBERTS and JAMES ROBERTS. 157a

CAPT. ffRANCIS YARDLEY plt agst JAMES LOPHAM deft to the next ourt.

CAPT: ffRANCIS YARDLEY plt agst THOMAS WILLOUGHBY deft referred vt Sup

CAPT: YARDLEY agst THOMAS ALLEN referred vt Sup^{x}

THOMAS ALLEN plt agst CAPT: YARDLEY deft referred vt Sup^{x}

ROBTE: EWENS plt agst GEORGE HEIGHAM deft referred vy Sup^{x}

158

PAYMENTS TO BE MADE OUT OF THE COUNTY LEVYES FOR THE PRESENT YEAR	1 tob
MR. JOHN HILL for Burgesses Charges	1860
MR. JOHN SIDNEY for his charges as Burgess	1700
MR. THOMAS BROWNE being High Shreive as by his account	2420
To MR. THOMAS IVY concerninge an Indians imprisonmt as by acct	600
Clerkes at Jamestown paid by MR. CONQUEST	60
More to him as pr account for ROBTE: PEIRSON his charges	1000
THOMAS LAMBERT as Collector for his arreares as p acct	959
THOMAS RAYNOLDS for his attendance upon the shreive uppon the proclayminge of the King	40
THOMAS TOOKER for Clerkes fees concerning PEIRSON as p account	100
To the Publique Levy	5808
THOMAS BROWNE the younger for four wolves heads	400
PETER SEXTON for 2 wolves heads	200
LINTON MOYSES for 1 wolfes head	100
MATHEW HOWARD for the like	100
JOHN MARTIN for the like	100
XPOFER RIVERS for the like	100
GEORGE KEMPE for the like	100
WILLIAM LANGLEY for the like	100
SIMON PEETERS for the like	100
JOHN GILHAM for 2 wolves heads	200
THOMAS ALLEN for one wolfes head	100
ANDREW WARNER for the like	100
MR. CAUSON for the like	100
WILLIAM BURGES for the like	100
JOHN WORKEMAN for the like	100
WILLIAM BASNETT for the like	100
SUMME TOTAL	16,647

158a

448 tytheable persons within this County.

MR. JOHN HILL appointed to be Collector of Tythes for the Western Branch of Lynhaven River from 76 tytheable persons and to pay

To MR. THOMAS BROWNE in full of account	2420
To THOMAS BROWNE JUNR: in pte for four wolves heads	385

158a 15 Nov 1650

MR. THOMAS LAMBERT appointed to be Collector of tythes from DANIELL TANNERS CREEK unto the Easterne and Southerne Branches of Lynhavven River from 114 persons and to pay: (should read Elizabeth River)

MR. JOHN HILL in full for Burgesses Chardges	(blank)
THOMAS BROWNE the younger in full for four wolves heads	"
MOYSES LINTON for one Wolfes head	100
PETER SEXTON for 2 wolves heads	200
MATHEWE HOWARD for one wolves head	100
XPOFER RIVERS for the like	100
JOHN HILL to himselfe for his arreres (sic) as Collector	959
GEORGE KEMPE for one wolves head	100
MR. SIDNEY in pte of his Chardges as Burgess	260
To salary	433
TOTAL	4332

CAPT: JOHN SIBSEY appointed to be collector of tythes from DANIELL TANNERS CREEK to CAPT: WILLOBYS from 54 tytheables and to pay:

159 MR: IVEY -blurred and illegible - in full as p account

WILLIAM LANGLEY for one Wolves head	100
SIMOND PETERS for the like	100
THOMAS RAYNOLDS for his attandance uppon the Shreive upon the proclayminge of the Kinge	0040
MR: CONQUEST in part of his account	XXX
To Sallary of 2052 at ten p cent	205

MR. LEMUELL MASON appointed to be Collector of tythes for the Little Creek from 66 tytheable persons and to pay:

THOMAS TOOKER for Clerkes Fees as per account in full	100
JOHN WORKEMAN for one Wolves head	100
WILLIAM BURGES for ye like	100
MR. CONQUEST in full of his account	53
To the Publique	1995
To Sallary 2508 at ten p cent	250

MR. MOSELEY appointed Collector of tythes for ye Western Shoare of Lynnhaven River from 91 tytheables and to pay:

JOHN GILHAM for killing of two Wolves	200
MR. SIDNEY in full of his Chardges as Burgess	1440
JOHN MARTIN for killinge one wolfe	100
To the Publique	1373
To Sallary	345
TOTAL	3458

MR. JOB CHANDLER appointed collector of tythes for the Easterne Shoare of Lynhaven River for 84 tytheables and to pay:

THOMAS ALLEN for killinge one Wolfe	100
ANDREW WARNER for ye like	100
WILLIAM BASNET for ye like	100
THOMAS CASSON for the (sic) like	100
To the Publique	2473
To Sallary	319
TOTAL	3192

159a

TO THE COMRS: OF LOWER NORFOLK: An Accounting concerning the wrecke of CAPT LUCK's ship to be exhibited unto me at the March Quarter Court next. Given at Berkeley farme under my hand 11 Nov 1650

WM: BERKELEY

GEORGE HORNER will dated 20 Aug 1650 No probate. Wife not named
Witnesses: HENERY (H)BRAKES and EDWARD(E)CRADWELL
Overseers: LEMUELL MASON and JOHN HOLMES
......being sicke in body...
unto my wife all household goods ....one calfe called Sherry and her heifer .... 2 men servants................................
unto my 3 children fower cowes, two bearinge cowe calves, one bull calve, one xxxxx, one bull of a yere and a halfe ould ....
to be equally divided between my 3 children and my wife to have the benefit ...... and the male encrease soe longe as they shall live with her and if any of my three daughters dye before they come to age ...... to be devided between their two sisters ...... there are also two bulls which I give unto my wife for provision for her house ..... my land called Crab Point to my wife. George Horner

160

(NOTE: The top of this page is torn and the following could be either a will or a deed of gift) .... unto SARAH WILLIAMS ... (cows with descriptions)...... until said SARAH arrive at the yeres of 16........
in case shee should dye before shee is at age to owne them, that then they should be equally divided amongst the rest of the children of ROGER WILLIAMS (this name should be WILLIAMSON) and JOHN CARRAWAYS that shall be livinge. Dated 31 Jul 1650
Wit: ROBTE: EYRE & SIMON (SH) HANCOCKE Signed: Richard Hafton

17 (Jun?) 1650 difference betwn: RICHARD JOANES Plt & THOMAS MARSH deft .... THOS: MARSH having left order with mee to doe therein as I should see cause accordinge to ye testimony brought before me by ye said JOANES, And it appearing unto mee by the deposicon of ROBTE: BOGGAS taken before me SAMUELL STOUGTER? also by testimony under ye hand of JAMES BRACK (BROCK?) That RICHARD JOANES has a dischardge signed with the name of THOMAS MARSH which did mencon 200 lbs tob received for use of MR: BRICE which dischardge ye sd JOANES delivered unto ZACHARY TAYLOR. I do therefore order that ye sd JOANES his bill due to the sd BRICE and alsoe pay unto ye sd JOANES .....& Court Chardges. JOHN HILL John Hill 160a

AT A COUNTY COURT HELD 15 (Dec 1650?)

PRESENT: xxxx xOHN SIBSEY MR: LEMUELL MASON
MR: JOHN HILL MR. WILLIAM MOSELEY
MR: THOMAS LAMBERT

(this page is torn)

LAWRENCE PHILLIPPS to pay 270 lb tob with Court Charges due unto THOMAS DADFORD by bill.

SIMON HANCOCKE hath made it appeare that there is due to him as assignee of EDWARD HALL, Chirurgeon from THOMAS WORKEMAN & NATHANIEL HAYES 940 lb tob with Caske .... WORKEMAN & HAYES to pay SIMON HANCOCKE

....There is due unto ANNE PHILLIPPS administrator of MATHEWE PHILLIPPS deceased, from JOHN PORTER (1?)17 lb tob with Caske being the remainder of a bill ......PORTER to pay with Court Charges.

JAMES SMITH was taxed for killing one hogge of HENERY WESTGATE ....
ordered that JAMES SMITH pay unto WESTGATE 700 lb tob and alsoe.......
EDWARD WILDER, he being the first informer thereof 100 lb tob.........

and SMITH to remaine in the Shreives hands untill he hath put in security .... with Court Charges.

..... It hath been playnely made appeare by HENRY WESTGATE as alsoe by confession that THOMAS PAXFORD, JOHN EYRES, GUY EVENS & JANE LATHAM, servants of MRS: ANNE PHILLIPPS widd: were confederates with JAMES SMITH in ye unlawfull killing of a hogge of ye sd HENRY WESTGATES. Therefore they are fined, each of them, to pay unto ye Comrs: of this Court for ye Countys use within one year after ye expiracon of their termes of service...........

161 (NOTE: This page is badly torn at the top, sides, and a strip out of the middle of the page. AGW)

MR: LEMUEL MASON shall receive ye saide Sowe xxxxxxx (the rest of this record is eligible and torn) xxxxxxxxxxxxxxxxxxxxxxxxxxxxxxxxxxxxxx

(JENY?) HILL widd: xxxx weake estate xxxxtornxxxxxxxx non ability xxxx (main)tayninge herself and her children ordered xxxxtornxxxxxx shall be quietly & xxxxxxtornxxxxxxxx possessed of ye estate of her husband deceased xxxxxxxxtornxxxxxxx without any further molestacon ....

THOMAS BRIDGES hath made it appeare that there is due unto him as agent xxxxtornxxxx (PET?)ER STYNNLAUDE, Governor of the Dutch Plantation xxxxtornxxxx FRANCIS YARDLEY 1400 lb tob & Caske xxxxx CAPT: ffRANCIS YARDLEY to pay with Court Charges. (Note: Your Editor feels sure that this is PETER STUYVESANT 1592-1672)

APT: ffRANCIS YARDLEY pltf & THOMAS ALLEN attorney of xxxtornxxx CANNON deft xxxxtornxxxx ordered that EDWARD CANNON & EDWARD HALL GENT: shall satisfie unto CAPT: ffRANCIS YARDLEY 400 lb tob or else one bulle .....

THOMAS ALLEN pltf agst CAPT: ffRANCIS YARDLEY deft concerning one steare & one heifer and ye sd CAPT: YARDLEY xxxxtornxxxx to put in security.

In the difference between CAPT: ffRANCIS YARDLEY plt & THOMAS WILLOUGHBY, JUNR: Attorney of THOMAS WILLOBY SENR: deft upon a full hearinge in Court of ye xxxx?xxxxx in question. It is ordered that THOMAS WILLOUGHBY satisffie and pay unto CAPT: ffRANCIS YEADLEY or his assigns 600 lb tob for ye use of ye orphants of CAPT: THURROWGOOD for satisfaccon of a mare colt. And alsoe xxxxtornxxxx satisfie unto ye sd YARDLEY (fall?) calve beinge borrowed by -(rest of this is faded)-

Peticon of ANNE WATKINS, servant of CAPT: THOMAS WILLOBYE, concerning her freedom. It is ordered that ye sd ANNE should be sett free, she satisfieinge and payenge unto THOMAS WILLOBYE JUNR:, Attorney of CAPT: THOMAS WILLOBY for 600 lb tob in consideracon of neglected service. And, shee, ye sd ANNE havinge unlawfully brought forth a Child duringe the tyme of her sd terme. And shee ye sd ANNE to put security for ye pformance aforesd otherwyse to serve ye sd THOMAS till shee procure it. And ye sd THOMAS WILLOBY to give unto ye sd ANNE /upon her security givinge/ the Corne and Cloathes which of right belonge unto her accordinge to the Custome of ye County or by Indenture.

161a (NOTE: Top of this page missing and some of the records torn eligible)

xxxxx attachment granted on estate of -missing- of THOMAS BRIDGE at ye Suite of ROBTE: EYRE attorney of RICHARD -torn- xxxx London xxxxxxxxxxx

SAVILL GASKIN & ANNE, his wife, were subponed unto the (Court) xxxxx of CAPT: ffRANCIS YARDLEY to testifye their knowledge in a cause xxx xxxtornxxxxx THOMAS ALLEN pltf ye sd CAPT: YARDLEY xxxxxtornxxxxxxxx they utterly refused to make their appearance. Therefore for their xxxxxxtornxxxxxx are fined 500 lb tob ....

Ordered that MR. LEMUELL MASON shall have full power and authority xxxxtornxxxx and take or any legall manner recon? all such debts and demands xxxxxtornxxxxx HENERY SEWELL, Orphan of HENERY SEWELL deceased be ye sd LEMUELL XXXtornXXXX givinge an account to this Court of his doeings therein ....

THOMAS WORKEMAN one of the Executors of ANNE HAYES xxxxxordered that WILLIAM ffANN?, STEPHEN KEY, THOMAS WSXXXX shall have full power to appraise ye estate of ye sd ANNE HAYES being first sworne by MR: LEMUELL MASON.........

HENERY SNAYLE pltf agst JOHN MARTIN deft to next Court.

ROBTS: EWENS plt agst GEORGE HEIGHAM deft to next Court.

COB HOWELL pltf agst ffRANCIS LAND deft to next Court.

EDWARD HALL Chirurgeon pltf agst THOMAS WILLOBY JUNR: Attorney of CAPT: THOMAS WILLOBY SENT: deft to next Court.

.... ye three causes dependinge betweene ffRANCIS LAND plt & COB: HOWELL deft to the next Court- 162

CAPT: ffRANCIS YARDLEY pltf agst xxxxxxtornxxxxx to the next Court.

RICHARD CONQUEST pltf agst THOMAS WORKEMAN executor of ANNE HAYES widow, decd deft to next Court.

RICHARD CONQUEST plt agst ROWLAND MORGAN deft to next Court.

ROGER ffLETCHER, Merchant decd...the Estate of in the hands of THO: BRIDGE. INVENTORY: dated 3 Nov 1650 pr RICHARD WAKE deceased by bill ye 13 Nov 1646 & Caske. JOHN SIBSEY by bill due 1646.
THOMAS BURBAGE by accoumpt in 1646 with Caske
RICHARD KENNAR decd by account 1646
xxtornxx BRADLEY decd xxtornxx at Chucketucke by bill
xxtornxx MOORE & JOSIAS SMITH by bill 3hh tob sent to England
xxxtornxxxxxxxxxxxxxxxxxxx WILLIAM ADDAMS by bill with Caske
MR: THOMAS BROWNE by remainder of account in 1646
MR: THOMAS IVEY by remainder of his bill 1646
MR: PEETER KNIGHT by bill with Caske.
MR. JOHN SIDNEY by bill with Caske

Tho. Bridge
THO: BRIDGE Total (faded)

ATT A COURT HELD AT ELIZABETH CITTY 18 Feb 1649/50

PRESENT: MR: ANTHONY ELLIOTT, MR: JOHN CHANDLER, LEIFT WILLIAM WORLICK, MR. JOHN ROBINS

Whereas: that CAPT: ffRANCIS YARDLEY hath bound on unto MR: WILLIAM HARRIS of ROTTERDAM and Company or their assignes 3 Negroes namely ffrancisco, Little Lewis and Antonio for paymt of 4278 lb tob & caske by the 20 November next. Notwithstanding ye casualty of the death of all or one of ye sd Negroes this acknowledgmt to stand firme, to bind ye said CAPT: YARDLEY as a Judgmt and uppon default of paymt Execucon to issue out either uppon ye sd Negroes of agst the sd CAPT: YARDLEY to the usuall Course of Lawe.

Recordat: (names not legible)

162a

ATT A QUARTER COURT HELD AT JAMES CITTY 30 Oct (1650?)
The Honorable WILLIAM BERKELEY, Gov.

PRESENT:	CAPT: SAMUELL MATHEWES	CAPT: WILLIAM CLAYBOURNE)	
	CAPT: HENERY BROWNE	CAPT: HUMPHREY HIGGINSON)	- ESQRS:
	MR GEORGE LUDLOE	CAPT: ffRANCIS MORRISON)	
	CAPT: BRIDGES FREEMAN	)	

It is ordered that MR: CORNELIUS LOYD deliver in the bond to CAPT: ffRANCIS YARDLEY Wherein MR: ARGIL YARDLEY ESQR: the sd CAPT: YARDLEY stand bound xxxxtornxxxx bond xxx 3402 lb tob to THOMAS BABB? the said debte beinge satisfied by ye said MR: ARGALL (sic) and that the Judgmt agst CAPT: YARDLEY in Lower (Norfolk County?) be reversed.
per mee THOMAS XXXXXX 9Name faded)

Received of WM: HOBSEN these bills as followeth:

1 bill of JAMES LOVE 366 lb tob		JOHN WATTFORD	247
1 bill of THOMAS HOLLOWELL	262	THOMAS TOMAS	669
1 bill of THOMAS BROWNE, GENT:	320	JOHN HORNE	2000
1 bill of WM: DAVENALL	277	JOHN PIPER	381
1 bill of JOANE YATES	341	EXPOFER RIVERS	394
1 bill of WATT HOWARD	326	MATHEWE READS	780
i bill of THOMAS WRIGHT	1810	THOMAS ALLENS	XXX
RICHARD YATES	1048	WILLIAM SHIPP	XXX
JOHN (RISCOMES?)	400	WILLIAM BATTAINE	XXX
THOMAS WRIGHTS	545	JOHN ASCOME	XXX
THOMAS DAVIES	200	JOHN GODFREY	XXX
MR: THOMAS LAMBERT	5390	THOMAS MEARES	XXX
RICHARD STERNELLS	460	RICHARD JENNINGS	XXX
WILLIAM BRUSE	360	ROBTE: BOWERS	XXX
THOMAS BAYLY	100	ffRANCIS HALE	XXX
		TOTAL	(Amounts are faded)

p mee ROGUM CROSSE p mee WM: JERMY

163

ATT A COURT HELD 15 JAN 1650/51

PRESENT:	CAPT: JOHN SIBSEY	MR: THOMAS LAMBERT)	
	MR: JOHN HILL	MR: RICHARD CONQUEST)	-COMRS:
	MR: LEMUELL MASON	)	

Attachmt granted HENERY BRAKES agst so much of the estate of THOMAS BUTTERES beinge departed out of this Collony for 100 lb tob with Caske and Court Charges.

Attachmt: granted CORNELIUS LOYDE agst Estate of JOHN MEARES for 1200 lb tob.

Attachmt granted WILLIAM DENHAM who intermarried with ELIZABETH ye late wife of WILLIAM BURDELL? agst so much of the estate of THOMAS BUTTERES beinge departed out of this Collony as shall satisfy 138 lb tob. HENERY BRAKES being first satisfied.

RICHARD CONQUEST hath impleaded THOMAS WORKEMAN one of ye executors of ANNE HAYES widd: deceased who was administrix of ROBTE: HAYES her husband deceased the sd CONQUEST having procured bills of Secretaries, Shreives & Clarkes for xxxxxxxx according to Act xxxxxxxxx to the sum of 500 lb tob xxxxx-x and being found due from the sd ROBTE: HAYES it is therefore ordered that WORKEMAN doe not at ye next Court pduce acquittances thereof that then Judgmt to passe agst him.

ffRANCIS LAND & COB HOWELL to meet at the house of SAVILL GASKIN there to make upp their accounts.

WHEREAS: JOHN WORKEMAN hath impleaded CAPT: ffRANCIS YARDLEY uppon an accon of battery and uppon full hearinge in Court & uppon testimony affirmed, it appeared that ye sd YARDLEY & WORKEMAN with sinxse? others were mett together in a combustion in a mutinous kind of manner contrary to the lawes of this Collony. They are therefore fined by this Court 100 lb tob a peice. And alsoe EDWARD STANDLEY, JOHN PARKER, and WILLIAM COOKE being then there present are fined 100 lb tob a peice for ye use of ye County. And alsoe EDWARD HALL Chirurgeon is fined 200 lb tob being then present and drawinge his sword amongst them to ye uses aforesaid .... if any further complaint ....may they be severely punished and each one to beare their owne charges.

SAVILL GASKIN pltf agst CAPT: ffRANCIS YARDLEY -xxfadedxx- It is by this Court ordered that ye sd CAPT: YARDLEY shall deliver -xxxtornxxx- Wherein the sd GASKIN stands engaged unto SARAH ye now wife of the sd CAPT: YARDLEY xxxfadedxxx the buildinge of an house to be camelled (sic) or else to give an aquittance thereof unto the sd GASKIN. 163a

RICHARD CONQUEST pltf agst CAPT: THOMAS WILLOBY to next court.

EDWARD HALL Chirurgeon to pay GEORGE HEIGHAM 2000 lb tob within 20 dayes.

GEORGE HEIGHAM stands indebted unto JOHN SIDNEY for the delivery of one man servant and as much broad clothe as shall make him a suite of cloathes. HEIGHAM to pay SIDNEY within 20 dayes.

... there is due uppon account 104 lb tob from JOHN SIDNEY unto GEORGE HEIGHAM .... SIDNEY to make paymt ..... within twenty dayes.

Peticon of CAPT: JOHN SIBSEY attorney of CAPT: RAPHE WORMELY xxtornxx of LUKE STUBBINGE deceased. WHEREAS: if appeareth that one HENDRICKE LIGHTHARTE .... in his lifetime stood indebted unto ye sd LUKE STUBBINGE ƀ 5/9 Ster: payable in Oct 1640 and one JOHN CORNELIUS having intermarried with the widd: of ye sd LIGHTHART ..... ordered that ye sd CORNELIUS before March Court next make it not appeare theforesd deft to be satisfied that then ye sd CORNELIUS to pay unto ye sd CAPT: JOHN SIBSEY the sd ƀ 5/9 with forbearance and Court Charges.

KATHERYNE PREISTHOOD?, late servant unto HENERY SEWELL deceased..... ordered that RICHARD CONQUEST GENTE: shall have full power hereby to take the Examacon (Examination) of the wife of ffRANCIS LAND concerning for what terme of yeres the sd KATHRYNE came into Collony for and to make a report thereto unto the next xxxxxxx and in the interim the sd KETHARYNE to remaine in the Custody of one JAMES SYMONDS.

163a 15 Jan 1650/51

EDWARD HALL Chirurgeon plt agst THOMAS WILLOBY to next Court.

164 SAVILL GASKIN for his contempt .... to pay fine of 500 lb tob and Court Charges. (This is blotted and faded with some of it illegible)

CAPT: JOHN SIBSEY hath made it appeare that there is due unto him from the estate of ROGER ffLETCHER deceased 364 lb tob with caske. CAPT: SIBSEY to be satisfied our of the sd estate in the hands of THOMAS BRIDGE administrator.

RICHARD CONQUEST Guardian of JOHN KENMAR an orphan pltf agst GEORGE HEIGHAM deft. Ordered that MR: THOMAS LAMBERT shall hereby .faded- to sweare and take the Examacon of TIMOTHY IVES and his wife concerning -faded- betweene RICHARD KENMAR deceased and ELIZABETH GLASCOCKE now ye wife of HEIGHAM and to make a report thereof at the next Court.

ROBTE: DARBY hath impleaded THOMAS WORKEMAN in this Court having a refference the last Court. DARBY not appearing ....DARBY to be contented and pay Court Charges.

ROWLAND MORGAN arrested to Court by the Shreive at the request of RICHARD CONQUEST GENT: and the Shreive neglectinge to take security ... and ROWLAND not appearing ..... Shreive to bringe ROWLAND or sufficient goods to next Court.

SAVELL CHARNICOE arrested to Court by RICHARD -faded- (CONQUEST) & EDWARD HALL GENT: being his security .... & CHARNICOE havinge fayled .... ordered ye sd HALL bringe in ye boddy or goods of ye sd CHARNICOE ye next Court to answere the sd CONQUEST otherwise to satisfye the debt.

Peticon of RICHARD KENMAR an Orphan, it is ordered that he have freedom to dispose of himselfe and what benefit he can make shall be to his own proper use without the molestacon of any.

CAPT: ffRANCIS YARDLEY pltf agst JAMES LOPHAM to ye next Court.

CAPT: YARDLEY pltf agst THOMAS WORKEMAN deft to ye next Court

164a (The item at the top of this page is no longer legible) xxxxxxxxxxxxxxxxxxxxxxxxxx is refferred to the next Court.

EDWARD HALL Chirurgeon pltf agst ROBTE: EY(RE) Attorney of JOHN PIGGOTT uppon ye peticon of ye sd EYRE is referred to the next Court.

Dated 12 Sep 1650 Recorded 14 Jan 1650/51 This bill bindeth me GEORGE HEIGHAM of Elizabeth River, my heirs &c..... to pay to ENSIGNE THOMAS LAMBERT of ye same place GENT: his heires &c...... the full and just some of 3626 sound merchantable tob in leafe and caske at or uppon ye last day of xxx Ensueing the date hereof. To the true pformance. Whereof I xxxxxxxxxxx doe bind over unto the foresd ENSIGNE LAMBERT as followeth vizt: xxxxxxxx for two yeres & upwards, JOHN HEBDON for 5 yeres & upwards, xxxxxxx for 8 yeres & upwards, six cowes two heifers and two steeres xxxxxxx acres of land beinge in ye Eastern Branch of Elizabeth River to have & to hold and enjoy the said Land, Cattle and Servants aforesd................. GEORGE HEIGHAM Geo: Higham
Wit: THOS: TOOKER

Recorded 16 Jan 1650/51. It was ordered ye 15 Dec 1650 that Mr. XXXX should devide the difference dependinge betweene THOMAS WORKEMAN xxxx of ANNE HAYES widd: deceased and ROWLAND MORGAN concerning a Sowe xxx piggs xxxxxx MORGAN to deliver the sowe and piggs unto ye sd WORKEMAN within two dayes. 165

Dated 18 Aug 1650 Recorded 15 Feb 1650/51. I, WILLIAM SCAPES of ROTTERDAM, Merchant, have made assigned &c..... JOSEPH (D?)EMMAS (or SEMMAS) & THOMAS LEE of ROTTERDAM my servants together or either of them to be my true Lawful Deputies & Attorneys for me & in my name to Deale and doe for me in all matters xxxxxxxxxx businesses whatsoever that I have to doe or to be done within the xxxxxxxx of America........
Wit: PRIMUS BOUSHERS & CORNELIC MONDEGNS Signed: Wm Scapes

Dated 12 Feb 1650/51 Recorded 15 Feb 1650/51. JOHN WHITE hath affirmed uppon oath before ye Court that BARBARA HOBSON wife of the said late deceased WILLIAM HOBSON her husband is whole Executrix and hath ordeyned RICHARD CHAPMAN her Lawfull Attorney..........Court of Nancimond County.
Teste: WM: HANDCOKE CL CUR Signed: JOHN WHITE 165a

Dated 12 Feb 1650/51 Recorded 15 Feb 1650/51. I ROBTE: SPRINGE have acknowledged uppon oath this lre (sic) of Attorney made by BARBARA HOBSON and that shee did make RICHARD CHAPMAN her full and Lawfull Attorney soe far as I know.

Dated 2 Aug 1650/51 REcorded 15 Feb 1650/51. ...I, BARBARA HOBSON of London widdow xxxxxxxxx of ye last will and Testament of WILLIAM HOBSON JUNIOR late Citizen of London, deceased, have ordeyned &c .... of London, Marriner my true & Lawfull Attorney &c....... faded......... GROSSE of the Island of Virginia beyond ye Seas xxxxxxxxxx and all such goods wares and Merchandizes as were left in ye hands and custody of ye said ROGER GROSSE by ye sd WILLIAM HOBSON & xxxxxxx the proper goods of the said WILLIAM And the same to returne, convey or cause to be returned and brought into England for ye aforesaid......................
Wit: JOHN COOK & ROBTE: SPRING Signed: Barbara Hobson 166

AT A COURT HELD 15 FEB 1650/51

PRESENT: CAPT: SAMMUELL MATHEWES — MAJOR mxxxxx
CAPT: JOHN SIBSEY — MR: JOHN HILL
MR: HENERY WOODHOUSE — MR: THOMAS LAMBART
MR: RICHARD CONQUEST — MR: WM: MOSELEY

CAPT: THOMAS WILLOBYE indebted unto JOHN RABLEY 2747 lbs of Neate tobacco with Caske. Ordered that THOMAS WILLOBYE the Younger, Attorney of ye sd CAPT: WILLOBY (sic) satisfie ye sd some in 10 dayes.

ANNE HAYES widd: deceased stood indebted unto CAPT: ffRANCIS YARDLEY 800 lb tob with Caske....- ordered uppon ye peticon of ye sd YARDLEY (that?) THOMAS WORKEMAN Executor of ye sd ANNE HAYES make paymt.

EDWARD HALL Chirurgeon pltf agst THOMAS WILLOBY xxxxxxxxxxx Attorney of CAPT: THOMAS WILLOBYE SENR: deft to the next Court.

LANCASTER LOVETT indebted unto BARTHOLOMEW HOSKINS 320 lb tob with caske. Ordered sd LOVETT to make paymt.

HENRY SNAYLE indebted unto CAPT: ffRANCIS YARDLEY 350 lb tob & caske. ...... SNAYLE to make paymt.

ROBTE: DAVYES hath arrested CORNELIUS SIMONSON to this Court & haveing not appeared....... DAVYES to be non-suited and pay SIMONSON 100 lb tob.

166a RICHARD CONQUEST pltf agst CAPT: THOMAS WILLOBYE Esq Deft............. uppon long debate in the business It was agreed and by this Court ordered that all Suits of Lawe should cease betweene ye sd CONQUEST and ye sd (WILLOBY?) untill ye returne of ye sd CAPT: WILLOBY (out?) of England, if in case ye sd CAPT: WILLOBY returne by ffebruary next xxxxtorn outxxxxxx but if it shall appeare that then ye sd CONQUEST to proceed.

ABSENT: CAPT: MATHEWES and MAJOR MORRISON

RICHARD CHAPMAN hath made it appeare to this Court that he is lawfull Attorney of BARBARA HOBSON widd who was Executrix of WILLIAM HOBSON deceased. And one ROGER GROSSE haveinge taken ires of Administration of ye sd WILLIAM HOBSONS estate. It is ordered the sd CHAPMAN satisfye unto ye sd GROSSE all such chardges and necessary expence said GROSSE have beene at by reason of ye said Administracon............GROSSE to deliver upp all writings to ye sd CHAPMAN concerninge (ye Estate?)

WILLIAM SHIPP to be satisfied out of the Estate of RICHARD KENMAR decd 500 lb tob xxxxxxxxxxxxfadedxxxxxxxxxxxx THOMAS LAMBERT being first satisfied.

Ordered that there be an equall division made of ye Estate of JOHN LANCKFIELD deceased between ye tree (sic - three?) Children of ye sd Lanckfield one of them beinge of age. And after division made THOMAS WORKEMAN to xxxxxxxxxxx ELIZABETH one of ye children of sd LANCKFIELD and her parte, NATHANIEL HAYES to xxxxxxx SARAH one other of ye sd children and her part and JAMES STERLINGE to enjoy ffRANCES one other of ye sd children and her parte for the xxxxxx one year they xxxxxxx giving an account to this Court thereon uppon demand. HENRY westgate, william ffANN, JOHN WORKEMAN and EDWARD HOLMES are thereby appointed to make the aforesd division.

ROWLAND MORGAN to make paymt to RICHARD CONQUEST of 700 lb tob xxxxxx present 300 and 400 the next crop.

167 ROBTE: EWENS (or EVENS?) pltf agst GEORGE HEIGHAM deft. Said EWENS be non suited and pay 20 lb tob unto sd HEIGHAM for Court Charges.

WILLIAM HILL non suited for non appearance agst WILLIAM BASNETT.......

It was ordered last Court that EDWARD HALL GENT: bringe ye Boddy or goods of SAMUELL CHARNICOE to this Court to answer RICHARD CONQUEST or otherwise satisfye the debt found due....... HALL havinge fayled HALL to pay (5)69 lb tob with Court Charges to CONQUEST.

Peticon of MARGRYE WICKESTEAD widd: declaring to this Court xxxxxxxx sake estate and her inability to maineteynne herselfe she being Greate (with child?) xx is ordered that ye sd MARGYRE shall quietly and peaceably possesse and enjoy all ye Estate xxxxxx late deceased husband. She paying his debts xxxxxxxxxx other molestation.

KATHERYNE PREISTHARD? late servant of HENERY SEWELL deceased shall serve her full terme yeres being appeare to xxxxxxxxx xxxxxxx she came into this Collony for ye sd terme And her tyme yet xxxxxxxx to be to the use of the Orphans of ye sd SEWELL and the sd KATHRYNE xxxxxx turne unto MR: LEMUELL MASON and at ye end of her terme to have xxxxxx as is the Custome

.... all as are indebted for or concerninge ye W(reck?) xxxxxxxxxx of CAPT: LUCKS SHIPP as well those arrested as not arrested should r(eceive?) their bills and put in security uppon demand otherwise to stand to ye xxxxxx of this Court.

It is further ordered that all such whome it concernes should meete ye 26 of this xxxxxx instant ffebr: at ye house of LAWRENCE PHILLIPPS about ye wrecke business of CAPT: LUCKS SHIPP.

Uppon peticon of CORNELIUS LOYD it is ordered that lres of Administration be granted unto him on ye Estate of CAPT: ROBTE: PAGE deceased, he being a great Credit(or?)........... 167a

Uppon ye peticon of CORNELIUS LOYD (Attorney or Executor? word is not legible) of EDWARD LOYD the order xxxxxxxx agst THOMAS CEELY dated 15 Feb 1647 on ye behalfe of xxxxxxx STAINSMERE is revived.

WILLIAM SMITH hath made it appeare...... that ROBTE HAYES deceased was in his lifetime indebted unto him 200 lb tob. THOMAS WORKEMAN Executor of MRS: HAYES who was administratrix of the sd ROBTE: HAYES make paymt thereof to SMITH.

ROBTE: LOVEDAY to make paymt of 845 lb tob due to RICHARD STERLINGE by bill together with Court Charges.

GEORGE MEE to pay 1500 lb tob with Caske due by bill with Court Charges to ffRANCIS LAND.

ROWLAND MORGAN to make paymt of 305 lbs tob with caske within tenne days with Court Charges to WILLIAM PEETERS.

...Ordered that there be a list made by JOHN SIDNEY and SIMON HANDCOCKE of all ye goods and debts belonginge to JOHN PIGGOTT, late in the hands of xxxxxx EYRE, deceased, Attorney of the said PIGGOTT or elsewhere. And that xxxxx give her (sic) best assistance therein. And ye said SIDNEY and HANDCOCKE xxxxxx where of there doings therein to this Court. And they to be xxxxxxxx their paines and care herein their reasonable chardges our of ye sd deceased Estate. And that the list to be taken within 5 or 6 dayes.

Ye Peticon of CORNELIUS SIMONSON showinge that MR: JOHN CHANDLER factor for the said CORNELIUS received 2 hh of tob of ROBTE: DAVYES then well condiconed and since much abused xxxxxx by the sd DAVYES .... therefore ordered that JOHN STRATTON and THOMAS Txxxxxxxxx beinge first sworne before MR: WOODHOUSE take a view thereof and make a report thereof to this Court.

CAPT: ffRANCIS YARDLEY pltf agst THOMAS WORKEMAN referred to next Court.

Ordered that lres of Administracon be granted unto ELIZABETH EYRE, widd: of the Estate of ROBTE: EYRE her late husband deceased. She entering into bond &c............. 168

CAPT: THOMAS BURBAGE assignee of XXXXXX xAYLES agst WILLIAM BASNETT referred to next Court.

Upon the peticon of ANNE PHILLIPPS widd: It is ordered that she xxxxx shall have ye tuicon and bringinge uppon (sic) of LEMUELL PHILLIPPS a Child (left?) (un)to her, by her late deceased husband during the Pleasure of this Court without the controulmt or molestacon of any others whatsoever.

THOMAS WORKEMAN Executor of ANNE HAYES deceased xxxxx and concerninge his allowance for his Disbursmts about the Estate...........ordered that he make upp a bill of xxxxxx nextourt.

(This record is badly damaged)THOMAS BULLOCKE Chirurgeon being gone out of this Collony CAPT: EDWARD WINDHAM shall have an (Extent?) agst ye Land of ye sd BULLOCKE untill he be fully satisfied the some of fower pounds with forbearance and Court Charges.

Ordered that THOMAS WORKEMAN notwithstandinge ye division of JOHN LANCKEFIELDS Estate should xxxxxxx the male increase of the Cattle to this fall xxxxxxxfor ye bringing up of ye children of ye sd LANCKEFIELD this last year...........

CERTIFICATE: to ANNE PHILLIPPS for 600 acres of land for transportation of 12 persons: MR: MATHEWE PHILLIPPS, Herselfe, MR: WILLIAM SALSBURY, MR: THOMAS BRIDGE, JANE LATHAM, ROSE CAULES, DUNCAN SHERAH (sic), GOWEN EVENS, JOHN AYRES, CONRARD CLOVERLY, JOHN THOMPSON and JOHN TAPP.

CAPT: YARDLEY pltf agst JAMES LOPHAM deft referred to next Corut on peticon of CAPT: YARDLEY.RICHARD CONQUEST agst GEORGE HEIGHAM to next Court at peticon of HEIGHAM.

CAPT: ffRANCIS YARDLEY assignee of JOHN MEARES agst EDWARD HALL GENT: referred vt supt.

168a AT A COURT HELD 26 FEB 1650/51

PRESENT: CAPT: JOHN SIBSEY MR: THOMAS LAMBERT
MR: JOHN HILL MR: RICHARD CONQUEST

Ordered that THOMAS WORKEMAN be first satisfied his Disbursemts as Executor to ANNE HAYES deceased and all such as by his bill appeare ....totall 723 lb tob.

The peticon of RICHARD RAGGETT shewinge whereas he waX xxxxxx lame did heretofore condicon with EDWARD HALL Chirurgeon to xxxxxx xxxteyne tyme if he would Cure him xxxxxxxxxxxxxxxxx Covennt? betweene them. The sd HALL havinge neglec(ted?) xxxxxx and as appear made no cure, accordinge to his condicon xxxxxxxx Ordered that ye sd RAGGETT have his freedom xxxxxxxxxxx unto ye sd RAGGETT 2 hh of tob xxxxxxxx with 20 dayes together with Court charges.

Recorded 3 Mar 1650/51. Due from ye Estate of ANNE HAYES widd: deceased unto THOMAS xxxxxxxxxx for 5 Tunne of Caske and 1 hoggs head.
To JOHN HOLMES 3 gallons and 3 qts Drames
To him for 2 pair of shoes for ye servants
To ENSIGNE LAMBERT for keeping ye cattle
To MR: BRAND for 3 paires of shoes & 2 pairs of Stockings
Paid to GEORGE ASHALL ye Tanner

To MR: ffOWLER for pease
To HENERY WESTGATE for sacke for my mother
To JOHN WORKEMAN for DRames at her Buriall
To LAURENCE PHILLIPPS for Dyett this year
To CAPT: YARDLEY for 2 capons for Lambs? rent
To NICHOLAS MASON beinge due from the Estate
To THOMAS TOOKER for Shreives fees
For 2 gallons of White wine at ye appraismt of the Estate
To SIMON HANCOCKE by order of Court.
TOTALL 2723 XXXXXX
(This was not signed. Usually three or four persons appraise an estate. Did such a few drink 2 gallons of white wine? AGW)

169

Dated 10 Oct 1650 REcorded 3 Mar 1650/51. WHEREAS ye 29 Oct 1650 it was ordered by this hono^ble Court that the xxxxxxente depending betweene CAPT: THOMAS WILLOBYE plt and CAPT: JOHN SIBSEY should be referred unto ye subscribers and in Obedience to ye sd Order we mett and hereby make our report as followeth: CAPT: JOSEPH JOHNSON peticoned as ye attorney of CAPT: WILLOBYE ESQR: for recovery of a debte of ŧ 190 Sterlinge to be due unto (him?) from ye estate of RICHARD WAKE deceased and pretendeth as Estate to be in ye hands of CAPT: JOHN SIBSEY as copartner with the sd WAKE And on motion of MR: xxxxxxx WHITBY ye attorny of ye sd CAPT: JOHN SIBSEY and desireinge CAPT: JOHNSON to xxxxxxxxxxxx to be due from ye sd WAKE unto xxxxxxxxxxx CAPT: THOMAS WILLOBY had his lres of administration granted unto him Wee xxxxxx find noe manifest proffe thereof And further demandinge of ye sd CAPT: xxxxxxxxxxxxx on (JOHNSON?). Whether or noe he could anyway make ys said debt appeare his answer xxxxxxx he had other papers which he would not produce untill CAPT: WILLOBYE his xxxxxxxxxxxxxxxxxx Whereuppon wee could proceede noe further. Dated 10 Oct 1650.

Signed: EDWARD BLAND
JOHN HARLOWE
THOMAS BUSHRODE
GEORGE HOBB (or LOBB?)

(NOTE: There are missing parts in this item. At the end of it I think it says, but cannot be sure, "Untill CAPT: WILLOBYE his return within this Country")

Dated 25 Dec 1631 (sic) Recorded 7 Mar 1650/51 This note doth certifie whereas there hath beene a former contract betweene RICHARD WAKE and JOHN SIBSEY xxxxxxx now they have xxxxxxxxx accoumpted and made over there rest due in bills ŧ 235/4/11 pence which bills are in ye hands of the said RICHARD with a bill of Exchange of ŧ 14 dated ye 13 Dec 1631 and the pduce of 8 hh of tob that is in the hands of the said RICHARD WAKE and alsoe a lre of Attorney made by ELIZABETH XXXXXXXXX ffurses? unto ye sd RICHARD WAKE for ye receiving of an account from ROBTE: HOWELL, all these somes abovemenconed are to be equally devided between RICHARD WAKE and JOHN SIBSEY there Executor or assignes................
Wit: RAPH GREGORY & THOMAS BURGIS p me Richard Wake 169a

Recorded 3 Mar 1650/51 per mee WILLM: JERMY. Cleared by me WILLIAM BARKER in the Shipp Americay? in the yere 1632 and the Shipp sett forth to Sea againe ŧ 640 Sterlinge and devided it amongst the

partners whereof MR: WAKE had hsi Eight part thereof ₺ 80 Sterlinge.
In the yere 1633 cleared ye same some of ₺ 640 Sterl: and the Shipp xxxxxxx to Sea all chardges paid.
In the yere 1634 I cleared ye same some of ₺ 640 and the Shipp xxxxxx all chardges paid.
In the yere 1635 I cleared ₺ 400 and the Shipp sett to xxxxx chardges paid.
In the Voyage 1636 RICHARD ORCHAR? (ARCHER?) then MAISTER to ye xxxxx nothinge gott, if anything nott much.
In the Voyage 1637 shee cleared ₺ 400 Ster: all chardges xxxxxxx
In the JOHN & BARBARA in the yere 16?? I cleared and paid MR: WAKE ₺ 3/16 cleare proffitt all chardges borne xxxxxxxx Voyage
I WILLIAM BARKER being aged 56 yeares or thereabouts Maister and parte owner of these Shipps make Oath to ye best of my knowledge all of these particulars abovementioned .
Jurate in Cur 10 ye 6 1647 (10 Aug 1647?) William Barker
Teste: HOLBY WYSE Clerk

170 (NOTE: This page is almost completely missing. All that can be read on this page is:)

day of Jun 1651

CAPT: LUCK, his Shipp

MRS: JOHN SIDNEY
MR: WILLIAM MOSELEY
MR: LEMUELL MASON
MR: WILLIAM WHITBYE

170a (NOTE: This page is missing except for the upper left hand corner. All that can be read is:)

JOHN (HANONOBLE?) of the Island of Barbadoes wanted by ye sd CORNEL: LOYD with ye table sorme?, bedsted and cupboard all xxxxxxx (This would be a will)

171 Dated 24 Mar 1651 Recroded 15 Apr 1651. SIR WILLIAM BERKELEY Kt Gov &c .....Commissioners should be appointed ...... for ye keepinge of County Courts six tymes in ye yere accordinge to ye Act of Assembly 1642 and oftener upon Extraordinary causes...... are here appointed to be ye present Comrs: of and for Lower Norfolk County:

CAPT: JOHN SIBSEY	MR: THOMAS BROWNE	Prs Coms:	CAPT: ffRANCIS YARDLEY
MR: RICHARD CONQUEST	MR. JOHN SIDNEY		MR: LEMUELL MASON
MR: EDWARD WINDHAM	MR: JOB CHANDLER		MR: THOMAS LAMBERT
MR: HENERY WOODHOUSE	MR: JOHN HILL		MR: WM: MOSELEY

Giving and granting unto you and any fower of you /whereof CAPT: JOHN SIBSEY, CAPT: ffRANCIS YARDLEY, MR. JOHN SIDNEY, MR: EDWARD WINDHAM, MR: HENERY WOODHOUSE and MR: JOHN HILL to be alwayes one/ full power and authority to heare and determine all suites and controversies
171a between pty and pty as Exceed ye value * of ₺ 10 Sterlinge or 1600 lb tob xxxxxxx neither shall it be lawfull for nay psons to appeale to ye Quarter Court at James Citty in any matters depending before you under the value of ₺ 10 Sterl: or 1600 lb tob any other wyse then is expressed in ye 68th Act of Assembly in March 1642 .... to take deposicons......................

(there is a lot more of this which seems a lot of repetition)
With all the Commissioners afore specified ye day and yere abovesaid took ye Oath of Spremacy and Allegiance together with the Oath for ye pformance of the Commissioners /Excepting MR: HENERY WOODHOUSE who was not Exxxxxxxxx per me WILLM: JERMY p me Willm Jermy

ATT A COURT HELD 15 APR 1651

PRESENT: CAPT: JOHN SIBSEY | MR: THOMAS LAMBERT
CAPT: ffRANCIS YARDLEY | MR: THOMAS BROWNE
MR: JOHN SIDNEY | MR: RICHARD CONQUEST
MR: EDWARD WINDHAM | MR: LEMUELL MASON
MR: JOHN HILL | MR: WM: MOSELEY

Attachmt is granted unto BARTHOLOMEW HOSKINS agst the Estate of JOHN PIGGOTT, Merchant for 1400 lb tob with Caske due uppon bill together with Court Charges. 172

JOHN PIGGOTT is indebted unto EDWARD HALL Chirurgeon One man servant with one bedd pillowe and rugge, one paire of Canvas Drawers, one New Canvas Sheet, one newe paire of shooes and stockings with all ye wearinge parrell belonging to ye sd servant for ye terme of fower yeres and to have xxxxxx beene delivered at or before ye Arrivall of ye last London Shipps next after ye date of the sd bill beinge ye 27 May 1650 And ye sd PIGGOTT havinge sayled in ye pmisses It is ordered that an Attachmt be granted to ye sd HALL agst soe much of ye Estate of ye sd PIGGOTT as shall become satisfactory for ye servant with Court Charges.

ROBTE: EYRE GENT: in his lifetime stood indebted unto SIMON HANDCOCKE One Man Servant about ye age of 18 or 24 sound with what clothes and beddinge he should bring in with him and to be delivered unto ye sd HANDCOCKE upon ye 25 Dec 1651.......the sd EYRE being since dead. It is by this Court ordered that ELIZABETH EYRE widd: Administratrix of ye sd ROBTE: EYRE her late husband shall within tenne dayes next ensueinge put in and give unto ye sd HANDCOCKE or his assigns sufficient and good security for ye pformance of the condicon aforesaid out of ye Estate of ye sd ROBTE: EYRE.

Uppon peticon of THOMAS ADDAMS who intermarried with ELLEN HORNER widd: late ye wife of GEORGE HORNER deceased, shee being a lame & impotent woman not fitt for travell. That LEMUELL MASON shall have full power to administer unto her an Oath for ye delivye (sic) unto this Court a true Inventory of ye estate of ye sd GEORGE HORNER.

Lres of Administration granted unto PEETER RIGGLESWORTH on ye Estate of JOHN PIPER deceased and being a great Creditor it being by consent of the widdowe PIPER late wife of ye sd JOHN PIPER..................

It beinge heretofore by this Court ordered that MR: JOHN SIDNEY & SIMOND HANDCOCKE should looke after and take care of ye estate of JOHN PIGGOTT Merchant late in ye hands of ROBTE: EYRE deceased ye sd PIGGOTT beinge out of this Country.........havinge done accordingly........... sd SIDNEY and HANDCOCKE be satisfied for their sd care & pains 300 lb tob out of the Estate of ye sd PIGGOTT with Court Charges.
Attachmt granted unto SIMON OVERZEE for soe much of ye Estate of WILLIAM WESTERHUSON Merchant as shall become satisfactory for £ 44/17/5 being a debt proven due by specialty and account.

Uppon ye peticon of SIMOND OVERZEE...........2400 lb tob with Caske due to him from HENERY WOODHOUSE for one Negro Man, five hh whereof was weighed & marked by JOB CHANDLER Attorney of ye sd OVERZEE....... sd WOODHOUSE refusinge to deliver sd 5 hh tob to ye sd OVERZEE. It is ordered that the Shreive make a deliverye.....................MR: WOODHOUSE make present paymt of the remainder to ye sd OVERZEE with Court Charges.

...... There is due from CAPT: YARDLEY 2192 lb tob of ould arreares for Levyes. It is ordered that ye Shreive shall receive ye same of CAPT: YARDLEY uppon MRS: PHILLIPPS account as Administratrix of MATHEWE PHILLIPPS deceased ye then Collector. CAPT: YARDLEY to be held accountable for what more he shalbe found in arreares by PHILLIPPS and if Overplus MRS: PHILLIPPS to be accountable to CAPT: YARDLEY and to be Ended the next Court.

Uppon peticon of THOMAS WORKEMAN Executor of ANNE HAYES wid: deceased he makinge it appeare to this Court by a bill of pticulars for Expend-xxxxxx about ye estate of ANNE HAYES that there is due unto him 310 lb tob. Ordered that WORKEMAN be satisfied out of ANNE HAYES Estate.

Uppon ye peticon of THOMAS WATKINS together with his wife at ye instance of GEORGE HEIGHAM subpened to this Court and have given attendance two dayes and humbly craves Chardges..........ordered that HEIGHAM satisfie unto WATKINS fower score l tob in consideration of his Expenses and losse of tyme.

GEORGE ASHALL ordered to pay 2200 lb tob & caske to CAPT: SAMUELL MATHEWES the 10 Oct next ensueinge.

It appeareth that there is due from CAPT: SAMUELL MATHEWES unto GEORGE ASHALL Tenne Jarres of cleene trayne Oile (sic) being formerly received by ye sd CAPT: MATHEWES of him ye sd ASHALL........therefore ordered that MATHEWES Make paymt thereof.....uppon the 10 Oct next ensueinge/ (NOTE: What was trayne oile? The dictionery says "Train oil - oil from a Marine animal such as a whale. Wonder what it was used for?)

173 Uppon ye peticon of ELIZABETH EYRE, wid: concerninge ye Estate of JOHN PIGGOTT Merchant late being in ye hands of ROBTE: EYRE her late husband deceased..........Is is ordered that MR: JOHN SIDNEY & SIMOND HANCOCKE should take into custody the foresd Estate there to remayne and rest untill ye comminge of ye sd PIGGOTT into this Country...............

THOMAS BROWNE ordered to pay ffRANCIS EMPEROR 1200 lb tob and Caske for a maid servant.

THOMAS BURBAGE Administrator of THOMAS OULDIS GENT: hath made it appeare by account under ye hand of ye sd OULDIS.....that there is due to him from WILLIAM BASNETT 800 lb tob. It is ordered if ye sd BASNETT doth not make it appeare ye next Court under ye hand of HENERY xxxxxxxxx late Shreive of Elizabeth Citty County that he was in Executon for the sd debt. Satisfied it and Cleared ye same Then ys sd BASNETT to pay ye sd 800 lb tob with forbearance and Court Chardges unto BURBAGE.

WILLIAM BASNETT ordered to pay 600 lb tob and Caske unto CAPT: THOMAS BURBAGE...... being due by bill together with forbearance & Court Chardges.

Uppon ye peticon of EDWARD LOYD shewinge that is ye yere he beinge made collector for ye Easterne Branch of Elizabeth River for ye receivinge of ye levyes. Due from the Inhabitants the account of which sd LOYD hath paid to this Court. And hath not received it of many Inhabitants as yet. Ordered ..... EDWARD LOYD ...... shall have full power to Distreyne (sic) ..... xxxxx hard to read xxxxxxxx.... Exceptinge one WM: HEATH...................

SIMOND OVERZEE assignee of JOHN JOHNSON to be paid 662 lb tob and Caske by JOHN COOKE with forbearance and Court Chardges.

Ordered that THOMAS WORKEMAN Executor of ANNE HAYES deceased make paymt of 1000 lb tob unto THOMAS CONYERS in full of dischardge of all demands whatsoever Due from ye Estate of ROBTE: HAYES deceased he ye sd CONYERS delivaringe upp unto ye sd WORKEMANS ustody one child alte of JOHN LANCKFIELDS deceased being an orphan.

CERTIFICATE: to HENERY BARLOWE for 50 acres for transportation of himselfe. 173a

THOMAS ALLEN to pay SAVILL GASKIN & his wife fower score lb tob for two days attendance at Court.

SAVILL GASKIN hath made it appeare that there is due to him 1140 lb tob for chardges Expended at a Court held for the Wrecke of CAPT: LUCKS SHIPP for ye Commissioners, Shreives, Clerkes and others xxxxxxxxxxxx Ordered that RICHARD CONQUEST GENT: for his satisfaccon Deliv: him upp our bill of STEPHEN KEYES wherein ye sd stand indebted unto ye Comrs: for ye sd Wrecke And if there be more than will satisfie ye sd GASKIN his debt then ye sd GASKIN to xxxxxxxx the overplus unto ye sd CONQUEST xxxxxx for ye use before specified.............

RICHARD CONQUEST administrator of JOHN KEMPE deceased hath made it appeare to this Court that there is Due to the Estate of sd KEMPE 414 lb tob from WILLIAM POWELL & also 40 lb tob sd CONQUEST for fees, And ye sd CONQUEST havinge from tyme to tyme accons (actions) against him ye sd POWELL for ye aforesd debts but would be xxxxxxx nor appeare. Ordered that ye sd CONQUEST shall have anxxxxxxxxxx the houses and Land of ye sd POWELL untill he be fully satisfied theforesd tobacco with forbearance and Court Charges.

WILLIAM SHIPP hath sett his name at ye Court Dore to give notice of his intended voyage for England this present Shippinge.

RICHARD CONQUEST pltf agst ANNE PHILLIPPS wid: administratrix of MATHEW PHILLIPPS deceased.......she has acknowledged that she hath received and made over 1791 lb tob a bill of pticulars pduced in Court appeareth which was due ye sd CONQUEST for Shreives Clerkes Secretaryes fees and a refference is granted untill the next Court.

DOROTHY OUBORNE wid: declaringe to this Court her poore and weake Estate and her nonability in gayninge herselfe a subssistance........ ordered that she shall quietly and peacably possesse and enjoy all ye Estate of her late deceased husband shee payinge his debts without any further molestacon.

Estate of THOMAS MORGAN to pay 2400 lb tob & Caske due by account to CAPT: YARDLEY.

EDWARD HALL Chirurgeon hath impleaded THOMAS WILLOBYE SENR: xxxxxxxxx having fayled to present? or any doe him xxxxxxx HALL to be non-suited and pay Court Chardges.

NATHANIELL HAYES plt agst THOMAS WORKEMAN deft uppon full hearinge It is ordered that ye sd WORKEMAN shall enjoy the Land in question accordinge to a writing pduced in Court under the hand of ROBTE: HAYES deceased without further molestacon.

The cause depending betweene RICHARD CONQUEST and CORNELIUS LOYD It is ordered that MR: LOYD bringe in ye nextCourt a sufficient dischardge under ye hand of CAPT: CLABORNE for the tobacco which was levied by the Shreiveupon the estate of ye sd CORNELIUS & then to be fully heard and determined

JOHN LOWNES hath spoken diverse words agst the larned (sic) Maties of ye Kinge. It is ordered that ye Shreive take LOWNES into his custody and him to deteyne untill he shall put in good security xxxxxxxxxxfor his psonall appearance at Jamestown ye 3 Jun Court next And that JAMES THELABALL and JASPER HOSKINSON be bound xxxxxx securities on his Maties behalfe.

CAPT: JOHN SIBSEY to make a deliverye of all such Cattle as are in his possession which were CAPT: PAGES, unto CORNELIUS LOYD Administrator of ye sd PAGE xxxxxxx and further xxxxxxx MR: LEMUELL MASON, THOMAS GOODRIDGE, THOMAS IVEY and TRUSTERAM MASON meete to morrow being the 17 Apr at ye house of MR: CONQUEST thereby him to be sworne and then to appraise thaforsd Cattle nowe at CAPT: SIBSEYES and soe xxxxxxxxx the rest as they come upp for present tobacco.

CERTIFICATE: to THOMAS WATKINS for 50 acres for transportation of SUSAN ffOSTER.

CERTIFICATE: to XPOFER BURSTALL for 50 acres for transportation of ELIZABETH BROWNE.

CERTIFICATE: to RICHARD JOANES for 100 acres for transportation of GEORGE WOOHAB and CHARLES HODGES.

ANNE PHILLIPPS pltf agst JAMES SMITH deft referred to next Court.

RICHARD PINNER agst RICHARD WOSTER file.(Note: this is complete entry)

JOHN HOLTON agst CAPT: ffRANCIS YARDLEY file.

174a JOHN WILLIAMS agst RICHARD CONQUEST file.

GEORGE HEIGHAM pltf agst RICHARD KINGE to nextCourt.

CORNELIUS LOYD agst RICUM (sic) CONQUEST file.

WILLIAM BASNETT agst THOMAS BURBAGE administrator of THOMAS OULDIS. referred vt sup.

RICHARD CONQUEST agst CORNELIUS LOYD referred vt sup.

CAPT: ffRANCIS YARDLEY Attorney of JOHN MEARES pltf and EDWARD HALL GENT: deft referred untill the next Court. MR: THOMAS CAUSON bindeth himselfe in a 1000 of tob to dischardge the sd MR: HALL of this accon and he will appeare the next Court to make answere thereunto.

AT A QUARTER COURT HELD AT JAMES CITTY 7 (Mar?) 1650/51
PRESENT: SIR WILLIAM BERKLEY Kt. Gov.
CAPT: HENERY BROWNE MR: RICH: BENNETT
CAPT: THOMAS PETTUS

MR: JOB CHANDLER is this day 7 (Mar?) 1650/51 chosen Shreive for Lower Norff: County and to be sworne the next County Court there held.
Test: ROB: HUBIRD Cl Cur

..... this Court MR: JOB CHANDLER was sworne Shreive for Lower Norff: County accordinge to the above order. And THOMAS TOOKER was sworne under Shreive. p me WILLM: JERMY

Constables chosen for this yere followinge 1651 by the Court vizt:
MARKES LEONARD from Danniell Tanners Creek to CAPT: WILLOUGHBYES
RICHARD JOANES for ye Westerne Branch of Elizabeth River
GEORGE HEIGHAM for ye Easterne Branch
HENER_ WESTGATE for Little Creek
JOHN MANNINGE for ye Southern Branch of Elizabeth River
RICHARD POOLE for ye Westerne Pte of Lynhaven
ROBTE: DAVYES for the Easterne Shoare of Lynhaven
It is ordered that everye one above chosen for Constables this yere following doe repaire to ye next adjacent Justice of the Peace of this County to be sworne accordingly. per me WILLM: JERMY

175

Recorded 18 Apr 1651 - MR: CHAPMAN his account for a man goeinge to Nancimond to fetch Rowle? tob.
for bringing his Chest from abroad
for a hat
for a bottle of Drames
for washinge, lodginge & Dyett for a moneth
TOTAL (all figures are faded)

There rest uppon ye ballance of Accompts betweene ROGER GROSSE and RICHARD CHAPMAN about the Estate of MR: HOBSON including a Debte of CHAPMANS 520 lb tob to be paid unto ye Estate by GROSSE.

THOMAS WORKEMANS account concerninge ye estate of ANN HAYES decd.
Recorded 18 Apr 1651
Imprimus for 20 dayes tyme at Sewall (several?) Courts xxxxxxxxxx
for myselfe and another 3 dayes at Kecotan
for losse of tyme about takinge the Inventory

14 Feb 1650/51 - MR: THOMAS LAMBERT & MR: CORNELIUS LOYD mett to Audette an account between MRS: ANNE PHILLIPPS administratrix of MATHEWE PHILLIPPS deceased and MR: RICHARD CONQUEST and since nothinge beinge done therein by reason of MR: CONQUEST his denyall to some pte of the sd account xxxxxxxxx these pticulars followinge are acknowledged to have been amde over and received by ye sd ANNE PHILLIPPS
of WM: LUCAS tob without Caske 302 of JOHN HOLMES 50
of MR: LO?E (or Hone?) without Caske 220 of SIMON PEETERS yet in 86
of LANCASTER LOVETT noe Caske 250 Dispute
of MRS: LIGHTHART without Caske 200 of MR: EDWARD HALL 285
of MR: ED: LOYD 1 hh cont: 380
SUMME TOTAL 1721

p me Tho Bridge

Recorded 18 Apr 1651 - These men whose names are underwritten havinge viewed ye Corpes of JOHN PIPER doe give in their verdict, that he bringe in drinche and beinge Dark put a Shoare, besides the landing place agst a bancke and could nott gett upp but lay downe to sleepe and ye tide came and Drowned him and this wee censure to be the cause of his death as witness our hands 12 Mar 1650.

PETER RIGGLESWORTH		RICHARD EASTWOOD
JOHN LOWNE		ROBTE: BOWERS
HENERY ROLLINES	JURY	PEETER BARNES
EDWARD MARMADETT		JOHN HARRIS
EWEN WEELETTS		

Sworne before me THOMAS BROWNE High Shreive

Recorded 18 Apr 1651 - A list of what goods MR: PIGGOTT left with MR: ROBTE: EYRE 27 May 1650:

Containing:

Callico	Shoes	Cotton
fish hookes	lininge	One Chest
stockings 14 pr men, womens & childrens		nayles
thredd	hooks & eyes	silk
&c		

These goods were left with CAPT: YARDLEY for MR: EYRE by MR: JOHN PIGGOTT & whether they were received wee cannot find but they come to 600 lb by MR: PIGGOTTS account.

The some in totall by MR: PIGGOTT his account is 406 lb

JOHN SIDNEY & SIMON HANDCOCKE

176

Recorded 18 Apr 1651 - A list of what bills MR: PIGGOTT left with MR: ROBTE: EYRE:

CAPT: SIBSEYS	400	MR: BURROWES bill	750
CAPT: YARDLEYS	2660	RICHARD WHITESHURST bill	2568
CAPT: WINDHAMS	1126	OLLIVER SPRYES bill	800
JOHN HOLMES	410	MR: HOANES (JOANES?) bill	345
WM: ffANNAS bill	650	WILLIAM WILSONS bill	371
SAVILL GASKINS	340	MR: CHANDLERS bill	1300
MR: SIDNEYS bill	360	MR: HEIGHAMS bill	350
GEORGE WILLIAMS bill	300	DOCT^{R} HALLS bill	600
PETER ASTONS bill	faded		
		SUMME TOTAL -faded -	

Bills taken by MR: EYRE -

LEWIS FARMALL	150	CAPT: WINDHAM by account	xxx
MR: MOSELEYS bill	540	MR: EYRES by account	xxx
JOHN CORNELIUS bill	287	MR: LOYDS bill	xxx
MR: KEELINGE his bill	281	DOCT^{r} HALLS bill	254
JOHN BIGGS bill	200	The some Total is	1753 1 tob
More left in goods -xxxxx faded xxxxxx -		Total	21684?

We find MR: ROBTE: EYRE his Estate Debtor to MR: PIGGOTT for goods sould and tobaccos received and made use of 2080

Recorded 15 Apr 1651 - Bills of debts and accounts to CAPT: ROBTE: PAGE left in ye hands of MR: MATHEWE PHILLIPPS 12 Jul 1649:

Bills of:

MRS: BUGIUS?	324	SIMON HANDCOCKE	82
GEORGE HORNER	116	JOHN ffINCH	120

PHILLIP POOLE	106	MR: EYRES	406
PHILLIPP LAND	630	MR: SAWYER	1395
MR: ROBT: HAYES	1000	2 bills of THOMAS HARTS	1400
ROBTE: JOANES	80	1 note of MR: MORRIS	12/6 pence

By Receipt of THOMAS LARIMORE 60 (?) Canvis, 8 gallons of Vinegar
ROBTE: SMITHS bill of ladinge
EDWARD GUNNELLS note to ROBTE: SMITH
ROBTE: GLASKOCK ingagemt to MR: GILLBANCKE? for 20 1 Sterling
MR: JAYTERS bond for ₶ 46 Sterling
MR: THOS: MEARES his bond for ₶ 37 Sterling
MRS. ANNE MARSHALLS ingagmt ₶ 11 Sterling
MR: THOMAS BUSHROODS bill ₶ 27 Sterling
MR: DAVID MANSFIELDS bill 400 176a
ffRANCES MASONS bill to PINCHER 200
PHILLIPP WESTON 398
by bill of Ditto 36
To ye bill of NEEDOMES 54
by SADLERS account 400
THO: SMITHS order in Court by ye bill of MR: MOORES 220
1 bill of MR: DANIELL BOUCHER 510
by i bill ANTHONY LINOYE 1500
to 1 bill of Dittoes 300
to 1 bill of JOHN (EBBS?) 1141
by a note of MR: WILLIAM BEARES (Meares?) p one bull value
MRS: KINOCOTT? lre of Attorney
MRS: KINICOTTS? order to MR: ROBTE PAGE
EATES? CASTER his order
BENJAMINE WHITE to JOHN WHITE
JOHN KEMPS bill 220
by 1 bill of THOMAS CLARKES 750
JOHN KINGS order of Court
MR: GRAFERES? lre
THOS: CLARKES order of Court
WM: WOLLFLYT his lre of Attorney
WM: JENNERS assigmt: to BRANDON
MR: LEMONS lre
WM: DODFORDS accountWM: JOHNSONS account
RICHARD HARDYRANES (sic) account
All which bills and accounts I, MATHEWE PHILLIPPS acknowledge to have received of CAPT: ROBTE PAGE ~~xxxxxxxx~~ bind myselfe to be accountable 12 Jul 1649.
Teste: THO: WHITE signed: MATH: PHILLIPPS
MORE: one engagmt of RICHARD TROWE for ye pceedinge voyage to Barbadoes and ye rest of ye Ilands and soe to London

ATT A COURT HELD 28 Apr 1651

PRESENT: CAPT JOHN SIBSEY)
CAPT: ffRANCIS YARDLEY)
MR: JOHN HILL)
MR: THOMAS BROWNE)

COMRS: MR: THOMAS LAMBERT
MR: RICHARD CONQUEST
MR: LEMUELL MASON

176a 28 Apr 1651

Attachmt: granted THOMAS IVY agst estate of LEONARD GUNNIS for 600 lb tob and Caske due uppon bill and account. sd GUNNIS having deserted this Collony.
Attachmt: granted LAURENCE PHILLIPPS agst estate of LEONARD GUNNIS for 200 lb tob ye sd GUNNIS having deserted this Collony.

Attachmt: granted unto WILLIAM ODEON agst the Estate of EDWARD PERKINS
177 & WILLIAM RICHARDSON for 2500 lb tob he makinge it appeare to be due.

HENERY BRAKES being Constable for ye Little Creed doe apprehend the boddyes of WILLIAM RICHARDSON & EDWARD PERKINS and to bringe them before CAPT: SIBSEY and there to presse boate and hands and to carry them aboard the Shipp called the Planter. MR: WILLIAM ODEON beinge Master and ye sd RICHARDSON & PERKINS havinge Deserted their service beinge hired by the sd ODEON ....

WHEREAS: heretofore an order was granted by this Court agst EDWARD HALL Chirurgeon unto RICHARD RAGGETT for 600 lb tob with Caske & Court costs. And ye sd HALL havinge fayld to pay the same accordingly And it being made appeare to this Court that ye sd RAGGED is since dead and that uppon his death xxxxxxxxxxx (will?) he gave ye sd 600 lb tob with Caske unto JOANE PAGGED (sic) (or Ragged?) his sister whX xxxxx intermarried with JAMES COLLINS xxxxx Ordered that the sd EDWARD HALL pay unto the sd COLLINS 600 lb tob with caske and Court Chardges.

MR: HILL hath this Court complained agst THOMAS TUCKER for not obeyinge his warrant uppon sight thereof. It is ordered that ye sd TOOKER xxxxx for his psonall appearance the next Court to answere his contempt xxxxxxxx sd TOOKER to make and deliver upp his account beinge xxxxxxxxx unto THOMAS BROWNE late High Shreive And alsoe to deliver upp all writings as of right belonge unto ye sd MR: THOMAS BROWNE.

At ye last Court ordered that the Shreive should take security for the psonall appearance of JOHN LOWNES at JAMES CITTY his answering of traiterous words by him spoken agst ye sacred Matie of ye King xxxxx now ordered that ye Shreive apprehend sd LOWNES and deteyne without bayle ssssss & caus (sic) his appearance before ye Gov: & Councill ye 3rd day of ye next Quarter Court to be held at James Citty.

CERTIFICATE: to JAMES THELABALL for 500 acres for transportation of ten psons: JOHN ARIS (HARRIS?), ROBTE: WINTER, WILLIAM ANNGER, ALEXANDER MAXXX, SARAH MUCHER, JOHN GLOVER, ANNE NEALE, JOHN MILLEGER, ANTHONY
177a WILKERSON and ALEXANDER MENSE.

SARAH SHIPP - Deed of Guift dated 15 Apr 1651 Recorded 29 Apr 1651. .... WILLIAM JULIAN, my late husband deceased did xx appoint me his sole executrix of his last will xxxx his then wife with all his Lands as a Deede of Guift. And whereas: I the sd SARAH xx have intermarried with WILLIAM SHIPP .... nowe out of the great love and affection which I bare unto my now husband WILLIAM SHIPP & his children xxxxxxxxxxx give and grant unto ANNE SHIPP the youngest daughter of WILLIAM SHIPP All that plantacon whereuppon I do now live ..... beinge in Elizabeth River .... with all that pte or dividend of land thereunto belonginge and all the houses &c .... to have and to hold .... after my decease /and not before/ .... and in case ye sd ANNE shall happen to dye

without issue the sd plantacon xxxxx unto MATHEWE SHIPP the youngest sonne of ye sd WILLIAM SHIPPE & to his heirs forever and if in case he shall happen to dye with out issue then ye aforesd Plantacon .... unto MARY SHIPP the Eldest daughter of ye sd MATHEWE SHIPP and in case she shall dye without issue .... yr sd Plantacon .....unto WILLIAM SHIPP the Eldest sonne of WILLIAM SHIPP............. 15 Apr 1651
Wit: LEMUELL MASON Signed: Fance (S) Shipp
Teste: WILLM: JERMY
This Deede of Guift was acknowledged in Court 28 Apr 1651. 178

ATT A COURT HELD 15 May 1651

PRESENT: CAPT: JOHN SIBSEY MR: THOMAS BROWNE
MR: JOHN HILL MR: LEMUELL MASON
MR: THO: LAMBERT

WHEREAS: the abovesaid COMRS: this day mett in and about ye givinge satisfaccon to the Governor and Councill about ye Wrecke of CEPT: LUCKS Shipp And here not appearinge soe many of ye Comrs: as were expected It is therefore thought .... ordered .... that all the Comrs: meete together ye 16 June next /being the day appointed for ye County Court? .... the Shreive to give notice thereof.

BARTHOLOMEW HOSKINS of Elizabeth River ..... Planter have freely given and delivered unto HENERY BARLOWE livinge in ye said River a Cowe Calve of a yere old which he hath marked .... (the Cattel mark is given)
Teste: RICHARD ffOSTER

Dated 14 Jun 1651 Recorded 23 Jun 1651 - .....-I JOHN MEREDITH, Shipwright Doe bind myselfe unto EDWARD CANNON and THOMAS ALLEN for their better security of a debte of 1723 lb tob and Caske....................
Wit: GRIFFON GWINN & GREGORY BEESTEE Signed: JOHN MIRIDITH. (sic)

Dated 15 Jun 1651 Recorded 17 Jun 1651 - .... I JOHN DYER of Linhaven doe ...... appoint JAMES LOPHAM of ye same place my true and lawful attorney..................... Signed: JOHN (D) DYER
Wit: JOHN MARTIN 178a

Dated 14 Jun 1651 Recorded 17 Jun 1651 - I WILLIAM DOVENALL of Elizabeth River, Planter doe owe & stand indebted unto RICHARD JOANES of the same place, Planter, all my cropp of tobacco and corne which I have nowe planted this yere 1651 as alsoe all other my goods and chattles whereof I am at present possessed to be paid unto ye sd RICHARD JONES or to xxxxxxxx heires &c xxxxxxxxxxxxxxxx14 June 1651

The condicon of the above obligation is such that the above bounden WILLIAM DOVENELL his heires &c shall well and truly save harmlesse & keepe undamnefied ye abovenamed RICHARD JONES his heirs &c for of and from all manner of trouble or molestacon concerninge one bill of Debt for 840 lb tob or thereabouts. Wherein ye sd RICHARD JONES together with ye sd WILLIAM DOVENELL standeth jointly and severally bound unto CAPT: LAMB and alsoe pay unto ye sd JONES 144 pownds of tob that their bond (with?) Obligation to be voyd and of none effect or else to stand and remain in full force.
Wit: JOHN HILL & THO: BROWNE Signed: WILLIAM (M) DOVENELL

178a 17 Jun 1651

Dated 26 Apr 1651 Recorded 17 Jun 1651 - JOHN MOY Debter to ROBTE: DAVYES By order of Court for forbearance and chardges allowed of ____________ (this is the way the sentence ends)
Wee whose names are underwritten have made an appraisement accordinge to order of Court of 5 head of attle for paymt of 1839 lb tob Due from JOHN MOYS Estate to ROBTE: DAVYES as witness our hands 26 Apr 1651

JOB CHANDLER
JOHN STRATTON
THO: ALLEN
JOHN MIRREDITH (sic)

Recorded 17 Jun 1651 - I can testifye that MR: ffERNAHAUGH and MR: EDWARD AHLL and MR: JOHN CRANWELL were all of them together at the ordinary at ROBTE: EWENS and for what they spent MR: ffERNAHAUGH gave ROBTE EWEN his bill for it which bill was burnt.

179 JOHN SUTTON John Sutton

Dated 12 Feb 1650/51 Recorded 17 Jun 1651 - These may testifye that to ye best of my knowledge and remembrance that MR: JOHN fferinhaugh was at ye Court at Nancimond ye 12 Feb 1648/9 being arrested at MR: HOUGH(ES?) suite and then he ye sd ffERINHAUGH and ROBTE: EWENS did present

heir accoumpts and MR: ffERINHAUGH past his bill to ROBTE EWEN for 693 lb tob but since that tyme his house was burnt and ye bill and other bills burnt in it but I know and remember this debte and was witness to ye sd bill and further saith not.
Teste: W: HANCOCKE Cl Court Nancimond Signed: JOHN SUTTON

Recorded 17 Jun 1651 - I was in company with MR: JOHN ffERINHAUGH when he made good xxx of this debte. I doe thinke in my consience that ye debte which ROBTE: EWENS demand is nothing just.
Teste: W: HANCOCK
Proved in Court before CAPT: THO: DEWE, MR: JOHN COTTON, MR: LAWSON (This is the Nancimond Court)

ATT A COURT HELD 16 Jun 1651

PRESENT: CAPT: JOHN SIBSEY, CAPT: ffRANCIS YARDLEY, CAPT: EDWARD WINDHAM, MR: JOHN HILL, MR: JOHN SIDNEY, MR: THOMAS LAMBERT, MR: THOMAS BROWNE, MR: RICHARD CONQUEST, MR: WILLIAM MOSELEY, MR: LEMUELL MASON

Ordered that JOHN PARKER make paymt of 910 lb tob with Caske unto SIMON OVERZEE with forbearance and Court Chardges.

JOHN CORNELISON arrested to this Court by ye Shreive at ye suite of ffRANCIS EMPEROR Atty of JOHN ALBERTSON.........sd CORNELISON not appearing ....Shreive to bring in the boddy or goods to the next Court.

179a RICHARD WHITEHURST Attorney of RICHARD ACKTON .... Ordered that ABRAHAM THOMAS, HENERY NICHOLLS, WILLIAM WILSON & JOHN CARRAWAY take a full veiwe of the land in question and that they make an equall division thereof betweene RICHARD ACKTON & ANDREWE NICHOLLS as well of the good land as the badd ...... accordinge as it is bounded by ye bill of sale pduced in Court and to deliver an account at the next Court.

It is ordered that ye non suite obteyned by THOMAS WILLOUGHBY atty of CAPT: THOMAS WILLOUGHBY agst EDWARD HALL Chir: the last Court stand voyd and of none effect........ referred to next Court.

.......by the confession of THOMAS WILLOUGHBY JUNR: and JOHN HOLMES that they tooke one boat xxxxxxx and oares out of the possession of JOB BEASLEY And that ye sd boate was xxxxxxx lost. .....therefore ordered by this Court that they pay xx unto THOMAS GOODRICH or his assigns beinge Atty of the sd BEASLEY 300 lb tob a peice with Caske ...... & ourt Chardges.

Judgmt acknowledged by WILLIAM ROBINSON xxxxxxxxxxxxxxxxxx MARTIN for ye paymt of 1150 lb tob with Caske.

It was ordered ye last Court that WILLIAM BASNETT did not xxxxxxxxx bringe in sufficient testimony under ye hand of one HENERY BATTS late Shxxxxxxxx (Shipwright see last Court) of Elizabeth Citty a full dischardge for ye clearinge of a debte of 800 lb tob .... due from sd BASNETT unto THOMAS OULDIS deceased by CAPT: THOMAS BURBAGE administrator of the sd OULDIS, that then BASNETT should satisfie ye sd debt with forbearance and Court Chardges and WILLIAM BASNETT having fayled .... it is ordered ye sd BASNETT satisfie ye sd 800 lb tob unto CAPT: BURBAGE.

ROBTE: EWEN hath made it appeare by sufficient Evidence .... that there was due to him from JOHN ffERINHAUGH in his life tyme TXX hundred ninety three pounds of tobacco by bill........Ordered that GEORGE HEIGHAM who intermarried with the relict of the sd ffERINHAUGH make paymt thereof.........

180

JOHN GRUNDRY hath made it appeare that there is due to him One boate of 20 foote by ye keele substancially wrought xxxxxx built with rough and clench and should have been delivered in Elizabeth River in Nov last past with fower oares, Mast, rudder and tiller as may appeare by a condicon under his hand being produced in Court and JOHN MERRIDITH having fayled in ye performance thereof. It is ordered that MERREDITH make paymt of thaforesd boate .... with forbearance and losse of tyme and Court Chardges within 30 dayes.

WILLIAM ROBENSON indebted together with ROBTE: EYRE GENT: decd unto JOHN MARTIN for 1160 lb tob and Caske beinge ye ppor (proportionable?) debte of ye sd EYRE xxxxxxxx ordered that ELIZABETH EYRE widow and relict of ROBTE: EYRE and administrator xxxxxxxx make paymt thereof unto WM: ROBENSON out of the estate of EYRE............

Uppon peticon of WILLIAM ROBINSON .... ELIZABETH EYRE widow and administratrix of ROBTE: EYRE to make paymt out of the estate of EYRE 794 lb tob due by bill.............

ELIZABETH EYRE widow and Administratrix of ROBTE: EYRE decd ordered to make paymt of xxxxxxxx 483 lb tob as by a bill........unto SIMON HANCOCKE out of ye estate. WILLIAM ROBINSON being first satisfied

WM: MOSELEY GENT: Attorney of RICHARD WOOLMAN made it appeare that there is due 1100 lb tob and Caske from ROBTE: EYRE decd. ELIZABETH widow and Administratrix to make paymt &c........... CORNELIUS LOYD .. 504 lb tob for 72 pounds of sugar ... ELIZABETH EYRE to make paymt the aforesd orders being first satisfied.........

180a 16 Jun 1651

Judgmt acknowledged by JAMES LOPHAM Attorney of JOHN DYER fore the paymt of 600 lb tob and Caske ye next cropp unto CORNELIUS LOYD GENT: he (Loyd) securinge ye sd DYER quiett and peacable possession of the land and houses thereon whereon he is now seated from CAPT: YARDLEY or his assignes untill ADDAM THURROWGOOD, an orphan, shall attayne to his full age of 21 yeres.

GEORGE HEIGHAM ordered to pay 20 lb tob each to ROBTE: YONGE & ANNE CARRAWAY.

Shreive to bring in ye boddy or goods of JOHN MERREDITH to answer TIMOTHY IVES the next Court.

Ordered that EDWARD HALL GENT: make paymt unto CAPT: ffRANCIS YARDLEY Atty of JOHN MEARES five hundred xxxxteene lb tob & Caske being the remainder of a bill of 800 lb tob due in 1642 with forbearance and Court Chardges the 20 Oct next ensueinge.

JOHN WILLIAMS pltf agst RICHARD CONQUEST deft to next Court.

RICHARD CONQUEST GENT: plt agst THOMAS BRIDGES deft to next Court.

At the peticon of ffRANCES LANCKFIELD it is ordered that THOMAS WORKEMAN redeliver unto JAMES STERLINGE all the male Cattle fallen since the devision of the Estate of JOHN LANCKEFEILD decd belonging unto the sd ffRANCES ....notwithstanding any order to the contrary .... WORKEMAN to bring in account to next Court of anything due to him from her ye sd ffRANCES.

181

(NOTE: Large pieces of this page are missing and what can be read follows. AGW):

EDWARD GUNNELL)
CAPT: JOHN SIBSEY) the next Court

due to JOB: BEASLEY
from JOHN PARKER about 2 paire of shooes
THOMAS GOODRICH to pay.

TO THE NEXT COURT: RICHARD CONQUEST agst JOHEM xxxxxxxx
JOHN HOLTON agst CAPT: ffRAN: YARDLEY
RICHARD PINNER agst RICHARD WORSTER
CORNELIUS LOYD agst RICHARD CONQUEST
RICHARD CONQUEST agst CORNELIUS LOYD

181a (Large pieces are missing)
xxxxxx CAPT: JOHN SIBSEY for a dead corpes cast uppon the shore beinge xxxxxxxxx wee suppose the servant of LAURENCE PHILLIPPS the corpse beinge much abused about the shoulder and xxxxxxx(what is left of this is not enough to make any sense)xxxxxxxxx

182 Only one word can be read on the tophalf of this page: PRESENT: (Which probably means a Court Date is missing)

800 hundred acres of Land on ye south side of ye Western Branch of Elizabeth River binding Northerly into the woods, Southerly into ye sd River Easterly uppon Merchants xxxxxgonexxxxxx Westerly uppon Muddy Creeke as by a pattent bearing date 2 (Nugent gives date p 50) Jun 1635 whereas CORNELIUS LOYD by his deede ye xxx Nov xxxx did give and grant

unto THOMAS EDWARDS 300 acres parte of ye sd land beginning at ye xxxxx of a little Creeke or branch which creeke is on ye East side of Parsimon Point next unto ye sd point and from thence Extendinge downe ye River-side 150 pole xxxxxxx Merchants Creeke for ye bredth with ye length into ye woods xxxxxxx whereas CORNELIUS LOYD xxxxxxxxxxx deedes dated 15 Nov 1649 did give and grant unto RICHARD xxxxxxxxx(the rest of this is missing.) xxxxxxxx

182a

(Most of this page is gone and whether or not this is a Deed or a Patent cannot be determined as too much is missing):

xxxx 500 acres of land xxxxxxxx all English Plantacons in America xxx
Wit: JOHN HILL & THOMAS BROWNE THO: TUCKER

183

(Only two small scraps are left of this page)

(in the margin) ORDER
SNAYLE

ROBTE: BOWERS to make paymt of 3 barrells of Indian Corne unto RICHARD STERNELL assignee of THOMAS GODBYE

183a

(There are only pieces of names left on this page)

184

(The top of page is missing and some holes in page. The writing is smudged and some is not legible.

JOHN CUSTIS who intermarried with ye relict of ROBTE EYRE to make paymt unto CORNELIUS LOYD (the beginning of this is missing. It must have been a debt of EYRE to LOYD)

JOHN CUSTIS who intermarried with ELIZABETH ye relict of ROBERT EYRE to pay unto LEWES ffARMALL 262 lb tob.

JOHN CUSTIS who intermarried &c to pay 226 lb tob to LAURENCE PHILLIPPS
THOMAS ADDAMS plt agst JOHN HOLMES deft. HOLMES to bring an
THOMAS ADDAMS plt agst JOHN HOLMES deft. HOLMES to bring an account to the next Court of what is due to him from ye Estate of GEORGE HORNER deceased

JOHN VINTON servant to CAPT: THOMAS WILLOUGHBY to receive 30 lashes uppon his bare backe for runninge away from his service and other misdemanors xxxxxx as by ye complaint of THOMAS WILLOUGHBY JUNR:

An Orphans Court to be held 16 Oct next.

Lres of administration granted to EDWARD HALL SENR: on ye estate of JOHN WOODWARD decd.

184a

THOMAS WILLOUGHBY JUNR: to put in security for his appearance before the ov: and Councill 1 Oct next xxx (this seems to be his appeal of some case xxxx top of item is missing) MR: LEMUELL MASON and CORNELIUS LOYD securities.

THOMAS WILLOUGHBY appealing a case to the Gov. and Councill xxxxxxxxx

CERTIFICATE: to JOHN GODFREY for 250 acres for trans: of 5 persons WILLIAM LUMBERS, (WILLIAM?) SHERMAN, SALLMELL, a Lad, SUSAN HALL & (See Nugent 260 says Hill) and ANNE COLEMAN.

184a Between Jun & Aug 1651
Dates lost in torn pages

CERTIFICATE: to XPOFER BURROWES 250 acres for trans: of 5 persons: HENXXX HALSTEAD, MARY TYLER, JOHN TOWNSEND, ELIZABETH CHURCHETH? & xxxMAS LAWSON. (This is not in Nugent)

Uppon peticon of EDWARD HALL SENR: requested that CAPT: ffRANCIS YARDLEY take ye deposicons of ELIZABETH CLERKE & ELIZABETH HATTERY? concerninge a will made by JOHN WOODWARD and psent them to the next Court.

The will of JOHN WOODWARD is mentioned.

JOHN LAULTOR (or HAULTON?) plt agst CAPT: ffRANCIS YARDLEY deft to next Court. LAWLTON to prove the deposicon of SAVIL GASKIN.

DAVY MARROLOE was by the Churchwardens presented for gettinge his now wife with child before marriage.......... torn................. to the next Court.

..... wife of HENERY SNAYLE & ELIZABETH wife of xxxxxxxxxxxxxxxxxxx (this item is torn) xxxx to next Court.

LAURENCE PHILLIPPS to make psonall appearance at the next Court.

185 CASES REFERRED TO THE NEXT COURT:
RICHARD CONQUEST plt GENT: agst JOHN DYER deft
xxxxxx ? xxxxx THOMAS BRIDGES
xxxxxx ? xxxxx CORNELIUS LOYD
CORNELIUS LOYD versus RICHARD CONQUEST

These are to certifie xx that according to my oath I psent DAVY MARROWE & his wife for gettinge her with child before he married her.
RICH: WHITEHURST

Dated 15 Aug 1651 Recorded 15 Aug 1651 - EDWARD HALL Chirur: appointing MR: SIMON OVERZEE, Merchant, his atty to sue & implead MR: THOMAS QILLOUGHBY Atty of CAPT: CAPT: THOMAS WILLOUGHBY xx any suite this present Court
Wit: EDW: WINDHAM EDW: HALL Chirur:

185a Dated 1 Aug 1651 Recorded (date is not ligeble) - I LEMUELL MASON of Lower Norfolk County doe hereby give and grant unto LEMUELL LANGLEY sonne to WILLIAM LANGLEY of Lower Norfolk County Planter being my godsonne one black heifer xxxxxxx with all the female increase xxxxx and the male increase to goe to ye sd WILLIAM LANGLEY toward the bringing upp of his sd sonne xxxxxxxx untill yr sd LEMUELL LANGLEY shall attain to the full age of 18 yeree .... then all the increase to go to his use ...... if he should dye .... then the heifer & increase to ye rest of the children of the said WILLIAM LANGLEY ..... equally divided among them. 1 Aug 1651
Wit: THO: LAMBERT, WILL: JERMY, RICH: PINNER

186 AT A COURT HELD 3 Oct 1651

PRESENT:	CAPT: JOHN SIBSEY		CAPT ffRANCIS YARDLEY
	MR: JOHN HILL	COMRS:	MR: THOMAS LAMBERT
	MR: THOMAD BROWN		MR: RICHARD CONQUEST
	MR: WILLIAM MOSELEY		MR: LEMUELL MASON

JOHN LOWNES ordered to pay unto CHRISTOPHER NEEDEHAM 1400 lb tob & Caske with Court Chardges.

JOHN LOWNES servant to pforme such worke as is specified in a condicon dated 3 Mar 1650 between COLL: ffRANCIS YARDLEY and the sd LOWNES..... by the next Court.
Uppon peticon of COLL: ffRANCIS YARDLEY that JOHN LOWNES put in good security for his appearance the next Court...... to prove such scandalouse termes and Expressions as ye sd YARDLEY hath declared agst him.

Court to be adjourned untill the 30 Oct 1651.

An Orphans Court to be kept the day after ye endinge of the sd County Court. p me WILLM: JERMY

186a

Recorded (date faded and smeared) Oct 1651 - It is agreed by and betweene CAPT: ffRANCIS YARDLEY of Linhaven and JOHN LOWNES of Elizabeth River. That WILLIAM EALE, brick layer and servant to MR: LOWNES shall well and substantially plaister white lyme and wash over ye Dyninge Roome, ye Yellowe roome & kitchinge & ye chamber over ye kitchinge and likewise mend and repair & wash out all the rest of ye roomes & chambers in ye house at Linhaven well & sufficiently as aforesd And to do and finish ye sd worke at such convenient tyme or tymes as ye sd CAPT: YARDLEY shall appoint with best convenience. Likewise ye sd WILLIAM EALE is to mend & repaire all ye Bricke worke about ye Dwellinge house at Keyconton without dores and to ruffe? cast ye same with lyme and gravell ye sd house being 50 foot longe and 20 foote wide and to doe and finish the same well ....YARDLEY findinge sd EALE Dyett and all matialls (materials?) necessary.......for ye sd worke......to be done in and about the two houses. And to find him a laborer to attend him dueringe ye tyme of his employmt. And is to begin and enter uppon ye sd work the 1 Apr 1650 & not to leave the same till it be all fully compleat....... YARDLEY is to pay unto JOHN LOWNES 1200 lb tob that his servant WILLIAK EALE shall well and sufficiently doe perfect and finish all and singler ye sd worke. JOHN LOWNES
If any Excepcons or differences shall happen...... to be determined by MR: CORNELIUS LOYD & MR: THOMAS MARSH
wit: EDW: WINDHAM
Bill is given for ye paymt of the 1200 lb tob & caske within specified And beare date with these presents 3 Mar 1650.
wit: EDW: WINDHAM

187

Recorded Nov 1651 - Depositions of EDWARD MOSSE & RICHARD RECKLES Ship Carpenters sworne....saith: ..... at ye instance of RICHARD RICHARDSON Merchant of ye good Shipp called ye Peter & ffRANCIS belonginge to ye Barbadoes Ixxxxxringe had a full view and search of ye sd Shipp doe declare that ye Sterne, post bilge & stepp of the foremast are altoget=her insufficient with many others .... She is in noe wayes fitt for Sea and to fitt her for Sea will cost far more than her value.
Teste: THOMAS LAMBERT Signed: EDWARD MOSSE & RICHARD RECKLES

ATT A COURT HELD 30 Oct 1651

PRESENT: CAPT: JOHN SIBSEY, MR: THOMAS LAMBERT, MR: THOMAS BROWNE, COLL: ffRANCIS YARDLEY, MR: JOHN SIDNEY, MR: JOHN HILL, MR: RICHARD CONQUEST, MR: WILLIAM MOSELEY

COLL: ffRANCIS YARDLEY, CAPT: EDWARD WINDHAM & LEMUEL MASON to take ye deposicons of MARY BRANITE? & MARY ASHALL as they are altogether unfit to travel in a cause betweene WM: PARRY & THOMAS BURBAGE.

AGNES HOLMES hath lately before COLL: YARDLEY much scandalized and abused ye wife of GEORGE HORNER deceased ....ordered AGNES HOLMES to make good her allegacons at the next Court. GEORGE HORNER'S wife intermarried with THOMAS ADDAMS.

Ordered that SIMOND HANDCOCK pay unto ELIZABETH BECKE 20 lb tob beinge at his instance subponed unto this Court toward her chardges.

187a COLL: ffRANCIS YARDLEY plt to be paid one half Anchor of Drames within one moneth by THOMAS WORKEMAN deft concerning the taking upp of a boate.

ROBTE: EYRE deceased in his lifetime stood indebted to JOHN YATES deceased. Upon peticon of JOANE YATES widow and administratrix of JOHN YATES deceased it is ordered that JOHN CUSTIS who intermarried with ELIZABETH ye relict of ROBTE: EYRE deceased shall pay out of EYRE'S estate 3 barrells of sound Indian corne and 40 lb tob shipped and smooth.

JOHN DYER to pay RICHARD CONQUEST 273 lb tob......beinge acknowledged by JAMES LOPHAM Atty of DYER.

The Cause between THOMAS WORKEMAN deft and COLL: ffRANCIS YARDLEY concerning ye cutting and countinge of certyne tymber WORKEMAN not to meddle with that nowe hewen untill further conclusions in the business.

Peticon of ANNE RICE ...... Ordered that JOHN DYER doe not strike nor any wayes make away the tob of ye sd ANNE untill further order.

JOHN WILLIAMS pltf to deliver a Sowe and half the increase to RICHARD CONQUEST deft.

188 (The first record on this page is too smeared to read.)

THOMAS SMITHERS in Open Court to aske the wife of HENERY WESTGATE for forgiveness for abusing her with scandalous and also pay WESTGATE 4 lb tob for his attendance at Court.

Ordered that THOMAS WORKEMAN deft. shall enjoy the Land in question accordinge to condicon made from ROBTE: HAYES deceased dated 30 Jan 1645/6. WORKEMAN to help NATHANIELL repair the fence about the necke of Land now planted.

THOMAS BRIDGE GENT: who intermarried with ye relict and administratrix of MATHEWE PHILLIPPS deceased hath brought an accon of account agst RICHARD CONQUEST GENT: which was pretended due to sd PHILLIPPS in his lifetyme. ....CONQUEST havinge cleared ye same uppon oath. And further it appeares that there is due to him 573 lb tob out of the Estate of PHILLIPPS......Ordered that BRIDGE make paymt out of ye estate of PHILLIPPS.

CORNELIUS LOYD appealing the differences between himself and RICHARD CONQUEST it is Ordered that they shall put in good security for their appearance the Sixt day of the next Quarter Court at James Citty.

MR: LEMUELL MASON in open Court undertaken for MR: LOYD his appearance.

Judgmt granted RICHARD CONQUEST GENT: Attor: of EDWARD GRYNELL agst estate of STEPHEN GEAREY now in the hands of CAPT: JOHN SIBSEY for ℔ 9 Sterlinge.

188a

RICHARD WESTER agst ROGER WILLIAMS ordered that ye Land in question be equally devided between sd WESTER and the children of the wife of sd. WILLIAMS being Orphans by RICHARD WHITEHURST, RICHARD ffOSTER, JOHN CHANDLER, HENERYNICHOLLS. MR: JOHN SIDNEY and WILLIAM MOSELEY are requested to be there present and to be done by the 23 Nov 1651

HENERY SNAYLE was ye last Court ordered to stand in the two parishes at ye tyme of devine service in Lynnhaven with a paper on his head then and there to acknowledge ye wronge he had done to JOSEPHE BIRCH .... uppon his submission ye Court doth with the consent of sd BIRCH remitt ye sd penance and orders that SNAYLE aske BIRCH forgiveness in Open Court for scandalous speeches...... being made to appeare false and to pay BIRCH 80 lb tob for two days appearance at Court together with his wife and Court Chardges.

JOHN WOODWARD deceased did in his lifetyme by his last will give unto ye child of ARTHUR EGLESTON one cowe .... and since WOODWARDS decease EDWARD HALL SENR: hath possessed himselfe of the sd cowe and her increase with divers other goods and refuseth to deliver the cowe HALL to deliver the cowe and her increase to Egleston for the use of his child.

RICHARD ffOSTER ordered to pay unto JOHN MARTIN 747 lb tob and Caske with forbearance and Court Chardges.

324 lb tob due to THOMAS BRIDGE from THOMAS TODD for Clerkes fees. Sd TODD havinge deserted the County an attachmt granted agst his estate in the hands of WILLIAM MOSELEY GENT:

189

THOMAS BRIDGES GENT: intermarried with ye relict and administratrix of MATTHEWE PHILLIPPS...... CAPT: ROBTE: PAGE deceased in his lifetyme was indebted to MATTHEWE PHILLIPPS 2410 lb tob by several specialtys and alsoe one Anchor of Drames. Ordered that CORNELIUS LOYD administrator of sd PAGE make paymt to sd BRIDGE out of ye estate of PAGE the sd LOYD being first satisfied.

WHEREAS: THOMAS MARSH GENT: hath received 7000 lb tob and upwards due to LAURENCE PHILLIPPS from divers of the inhabitants of this County amd refuseth to give an account......MARSH having deserted this Collony and carried away many which are indebted unto sd PHILLIPPS....... Attachmt granted PHILLIPPS agst estate of MARSH for the 7000 lb tob and those due from such as MARSH has transported out of this Collony.

RICHARD CHAPMAN agst ROGER GROSSE uppon balance of accounts......... there remains due from ROGER GROSSE to the Estate of MR: HOBSON 520 lb tob and Caske. GROSSE ordered to make paymt unto RICHARD CHAPMAN.

At the peticon of RICHARD WESTER, JOHN CARRAWAY ordered yo pay his share of the debt due to RICHARD PINNER as per order of the last Court.

189a 30 Oct 1651

CORNELIUS LOYD and RICHARD CONQUEST (this record is blotched and not legible) MR: DURAND ....next Court.

Orphans Court to be held 27 Nov 1651.

Ordered for the prevencon of further molestacons that the Shreive take up JOHN LOWNES and him safely to deteyne without bayle and to deliver him to James Citty the first day of March Court to answer to heynous offences agst his Maties and alsoe the Comrs:

CERTIFICATE: to SAVILL GASKIN for 150 acrés for transportation of 3 psgrs (passengers?) ANNE BYARD, DONKINGE GLASSE, & MARGARETT HODGES, SAVILL GASKIN hath in Open Court assigned his rights over to JAMES STARLINGE.

CERTIFICATE: to LANCASTER LOVETT for 200 acres (see Nugent 220) for transportation of 4 persons, JAMES ffLAHARTIE, GARRETT BURREY, SARAH THOMPSON & JOHN KIRKE. In the margin is written: Certificate LOVETT assigned to ffOUNTAYNE and delivered. (see also Nugent 331 - ROGER FOUNTEINE - his land described with the same headrights as listed in this Certificate.)

CERTIFICATE: to JOB CHANDLER for 300 acres for transportation of 6 persons. JOB CHANDLER, ALLEXANDER SIMCOCKS, DANIELL GORDAN, ARCHIBALD WAHOOPE, ROSE SPRINGE, HUMFREY TWIDLEY and ye sd JOB CHANDLER hath in open Court assigned said Rights unto LANCASTER LOVETT. In the Margin: Certificate to CHANDLER Assigned by LOVETT to
190 ffOUNTAYNE.

CERTIFICATE: to JOHN WALFORD for 50 acres of Land for transportation of JUDITH WATSON.

CERTIFICATE: to THOMAS WILLOUGHBY JUNR: for transportation of 7 persons JANE LATHAM, ANN WHITE, EDWARD NICKSON, JOHN DAVYES, JOHN NEEBY, JOHN POTTER and JOHN PEADE and ye sd WILLOUGHBY hath in open Court assigned over his rights to ENSIGNE KEELINGE.

CERTIFICATE: ti THOMAS WILLOUGHBY JUNR: for 850 acres of land for transportation of 17 persons: RICHARD BARKER, ffRANCIS DENES, ffRANCIE VAUGHAN, AMBROSE ALFORD, WILLIAM CHURCHMAN, THOMAS BATELY, WILLIAM CREATEN, MAUDLIN PARKER, WM: ANISON, JOANE SMITH, TOBIAS INMAN, MANUELL DELVEERE, WILLIAM DEANE, ANNE WATKINS, THOMAS SEELY, HENERY HOWSER and JOHN VINTON ..... all of which rights the sd WILLOUGHBY HATH IN OPEN COURT assigned over unto JOHN MARTIN.

CERTIFICATE to THOMAS KEELINGE for 250 acres of land for transportation of 5 psons: JAMES LYNCEY, HENERY BOND, ROBTE: SORRELL, ffRANCIS SURE and ELIZABETH BILLINGS. (see Nugent 220 for a description of the land)

CERTIFICATE: to WILLIAM BASNETT for 450 acres for trans: of Nyne psons: ROBTE: PEIRSOPHER AND HIS SONNE JOHN HASNETT, THOMAS DICKSON, MARTIN COLE, ANNE MORRIS, ELIZABETH BOUDEN, GILBERT ffOUCH and RICHARD SUTTON. (see Nugent 362)

Cases referred to the Next Court:
COLL: ffRANCIS YARDLEY agst JAMES LOPHAM
WILLIAM HILL agst WILLIAM BASNETT file

CASES REFERRED TO THE NEXT COURT:

GEORGE HEIGHAM agst SIMON HANCOCKE
THOMAS EVERAGE agst COLL: ffRANCIS YARDLEY
CORNELIUS LOYD agst LANCASTER LOVETT file
JOHN ROBINS administrator of EDWARD MOORE & JOHN SIBSEY file
Carbordue? RIGAN & RICHARD CONQUEST administrator of JOHN KEMPE
Teste WILLM: JERMY

190a

The pticular accompts to be out of the County Levyes for the present year...... (the amounte are blurred)
TO THE PUBLIQUE:
WILLIAM COOKE for one Wolfe killinge
RICHARD ffOSTER for the like
DUKE MARRINGTON for the like
the SHREIVE towards a prison 0460
MR: JOHN HILL for Burgesses charges last year
MR: BROWNE late Shreive for boate hire
THOMAS TUCKER -or makinge upp ye last yeres levy
MR: CORNELIUS LOYD for Burgesses charges
MR: BARTHOLOMEW HOSKINS for the like
him more for his mans attendance at Jamestowne
MR: EDWARD LOYD for arreares in full
MR: SIDNEY for Burgesses Charges last year
The now Shreive in full of his account
WILLIAM JERMY in full
By tobacco for powder
For sallary TOTAL 29,930

Satisfaccon of the aforesaid some of 29930 lb tob.
It is ordered that their be Levyed of every Tytheable pson within this County...... accordinge to the lists given in 461 at 65 lb tob per poll amounts to ye some of 29965 being overplus 35 lb tob.

CAPT: JOHN SIBSEY appointed to be Collector from Daniel Tanners Creeke to CAPT: WILLOUGHBYES from 43 tytheable psons........ 2795
and pas (sic) as followeth:

To the Shreive towards a Prison	460	
To the Publique in gte?	2081	
To himselfe for sallary	254	
		2795

NOTE: The jump in page numbers is a mistake for B 200 is a continuation of B 190a There do not seem to be any pages missing. AGW 200

MR: JOHN HILL appointed collector for ye Westerne Branch of Elizabeth River from 65 tytheable psons at 65 lb tob p poll amounts to 4225 lb tob and is to pay as followeth:

To himselfe as Burgess last yere	2022	
To MR: BROWNE late Shreive for boate hire	0760	
To THOMAS TUCKER for makinge upp ye last yeres levy	0150	
To MR: CORNELIUS LOYD as Burgess this yere in pte	0909	
For sallary at 10 lb p cent	0334	
	TOTAL	4225

200 30 Oct 1651

CAPT: LEMUELL MASON appointed Collector for ye Little Creek from 79 tytheable psons at 65 lb p poll which amounts to 5135

And is to pay as followeth:

To the publique in pte	4669	
for sallary at 10 lb p cent	0466	
TOTAL		5135

COLL: ffRANCIS YARDLEY is appointed Collector for the Westerne Shoare of Lynhaven from 102 tytheable psons at 65 p poll which amounts to 6630

And is to pay as followeth:

ffor powder	2766	
To WILLIAM COOKE for killinge one Wolfe	0100	
To the Publique in pte	3161 1/2	
for Sallary at 10 lb p cent	0602 1/2	
TOTAL		6630

COLL: JOHN SIDNEY is appointed Collector for the Easterne Shoare in Lynhaven from 68 tytheable psons at 65 p poll which amounts to 4420

and is to pay as followeth:

To the Publique in Pte	4018 1/2	
for sallary at 10 lb p cent	401 1/2	
TOTAL		4420

200a

LEIFT THOMAS LAMBERT appointed collector for ye Eastern and Southern Branches in Elizabeth River from 104 tytheable psons at 65 p poll which amounts to 6760

And is to pay as followeth:

To MR: BARTHOLOMEW HOSKINS in full for Burgesses charges	1170	
To LEIFT: COLL: SIDNEY in full	1350	
To ENSIGNE WILLIAM JERMY	0350	
To LEIFT: ffOSTER for killinge one woolfe	0100	
To ye Shreive in full of his account	0410	
To DUKE MARRINGTON for one woolfe killinge	0100	
This name is written thusly: Marrington		
To MR: CORNELIUS LOYD full of account	0091	
To MR: EDWARD LOYD in full of arreares	0091	
To MR: EDWARD LOYD in full of arreares	0110	
To the Publique in full	2270	
for sallary at 10 lb p cent	0595	
Surplus	0214	
TOTAL		6760

Ordered by Court whereas there is one halfe bushell of Indian Corne to be paid to ye Governor for every tytheable pson throughout the County.................. Teste: WILLM: JERMY

201 Recorded 30 Oct 1651 - RICHARD JOANES Constable for ye Westerne Branch of Elizabeth River present THOMAS BUCKMASTER a delinquent halfe an Acre of Corne according to Act of Assembly.

Recorded 3 Nov 1651 - I, WILLIAM LUCAS of Lynhaven doe confesse to have given and delivered unto WILLIAM BASNET the yonger, ye sonne of WILLIAM BASNETT of Lynhaven a cowe calve-........29 Oct 1651.......
Wit: JOHN (X) CCANVER?

Wm Lucas

Dated 15 Oct 1651 Recorded 3 Nov 1651 - By ye Governor of Virginia WHEREAS: JOHN LOWNES is arrested of heynous matters and ye witnes not hearinge of the Adjrmt (adjournment) of ye Court by reason of my sickness and not knowinge whether God will restore my health by ye next appointed tyme........LOWNES case to be put off til March Court and he and the Witness have notice of it. WILLIAM BERKELEY

Dated 15 Oct 1651 Recorded 3 Nov 1651 - COLL: YARDLEY this villayn LOWNES hath wronged me more then you (know?) for God is my witness. I scarce ever chandged three words with him but what concerned his owne ill carriage and some questions concerninge ye last Dutch Shipp of whose arrivall he brought notes what MR: WHITBY sayes I knowe not, but I believe I knowe him as well as any man does. Pray be assured I will doe nothinge unworthy myself or you.

Your faithfull frend and Servant
WILLIAM BERKELEY 201a

Dated 11 Nov 1651 Recorded 12 Nov 1651 - Wee whose names are underwritten were Arbitrators indifferently chosen to arbitrate all matters in difference betweene RICHARD RICHARDSON Merchant of ye Good Shipp called ye Peter and ffrancis belongeing to ye Barbadoes And MATHEWE WHITE, HENERY ffARR and JOHN WILFORD passengers in ye sd Shipp. We conclude as followeth:
In difference betweene RICHARD RICHARDSON & JOHN WILFORD. RICHARDSON shall deliver unto ye sd WILFORD all his goods, WILFORD payeing unto RICHARDSON £ 19/17/6 to be paid in Merchantable Tobacco at 20 Shillings ye hundred with caske, And in respect ye sd Shipp is not able to pforme her voyage.......ye sd RICHARDSON shall pay 40 shillings unto WILFORD towards his transportation to his port And to pay such damages as ye sd WILFORD shall make appeare he is dampnified in his sd goods.

In the difference betweene RICHARDSON and MATHEWS WHITE - We ...... conclude that WHITE shall have all his goods, he payeing RICHARDSON £ 11/12/6 according to bill of Ladinge (to be paid in tobacco as above) As RICHARDSON has not pformed his voyage according to his bill of Ladinge. It is agreed he shall pay WHITE for his transportation to his port £ 3/12/6 in tob at ye above rate...... 202

In difference betweene HENERY ffARR and RICHARDSON we conclude RICHARDSON and ffARR enter each to other a bond of 2000 lb tob with condicon to stand to ye arbitracon and finall determinacon of THOMAS LAMBERT and JOHN LOWNES GENT: within 20 dayes. To all of the above we have hereunto sett our hands THO: LAMBERT
BARTHO: HOSKINS
JOHN LOWNES
WILL: JERMY

Dated 20 Jan 1650/51 Recorded 18 Dec 1651 -
I THOMAS MARSH of Virginia Merchant appoint FRANCIS EMPEROR Merchant my true and lawfull Deputy and Atturney. THOMAS (MARSH?)
Wit: WM: MOSELEY 202a
PETER KENRTRIE?
JACOBUS CARPENEELL?

202a 18 Dec 1651

JUDITH BRICE alias HICKES now ye wife of ROBTE: BRICE of ye town and County of Southton, Marriner, formerly ye wife of MICHELL HICKES of ye same towne and County deceased and ye naturall and lawfull Mother of STEPHEN HICKS late of Virginia.....deceased ....Whereas ye sd STEPHEN HICKS lately dyed intestate, being seized and possessed of ye tyme of his death of a certryne psonall estate in Virginia......
203 ye administration which doth of right Lawfully belonge unto ye sd JUDITH BRICE ye mother of ye sd STEPHEN HICKES.......... for divers good causes &c ye sd JUDITH BRICE doth (appoint) HENRY BARLOWE & RAPH BARLOWE of Elizabeth City in Virginia Merchants, joyntly or severally her true & lawfull .... Attorneys .... to take Administration of all and singular ye estate of STEPHEN HICKES.....
203a Wit: WM: STANLEY
RIC: STANLY
JOH: SHEPPARD (Servant)

JUDITH (mark) BRICE

Dated 14 Jul 1650 Recorded 27 Dec 1651 - We whose names are subscribed doe certifie .... that JUDITH BRICE als HICKS who hath subscribed ye lre of Attorney before goinge is and soe hath beene......known to be ye naturall and lawfull Mother of STEVEN HICKS..........who went from the town of Southampton in England into Virginia about 16 or 17 yeres now last past or thereabouts...... wee have hereunto sett our hands And in further confirmacon and testimony of I ye Mayor of ye towne of Southton .... have caused my seale of office to be hereunto put

CHARLES WALLESTON, Mayor

WIT: JAMES CAPEKIN, PETER SIALE, PETER CHUNGSON, ROBTE: WROTH
204 Recorded 27 Dec 1651 - STEPHEN ye sonne of MICHALL HICKS was Baptized the 23 Sep 16(20?) as it is registered uppon the Churches booke of ye parish of St: Michalls in Southton where his mother that was then JUDITH HICKS nowe JUDITH BRICE yet liveth. Witness my hand

JOHN (TOMS?) Minister of ye sd Parish

ATT A COURT HELD 15 Dec 1651

PRESENT: COLL: ffRANCIS YARDLEY, MR: JOHN HILL, MR: THOMAS LAMBERT, MR: THOMAS BROWNE, MR: RICHARD CONQUEST, MR: WM: MOSELEY, MR: LEMUELL MASON

(NOTE: No items recorded between this Court and the following Quarter Court AGW)

ATT A QUARTER COURT HELD AT JAMES CITTY 6 Nov 1651
SIR WM: BERKELEY Kt. Gov.

SIR THOMAS LUNSFORD GENT:, COLL: SAM: MATHEWES, COLL: WM: BERNARD, COLL: THO: PETUS, COLL: GEORGE LEDLOWE, ADJUTANT ffREEMAN, COLL: HILL, MAJOR WM: TAYLOR

WHEREAS: the Governor hath noted the Civell Demeanor and Good behavior of MR: CORNELIUS LOYD and his truth and honesty, to his Ma[tie] which hath beene proved by his Late modest carriage to ye uttermost of his power .... Ordered that he be received againe into ye Commission of Lower Norffolke County and to take his place as formerly.

Teste: JOHN JENNINGE Clerk Council

..... MR: CORNELIUS LOYD was sworne Comr: ...... accordinge to ye tenor of ye above sd order. Teste: WILL: JERMY ClCur

204a

(NOTE: The above is all that came under the Quarter Court - we are now back in Lower Norfolk County Court of the 15th of Dec. AGW)

MORE PRESENT: CORNELIUS LOYD Comr:

CAPT: MATHEWE WOOD agst RICHARD RICHARDSON, Merchant of the Shipp called the Peter & ffrancis belonginge to ye Barbadoes CAPT: MATHEWE WOOD was hired unto the sd Shipp at ye Barbadoes as Master thereof and was to have ₺ 5 per moneth money Ster: for soe longe (a) tyme as he should be there imployed. And was bound to Virginia and New England and soe back againe and in respect of ye insufficiency of ye sd Shipp they can goe noe further ...... cause by this Court being fully heard ...... ordered that RICHARDSON pay unto WOOD ₺ 5 per moneth for every moneth ye sd WOOD hath been imployed in ye sd Shipp, to be paid in sugar at ye rate of 6 pence by the pound .... he ye sd WOOD allowinge 10 pounds in the hundred for Shrinckage and allowinge fraught and further RICHARDSON to pay & allowe WOOD one moneth pay more after ..... towards his chardges for his transportation and to give WOOD a full dischardge.........

MATHEWE ffASSETT hath made it appeare that there is due to him from RICHARD RICHARDSON of ye Shipp called Peter & ffrancis belonging to Barbadoes ye some of ₺ 16/10 mony Ster: for 6 moneths imploymt in ye sd Shipp being hired at 55 shillings per moneth ....RICHARDSON to make paymt in Sugar at 6 pence per pound ffASSETT allowinge Shrinckage at 10 lb in ye hundred and fraught............ and one moneths more pay for and towards his transportation (back to Barbadoes) and to give him a full dischardge.

(This folio is numbered 206 but is really 205) -------------------- 205

THOMAS SAYER indebted unto HENRY BARLOWE 2000 lb tob by bill. Ordered that SAYER make paymt unto BARLOWE for the use of JUDITH BRICE als HICKS in England.

ANTHONY SIZEMAN plt agst JOHN HOLMES deft to the next Court.

Ye last Court uppon peticon of ARTHUR EGLESTON an order was granted him agst EDWARD HALL SENR: for ye delivery of one Cowe and her increase unto EGLESTON which he made appeare was given him for ye use of his child by JOHN WOODWARD deceased his last will ...... & HALL appearing this Court & uppon oath a Collatterall will made by ye sd WOODWARD. Therefore ordered that ye aforesd order be reversed and stand to noe effect. HALL to enjoy ye sd Cowe untill EGLESTON prove the Contrary.

Ye last Court EDWARD HALL was fined 350 lb tob for his contempt not lettinge his man servant appeare, being lawfully subpenoed......... HALL submitting himselfe by acknowledgmt of his error ...... ordered that the fine be remitted.

JOSEPH BIRCH at the instance of JOHN HOLMES he lent one boate to a Dutchman and that his boate was by him splitt and proving it by oath that he could not have it mended for 200 lb tob. Therefore ordered that sd HOLMES make paymt unto BIRCH 210 lb tob towards repaie of boate.

205a

WILLIAM EALY Indebted unto RICHARD CONQUEST GENT: 594 lb tob and GEORGE MIGH hath transported sd EALY out of this Collony. CONQUEST granted an attachmt agst Estate of GEORGE MIGH........

WILLIAM LANGLEY to make paymt of 245 lb tob as alsoe 3 barrells and a halfe of Indian Corne due fower yeres to RICHARD CONQUEST.

Attachmt granted THOMAS LAMBERT agst Estate of THOMAS DAVIS for 582 lb tob and Caske due by bill......

JOHN MARSHALL ordered to pay 571 lb tob with caske by bill unto GEORGE HEIGHAM

THOMAS TUCKER to pay RICHARD STERNELL 965 lb tob with caske

COLL: ffRANCIS YARDLEY deft and JAMES LOPHAM pltf to next Court.

206

Presentmt of RICHARD JOANES Constable: GEORGE MERRICKE was by this Court fined ..... 500 lb tob for beinge deficient in planting one acre of Corne for ye uses of ye Act of Assembly. MERRICKE......... humbly shewinge that his partner fell sicke. Whereby pte of the land planted was left of and benne much damnified by hoggs .... in respect to his poverty the Court remitts ye fine.

THOMAS TUCKER to make full paymt unto RICHARD BECKE 303 lb tob in 20 dayes.

THOMAS TUCKER shall satisfie THOMAS GODBYE 230 lb tob within 20 dayes.

Attachmt granted JOHN HOLMES agst Estate of WILLIAM PEETERS for 210 lb tob .... for One boate lent ye sd PEETERS and beinge out of this Collony....

Cause betweene ffRANCIS YARDLEY Atty of EDMONDS and JAMES LOPHAM concerning the paymt of 5 barrels of Corne. Ordered that if LOPHAM make it not appeare next Court that MR: THOMAS DAYNES gave him order to sell ye sd corne being due by bill to MR: EDMUNDS then LOPHAM to pay accordinge to the specialty.

Uppon gull hearinge of the cause betweene THOMAS ADDAMS & AGNES HOLMES wife of JOHN HOLMES ..... ordered that HOLMES pay all the Court harges due.

206a

It is by this Court ordered for divers reasons to them knowne that the Shreive take ye boddy of AGNES HOLMES and her to deteyne in his custody untill March Court next to be held at James Citty then and there to deliver her upp to ye Shreive .... it is alsoe left to ye Shreive whether he will take bayle or not in respect ye sd AGNES is both a Lame and diseased woman.

Cause between GEORGE HEIGHAM plt & SIMOND HANDCOCKE deft referred untill ye next Court.

Due to THOMAS ADDAMS uppon account 1000 lb tob from JOHN HOLMES. Ordered that HOLMES make paymt thereof.....& further what ye sd HOLMES can make appeare due from ADDAMS is to be satisfied by ADDAMS

CAPT: WILLIAM CLAYBORNE non suited for non appearance agst CAPT: MATHEWE WOOD.

WM: PARRY nonsuited for non appearance agst THOMAS WRIGHT.

CAPT: JOHN SIBSEY Atty of CAPT: RAFFE WORMELEY ESQ: Administrator of LUKE STUBBINGE deceased formerly obteyned an Order agst JOHN CORNELIUS who intermarried with ye relict of HENDRICKE LIGHTHARTE for ℔ 5/9 mony Sterlinge with forbearance & Court Chardges CAPT: WORMELEY being since deceased It is ordered that ye sd CORNELIUS pay thaforesd some unto CAPT: SIBSEY being the Atty of AGATHA WORMELEY the relict of CAPT: WORMELEY deceased.

At a Court held 15 Nov 1650 it was ordered that ANNE PHILLIPPS widow 207
should have an attachmt agst Estate of JOHN CLAUSON deceased for 1003 lb tob with Caske and Court Chardges uppon the petition of THOMAS BRIDGE GENT: who intermarried with ye sd ANNE PHILLIPPS the order if revived.

Formerly ordered that RICHARD CONQUEST GENT: Administrator of JOHN KEMPE deceased should satisfie unto XOPHER BURROWES 1200 lb tob for chardges and Expenses disbursed about ye sd KEMPE in ye tyme of his sickness...... & now ye sd BURROWES ath bought certeyne goods at ye Outcry to ye value of 369 lb tob and other goods that he deteyned in his custody to ye valewe of 685 lb tob the totall 1054 lb tob ..... ye Court conceivinge if they had been sold at Outcry would have pcured 1200 lb tob therefore ordered that the 1054 lb tob be in full satisfaccon..... and BURROWES to give a full discharge unto ye Adm:

CERTIFICATE: to WILLIAM DAYNES for 300 acres for transportation of 6 negroes.

CERTIFICATE: to EDWARD HALL the ELDER for 400 acres for the transportation of 8 psons: DANIELL NEEDHAM, JOHN JENKINS, DANIELL DOONE, ANNE GRAVES, WILLIAM WHITE, ELIZABETH LUTTEBELL (Nugent gives Huttibell p 287), JOHN WHITE & KATHERINE SIMPSON. (Nugent 287 gives 398 acres and a description of the land)

CERTIFICATE: to HENERY WOODHOUSE GENT: for 400 acres for transportation of 8 psons: JOHN SMITH, PETER WHITE, EDWARD PARRETT, JAMES RICCARD, MARY a maid servant, JOHN HOPWOOD (Nugent says HOPSWOOD), DERBIS SEXTON (Nugent says DORCAO SEYTON) and HONA MARIA HENDRICKSON (Nugent 287 says 300 acres and "last two assigned to WM: CAPPS")

CERTIFICATE: to THOMAS ALLEN for 250 acres for trans: of 5 psons: 207a
himselfe, GRIFFON GWIN, GEORGE BEASLEY, HENERY SHADE, and SARAH a maid servant.

CORNELIUS LOYD GENT: pltf agst LANCASTER LOVETT deft referred to next Court.

EDMUND LILLEY & THEOPHILIS HONE deft - file

CORNELIUS LOYD & JOHNSON BENNETT - file

Quinto Dec 1651 - The markes ordered to be recorded of: RICHARD KINGE, JOHN PARTER JUNR:, JOHN PORTER SENR, WILLIAM JERMY.

(Note: this seems to be a letter) - Ordered to be recorded. 208
CAPT: JOHN SIBSEY xxxxxxx ye 8th of this instant xxxxxxxxx to my ands. Wherein you acquaint me xxxxxxxxxxxxxx from HENDRICK LIGHTHART

who stood indebted to my deceased husband MR: LUKE STUBBINGE fir ƀ 5/9 but since ye death of sd LIGHTHART it appeareth due from JOHN CORNELIUS agt: whom you have obteyned order for ye sd debte. These are humbly to request you and authorize you to psecute your course begun. And uppon non paymt to bringe sd CORNELIUS to Execucon..... .... or to doe or act according to your wisdom .... for my best benefitt .... And doe return you many thanks for your good office of Love to my dear and late deceased husband and myselfe.

17 Nov 1651 Your reall frend and servant
Teste: ROWE BURNEHAM AGATHA WORMELEY

ELIZABETH CLARKE aged 17 yeres or thereabouts saith: That MR: HALL & JOHN WOODWARD were in discourse about ye Cowes soe MR: HALL asked him if he would give HUMPHREY all his cowes & he said his conscience did tell him that he should be as good by his word to HUMPHREY ever since he was affected with him, then he said he would give HUMPHREY 3 Cowes and the firle the redd heifer and this was a moneth after he made his will or thereabouts and further saith not.

ELIZ: (a) CLARKE

ELIZABETH HABBERELL sworne saith the same.

ELIZ: (H) HATTERELL

29 Nov 1651
Wit: ffRAN: YARDLEY & EDWARD WINDHAM

208a

Dated 29 Dec 1651 Recorded 17 Jan 1651/2 - THOMAS TUCKER of Elizabeth River for 620 lb tob have sould JOHN HARRIS of ye same place, Planter, one owe and one blacke owe.
Wit: ffANIE ffLINTON & RICHARD VINNERT Tho: Tooker

Recorded 15 Jan 1651/52 - Received by mee RICHARD PINNER of GEORGE ACKERLY 300 lb tob for a debte formerly due to MR: PHILLIP CONERS of Kent. I say received by mee.

RICH: PINNER

ATT A COURT HELD 15 Jan 1651/52

PRESENT: CAPT JOHN SIBSEY, MR: CORNELIUS LOYD, COLL: ffFRANCIS YARDLEY, MR: JOHN HILL, MR: JOHN SIDNEY, MR: THOMAS LAMBERT, MRS: THOMAS BROWNE, MR: RICHARD CONQUEST, MR: WILLIAM MOSLEY

This Court MR: HENERY WOODHOUSE tooke the Oath of Allegiance and was Sworne Commissioner for this Court.

209

MORE PRESENT: MR: HENERY WOODHOUSE

Probate of the last will and testament of ROBTE: POWERS Clerke deceased is granted unto ROBTE: POWES his sonne being sole executor named in ye sd last will and testament.

Lres of administracon granted unto ROGER ffOUNTAYNE on ye Estate of JOHN GILHAM decd he beinge a great creditor.

The said ROGER ffOUNTAYNE, ffRANCIS LAND & JOHN COOKE in open Court became bound to the abovesd Comrs: in 20,000 lb tob severally for ye bringinge in of a true inventory of JOHN GILHAM to the next Court.

Ordered uppon peticon of ROGER ffONTAYNE that JOHN MARTIN, ffRANCIS LAND & JOHN TAYLOR & LANCASTER LOVETT shall have full power for ye appraisinge of the Estate of JOHN GILHAM with all convenient speed. They first being sworne by MR: HENERY WOODHOUSE.

ROGER ffOUNTAYNE adm: of JOHN GILHAM deceased to make paymt of 900 lb tob to RICHARD CONQUEST sd Adm: being first satisfied.

Attchmt granted HENERY BRAKES agst Estate of JOHN GILHAM deceased for so much as BRAKES shall make appeare due by bil...........

JOHN GILHAM in his lifetime stood indebted to WILLIAM VINCENT by bill 209a
433 lb tob and Caske the adm: ROGER ffONTAYNE to make paymt after satisfying the sbove sd creditors.

LANCASTER LOVETT stood indebted unto CAPT: PAGE deceased by bill 1000 lb tob and that 300 lb tob was satisfied and ye rest remayne still due....... LOVETT to make paymt of 700 lb tob unto CORNELIUS LOYD Adm: of PAGE.

Divers complaints of severall misdemeanors of JOHN BRADLEY servant to GEORGE HEIGHAM. It is ordered that BRADLEY receive 20 good Lashes uppon his beare back.

Difference betweene ANTHONY SIZEMAN & JOHN HOLMES ...... it is ordered that SIZEMAN be sett free from ye sd HOLMES and to have his Corne & Cloathes accordinge to ye Custome of ye County..... SIZEMAN havinge served HOLMES ye full terme he was bound for in England........

Attachmt granted THOMAS WRIGHT agst Estate of GEORGE LOBB in ye hands of RICHARD CHAPMAN for 300 lb tob. 210

JANE LATHAM hath made complaint to this Court of her ill usage by her master MR: THOMAS WILLOUGHBY uppon the hearinge of the motion it is ordered that she return to her masters house there to doe her service in such manner as she ought to doe untill ye next Court. And then MR: WILLOUGHBY & JANE LATHAM to appeare and to bringe such witnesses as can speake in ye difference betweene them, and MR: WILLOUGHBY there to produce ye ropes he strucke ye sd LATHAM

Attachmt granted to THOMAS BUSHRODE agst Estate of WILLIAM BASNETT for 1400 lb tob being due by bill..........

CERTIFICATE: to RICHARD PINNER for 150 acres for trans: of himselfe, MILICENT SIMONDS AND SARAH TERY.

NATHANIELL HAYES shewinge ye there was due to him from JOHN KENMAR decd 1163 lb tob for certayne commodities had by Kenmar in his lifetyme of sd HAYES & For funeral chardges expended by HAYES.......... Ordered that HAYES receive & be satisfied out of ye cropp of ye sd JOHN KENMAR 1100 lb of tob with caske in full........ and HAYES to bring in an account of the whole estate at next Court and ye remainder to be disposed of as the Court thinks fit.

THOMAS DAVYES to make paymt of 520 lb tob due by bill to ffRANCIS LAND.

WILLIAM DAYNES Atty of LEWE (or HEWE) WILSON shewinge that ROBTE: EYRE GENT: in his lifetime stood indebted unto LEWE WILSON by bill 300 lb tob and caske........ rest yet unsatisfied is testified by MR: CORNELIUS LOYD therefore ordered that JOHN CUSTIS who intermarried with ye relict and Administratrix of ye sd EYRE make paymt thereof out of ye estate of EYRE........

JOHN RABLEY to be non suited at peticon of ffRANCIS LAND deft for his non appearance.
Attachmt granted JOHN HOLMES agst Estate of WILLIAM PEETERS for 350 lb tob with Caske and Court Charges ordered in lewe of damages sus-teyned by ye lending of one boate unto PEETERS and sd PEETERS being out of this County.

Attachmt granted WILLIAM HILL agst Estate of WILLIAM BASNETT for 1000 lb tob unless BASNETT makes anything contrary appeare ye next Court

Due to JOHN HOLMES out of ye Estate of JOHN GILHAM decd 320 lb tob and Caske .... ordered that ROGER ffOUNTAYNE Adm: of GILHAM make paymt thereof.......

211 At a Court held 30 Oct last past an Attachmt was granted unto THOMAS" RIDGE agst ye estate of THOMAS TODD for 324 lb tob ..... Judgmt is awarded for the 320 lb tob agst ye estate of TODD in ye hands of MR: WILLIAM MOSELEY.

At ye last Court an Attachmt was revived by THOMAS BRIDGE agst Estate of JOHN CLAUSON decd in ye hands of ye sd BRIDGE for 1003 lb tob and Caske..... Judgmt awarded if MR: WHITBYE sheweth nothinge contrary ye next Court.

At a Court held 25 Feb 1649 Judgmt was granted THOMAS BRIDGE agst GEORGE HEIGHAM for 1767 lb tob ... at peticon of BRIDGES Judgmt is revived.

Judgmt is confessed by THOMAS TOOKER Atty of JOHN WILLIAMS for 300 lb tob with Caske unto CORNELIUS LOYD GENT: being due by bill.

COLL ffRANCIS YARDLEY plt & JAMES LOPHAM deft referred to nest Court.

Certayne business belonginge to this Court you shall find recorded in the next book.

p me WILLM: JERMY

p me Willm Jermy Chmn Supra

NAME INDEX

IMPORTANT: Please that this index is to the folio numbers of the original Book "B", and not the page numbers of this book. This has been done to facilitate the ordering of copies of the original records from the Virginia State Library. Lower Norfolk County has not been indexed inasmuch as this book is Lower Norfolk County Record. Use your imagination when searching names as the Clerks wrote them as they heard them, not as they should be spelled in many cases. I have found EVRG as the spelling for the name Etheridge. Don't forget they used the broad A in those days. The same name can be spelled many different ways in these records.

L

M

N

O

P

Q

R

PLACE

Inasmuch as Lower Norfolk County appears on the majority of pages it is not indexed.

NOTE: page numbers refer to those of the original record book and not to the pages of this book.

SUBJECT

ABREVIATIONS

* = is placed where the page begins sometimes in the middle of sentences.

Dates = all dates are given: day/month/year. All months abreviated to 3 letters.

: = where used incorrectly after partial words indicates the word is abreviated thusly in original record. Or an unfinished name.

( ) = Brackets indicate the words contained therein are those of the editor.

XXXX = words or sentences faded or missing or illegible.

// or [ ] = parenthesis as used in the original records.

.... = omitted by the editor as being repetitious or inconsequental

(X) or (mark) or (initials) = The mark of the person signing

~~XXXXXX~~ = crossed out in original record

accon = action
adm = administration
agst = against
appr = appraiser or appraisal
arb = arbitrator
atty = attorney
Burg: = Burgesses
Cert: = certificate
ClCur = Clerk of Court
Col = collector also Colonel
Coll: = Colonel
Comp^{tts} = Complainants
Comr: = Commissioner
dau = daughter
DB = deed book
D Cl = Deputy Clerk of Court
Deft: = defendant
est = estate
exix: = executrix
exor: = executor
hh = hogshead (of tobacco)
jdgmt: = judgement
LNco = Lower Norfolk County
1 tob = pownds (pounds) of tobacco
MB = Minute Book
NW = nun will or nun-cupative will
p = per, pre, pro &c also personal,(psonal in records)
pish = Parish
Plt^{ff}: = plaintiff
Prish: = Parish
sd = said
Sec: = security
th = thence
trans: transported
VM = Vestryman
wch = which
wd = will dated
wp = will probated or proved
wid: = widow
wit: = witness
y^{t} = yet

DATES COURT HELD

Date	Page
2 Nov 1646 (first date in book)	1
10 Oct 1646 (Quarter Court) (in James Citty)	6
16 Nov 1646	8a
17 Nov 1646	10
18 Nov 1646	10a
15 Dec 1646	15a
20 Jan 1646/47	20a
30 Jan 1646/47	24
29 Dec 1646 Court held for Nancemond	25
15 Feb 1646	25
16 Feb 1646	28a
10 Aug 164X Court held at house of Robert Partin in co. of Isle of Wight	32a 33
22 Mar 1647	33
31 Apr 1647	33a
27 Aug 1646 Court held at Eliza- City	33a
5 Mar 1646/7 Quarter Court held at James Citty	37
xx Apr 1647	37a
15 Jun 1647	39a
15 Jun 1647 "at a County Court" Burgesses present Must mean James City	39a
15 Jun 1647	40a
13 Jul 1647 Capt. Wm. Claiborne presided at these last 3 courts.	48
16 Aug 1647	50
17 Aug 1647	52
22 Apr 1647 Held at Deepe Creek Recorded 6 Oct 1647	53
14 Oct 1647 Adjourned to the 15 Dec because of the Assembly.	53
10 Nov 1647 - Recorded 10 Dec 1647 Members of Assembly present	53a
15 Dec 1647	53a
16 Dec 1647	55a
20 Jan 1647/8	61a
20 Jan 1647/8 The handwriting changes here.	61a
15 Feb 1647/8	64a
20 Feb 1647/8	67a
3 Mar 1647/8 Quarter Court at James Citty	
21 Dec 1647 Note date out of place. Court held at howse of Peter Talbot	70
7 Apr 1648	70a
15 Apr 1648	70a
14 Jun 1648 Appointed for an Orphans Court	72
15 Jun 1648	76a
Court adjourned until	
15 Jul 1648	76a
15 Aug 1648	82a
3 Apr 1645 (or 1648?) Quarter Court at James City	84a
27 Apr 1648 James City	85
28 Feb (1647?)	85
24 Aug 1648	86
1 Sep 1648 Quarter Court	87
2 Oct 1648 Vestry Meeting	88
2 Oct 1648 Recorded as before	88a
15 Oct 1648 To be held	88a
6 Oct 1648	88a
3 Nov 1648	89a
15 Nov 1648	90
16 Nov 1648	91
16 Nov 1648 Accts. to be paid	92a
15 Dec 1648	102a
Becaus of Assembly 10 Feb next County Court to be held 15th day xxxxx to the 1 day of Feb.	
16 Dec 1648 Recorded	103a
1 ffeb 1648/9	104
15 Feb 1648/9	105
17 Feb 1648/9	107
20 Mar 1648	109a
6 Apr 1649 Recorded	111a
9 Apr 1649 Quarter Court at James Citty	112
16 Apr 1649	112a
19 Apr 1649 Held at Linhaven at House of Savill Gaskin.	114
14 May 1649 "for Eliza. River Parish"	115
30 May 1649 Recorded	116a
15 Jun 1649	117
16 Nov 1648 Date out of place	119
31 Jul 1649	120
15 Aug 1649	120a
1 Oct 1649	123
31 Oct 1649 at ye house of Thomas juies (Ivies)	124a
20 Nov 1649 at Mr. Ivies	129
30 Nov 1649	130
19 Dec 1649 at Mr. Ivies	130a
12 Jan 1649/50 at house of Mris An Phillipps,wid	132a
15 Feb 1649/50 a. Lau: Phillipps	134
25 Feb 1649/50 at Lau:Phillipps	135
27 Feb 1649/50 Orphants Court at ye house of Mris Anne Phillipps	137a
26 Mar 1650	140
13 Mar 1649 Quarter Court at James Citty	142
28 Mar 1650 At an Orphants Court	142a
18 Jun 1650	146
19 Jul 1650	151a
15 Aug 1650	152
15 Oct 1650	154
1 Nov 1650	154
15 Nov 1650	156a
15 (Dec?)	160a
18 Feb 1649/50 at Eliza. Citty	162
30 Oct xxxx Quarter Court at James Citty	162a
15 Jan 1650/51	163
15 Feb 1650/51	166
26 Feb 16xx	168a
15 Apr 1651	171a
7 (Mar?) 1650/51 Quarter Court at James Citty	174a
28 Apr 1651	176a
15 May 1651	178
16 Jun 1651	179
Jul?	182
3 Oct 1651	186
30 Oct 1651 Next Court to be held	186
30 Oct 1651	187
15 Dec 1651	204
6 Nov 1651 Quarter Court at James Citty	204
15 Jan 1651/52	208a

www.ingramcontent.com/pod-product-compliance
Lightning Source LLC
Chambersburg PA
CBHW071222290426
44108CB00013B/1259

* 9 7 8 0 8 0 6 3 4 5 6 0 4 *